COLLECTION CONSTITUTIONAL LAW

Directed by
Domingo García Belaunde

Edited by
Carlos Antonio Agurto Gonzáles
Sonia Lidia Quequejana Mamani
María-Pía Guadalupe Díaz Díaz
Benigno Choque Cuenca

ALLAN R. BREWER-CARÍAS
Emeritus Professor of Law, Central University of Venezuela
Fellow, Trinity College, and Simón Bolívar Professor,
University of Cambridge, UK (1985-1986)
Vice President, International Academy of Comparative Law (1982–2010)

JUDICIAL REVIEW IN COMPARATIVE LAW

COURSE OF LECTURES, CAMBRIDGE

1985–1986

editorial jurídica venezolana

Ediciones Olejnik

Title of book:
JUDICIAL REVIEW IN COMPARATIVE LAW.
COURSE OF LECTURES, CAMBRIDGE 1985-1986

Huérfanos 611, Santiago - Chile
E-mail: contacto@edicionesolejnik.com
Web site: http://www.edicionesolejnik.com

ISBN: 978-956-392-973-7

Diseño de Carátula: Ena Zuñiga
Diagramación: Luis A. Sierra Cárdenas

La primera edición de Ediciones Olejnik fue impresa en Argentina, 2021

La reimpresión en coedición entre Ediciones Olejnik y Editorial Jurídica Venezolana fue impresa por Lightning Source, an Ingram Company, para Editorial Jurídica International Inc., 2021

ÍNDICE

PREFACE
WITH SOMME COMMENTS ON THE 2016-2017 JUDICIAL REVIEW «BREXIT» CASE BEFORE THE CONSTITUTIONAL JUDGES OF THE UNITED KINGDOM

PART ONE
THE MODERN STATE SUBMITTED TO THE RULE OF LAW (ÉTAT DE DROIT)

PART TWO
PROCESS OF CONSTITUTIONALIZATION OF THE ÉTAT DE DROIT

PART THREE
THE FOUNDATION OF JUDICIAL REVIEW OF THE CONSTITUTIONALITY OF LEGISLATION

PART FOUR
THE DIFFUSE SYSTEM OF JUDICIAL REVIEW

PART FIVE
CONCENTRATED SYSTEMS OF JUDICIAL REVIEW

ADDENDUM
CONSTITUTIONAL COURTS AS POSITIVE LEGISLATORS IN COMPARATIVE LAW

In memory of my dear friends and distinguish
Scholars: *Mauro Cappelletti* (Italy),
Louis Favoreu (France)
and *Hector Fix Zamudio* (Mexico),
pioneers in the study of Judicial Review in Comparative Law.

PREFACE

WITH SOMME COMMENTS ON THE 2016-2017 JUDICIAL REVIEW «BREXIT» CASE BEFORE THE CONSTITUTIONAL JUDGES OF THE UNITED KINGDOM

I

This book on *Judicial Review in Comparative Law*, is the original version of the text I wrote for the Course of Lectures I gave as *Simon Bolivar Professor* of the University of Cambridge in 1985-1986, in the *LL.M. Course* at the Faculty of Law, University of Cambridge, UK. My appointment for the *Simon Bolivar Chair in Latin American Studies* was proposed by Professors C. J. Hamson and A. Jolowicz, both members of the International Academy of Comparative Law and Professors at the Faculty of Law of the University of Cambridge. At their initiative, at that time, I was also elected *Fellow of Trinity College*.

The text of the lectures was written during that year, basically working at the University Library, in my Room in Angel Court at the College, and in the small Library I had in the Goodhard Professor House, in Trumpington Road, where I had the privilege of staying with my family during my tenure.

The *Simón Bolívar Chair* was established in 1968 with a grant from the Venezuelan government, for the purpose of bringing each year to Cambridge «a distinguished Latin American scholar or intellectual». Like all other Professors at the University, each holder of the Chair is assigned to the Faculty most appropriate to his academic interests and is elected a Fellow of a College. The Professor is also usually closely associated with the work of the Centre of Latin American Studies of the University.

I was the first *Legal* scholar to be appointed to held such important Academic Chair, having been preceded by a group of very distinguish scholars in other scientific or academic fields: *Science*: Arnaldo Gabaldón, Marcel Roche, Tulio Arends; *History*: Alvaro Jara, Pedro Grases, Sergio Villalobos; *Economics*: Celso Furtado; *Anthropology*: Ignacio Bernal; *Sociology*: Pablo González Casanova, Fernando Henrique Cardozo (President of Brazil 1995-2002); *Political Science*: Ramón Escovar Salom; and *Literature*: Octavio Paz, (Nobel Prize in Literature 1990), Mario Vargas Llosa (Nobel Prize in Literature 2010). I even was immediately succeeded by Carlos Fuentes, another very distinguished writer and novelist.

Unlike the previous appointees, I was the first *Simon Bolivar Professor* to which the University asked to give a full regular course at a Faculty, in my case, in the LLM Program of the Faculty of Law, a task that I gladly accepted. The result are the Lectures that make up this book on *Judicial Review*, that is, the power of judges to control the constitutionality of State acts, particularly of Legislation; a subject that not only was very important at the time but continue to be one of the most important subjects of contemporary constitutional law, as well as the most distinctive feature of all democratic constitutional systems, being very suitable to be analyzed in comparative law.

All over the world, in all democratic States, independently of having a legal system based on the common law or on the civil law principles, the courts - special constitutional courts, supreme courts or ordinary courts - have the power to decide and declare the unconstitutionality of legislation or of other State acts when a particular statute violates the text of the Constitution or of its constitutional principles.

This power of the courts is the consequence of the consolidation in contemporary constitutionalism of three fundamental principles of law: *first*, the existence of a written or unwritten constitution or of a fundamental law, conceived as a superior law with clear supremacy over all other statutes; *second*, the «rigid» character of such constitution or fundamental law, which implies that the amendments or reforms that may be introduced can only be put into practice by means of a particular and special constituent or legislative process, preventing the ordinary legislator from doing so; and *third*, the establishment in that same written or unwritten and rigid constitution or fundamental law, of the judicial means for guaranteeing its supremacy, over all other state acts, including legislative acts.

Accordingly, in democratic systems subjected to such principles, the courts have the power to refuse to enforce a statute when deemed to be contrary to the Constitution, considering it null or void, through what is known as the diffuse system of judicial review; and in many cases, they even have the power to annul the said unconstitutional law, through what is known as the concentrated system of judicial review.

The former, is the system created more than two hundred years ago by the Supreme Court of the United States, and that so deeply characterizes the North American Constitutional system. The latter system, has been adopted in constitutional systems in which the judicial power of judicial review has been generally assigned to the Supreme Court or to one special Constitutional Court, as is the case, for example, of many countries in Europe and in Latin America. This concentrated system of judicial review, although established in many Latin American countries since the 19th century, was only effectively developed particularly in the world after World War II following the studies of Hans Kelsen.

In Democratic States, in addition, the courts have the specific power to protect and guaranty the constitutional and fundamental rights of citizens declared in the text of the Constitutions or in International Treaties on Human Rights, which in many countries even have constitutional rank and value. The fact is that in all countries, some sort of specific judicial review means of protection have been developed in order to immediately guarantee constitutional rights, being them or specific injunctions (for example the «civil rights injunction»), or special actions like the well-known «amparo» action or proceeding established in almost all Latin American countries as well as in Spain or Germany. These injunctions or protective actions are also part of the judicial review system of many countries.

The Cambridge Course and the Lectures that make up this book precisely deals with this subject of Judicial Review, considered from a constitutional comparative law perspective, written at a time in which the subject already had started to be analyzed in comparative law by a few dear friends and distinguished scholars like Mauro Cappelletti (Italy), Louis Favoreu (France) and Hector Fix Zamudio (Mexico), to the memory of whom this edition is dedicated.

Of course, during the past thirty years many changes have occurred in the world on these matters of Judicial Review, in particularly in Europe and specifically in the United Kingdom, where these Lectures were delivered. Nonetheless, I have decided to publish them hereto in its integrality,* as they were: the written work of a law professor made as a consequence of his research for the preparation of his lectures, not pretending to be anything else, but the academic testimony of the state of the subject of judicial review in the world in 1985-1986.

II

Nonetheless, in this Preface, as a sort of specific update, I have decided to refer to the matter in the United Kingdom, commenting the especially important *«Brexit» Case* decided by the Constitutional Judges of the country, specifically through the decision of the High Court of Justice of November 3, 2016, confirmed by the Supreme Court in decision dated January 24, 2017.**

In fact, one of the most important decisions on constitutional law adopted by the courts of the United Kingdom has been the one issued by the High Court of Justice on the 2d of November 2016, ratified by the Supreme Court of the United Kingdom on 24th of January, 2017, with regard to the *«Brexit case»*, that is, concerning the United Kingdom's withdrawal from the European Union (finally materialized on January 2021) as a result of the referendum held on this matter on June 23, 2016. This political decision may be the most important decision adopted to this date within the framework of European regional integration, which, since its inception, has been a political process generated hand in hand with constitutional law.[1]

---

* This original version of the Course of Lecture was included in my book: *Études de droit public compare,* Académie Internationale de Droit Comparé, Éditions Bruylant, Bruxelles 2001, pp. 525-934; and also, in my book: *Judicial Review. Comparative Constitucional Law Essays, Lectures and Courses (1985-2011),* Fundación de Derecho Público Editorial Jurídica Venezolana, Caracas 2014, 1197 pp. An abridged and edited version of the Course of Lectures was published by Cambridge University Press in 1989: *Judicial Review in Comparative Law* (Foreword by J. A. Jolowicz), Cambridge Studies in International and Comparative Law. New Series, Cambridge University Press, Cambridge 1989, 406 pp.

** These comments are based on the paper I wrote for the Presentation made before the *European Group of Public Law (EGPL),* Annual Reunion, 2018, Athens 7-8 September 2018; published as: «The «Brexit» Case Before the Constitutional Judges of the United Kingdom: Comments regarding the Decision of the High Court of Justice of November 3, 2016, confirmed by the Supreme Court in Decision dated January 24, 2017», in *Revue européenne de droit public, European Review of Public Law,* ERPL/REDP, vol. 31, No 1, Spring/Printemps 2019, European Group of Public Law (EGPL), pp. 77-103

1 See Allan R. Brewer-Carías, «Constitutional Implications of Regional Economic Integration» (General Report, XV International Congress of Comparative Law, International Academy of Comparative Law, Bristol September 1998), in Allan R. Brewer-Carías, *Études de Droit Public Comparé,* Bruillant, Bruxelles, pp. 453-522. Also see Allan R. Brewer-Carías, *Las implicaciones constitucionales de la integración económica regional,* Cuadernos de la Cátedra Allan R. Brewer-Carías de Derecho Público, Universidad Católica del Táchira, Editorial Jurídica Venezolana, Caracas 1998.

Our intention in this comment is to give an account of the most relevant contents of such decisions in light of contemporary constitutional principles, particularly those regarding the separation of powers pertaining to relationships between Parliament and the Executive Branch of the Government according to the principles of parliamentary sovereignty and the limitations of the Crown's prerogative powers on regulatory matters.

I. SOME PRINCIPLES OF BRITISH CONSTITUTIONALISM

While it is true that the United Kingdom does not have a Constitution to be found entirely in a written document adopted by the people according to principles deriving from modern constitutionalism,[2] this does not mean there is an absence of a constitution or constitutional law. On the contrary:

> «the United Kingdom has its own form of constitutional law, as recognized in each of the jurisdictions of the four constituent nations. Some of it is written, in the form of statutes, which have particular constitutional importance. Some of it is reflected in fundamental rules of law recognized by both Parliament and the courts. These are established and well-recognized legal rules which govern the exercise of public power and which distribute decision-making authority between different entities in the State and define the extent of their respective powers».[3]

The foregoing is not something that has been said in any writings or book on the constitutional law of the United Kingdom or on comparative constitutional law, but was stated by the High Court of Justice *(Queen's Bench Division, Divisional Court*) of the United Kingdom, in its decision of 3rd of November, 2016, issued in *Gina Miller* et al. v the *Secretary of State for Exiting the European Union,*[4] precisely to decide on a constitutional matter, none other than to determine whether under the constitutional order of Great Britain it was possible for the Government, in exercising the Crown's prerogative powers and without the intervention and prior decision of Parliament, to decide to serve notice on the European Union, under Article 50 of its Treaty, of the decision on the United Kingdom's withdrawal from said Union, pursuant to the people's recommendation expressed in the referendum of 23 of June, 2016. Said referendum was carried out according to the Law approved by the Parliament in 2015 (*European Union Referendum Act 2015*), on the matter of whether the United Kingdom should remain or withdraw from the European Union,[5] the people's response having been, as is known, that the United Kingdom should withdraw from said Union.

To decide on the proposed constitutional matter, the High Court confirmed that in the United Kingdom, as a constitutional democracy, the bodies of the State are subordinated to the rule of law, wherefore the courts of the United Kingdom, as stated by the High Court itself, have a:

---

2 See Allan R. Brewer-Carías, *Principios del Estado de Derecho. Aproximación Histórica,* Cuadernos de la Cátedra Mezerhane sobre democracia, Estado de derecho y derechos humanos, Miami Dade College, Editorial Jurídica Venezolana International, Miami 2016, pp. 38 ss

3 Case *Gina Miller* et al. v *the Secretary of State for Exiting the European Union* (Case No: CO/3809/2016 and CO/3281/2016). See the text of the decision: https://www.judiciary.gov.uk/judgments/r-miller-v-secretary-of-state-for-exiting-the-european-union-accessible/

4 *Idem*

5 See http://www.legislation.gov.uk/ukpga/2015/36/contents/enacted/data.htm. The question in the referendum was: «*Should the United Kingdom remain a member of the European Union or leave the European Union?*».

«constitutional duty fundamental to the rule of law in a democratic state to enforce the rules of constitutional law in the same way as the courts enforce other laws».

This statement by the High Court is without doubt one of the clearest acknowledgements by the British judicial bodies regarding the existence of a constitutional jurisdiction in the United Kingdom,[6] based on which the High Court, exercising its power of judicial review, confirmed that in order to decide on this specific case, it was precisely called upon to:

«apply the constitutional law of the United Kingdom to determine whether the Crown has prerogative powers to give notice under Article 50 of the Treaty on the European Union to trigger the process for withdrawal from the European Union».

All this set clear that the United Kingdom has a constitution as supreme rule that prevails over State bodies decisions, and that the courts have judicial review powers over State decisions.[7]

II. THE «BREXIT» CASE

The case of *Gina Miller et al. v the Secretary of State for Exiting the European Union* before the High Court was, therefore, a typical constitutional proceeding or judicial review of the constitutionality of the Government's decision,[8] in this case of a preventative nature, in view of the British Government's official announcement that was made public after the governmental readjustment caused by the outcome of the referendum, to give notice to the European Union of the United Kingdom´s withdrawal therefrom.

In this proceeding, the High Court based its decision on the consideration that the *European Communities Act* of 1972 (*ECA 1972*),[9] which made the community law effective in the national legal system of the United Kingdom, was a constitutional law to which the Government was subject and which it could in no way modify by exercising the Crown's prerogative powers.

The constitutional rank («constitutional statute») of the Act, according to the High Court, was confirmed in due time by the House of Lords in *R* v *Secretary of State for Transport, ex p. Factortame Ltd* [1990] 2 AC 85, deeming that the ECA 1972 was in force as long as it remained in the statute book, granting a direct and prevailing effect to the law of the European Union over the primary domestic or national legislation. That is, by virtue of the *ECA 1972*, the national courts give full effect to the law of the European Union as part of the internal law applied by them.

As Lawton LJ stated in *Thoburn v Sunderland City Council* [2003] QB 151 (DC) at [62], quoted in the decision: «It may be there has never been a statute having such profound effects on so many dimensions of our daily lives», considering the ECA 1972:

---

6 I anticipated this some years ago when analyzing the situation of the constitutional courts in comparative constitutional law. See Allan R. Brewer-Carías, *Constitutional Courts as Positive Legislators in Comparative Law*, Cambridge University Press, New York 2010, p. 25

7 Something that had not been readily accepted some decades ago. See Allan R. Brewer-Carías, *Judicial Review in Comparative Law*, Cambridge University Press, Cambridge 1989.

8 See, in general, regarding constitutional proceedings: Allan R. Brewer-Carías, *Derecho Procesal Constitucional. Instrumentos para la Justicia Constitucional*, Editorial Jurídica Venezolana International, 2015.

9 See in http://www.legislation.gov.uk/ukpga/1972/68/contents

«as a constitutional statute, having such importance in our legal system that it is not subject to the usual wide principle of implied repeal by subsequent legislation. Its importance is such that it could only be repealed or amended by express language in a subsequent statute or by necessary implication from the provisions of such a statute. Similarly, the ECA 1972 was described as one of a number of constitutional instruments by Lord Neuberger of Abbotsbury PSC and Lord Mance JSC in R (Buckinghamshire County Council) v Secretary of State for Transport [2014] UKSC 3; [2014] 1 WI.R 324. at [207]».

Said parliamentary law, of a constitutional rank, sealed the incorporation of the United Kingdom into the European Community, which was materialized on the 1st of January 1973, and was enacted as a result of the condition established in the Community's law: that in order for the same to be incorporated into domestic law, it should be approved by a primary legislation in each State. As stated by the High Court in its decision,

«the Crown could not have ratified the accession of the United Kingdom to the European Communities under the Community Treaties unless Parliament had enacted legislation. Legislation by Parliament was needed to give effect to EU law in the domestic law of the jurisdictions in the United Kingdom as was required by those Treaties and as was necessary to give effect in domestic law to the rights and obligations arising under EU law».

The constitutional proceeding before the High Court, questioning the possibility that the Government could decide alone on the United Kingdom's withdrawal from the European Union, was brought by a British citizen who filed an action equivalent to the so-called *acción popular de constitucionalidad* for judicial review of constitutionality in Latin American law.[10] The *actio popularis* was filed precisely against the Government's purported intention to give such notice, and the court recognized such citizen's legal standing since such challenge could be brought by everyone in the United Kingdom or with British citizenship whose interests might be affected if the notice to withdraw from the European Union were served. The claimant in the proceeding was joined by other persons and lawyers dealing, among others, with matters of parliamentary sovereignty; the impact that such notice would have on the freedom of movement rights under the EU Law of British citizens who lived in other member States and had access to public services there; and how would the immigration status of persons living in the United Kingdom be affected as a result of the notice under Article 50.

It was accepted that the defense of this case be conducted by the U.K.'s Secretary of State for Exiting the European Union, considering that it was the appropriate body to act in the name of the Government on behalf of the Crown, thus covering the action by any other minister of the government.

---

10 See Allan R. Brewer-Carías, «Acción popular de inconstitucionalidad», in Eduardo Ferrer Mac-Gregor, Fabiola Martínez Ramírez, Giovanni A. Figueroa Mejía (Coordinadores), *Diccionario de derecho procesal constitucional y convencional*, Poder Judicial de la Federación, Consejo de la Judicatura Federal, Universidad Nacional Autónoma de México, Instituto de Investigaciones Jurídicas, Serie Doctrina Jurídica, N° 692, pp. 232-233.
Something that was not readily accepted some decades ago. See Allan R. Brewer-Carías, *Judicial Review in Comparative Law*, Cambridge University Press, Cambridge 1989.

III. THE CONSTITUTIONAL MATTER POSED

The matter posed by the plaintiffs to the High Court was that:

«it is a fundamental principle of the UK constitution that the Crown's prerogative cannot be used by the executive government to diminish or repeal rights under the law of the United Kingdom (whether conferred by common law or statute, unless Parliament has given authority to the Crown (expressly in or by necessary implication from the terms of an Act of Parliament) to diminish or abrogate such rights».

The plaintiffs also argued that one cannot find any express or implicit word in the *ECA 1972* or in any other subsequent legislation related to the European Union, whereby Parliament would have conferred such authority to the executive government to start the process of terminating the European Union Treaty; and that Parliament did not grant any authority to the Crown in the *Referendum Act of 2015*, to serve the notice referred to in Article 50 of the Treaty on the European Union.

This was, as stated in the decision, a «pure matter of law» that was deemed entirely justiciable under the United Kingdom constitution, which, of course, had nothing to do with the merits or demerits of the decision to exit the European Union, which the Court deemed to be «a political issue»[11] beyond its jurisdiction.

The justiciable matter, as inferred from the plaintiffs' allegations, was ultimately to determine whether under the constitutional law of the United Kingdom, the Government, in exercising the Crown's prerogative powers and without Parliament's intervention, could serve, pursuant to Article 50 of the Treaty on the European Union, the official notice of the governmental decision to exit the same; basing this on the assumption, which had been accepted by the parties, that neither the *Referendum Act of 2015* nor any other Act of Parliament had conferred upon the Government any legal authority other than the prerogative powers of the Crown, that would enable it to give said notice under Article 50.

On the other hand, the Court also stated that the system governing the European Community's procedure for a State to exit the European Union implies that once a State gives notice of its decision under Article 50 of the Union's Treaty, there starts to run a term of two years to negotiate a withdrawal agreement. This notice, as accepted by the Government in the proceeding», cannot be subject to conditions such as, for example, the Parliament's approval. The consequence of this notice according to Article 50 was, as noted by the Court, that upon completing the State's process for exiting the European Union, British citizens will unavoidably lose some of the rights sanctioned in the law of the European Union, which precisely were included in the domestic law of the United Kingdom by the *ECA 1972*.

IV. CONSTITUTIONAL PRINCIPLES OF THE UNITED KINGDOM CONSIDERED

In deciding the case, the High Court analyzed the «constitutional principles» of the United Kingdom, highlighting what it stated to be the most fundamental

---

[11] The Court added in its decision that the same «cannot interfere *in* the government's policies, because government policy is not law. The policies to be applied by the executive branch of the government and the merits or demerits of the exit are matters of political opinion to be settled through a political process».

rule of the UK's constitution: «that Parliament is sovereign and, as such, can make and unmake any law it chooses;» one of the aspects of Parliament's sovereignty, established hundreds of years ago, being that the Crown - that is, the Government - cannot exercise its prerogative powers to repeal legislation enacted by Parliament.

The Court deemed that this principle was of the utmost importance when analyzing the context of the general rule on which the Government sought to base its argument in this case, which was the executive branch's competence, in exercising Royal prerogative powers, to conduct international relations and enter into or denounce treaties on matters deemed to fall within the scope of such prerogative powers.

The High Court deemed that such a general rule actually exists, but is only valid on the international scope, not having such prerogative any effect on the domestic law established in the legislation enacted by Parliament. Citing Lord Oliver of Aylmerton in his presentation in the *Tin Council case, J.H. Rayner (Mincing Lane) Ltd* v *Department of Trade and Industry* [1990] 2 AC 418, at 499E-500D, the High Court deemed that

> «as a matter of constitutional law of the United Kingdom, the Royal Prerogative, whilst it embraces the making of treaties, does not extend to altering the law or conferring rights upon individuals or depriving individuals of rights which they enjoy in domestic law without the intervention of Parliament».

Lord Oliver of Aylmerton concluded by stating the principle that «a treaty is not part of English law unless and until it has been incorporated into the law by legislation».

Therefore, in deciding, the High Court stated - which the Government accepted and argued in a positive way -, that if the notice were served pursuant to Article 50, this would inevitably alter the effects of domestic law in the sense that the legal provisions of the European Union that Parliament had made part of domestic law by enacting the *ECA 1972*, in due time would thereupon cease to be effective.

The Government's main allegation to counteract this reasoning was that it should be assumed that Parliament, when enacting the *ECA 1972*, had the intention to consider that the Crown would retain its prerogative powers to decide on the United Kingdom's exiting the Treaties on the European Community (then, the Treaty on the European Community), and also that the Crown would have the power to decide whether the law of the European Union should continue to be in effect in the sphere of the domestic law of the United Kingdom. The High Court did not accept this reasoning in its decision, but rather deemed that there were no grounds for this in the *ECA 1972*, dismissing it and accepting the arguments brought forth by the plaintiffs, on the basis of the language used by Parliament in said Law, on the constitutional principle of Parliament's sovereignty, and on the Crown's lack of power to change domestic law by exercising its prerogative powers.

Based on these arguments, the High Court of Justice decided that the Government of the United Kingdom had no power based on the Royal prerogative power to serve the notice contemplated in Article 50 of the Treaty on the European Union for the United Kingdom to withdraw from or exit the European Union.

V. A LESSON ON THE CONSTITUTIONAL LAW OF THE UNITED KINGDOM

Besides the importance that the decision by the High Court of Justice of the United Kingdom had for the European community law and for the future of the European Union, the decision of 3rd of November, 2016, is of special importance for those interested in constitutional law, particularly Continental and Latin American law, because the same is in itself, as stated, a clear lesson on the contemporary constitutional law of the United Kingdom, particularly with regard to the rules governing the relationship between the legislative and executive powers, established on the basis of the constitutional principles of parliamentary sovereignty and the prerogative power of the Crown.

1. *Principle of Sovereignty of the Parliament of the United Kingdom*

In fact, as argued by the High Court, the primary rule of the United Kingdom's constitutional law is the principle of the sovereignty of Parliament, that is of the «Crown in Parliament», which is sovereign, so that the legislation enacted «by the Crown with the consent of both Houses of Parliament is supreme».

Consequently, only Parliament can enact the primary legislation of the United Kingdom and change the laws however it may decide, there being no law above the primary legislation, with the sole exception of cases in which Parliament itself has expressly provided that this be otherwise; as It was precisely the case of the ECA 1972, whereby it granted precedence to the law of the European Union over the acts of Parliament.

But, even in those cases, Parliament continues to be sovereign and supreme, and to have full powers to remove any authority or rank given to other laws by means of previous primary legislation.

To summarize, the Court concluded that, «Parliament has the power to abrogate the *ECA 1972*, if it so resolves», going on to review the traditional doctrinal principles of British constitutional law, starting with what it considered the leading doctrine contained in the book of professor A.V. Dicey, *An Introduction to the Law of the Constitution*, where he explains that the parliamentary sovereignty principle means that Parliament has:

> «the right to make or unmake any law whatever; and further, that no person or body is recognised by the law of England as having a right to override or set aside the legislation of Parliament».[12]

In the opinion of the High Court, this means, among other things, that a law cannot be said to be invalid because it is opposed to the electorate's opinion, since as a legal principle:

> «The judges know nothing about any will of the people except in so far as that will is expressed by an Act of Parliament and would never suffer the validity of a statute to be questioned on the grounds of its having been passed or being kept alive in opposition to the wishes of the electors».[13]

This Parliamentary sovereignty principle, as stated by the High Court, has been recognized in many cases by leaders of the highest judicial authority, wherefore,

---

[12] Quoted by the Court: «p. 38 of the 8th edition, 1915, the last edition by Dicey himself; and see chapter 1 generally».

[13] Quoted by the Court: «*ibid.* pp. 57 and 72».

since it is an accepted principle, it has merely quoted the presentation made by Lord Bingham of Cornhill in *R (Jackson) v Attorney General* [2005] UK HI. 56; [2006] 1 AC 262 at para., stating that «the bedrock of the British constitution... is the supremacy of the Crown in Parliament.»..

2. *On the matter of the limits of the Crown's prerogative powers*

As to the powers of the Crown pursuant to its prerogative (often referred to as «regal prerogative»), the Court touched on its extension, considering that such «prerogative powers are the residue of discretionary or arbitrary authority, which at any given time is legally left in the hands of the Crown», citing in support thereof what was stated by Lord Re in *Burmah Oil Co (Burma Trading) Ltd* v *Lord Advocate* [1965] AC 75, at 101:

> «The prerogative is really a relic of a past age, not lost by disuse, but only available for a case not covered by statute».

With regard to the prerogative, the Court stated that an important aspect of the Parliamentary sovereignty principle is that the primary legislation is not subject to replacement by the Crown by exercising its prerogative powers; further adding that the «constitutional limits» on such powers are even more extensive, considering that the Crown has those prerogative powers only when they are recognized by the common law and their exercise is only effective within the limits acknowledged thereby. Beyond these limits, the Crown has no power to alter laws, whether they be part of common law or the legislation.

The Court stated that the subordination of the Crown, and particularly that of the executive Government, to the law, is the foundation of the rule of law in the United Kingdom, with its roots settled much before the war between the Crown and Parliament in the 17th Century, which was finally confirmed, as heretofore acknowledged, in the agreement reached after the Glorious Revolution of 1688.[14]

To support this statement, the Court then cited what Sir Edward Coke referred as his opinion and that of contemporary judges of renown regarding the *The Case of Proclamations* (1610) 12 Co, Rep. 74, in the sense that «The King by his proclamation or other ways cannot change any part of the common law, or statute law, or the customs of the realm», and that «the King hath no prerogative, but that which the law of the land allows him».

This, in the opinion of the High Court, was confirmed in the first two parts of the First Section of the Bill of Rights of 1688, to wit:

> «Powers of suspension: The pretended power of suspending the laws and dispensing with laws by regal authority without consent of Parliament is illegal.
>
> Late dispensing power - That the pretended power of dispensing with laws or the execution of laws by regal authority as it hath been assumed and exercised of late is illegal».

---

[14] See comments that I made on this matter in Allan R. Brewer-Carías, *Reflexiones sobre la revolución norteamericana (1776), la revolución francesa (1789) y la revolución hispanoamericana (1810-1830) y sus aportes al constitucionalismo moderno*, 2ª Edici0n Ampliada, Serie Derecho Administrativo No. 2, Universidad Externado de Colombia, Editorial Jurídica Venezolana, Bogotá 2008.

This legal stance, as the High Court recalled, was summarized by the *Privy Council,* in *The Zamora* [1916] 2 AC 77, at 90, as follows:

> «The idea that the King in Council, or indeed any branch of the Executive, has power to prescribe or alter the law to be administered by the Courts of law in this country is out of harmony with the principles of our Constitution. It is true that, under a number of modern statutes, various branches of the Executive have power to make the rules having the force of statutes, but all such rules derive their validity from the statute which creates the power, and not from the executive body by which they are made. No one would contend that the prerogative involves any power to prescribe or alter the law administered in Courts of Common Law or Equity...».

The High Court considered these principles to be generally accepted, hence deeming it unnecessary to explain them in greater detail, and on the basis thereof it analyzed the matter of the Crown's power to make and unmake treaties, with reduced effects in the international sphere and no effects on domestic law, as explained above.

VI. CONSTITUTIONAL INTERPRETATION AND CONSTITUTIONAL CONTROL

With this, the Court went on to exercise its constitutional oversight over the Executive's intention to issue the notice contemplated in Article 50 of the Treaty on the European Union, deemed to be a constitutional law, without the intervention of Parliament, for which the Court set a series of criteria on constitutional interpretation.

1. *The principle of the presumption of constitutionality of Acts of Parliament*

The first one was the classical criterion of the presumption of constitutionality of Parliament's acts, in the sense that where constitutional principles are strong, there is a presumption that «Parliament legislates in conformity with them and not to undermine them», citing multiple judicial decisions in support thereof, for example, considering that there is a strong presumption against Parliament being deemed to have intended to give retrospective effect to a legal provision, even if the language used in the statute might appear to create such effect; as well as with regard to the territorial effects of statutes. There is also strong presumption that Parliament does not intend to preclude access to the ordinary courts for determination of disputes.[15] The High Court continued its reasoning stating that:

> «All these presumptions can be overridden by Parliament if it so chooses, but the stronger the constitutional principle the stronger the presumption that

[15] Quotes by the Court: «see, for example, *Anisminic Ltd v Foreign Compensation Commission* [1969] 1 AC 147. Another example, debated at some length at the hearing, is the principle of legality, i.e. the presumption that Parliament does not intend to legislate in a way which would defeat fundamental human rights: see R v *Secretary of State for the Home Department, ex p. Pierson* [1998] AC 539 at 573G, 575B-G (Lord Browne-Wilkinson) and *R* v *Secretary of State for the Home Department, ex p. Simms* [2000] 1 AC 115, 131D-G (Lord Hoffmann). see, for example, *Anisminic Ltd v Foreign Compensation Commission* [1969] 1 AC 147. Another example, debated at some length at the hearing, is the principle of legality, i.e. the presumption that Parliament does not intend to legislate in a way which would defeat fundamental human rights: see R v *Secretary of State for the Home Department, ex p. Pierson* [1998] AC 539 at 573G, 575B-G (Lord Browne-Wilkinson) and *R* v *Secretary of State for the Home Department, ex p. Simms* [2000] 1 AC 115, 131D-G (Lord Hoffmann)».

Parliament did not intend to override it and the stronger the material required, in terms of express language or clear necessary implication before the inference can properly be drawn that in fact it did so intend. Similarly, the stronger the constitutional principle, the more readily can it be inferred that words used by Parliament were intended to carry a meaning which reflects the principle».

This interpretation was important, in the opinion of the High Court, because the Secretary of State, in his argument when interpreting the *ECA 1972* omitting part of the constitutional background referred to above, alleged that it was up to the appellants to identify the express language in the statute that eliminated the Crown's prerogative with regard to the conduct of international relations on behalf of the United Kingdom. That is, the Secretary of State alleging in his defense that it was necessary to find an express and, in any event, clear language that evidenced that Parliament had the intention to remove the Crown's prerogative power to take the necessary steps for the United Kingdom to withdraw from the European Communities and the Treaty on the European Community.

In making this allegation, in the Court's view, the Secretary of State did not assign in his analysis of the *ECA 1972*, any value to the constitutional principle that, only when Parliament legislates otherwise, the Crown's prerogative powers cannot be used to amend the law of the land.

Consequently, the High Court dismissed the allegations of the Secretary of State on the grounds of two constitutional principles.

2. *The principle that the Crown has no prerogative power to alter domestic legislation*

First, the constitutional principle that the Crown has no prerogative power to alter domestic legislation, which in the opinion of the High Court, is the result of an especially strong constitutional tradition of the United Kingdom and the democracies which follow that tradition.[16] The principle evolved through the long struggle referred to above, which asserted parliamentary sovereignty and restricted the Crown's prerogative powers. For this reason, the High Court deemed that it would have been surprising if, in light of that tradition, Parliament, as the sovereign body under the Constitution, should have intended to leave the continued existence of all the rights it introduced into domestic law by enacting the *ECA 1972* subject to the choice of the Crown, in exercising its prerogative powers, either to allow the Community Treaties to continue in place or to have the United Kingdom withdraw therefrom. The High Court added, as Lord Browne-Wilkinson put it in *R* v *Secretary of State for the Home Department, ex p. Fire Brigades Union* [1995] 2 AC 513 at 552E:

> «It is for Parliament, not the executive, to repeal legislation. The constitutional history of this country is the history of the prerogative powers of the Crown being made subject to the overriding powers of the democratically elected legislature as the sovereign body».

In this context, the High Court also deemed it relevant to bear in mind the profound effects which Parliament intended to produce on domestic law by enacting the *ECA 1972*, which precisely has led to its being identified as a «statute of special

[16] Quote by the Court: «see for example the New Zealand decision in *Fitzgerald v Muldoon* [1976] 2 NZLR 615 at 622).'

constitutional significance», wherefore due to the profound and extended legal changes it brought about, it is especially unlikely that Parliament intended to leave their continued existence in the hands of the Crown through the exercise of its prerogative powers. Parliament having taken the major step of setting the direct and prevailing effect of the EU law in the national legal system, by passing the *ECA 1972* as primary legislation, it was not plausible to suppose that Parliament intended that the Crown be able, through its own unilateral action pursuant to its prerogative powers, to eliminate its effect.

Moreover, the High Court stated that the *ECA 1972*, as a constitutional statute was such that Parliament was deemed to have made it exempted from the operation of the usual doctrine of implied repeal by enacting the subsequent inconsistent legislation.[17] To the contrary, no part of the Law could be repealed if Parliament did not clearly state such repeal in a subsequent legislation, that is to say, that it was what it wishes to do. The High Court concluded by stating that:

> «since in enacting the *ECA 1972* as a statute of major constitutional importance, Parliament has indicated that it should be exempt from casual implied repeal by Parliament itself, still less can it be thought to be likely that Parliament nonetheless intended that its legal effects could be removed by the Crown through the use of its prerogative powers».

3. *The principle that the conduct of international relations is a matter for the Crown with no effect on domestic law*

The second constitutional principle referred to by the Court in deciding was the above-mentioned principle that the conduct of international relations is a matter for the Crown through the use of its prerogative powers, and that those powers have no effect on domestic law, it being a principle accepted by the courts that this is a field of action left to the Crown without the interference of Parliament. But the justification for a presumption of non-interference with the Crown's prerogative in the conduct of international affairs is substantially impaired in the case at issue, in which the Secretary of State, to the contrary, stated that he could bring about major changes by exercising the Crown's prerogative powers, and this was rejected by the Court.

The High Court's conclusion when interpreting the *ECA 1972* in light of the constitutional background referred to above, sets it clear that Parliament's intention when enacting that Law and introducing the law of the European Union into domestic law was that this could not be undone by the Crown through its prerogative powers. That is, the enactment of the *ECA 1972* precluded the Crown's prerogative powers to decide on the United Kingdom's exiting the Treaties on the Community and affect the rights of citizens thereunder by serving the notice set in Article 50 of the Treaty on the European Union; consequently, rejecting the allegations made by the Secretary of State.

Finally, the High Court referred to the *Referendum Act of 2015* regarding the UK and the European Union, agreeing with the fact that the Secretary of State did not argue that the same allegedly granted statutory power to the Crown to serve the notice under Article 50 of the Treaty on the European Union, for this allegation would be untenable as a matter of statutory interpretation.

---

[17] Quote by the Court: «see *Thohurn v Sunderland City Council*, at [60]-[64], and section 2(4) of the ECA 1972».

In the opinion of the High Court, the *Referendum Act of 2015* was interpreted in light of the basic constitutional principles of Parliamentary sovereignty and representative democracy applied in the United Kingdom, which lead to the conclusion that a «referendum on any topic can only be advisory for the lawmakers in Parliament unless very clear language to the contrary is used in the referendum legislation in question», but no such language was found in the text of the Referendum Act of 2015.

Moreover, in the case of the *Referendum Act of 2015*, the High Court recalled that the relevant act:

> «was passed against a background including a clear briefing paper to parlamentarians explaining that the referendum would have advisory effect only. Moreover, Parliament must have appreciated that the referendum was intended only to be advisory as the result of a vote in the referendum in favour of leaving the European Union would inevitably leave for future decision many important questions relating to the legal implementation of withdrawal from the European Union».

In any event, the High Court concluded in its judgment that it «did not question the importance of the referendum as a political event, the significance of which will have to be assessed and taken into account elsewhere», finally deciding that «the Secretary of State has no power under the Crown's prerogative, to issue the notice pursuant to Article 50 of the *Treaty on the European Union* for the United Kingdom to exit the same».

VII. CONFIRMATION OF THE DECISION OF THE HIGH COURT OF JUSTICE BY THE SUPREME COURT OF THE UNITED KINGDOM

The decision of the High Court of Justice of 3rd of November, 2016, after being appealed by the Government, was confirmed by the Supreme Court of the United Kingdom in a judgment issued by a majority of 8 to 3, on 24th February, 2016 (Case: *R (on the application of Miller an another) v Secretary of State for Exiting the European Union)* ([2017 UKSC 5) (UKSC 2016/0196),[18] ratifying that in this case, it was necessary that an Act of Parliament authorize the Ministers to give notice of the decision on the United Kingdom's exit from the European Union.

It should be noted that after the High Court's decision of November 3, 2016, and having filed the appeal, on December 7, 2016, the House of Commons adopted a resolution calling upon the ministers to give by March 31, 2017, the relevant notice on the United Kingdom's withdrawal from the European Union, in accordance with Article 50 of the Treaties. However, in the opinion of the Supreme Court, with what the Government agreed upon in the proceeding, it was only a political decision that in no way affected the matters arising from the appeals in the proceeding.

Among such matters, the most important that was considered to decide the appeal was the Supreme Court's holding that the terms of the *ECA 1972*, which gave effect to the United Kingdom's becoming a member of the European Union, were inconsistent with the claim that Ministers could exercise any power regarding

[18] See text of the decision in: https://www.supremecourt.uk/cases/docs/uksc-2016-0196-judgment.pdf See press information on the decision in https://www.supremecourt.uk/cases/docs/uksc-2016-0196-press-summary.pdf

the exit of the United Kingdom from the Treaties on the European Union without Parliament's prior authorization.

In the Court's opinion, Section 2 of the *ECA 1972* authorized a dynamic process whereby the law of the European Union became a source of law of the United Kingdom, prevailing over the application of all other sources of the domestic law thereof, including the statutes. Therefore, while the *ECA 1972* remained in force, its effects were those of making the law of the European Union as an independent and prevailing source of domestic law. The Supreme Court also deemed that the *ECA 1972* brought about a partial transfer of law-making powers and assignment of legislative competences by Parliament to the institutions of the European Union, except and until Parliament otherwise decided. This implied that the domestic law of the United Kingdom would change when it ceased to be a member of the Treaties on the European Union, and that the rights arising from the community's law that were enjoyed by the residents of the United Kingdom would be affected.

The Supreme Court analyzed the Government's argument that the *ECA 1972* had not excluded the Ministers' power to withdraw the United Kingdom from the Treaties on the European Union, and that Section 2 of the Law set forth for the exercise of such power when giving effect to the law of the European Union only and up to the moment that the power to decide on the exit was to be exercised. However, the Supreme Court indicated that there was a vital difference between the changes that could occur in the law of the United Kingdom as a result of changes in the law of the European Union, and the changes that could result from exiting the Treaties on the European Union. In the latter case, if the relevant notice was served, the unavoidable result was due to be a fundamental change in the constitutional framework of the United Kingdom, for this would imply as indeed has implied, the elimination of the sources of law of the European Union in the domestic sphere.

In the Supreme Court's view, such a change in the constitution of the United Kingdom was due to be effected through parliamentary legislation. Furthermore, the fact that the United Kingdom's exiting the European Union implied the elimination of certain domestic rights enjoyed by the residents of the United Kingdom, made it impossible for the Government to decide to exit the Treaties of the European Union without Parliament's prior authorization.

Of course, when Parliament enacted the *ECA 1972*, it could have authorized the ministers to decide on the United Kingdom's exit from the Treaties on the European Union, in which case, however, this possibility would have to be clearly set forth in the express text of the Law, which did not occur. To the contrary, not only was there no clear wording on this matter, but the provisions of the *ECA 1972* itself expressly stated that ministers do not have such power. And the fact that ministers were accountable to Parliament for their actions was not a useful constitutional answer to settle the matter at issue, especially if the power to act did not exist, and if the decision would irrevocably void Parliament itself from acting.[19]

In any event, in the opinion of the Supreme Court, the subsequent legislation related to the European Union enacted after 1972, including the introduction of

[19] Quote by the Court: «The Supreme Court of the United Kingdom Parliament Square London SW1P 3BD T: 020 7960 1886/1887 F: 020 7960 1901 www.supremecourt.uk».

parliamentary controls with regard to decisions adopted by ministers at the level of the European Union with regard to the competencies thereof or the process for creating community regulations, although not to give the notice contemplated in Article 50 of the Treaties, was entirely consistent with Parliament's assumption that there was no power to decide the United Kingdom's exit from the Treaties in the absence of a statute that authorized it.

Finally, the Supreme Court, in its decision, also referred to the 2016 referendum, considering that while it was an event of great political importance, its legal meaning was that established by Parliament in the Law that authorized it, and the Law merely provided for it to be carried out, but did not specify its consequences. Therefore, the Supreme Court deemed that the changes in law required for implementing the results of the referendum could only be made in the sole manner permitted by the constitution of the United Kingdom, that is, by means of legislation.

The outcome of this entire constitutional proceeding carried out before the bodies competent to exercise the Constitutional Jurisdiction in the United Kingdom was, therefore, that the exit thereof from the Treaties on the European Union could only be settled by an act of Parliament deciding on the matter, and that the political recommendation expressed in the 2016 referendum had no constitutional legal effect.

This was the criterion set forth in their decisions both by the High Court of Justice and the Supreme Court of the United Kingdom, in a proceeding for judicial review or constitutional control, rejecting the possibility for the Executive to have any competence to make this decision without Parliament's prior authorization.

VIII. OUTCOME OF THE JUDICIAL REVIEW PROCEEDING AND ITS CONSTITUTIONAL CHALLENGES

The general conclusion of this entire constitutional proceeding carried out before the competent Courts in the United Kingdom on matters of Judicial Review was, therefore, that the exit from the Treaties on the European Union could only be decided through an act of Parliament - as it was finnaly decided - , and that the political recommendation expressed in the 2016 referendum had no constitutional or legal obligatory effect.

This was the criterion set forth in their decisions both by the High Court of Justice and the Supreme Court of the United Kingdom, in the proceeding for judicial review or constitutional, rejecting the possibility for the Executive to have any competence to make this decision without Parliament's prior authorization.

The immediate consequence of the judicial decisions was that on 16 of March 2017, at the request of the Government, the Parliament passed the *European Union (Notification of Withdrawal) Act 2017*, conferring «power on the Prime Minister to notify, under Article 50(2) of the Treaty on European Union, the United Kingdom's intention to withdraw from the EU».[20] The Prime Minister interpreted such Act of Parliament, as she explained in the letter dated 29 of March 2017 that she sent to Donald Rusk, President of the European Union, triggering Article 50 of the European Union Treaty,[21] as an Act that «confirmed the result of the referendum by voting

[20] See in http://www.legislation.gov.uk/ukpga/2017/9/contents/enacted/data.htm

[21] See in https://www.gov.uk/government/publications/prime-ministers-letter-to-donald-tusk-triggering-article-50/prime-ministers-letter-to-donald-tusk-triggering-article-50

with clear and convincing majorities in both of its Houses for the European Union (Notification of Withdrawal) Bill».

That is why in her statement she made before the Parliament that same day, she began by saying that: «On 23 June last year, the people of the United Kingdom voted to leave the European Union», explaining that although «that decision was no rejection of the values we share as fellow Europeans», and that «the referendum was a vote to restore, as we see it, our national self-determination», she insisted that the government was acting «on the democratic will of the British people, « and that «the United Kingdom is leaving the European Union» « in accordance with the wishes of the British people».[22]

The *European Union (Notification of Withdrawal) Act 2017* was fallowed by the *European Union (Withdrawal) Act 2018*, devoted to repeal the *European Communities Act 1972*, on exit day, and also to make other provision in connection with the withdrawal of the United Kingdom from the European Union.[23]

In any case, due to the emphasis that was given by the Prime Minster in supporting the government decision to exit the European Union, to the will of the people as expressed in the 2016 Referendum, a group of British citizens residing in other Member States of the European Union (Susan Wilson & Others Complains representing various associations named *Bremain in Spain, Fair Deal Forum, British in Italy, and Brexpats*), recently filed (13 of August 2018) before the High Court of Justice (Queen's Bench Division, Administrative Court) a new claim for Judicial Review against the Prime Minister; seeking from the Court to declare that «the Referendum result» as well as the «Decision and Notification are vitiated by reason of corrupt and illegal practices in the Referendum».[24]

As stated in the Complaint:

> «The Prime Minister and the Secretary of State have repeatedly stated the basis for the Prime Minister's decision to withdraw the UK from the EU was that a majority of those who voted in the referendum voted in favor of leaving the EU and the Government had promised to honor the result of the referendum.
>
> It follows that the basis for the Prime Minister's decision to withdraw and notify was her understanding that there had been a lawful, free and fair vote which had produced a result of 51.89% of those voting, voting in favor of the UK leaving the EU (or 34.73% of the voting public, turnout according to the Electoral Commission)».[25]

The Claimants argued that the Prime Minister was obliged to exercise its powers according to the *European Union (Withdrawal) 2017 and 2018 Acts*, in a «lawfully

---

22 See in https://www.gov.uk/government/speeches/prime-ministers-commons-statement-on-triggering-article-50

23 See in http://www.legislation.gov.uk/ukpga/2018/16/introduction/enacted

24 See the document on the case, Susan Wilson & Others Claimants , and The Prime Minister Defendant, Grounds For Judicial Review (Croft Solicitors) 13 August 2018 in http://www.croftsolicitors.com/wp-content/uploads/2018/08/239484-Grounds-for-Judicial-Review-and-Statement-of-Facts.pdf. See also the information in: http://www.croftsolicitors.com/croft-solicitors-are-representing-clients-in-a-court-challenge-against-brexit-on-the-ground-of-the-breaches-of-electoral-law-of-the-campaigns-during-the-2016-referendum/

25 Idem.

and rationally» way, subjected to «public law principles, in accordance with: (i) the principle of legality; (ii) common law principles of constitutionality;» and (iii) «in accordance with the UK's constitutional requirements» and among them, the «well established principles which value and seek to preserve the integrity of democracy, including the voting process, as well as lawful decision-making».

In the case of the Referendum, the Claimants argued that «it is now clear that it was not conducted in accordance with the UK's constitutional requirements, including the express statutory provisions regulating campaigning in the Referendum», founding its arguments on two *Reports by the Electoral Commission* (May and July 2018),[26] referred to «corrupt and illegal practices» followed in the process of the Referendum.

For all those reasons the Complaints argued that having the Prime Minister «repeatedly emphasized» that her Decision to withdraw from the EU was «based solely upon the outcome of the Referendum», relying upon its outcome, that «factual premises» «can now be seen to be flawed by reason of the said corrupt and illegal practices».

Consequently, the Complaints concluded that being «now known», that the result of the Referendum was «vitiated by corrupt and illegal practices», then «the basis of the decision made by Prime Minister [is] thereby fundamentally undermined», in the sense that «neither the decision nor notification under Article 50 was in accordance with the UK's constitutional requirements», eventually «respectfully» inviting the Court «to grant the relief sought or such relief as it may think fit».

Nonetheless, if the High Court in its ruling of 2016 decided that in the United Kingdom, a law cannot be invalid because it is opposed to the electorate's opinion, it seemed that in this new case, the outcome could be in the same line, following what was stated by the High Court in 2016, when it affirmed that:

> «The judges know nothing about any will of the people except in so far as that will is expressed by an Act of Parliament and would never suffer the validity of a statute to be questioned on the grounds of its having been passed or being kept alive in opposition to the wishes of the electors».

In any case, after countless political events, on 23th January 2020, Parliament sanctioned the *European Union (Withdrawal Agreement) Act 2020* to implement the agreement between the United Kingdom and the EU under Article 50(2) of the EU Treaty which sets out the arrangements for the United Kingdom's withdrawal from the EU.[27] An finally, after months of endless negotiations, the United Kingdom and European Union finally agreed a deal defining their future relationship, which came into effect at 23.00GMT on 31 December 2020.

---

[26] «50.1 Report on an investigation in respect of the Leave.EU Group Limited (Concerning pre-poll transaction reports and the campaign spending return for the 2016 referendum on the UK's membership of the European Union) dated 11 May 2018 («the Leave.EU Report»). 50.2 Report of an investigation in respect of Vote Leave Limited, Mr Darren Grimes, BeLeave, Veterans for Britain (Concerning campaign funding and spending for the 2016 referendum on the UK's membership of the EU), dated 17 July 2018 («the Vote Leave & Others Report»)». In *Idem*

[27] See the text at: https://www.legislation.gov.uk/ukpga/2020/1/enacted/data.htm

III

Finally, in this book, and as a general update on these matters of Judicial Review in Comparative Law, in particular regarding the role of Constitutional Courts, acting as «Positive Legislators», observed during the past decades, I am including as an *Addendum* the text of the oral Presentation I made of my *General Report* on that subject of *«Constitutional Courts as Positive Legislators»*,[28] which I delivered at the - *International Congress of Comparative Law* of the International Academy of Comparative Law held in Washington DC. in July 2010.[29]

New York, 1rst February 2021

[28] See the text of the General Report and of all the National Reports I received, in Allan R. Brewer-Carías, *Constitutional Courts as Positive Legislators*, Cambridge University Press New York, 2011, 933 pp..

[29] See Allan R. Brewer-Carías, «Constitutional Courts as Positive Legislators», in Karen B. Brown y David V. Snyder (Editors), *General Reports of the XVIIIth Congress pf the International Academy of Comparative Law- Rapports Généraux du XVIIIème Congrès de l'Académie Internationale de Droit Comparé*, Springer, 2012, pp. 549-569.

INTRODUCTION

Judicial Review, in its original North American sense, is the power of courts to decide upon the constitutionality of legislative acts, in other words, the judicial control of the constitutionality of legislation.

It has been said that judicial review is the most distinctive feature of the North American constitutional system[1] and we must add that, in fact, it is the most distinctive feature of almost all the constitutional systems in the world today. All over the world, with or without similarities to the North American system of judicial review, the courts -special constitutional courts or ordinary courts- have the power to declare a law unconstitutional. Accordingly, they have the power to refuse to enforce it, because it is considered null or void, and in some cases, they have the power to declare the annulment of the said unconstitutional law.

As we all know, the system of the United Kingdom is quite different, and we could even say that the main feature that also distinguishes the British constitutional system is precisely the lack of judicial review of legislation. Perhaps that is why Professor D.G.T. Williams of this Faculty said:

> «Most British judges and the vast majority of British lawyers must have had little or no contact with the problems and workings of judicial review».[2]

This substantial difference between the constitutional systems of the United Kingdom and, in general, the other constitutional systems in the world derives from a few but very important principles, unique to the British constitution, and influencing all of them. It is the principle of the sovereignty of Parliament, called by Dicey the «secret source of strength of the British constitution» or «element of power which has been the true source of its life and growth».[3]

This principle, with all its importance in constitutional law in Great Britain, is, at the same time, the most powerful obstacle to judicial review of the constitutionality of legislation. It implies that even if it is true that the courts in this country are the ultimate guarantors the rule of law, they are bound to apply an Act of Parliament whatever view the judges take of its morality or justice, or of its effects on important individual liberties or human right.[4] And this is because of the

---

1 E.S. Corwin, «Judicial Review», *Encyclopaedia of the Social Sciences*, Vol. VII-VIII, p. 457.

2 D.G.T. Williams, «The Constitution of the United Kingdom», *Cambridge Law Journal*, 31, (1) 1972-B, p. 277.

3 A.V. Dicey, *England's Case Against Home Rule* (3rd. ed. 1887), p. 168 quoted by D.G.T. Williams, *loc. cit.*, p. 277.

4 T.R.S. Allan, «Legislative Supremacy and the Rule of Law: Democracy and Constitutionalism», *Cambridge Law Journal*, 44, 1, 1985, p. 116.

absence of a written constitution in the modern constitutional form, with its entrenched declaration of fundamental rights and liberties.

It will suffice at this point to quote the words of Lord Wilberforce in the House of Lords case of *Pickin* v. *British Railways Board* in 1974, in a conclusive way regarding the consequences of parliamentary sovereignty and also concerning the absence of judicial review of legislation. In that particular case, it was stated:

> «The idea.... that an Act of Parliament, public or private, or a provision in an Act of Parliament, could be declared invalid or ineffective in the courts on account of some irregularity in Parliamentary procedure, or on the ground that Parliament in passing it was misled, or on the ground that it was obtained by deception or fraud, has been decisively repudiated by authorities of the highest standing from 1842 onwards. The remedy for a Parliamentary wrong, if one has been committed, must be sought from Parliament, and cannot be gained from courts».[5]

Therefore, this course on *Judicial Review in Comparative Law* naturally will not be related to the British constitutional system and could not be written from a British lawyer's point of view. Rather, it will be, and ought to be, a course on comparative foreign law on the subject in which we will study the most important systems of judicial means and actions that could be brought before the courts by individuals to obtain control of the legislation by the courts.

Because they are means which can also lead to judicial control of the constitutionality of legislation, we will also study the most important actions that could be brought before the courts by individuals for the defense and protection of their fundamental freedoms and rights established in the constitution.

In this respect, the course will be divided into six parts. In the first part, we will study the concept of what is called in continental and Latin-American law, l'*État de droit*, *Estado de Derecho*, *Stato di diritto* or *Rechtstaat*; terms that do not have an exact equivalent in English. The expressions *legal state*, state *according to law* or *rule of law* have been used for the same purpose, though we think there is no real equivalent.

In this first part, we will study the main features of the modern *État de droit*, and in particular, the consequences of the limitation and distribution of state powers; the principle of legality, as a basic concept more related to the idea of the English concept of the rule of law; and the establishment of entrenched fundamental liberties and rights. All these features are related to the process of the constitutionalization of the *État de droit*, which we will refer to in the second part with particular historical references to the process of constitutionalization or constitutionalism in North America, France and Latin America in the late eighteenth and early nineteenth centuries. This concept of the state according to the law, old and new, is the one that leads us, in the non British contemporary constitutional systems, to the possibility of a judicial review of all the acts of the state, including, the judicial control of the constitutionality of legislative acts.

In the other four parts of the course, we will study in particular the judicial review of the constitutionality of legislation, which can be considered as we

---

5 A.C. 765 (1974)- See the text also in O. HOOD PHILLIPS, *Leading Cases in Constitutional and Administrative Law*, London 1979, pp. 1-6. See the comments in P. ALLOTT, «The Court and Parliament: Who whom?», *Cambridge Law Journal*, 38, 1, 1979, pp. 80-81.

mentioned, one of the main consequences of the constitutionalization of the modern *État de droit*.

This judicial review of the constitutionality of legislation, in other words, of laws and other legislative acts, requires at least three conditions for it to function in a given constitutional system. In the first place, it requires the existence of a written constitution, conceived as a superior and fundamental law with clear supremacy over all other laws. Secondly, such a constitution must be of a «rigid» character, which implies that the amendments or reforms that may be introduced can only be put into practice by means of a particular and special process, preventing the ordinary legislator from doing so. And thirdly, the establishment in that same written and rigid constitution, of the judicial means for guaranteeing the supremacy of the constitution, over all other state acts, including legislative acts.

Judicial review of legislation as the power of courts to decide upon the constitutionality of legislation has been considered one of the main contributions of the North American constitutional system to the political and constitutional sciences.[6] However, the so-called «American system» of judicial review is not the only one that exists in present constitutional law. There is also the so called «Austrian system» of judicial review, originally established in the 1920 Austrian constitution and the mixed systems, mainly in Latin America, that have adopted the main feature of both the American and Austrian systems.

The main distinction between both systems of judicial review of legislation, the American and the Austrian systems is based on the judicial organs that can exercise this power of constitutional control: The «American system» entrusts that power of control to all the courts of a given country. It is for this reason that the system is considered to be a decentralized or diffused one. On the contrary, the «Austrian system» entrusts the power of control of the constitutionality of laws either to one existing court or to a special court, and it is therefore considered a centralized or concentrated control system.

In the course, we will study the most important systems of each of those two types of judicial review. Within the «American system», we will analyze not only the North American system, but also a few of those systems that have been influenced by it including various Latin-American systems, such as the Mexican, and Argentinean systems. We will also study others that have developed in many of Britain's former colonies such as Canada, Australia and India, and those that over a certain period were influenced by the North American system such as the Japanese constitutional system in 1947.

Within the so-called «Austrian system» we will examine the most important continental European systems of constitutional courts or tribunals, such as the Austrian, the German, the Italian and the Spanish. We will also consider, although it is an incomplete centralized system, the French constitutional council system and its very important recent developments.

However, there are also mixed systems of control of the constitutionality of legislation. They combine the decentralized systems, characterized by the assignment of power of control to all judges with the features of the centralized system that

---

6 J.A.C. GRANT, «El control jurisdiccional de la constitucionalidad de las leyes: una contribución de las Américas a la Ciencia Política», *Revista de la Facultad de Derecho de México*, 45, 1962, pp. 417-437.

empower the Supreme Court to declare the annulment of any particular law by means of a «popular action» that can be brought before the Supreme Court by any individual. The Colombian and Venezuelan systems offer good examples of this and also in an incomplete form, does the Swiss system. We will analyze individually and comparatively the most important of all those systems of judicial review or control of the constitutionality of legislation.

Finally, we will also study particular aspects of the control of constitutionality, related to fundamental liberties and rights. As we have already mentioned, one of the main features of the process of constitutionalization of the *État de droit* has been the formal establishment of an entrenched declaration of fundamental liberties and human rights in written constitutions with adequate guarantees. Within such guarantees, there are judicial means for the protection of such liberties and rights, in particular special judicial actions, claims or writs established for that purpose by a given legal order.

Apart from the classic «writ of habeas corpus», there are the special «action for protection» (*amparo*) of fundamental rights developed since the last century in most Latin American countries, including the universally known *juicio de amparo* - literally «judgment of protection»- of Mexico, and the recently developed equivalent recourse for protection in continental Europe, particularly in Germany and Spain. We will refer to all those institutions as a means for judicial review of legislation.

Therefore, this course will refer to judicial review of the constitutionality of legislative acts in comparative law in legal systems other than the system of Great Britain, where the control of the constitutionality of acts of Parliament by the courts is inconceivable and the protection of fundamental rights is ensured by the courts by means of ordinary remedies of common law and equity and not by special judicial means.

PART ONE

THE MODERN STATE SUBMITTED TO THE RULE OF LAW (ÉTAT DE DROIT)

I. THE MODERN ÉTAT DE DROIT

The subject of judicial review or judicial control over the exercise of power is, undoubtedly, one of the basic and most characteristic elements of all contemporary states. Due to the submission of the state to the rule of law, one can say that at present time, all states have some system of judicial control or review over activities resulting from the exercise of public powers. In this respect we can also say that the concept of judicial review over the exercise of power is essentially related to the classical but current concept of what in English terminology is known, as we have already mentioned, as the state according to law or the state according to the rule of law, equivalent to the German *Rechtstaat*, the French *État de droit*, the Spanish *Estado de Derecho* and the Italian *Stato di Diritto*. This concept of the state according to law is based on the principle that not only must all the power of the public bodies forming the state stem from the law, or be established by law, but also that those powers are limited by law.

According to this concept, the law becomes, as far as the state is concerned, not only the instrument whereby attributions of its bodies and officials are established, but also the instrument limiting the exercise of those functions. Consequently, the *État de droit*, or state according to the rule of law, is essentially a state with limited powers and subject to some form of judicial control. This obviously, has numerous connotations in the evolution of the modern state and also presents features peculiar to each of the major contemporary legal systems.

That is why we have considered it necessary, before studying the systems of judicial review in comparative law, to begin by detailing some of the characteristic elements of the *État de droit* in the modern world and briefly reviewing its historical evolution.

In the continental legal systems, in the course of the historical evolution of the modern state, as opposed to the Absolute state and the economic doctrine of mercantilism that sustained it, the *État de droit* emerged together with liberalism, which also sustained it. The historical event which marked the transition from one political -economic system to another was the French Revolution (1789). However, the change took place following a theoretical preparation that lasted for several decades prior to the Revolution.

Naturally, we do not intend to enter into a historical analysis of the evolution of the *État de droit* as one of the phases of the modern state. we believe, however, that it is essential to refer to certain aspects of that evolution so as to explain the basis of judicial control of the exercise of power in the modern world.

The *État de droit is*, as we have said, a state according to law, or to put it in a better way, a state whose power and activity are regulated and controlled by legal rules. Basically, therefore, the *État de droit* consists of the rule of law; law understood, in this context, to mean the normative acts which make up the legal order of the state.

Seen from this standpoint, the *État de droit* as a state with powers regulated and limited by the law and other legal instruments is the opposite of any form of absolute or Totalitarian state. That is to say, it is the opposite of any type of state possessing unlimited power, in the sense of power not subjected to legal control, or at least, insufficiently regulated and subject to law.

Therefore, the ideas of judicial control of state activity and limitation of state power by subjection to the law emerge as the central concepts involved in the *État de droit* always related to the fundamental rights and liberties.

In line with the foregoing, it can be said that the *État de droit* is characterised by the following fundamental principles:

In the first place, there is the principle of limitation of state power by the classical division into the legislative, executive and judiciary, to guarantee liberty and to curb possible abuse of one power in relation to another; and the consecration of the necessary autonomy of the Judiciary, even to control the submission of the state to the law.

The second principle that characterizes the *État de droit* is that of the rule of law, that is to say, the subjection of the state to the law, not only to formal law, but also to all the sources of the legal order of a given state. This implies, therefore, that all state bodies are subject to the law of that same state, and particularly to the law as enacted by Parliament. This has especially given rise to the principle of legality applied to government or administrative actions, according to which, the administration must act in accordance with the law and can be judicially controlled to that end. Consequently, a series of procedures has been established for the purpose of controlling administrative action in particular, but also to control the constitutionality of laws, as protection against despotism on the part of the legislative power.

These principles have led to others inherent in the *État de droit*: On the one hand, that of the primacy of the legislation regulating all state activity, both of the executive and of the judiciary, the law being understood in this context, basically, to mean the formal law, that is to say, laws drawn up by the legislative bodies of the state (Parliament); and on the other hand, the establishment of a hierarchical system of the legal order and consequently of the various rules comprised therein. This system classifies the different rules in various ranks, according to their respective sphere of validity, usually in relation to a supreme or higher law, which is the constitution.

The third principle that identifies the *État de droit* is the recognition and establishment of fundamental rights and liberties, as a formal guarantee contained in constitutional texts and providing for their effective enjoyment as well as political and judicial means of control to ensure such enjoyment.

These are all principles or expressions of a common objective essential to the *État de droit*: The limitation of power, which emerged in contrast to the unlimited power of the Absolute monarch in what has been considered the first historical form of the continental modern state, namely the absolute state.

Indeed, it can be said that the modern state came into being when the feudal regime was dissolved as a result, among other factors, of a process of centralization of power, giving rise to the European continental monarchies, in which political power was concentrated in a Sovereign, as a superior political unit in contrast with the territorial dispersal of power characteristic of feudalism. Thus the modern state came into being as an absolute state, a concept in which the idea of concentration of power was added to that of the absolute and perpetual sovereignty of the monarch, constituting supreme, absolute and perpetual power over the citizens of a republic.

Thus, Bodino[1] or Bodin, in his *Six Books of a Commonwealth* published in 1576, translated into English in 1606 and once used as a textbook in Cambridge,[2] referred to Sovereignty as a condition for the existence of a state (a Commonwealth) by including it in his definition. He said:

A Commonwealth may be defined as the rightly ordered Government of a number of families, and of those things which are their common concern, by a sovereign power.

Sovereignty is that absolute and perpetual power vested in a commonwealth which in Latin is termed *majestas*...[3].

The modern state, represented in this sovereign monarchy, was what Hobbes termed the Leviathan (1651) the unitary personification of a multitude of men.

In Hobbes own words:

> «A multitude of men are made one person, when they are by one man, or one person, represented: so that it be done with the consent of every one of that multitude in particular. For it is the unity of the representer, not the unity of the represented that make the person one. And it is the representer that bears the person and but one person; and unity, cannot otherwise be understood in multitude».[4]

This *Leviathan*, is no doubt, the Modern state.[5]

During the seventeenth and eighteenth centuries, this modern state was identified as we said with the absolute monarchies of the continent, in which all power was concentrated in one person, «the king», who exercised it in an unrestricted manner. Moreover, sovereignty was a personal attribute of the Monarch,

---

1 I. BODIN, *The Six Books of a Commonwealth*, London 1606 (ed. by Kenneth Douglas MC RAE), Cambridge, Mass 1962, Book I, Clap. VIII, p. 84.

2 P. ALLOTT, «The Courts and Parliament: Who whom?, *Cambridge Law Journal*, 38, (1) 1979, p. 104.

3 Quoted by P. ALLOTT, *loc. cit*, p. 104 from trans. Tooley (1960), Chaps. I and VIII of Book I.

4 T. HOBBES, Leviathan (ed. John Plamenatz), London 1962, Chap. XVI, p. 171. *Cf.* M. M. GOLDSMIDT, *Hobbes' Science of Politics*, NY 1966, p. 138.

5 A. PASSERIN D'ENTRÈVES, *The Notion of the State. An Introduction to Political Theory*, Oxford 1967, p. 11.

and for this reason he was totally exempt from control in the exercise of his power, in view of his divine origin.[6] The monarch had only one duty, namely that of ensuring public order and the happiness of his subjects in the interest of the state, which is the reason for the existence not only of the recourse to *Raison d'État*,[7] but also of the exercise of the full powers characteristic of absolutism, in which the monarch was exempt from responsibility.

This exemption from responsibility is reflected in the classical expression «The crown can do no wrong» or *le roi ne peut mal faire*.

In systems such as the English one, this did not change until 1947, when, following the *Crown Proceeding Act*, it became possible to hold the Crown responsible before the Courts.[8] In any case, in the absolute state, the subject had no rights vis-à-vis the monarch; his only duty was to obey.

By contrast with the continental systems, the British experience is special. As Jennings stated, absolutism never developed in English history, except for a brief period under the Commonwealth, (1653) and even then, only moderately.[9]

Since the beginning of the thirteenth century, the king's authority in England was limited by his barons and that struggle is clear in the Magna Carta of 1215, considered the origin and source of English constitutional law.[10] This Great Charter, as is well known, did not legislate for Englishmen generally, but really attempted to safeguard the rights of different classes according to their different needs, and therefore, churchmen, lords, tenants, and merchants were separately provided for.[11] Even though the Magna Carta with its clauses placing limitations upon arbitrary power, has been considered the first attempt to express in precise legal terms some of the leading ideas of constitutional government in England, its interpretation by lawyers, historians and politicians and mainly by the courts, has subsequently led to the consideration of the document as a mean of safeguarding people's liberties even if the *liberi homines* were originally excluded from its clauses.[12]

Subsequently, kings had to fight against the landowners, and they did not always win. When the feudal lords disappeared, there was already a Parliament strong enough to limit royal authority, take over part of the king's power, discuss its limits and even, at times, to destroy a king whose ideas and actions transcended the limits considered reasonable by Parliament.[13]

In this context, the Revolution of 1642 was not really a social revolution, like the French, aimed at destroying a despotic system of government and the society

---

6 *Idem* p. 44-202.

7 *Idem* p. 44.

8 J.A. JOLOWICZ, «Torts», *International Encyclopaedia of Comparative Law*, Vol. XI, Chap. 13, (Procedural Questions), p. 13-41; H.W.R. WADE, *Administrative Law*, Oxford 1971, p. 17.

9 I. JENNINGS, *The Law and the Constitution*, London 1972, p. 46. «No King of England has ever been regarded by his contemporaries as an Absolute Monarch. The very concept is unknown in English Law», I. JENNINGS, *Magna Carta*, London 1965, p. 13. King Charles I in the trial opened in Westminster Hall 20-1-1649 refused to plead, as he would not recognize the jurisdiction of the Court or indeed of any court. He said, «The King cannot be tried by any superior jurisdiction on earth». On 21-1-1649 he was sentenced to dead. See M. ASHLEY, *England in the Seventeenth Century*, 1972, p. 89.

10 W. HOLDSWORTH, *A History of English Law*, Vol. II, Fourth Ed., London 1936, Reprinted 1971, p. 209.

11 *Idem* p. 211.

12 *Idem* p. 211.

13 I. JENNINGS, *The Law and the Constitution*, *cit.* p. 46-47.

on which it was based. Fundamentally, it was the result of a political struggle between king and Parliament.

The result of the Civil War that developed in England from the year 1642 and lasted 18 years was to make personalized monarchies impossible in future as well as to impede Parliament from attempting to perpetuate itself in defiance of public opinion. Thus, when the monarchy was restored after the Civil War, the whole position both of the monarchy and of Parliament had been altered.

Particularly after that Revolution, Parliament attained a position in the state which it had never possessed before, in the sense that it became as permanent a part of the government as the king himself, no longer a body to be called occasionally to assist king's government by sanctioning new legislation.[14]

It must be stated also that if it is true that as a result of that Revolution the authoritative position of Parliament had been secured, so had the supremacy of the law and mainly because of the increased national desire to see the law really supreme after the nation's experience under the Protectorate which had constantly found itself needing to violate the law.

That is why Sir William Holdsworth in his book *A History of English Law* said that the alteration of the relationship between king, Parliament and the courts and consequently of the executive, legislative and judicial powers led them to begin to assume the legal position which they hold in modern law.[15] That was undoubtedly facilitated because of the enactment of the *Instrument of Government* or 1653, considered to be the first written constitution in the modern world[16] in the sense of a higher law not to be modified by Parliament.

However, the political developments in England up to the Restoration led eventually to the final victory of Parliament in 1689 regarding the other powers of the state.

With this Parliamentary supremacy, it can be said that the rule of law system, in the liberal sense, has existed in England, and it was, as a matter of fact, an Englishman, John Locke, theoretician of the English Revolution, who laid the basis for the doctrine of the Liberal state, which had so much influence on continental law, and on the notion of the modern *État de droit*.

As we have previously said the modern *État de droit* is characterized by a few but very important features that have been developed over the last two centuries, and we think it is worthwhile studying, for our purpose of further analysis, judicial review or protection of the constitution.

We want to analyze the main features or characteristics of the *État de droit* classifying them into three different parts: firstly, the limitation of state power as a guarantee of freedoms; secondly, the submission of the state to the rule of law, that is to say in continental law terms, to the principle of legality; and thirdly, the establishment of fundamental rights and liberties in a constitution.

II. LIMITATION OF POWER AS A GUARANTEE OF LIBERTY

The first feature of the state according to law is the existence of a system of division or separation of powers. This means that Parliament or the legislative

---

[14] W. HOLDSWORTH, *op. cit.*, Vol. VI, p. 161-162.

[15] *Idem* p. 163.

[16] P. ALLOT, *loc. cit.*, p. 97.

power draws up the legal rules, and the administrative and judicial bodies are responsible for enforcing them. This system of separation of powers, or rationalization of power, is also established as a guarantee to citizens of their respective rights, considering as legislators, in the strictly formal sense, only those elected bodies aimed at representing the people. Consequently, the executive body, despite the normative faculties with which it is endowed, cannot be considered as legislator, in the sense of drawing up rules which might, for example, limit individual rights and guarantees.

Furthermore, this system of separation of powers contains a fundamental component, namely the autonomy and independence of judges, which also serves to guarantee individual rights. Consequently, neither person holding legislative office, nor the executive can be considered as judges.

However, in the *État de droit* regime, the system of separation of powers is not absolute and rigid, since there are numerous interrelations between the various state bodies, which must exercise mutual control and limitation, through the so-called system of weight and counterweight, or checks and balances, which, in fact, balances the system of state power. This system is characterized by several factors one of which is the supremacy of the legislative power, as creator of the law vis-à-vis the executive and the judiciary, who are responsible for enforcing that law. But this primacy of the legislator is not necessarily tantamount to sovereignty, and to avoid absolutism on the part of the legislator, or what has been called «elected dictatorship»,[17] the legislative power is necessarily subjected to the constitution. Thus, since the Legislator is limited by the constitution, a system must be set up to control the constitutionality of his acts, either by ordinary courts or by special courts, to guarantee the constitutionality of the laws.

But in this system of separation of powers, as we have already pointed out, the independence of the judiciary vis-à-vis the legislator and the executive is a fundamental element of the *État de droit* to such an extent that one can say that the genuine state according to the law is the one in which judges are autonomous and independent and, naturally, the one in which procedural guarantees exist, to avoid abuse of authority on the part of the judges.

Now, this principle of the separation of powers is at the very origin of the *État de droit*, as conceived by the theoreticians of absolutism, particularly Locke, Montesquieu and Rousseau.

1. Theoretical Backgrounds

In effect, John Locke, in his *Two Treatises of Government* (1690), became the first ideologist of the reaction against absolutism when he advocated the limitation of the monarch's political power. He based his proposal on the consideration of man's natural condition and the social contract of the society, which gave birth to the state. In Locke's opinion, the reason why men enter into a social contract is to preserve their lives, liberties and possessions, the three basic assets that he regards,

---

17 HAILSHAIN, *Elective Dictatorship*, 1976, quoted by P. ALLOTT, «The Courts and Parliament: Who whom? *Cambridge Law Journal*», Vol. 38, 1, 1979, p. 115. Hogg also has said that Parliament lead become «virtually an elective dictatorship. The party system makes the supremacy of a government like, the present, automatic and almost unquestioned». Quoted by M. ZANDERS, *A Bill of Rights?*, London 1980, p. 5.

in general, as «property». And it is this «property» that gives men political status. In Locke's own words:

> «For liberty is to be free from restraint and violence from others which cannot be, where there is no Law: But freedom is not, as we are told, a liberty to dispose, and order, as he wishes his person, action, possessions, and his whole Property».[18]

Naturally, this social contract as conceived by Locke, changed man's natural condition, and could not give rise to the formation of a government under which men would be placed in a worse situation than they had previously been in. Consequently, an absolute government could not even be considered legitimate as a civil government was. If the state emerged as a protector of «natural rights» which did not disappear with the social contract, their actual disappearance due to the action of an absolute state would justify resistance to the abuse of power.[19]

Now within the measures designed to rationalize and limit power, Locke developed his classical distribution of state functions, some of which he regarded as powers. In paragraph 131 of his book *Two Treatises of Government*, Locke said the following:

> «And so whoever has the legislative or supreme power of any Common-wealth, is bound to govern by established standing Laws, promulgated and known to the people and not by Extemporary Decrees; by indifferent and upright Judges, who are to decide Controversies by those Laws; and to employ the force of the Community at home, only in the Execution of such Laws, or abroad to prevent or redress Foreign Injuries, and secure the Community from Inroads and Invasions».[20]

So, Locke distinguished four state functions, that of legislating, of judging, of employing forces internally in the execution of the laws and of employing those forces abroad, in defense of the community. He gave the name of *legislative power* to the first function, that of making the laws «to which the other powers are, and must be subordinated»[21] as he said. The third function he called the *executive power*, which involved «the execution of the municipal laws of the society within the latter and above its parts»[22] or components. The fourth function he called the federative power, which includes «the power of war and peace, leagues and alliances, transactions with all persons or communities outside the state».[23]

Of all the functions he assigned to any sovereign state, the only one which he did not regard as a «power» was the *function of judging*, with respect to which Peter Laslett, in his introduction to Locke's book, indicates that «it was not a separate power, but a general attribution of the state».[24]

In this effort to rationalize state functions, the novelty of Locke's thesis lies in the distinction between the faculty of legislating and that of employing the forces

18 J. LOCKE, *Two Treatises of Government* (ed. Peter Laslett), Cambridge 1967, paragraph 57, p. 324.
19 *Idem*, p. 211.
20 *Idem*, p. 371.
21 *Idem* paragraphs 134, 149, 150, p. 384, 385. Peter LASLETT commentaries, «Introduction», p. 117.
22 *Idem*, p. 117.
23 *Idem*, p. 383. In relation to the name given by LOCKE to this power he said: «if any one pleases. So the thing be understood, we are indifferent as to the name». *Idem*, p. 383.
24 P. LASLETT, «Introduction», *loc. cit.*, p. 118.

in the execution of the laws. In this context, it was not necessary to individualize the power of judging, which, particularly in England, was a traditional state function.

In any case, it is important to note that Locke confined himself to rationalizing and systematizing the functions of the sovereign state but did not actually formulate a theory on the division of powers, much less their separation. What is more, no thesis can be inferred from Locke's work to the effect that the power of the state had to be placed in different hands to preserve liberty or guarantee individual rights, whilst allowing for the parts to coincide.[25] He did however admit that if the powers were placed in different hands, a balance could be achieved; as he stated in his book: «balancing the Power of Government, by placing several parts of it in different hands.[26]

Perhaps then, Locke's fundamental contribution to the principle of the division of power lay in his criteria, according to which the executive and federative power must necessarily be in the same hands.[27] Also, his criteria of the *supremacy of the legislative power* over the others, to the extent that both the executive function and that of judging had to be performed in execution of, and in accordance with the laws adopted and duly published.[28] For Locke, this supremacy of the legislative power was precisely the consequence of the supremacy of Parliament over the monarch, resulting from the 1689 Revolution which, *supremacy*. We have mentioned, is the most characteristic feature of English public law, compared to continental systems.

This theory of the division of power, that had such a great influence on modern constitutionalism, mainly because of its conversion from the «division of power» to the «separation of power» both in the French Revolution and in the American and Latin-American Revolutions, had its fundamental formulation in Montesquieu's equally well known work.

According to Montesquieu, political liberty only existed in those states in which the power of the state, together with all corresponding functions, was not in the hands of the same person or the same body of magistrates.[29] That is why, in his famous work *De l'Esprit des Lois*, he insisted that «it is an eternal experience that any man who is given power tends to abuse it; he does so until he encounters limits... In order to avoid the abuse of power, steps must be taken for power to limit power».[30]

From his comparative study of the various states existing at the time (174 8), Montesquieu reached the conclusion that England was the only state, the direct aim of which was political liberty. That is why, in the well-known Chapter VI of Volume XI of his book, he undertook to study the «constitution of England», and from that study he formulated his theory of the division of power into three categories:

> «Legislative power, power to execute things which depend on international law, and power to execute things which depend on civil lawn the first case,

---

25 *Idem*, p. 117-118.

26 *Idem*, p. 107, 350.

27 *Idem*, p. 118.

28 M.J.C. VILE, *Constitutionalism and the Separation of Powers*, Oxford 1967, p. 36. (LOCKE: «There can be one supreme power, which is the legislative, to which all the rest are and must be subordinated», «for what can give laws to another, must need be superior to him», Chap. XIII, p. 149-150).

29 A PASSERIN D'ENTRÈVES, *The Notion of the State. An introduction to Political Theory*, Oxford 1967, p. 120.

30 MONTESQUIEU, *De l'Esprit des Lois* (ed. G. Truc), Paris 1949, Vol. I, Book XI, Chap. IV, p. 162-163.

the prince or magistrate makes laws for a period of time or forever. In the second case, he makes peace or war, sends or receives ambassadors, establishes security, takes measures against invasion. In the third case, he punishes crimes, or settles disputes between individuals. The latter we shall call the power to judge, and the other simply the executive power of the state».[31]

Following Locke's example, Montesquieu defined various state functions or faculties, rather than division of power: the function of making laws, that of judging and that of executing laws, the latter encompassing what Locke called executive and federative power.

However, the novelty of Montesquieu's division of power, and what distinguishes it from Locke's approach, is, on the one hand, his proposal that to guarantee liberty, the three functions must not be in the same hands. On the other hand, that in the division of power, they were to *be* on an equal footing, otherwise power could not curb power. In the same Chapter VI of Volume XI of De 1'Esprit des Lois, Montesquieu expressed the following opinion:

> «When legislative power and executive power are in the hands of the same person or the same magistrate's body, there is no liberty... Neither is there any liberty if the power to judge is not separate from the legislative and executive powers... All would be lost if the same man, or the same body of princes, or noblemen or people exercised these three powers: that of making the laws, that of executing public resolutions and that of judging the wishes or disputes of individuals».[32]

As a result of all this, Montesquieu stated:

Those princes who wanted to become despots, always began by taking possession of all the magistracies.[33]

Underlying this whole conception, there was also, of course, the concept of liberty, seen from the same standpoint as Locke. Montesquieu even said, in terms very similar to those used by Locke:

> «It is true that in democracies the people seem to do what they want; but political liberty does not consist of doing what one wants. In a state, that is to say, in a society in which laws exist, liberty can only consist of being able to do what one should want to do, and not being obliged to do what one should not want to do».[34]

But in contrast to what existed according to the English constitution which he *was then* analysing, Montesquieu's concept involved no proposal whatsoever that any particular public authority should have priority over another. It is true that by defining the legislative authority as the «general will of the state» and the executive

---

31 *Idem*, Vol. I, pp. 163-164.

32 *Idem*, Vol. I, p. 164. In the same Chap. VI, Book XI MONTESQUIEU added that «Were (the judiciary power) joined with the legislative, the life and liberty of the subject would be exposed to arbitrary control; for the judge would, be then the legislator. Were it joined to the executive power, the judge might behave with violence and oppression». *Cf.* Ch. H. MCILWAIN, *The High Court of Parliament and its Supremacy*, Yale 1910, pp. 322-323.

33 *Idem*, Vol. I, p. 165.

34 *Idem*, Vol. I, Book XI, Chap. III, p. 162.

authority as the «execution of that general will»,[35] it could be inferred that the latter, as far as the execution itself was concerned, was to submit to the will of the former, but not, of course, in the sense of political subordination. On the contrary, he conceived the three authorities as being so equal that they could act as a mutual restraint, as the only possible form of co-operation for the maintenance of political liberty. That is why Montesquieu concluded with his famous proposal: «these three powers should constitute a rest, or inaction. But since, as all things, they must necessarily move, they will be forced to move in concert».[36]

It is clear, in any case, that Montesquieu's concept like Locke's theory was devised for Absolutism. Both were theoreticians of absolutism. That is why their concepts of the division of the sovereign's power were a legal doctrine rather than a political postulate. In other words, the theory does not answer the question about who is to exercise sovereignty, but how power should be organized to achieve certain objectives.[37]

But in addition to Locke's and Montesquieu's contributions to the definition of the limitation of power, in the political theory, which led to continental reaction against the Absolute state, and the appearance of the *État de droit*, Rousseau's concept of law occupies a place of paramount importance. This concept subsequently led to the postulate of the submission of the state to the Law, which is of its own making. That is to say, it gave rise to the principle of legality and consolidation of the *État de droit* itself.

In effect, as Rousseau himself said, the social pact or contract is the solution to the problem of finding a form of association: «which defends and protects, with the whole common force, the person and goods of each member of the association, and in which each person, united with all, nevertheless obeys only himself and remains as free as before».[38]

Thus, he said, «the transition is made from the natural to the civil state».[39] But, as Rousseau himself pointed out, «through the social pact we have given birth to the political body; we must now endow it with movement and a will, through legislation».[40]

Thus, -and this was the novelty of his proposal- it is the law, as a manifestation of the sovereign state resulting from the social pact, which sets the state in motion and provides it with the necessary will, since it is a question of «acts resulting from the general will and dealing with a general issue». Thus Rousseau not only built up the theory of the law as an «act of the general will», to which the conduct of the state itself and that of private individuals must be subjected, but he also established the principle of the generality of the law, which was to subsequently lead to the reaction against privileges, which is another basic element of the *État de droit*.[41]

However, Rousseau limited state functions to two: the making of laws and their execution, to which he applied the same terminology as Montesquieu:

---

35 *Idem*, Vol. I, p. 166.
36 *Idem*, Vol. I, p. 172.
37 A. PASSERIN D'ENTRÈVES, *op. cit.*, p. 121.
38 J.J. ROUSSEAU, *Du Contract Social* (ed. Ronald Grimsley), Oxford 1972, Book I, Chap. IV, p. 114.
39 *Idem*, Book I, Chap. VIII, p. 119.
40 *Idem*, Book II, Chap V, p. 134
41 *Idem*, Book II, Chap, V, p. 136.

legislative power and executive power.[42] Nevertheless, it is not a question here either of a doctrine of separation of powers, but, along the same lines as Locke and Montesquieu, a doctrine of the division of one single power that of the sovereign, resulting from the social pact or from the integration of the general will.[43]

Neither was Rousseau in favor of placing the two functions of power -the expression of the general will by means of laws and the execution of those laws- in the same hands. So, adopting the same approach as Montesquieu, he also recommended that different bodies exercise them, although, unlike Montesquieu, he insisted on the need for the subordination of the body executing the law to the body making it. This, in Locke's approach and in the English system, was to ensure the subsequent supremacy of the legislation and the law, developed later in Europe. Furthermore, the supremacy of the law was to be the corner stone of public law within the framework of the *État de droit* in Europe, allowing the development of the principle of legality, particularly with regard to government.

In this respect Rousseau agreed with Montesquieu. Rousseau in fact stated: «Therefore, we understand a Republic to be any state which is governed by laws».[44] Montesquieu, for his part defined the «state» as «a Society in which laws exist».[45] Which is also a declaration of the fact that the existence of laws was a fundamental requisite for the existence of the state.

2. The American and French Revolutions

It can generally be said that the writings of Locke, Montesquieu and Rousseau made up the whole theoretical and political arsenal for the reaction against the absolute state and its replacement by the state according to law based on the separation of powers, as a guarantee of liberty. That reaction was to occur in Continental Europe, with the French Revolution (1789), and in North America, with the Independence (1776), based on the exaltation of individualism and liberty.

In effect, all the political theories previously y mentioned were based on the analysis of man's natural situation and the achievement of the social pact or contract which established a sovereign as a mechanism for the protection of liberty. This was the basis for the subsequent exaltation of individualism and the political consecration of rights, not only of the citizens of a particular state, but also those of man, with the consequent construction of political and economic liberalism.

It was also considered necessary for the power of the state, as a product of the social pact, to be divided and rationalized, to prevent its abuse by the sovereign. To that end, state functions were systematized and power was divided, thereby paving the way for the adoption of a different and more radical formula: that of the «separation of powers», as a *guarantee* of liberty.

As Madison pointed out at the beginning of American constitutionalism:

> «The accumulation of all powers, legislative, executive, and judiciary in the same hands, whether of one, a few, or many, and whether hereditary, self-appointed or elective, may justly be pronounced the very definition of Tyranny».[46]

---

42 *Idem*, Book III, Chap, I, p. 153.

43 R. GRIMSLEY, «Introduction», in ROUSSEAU, *op. cit*, p. 35.

44 *Idem*, Book III, Chap. VI.

45 MONTESQUIEU, *op. cit.*, Book XI, Chap. III, p. 162.

46 J. MADISON, *The Federalist* (ed. B.F. Wright), Cambridge, Mass 1961, Nº 47, p. 336.

That is why the principle of the separation of powers was one of the essential elements of the American constitution. For example, the constitution of Massachusetts (1780) contained categorical expressions:

> «In the government of this Commonwealth, the legislative department shall not exercise the executive and judicial powers, or either one of them: The executive shall never exercise the legislative and judicial powers, or either one of them: The judicial shall never exercise the legislative and executive powers, or either one of them: to the end it may be a government of laws not of men».[47]

Moreover, the sovereign's power was considered to be updated by the production of laws, which were believed to be not only indispensable for the existence of the state itself, but also a guarantee of civil and political liberty. And the legislative function occupied a superior position to that of the other executive functions.

Consequently, in this concept arising out of the French Revolution, all acts, both of the Sovereign and of private individuals, were subjected to the law, understood to be an act of the general will. This gave rise to the principle of legality.

The *État de droit* and liberalism are, therefore, based on the concepts of liberty, separation of powers, supremacy of the law and the principle of legality. As a result, the essence of the *État de droit* from the beginning, in contrast to the absolute state, lies in the principle of the submission of the state and its administration to legality, which is to say, the necessary regulation of the state by the law, which must set limits on power.

However, such submission was not always guaranteed definitively in European countries and in all those, which adopted the *État de droit* model. At the beginning, for example, the separation of powers in France presented the non-interference of one power with another in such a fashion that the judicial power could not guarantee individuals that government would be submitted to legality. Proof of this was the famous Law of Judiciary Organization of 16-24th of August 1790, which specified:

> «Judiciary functions are and shall always be separate from administrative functions. Any interference by judges in the activities of the administrative bodies, or any summons issued to the administrators by the said judges, for reasons relating to their functions, shall constitute a breach of duty».[48]

Subsequently, the Law of 16 *Fructidor* of the year III (1795) ratified that:

> «The Courts are forbidden, under penalty of law, to take cognizance of administrative acts, whatever their nature».[49]

---

47 Art. XXX. *Massachusetts General Law Annotated*, St. Paul, Minn. Vol. 1-A, p. 582. In 1776, the constitution of Virginia, also had a declaration on separation of powers, considered as «The most precise statement of the doctrine which had at that time appeared». M.J.C. VILE, *Constitutionalism and the Separation of Powers, cit.*, p. 118. Article III of that constitution stated: «The Legislative, Executive and Judiciary departments, shall be separate and distinct, so that neither exercise the potters properly belonging to the others; nor shall any person exercise the powers of more than one of them at the same time, except that the Justice of the County Courts shall be eligible to either House of Assembly».

48 J. RIVERO, *Droit Administratif*, Paris 1973, p. 129; J.M. Auby et R. DRAGO, *Traité de contentieux administratif*, Paris 1984, Vol. I, p. 379.

49 J. RIVERO, *op. cit.*, p. 129.

As a result, the evolution of administrative jurisdiction in France, as jurisdiction separate from the judicial order for judging the government itself, constituted an extreme form of separation of powers. If the government or administrators were to be judged, a special jurisdiction, different and separate from the judicial power, had to be set up and that developed through a lengthy process which led, eventually, to the establishment of the *Conseil d'Etat*.

On the other hand, in the concept of Parliament and the law resulting from the French Revolution, any kind of control over the constitutionality of the laws in continental Europe was inconceivable, and this continued to be the case up to the beginning of the present century. As we will see, there is still no system of direct control over the constitutionality of the laws in France, and it was only in the post-war periods the twenties, and later in the forties, that a system of this kind was developed in other European countries, but which is still inconceivable in the British legal system.

In any case, throughout the last century and during the present one, the evolution of the principle of the separation of powers and the primacy of the legislator has shown a growing tendency both towards the submission of the state and all its bodies to the law and to legality, and towards the establishment of judicial controls to that end, either by means of special tribunals separate from judicial power, or by the use of the courts of the judiciary itself. This submission and controlled, *inter alia*, to the very birth of administrative law in Europe and even in England, as an autonomous branch of the legal sciences as at the end of the last century.

The struggle for the submission of government to legality is an irreversible victory of the *État de droit* and has been implanted throughout the world nowadays.

The characteristics of the separation of powers naturally vary from one country to another and its original justification as a guarantee of liberty has been forgotten. In many cases it has been used for purposes never originally envisaged. In England for example, the separation of powers was maintained, but for the purposes of the supremacy of Parliament over the various state bodies, that is to say, to subject the courts and tribunals to Parliament, and even to allow the courts the possibility of controlling the administrative authorities. The same doctrine also prevailed in the United states of North America, but for the purpose of clearly separating the executive and legislative functions, and enabling the Supreme Court to even declare acts of Congress invalid, whereas in France, the principle was used to make the legislative power supreme, but taking the separation to the extreme of preventing ordinary courts from controlling the legality of administrative acts, and eliminating any possibility of controlling the constitutionality of the legislator's acts.[50]

The North American constitution can indeed be considered a classical example of the division of powers, although it contains no precept specially designed for that division. The principle is, however, patent in several rules stipulating, for example, that all legislative powers are entrusted to Congress; that executive power is granted to the president; and that the judicial power of the United states is in the hands of the Supreme Court.[51] The rigidity of the division of powers is also evident

---

50 I. JENNINGS, *The Law and the Constitution*, London 1972, p. 25-28.
51 Arts. 1,1; 2,1 and 3,1.

from the fact that the Cabinet is absolutely independent from Congress, with which it has no formal communication.[52]

The principle has, however, undergone several changes, due to the constitution itself, to judicial interpretation, and to constitutional practice. In the first place there is, together with the principle of the separation of powers, a system of checks and balances, whereby the Executive has some participation in legislative power by veto and the annual address to Congress and in judicial power through the prerogative to pardon. Regarding the executive's right to appoint offices and ratify treaties, this requires the consent of the legislator, who also performs judicial functions in cases of impeachment, and is responsible, within the limits of the constitution, for the organization of judicial power. Finally, the courts are authorized to establish their rules of procedure, which is undoubtedly a legislative function, and they have also developed the power even to control the actions of Congress itself.[53]

3. The Sovereignty of Parliament

But in the concept of the separation of powers as a system of distributing power in such way that power curbs power, the English system was at variance.

Despite Montesquieu and all the literature produced in the eighteenth century with reference to England, as a living example of the separation of powers, the fact is that such separation has never been a reality and the situation at that time was, and has always been, that of the *heureux mélange* -the successful mixture- to which Voltaire referred.[54]

Be that as it may, British constitutional history shows a series of groups and institutions contending the domination and participation in state power. This has brought about the phenomenon of a balance of powers, which has constantly given rise to a system of restriction and counter-restriction, although in the United Kingdom one power has always prevailed over the others. In general, the predominant power has been that of Parliament, but it fact the predominant power has been considered to be that of the government, due to its control over the House of Commons and to the practice of delegated legislation.

In this sense, Philip Allott in an article published a few years ago in the Cambridge Law Journal stated:

> «The Executive has acquired an overall position of dominance, extending its authority in all three of the functional branches of Government -legislative, executive and judicial-. Above all, it has acquired a practical control over the House of Commons in Parliament, from which it has virtually excluded the House of Lords as a countervailing power».[55]

This fact has been pointed out by almost all the constitutional lawyers of the United Kingdom[56] and that is why Wade and Phillips in their book on constitutional and Administrative Law pointed out that «In absence of a written constitution,

---

52 M. GARCÍA-PELAYO, *Derecho constitucional comparado*, Madrid 1957, p. 350.

53 *Idem*, p. 350 and 351. In general, A and S. TUNC, *Le système constitutionnel des Etats Unies d'Amérique*, 2 vols. Paris 1954.

54 Quoted by M. GARCÍA-PELAYO, *op. cit.*, p. 283. *Cf.* G. MARSHALL, *Constitutional Theory*, Oxford 1971, p. 97.

55 P. ALLOTT, *loc. cit.*, p. 115.

56 For example, T.R.S. ALLAN has noted out that «the political consequence of the legal arrangement (that perceive the constitution as a legal order subject to, and dominated by, an unrestrained and

there is no formal separation of power in the United Kingdom».[57] and particularly between the legislative and the executive power; that the practical needs of the parliamentary government have obliged Parliament to trust governmental policy and accept the cabinet's wishes as far as the legislative program is concerned, but retaining the right to amend, criticize, question and ultimately to annul, and also that practical needs have demanded considerable delegation to the executive of the power of rule regulation.[58]

But in spite of these facts, it is certainly clear that in the United Kingdom legal system, the idea of parliamentary sovereignty has been traditional, breaking with the continental and American principle of separate powers, which mutually curb each other.

This principle of parliamentary sovereignty is characterized *inter alia,* by the following elements:

In the first place, because of the absence of any formal distinction between constitutional and ordinary laws, which implies that in the absence of a written constitution, Parliament can, at any time, institute, by the ordinary method of law-making, reforms of a constitutional nature. Therefore, «the authority of Parliament to change the law is unlimited» and «since the sovereignty of Parliament is recognised by law, -said T.R.S. Allan, in an article published in the last issue of *The Cambridge Law Journal,*- it would be contrary to the rule of law to deny full force to enactments which change existing law».[59]

The second element that characterizes the principle of sovereignty of Parliament is the absence of any possibility of control over parliamentary activity. This implies that there is no court competent to decide upon the constitutionality of laws or acts of Parliament. Consequently, any act of Parliament, whatever it's content, must be applied by the courts of justice, and in no case can those courts fail to apply the said rules.

As Dicey said at the very beginning of his *An Introduction to the Study of the Law of the Constitution,*

> «The principle of Parliamentary sovereignty means neither more nor less than this, namely, that Parliament... has, under the English constitution, the right to make or unmake any law whatever; and, further, that no person or body is recognized by the law of England as having a right to override or set aside the Legislation of Parliament».[60]

---

all-powerful sovereign: the Parliament) is the overwhelming authority of a government with a majority of seats in the House of Commons», and that «It is this concentration of power which is seen as a threat to fundamental rights and liberties constitutional restraints are therefore needed to protect such rights from irresponsible legislative encroachment; the need is to counteract the «helplessness of the law in face of the legislative sovereignty of Parliament» (Sir Leslie Scarman), in «Legislative Supremacy and the rule of Law: Democracy and constitutionalism», the *Cambridge Law Journal,* Vol. 44, (1), 1985, pp. 111-112.

57 E.C.S. WADE and G. GODFREY PHILLIPS, *Constitutional and Administrative Law,* (9th ed. by A.W. BRADLEY), London 1985, p. 53.

58 *Idem,* p. 49, 564.

59 T.R.S. ALLAN, *loc. cit.,* p. 122.

60 A.V. DICEY, *An Introduction to the Study of the Law of the Constitution,* (Introduction by E.C.S. WADE), 10th Ed. 1973, p. 39-40.

And regarding the courts, in the case of R. v. Jordan in 1967, a Divisional Court stated clearly that as Parliament was supreme, «there was no power in the courts to question the validity of an Act of Parliament».[61]

We have also mentioned the particularly important decision of the House of Lords, made in 1974 in the case of the *British Railways Board* v. *Pickin* in which Lord Reid stated that:

> «The idea that a court is entitled to disregard a provision in an Act of Parliament on any ground must seem strange and startling to anyone with any knowledge of the history and law of our constitution», adding, «no court of justice can inquire into the manner in which (an Act) was introduced into Parliament, what was done previously to its being introduced, or what passed in Parliament during the various stages of its progress through both Houses of Parliament»,
>
> and concluding precisely that:
>
> «The function of the Court is to co construe and apply the enactments of Parliament. The court has no concern with the manner in which Parliament or its officers carrying out its Standing Orders perform these functions».[62]

The third point that emerges from the principle of the supremacy of Parliament is that the law created by Parliament, that is to say, *the statutes*, have primacy over common law and over any form of legal creation. As stated by the Chancery Division in the case of *Cheney* v. *Conn (Inspector of Taxes)* in 1968:

> «What Statute says and provides is itself the law, and the highest form of law that is known to this country. It is the law which prevails over every other form of law, and it is not for the Court to say that a parliamentary enactment, the highest law in the country, is illegal».[63]

The fourth principle derived from the sovereignty of Parliament is that of the power of Parliament to prevail over judicial decisions themselves, since a bill could even be approved for the purpose of legalizing an illegal act, or exempting somebody from the legal consequences of a committed act. This is why it is said that «the legal authority of Parliament is absolute, not limited».[64]

For instance, Parliament's term of office, according to one of the conventions, is five years, but this period might be extended. Parliament can also regulate succession to the Throne, exclude persons who are not members of a particular religion, limit royal prerogatives, change the state religion, in short, make any decision with no limitation whatsoever. The principle implies that any act of Parliament can always be revised and changed by a subsequent act, either expressly or, in the case of conflict, implicitly. Consequently, important acts of Parliament such as the Habeas Corpus Act 1679, the Bill of Rights 1689, the Act of Settlement 1700, the Statute of Westminster 1931 and even the European Economic Communities Act 1972 can very well be revised by Parliament. No special majority is needed for this.[65]

---

61 O. HOOD PHILLIPS, *Leading Cases in Constitutional and Administrative Law*, London 1979, p. 1.

62 *Idem*, p. 2-5.

63 *Idem*, p. 28. That is why, we think, George Winterton said that «the rule of law comes to mean rule of law as enacted by Parliament, and not the rule of the ancient common law «, in «'the British Grundnorm: Parliamentary Supremacy re-examined», *The Law Quarterly Review*, Vol. 92, 1976, p. 596.

64 T.R.S. ALLAN, *loc. cit.* p. 129. Also see E.C. WADE and G. GODFREY PHILLIPS, *op. cit.*, pp. 61-62.

65 H.W.R. WADE, *Administrative Law*, 5th ed. Oxford 1984, p. 27.

Parliamentary sovereignty, in this form, is without doubt, one of the most important features of the constitutional system of the United Kingdom.

One of the consequences of parliamentary sovereignty, as pointed out by Prof. H.W.R. Wade, is that there are no constitutional guarantees, in the United Kingdom neither is there anything similar to what happens with written and rigid constitutions, which can only be changed by special procedures. This is undoubtedly an exception in the modern world, since most countries, even in the English-speaking world have a written constitution represented by a formal document, protected, as a fundamental law, against any attempt by simple majorities to introduce reforms.[66]

However, not only are constitutional guarantees nonexistent in the United Kingdom, nor does it seem possible to create them, as Prof. H.W.R. Wade said, since, if an ordinary act of Parliament can reform any law, then it is impossible for Parliament itself to declare a law or statute to be non-reformable, or only reformable subject to certain conditions. In other words, Parliament cannot modify or destroy its own «continuing sovereignty» for the courts will always obey its commands.[67]

In any case, parliamentary sovereignty in the United Kingdom as it exists today, has a profound effect on the position of judges. They are not guardians of a constitution or of constitutional rights, with, for example, power to declare certain legislative acts unconstitutional, as is the case with the Supreme Court of the United states.

That is why, no entrenched Bill of Rights can be adopted in this country. The adoption of it would, of course, involve the exercise of judicial review by the courts, that is to say, the power of domestic courts to protect certain fundamental freedoms even against the legislature itself,[68] and that would be against the principle of the sovereignty of Parliament.

Sir Ivor Jennings summarized the consequences of this main principle of the constitution of this country saying that parliamentary sovereignty essentially means two things. In the first place, it means that Parliament can legally pass legislation dealing with any matter: in Ivor Jennings words,

> «Parliament may remodel the British constitution, prolong its own life, legislate ex-post facto, legalize illegalities, provide for individual cases, interfere with contracts and authorize the seizure of property, give dictatorial powers to the Government, dissolve the United Kingdom or the British Commonwealth, introduce communism or socialism, or individualism or fascism, entirely without legal restriction».[69]

That is to say that as there is no written or rigid constitution in the United Kingdom, Parliament is not limited by any text or superior fundamental rule. So, there is no possibility of exercising any kind of judicial control over the conformity of Parliamentary acts with a higher law, which means in our perspective that the principle of the rule of law is not applicable to Parliament.

---

66 *Idem*, p. 28.

67 *Idem*, p. 28. See also G. WINTERTON, *loc. cit.*, p. 597.

68 D.G.T. WILLIAMS, «The constitution of the United Kingdom», *The Cambridge Law Journal*, 31, (1), 1972-B, p. 279.

69 I. JENNINGS, *The Law and the Constitution, cit.*, p. 147.

4. The Distribution of Power

The idea of the state according to law with or without parliamentary sovereignty is based on the concept of the limitation and distribution of power, which may be observed in three aspects.

In the first place, it can be observed in a distribution of power between the state itself, on the one hand, and individuals or citizens on the other, in the sense that a sphere of liberty is established for individuals and citizens, even as a fact existing prior to the state. This implies limitations to state powers, in the sense that the faculty of the state to invade the sphere of fundamental rights is, in principle, limited.

This is true, in a certain way even in the United Kingdom with Parliamentary supremacy, the absence of an entrenched Bill of Rights and the unthinkable judicial review of legislation. As Winterton pointed out:

> «For centuries, and certainly at the time of the 1688 Revolution, the concept of practically «inalienable» personal liberties has been a very strong feature of the British constitution: it is implicit in the British concept of the Rule of Law and has led to the doctrine of natural justice in administrative law, as well as the rules for interpreting statutes so as not to threaten individual liberty».[70]

The second aspect of the distribution of power in the *État de droit* relates to its organization by means of a principle of distribution of power between constituent and constituted power. Constituent power belongs and corresponds to the people who are sovereign and is reflected in a constitution, so that constituent act can only be taken by the latter, in accordance with the provisions of the constitution itself. Thus the bodies of the constituted power cannot invade the activities which correspond to the constituent power established in the constitution, and that is why all invasions of those activities invalidate acts taken in such a way.

Third and last, this principle of the distribution of power in the *État de droit* also refers to the organization of state power itself in the sphere of constituted power, by means of a system of division of power consisting of a series of attributions to the different state bodies.

This principle of organization or distribution of power has two connotations: in the first place, the classical horizontal division or separation of powers, that distinguish the various branches of public power in a nation, between the legislative, the executive (government and administration) and the judicial bodies. The aim of this division and distinction is to establish reciprocal restrictions and controls between the various state powers, and they are normally established in the constitution.

In addition to this, there is a second, vertical connotation that seeks a distribution of state power among its different territorial levels, resulting, for example, in the Federal state or politically decentralized forms of state. In these, the different territorial levels (national, federate states or Regions and Municipalities) exercise part of the public power, also within a system of distribution of jurisdictions established by the constitution.

---

70 G. WINTERTON, *loc. cit.*, p. 599.

These three forms of distribution and limitation of state powers bring in constitutional matters, and necessarily lead, when adopted by a state, to a system of judicial review to control the illegitimate invasions or interferences of one of such powers in the sphere reserved to the other. That exists, more or less in the constitutional system of the Western World today, because these countries have written and rigid constitutions with a formal declaration of fundamental rights and have either a federal organization or other systems of political decentralization.

In the constitutional system of the United Kingdom there is, on the contrary, no entrenched Bill of Rights, though the judicial protection of fundamental rights cannot imply the invalidation of acts of Parliament. No distinction is made between constituent and constituted powers due to the absence of a written constitution and the principle of sovereignty and supremacy of Parliament, though there is no control over the constitutionality of Parliamentary acts. Finally, the constitutional system is a unitarian one, with no power distributed in territorial units that could restrain the powers of Parliament, though there is no control of constitutionality of the vertical distribution of power.

III. SUBMISSION OF THE STATE TO THE LAW

The second main feature of the concept of the *État de droit* is the submission of the state to the law, which implies that all the actions of the public bodies of a given state and its authorities and officials must be carried out subject to the law and within the limits set by the law. Hence, there is the expression state according to the rule of law or in the Continental sense *État de droit*.

This principle is, perhaps, one of the main features of legal system today, although there are certainly as many interpretations as there are legal systems and even authors. It is also referred to by various expressions: For instance, as we said, in the Continental and Latin-American legal systems, this principle of the submission of the state to the law is commonly identified with the «principle of legality»; in the American system, with the whole idea of constitutionalism or government under the law; and in the British constitutional system by the classical expression «rule of law».

All these expressions ultimately mean that state bodies should be subject to the law, although it is certain that these assertions do not always have the same meaning and scope in every system.

For instance, Sir Ivor Jennings said that the rule of law or government according to law, means «that all power came from the law and that no man, be he King or Minister or private person, is above the law».[71]

But we may ask what about the sovereign, and in the case of the British constitution, what about Parliament? Jennings referred to «the Government according to law», and we could ask: does he include Parliament in that expression? can we say that the whole principle of the state according to the law or submitted to the law, that is to say, that all power of state bodies came from the law, is also applicable to the British constitutional system? Or is it true that in general terms, the rule of law in the British legal system is rather a principle related to government, in the sense that the executive must be enforced by the courts, and is not a principle related to Parliament?

---

[71] I. JENNINGS, *Magna Carta*, London 1965, p. 9.

1. The Sovereign and the Law

We think we can start our approach to the analysis of this principle of the submission of the state to the law, as one of the main features of modern constitutionalism, by following the statement made by Prof. H.L.A. Hart in his book, *The Concept of Law*, when he said:

«Whenever there is law, there is a sovereign incapable of legal limitation».[72]

Consequently, in all modern legal systems, we can distinguish two powers: that of the constituent, that is to say, the sovereign body, and that of the constituted, formed by all the state organs. This is, as we have seen, one of the main consequences of the principle of limitation of state power: the division in a given society between the constituent and the constituted power, bearing in mind that the constituent power is in the hands of the sovereign, who exercises it with no legal limitation whatsoever, and that all the constituted powers are, on the contrary, limited above all by the rules laid down by the sovereign or constituent body. That is why this sovereign said Hart, «makes law for his subjects and makes it from, a position outside any law». Therefore, «there are, and can be, no legal limits on his law-creating powers». He concluded by saying «the legally unlimited power of the sovereign is his definition».[73]

In similar terms, C.M. McIlwain, speaking on the sovereign said: «it is the highest body legally able to make rules for the subject, and itself free of the law».[74]

If we therefore accept this theory, and the principle that in all legal order there is a sovereign not submitted to the law or legal limitations, how can we talk about the *État de droit* or the state submitted to the law?

This question leads us again to the problem of sovereignty and the sovereign and in particular, to the task of identifying within the bodies and organs of the state, which one is the sovereign and therefore, not subjected to the law.

In a democracy, as Austin stated, and this is in the essence of the *État de droit* it is not the elected representatives who constitute or form part of the sovereign body but the electors. Hence in England, Austin said, «speaking accurately, the members of the House of Commons are merely trustees for the body by which they are elected and appointed: and consequently, the sovereignty always resides in the king's peers and the electoral body of the Commons». Similarly, he held the opinion that in the United States, sovereignty of each state of the Federal Union, «resides in the state's government as forming one aggregate body, meaning by a state's government not its ordinary legislature but the body of citizens which appoints its ordinary legislature».[75]

With regard to this distinction in a democracy, between the sovereign itself, the people, and the organs of the state, the Germans have made a useful distinction

---

72 H.L.A. HART, *The Concept of Law*, Oxford 1961, p. 70. On p. 65 asserts: «in every society where there is law there is a Sovereign» ... «everywhere the existence of law implies the existence of such a. sovereign».

73 *Idem*, p. 64-5.

74 C.M. MCILWAIN, *Constitutionalism and the Changing World*, Cambridge 1939, p. 31.

75 J. AUSTIN, *The Province of Jurisprudence Determined* (ed. H.L.A. HART), London 1954 Lec. VI, p. 230, 231, 251, quoted by H.L.A. HART, *op. cit.*, p. 72.

between what they choose to call the sovereign and the sovereign organ. (*Trager der Staatgewalt* or *Staatorgan*).[76] The sovereign that is to say the electoral body, has no legal limitations as a constituent power, but the sovereign organs not only have limitations imposed on them by the constituent power in the constitution, but are also subject to various types of control, even the political one by the same people who set them up, throughout for instance, by referendum.

In this perspective, we must again consider the concept of parliamentary sovereignty. In this respect, Hart points out the following alternative:

> «There could only be legal limits on legislative power if the legislator were under the orders of another legislator whom he habitually obeyed; and in that case he would no longer be sovereign. If he is sovereign he does not obey any other legislator and hence there can be no legal limits on his legislative power».[77]

And that is, precisely, the main question. Is the legislative organ legally bound to observe constitutional restriction imposed by a constituent power, that is to say, by the people as sovereign? In that case, the legislative body would not then be the sovereign but only the sovereign organ, Conversely is the legislative body in a state, free of the Law and therefore with no constitutional or legal limits to its power because it is the only body that established the law of a country, without legal restriction? In this case it would be the sovereign itself.

We must generally accept that in the modern world, almost all legal systems establish legal limitations on the exercise of legislative organ power, normally incorporated in a written and rigid constitution, and do not identify the sovereign with that legally limited legislator or Parliament but rather with the people as an electoral body.

«Austin himself did not identify the sovereign with the legislature even in England» Hart said. This was his view although the queen in Parliament is, according to normally accepted doctrine, free from legal limitations on its legislative power, and so is often cited as a paradigm of what is meant by «a sovereign legislature» in contrast with Congress or other legislatures limited by a 'rigid' constitution».[78]

But in spite of this general principle of the sovereignty of Parliament in the British constitution in the legal state perspective as state subjected or submitted to law, even in the United Kingdom as a democracy, we must admit that the sovereign is in fact not really Parliament but the people of this country, as an electoral body. And that the real difference between the British constitution and the other constitutional systems in the world, is that of the degree of delegation of sovereign power given by the people to the legislative organ, in other words, «the manner in which the sovereign electorate chooses to exercise its sovereign power».[79]

Professor Hart pointed out the distinction in the following passages from his book:

> «In England, ... the only direct exercise made by the electorate of their share in the sovereignty consists in their election of representatives to sit in Parliament

---

[76] C.M. McILWAIN, *op. cit.*, p. 31.
[77] H.L.A. HART, *op. cit.*, p. 65.
[78] *Ibid*, p. 72.
[79] *Ibid*, p. 72.

and the delegation to them of their sovereign power. This delegation is, in a sense, absolute since, though a trust is reposed in them not to abuse the powers thus delegated to them, this trust in such cases is a matter only for moral sanctions, and the courts are not concerned with it, as they are with legal limitations on legislative power».[80]

By contrast, Hart added:

«In the United States, as in every democracy where the ordinary legislative is legally limited, the electoral body has not confined its exercise of sovereign power to the election of delegates but has subjected them to legal restrictions. Here the electorate may be considered an «extraordinary and ulterior legislature» superior to the ordinary legislative which is legally «bound» to observe the constitutional restrictions, and, in cases of conflict, the courts will declare the acts of the ordinary legislature invalid. Here then, in the electorate, is the sovereign free from all legal limitations which the theory requires».[81]

Then we can conclude by saying that this principle of the *État de droit* or of the state according to the law, implies that the sovereign body which has no legal limitations, can only be the people as electorate, and therefore that all state organs or bodies are subject to the law.[82] And law here means not only what we call in the continental systems «formal law», that is to say, a statute or act of Parliament, but also all the rules that constitute the legal order, in its hierarchical frame work with the constitution as the supreme norm or *grundnorm*.

In the constitutional systems with written constitutions, therefore when we referred to the state according to or subject to the law, in the word law, we must include all the sources of the legal order: the constitution itself and all the other norms deriving there from. On the contrary, the sense of the term «law» in the expression «rule of law» in the constitutional systems with non-written constitutions, basically means, «rule of law as enacted by Parliament»,[83] which in principle, with its sovereignty delegated by the sovereign has no legal limits on its activity.

And we say in principle, because in spite of everything that is said about the unlimited, absolute, omnipotent, all-powerful or unrestrained powers of Parliament that we find in almost all written works about constitutional law in Britain, it must be admitted that Parliament has in fact lot of limitations, precisely those that have kept the British constitution more or less unaltered since the end of the Glorious Revolution and the Declaration of Rights in 1689.

Lolme's famous statement that «Parliament can do everything but make a woman a man and a man a woman»,[84] although not entirely impossible nowadays, is no more than an exaggeration tending to mean that Parliament has no legally entrenched limits upon its actions, because of the absence of a written and rigid constitution. But it does not mean that there could be arbitrariness in the exercise of Parliamentary Powers, and that in certain aspects, in political practice, there are absolutely no limits over Parliaments.

---

80 *Ibid*, p. 73.

81 *Ibid*, p. 73.

82 J.D.B. MITCHELL, *Constitutional Law*, Edinburgh 1968, p. 62.

83 G. WINTERTON, «The British Grundnorm: Parliamentary Supremacy re-examined», *The Law Quarterly Review*, 92, 1976, p. 596.

84 I. JENNINGS, *Parliaments*, Cambridge 1961, p. 2.

Firstly, there are some Acts of Parliament that can be considered at least from the perspective of constitutional law, as «constituent documents» limiting parliamentary action. In this respect, J.D.B. Mitchell qualified as «constituent documents» the Acts of Union of 1707 and the Ireland Act of 1800, even though the limitations imposed by them upon Parliament -he said-, are established «in such a way that any infringement of them is improbable».[85] He also mentions as limits upon Parliament, those established by convention, that is to say, habits of thought which are the product of Parliamentary life. Like that related to the «doctrine of mandate» which states that a government which has lost general support in the country should not force major legislation through Parliament shortly before an election, even though such legislation may have been in its electoral program.[86]

There are, moreover, limits in political practice, imposed y Parliament itself, that undoubtedly bind other Parliaments, in such a way that Parliament cannot reverse what a previous Parliament had done. For instance, one cannot imagine that Parliament could reverse the Statute of Westminster 1931, which limits the power of Parliament to legislate over a dominion without its consent;[87] nor can one imagine that Parliament could reverse the acts granting independence to the dominions or territories overseas and thus try to take away their independence.[88]

In the same context, discussions have taken place concerning the primacy of European community law in relation to domestic statutes, both before and after the European Communities Act 1972 was passed. In accordance with that Act, Community law must have primacy over domestic law, and therefore, Parliament must not enact future acts that conflict with Community Law, unless it amends the European Community Act itself. While the United Kingdom remains a member of the Community, in would be difficult in practice, for Parliament to exercise its legislative power through acts contradicting the application of Community Law.[89]

On the other hand, we can also say that limitations upon arbitrary powers have been fixed in the national tradition of this country, and perhaps it has been because of the absences of real threats against the constitution that the need to establish entrenched limits to the power of Parliament has not arisen.

As J.M. Snee pointed out in a Conference held in Harvard Law School on the occasion of the Bicentennial of John Marshall, in 1955:

---

85 J.D.B. MITCHELL, *op. cit.*, p. 69-75.

86 *Ibid*, p. 56, 66, 67.

87 Section 4 of the Statute of Westminster, provides: «No Act of Parliament of the United Kingdom passed after the commencement of this Act shall extend, or be deemed to extend, to a Dominion as part of the law of that Dominion, unless it is expressly declared in that Act that that Dominion has requested, and consented to, the enactment thereof». *Cf.* C. TURPIN, *British Government and the Constitution*, London 1985, p. 27. In a contrary sense, Ilamish R. GRAY said that «The general tendency of constitutional lawyers is to reject the interpretation of section 4 which requires Parliament as a matter of law to act in a particular way for any particular purpose», in «The Sovereignty of the Imperial Parliament», *The Modern Law Review*, 23 (6), 1960, p. 647.

88 For example, The Zimbabwe Act, 1979, Section I (2) provides: «On and after Independence Day Her Majesty's Government in the United Kingdom shall have no responsibility for the government of Zimbabwe; and no Act of the Parliament of the United Kingdom passed on or after that day shall extend, or be deemed to extend to Zimbabwe as part of its law'. *Cf.* C. TURPIN, *op. cit.*, p. 27.

89 *Cf.* F.A. TRINDADE, «Parliamentary Sovereignty and the Primacy of European Community Law», *The Modern Law Review*, 35 (4), 1972, p. 375-402; S.A. DE SMITH, «The Constitution and the Common Market: a tentative appraisal», *The Modern Law Review*, 34 (6), 1971, p. 597-614; H.W.R. WADE, «Sovereignty and the European Communities», *The Law Quarterly Review*, 88, 1972, p. 1-5.

> «No British Parliament today would dare to put into practice the statement made by Lord Chancellor Northington in 1766 during the debate on the repeal of the Stamp Act:
>
> Every Government can arbitrarily impose laws on all its subjects; there must be a supreme dominion in every state: whether monarchical, aristocratic, democratic, or mixed. And all the subjects of each state are bound by the laws made by government».

Nonetheless, the absolute supremacy of Parliament remains the orthodox doctrine of English constitutionalism, as expressed by Sir Hartly Shawcross in a speech reported in *The Times* 13 May 1946:

> «Parliament is sovereign; it can make any laws. It could ordain that all blue-eyed babies shall be destroyed at birth; but it has been recognized that it is no good passing laws unless you can be reasonably sure that, in the eventualities which they contemplate, these laws will be supported and can be enforced.
>
> The English, of course, with an irritating but sublime confidence in their institutions are sure that no Parliament would so act».[90]

This confidence is largely justified in the United Kingdom even though there is no judicial review or control of the constitutionality of acts of Parliament, mainly because of the continuity of constitutional rule in the last three hundred years. Also, because in spite of the absence of judicial review of Statutes as Professor A. Goodhart pointed out twenty years ago,

> «Judges, however, usually manage to get their own way: The House of Lords has been able to attain some of the same results which in the United states, are achieved by the first ten amendments. By a convenient fiction it assumes that Parliament always intends that its statutes will accord with natural justice; no statute will therefore be constructed to be retrospective or to deprive a person of a fair hearing or to prevent freedom of speech unless Parliament has so provided in the most specific terms».[91]

Accordingly, one can agree that some kind of limitation upon parliamentary power to enact legislation, in the United Kingdom has been developed by means of judicial interpretation, based on presumptions. So, as Prof. J. D. B. Mitchell said:

> «A statute is presumed, in the absence of clear words to the contrary, not to take away property without compensation, not to exclude the jurisdiction of the court, not to be retrospective, not to impose taxation».[92]

It has also been considered that precisely through such presumptions, effective protection can be given to fundamental rights and liberties, and therefore, arguments had arisen in the sense that with this presumption of interpretation it is uncertain that the enactment of a formal Bill of Rights as part of English law would achieve better protection of traditional liberties. On the contrary, T.R.S. Allan said,

---

90 J.M. SNEE, S.J. «Leviathan at the Bar of Justice», in A.E. SUTHERLAND (ed.), *Government under Law*, Cambridge, Mass 1956, p. 106-107.

91 A.L. GOODHART, «Legal Procedure and Democracy», *The Cambridge Law Journal*, 22,1, April 1964, p. 52. *Cf.* J.D.B. MITCHELL, *op. cit.*, p. 13.

92 J.D.B. MITCHELL, *op. cit.*, p. 66.

«A common law presumption which commands the loyalty of the judges is as powerful an instrument for interpreting legislation so as to safeguard individual liberties as an enacted Bill of Rights».[93]

However, in most other countries, the people or the electorate sovereign do not unluckily always have the confidence English people have in their own legislative organ or in presumptions of interpretation. On the contrary, experience abroad has shown that it has been precisely because of the actions of Parliaments, dominated by circumstantial majorities, that the worst attacks against human rights have been committed. On the other hand, in other countries the sovereign does not unluckily fear fictions or presumptions, duly applied, as a means of judicial protection of human rights. Whereas the majority of other countries today[94] feels the need to establish a written and rigid constitution, with an entrenched declaration of fundamental rights and liberties, precise dispositions for the limitation and distribution of state powers, mainly of the legislator and of the executive, and giving judges substantial power of control over the submission of all state organs to the constitution and to the law. From there comes the concept of the legal state.

2. The Law and the Legal Order

As we said at the beginning, in this expression, *État de droit* or state according to the law, or simply «the rule of law» mainly in legal systems with written constitutions the world «law» must be understood, not only in the sense of acts of Parliaments, Congress or legislative bodies, that is to say, Statutes in English terminology, but in the broader sense of legal order, comprising all the norms that regulate a given society according to its political constitution. In the same broader sense the expression «principle of legality» used in continental law, as equivalent to the rule of law, must be understood.

Therefore, «legality», in contemporary constitutional law is not only the submission to «formal law» as an act passed by the legislator, as it used to be in the last century in relation to administrative actions and as a consequence of the principle of the supremacy of the law, but means today submission to law as the legal order, including, the constitution and other deriving sources of law. Furthermore, in the contemporary world, the rule of law or the principle of legality not only refers to the submission of the executive to law controlled by the courts, but also the submission of all the state organs to the laws that regulate its functioning. In this sense, the principle of legality or the rule of law applicable to Parliament or to the legislative body, in systems with written constitution, are the rules contained in that constitution.

However, as we said from the historical point of view, the principle of legality in continental Europe was understood in the restricted sense. It was considered that, if the state was to be subject to the law, «law» in this expression was understood in its formal sense to mean an act issued by the legislator, considered to be the body representing the people, and as the expression of the general will.

---

93 T.R.S. ALLAN, «Legislative Supremacy and the Rule of Law: Democracy and Constitutionalism», *The Cambridge Law Journal*, 44, (1), 1985, p. 135.

94 With the exemption of the United Kingdom, New Zealand and Israel, all other countries of the world have written constitutions. *Cf.* O. HOOD PHILLIPS, *Reform of the Constitution*, London 1970, p. 4; F.M. AUBURN, «Trends in Comparative Constitutional Law», *The Modern Law Review* 35 (2), 1972, p. 129.

In this sense, the law as an act of the legislative body, was what Locke used to define the liberty of man under the law: He said:

> «The liberty of man in society is to be under no other legislative power but the established, by consent, in the commonwealth; nor under the dominion of any will or restraint or any law, but what that legislative shall enact according to the trust put in it».[95]

Also, law, as the expression of the general will, in Rousseau's terminology was that enacted by the legislator.[96]

In this sense, the French Declaration of the Rights of Man and Citizen of 1789 was drafted and in which article 6 states the following:

> «The Law is the expression of the general will; all citizens have the right to participate personally, or through their representatives, in its formation».[97]

Undoubtedly, in France during the last century (19th century) and throughout the present one (20th century), in general this restricted sense has generally been the one of the term «law» referred to the principle of legality.

For instance, Raymond Carré de Malberg, one of the most important and classical constitutional writers of the beginning of this century, wrote the following, about the formal criteria for the definition of law:

> «The parliamentary act of legislation resembles the work of an organ enjoying, in regard to the formulation of the laws, an exclusive special power, and in this sense, it constitutes an act of the state power».

And he added,

> «In the assembly of the deputies representing the Nation, the citizens themselves, all the citizens, in their capacity as constituent members of the nation are represented and thus participate in making laws».[98]

In this tradition, the law, as an expression of the general wills enacted by Parliament, was the fundamental guarantee of liberty. Moreover, the laws proposed for the limitation of power at the time of the beginning of the *État de droit* and after the French Revolution, were not as far as their contents were concerned, the statutes or laws usually approved by today's Parliaments, but «laws of liberties»[99] that is to say, laws designed to enable the members of the social body to evolve freely mainly because of the fact that the state had, as its main function, to enable the exercise of liberties by the citizens. That was the essence of liberalism in its political perspective, and in this regard, the Declaration of the Rights of Man and the Citizen stated:

---

95 J. LOCKE, *Two Treatises of Government* (ed. Peter Laslett), Cambridge 1967, Chapter 4.

96 J.J. ROUSSEAU, *Du Contrat Social* (ed. Ronald Grimsley), Oxford 1972, Book II, Chap V, p. 136–; Book III, Chap IV, p. 163.

97 See in W. LAQUEUR and B. RUBIN, *The Human Rights Reader*, 1979, p. 119. *Cf.* G. DE RUGGEIRO, *The History of the European Liberalism*, Boston 1967, p. 67.

98 Carré DE MALBERG, *La loi, expression de la volonté générale*, 1931, quoted by M. LETOURNEUR and R. DRAGO, «The Rule of Law as Understood in France», *American Journal of Comparative Law*, 7, 1958, p. 148.

99 E. GARCÍA DE ENTERRÍA, *Revolución francesa y administración contemporánea*, Madrid 1972, p. 16.

«The aim of every political association is the preservation of the natural and inalienable rights of Man; these rights are liberty, property, security and the resistance to oppression.

Liberty consists of the power to do whatever is non injurious to others; thus, the enjoyment of natural rights of every man has for its limit, only those that assure other members of society the enjoyment of those same rights; such limits may be determined by the law».[100]

This restricted meaning of the term law, as a formal law, in the definition of the principle of legality has been followed in contemporary times by French administrative writers[101] even though some followed the broader sense of the law, as «legal order», in the definition of the principle of legality[102] or of what Hauriou once called the *bloc legal* or *bloc de la legalite* [103].

In any event, the reason for this narrow sense of the law regarding the principle of legality in France, even in modern times and in spite of the written constitutions adopted by that country since 1791, is that it has normally been formulated in relation with the control of the executive or administration, due to the traditional concept in France of the supremacy of the law, and also to the traditional absence of any protection given to the people against legislative actions contrary to the constitution[104] with the exception of the recent development of the control of the constitutionality of laws by the constitutional Council.

In effect, with the development of the judicial control of the constitutionality of laws in France, thanks to the functioning of the constitutional Council and its recent decisions, and with the spreading of the American and Austrian models of judicial review of the constitutionality of legislative acts in legal systems with written constitutions, the difference between the constitution, as constituent rule and the law, meaning act of Congress or of the legislative power, subordinate to the former, is now accepted, and with it, the expansion of the principle of legality or rule of law.

In this perspective, the acts of the legislative body are *per se* derivative norms of the constitution and therefore subordinate to it. Consequently, the rule of law or the principle of legality in the contemporary *État de droit* also comprises the «rule of the constitution» or the «principle of constitutionality», and therefore those acts issued in direct execution of the constitution are submitted to it and can be controlled; hence the judicial control of the constitutionality of laws.

Now, two things we must pick up from what we have said:

First, that the principle of legality or rule of law in our context is referred to the state, namely to all state organs and powers, and not only to one mainly the

---

[100] Arts. 2 and 4. See in W. LAQUEUR and B. RUBIN, *op. cit.*, pp. 118–119.

[101] Ch. EISENMANN, «Le droit administratif et le principe de legalité», *Etudes et documents*, Conseil d'Etat, N° 11, Paris 1957, p. 25–40; N. LETOURNEUR and R. DRAGO, *loc. cit.*, p. 149.

[102] A. DE LAUBADÈRE, *Traité elémentaire de droit administratif*, Paris, N° 369; G. VEDEL, *La summission de l'administration a la loi* (extrait de la *Revue Al Ouanoun Wal Igtisad*, 22e année, Le Caire) no. 26, 31, 47, 58, 94, 165, 166, quoted by Ch. EISENMANN, *lot.cit.*, pp. 26–27.

[103] Ch. EISENMANN, *loc. cit.*, p. 26.

[104] A. TUNC, «Government under Law: a Civilian View» in Arthur E. SUTHERLAND (ed.), *Government under Law*, Cambridge, Mass 1956, p. 43.

executive or administrative power. As a result in a state with a written constitution, the legislative body is also bound by the principle of legality or the rule of law, in the sense that its activities are legally limited and, therefore, it can also be judicially controlled in most countries as is the administration.

Second, we must also stress that in the expression principle of legality or rule of law, the term «law» must be understood in the broader sense of legal order and not in the formal sense of act of Parliament or statute, thus comprising the constitution itself, the formal laws, and all the norms established in a legal system deriving from the constitution.

This approach leads us to the need to identify the basic trends of a legal system to determine which norms are applicable to each organ of the state, in other words, to establish the confines of the legality to which the various organs of the state are submitted.

In this sense, we must say above all that in all legal systems[105] in general, a distinction between those rules which form the constitution itself, as a higher positive law, and on the other hand, those provisions or rules of law which may be made by an authority delegated by the constitution exists and must exist. In other words, a distinction must be established between constituent law and ordinary legislation.

As McIlwain pointed out when referring to Bodin's thoughts on the matter:

> «There is and there must be, in a every free state, a marked difference between those laws which a government makes and may therefore change, and the one which make the Government itself. The Government... is «free of the law» (said Bodin)... but by this he meant free only of the ordinary laws which the government itself has made or may make. He does not include among these laws, the fundamental principle of the constitution under which the government itself comes into being, which defines, and sets bounds to the supreme organ in the government so created... The... supreme authority established and defined by a fundamental law is bound absolutely by that law, though he is free of all other laws».[106]

This distinction between constitutional rules of law and ordinary legislation, we stress, is of a fundamental character in modern constitutionalism, mainly of course, in written constitutional systems. If, as we have said, the principle of legality is that of the conformity or of the submission of all state acts to the law, in other words, the principle according to which all the activities of a state must conform to the Law, it is undoubtedly necessary to determine which is the rule of law which each act of the state must conform to. For this purpose, the rules of law that comprise a legal system, are deliberately or spontaneously, usually organized in a hierarchical way, so that there are norms of superior level that prevail over norms of inferior level.

3. Hierarchical or Graduated Legal System and the Confines of the Principle of Legality

Kelsen's theory of a legal system as a hierarchy of norms is without doubt, a useful method for identifying the hierarchical relation between the rules of law

[105] G. MACCORMACK, «Law and Legal System», *The Modern Law Review*, 42 (3), 1979, p. 285-290: «Legal system» understood as a collection of rules of law that have in common their interrelation in a particular order, mainly hierarchical.

[106] Ch. H. MCLLWAIN, *Constitutionalism and the Changing World*, Cambridge 1939, p. 73.

composing a legal system. In this sense, each norm belonging to the system usually has its derivation in another norm, ending the chain of derivation in a *Grundnorm* or constitution, which is the ultimate reason for the existence of all the norms of the whole system.

When sneaking of «derivation» Kelsen referred to the mode of creation of norms, in the sense that a norm is always created according to a power established by another norm.[107]

Kelsen said:

> «A plurality of norms or of rules of law constitute a unity, a system or an order when their validity depends on, in the final analysis, a unique rule or norm. This fundamental norm is the common source of validity of all the rules or norms that belong to the same order and form its unity. A rule of law thus belongs to a given order only when the possibility exists of making its validity depend on the fundamental norm that is on the foundation of this order».[108]

This theory of the graduated systemization of the legal order in a hierarchical way, with the constitution at the apex was developed by Adolf Merkl, from the same so-called «school of Vienna» to which Hans Kelsen also belonged, mainly on the grounds of administrative law.[109] We refer to it, because it give us a good method of logical order for constructing a legal system containing the various normative levels involved in a legal order of any state at a particular point in time. It also provides us with a logical explanation for the formal validity of each of those normative levels. It also gives us the formal confines of the «legality» of each act of the state organs, related to the leveled position of each norm that is created in that legal system.

In effect, the positive law of any state, at a given point in time, consists not only of the laws as formal acts of Parliament, but also of other normative bodies, such as delegate legislation, regulations, customs, the general principles of law and a whole series of other rules, including case law, certain specific and individualized ones such as contracts, court judgments and various types of administrative acts and provisions. All these precepts that make up the legal order in force at a given time not only have different origins but also different ranks, and it is not a question of considering them as co-coordinated rules in juxtaposition.[110] On the contrary, every legal order has a hierarchical structure, with its rules distributed in various strata, more or less one above the other. But within this hierarchy, there must necessarily be a formal connection between the rules, because they are linked organically, despite their different origins and characteristics.

Consequently, the legal order cannot be interpreted as a mere inorganic and disorderly aggregate of components, or simply as a chance juxtaposition of rules.

---

107 H. KELSEN, *General Theory of Law and State*, trans. Wedberg, rep. 1901, p. 110 et seq., quoted by G. MacCormack, *loc. cit.*, p. 286.

108 H. KELSEN, *Pure Theory of Law*, Chap. IX; *Teoría pura del derecho*, Buenos Aires 1981, p. 135.

109 It was Adolf MERKL, from the same 'School of Vienna' who developed the legal system as a hierarchy of norms in the grounds of administrative law. See A. MERKL, *Teoría general del derecho administrativo*, Madrid 1935, p. 7-2. See also H. KELSEN, «La garantie juridictionnelle de la constitution (La Justice constitutionnelle)», *Revue du droit public et de la science politique en France et a l'ètranger*, Paris 1928, pp. 197-257.

110 H. KELSEN, *Teoría pura... cit.*, p. 147.

On the contrary, to fully understand the legal order of a state, all such components must be arranged in hierarchical order, so that they form a legal system, with various types of norms unified and related. That is to say, they must follow a systematic order, with relations of co-ordination and dependence between the different parts.

Now, as we have said, the principle, which establishes the relationship between all those legal rules of such varied origin, rank and scope, shaping them into a system, is the existence of a common basis of validity, in the form of a fundamental or superior rule. Thus, a set of rules of law constitutes a relatively independent legal system when the justification or validity of them all has its derivation in a single rule, on which they are all formally based. And this single rule is referred to, in relation to all the others, as the fundamental rule or the constitution.

This method of the construction of the legal order in force by means of a graduated system of rules is based on the fact that the creation of a legal rule is always founded on another legal rule. One can, therefore, speak of a superior rule and of an inferior one. For example, the establishment of ordinary laws or acts of Parliament is regulated by the constitution; the decision as to who is to enact delegate legislation and how it is to be enacted, is regulated by certain formal laws. Then judicial decisions and their procedural rules are subject to previous legal rules established in formal law and delegate legislation. Likewise, the validity rules of administrative acts are established in ordinary laws, delegate legislation and other general regulations, and so on.

Thus, the principle of the internal connection of a legal system consists of basing the validity of certain rules on the validity of others. According to this method, it can be said that each category of rules is based on others of higher ranking, and at the same time, serves as the basis for others of lower ranking. Consequently, the whole legal order in force constitutes a system, which is graduated in hierarchical structures, and in which each link depends on others while supporting others.

In accordance with this method, the validity of all the rules of a given legal order, ultimately, stems from the constitution, the latter being understood to mean the rule which regulates the whole structure of the legal system, which is at the apex of the legal order and on which, finally, the latter is based.

This method referring to the forms of submission of state organs and activities to the rule of law is not only applicable to legal orders with written constitutions, but also applies to those systems with unwritten constitutions. In the former, the application of the theory of the graduated or hierarchical system of rules is evidently clear, precisely because a formal constitutional document established as a supreme constituent rule exists. Whereas in other legal systems without written constitutions the process of systemization of the legal order is much more complicated, and that is why the legal system here consists of an amalgam of heterogeneous rules, established in statutes and common law,[111] which are applied by courts as rules of law, also including ancient laws enacted centuries ago, conventions, delegate legislation and so on.

---

111 «The law is today an amalgam of common law and statute law of such an interdependent kind that it is often difficult to say whether a particular result is determined by the statute or by ordinary case Law». P.S. ATIYAH, «Common Law and Statute Law», *The Modern Law Review*, 48, (1), 1985, p. 5.

In either case, the formal systemization of a legal order is nevertheless indispensable to the determination of the scope of application of the law to state bodies, because in both cases, situations very often arise in which two provisions, antagonistic in their content, apparently claim to be in force. In such cases it will always be necessary to find out which of the two is in force, to determine which one ranks higher or lower in the event of conflicts between two or more rules of law, which appear to be in force, and which state body is competent to decide which one is in force and which one is not.

In short, to solve the issue of the formal validity of the precepts applied to state bodies, it is necessary to formally systematize the whole set of rules of law in a unified structure, from the logical point of view. And that is precisely the reason why the method of the graduated system of rules of law provides an appropriate tool.

With this method, in the overall analysis of the legal order, it is possible to distinguish between those acts of state whose execution is immediately related to the constitution, that is to say, which are issued directly on the basis of constitutional powers, and those, whose execution is not directly related to the constitution and which are actually issued on the basis of powers that establish rules of law inferior to the constitution.

Among the acts immediately related to the constitution are, primarily, the «formal laws», that is to say, acts of Parliament issued in accordance with the provisions of the constitution, as well as formal acts of a legislative nature, drawn up by the politically decentralized territorial entities. For example, in a Federal state, there are the laws issued by the legislative bodies of the member states of the Federation; or the formal acts, also of a legislative nature, of the local and municipal authorities, when the latter have political autonomy.

In all such cases, the laws as formal acts of the legislative bodies constitute a direct exercise by them of a competence contained in the constitution of the state itself. Therefore, they are produced on the basis of a competence established in the constitution and exercised in direct execution of the constitution.

That is why we have said that in relation to acts of Parliaments, for instance, the rule of law that establishes limitations on its activities is the «rule of the constitution», in the sense that in a written constitutional system, the legislative body finds its confines of legality in the norms of the constitution. The principle of legality in relation to the legislative body, therefore, implies submission to the constitution, and judicial control over its acts can only be of a constitutional character.

In legal systems with written constitutions not only are the formal laws acts of direct execution of the constitution, but there are also acts of Parliament which are issued on the basis of attributions provided for directly in the constitution, and which are not defined as «formal laws» because they are not instruments regulating the conduct and activities of individuals, as is the case of normative parliamentary acts that regulate the organization and procedures of the legislature internally. They are what are called *interna corporis*, that is to say, acts that regulate the functioning of the Houses.

Parliament can also pass other acts, which are not «formal laws» nor acts with internal effects, and which are also issued on the basis of the direct execution of constitutional attributions. In many written constitutions, in effect, and because of the check and balance system of the separation of powers, a multitude of legislative interventions in executive activities has been established in a way that certain executive acts require, as a condition of validity, the approval of Congress or of the Legislative Assembly. That happens, for instance, in the appointment of some high-ranking state officials in domestic administration or in the diplomatic corps; in contracting foreign loans or in the approval of various budget modifications. In many countries, the executive requires the approval, or the authorization of Congress, before taking any such actions.

All these acts of Parliament, even though they are not formal laws, enjoy the same formal hierarchy as the formal Law, in the sense that they are only submitted to the constitution, which regulates them. They are, therefore, subject to the principle of legality but in the sense of subjection to the constitution and can also be judicially reviewed to enforce the constitutional rule to which they must be in accordance.

In these constitutional systems of written constitutions, this fundamental document also attributes in some cases direct powers to the head of state to exercise certain activities, which are not subject to regulation by the ordinary legislator. In such cases, there is the question of powers attributed by the constitution to the head of state, or of government, who exercises them, precisely, on the basis of those constitutional attributions, which can neither be regulated nor limited by the legislator through acts of Parliament.

Here it is a question of acts which normally concern the «government» in the political sense, and which are reserved for the head of state or of government. It is what is termed in European continental law «acts of government» or «political acts», more or less equivalent to the North American notion of «political questions», which, being acts of direct execution of the constitution, are not submitted to regulation by formal law, and are exercised by the head of state, based on the direct provisions of the constitution. Consequently, these acts of government also rank equal to formal laws, and they are only subject to what is established by the constitution, which determines its confines of legality.

Because of the traditional absence of judicial control of the constitutionality of state acts, and because of the limited power conferred upon the administrative judicial courts or tribunals in France and in other continental European countries, the doctrine of the *actes de gouvernement* or «political acts» as an exception to the principle of legality was developed during this century in the sense that they were not subject to judicial control by the administrative judicial courts.

In France, the decisions of the *Conseil d'État* declaring its incompetence to control such acts, led to the development of that doctrine, establishing a distinction between administrative action, which should be subject to judicial control, and governmental action, which was not subject to such control. This governmental action was progressively reduced to basically two fields: the acts of the head of state or of government in relation to the legislative body, for instance the power of the executive to submit bills to the legislature, and acts concerned with international relations, for example, the process of making or denouncing a treaty.[112] On the contrary, in a legal system with judicial review of the constitutionality of state acts, these «acts of government» if it is true that they would escape judicial review of the

112 A. TUNC, «Government under Law: a Civilian View», *loc. cit.*, pp. 46–47.

administrative judicial court because they are not subject to «formal law» and they are not administrative acts, they would nevertheless be subject to judicial control of the constitutionality. Here, again those acts of the head of state or of government are undoubtedly subject to the principle of legality, but here also legality means constitutionality (submission to the rule of the constitution). Therefore, if there were no system of judicial review of constitutionality, ordinary courts for administrative judicial control acts would declare their incompetence to control these on the grounds of unconstitutionality and not because they would have been an exception to the rule of law. Here again, in relation to each state act, the question is of the definition of the confines of what legality means to them, so as to establish its validity conditions.

In addition to the so called «acts of government» within the acts of the head of state or of government, in direct execution of the constitution, we can also add the so-called «decree laws», which rank equal to the «formal law» and which are produced in those cases in which the constitution attributes certain legislative powers to the executive power, that is to say, to the head of state. In such cases it is not simply a matter of delegating legislation, but it is a question of acts with the force of «formal law», as far as their rank and content are concerned, and not issued by the ordinary legislator or by Parliament, but by the head of state or of government.

By virtue of their legislative content, these are normative acts of government which are also issued in direct execution of the constitution, on the basis of power established directly by the constitution, or on some occasions, delegated by Parliament in accordance with the provisions of the constitution. In such cases, the Decree-laws have the same hierarchy as ordinary formal Laws; although, by virtue of their content, ordinary formal law enacted by Parliament could replace them.

In all these cases, acts issued by constitutional bodies are acts in direct execution of the constitution and are, therefore, submitted only to the constitution. The principle of legality of the *État de droit*, that is to say, the necessary submission of state bodies to the law, as far as these constitutional bodies and acts issued in execution of the constitution are concerned, is tantamount to submission to the constitution. As we have already said, in these cases, «legality» is equivalent to «constitutionality» for Parliament and for the head of state, or government, in other words, submission to the constitution, or action in conformity with the rules established by the constitution and within constitutional limits.

Nevertheless, in the formal systematization of the legal order, within this graduated system of production of rules and their execution, apart from all those acts issued in direct execution of the constitution, the rest of the state bodies, particularly in the administrative and judicial field, exercises its powers not in direct execution of constitutional rules, but rather in direct execution of the «legislation», that is to say of the formal laws or acts of parliament and even acts of government or decree-laws issued by the appropriate constitutional bodies, in turn, in direct execution of the constitution.

Thus, all administrative activities are ultimately acts in immediate execution of the «legislation», and mediate execution of the constitution, that is to say, in direct execution of the «legislation» and indirect execution of the constitution.

Consequently, the extent of the administration's submission to legality in the *État de droit* is greater than that of the submission to the rule of law of the supreme state bodies. Congress or Parliament is submitted to the constitution and also when the head of state or of government issues an act of government, he is only restricted by the constitution; whereas the administrative bodies and authorities are involved in a much more extensive area of legality, since they are submitted to the «legislation» and execute it. That is why in this field the principle of legality has taken on the meaning it normally has in relation to administrative action in the contemporary state.

This approach to the graduated system of legal order for the analysis of legal systems, as we have said, has enormous implications in the area of judicial control of the activities and actions of the state.

In effect, it would be no use formulating the principle of legality in the *État de droit,* in the sense of submission of the state to the rule of law, if some mechanism were not set up, whereby individuals could control the effective submission of state bodies to the law, by court action. This obviously leads us to the two major aspects of judicial review in the modern world, which are, of course, conditioned by the degree of execution of the acts of state vis-à-vis the constitution.

In effect, in those systems in which a written constitution exists, the maximum demonstration of the principle of legality is reflected in the establishment of two major systems of judicial control over the exercise of power: the control of constitutionality and the control of legality in the strictest sense of the term.

In the case of state acts issued in direct execution of the constitution, that is to say, acts of Parliament, such as statutes or *interna corporis*; or acts of the head of state or of government, such as acts of government, issued on the basis of powers granted directly and exclusively by the constitution, these must be subject to some system of judicial control of constitutionality for it, to be a *État de droit* in the fullest sense of the term.

It is to this end, for example, that constitutional tribunals have been set up in the European continental states, as constitutional bodies, with the basic aim of controlling the constitutionality of state acts issued in direct execution of the constitution.

The constitutionality of laws and acts as pertaining to the internal regulations of Parliament has been especially controlled, as well as that of acts of government and decree-laws.

It is not by chance that the countries in Europe in which the first constitutional tribunals were set up were precisely those in which the organization of the constitutional system was directly influenced by Kelsen's theory of a legal system as a hierarchy of norms. The precise purpose of these tribunals was to judge cases of unconstitutionality of state acts issued in direct execution of the constitution. That was the situation in Austria and Czechoslovakia in 1920, where the constitutions and legal systems of those countries were directly influenced by the doctrine of the Viennese School. But it was not until the nineteen-forties that constitutional tribunals were established in continental Europe, to judge the constitutionality of laws and acts of government, particularly those having the force of law.

On the other hand, we must stress that precisely because of the absence of a constitutional body entrusted with the control of the constitutionality of state acts in direct execution of the constitution, together with the expansion of the principle of legality in relation to administrative acts, this led, in many cases, to a distortion of the situation of the *État de droit*. Such distortion can be seen in the development of the previously mentioned doctrine of the «act of government» or «political act», aimed at excluding the judgment of the legality of certain state acts issued by the head of state from the competence of the administrative judicial courts. Thus, the famous doctrine of the «acts of government» in French law, or «political acts» in Italian or Spanish law, which was developed long before constitutional tribunals were established in those countries. As we have said, according to that doctrine, it was supposed that there were certain executive acts that, although improperly considered as administrative acts, were not, however, submitted to the control of legality by the administrative judicial courts. This was because they were considered to have been formulated initially for political reasons, or later, when the day of that doctrine was coming to an end, because it was considered that they referred to issues stipulated directly in the constitutions with reference to the relations between the different state powers or constitutional bodies, or to other states in the international order.

As we said, such acts were actually exempt from submission to administrative judicial control or from control of administrative legality, not because they were administrative acts issued for political reasons but because, contrary to what was asserted, they were not really administrative acts. In effect, they were acts of government issued in direct execution of the constitution, and the only control to which they could be submitted was the control of constitutionality, that means submission to the rule, which was executed by their issuance, namely, the constitution itself. Since there was no control of the constitutionality of state acts in those countries, there could be no judicial control over such acts, which contributed to the distortion of the doctrine of the «act of government». In countries such as Spain and Italy, the subsequent establishment of control over the constitutionality of laws and executive acts with the force of laws resulted in the reduction or disappearance of the doctrine of the judicial immunity of political acts. They now come under the control of the constitutional tribunals.

In France, since there is no genuine control of the constitutionality of acts in execution of the constitution yet, the doctrine of the exemption of «acts of government» from judicial control still exists, giving rise to an area which is immune to the control of legality typical of the *État de droit*.

Now, in the United Kingdom legal system, in the absence of a written constitution, in the sense of a formal document of the nature of a fundamental law governing the basic principles of the actions of state bodies and establishing a set of entrenched rights and constitutional guarantees, there can be, of course, no judicial control over the constitutionality of certain acts. Consequently, when there is no written constitution, in a graduated legal system, there is nothing in the nature of a fundamental rule or constitution to serve as a source of validity of lower-ranking laws.

In the absence of any such formal constitution serving as a fundamental law, as we have seen the sovereign act in the British system is precisely the act of Parliament; hence the principle of parliamentary sovereignty which implies that as Parliament is not submitted to any superior rule, it produces the superior rules itself. In this sense, an act of Parliament is not submitted to any other rule, and its constitutionality could not, therefore, be controlled with respect to any formal document.

Consequently, in the British legal system, a control of the constitutionality of acts of Parliament is inconceivable in the terms provided for in continental, European or American legal systems. Hence, the establishment of a precise hierarchy in the production of rules of law is also very difficult, since there is no such written constitution and finally the supreme rule is the rule of Parliament. Besides, there are no degrees of validity among statutes.[113]

Nevertheless, in relation to the legal order below the acts of Parliament we think a system of a graduated or hierarchical legal order can, in fact, be developed and that it is possible to establish a systematization more or less of the entire legal order, based, naturally, on the concept of the superiority of acts of Parliament.

In any case, apart from acts issued in direct execution of the constitution in graduated legal systems which have given rise to the systems of judicial control of constitutionality, it is evident that the principle of legality plays a more important role at the second level of execution of the legal order, that is to say, those state acts issued in direct execution of the «legislation, or in indirect execution of the constitution. Here the principle of legality has developed in the fullest sense of the term, particularly in connection with the administration, both in the continental European and in the United Kingdom legal systems, giving rise to the judicial control of the legality of administrative acts or action, and therefore, to administrative law itself.

But this principle of legality, mainly in legal systems with written constitutions implies, of course, not only that the executive or administrative power is subject to the rule of law, but that the other organs of the state, including the legislative organs, are also subject to the rule of law. Therefore, what the rule of law is all about, in relation to which each state organ is submitted, varies and has a different confine or ambit, depending on the position that each norm or state act has in the hierarchical legal system. That is why, for the legislator, legality means constitutionality or submission to the constitution; as for the head of the state, with regard to acts of government, legality also means subjection to the constitution. In such cases, they are adopted in direct execution of the constitution, without the interference of acts of Parliament, so that they are submitted only to the constitution.

4. Principle of Legality and the Executive

As far as executive and judicial powers are concerned, the principle of legality or the rule of law has a wider sense. It includes not only the constitution itself, but also all state acts with a general and normative character, and especially those of «legislative» level that include not only acts of Parliament, but also all other state acts with the same legal force, as are those acts of the head of state issued within its constitutional powers. In the principle of legality related to the executive all the other sources of legal rules that bind administrative action are also included as well as the general principles of law, or principles of natural justice that are to be observed by public administration.

In this respect, it is obvious, in the contemporary public legal systems, that the principle of legality in relation to the executive and to administrative of action, is in fact, of more importance.

---

113 *Halsbury's Laws of England*, 4th Ed. London 1974, Vol. 8, p. 531.

However, in the evolution of the contemporary state, the principle of legality was traditionally referred to the submission of the administration to the law, in the sense of «formal law», that is to say, acts issued by Parliament, it being understood by this that public administration always had to act on the basis of a pre-existent rule of law.

But, in continental legal systems, this principle of legality originally confined to submission to the formal law has been expanded to the extent that the term «legality» has become synonymous to legal order, in the sense that in a graduated legal system, the administration must be submitted to all the superior rules governing its activities. In this context, therefore, law is not just law in the formal sense, but it also includes international treaties signed by the respective states, delegate legislation and other resolutions of a general nature, as well as decree-laws and any other normative sources of law applied to the administration, including, the general principles of law.

Naturally, this principle of legality referring to public administration has been particularly implemented by the establishment of a system of control of the administration through the courts, either the ordinary courts or special administrative judicial courts, and by the establishment of the principle of the responsibility of the state, particularly for damage caused to individuals by state actions.

In short, the principle of legality in relation to the executive implies the establishment of a system of judicial review of administrative actions; that is to say, it demands the establishment of a system of administrative justice to control the submission of public administration, precisely, to legality.

In this sense, in the *État de droit*, unlike the situation in absolutist regimes, the activities of the administration are subject to complete judicial supervision through the judicial mechanisms provided for in ordinary law, or established in a particular administrative law system, and implemented through actions granted to individuals, to control any legal infractions which may be committed by the administration itself.

Occasionally, the theory of discretionary powers opened a void in the principle of legality, but, little by little, the progressive judicial control of these discretionary acts has been allowed with the result that, despite the liberty granted to the administration to make decisions, such acts are also submitted to a judicial control of legality. They are no longer considered in any country as an exemption to the principle of legality as was originally thought mainly under French administrative law.

When granting discretionary powers, the law lives the administration certain amount of freedom to take the most convenient action or decision according to its own interpretation. But it has been accepted and established through the judicial control of administrative action, that discretionary power has limits, and cannot transform itself into arbitrariness. Therefore, various limits to the exercise of discretionary power have been identified in continental European administrative law, derived from the principles of proportionality, rationality, non-discrimination, equity and justice.

It has also been accepted that the use of discretionary powers by the administration cannot lead to the violation of the general principles of administrative procedure, in particular, those connected to the right to a fair due process of law, granting the general right to citizens to look for their own defence. A demonstration of this is the right to a hearing before an administrative action could be taken, so that the individual who may be affected by that such a decision could have the opportunity to express his position regarding the administrative action and argue his rights.

All these principles leading to limiting discretionary power, even though originated in case law, have frequently been formally established in various countries in formal laws relating to administrative procedures. Venezuela can serve as an example of this process of formalization of the limits to discretionary power. Its Administrative Procedures Act of 1981[114] for instance, states in article 12:

> «*Art. 12.* When a norm of a Statute or of a general regulation issued by the Executive, leaves an administrative measure or decision to be made by the competent authority on his own understanding such a measure or decision must maintain due proportionality and adequacy with the facts and aims established in the norm, and follow all the procedural rules and formalities needed for its validity and effectiveness».

That is to say, when an administrative authority has been granted by an act of Congress or by a general executive regulation, enough liberty to take any measure or make any decision based on its own understanding of the circumstances and timing of the given action, it must, first, respect the principle of proportionality of the administrative action; second, it must seek the aims for which the discretionary powers were granted; third, it must observe the due fitness of the facts within such rules established in the norm; and fourth, it must always respect the procedural steps required for the validity and effectiveness of the administrative action.

Thus, the first limit of the discretionary power in that law is the duty imposed by it on all administrative authorities to respect due proportionality between the facts that motivated the administrative actions, and the consequences established in the latter. In that respect, if the norm authorises the administrative organ, for example, to apply a fine or penalty measured against two extremes, in accordance with its appreciation of the gravity of the offence, the action, that is to say, the fine or penalty imposed must have some proportion with the actual facts which occurred and which causes the administrative action deriving from rationality justice and equity.

This principle of proportionality as a limit to discretionary power leads to another, the principle of equality and nondiscrimination, in the sense that if in relation to a given fact a measure has been taken or a decision has been made against an individual, the same measure or decision must be made against other individuals, if the facts coincide. Of course, this also implies that the principle of impartiality as a general principle of administrative action, is also a limit on discretionary power.

But the norm of the Venezuelan Administrative Procedures Act that we are referring to as an example, also establishes as a limit on discretionary power, the need for a administrative authority to try to attain when taking a measure or making a decision, the aims established in the norm when granting power to public

---

114 A.R. BREWER-CARÍAS, *El derecho administrativo y la Ley orgánica de procedimientos administrativos*, Caracas 1982, p. 379-414.

administration. Any deviation in obtaining or pursuing those aims can lead to judicial control of the administrative action by means of illegality, though the so called *détournement de pouvoir* in French administrative law.

Moreover, that same article of the Venezuelan Administrative Procedure Act established, also as a limit upon discretionary powers, the due fitness of the actual facts that motivated an administrative action with the ones established in the particular norm. That means that public authority must first determine the fact that had occurred; second, it must prove them, through the usual or technical means required; and third, it must qualify them appropriately, and finally, the facts must coincide with the ones established in the norm authorizing the action. All these steps must be taken in accordance with the already mentioned principles of equality, impartiality and justice, so that any violation thereof leads to illegality.

Finally, the norm states that in the use of discretionary powers by public administration the administrative organ must always respect the procedural steps normally required for the validity and effectiveness of the administrative action. Within these procedural rules, we must underline the right to defend oneself that must be guaranteed in all administrative actions and which derives from the constitution itself. This right of every citizen to look for his own defense leads in the Administrative Procedures Act of Venezuela, to the formal establishment of a few other and derivative rights of the individual vis-à-vis public administration. For instance, the right to be heard always before a decision can be made that affects his rights and interests; the right to participate in administrative procedures that could affect those rights and interests; the right to be formally and personally notified of every decision that may affect him; the right to have access to all official documents filed in the dossier concerned and the right to copy those documents; the right to present evidence before the public administration in one's own defense; and the right to be notified of the means of appeal or other actions that the individual can use for his defense whether administrative or judicial.[115]

Therefore, as we can deduct from this example of a formal establishment of limits on discretionary powers by statute and not only by means of case law, the principle of legality related mainly to administrative action, has expanded considerably. All such limits on the discretionary powers of the executive, although now established, as we have seen from the Venezuelan example in particular laws or statues, have undoubtedly been developed through judicial decisions, (case law), even in civil law legal systems.

Of course, in common law legal systems, these limits have also been established in case law, particularly through the principles of natural justice.[116]

All these systems have in common the exclusion of the consideration of discretionary power as an exemption of the principle of legality or the rule of law, as well as the acceptance that even in its discretionary power granted by law, administrative action is entirely submitted to the rule of law.

But in relation to this exemption to the principle of legality as it was treated in continental European legal systems, a few decades ago, the same can be said of so-called government or political acts.

---

115 *Ibid*, p. 112-118.

116 See in general, P. JACKSON, *Natural Justice*, London 1979, p. 224.

As we have said, in continental Europe, certain acts of the executive, such as political acts, were traditionally seen as being exempt from submission to legality. Nevertheless, even though such acts cannot be considered as administrative acts, not only has the Legal state made an effort to gradually reduce the number of such political acts exempt from control, but with the establishment in continental Europe of constitutional tribunals, it has been possible, in some countries to control the constitutionality of such acts of government, as acts in direct execution of the constitution.

In short, all the activities of the executive must be submitted to the principle of legality and must, therefore, be submitted to judicial review. Because of this, it is possible to demand that the administration be held responsible for damages caused by its actions. Of course, when we say that all activities of the executive must be submitted to the law, this naturally also includes all the normative activities of the executive itself, such as, regulations and different forms of delegated legislation, which are also submitted to review by independent judicial bodies.

5. The Rule of Law and Dicey's Concepts

As we said at the beginning, in the United Kingdom legal system, what the continental European legal systems call the principle of legality is included under the general term of «rule of law». It is true that this «rule of law» generally means the same as the *État de droit* for continental states, that is to say, it is the laws that govern, not men.

However, there is perhaps a radical historical difference between the two systems: whereas the *État de droit* came into being on the continent as a rational system substituting the *Ancien Régime*, the «rule of law», since monarchical absolutism was unknown in England, is causally linked to the medieval doctrine of the *Reign of Law* in the sense that law, whether it be attributed to supernatural or human sources, ought to rule the world.[117]

Therefore, as Professor E.C.S. Wade said, Dicey did not invent the notion of the rule of law[118] but was the first writer to systematize and analyze the principle. That is why we think it is impossible to refer to the rule of law in the United Kingdom, without referring in one way or another to Dicey's approach, which has tended to govern modern discussion, on the subject.[119]

According to Dicey's classical definition, the rule of law means three things: the absolute predominance of the law; equality before the law; and the concept according to which the constitution is the result of the recognition of individual rights by judges.

With regard to the first meaning, Dicey stated that by rule of law,

> «We mean... that no man is punishable or can be lawfully made to suffer in body or goods except for a distinct breach of law established in the ordinary legal manner before the ordinary courts of the land. In this sense, the rule of law is contrasted with every system of government based on the exercise by

[117] W. HOLDSWORTH, *A History of English Law*, Vol. II, London 1972, p. 121. *Cf.* E.C.S. WADE, «Introduction» to A.V. DICEY, *An Introduction to the Study of the Law of the Constitution*, London 1973, p. xcii.
[118] E.C.S, WADE, «Introduction», *loc. cit.*, p. xcii.
[119] J.D.B. MITCHELL, *op. cit.*, p. 53.

persons in authority of wide, arbitrary, or discretionary powers of constraint».[120]

As Dicey himself stated, in this sense, the rule of law means:

> «The absolute supremacy or predominance of regular law as opposed to the influence of the arbitrary power, and excludes the existence of arbitrariness of prerogative, or even wide discretionary authority on the part of the Government. Englishmen are ruled by the law, and by the law alone; a man may with us be punished for a breach of law, but he can be punished for nothing else».[121]

In relation to this first meaning of the rule of law, we must observe that, as we have said, discretionary powers granted to government by the law is not necessarily equivalent to arbitrariness, on the contrary the government itself has limits in its exercise.

We must also observe when considering this first meaning of Dicey's rule of law, that whilst it is true that the government lacks arbitrary power, it is clear, however, that that power lies on Parliament, since, unlike the legislative bodies of other countries, Parliament's powers are not limited by a constitution. Consequently, the British Parliament, by virtue of its sovereignty, possesses, in principle, unlimited-powers, not only to establish general rules, but also individual rules with any content.

Arbitrary regulation is not, therefore, constitutionally excluded, although, in principle, it must take the form of an act of Parliament or be authorized by such an act. But bearing in mind government's factual supremacy over Parliament, because of the fact that the latter's decisions are determined by the former owing to the party system, the result is that the decision on measures is actually made, in the last resort, by the government, which may request action from Parliament, even after having taken such measures. Thus, for example, it has been said Parliament ratified and legalized in 1931 a series of illegal acts issued by the Cabinet with reference to the abolition of the gold standard. In this case, the arbitrary power of Parliament served to sanction illegal acts.[122]

According to Dicey, the rule of law also means legal equality. In this sense, Dicey wrote:

> «We mean in the second place, when we speak of the rule of law as a characteristic of our country, not only that with us no man is above the law, but (what is a different thing), that here every man, whatever be his rank or condition, is subject to the ordinary law of the realm and amenable to the jurisdiction of the ordinary tribunals».[123]

However, in explaining this second meaning, he went further, also applying the concept to government officials. He said:

> «It means, again, equality before the law, or the equal subjection of all classes to the ordinary law of the land administered by the ordinary law courts. The

---

120 A.V. DICEY, *op. cit.*, p. 188.

121 *Ibid*, p. 202. In this concept, regular law is understood to mean statute law and common law, but the former has supremacy over the latter.

122 I. JENNINGS, *The Law and the Constitution, cit.* p. 57-58

123 A.V. DICEY, *op. cit.*, p. 193.

rule of law in this sense excludes the idea of any exemption of officials or other from the duty of obedience to the law which governs other citizens or from the jurisdiction of the ordinary tribunals».[124]

In this sense, Dicey's concept of the rule of law, ecludes the idea of any exemption in favor of public officials or other individuals, and naturally also excludes any idea of administrative judicial special courts in the French manner.

As a consequence of this statement, is his famous mistaken approach to «administrative law», which concludes that «there can be with us nothing really corresponding to the «administrative law», *droit administratif* «or the «administrative tribunals» (*tribunaux administratives*) of France.[125]

Dicey really denounced what he understood French administrative law to be. He said that the *droit administratif* rested at bottom on various «leading ideas alien to the conceptions of modern Englishmen», and within which he referred to the idea:

> «That in France, the government and every servant of the Government, possesses, as representative of the nation, a whole body of special rights, privileges, or prerogatives as against private citizens, and that the extent of these rights, privileges or prerogatives is to be determined on principles different from the consideration which fix the legal rights and duties of one citizen towards another».[126]

All these privileges and prerogatives referred to by Dicey lead to what he considered to be the main one in the French system: the existence of special administrative courts to judge public bodies and officials ranked in a separate system of judicature different to the judicial power, having at its apex not the *Court de Cassation* but the *Conseil d'État*.

It has long been realized in Great Britain that Dicey's picture of administrative law was wrong[127] and that legal equality does not mean that the state bodies would be submitted to the same laws applicable to ordinary citizens. As Professor J.D.B. Mitchell stated:

> «While the subjection of officials to law is desirable, it does not follow that this should in all cases, or generally, be a subjection to the law which is applicable to the ordinary citizen» (because)... it is clear that the powers of government cannot be those of an ordinary citizen... and that as far as rights are concerned public bodies and public officials cannot be governed by the ordinary law».[128]

Therefore, if it is desirable that the executive must in principle be subject to the same law as that governing the citizens, this does not, of course, exclude the possible need for the government, in view of its very nature, to have special prerogatives and powers. What the principle of the rule of law actually requires is

---

124 *Ibid.* p. 202-203.

125 *Ibid.* p. 203.

126 *Ibid.* p. 336-337. «An individual in his dealing with the state does not, according to French ideas, stand on anything like the same footing as that on which he stands in dealing with his neighbor», p. 337.

127 H.W.R. WADE, *Administrative Law*, Oxford 1984, p. 25.

128 J.D.B. MITCHELL, *op. cit.*, p. 58.

that the government be granted no unnecessary privileges or exemptions in relation to ordinary laws. In this respect, for example, the fact that the crown could not be taken to court on the grounds of responsibility constituted an unnecessary privilege, which was eliminated in 1947 by the Crown Proceeding Act.[129]

In any event, in relation to this second meaning of the rules of law as developed by Dicey, we can conclude by saying that it really implies that government bodies should be subject to the law. In this same sense, we can say based on the principle of the sovereignty of Parliament, that is to say, that Parliament, in its capacity as the legislature, is sovereign and exempt from any legal control, that the principle of the rule of law means, that all government actions must be carried out in accordance with the law. In particular, when applied to administrative or governmental authorities, it implies that all of such authorities, when issuing any act, must do so by means of an authorization granted in a law that, in general, must be understood to be an act of Parliament. In other words, the rule of law implies that any government act, which may affect some individual rights or liberties, must be carried out strictly under the authority of an act of Parliament.

But the principle of the rule of law does not consist solely of submission to formal law. It also implies, as we have seen, the need for the administrative authority to submit to the principles and rules which limit any discretionary power granted to the said authority by an act of Parliament. That is the reason why it has been said that the principle of the rule of law was developed in relation to the administration, on the basis of judicial limitations upon the powers which may have been granted to the administrative authorities by acts of Parliament.[130] The object of all this is to prevent and avoid abuse in the exercise of discretionary powers.

In addition to the foregoing, the principle of the rule of law, as a specific manifestation of the *État de droit* and of the principle of legality in the United Kingdom legal system, implies that claims brought by individuals against administrative and government acts and officials must be judged by the judicial authority, that is to say, by judges completely independent of the executive bodies. Naturally, the principle of legality does not necessarily require that these judicial bodies that control administrative actions be separate from the ordinary judicial bodies. What legality and the state according to law demand is that control be exercised by judicial bodies, and in the countries with common law systems particularly in the United States and the United Kingdom, disputes between the administration and individuals are settled by the ordinary law courts.[131]

Thus, contrary to the practice in the French system, in which disputes relating to the control of the legality of administrative action are brought before administrative courts organized separately from the judicial hierarchy, but independent of the government, in the British system, the right to have the public administration appear before ordinary courts and independent judges, in matters of control of legality, is one of the most important elements of the concept of the rule of law.

---

129 H.W.R. WADE, *op. cit.*, p. 24.

130 L.L. JAFFE and E.G. HENDERSON, «Judicial Review and the Rule of Law: Historical Origins», *The Law Quarterly Review*, 72, 1956, pp. 345-364. See in general, B. SCHWARTZ and H.W.R. WADE, *Legal Control of Government*, Oxford 1978, p. 350.

131 J.M. EVANS, *de Smith's Judicial Review of Administrative Action*, Fourth Ed., London 1980, p. 11.

The third meaning of the rule of law according to Dicey is that the constitution was the result of the recognition of individual rights by judges, and therefore, that these rights were not the result of a written constitution.

Dicey explained this third meaning of the rule of law as follows:

> «We may say that the constitution is pervaded by the rule of law on the grounds that the general principles of the constitution (as for example the right to personal liberty, or the right of public meeting) are with us the result of judicial decisions determining the rights of private persons in particular cases brought before the courts; whereas under many foreign constitutions the security (such as it is) given to the rights of individuals results, or appears to result, from the general principles of the constitution».[132]

In other words, he described this third meaning of his conception of the rule of law by saying that this expression.

> «May be used as a formula for expressing the fact that with us the law of the constitution, the rules which in foreign countries naturally form part of a constitutional code, are not the source but the consequence of the rights of individuals, as defined and enforced by the courts».[133]

We do not think that this third meaning can be sustained firmly nowadays. The rights of individuals that a state have to ensure and protect today are not only personal liberties such as free speech which Dicey was concerned with but rather, rights such as the protection of physical well-being, having a proper home, being educated, having social security, a proper environment, etc., that cannot be the creation of judge-made law, on the contrary it requires complex legislation.[134] That is to say, «the common law does not assure the citizens economic or social wellbeing».[135]

Therefore, if it is true that ordinary courts continue to play a fundamental role in the protection of individual rights, it is also true that statutory regulations are required for the enforcement of such rights. Thus, they cannot only be the result of the courts enforcement but also undoubtedly of their establishment in acts of Parliament. Also, we have to bear in mind the primacy of statutory law over common law, thus the latter can always be modified by Parliament, and the most fundamental liberties may be removed by statute.

Thus, Dicey's faith in the common law as the primary legal means for the protection of citizen's liberties against the state has been superseded and the experience of many western countries with entrenched declarations of human rights imposing legal limits upon the legislature to infringe it, has proved to be of value.

Anyway, despite the well-known expansion of Dicey's concepts, particularly in regard to his distrust of administrative law, this discipline widely developed in this country during the present century (20th century), and within its own rules, new concepts arose regarding the rule of law, always related to governmental action and more closely to the principle of legality developed in continental Europe.

---

132 A.V. DICEY, *op. cit.*, p. 195.
133 *Ibid*, p. 203.
134 J.D.B. MITCHELL, *op. cit.*, p. 54-55.
135 E.C.S. WADE and G. GODFREY PHILLIPS, *Constitutional and Administrative Law*, London 1982, p. 89.

In order to understand this change, it will suffice to recall here two of the new and recent approaches to the matter.

The first is the concept developed by Professor H.W.R. Wade in his well-known book on *Administrative Law*, in which he identified five different although related meanings of the rule of law. First, that all governmental action must be taken according to the law, in the sense that all administrative acts that infringe individual rights must be authorized by law. Second, that government should be conducted within a framework of recognized rules and principles that restrict discretionary power, in the sense that an essential part of the rule of law is that of a system of rules for preventing the abuse of such discretionary power. Third, that disputes as to the legality of acts of government are to be decided upon by courts that are wholly independent of the executive, which in this country are the ordinary courts of law. Fourth, that the law should be even handed between government and citizen, in the sense that even though it cannot be the same for both, the government should not enjoy unnecessary privileges or exemptions from ordinary law. And fifth, outside the sphere of public administration, the rule of law means that no-one should be punished except for legally defined crimes, a principle that applies, however, to administrative action in the sphere of administrative sanctions.[136]

In another more descriptive perspective, Joseph Raz enumerated a few principles, which can be derived from the basic idea of the rule of law, which undoubtedly complement the previously mentioned view of Professor Wade. Those principles are as follows: All laws should be prospective, open and clear; laws should be relatively stable; the making of particular laws should be guided by open, stable, clear and general rules; the independence of the judiciary must be guaranteed; the principles of natural justice must be observed; the courts should have review powers over the implementation of those principles; the courts should be easily accessible; and the discretion of the crime prevention agencies should not be allowed to hinder the law.[137]

All these meanings or principles related to the concept of the rule of law, in the British constitutional system and since Dicey's conception, are, of course, mainly related to the activities of the executive or government, and mainly to administrative action. Parliament, because of its sovereignty, is not included in the principle.

Therefore, because of the absence of a written constitution and the already mentioned principle of parliamentary sovereignty, Parliament, has in fact no entrenched law to which it must be kept submitted. Thus, it has no legal limits upon its activities, and its acts cannot be judicially reviewed because no court has the power to control their constitutionality. Here lies the real difference, nowadays, between the concept of the rule of law in the British constitutional system and the principle of legality in the legal states of continental Europe and America.

In continental Europe and America, the concept of the principle of legality also includes the legislative in the sense that Congresses, General Assemblies or Parliaments are , in general, submitted to and limited by the constitution, established as a written and rigid higher law, and that submission is judicially controlled by ordinary or special courts with sufficient power in some cases, even to annul unconstitutional laws.

---

136 H.W.R. WADE, *op. cit.*, p. 22, 24.

137 J. RAZ, «The Rule of Law and its Virtue», *The Law Quarterly Review*, 93, 1977, p. 198-202.

Up to now, we have referred to two principles of the *État de droit* in the contemporary world, that of the distribution and limitation of state powers, and that of the submission of all state bodies to the principle of legality or the rule of law.

Now I want to refer to the third of the main features of the *État de droit* that of the establishment of an entrenched bill of rights normally in a written constitution, that historically has always been essential to the notion of the *État de droit* and, of course, to liberalism.

IV. THE DECLARATION OF FUNDAMENTAL RIGHTS AND LIBERTIES

In effect, as we said, the third characteristic of the *État de droit* is the establishment of a set of fundamental rights and liberties, normally enumerated in a formal declaration of constitutional rank or in a written constitution, in an entrenched way and with the necessary guarantees and legal security to prevent its violation by the state itself.

In this sense, the first characteristic of this formal establishment of fundamental rights is that it is one of the main consequences of the already mentioned principle of the distribution of powers essential to the state according to law.

We have said that the distribution of power finally reveals itself in three ways: first, in a distribution of power between the citizen and the state; secondly, in a distribution of power between constituent and constituted powers; and thirdly, in a distribution of power within the constituted power in a horizontal or vertical way, giving rise to the classical separation of state powers or to a politically decentralized form of the state.

The first form of distribution of powers, between citizens and the state is, precisely, the one related to the establishment of fundamental rights and liberties: the *État de droit* or state according to law always implies that there is a sphere of liberties granted to citizens out of reach of the state, and that the state also has powers and prerogatives to ensure its functions, ruled by particular rules different to those applied to individuals. This distribution of power between citizens and state, implying the formal establishment of fundamental rights and liberties for the former, must be, of course, of an entrenched form, resulting from a constituent power, and, therefore, not subject to amendment by ordinary legislation.[138]

In any case, the constitutional establishment of fundamental rights appears as a central element of liberalism, as a result of the distinction between state and society and of course of the *État de droit*. In the latter, its aims are considered as being the protection, guarantee and fulfillment of human rights and fundamental liberties, contrary to those of the absolute or totalitarian state, where these rights do not exist.

That is why at its origin, the distribution of power between a citizen's sphere of liberties and state powers lead to the concept in which, in principle, individual liberty was unlimited, whereas the powers of the state were limited, precisely because the state was set up for the protection of the former.

---

[138] As O. HOOD PHILLIPS said: «The provision that cannot be amended by ordinary legislative procedure are said to be «entrenched». *Reform of the Constitution*, London 1970, p. 3.

1. Theoretical Backgrounds and Historical Antecedents

This conception lies beneath the whole construction of the *État de droit* from the very beginning of its philosophical background, and again, we must recall Locke's concepts in his *Two Treatises of Government* (1690), without doubt, the great classic of the most liberal tradition, and the book that most influenced the birth of the *État de droit*.

In effect, the establishment of a political or civil society according to Locke, as opposed to absolute monarchy, implies an agreement between men,

> «To join and unite into a community for their comfortable, safe, and peaceful living one among the other, in a secure enjoyment of their properties and a greater security against any that are not of it».[139]

Thereof, the power granted to the commonwealth, and in particular to the legislative, -he said-,

> «Is not, nor can possibly be absolutely arbitrary over the lives and fortunes of the people, for it being but the joint power of every member of the society given up to that person or assembly which is legislator, it can be no more than those persons had in a state of nature before they entered into society and gave up to the community; for nobody can transfer to another more power than he has in himself, and nobody has an absolute arbitrary power over himself, or over any other, to destroy his own life, or take away the life or property of another. A man, as has been proved, cannot subject himself to the arbitrary power of another; and having in the state of nature no arbitrary power over the life, liberty, or possession of another, but only so much as the law of nature gave him for the preservation of himself and the rest of mankind, this is all he does or can give up to the commonwealth, and by it to the legislative power, so that the legislative can have no more than this. Their power, in the utmost bounds of it, is limited to the public good of the society. It is a power that has no other end but preservation, and therefore can never have a right to destroy enslave, or designedly to impoverish the subject».[140]

On this basis, Locke defined the «end of government» as «the good of mankind», and stated that «all the power government has is only for the good of the society». Therefore, opposed to civil society was the absolute arbitrary power or government without settled standing laws. Those, he said,

> «Can neither of them consist with the end of society and government which men would not quit the freedom of the state of nature and tie themselves up under, were it not to preserve their lives, liberties, and fortune, and by stated rules of right and property to secure their peace and quiet. It cannot be supposed that they should intend, had they a power so to do, to give to anyone, or more, an absolute arbitrary power over their persons and estates, and put a force into the magistrates' hand to execute his unlimited will arbitrarily upon them. This -he ended- were to put themselves into a worse condition than the state of nature, wherein they had a liberty to defend their right against the injuries of others and were upon equal terms of force to maintain it, whether invaded by a single man or many in combination».[141]

---

[139] J. LOCKE, *Two Treatises of Government*, quoted in W. LAQUER and B. RUBIN ed., *The Human Rights Reader*, New York 1979 p. 64.

[140] *Idem*, p. 65.

[141] *Ibid*, p. 66.

The conclusion of all this conception regarding to fundamental rights, or «property», as Locke identified them, was that,

> «The supreme power cannot take from any man part of his property without his own consent; for the preservation of property being the end of government and that for which men enter into society, it necessarily supposes and requires, that the people should have property».[142]

In this perspective, as we have seen, all the construction of the *État de droit* apparatus as opposed to that of the absolute state was based on the idea of the existence of man's liberties, that were inalienable and which cannot be renounced, and that the state was to be set up for the protection and maintenance of such liberties.

In this same sense, the other two theoreticians of the state, whose ideas helped the setting up of the liberal state, are clear and eloquent. Rousseau when referring to the nature of the rights of citizens, said:

> «To renounce one's liberty is to renounce one's quality as a man, the rights and also the duties of humanity... such a renunciation is incompatible with man's nature, for to take away all freedom from his will is to take away all morality from his actions. In short, a convention which stipulates absolute authority on the one side and unlimited obedience on the other is vain and contradictory».[143]

Montesquieu, for his part, argued, as we have seen, that «political liberty» was to be found only in «moderate governments», that is to say, those where «there is no abuse of power»,[144] and those only exist in systems -he thought-, like the English, where power checked power. Thus there is his theory of the distribution of power as a pre-requisite for political liberty.

In this context, England again had a long tradition, and even though the idea of «natural rights» has been said to be «strictly an (English) commodity for export, particularly to France, and to the American colonies»,[145] the truth is that it had a tremendous influence both on English tradition of liberty and abroad.

The *Magna Carta* of 1215 is often referred to as the first declaration of fundamental rights. But in reality this Charter was the result of the struggle between the centripetal and centrifugal feudal forces, that is to say, on the one hand the king's forces, particularly as a result of the tyranny of King John, and the established central institution which administered a common law; and on the other hand, the forces of the barons of the kingdom, which sought disintegration which would mean independence and power, as well as the combined forces of landowners, ecclesiastics and traders.[146]

As a result of that struggle, the Great Charter was a formal charter in the feudal sense, that is to say, a free grant by the king. In fact, however, it resulted in

---

142 *Ibid*, p. 67

143 J.J. ROUSSEAU, *The Social Contract*, quoted in W. LAQUER and B. RUBIN (ed.), *op. cit.*, p. 70.

144 MONTESQUIEU, *The Spirit of Laws*, quoted in W. LAQUER and B. RUBIN (ed.), *op. cit.*, p. 68-69.

145 K. MINOGUE, «The History of the Idea of Human Rights», in W. LAQUER and B. RUBIN (ed.), *op. cit.*, p. 6.

146 W. HOLDSWORTH, *A History of English Law*, Vol. II, London 1971, p. 207-208. *Cf.* F.W. MAITLAND, *The Constitutional History of England*, Cambridge 1968, p. 67.

a code for reforming laws passed by the whole body of barons and bishops and thrust upon a reluctant king.[147] That is why it opened a new chapter in English history and has been seen as the origin and source of English constitutional law.[148]

But, as we mentioned, the Great Charter is one of many formal examples of stipulations between the king and the feudal knights; in that sense, it was a *stabilimentum* or an enactment formulated by the king, church, barons and merchants as partners in the legislative powers of the nascent state, contained in a probatory document called a Charter. Thus, the Charter set forth a series of rights of a heterogeneous nature, all relating to the different classes participating in its enactment. Its clauses were classified into five groups; those granting the liberty of the church; those dealing with what is called feudal grievances; those relating to trade; those relating to central government; and those that placed limitation upon arbitrary power.[149]

In reality, therefore, the Great Charter contained nothing resembling a general declaration of fundamental rights of the English people. The freemen whose rights the document refers to were not all but just a fraction of Englishmen, particularly the barons, and if it is true that in some clauses the Magna Carta mentioned all *liberi homines* in a sense that could include the villain, as Sir William Holdsworth said,

> «It is fairly clear that they were thus protected, not because it was intended to confer any rights upon them, but because they were the property of their lords, and excessive amercements would diminish their value».[150]

Thus, if it is true that the Magna Carta guaranteed all freemen certain rights of protection against the abuse of royal power, this is something quite different from a modern declaration of the rights of man and the citizen. In those days, only the Barons were *liberi homines*; they alone were *liberi* and they alone were considered as *homines*. Thus, historically speaking, the Magna Carta was an agreement between a feudal aristocracy and its king, to whom it renewed its homage in exchange for guaranteed rights. In that context the Magna Carta's 63 chapters contained limitations on the judiciary for example, the affirmation that no freeman could be imprisoned or arrested, except by a legal court, composed of people of his own class, or in accordance with the law of the land; limitations upon taxation power, and above all, the establishment of a resistance committee in the event of failure to maintain these prescriptions.

Thus, there is no reference in the Magna Carta to the people as a whole, and this could not be otherwise, since such a reality had not yet made its appearance in history. Naturally, those historical facts do not detract from its crucial importance in British constitutional history, due basically to the symbolic association attached to it.

What is true, is that the modern concept of fundamental rights, related originally to the idea of natural rights, only appears in more modern times after the medieval age finished in the course of the sixteenth century, and when the idea

---

[147] F.W. MAITLAND, *op. cit.*, p. 67.
[148] W. HOLDSWORTH, *op. cit.*, Vol. II, p. 209.
[149] *Idem*, p. 212.
[150] *Idem*, p. 212.

of duty gave way to the idea of rights[151] and due, as we have seen, in political theory to the theoreticians of the absolute state. Thus, the first formal expression of this new concept can be found in the writ of *Habeas Corpus* developed by English courts, precisely because of the influence and interpretation of the Magna Carta. As Sir William Holdsworth pointed out:

> «Whether or not the famous clause of Magna Carta, which enacted that 'no free man shall be taken or imprisoned or diseased or exiled or in any way destroyed except by the lawful judgment of his peers or by the law of the land', was intended to safeguard the principle that no man should be imprisoned without due process of law, it soon came to be interpreted as safeguarding it. Because it was interpreted in this way, it has exercised a vast influence, both upon the manner in which the judges have developed the writs which could be used to safeguard this liberty, and upon the manner in which the Legislature has assisted that development».[152]

And precisely, the Habeas Corpus Act of 1679 is perhaps the first formal law in modern times related to a fundamental right, that of personal liberty, although it was applied only to detention for 'any criminal or supposed criminal matters'. It was passed to secure that persons detained on criminal charges were brought speedily to trial and to ensure that the power to detain persons on criminal charges was not abused.[153]

The first formal act that refers to fundamental liberties in a wider sense in modern time is undoubtedly the *Bill of Rights* of 1689, enacted at the end which of the English Revolution of 1688-1689, and which marks the ultimate triumph of Parliament in its struggle against the crown.

This act of Parliament, adopted by the new true Parliament which resulted from the Convention Parliament in 1689, gave undoubted legal authority to all the provisions contained in the Declaration of Rights presented in February 1689 to Prince William and Princess Mary of Orange when the convention offered them the crown of England, and which contained all the major resolutions of the convention. Therefore, its contents, more than just a statement of rights, have been considered as a political document containing 'the rights of the nation'[154] as had previously been established by legislation.[155]

Regarding rights, however, the Bill of Rights gave legal effect to those rights mentioned in the Declaration by means of a provision stating that:

> «All and singular the rights and liberties asserted and claimed in the said declaration, are the true, ancient, and indubitable rights and liberties of the people of this Kingdom, and so shall be esteemed, allowed, adjudged, deemed, and so taken to be».[156]

---

151 «A common and useful way of describing the change from the medieval to the modern world is to say that the idea of *duty* gave way to the idea of right». K. MINOGUE, *loc. cit.*, p. 5.

152 W. HOLDSWORTH, *op. cit.* Vol. IX, London 1966, p. 104.

153 E.C.S. WADE and G. GODFREY PHILLIPS, *Constitutional and Administrative Law*, ninth edition by A.W. BRADLEY, London 1980, p. 456.

154 L.G. SCHWOERER, *The Declaration of Rights, 1689*, 1981, p. 19, 291.

155 That is why W. HOLDSWORTH considered that in the Bill of Rights there is no «statement of constitutional principles», *op. cit.*, Vol. VI, London 1971, p. 241.

156 Quoted by P. ALLOT, «'The Courts and Parliament: Who Whom?, *The Cambridge Law Journal*, 38 (1), 1979, p. 98.

But in fact, the Declaration of Rights cannot only be thought of as a document tending only to restore the old and acknowledged rights of Englishmen which had been grievously violated by King James II. It must also be regarded, like the Bill of Rights, as a radical reforming document in the sense that it resolved long-standing disputes in ways favorable to Parliament and the individual, and according to the libertarian political principles that the Revolution embodied.

As L.G. Schwoerer stated in his study of the Declaration of Rights 1689, that Declaration and the Bill of Rights:

> «Dealt with royal prerogatives that lie at the very heart of sovereignty; royal power respecting law, military authority, and taxation. They sought also to strengthen the role of Parliament, by claiming the rights of free election, free speech, free debate, free proceedings, and frequent meetings. And they guaranteed rights to the individual - to petition the King without fear of reprisal, to bear arms (under certain restrictions)' and to be protected against certain judicial procedures (excessive bail, excessive fines, cruel and unusual punishments, and the granting and promising of fines and forfeitures before conviction)».[157]

In so doing, this document must be thought of as the necessary ingredient of the Revolution 1688-1689 so as not to be seen as a simple *coup d'Etat*. On the contrary, the Revolution has been thought of as real, not only because it destroyed the essential elements of the *ancien regime*, but also because it also restored certain rights which had been assaulted by the Stuarts and, in resolving certain long-term controversies, it created a new kingship. Thus in the new political system which was born, the principles of divine-right monarchy, the idea of direct hereditary succession, the prerogatives of the king over law, the military, taxation and judicial procedures which were to the detriment of the individual, all underwent radical changes; and Parliament definitively gained supremacy in its struggle against the king.

This revolution has been considered by Schowerer as:

> «The greatest, in the sense of being the most effective, of the revolutions that occurred in early modern European history. And its legacy was ongoing in the revolution (and the document accompanying it) that occurred at the end of the eighteenth century in the American colonies».[158]

The importance of the Bill of Rights 1689, therefore, lies in two principal aspects: first, because it paved the way for the transition from the ancient system of class rights towards modern individual rights in the sense that the Bill of Rights declared individual rights not of some privileged classes but of English people as a whole; and second, because of its influence in the first declarations of fundamental rights in modern times, those of the English colonies of North America.

2. The American and French Declarations and Their Influence

In fact, it has been considered that the first of the formal declarations of individual rights in the modern constitutional sense are the bills of the American colonies. They differed from the English precedents, mainly because in establishing

---

[157] L.G. SCHWOERER, *op. cit.*, p. 283.
[158] *Idem*, p. 291.

those rights, they did not refer to rights based on the common law and tradition, but rather to the rights derived from human nature and ratio. Thus the rights declared in the Bill of Rights of those colonies were natural rights which «do pertain to... (the people) and their posterity, as the basis and foundation of government» as the Virginia Declaration of Rights, 12-6-1776 stated.[159]

In the brief preamble to that Declaration, the relation between natural rights and government was clearly established, and thus the direct influence of Locke's theories in the sense that political society forms itself upon those rights as the basis and foundation of government.

The first three sections of the Declaration clearly followed these ideas:

«*Section 1*: That all men are by nature equally free and independent and have certain inherent rights, of which, when they enter into a state of society, they cannot by any compact, deprive or divest their posterity; namely, the enjoyment of life and liberty, with the means of acquiring and possessing property, and pursuing and obtaining happiness and safety.

Section 2: That all power is vested in, and consequently derived from, the people; that magistrates are their trustees and servants and at all times amenable to them.

Section 3: That government is, or ought to be, instituted for the common benefit, protection, and security of the people, nation, or community; of all the various modes and forms of government, that is best which is capable of producing the greatest degree of happiness and safety, and is most effectually secured against the danger of maladministration; and that, when any government shall be found inadequate or contrary to these purposes, a majority of the community hath an indubitable, inalienable, and indefensible right to reform, alter, or abolish it, in such manner as shall be judged most conducive to the public weal».[160]

In addition, Section 4 established the prohibition of privileges and Section 5 prescribed the separation of powers and the temporal condition of public offices.

From these sections in the Declaration, the theory of the social contract or pact, based on the existence of inherent and inalienable rights of man is clear; and the democratic basis of government also as its best and must just form, thus the theory of democratic representation through free elections (Section 7); and the right of resistance, a product itself of the social pact.

The other eleven sections are devoted to regulating a few fundamental rights, among which are the right to a speedy trial, with due guarantees; the right not to be condemned to excessive fines or to cruel and unusual punishment, and the freedom of the press.

The same fundamental liberal principles of the Virginia Declaration can also be found in the Declaration of Independence of the United States of America, approved less than one month later (4-7-1776). It stated:

---

159 See the text in J. HERVADA and J.M. ZUMAQUERO, *Textos internacionales de derechos humanos*, Pamplona 1978, p. 25.

160 *Idem*, p. 27-29.

«We hold these truths to be self-evident. that all men are created equal; that they are endowed by their Creator with certain unalienable rights; that among these are life, liberty, and the pursuit of happiness; that, to secure these rights, government is instituted among men, deriving their just powers from the consent of the governed; that, whenever any form of government becomes destructive of these ends, it is the right of the people to alter or to abolish it and to institute new government, laying its foundation on such principles/ and organizing its powers in such form, as to them shall seem most likely to effect their safety and happiness».[161]

These declarations, undoubtedly, marked the beginning of the democratic and liberal era of the modern state according to law although the 1787 constitution of the United states did not contain a declaration of fundamental rights, it nevertheless constituted one of the main characteristics of American constitutionalism, that influenced modern constitutional law.[162] The 1787 constitution was criticized for the fact that it did not include a statement of fundamental rights, but that lack was resolved two years later when ten amendments to the constitution were drafted by the first Congress and approved on 25 September 1789 just one month after the French Declaration of the Rights of Man and Citizen.[163]

In effect, on 27 August 1789 the representatives of the French People, organized in the National Assembly, approved a Declaration of the Rights of Man and the Citizen, where all the fundamental rights of man were recognized and proclaimed in seventeen articles. The undoubted influence upon it of the American Declarations was decisive, particularly in the principle itself of the need of a formal declaration of rights, and in its contents. The mutual influences between the two continents at the time are well known: the French philosophers, including Montesquieu and Rousseau were studied in North America; French participation in the War of Independence was important; Lafayette was a member of the drafting committee of the Constituent Assembly which produced the French Declaration and who submitted his own draft based on the Declaration of Independence and the Virginia Bill of Rights; the *repporteur* of the constitutional Commission proposed «transplanting to France the noble idea conceived in North America»; and Jefferson himself was present in Paris in 1789, having succeeded Benjamin Franklin as American Minister to France.[164]

Anyway, the main objectives in both declarations were the same: to protect the citizen against arbitrary power and to establish the rule of law.

However, it is certain that the French Declaration was, of course, more directly influenced by the thoughts of Rousseau and Montesquieu. The drafters of the Declaration took from Rousseau the principles of considering the role of society as being related to the natural liberty of man, and the idea that the law, as the expression of the general will passed by the representatives of the nation, cannot be an instrument for oppression. They also took from Montesquieu his fundamental distrust of power, and therefore, the principle of separation of powers.[165] Of course,

---

161 *Idem*, p. 37.

162 Ch. H. McIlwain, *Contitutionalism and the Changing World*, Cambridge 1939, p. 66.

163 See the text in W. Laqueur and B. Rubin, *op. cit.*, p. 106-118. *Cf.* A.H. Robertson, *Human Rights in the World*, Manchester 1982, p. 7.

164 J. Rivero, *Les libertes publiques*, Paris 1973, Vol. I, p. 45; A.H. Robertson, *op. cit.*, p. 7.

165 J. Rivero, *op. cit*, p. 41-42.

the rights proclaimed in the Declaration were natural rights of man, thus inalienable and universal. These were not rights that political society granted, but rights belonging to nature inherent in human beings.

This conception is clear in the text of the Declaration issued by the representatives of the French people, by «considering that the ignorance, forgetfulness or contempt of the rights of man are the sole causes of public misfortunes and of the corruption of government». The Declaration was, then, a perpetual reminder of the «natural inalienable and sacred rights of man».[166]

The first articles of the Declaration that recognized and proclaimed the rights of man and citizen, were, undoubtedly, a sort of compilation of all the liberal principles based on the ideas of Locke, Montesquieu and Rousseau, and concretized in the American Revolution. They were:

«1. Men are born and remain free and equal in rights; social distinctions may be based only upon general usefulness.

2. The aim of every political association is the preservation of the natural and inalienable rights of man; these rights are liberty, property, security, and resistance to oppression.

3. The source of all sovereignty resides essentially in the nation; no group, no individual may exercise authority not emanating expressly therefrom.

4. Liberty consists of the power to coo whatever is not injurious to others; thus the enjoyment of the natural rights of every man has as its limits only those that assure to other members of society the enjoyment of those same rights; such limits may be determined only by law.

5. The Law has the right to forbid only actions which acre injurious to society. Whatever is not forbidden by law may not be prevented, and no one may be constrained to do what it does not prescribe.

6. Law is the expression of the general will all citizens have the right Lo concur personally, or through their representatives in its formation; it must be the same for all, whether it protects or punishes...

16. Every society in which the guarantee of rights is not assured, or the separation of powers not determined, has no constitution at all».[167]

The rest of the Declaration concerned with individual rights, for instance, the principle *nullum crimen nulla poena sine legge*; the presumption of innocence until a declaration of guilt; the right of free expression and to free communication of ideas and opinions, considered in the Declaration as «one of the most precious of the rights of man»; and the right to property considered «sacred and inviolable».

We could say that the whole process of the development of the *État de droit* on the basis of this third, general feature, of the establishment of a declaration of rights, took its lead from these two formal declarations, the American and the French, subsequently incorporated into written constitutions.[168] They first had an impact in Latin America, long before in other European countries.

---

166 See the text in J. HERVADA and J.M. ZUMAQUERO, *op. cit.*, p. 39-40; W. LAQUEUR and B. RUBIN, *op. cit.*, p. 118.

167 *Idem*, pp. 41-49 and pp. 118-119.

168 The French declaration was incorporated in the preamble to the constitution of 1791.

In this sense, what can be considered as the third formal declaration of rights by an independent state in constitutional history was the Declaration of Rights of the People adopted by the Supreme Congress of Venezuela in 1811 four days before the formal Independence Act of the 5th July 1811 was issued.[169] The content of that Declaration followed the French one but in much more detail in its enumeration of rights, including new ones in relation to the previous American and French Declarations, such as the right to industrial and commercial freedom and the freedom to work; the right to consider ones home as inviolable, and the right to petition before authority without limitation. The Declaration was also incorporated as a final Chapter of the first of all Latin-American constitutions, the Venezuelan one of 21st December 1811 in 59 articles.[170]

Afterwards, the declarations of fundamental rights by all the newly the independent states of Latin America at the beginning of last century spread as a basic constitutional feature of our countries.

In any case, it must be said that in general, the American -North American and Latin-American- and the French declarations of rights were different in their content and meaning.

In the French Declaration, it was not a case of establishing a new state but of the continuation of a national state already in existence. Therefore, the concept of the citizen was taken for granted whereas in the American Declarations, new states were being built upon a new basis. In consequence the purpose of the French Declaration, as stated in its introduction, was to solemnly remind all members of the community of their rights and duties. Hence the new principle of individual liberty appeared only as an important modification within the context of a political unity already in existence.

Whereas in the North American and Latin-American declarations, the enforcement of rights was an important factor in the independence process, and thus of the building of the new states upon a new basis, particularly the principle of the sovereignty of the people with all its democratic content. Therefore, on the American Continent, the solemn Declaration of Fundamental Rights signified the establishment of principles on which the political unity of the nations was based, and the validity of which was recognized as the most important supposition in the emergence and formation of that unity.

In any case, after this process developed during the first decades of the last century (19th century), we can say that the general declaration of fundamental rights and liberties became normal practice all over the world. Therefore, it is difficult to find in the last and present centuries (19th and 20th century) written constitutions without a declaration or an enumeration of fundamental rights including not only the traditional liberties of men, but also the new social and economic rights developed during this century (20th century) within the framework of the welfare state.

The general situation today is that declarations of fundamental rights have existed and exist in almost all countries, particularly as a part of their written constitutions. Moreover, after the horrors that were seen during the World War II, those declarations have even been internationalized not only as simple declarations

---

169 See the text in A. R. BREWER-CARÍAS, *Las Constituciones de Venezuela*, Madrid 1985, pp. 175-177.

170 *Idem*, p. 196-200.

without the means to enforce them, like the Universal Declaration of Human Rights and the American Declaration of Rights and Duties of Man, both of 1948, but also as formal international conventions and treatises, like the International Pacts of Civil and Political Rights and on Economic, Social and Cultural Rights 1966; the European Convention for the Protection of Human Rights and Fundamental Freedoms 1950; and the American Convention on Human Rights 1969, texts that in most of the countries that ratified them, are considered as formal laws and as part of the law of the land.[171]

In any case, what can be considered as a particular feature of the declarations of rights in the Legal state is that in general they were and are normally incorporated in written constitutions. Besides, those written constitutions had been and are also rigid, therefore the declarations of fundamental rights are normally entrenched declarations in the sense that the ordinary legislator cannot eliminate or modify their contents.

Of course, not all the rights contained in those declarations as fundamental ones are formally established in the same manner. Some of them, particularly traditional individual rights, like the right to live, are established in an absolute way in the sense that no legislation can be passed limiting its enjoyment. On the contrary, other rights are established in a way that the constitution itself allows for the possibility of the Legislator to regulate or limit those rights but only within the limits established in the constitution. However, in some cases, the constitutional authorization for the legislative power to regulate certain rights is established in a way that legislation must be passed for its effective enjoyment. That happens in some countries, where for instance, the right to strike in public services can only be exercised in cases expressly established in a law.

In any case, the establishment of an entrenched declaration of fundamental rights and freedoms, in a written and rigid constitution, implies that the first and most important guarantee of those rights is the principle of a «legal reserve» in favor of the legislative power for their regulation and limits according to what is determined in the constitution. That means, in all cases in which the constitution allows possible further regulation and limits to the enjoyment of rights, that those regulations and limits can only be established through formal laws or acts of Parliament. Therefore, the executive itself cannot set any limit whatsoever on constitutional rights. Only exceptionally, in the constitutional systems that allow the possibility for Parliament to delegate legislative powers to the executive, can it be possible, within the limits of the delegation, for the executive through delegate legislation or decree–Law, to establish regulations in relation to some rights.

Thus, within the concept of the state submitted to law, the principle relating to individual rights and liberties, which stipulates that an *État de droit* is one in which the state can only intervene in the sphere of individual liberties based on a formal law, has a special meaning. A state according to law is, therefore, one in which intervention in individual liberties is only possible through formal law, and in which the administration cannot, therefore, invade this reserve granted to formal law.

---

171 See the text in M. TORRELLI and R. BAUDOUIN, *Les droits de 1'homme et les libertes publiques par les textes*, Montreal, 1972, p. 388; J. HERVADA and J.M. ZUMAQUERO, *Textos internacionales de derechos humanos*, *cit.*, p. 994.

This concept of the *État de droit* is evidently built against the administration, bearing in mind that only a state in which all administrative actions are subject to the law is really an *État de droit*. That is why the principle of legality related to the administration has been so characteristic of this concept of the state, together with the consequent establishment of a series of guarantees against abuse of power by the administration.

Naturally, in this concept of the *État de droit*, in which the law has supremacy over the administration and in which individual rights can only be regulated by the law, there is another fundamental characteristic, namely that of judicial independence, which is the only instrument capable of guaranteeing adequate judicial control over the exercise of power by the administration. Hence the definition of the *État de droit* as one in which judicial control of the administration exists, also referred to as a «state of Justice».

Therefore, in the constitutional *État de droit* or state according to the rule of law, the establishment and regulation of constitutional rights with or without possible further regulation by the legislator, implies the need of a system of guarantees of such rights: on the one hand, as already explained, guarantees of regulation and limitation through the so-called «legal reserve», and on the other guarantees against abuse of public powers in relation to those rights, through judicial mechanisms ensuring their implementation, either by means of the ordinary judicial remedies or through special ones, like the writ of *habeas corpus*, concerning individual liberty, or through special «actions of protection» to protect all constitutional rights or, in general, the means for the judicial control of the constitutionality of laws which may violate those rights.

3. The Situation of Fundamental Rights in the British Constitutional System

England has rightly been called the land of liberalism: Locke was English, Montesquieu's system is based on his interpretation of the English constitution; and from the point of view of positive law, the declarations of rights have their antecedents in English constitutional history. Because of those antecedents, in general, liberal democratic constitutions nowadays normally contain a declaration of rights. However, in the United Kingdom, in the absence of a written constitution, and apart from references to historical statutes, there is no declaration or special code relating to fundamental rights; therefore. as Sir Ivor Jennings has said, «there are no fundamental rights» and «there is no special protection for «fundamental rights».[172]

Consequently, the rights of the British people equivalent, of course, to those established elsewhere in entrenched declarations, are based on two assumptions: in the first place, that citizens can do or say anything, provided it is not an infringement of a law or of other citizens' rights; and in the second place, that the authorities can only do what is permitted by statutory or common law.[173] Consequently, in the United Kingdom legal system, rights are expressed, in principle, not positively, but negatively. Hence, strictly speaking, rather than rights they are liberties.

That is why, as E.C.S. Wade and G. Godfrey Phillips pointed out «the approach of the law in Britain to the citizen's liberty has often been to treat it as a residual

172 I. JENNINGS, *The Law and the Constitution*, London 1972, p. 40, 259.

173 M. GARCÍA PELAYO, *Derecho constitucional comparado*, Madrid 1957, p. 278.

concept: The citizen may go where he pleases, and do or say what he pleases provided he does not commit a criminal offence or infringe the rights of others».[174] Accordingly, we can say that in the system of this country, the principle is that «anything is lawful which is not unlawful», in other words, «it is lawful to do anything which is not unlawful or which cannot be prohibited by public authorities».[175] Therefore, the essence of the provisions related to fundamental rights regulation in Britain is founded upon whom can establish unlawful actions or prohibit them. Naturally, these limits must be found primarily in legislation, that is to say, in Acts of Parliament.[176]

It was precisely this negative approach to fundamental rights in England that led Dicey to establish a contrast between the continental and the English constitutions, as we have seen, saying that on the continent, individual rights result, or appear to result, from the general principles of the constitution», whereas in England, «the general principles of the constitution (as for example the right to personal liberty, or the right of public meeting) are... the result of judicial decisions determining the rights of private persons in particular cases brought before the courts». As a result of which, -Dicey concluded- «the rules which in foreign countries naturally form part of a constitutional code, are not the source but the consequence of the rights of individuals, as defined and enforced by the courts».[177]

Dicey's views in relation to the situation of this country were expressed exactly one hundred years ago. The first edition of *An Introduction to the Study of the Law of the Constitution* was published in 1885. At that time, the role of Parliament and the Courts was quite different from today, and moreover, we have to consider the impact upon fundamental rights of the Welfare state or the Social *État de droit* as it is called in Continental Europe.

As makers of law Professor J.D.B. Mitchell said, «the courts have declined in importance. In part this is the obvious result of the development of Parliament, in part it is the result of changes in ideas about the functions of a state».

Moreover, he added,

> «The development of the Welfare state has meant that rights with which individuals are increasingly concerned, protections or hedges against poverty, ill health, and the like, cannot be the creation of judge-made law as could be the -rights of speech, etc., with which Dicey was concerned. These newer rights can only be the result of complex legislation».[178]

And it has been so, even though the role of ordinary courts continues to be important as the ultimate guardians of fundamental rights, and not as their creators.

---

174 E.C.S. WADE and G. GODFREY PHILLIPS, *Constitutional and Administrative Law*, ninth edition by A.W. BRADLEY, London 1982, p. 441.

175 I. JENNINGS, *op. cit.*, p. 41, 262. «It asserts the principle of legality, that everything is legal that is not illegal».

176 Delegated Legislation in relation to fundamental rights, in principle, is only Possible in cases of state of emergency in accordance with the Emergency Powers Act 1920. E.C.S. WADE and G. GODFREY PHILLIPS, *op. cit.*, p. 567.

177 A.V. DICEY, *An Introduction to the Study of the Law of the Constitution*, with an «Introduction» by E.C.S. WADE, 1973, p. 195, 196, 203. See also WADE comments, p. CXVIII.

178 J.D.B. MITCHELL, *Constitutional Law*, Edinburgh 1968, p. 55.

Nevertheless, despite all the British tradition, discussions have been held in the United Kingdom particularly during the last two decades, on the need and possibility of the enactment of an entrenched Bill of Rights.

The principal argument for a Bill of Rights is to restrain excess or abuse of power by public authorities, and it has been thought that with a Bill of Rights, the power to bring legal actions against the state and agencies of government will improve, in other words, it has been thought that a Bill of Rights is potentially a more fruitful source of remedies.[179]

This arguments in favor of the enactment of a Bill of Rights has been summarized by P.S. Atiyah, as follows:

> «That there ought to be, and are, certain basic human rights which ought not to be at the mercy of a government and legislature; that -governments and legislatures derive their power from the people, and that the people cannot be assumed to have granted away unlimited and despotic powers just because they have elected a Parliament (by a process set by Parliament itself); that a majority of the people is no doubt entitled to elect a majority government and parliament to represent their views, but this does not give, and ought not to give, that government and parliament unlimited power to oppress the minority or minorities; and that at the very least, the basic structure of the democratic process- which alone gives legitimacy to the power of governments and parliaments ought to be entrenched so as to be unalterable by Parliament».[180]

Evidently, these arguments in favor of the enactment of a Bill of Rights in Britain, that follow the most orthodox liberal tradition, must take into account the well-known principle of Parliamentary sovereignty. An entrenched Bill of Rights would limit the powers of the ordinary legislator to modify it, which is contrary to the main principle of the British constitution. On the other hand, a Bill of Rights formally entrenched in the constitution would mean that judges would become the ultimate arbiters of the powers of Parliament, and that, -it has been said- would be disastrous unless judges could be persuaded to alter their traditional methods of interpretation. «For traditional and crabbed methods of interpretation -P.S. Atiyah said-, could often lead to the invalidation of legislation which is absolutely necessary to keep pace with changing values or conditions; huge tensions would then build up in the legal and political system, and general discredit could be thrown on the law».[181]

The main arguments against the enactment of a Bill of Rights have been exposed, clearly summarized and critiqued by Michel Zander in his pamphlet entitled *A Bill of Rights?*,[182] originally published ten years ago (1975). Among those arguments we may point out the following:

In the first place, it has been said that a Bill of Rights is an «un-British way of doing things»,[183] based on the well-known apprehensiveness to written constitutions

---

179 M. ZANDER, *A Bill of Rights?*, London 1985, p. 27.
180 P.S. ATIYAH, *Law and Modern Society*, Oxford 1983, p. 109.
181 *Idem*, p. 111.
182 London 1985, p. 106.
183 *Idem*, p. 43.

or constitutional documents, that in constitutional law derives from Dicey's concepts. To say that a Bill of Rights is «un-British» says M. Zanders, «is to show an ignorance of history».[184] In fact, as we have seen, this country invented the in Bill of Rights with the Magna Carta in 1215 and the Bill of Rights in 1689; it influenced the Declaration of Rights in the American Colonies 1776 and the content of the first ten amendments of the North-American constitution (1789); and in more recent times, the United Kingdom has been the main exporter of the ideas of fundamental rights and freedoms established in an entrenched way, to the Commonwealth countries on a scale without parallel in the rest of the world.[185] All the countries of the Commonwealth, except New Zealand, have written constitutions and a formal declaration of fundamental rights.

The second argument against the enactment of a Bill of Rights is that it is not needed because human rights are adequately protected in Britain. This has also been the main argument used to justify[186] why the European Convention on Human Rights has not been transformed into domestic law in the United Kingdom. «At the time of ratification, -Drzemczewski said- the government of the day assumed that domestic law was in full conformity with the Conventions provisions, and successive governments have since that time expressed the opinion that the rights and freedoms enumerated are in all cases already secured in domestic law».[187] In relation to this argument, Professor Zander, bearing in mind that in Britain a system of remedies rather than of rights exists, said that «the existing ways of getting remedies all leave much to be desired»,[188] and in fact, as Anthony Lester pointed out in his recent article about the isolation of the United Kingdom concerning fundamental rights and the European Convention, «no other country which belongs to the convention systems has been faced with so many cases» of importance, adding:

It is not the sheer volume of cases which is so telling, but the proportion of cases declared admissible by the commission and of cases decided against the United Kingdom.[189]

The third argument against the enactment of a Bill of Rights is based on the principle of sovereignty of Parliament, as we have seen. A Bill of Rights needs to be entrenched, and that would restrict Parliament's freedom to legislate in the future. As professor O. Hood Phillips said:

> «The primary characteristic of our constitution is the legislative supremacy of Parliament. This means that Parliament can pass a law on any subject matter, even. of a fundamental constitutional nature and can do so by the ordinary procedure of an Act of Parliament... this legally unlimited power of Parliament to make laws on any subject matter is a corollary of the absence of «entrenched»

---

184 *Ibidem*, p. 44.

185 A. LESTER, «Fundamental Rights: The United Kingdom Isolated?» *Public Law*, spring 1984, p. 56, 57; M. ZANDERS, *op. cit*, p. 28-30. To realize the extent of this contribution, we only have to mention the amendments adopted by the British Parliament in 1982, in regard to the British. North American Act 1867, renamed in 1982 the constitution Act 1867, in which the Canadian Charter of Rights and Freedom was included at the same time in which the last vestige of the colonial relationship with regard to constitutional amendments in Canada disappeared.

186 M. ZANDERS, *op. cit.*, p. 45.

187 Q.Z. DRZEMCZEWSKI, *European Human Rights Convention in Domestic Law. A Comparative Study*, Oxford 1985, p. 178.

188 M. ZANDERS, *op. cit.*, p. 45.

189 A. LESTER, *loc. cit.*, p. 65.

provisions and of the flexible nature of the British constitution. It also follows that we have no strictly fundamental rights».[190]

Along the same line of thought, Professor H.W.R. Wade says:

«...The one inherent limit on (Parliamentary omnipotence, which is the consequence of that omnipotence itself, is that the Parliament of today cannot fetter the Parliament of tomorrow with any sort of permanent restraint, so that entrenched provisions are impossible».[191]

But in practice even this substantive formal argument is not really an obstacle to an entrenched Bill of Rights. Anthony Lester said in his article:

«Normally only the very young have fantasies of omnipotence. Growing up involves accepting the necessity for laws, rules and limits. A mature Parliament would not insist upon the continuous assertion of its fanatical absolute powers at the expense of individual justice. A, mature Parliament would use its sovereign law-making powers to confine those powers within proper constitutional limits.[192]

In any case, the fact is that even if a Bill of Rights were adopted in an entrenched way, that would only imply that the provisions of the Bill of Rights would prevail unless subsequent enactment explicitly stated otherwise, which would not prevent the express will of Parliament from prevailing in the end. It would mean, however, «that the courts could strike down a statute as being contrary to the Bill of Rights unless it contained an express provision modifying the Bill of Rights to that extent».[193]

This leads us to a final argument against the enactment of an entrenched Bill of Rights in this country, related to the powers of courts to review acts of Parliament. As Professor D.G.T. Williams pointed out:

«An entrenched Bill of Rights would, of course, involve the exercise of judicial review by English and other courts of the United Kingdom, in the sense that would entrust domestic courts of a blank check to protect certain fundamental freedoms even against the legislature itself».[194]

Therefore, the real problem of a Bill of Rights, adopted in the ordinary, constitutional way of impeding its modification by ordinary legislation, in a constitutional system like the British one, is that it could imply the powers of courts to review the conformity of acts of Parliament with that Bill which could not be acceptable in the British constitutional system, unless greater modification of the constitution itself took place.

All these arguments could be overcome if the United Kingdom limited its search for establishing a positive code of rights and freedoms, by granting domestic status to the European Convention on Human Rights and therefore, allowing the courts to apply and interpret the Convention and to secure speedy and effective

[190] O. HOOD Phillips, *Reform of the Constitution, cit*, p. 11, 12.
[191] H.W.R. WADE, *Constitutional Fundamentals*, London 1980, p. 25.
[192] A. LESTER, *loc. cit.*, p. 71.
[193] M. ZANDERS, *op. cit.*, p. 70.
[194] D.G.T. WILLIAMS, «The Constitution of the United Kingdom», *The Cambridge Law Journal*, 31, (1), 1972, p. 277.

domestic remedies for the citizens of this country against the violation of their fundamental human rights.[195] This, it seems, is the best alternative to the matter today,[196] although it involves a number of questions regarding relations between international law and English law and the interpretation of the Convention in English law.[197]

In any case, if it is true that because of the absence of a declaration of rights protected by a constitutional supra-legality in the United Kingdom, there are in general no legal guarantees whatsoever for the existence of those rights faced with the will of Parliament, and this fact can lead both, to an expansion of the field of forbidden activities and to the granting of ample powers to authorities, the discussion in some respects is definitely a theoretical one.

The validity of rights in this country, at least from the point of view of a foreign lawyer, is inseparable from the total structure of the British constitution. Consequently, abolishing freedom and liberties would be tantamount to abolishing the entire British constitution, which makes no sense.

In any event, what we wanted to point out is that in the modern *État de droit*, further to the limitation of powers and the submission of all state organs to the rule of law, its third main feature is the existence of a formal declaration of fundamental rights and liberties, normally of an entrenched character and embodied in a written constitution. This is the general trend in today's constitutional law, with the exception, on this last point, and at least formally, of the United Kingdom constitutional systems, because of the absence of a Bill of Rights.

We have to refer now to the three main features or characteristics of the *État de droit* or state according to law at the present time, and to its development.

We have analyzed the principle of limitation of powers, from its original conception as a division of powers to its final constitutional consecration as separation of powers. We also mentioned the various interpretations of this separation that each country can make, and finally we stressed the three meanings of the principle in the contemporary *État de droit*: the division of powers between state powers and the rights and liberties of citizens; the division between constituent and constituted powers; and within the latter, the division or separation of powers, in the horizontal way between legislative, executive and judiciary, and in the vertical way, between the different levels of political decentralization when it exists.

We have also seen the main consequences of the second leading feature of the *État de droit*: namely the submission of state organs to the rule of law, which led us not only to the analysis of the legal system as a hierarchical legal order with a written constitution at its apex, as generally exists in almost all countries to the world today, but also to establish the contrast with the British constitutional system, where the principle of the sovereignty of Parliament prevails over any other rule. In any case, we have seen how the submission of the state to the rule of law, in systems with or without written constitutions, has brought about the development of the principle of legality, and the reduction of its former exceptions, particularly on the sphere of discretionary powers.

---

195 A. LESTER, *loc. cit.*, p. 66.
196 M. ZANDERS, *op. cit.*, p. 83-89.
197 J. JACONELLI, *Enacting a Bill of Rights. The Legal Problems*, Oxford 1980, p. 270-277.

Finally, we have also considered the third feature of the *État de droit*, namely the adoption of an entrenched declaration of fundamental rights and freedoms, and its historical development, and expansion all over the world, and the particular problems it poses for the British constitutional system.

Now, the development and adoption of these three elements of the Modern *État de droit* with all the diversities peculiar to each legal system, have been followed, in one way or another, by a process of constitutionalization, generally reflected by its incorporation in a written and often rigid constitution, as a fundamental and basic norm of the legal system. That is why the process of constitutionalization of the *État de droit* has been considered another of its basic aspects.

We now want to refer to that process of constitutionalization, particularly from a historical point of view, and its direct consequence namely, judicial review.

PART TWO

PROCESS OF CONSTITUTIONALIZATION OF THE ÉTAT DE DROIT

I. THE WRITTEN CONSTITUTIONAL PROCESS

The consolidation and further development of the *État de droit* from the beginning of the last century is, undoubtedly, closely related to the process of constitutionalization of the state. This process was characterized by the establishment of a system of norms of a higher level in a given legal order, containing in a global way, the basic rules related to the fundamental functions of the state, its different organs and powers and its interrelations, and related to the fundamental rights and liberties of the citizens.

Thus, the constitutionalization of the state according to law, started two hundred years ago with the introduction of written constitutions in the practice of politics. These written constitutions were conceived as formal documents containing the will of the people considered as sovereign in regard to the political organization of a nation. As a consequence of this process, the organs of the state, including kings and parliament, were converted, precisely, into such organs of the state, and sovereignty was in general depersonalised and attributed to the people represented by those organs.

During the last two centuries, after the approval of the first of the written constitutions of modern times, the Constitution of the United States of America in 1787, the practice of written constitutions had spread and written constitutions exist in almost every country in the world today, with very few exceptions, among which is that of the United Kingdom. Of course, the fact that in this country and in a few others such as Israel or New Zealand there is no written constitution, does not mean that there is no constitution at all. On the contrary, in these countries a collection of rules exists, partially written, partially unwritten, which establishes, regulates and governs its government.[1] Thus the constitutionalization of the state according to law has also taken place in constitutional systems with no written constitutions.

In any case, this process of constitutionalization of the *État de droit*, reflected in a constitution, has produced a system of guarantees of individual liberties, which are specified in the recognition of fundamental rights; the establishment of the

---

[1] M.C. WHEARE, *Modern Constitutions*, Oxford 1966, p. 1, 2.

division of powers; provision for the people's participation in legislative power by means of popular representation; and submission of the state to the rule of law. Most important of all in the context of modern constitutions, it has produced a system that responds to a political decision of society, adopted by the people, as a constituent power through a particular constituent assembly.

In particular, the principle of separation of powers, with its distinction between legislative, governmental and administrative bodies and courts of justice, has been considered a necessary content of any constitution since the eighteenth century, except in socialist countries, because it is thought, in itself, to be the organic guarantee against abuse of power on the part of the state. We have only to remember the article 16 of the 1789 French Declaration of the Rights of Man and the Citizen, which reads as follows:

> «Every society in which the guarantee of rights is not assured, or the separation of powers not determined has no Constitution at all».[2]

As we have said, the first written constitution in modern times was the American Constitution of 1787, the United States being the first common law country to have parliamentary sovereignty replaced by the paramount law of a constitution given by the people, and its enforceable fundamental rights.[3] Indeed, the idea of a higher and fundamental law established as a social contract had also English origins and antecedents in the process of colonization.

The higher law background of the American Constitution,[4] can be traced back to the medieval doctrine of the supremacy of law, drawn from the pages of the works on the laws of England, by the greatest English medieval lawyer, Bracton (1569) mainly interpreted by Sir Edward Coke. This principle led to a reaction against the doctrine of the divine right of kings, based on the doctrine of divine origin of law upon which the basis of civil society is built, and on the principle that law is supreme above king and people equally.[5]

1. Historical Origins

Written constitutions of modern times, one can say, do not have their formal historical origins in the medieval charters, but particularly in the *Instrument of Government* (1653), considered to be the first written constitution in constitutional history.

Nevertheless, the remote antecedents of written constitutions can be found in the medieval formal pacts made between a prince and his vassals, or a prince and popular representation, which was subsequently taken as the expression of the will of the people.

Certainly, in the Middle Ages, these written agreements, which were called charters, were established between the Princes and their barons. The most famous of them is the *Magna Carta* of 1215. However, these documents were not constitutions in the modern sense of the word, although their legal nature has been interpreted

---

2 See in W. LAQUEUR and B. RUBIN, *The Human Rights Reader*, 1979, P. 120.

3 A. LESTER, «Fundamental Rights: The United Kingdom Isolated», *Public Law*, 1984, p. 58.

4 See in general, F. CORWIN, «*The Higher Law*» *Background of American Constitutional Law*, New York 1955

5 T.F.T. PLUCKNETT, *A Concise History of the Common Law*, London 1956, p. 49.

in various ways. They have been termed laws, because they were issued by the king and took the form of royal concessions, and as such, they have even been described as public law contracts. They have also been present throughout British history, acting either as a factor of real integration, or as the ideological content of competition between parties, or as a symbol of the parliamentary party. And as of the eighteenth century, they even symbolized the spirit of the constitution in its entirety.

Actually, the Magna Carta was the result of a resistance movement by the privileged barons against the crown policy during the reign of King John (1199-1216).[6] It was just one of the many general charters established between the prince and his barons, guaranteeing them privileges in exchange for certain commitments on their part, which were created in feudal times.

Consequently, none of the distinctions belonging to modern constitutional law can be applied to medieval relations. The Magna Carta was a *stabilimentum*, that is to say, an agreement or stipulation lacking any precise sense of political law. The fact that it was in writing is no argument in favour of a constitution, and its very name, Magna Carta, is not explained historically by the fact that it contained a fundamental law in the sense of modern constitutions; it was a popular description to distinguish it from the *Carta Foresta* or Chart of the Forest of 1217 relating to hunting rights.[7]

The original name of the Magna Carta was *Cartam Libertatis* or *Carta Baronum*. It was only centuries later, during the Revolution, with Parliament's struggle against the absolutism of the Stuarts, that the modern sense was attributed to it, making it the origin of a Liberal constitution. But as Carl Smith has pointed out, it would be a historical error to see, even if only by approximation, anything in it analogous to a modern liberal or democratic constitution.[8] Nevertheless, in medieval times, it was considered to be an unalterable, fundamental and perpetual[9] part of the enacted law, and was confirmed by different kings more than thirty times thus being an important part of the progress of common laws.[10]

In the same English context, the first example of a modern written constitution is undoubtedly the *Instrument of Government* 1653, which was the result of the only real break that had occurred in English constitutional history and its political continuity.[11]

In effect, the Great Civil War, which started in 1642 and divided the country into Parliamentarians and Royalists, can be thought of as the final step in the long struggle between the parliament and the king. With its religious, economic and political causes and mutual accusations of breaking and subverting the fundamental law,[12] it brought about the execution of King Charles I, the destruction of the whole system of central government and the assumption of the government of the country by the Long Parliament (1649-1660).

6 See in general, I. JENNINGS, *Magna Carta*, London 1965, p. 9.
7 W. HOLDSWORTH, *A History of English Law*, Vol. II, 1971, p. 207, 219.
8 C. SCHMIDT, *'Teoría de la Constitución* (Spanish ed), México 1961, p. 52-53.
9 Ch. H. MCILWAIN, *The High Court of Parliament and its Supremacy*, Yale 1910, p. 64-65.
10 W. HOLDSWORTH, *op. cit.*, Vol. II, p. 219.
11 M.C. WHEARE, *Modern Constitutions*, Oxford 1966, p. 9. *Cf.* J.D.B. MITCHELL, *Constitutional Law*, Edinburgh 1968, p. 27.
12 M. ASHLEY, *England in the Seventeenth Century*, London 1967, p. 76, 79, 80, 82.

Charles I went on trial and was executed in January 1649, and soon afterwards the monarchy and the House of Lords were abolished and England was named a Commonwealth or free state, under the control of the Army and of Oliver Cromwell.[13] Parliament carried out the wishes of the army, except when setting a limit on its own powers and its own existence. After long and futile negotiations, Cromwell finally dissolved Parliament by force in 1653. To take its place, he invited a number of proven Puritans to form an Assembly of Saints that shortly afterwards resigned their powers and gave back their authority to Cromwell. Then the Council of army officers produced a written constitution for the government, known as the Instrument of Government 1653,[14] which shows all the features of a constitution as we understand it today.

The Instrument of Government made Oliver Cromwell «Lord Protector» of the Commonwealth of England, Scotland and Ireland, which he had united under one government. It conferred executive powers upon the Protector assisted by a Council of State containing both civilian and military members conceived as a body independent of both Protector and Parliament, that was to be elected including representatives of Scotland, Ireland and England.[15] However, when the Parliament met, not all its members accepted the «fundamentals» of the Protectorate Government and refused to accept the constitution under which it was assembled. Eventually it was dissolved mainly because it attempted to deprive Cromwell of sole control over the army; and Cromwell again found himself obliged to rule by means of the army.[16] This happened again and again until his death in 1658. As Sir William Holdsworth said of Cromwell: «He was the only man who could control the army, and consequently, the only man who could have any chance of establishing civil, as opposed to, military government».[17] Therefore, King Charles II was restored soon afterwards by a new Parliament under the terms of the Declaration of Breda 1660, which contained four principles or conditions: a general amnesty, liberty of conscience, security of property and payments of arrears to the army.[18] This Declaration was, indeed, not a constitution in the sense of the Instrument of Government, because in fact the Restoration meant a return to the old form of government, and no constitution was needed to that end. As K.C. Wheare said:

> «Those who speak of an unbroken line of development in the history of English government... have a good deal of truth on their side. There was a break and an attempt to make a fresh start with a Constitution, but it failed, and the former order was restored».[19]

As we have said, the Instrument of Government (1653) and its modifications mainly through the Humble Petition and Advice[20] has been unanimously considered as the first written constitution in constitutional history of modern times. The immediate purpose of it was to establish a permanent and inviolable rule vis-à-vis the changing majority resolutions of Parliament. In all governments, Cromwell said, something fundamental is required, something like a Great Charter which is

---

13 *Cf.* W. HOLDSWORTH, *op. cit.*, Vol. VI, p. 146; M. ASHLEY, *op. cit.*, p. 91-92.
14 W. HOLDSWORTH, *op. cit.*, p. 146; M. ASHLEY, *op. cit*, p. 106.
15 W. HOLDSWORTH, *op. cit.*, p. 154-155.
16 W. HOLDSWORTH, *op. cit.*, p. 147; M. ASHLEY, *op. cit.*, p. 102.
17 W. HOLDSWORTH, *op. cit.*, p. 148.
18 *Ibid*, p. 165.
19 K.C. WHEARE, *op. cit.*, p. 10.
20 W. HOLDSWORTH, *op. cit.*, p. 157.

permanent and invariable, or if you wish, absolutely invulnerable. For example, the stipulation that Parliament can never declare itself to be a permanent corporation was, in Cromwell's opinion, one such fundamental principle.[21]

Thus, historically speaking, one can say that the idea of a constitution arose out of the need to formally determine the composition or fundamental functions of the instruments of government. It is generally a sign of order, following institutional chaos created by a great political or social revolution, when a nation is liberated from a foreign conqueror, or when a nation is formed by the merging of small political units. It is on such occasions of historical and political decisions to reorganize or create a state that constitutions have come into being.

As Jennings has pointed out, that need arose in England in 1653, when the Parliament, having created an army to destroy the king, was destroyed by its own creation.[22] In this sense, the *Instrument of Government, which* made Cromwell *Lord Protector* and established a new legislature, was the first and only example of a written constitution in England. It only remained in force for a few years, and almost survived Cromwell himself.

However, this constitution anticipated many of the constitutional developments of the nineteenth and twentieth centuries. As Sir William Holdsworth pointed out, this Instrument of Government and its immediate modifications:

> «Were the first attempt that Englishmen had made to construct a written constitution, and therefore they raised for the first time all the problems connected with its construction. Thus, we get the idea of a separation of powers as a safeguard against the tyranny both of a single person and a representative assembly; the idea of stating certain fundamental rights of the subject; and the idea of rendering these rights permanent, by denying validity to any legislation which attempted to affect them».[23]

In any case, with that sole exception, England has never had a written constitution, which, I insist, does not mean that it has no constitution. The institutions required for the performance of various functions of the modern legal state have been set up in the United Kingdom, in keeping with political needs and following a permanent process of invention, reform and transformation. Hence Jennings' statement:

> «If a Constitution consists of institutions and not of the paper that describes them, the British Constitution has not been made, but has grown, and there is no paper.[24]

2. The American Constitution (1787)

The modern practice of written constitutions actually began in the United States of America when the colonies separated from England, declaring themselves independent States (1776) and formulating their constitutions in writing. A Continental Congress in 1776 even invited all the colonies of the Union to draw up their own constitutions, as a political decision of the people.[25]

---

21 Quoted by C. SCHMIDT, *op. cit.*, p. 45.
22 I. JENNINGS, *The Law and the Constitution*, London 1972, p. 7.
23 W. HOLDSWORTH, *op. cit.*, p. 157.
24 I. JENNINGS, *op. cit.*, p. 8.
25 A.C. MCLAUGHLIN, *A Constitutional History of the United States*, New York 1936, p. 106-109.

The movement towards independence from England began in the United States long before independence was finally declared in 1776, and the independent spirit developed through the colonial assemblies, which had grown in power and influence during the first half of the eighteenth century, by resolving many of the colonists' problems at local level.[26] This assembly spirit was undoubtedly one of the main factors in the independent process. That is why the Declaration and Resolves of the First Continental Congress, 14 October 1774, bearing in mind that «assemblies have been frequently dissolved, contrary to the rights of the people, when they attempted to deliberate on grievances, resolved that 'the inhabitants of the English colonies in North America, by the immutable laws of nature, the principles of the English constitution, and the several charters or compacts», had their own rights, among which was:

> «A right peaceably to assemble, to consider their grievances, and petition the king; and that all prosecutions, prohibitory proclamations, and commitments for the same, are illegal».[27]

Therefore, the process of separation of the English colonies in America from the mother country took place on the basis of two fundamental elements: the process towards independence of each one of the colonies, through their own representative governments; and the process towards the unity of the colonies, through the continental congresses. According to what was said by one of its principal protagonists, John Adams, «The Revolution and the Union developed gradually from 1770 to 1776».[28]

During that period, it was initially a process of intercolonial agreements designed to establish economic boycotts in resistance to the tax pretensions of England. In this context, the first joint meeting of historical and constitutional significance between these colonies was the New York Congress of 1765, which met to demonstrate the colonies' rejection of the Stamp Act passed by the English Parliament on 22 March 1765. This Act placed stamp duties on all legal documents, newspaper pamphlets, college degrees, almanacs, liquor licences and playing cards, and aroused hostility that spread in the colonies.

Besides the social and economic causes of this rejection, the political reaction was based on the cry «no taxation without representation». Thus the 3rd, 4th and 5th rights declared in the Resolutions of the Stamp Act Congress 19 October 1765 stated:

> «3rd That it is inseparably essential to the freedom of a people, and the undoubted rights of Englishmen, that no taxes should be imposed on them, but with their own consent, given personally, or by their representatives.
>
> 4th. That the people of these colonies are not, and from their local circumstances, cannot be represented in the House of Commons in Great Britain.
>
> 5th. That the only representatives of the people of these colonies, are persons chosen therein by themselves; and that no taxes ever have been, or can be constitutionally imposed on them, by their respective legislatures».[29]

---

26 R.L. PERRY, (ed.), *Sources of our Liberties. Documentary Origin of Individual Liberties in the United States Constitution and Rights*, 1952, p. 261

27 *Idem*, p. 287, 288.

28 Quoted by M. GARCÍA-PELAYO, *Derecho constitucional comparado*, Madrid 1957, p. 325.

29 R.L. PERRY (ed.), *op. cit.*, p. 270.

In this Congress although a «due subordination to that august body, the Parliament of Great Britain», was declared, its representative character was questioned on the grounds that the taxes established in the Stamp Act had not been approved by the Colonial Assemblies. England annulled the Stamp Act, but imposed a series of customs duties on colonial products.

By 1774, it had become clear that the problems of individual colonies were really the problems of them all, and that brought about the need of united action by the Colonies, with the result that Virginia proposed that an annual Congress be held to discuss the joint interests of America. Thus, in 1774 the First Continental Congress met in Philadelphia with representatives from all the colonies, except Georgia.

The main political element discussed in the congress was the authority the colonies should concede to the Parliament, and on what grounds: either the law of nature, the British Constitution or the American charters.[30] It was decided that the law of nature should be recognized as one of the foundations of the rights of the colonies, and therefore not only the common law. Thus, the Congress declared, as a Right of the inhabitants of the English Colonies in North America, in the same sense of the Resolutions of the Stamp Act Congress:

> That the foundation of English Liberty, and of all free government, is a right in the people to participate in their legislative council; and as the English colonists are not represented, and from their local and other circumstances, cannot properly be represented in the British Parliament, they are entitled to a free and exclusive power of legislation in their several provincial legislatures, where their rights of representation can alone be preserved in all cases of taxation and internal polity, subject only to the negative of their sovereign, in such manner as has been heretofore used and accustomed».[31]

Thus, in these resolutions, loyalty to the king was maintained, but the parliament was denied competence to impose taxes on the colonies.

As a result of this Congress, economic war was declared with the suspension of imports and exports to England. The economic war rapidly became a military one and the Congress met again in Philadelphia and adopted the «Declaration of the Causes and Necessity of Taking up Arms» of 6 July 1775, as a reaction against the «enormous», and «unlimited power» of the Parliament of Great Britain. Therefore, the American Revolution can be considered a revolution against the sovereignty of the English Parliament.

One year later, the second continental Congress, in its session of 2 July 1776, adopted a proposition whereby the colonies declared themselves free and independent:

> «That these United Colonies are, and of right, ought to be, Free and Independent States; that they are absolved from all allegiance to the British Crown, and that all political connexion between them, and the state of Great Britain, is, and ought to be, totally dissolved».[32]

---

30 Ch. F. ADAMS (ed.) *The Works of John Adams*, Boston 1850, II, p. 374 quoted by R.L. PERRY, *op. cit.*, p. 275.

31 R.L. PERRY (ed.), *op. cit.*, p. 287.

32 *Idem*, p. 317.

The Congress agreed to draw up a declaration proclaiming to the world the reasons for the separation from its mother country, and on the 4th July, the Declaration of Independence was adopted, in formal ratification of the act already executed.

This document is of universal historical interest, for it was the first time that juridical-political-rationalist legitimacy had made its appearance openly in history. There was no longer the recourse to common law, nor to the rights of Englishmen, but exclusively to God and to the laws of nature. There was no longer the recourse to the Bill of Rights, but to self-evident truths, namely:

> «That all men are created equal; that they are endowed, by the Creator, with certain unalienable rights; that among these are life, liberty, and the pursuit of happiness. That to secure these rights, Governments are instituted among men, deriving their just powers from the consent of the governed; that whenever any form of government becomes destructive of these ends, it is the right of the people to alter or to abolish it, and to institute a new government, laying its foundation on such principles and organizing the powers in such form, as to them shall most likely effect their safety and happiness».[33]

Consequently, anything, which was not rationally adapted to the objectives established, was unjustified and illegitimate, and, the state was also organized in the most adequate way to achieve the said objectives.

Apart from the importance of this document for the United States, it is undoubtedly also of universal significance: its basic premise, as a syllogism, is constituted by all those acts of the crown which, according to Locke, define tyranny, and the conclusion of the syllogism is obvious: by violating the pact uniting him to his American subjects, the king had lost all claim to their loyalty, and consequently, the colonies became independent states.

Obviously, once the colonies had acquired their independence, they had to regulate their own political organization. Moreover, after the king's proclamation of rebellion on 23 August 1775, the Congress just before the Declaration of Independence urged all colonies to form separate governments for the exercise of all authority. It resolved:

> «That it be recommended to the respective assemblies and conventions of the United Colonies, where no government sufficient to the exigencies of their affairs has been hitherto established, to adopt such government as mall, in the opinion of the representatives of the people, best conduce to the happiness and safety of their constituents in particular and America in general».[34]

Thus, the Bill of Rights and the Constitution or Form of Government of Virginia were adopted on 12 June 1776, and the other Constitutions of the States were adopted after the Declaration of Independence until 1787.

These colonial constitutions were of fundamental importance both for constitutional history in general and for the history of the United States itself, since they undoubtedly represented the triumph of the rational normative concept of the constitution, which could already be glimpsed in the Declaration of Independence. Furthermore, there were written systematic and coded constitutions, many of which

---

33 *Idem*, p. 319.

34 *Idem*, p. 318. A.C. MCLAUGHLIN, *op. cit.*, p. 107-108.

were preceded by a table of rights inherent in human beings. In accordance with that table of rights the organic part of the constitution was set, adopting, naturally, as a fundamental principle the division of powers, which also made its entry for the first time in constitutional history with the principle of the sovereignty of the law.

Therefore, the rational normative concept of the constitution, with its table of rights, its division of powers, its sovereignty of the law, its distinction between constituent and constituted power, and its division of the constitution into a dogmatic and organic part, comes from America and its colonial constitutions, from where it proceeded to Europe, to the French Declaration of 1789, and through it, to modern constitutional law.

The idea of a Confederation or Union of Colonies was also formulated at the same time as the Declaration of Independence, thereby satisfying the need for a political union mainly derived out of the conduct of the war. Hence the adoption by the Congress, on 15th November 1777, of the «Articles of Confederation» is considered to be the First constitution.[35] It established a confederation and perpetual union between the States, the aim of which was the «common defence, the security of their Liberties and their mutual and general welfare»[36] in a system in which each state retained «its sovereignty, freedom and independence»[37] and any power, jurisdiction and right not expressly delegated to the United States in Congress.

The result was that the sole body of the Confederation was the Congress, in which each state had a vote. Consequently, the Confederation lacked direct taxation power, depended economically on the contributions of the States, had no executive body and only an embryonic form of judicial organization. Despite its weakness, the Confederation succeeded in carrying on the war for 7 years until it won. Following the victory, the precariousness of the Confederation made it necessary to establish a greater power to achieve national integration and a Federal Convention was called to meet, «for the sole and express purpose of revising the articles of Confederation».[38]

This led in 1787 to the adoption by the Congress of the Constitution of the United States that was the result of a series of general compromises[39] between the political and social components of the independent colonies, of which the following are the most outstanding:

In the first place, the compromise between Federalists and Antifederalists, which provided the Union the necessary competences for its existence, while maintaining the autonomy of the Federate States. From this compromise emerged the form of the Federal state,[40] which appeared for the first time in constitutional history as a political organization of States, through a system of political decentralization or vertical separation of powers. This compromise was one of the main contributions of the North American Constitution to modern constitutional law.

---

35 R.B. MORRIS, «Creating and Ratifying the Constitution», *National Forum. Towards the Bicentennial of the Constitution*, fall 1984, p. 9.

36 A.C. MCLAUGHLIN, *op. cit.*, p. 131.

37 *Idem*, p. 137; R.L. PERRY, (ed.), *op. cit.*, p. 399.

38 R.L. PERRY (ed.), *op. cit.*, p. 401.

39 M. GARCÍA-PELAYO, *op. cit.*, p. 336-337.

40 R.B. MORRIS, *loc. cit.*, p. 12, 13; M. GARCÍA-PELAYO, *op. cit.*, p. 336; A.C. MCLAUGHLIN, *op. cit.*, p. 163.

The second great compromise reflected in the constitution was, as a result of a long brewing confrontation, the compromise between large and small States of the Union regarding representation. That is to say, between a Congress in which the States would be represented in proportion to their population and a Congress with a confederate type of representation. The result was a bicameral system in which the House of Representatives was to be made up of a number of deputies proportional to the population of each state, whereas the Senate would comprise two representatives per state, regardless of its size, thus providing equality among the states.[41]

In relation to the latter, the third compromise of the Constitution was that between the North and the South, that is to say, the compromise between free states and pro-slavery states, according to which the slave population was estimated at three fifths in relation to the white population for the purposes of determining the population of each state, both for the appointment of representatives and for tax purposes.

The great slavery issue was also to produce a fourth compromise concerning the question of import and export duties and, therefore, on the import of slaves or its abolition. The middle ground solution led to the adoption of a clause impeding the Congress from making any decision prohibiting slave importation for twenty years, until the year 1808.[42]

The fifth compromise that we can identify in the American Constitution is that between democracy and the interests of the ruling classes, to avoid despotism when voting. Thus, limited mechanisms for voting were established, based on private property, as well as a mechanism for direct election of representatives to the House of Representatives as established by each state, and indirect election to the Senate.

The last and final compromise reflected in the constitution was the establishments of a system of separation of powers at federal level, thus, a check and balance system. Therefore, in addition to the legislative body, a strong presidency was provided for, to be occupied by a President elected for four years, by means of a system of indirect suffrage; and a Supreme Court was created, made up of judges elected for life by the two bodies furthest from the masses, the president and the Senate, being granted power to declare the unconstitutionality of acts issued by the other powers against the constitution. Separation of powers and judicial review of the constitutionality of legislative acts are another two main contributions of the American constitution to modern constitutional law.

In addition to these compromises of the constitution of the United States, we must turn our attention to another two main contributions of America to constitutional law: First, constitutionalism itself, in the sense of the adoption of all those compromises of forms of government in a written constitution as fundamental law, and second republicanism, as an ideology of the people against monarchy and hereditary aristocracies,[43] based on political representation.

Eighteenth century Americans decided upon revolution to repudiate royal authority and to erect a republic in its place. Thus, Republicanism and to become

---

41 M. GARCÍA-PELAYO, *op. cit.*, p. 336; R.B. MORRIS, *loc. cit.*, p. 10; A.C. MCLAUGHLIN, *op. cit.*, p. 179.

42 R.B. MORRIS, *loc. cit.*, p. 11; A.C. MCLAUGHLIN, *op. cit.*, p. 185.

43 G.S. WOOD, «The Intelectual Origins of the American Constitution», *National Forum, cit.*, Fall 1984, p. 5.

republican was what the American Revolution had been about. That is why «the people» who then became the sovereign in constitutional history gave the constitution.

The constitution adopted in 1787, however, was conceived basically as an organic document, regulating the separation of powers within the organs of the new state, both horizontally and vertically among the legislative, the executive and judicial powers and between the states and the United States in accordance with the federal System.

In spite of the colonial antecedents, and of the proposals made in the Convention, it did not contain a Bill of Rights, except the right to representative government. The protests of the opponents of the new Federal system, led particularly by the anti-federalists, during the ratification process brought about the adoption of the First Ten Amendments to the Constitution, on the 15th December 1791, containing the American Bill of Rights.[44]

3. The French Constitution (1791)

After the American Revolution, the constitutionalization of the Legal state was followed by the French Revolution 1789 and the adoption of the third constitution in the world, the French one dated 3 September 1791, the Polish Constitution promulgated on the 3rd May of the same year, 1791, being the second.[45]

Two years after the approval of the American Constitution and thirteen years after the Declaration of Independence of the United States, the French Revolution (1789) developed into a social revolution aimed at liquidating the *Ancient Regime*, represented by an absolute and personal monarchy.[46] The problem here, was not how to find a common denominator between thirteen independent states and build a new state from the remains of the English colonies as was the case in the American constitutional process, but rather, how to transform an over-centralized state constructed around the old French monarchy, where the state was the monarch (*L'État c'est Moi*), into a new form of state in which the people, through the concept of the nation, were to participate. A revolution was needed, and its first result was the weakening of the monarchy itself.

After 14th July 1789, two main decisions were made by the French National Assembly: the abolition of seigniorial rights on 4th August and the Declaration of the Rights of Man and of the Citizen on 26th August, both in 1789. Two years later, the First French Constitution of 3rd September 1791 was adopted, which even though still a monarchical constitution, it conceived the king as a delegate of the nation and subject to the sovereignty of the Law. The fact was that from that process onwards, the state was no longer the king, as an absolute monarch, but the organized people in a Nation subject to a constitution.

The Constitution of 1791 adopted a structure which later proved to be classical for the development of modern constitutional law, and which has been witnessed in some of the American States' constitutions. This structure established a clear

---

44 See the text in R.L. PERRY (ed.), *op. cit.*, pp. 432-433.

45 A.P. BLAUSTEIN, «The United States Constitution. A Model in Nation Building», *National Forum, cit.*, p. 15.

46 A. DE TOCQUEVILLE, *The Old Regime and the Revolution* (L'Ancien Régime et la Revolution)

distinction between a dogmatic part, containing individual rights and the limits and obligations of the state power, and an organic part, establishing the structure, attributions and relations between the various state bodies.[47]

The Constitution began with the Declaration of the Rights of Man and of the Citizen, already adopted by the Assembly on 26th August and approved by the king on the 5th October 1789. This text was inspired by the Declarations of the American States recently emancipated from England, mainly the Virginia Bill of Rights (1776). However, this does not mean that the Declaration was not basically a French one, a pure work of rationalism, inspired directly by the thoughts of Rousseau and Montesquieu.[48]

This Declaration of Rights that preceded the constitution can be characterized by the following major features: In the first place, its content constituted a formal adhesion to the principles of natural law and to the «natural» rights with which Man is born, so that the Law simply recognizes or declares them, but does not establish them. Thus the declaration had a universal character. It was not a declaration of Frenchmen's rights but the acknowledgement by the revolutionaries, of the existence of the fundamental rights of man, for all time and for all States. That was why De Tocqueville compared the political revolution of 1789 with a religious revolution, by saying that in the fashion of great religions, the political revolution established general rules, and adopted a message that spread abroad. This important aspect of the Declaration is related to the fact that the rights declared were natural rights.[49]

Secondly, under Rousseau's influence, the Declaration was based on man's natural bounty, which implicitly rejected the idea of original sin, for as it stated:

> «Ignorance, forgetfulness and contempt of the rights of Man are the sole causes of public misfortunes and of the corruption of governments».

Thirdly -and this is fundamental- from the legal and political point of view, the powers of the state were limited, inasmuch as it had to act within the limits imposed on it by such rights and consequently, under the sovereignty of the law, a principle which is established in the constitution.

Moreover, both the Declaration of Rights and the constitution itself were based on the affirmation of national sovereignty, introducing a concept which has been fundamental in French constitutional law, as it marked the beginning of a new basis for the legitimization of state power, as opposed to the monarchical legitimacy of the past, as well as a new assumption for the reorganisation of state bodies.

In the French Constitution, the idea of the nation emerged for the purpose of depriving the king of his sovereignty; but as sovereignty existed only in a person who exercised it, the concept of the nation emerged, as a personification of the people. To use Berthelémy's words:

> «There was a sovereign person who was the King. Another sovereign person had to be found to oppose him. The men of the Revolution have found that

[47] M. GARCÍA-PELAYO, *op. cit.*, p. 463.

[48] J. RIVERO, *Les Libertes Publiques*, Vol. I, Paris 1973, p. 38-42.

[49] A. DE TOCQUEVILLE, *op. cit.*, quoted by Y. MADIOT, *Droits de l'Homme et Libertes Publiques*, Paris 1976, p. 46.

sovereign person in a moral person: the Nation. They have taken the Crown away from the King and have placed it on the head of the Nation».[50]

But the nation in revolutionary theory was identified with what Sièyes called the «Third Estate». The Third Estate in the revolutionary States-General, compared to the other two «estates» (the nobility and the clergy), was the lower state or the nation as a whole. *Quest-ce que le Tièrs?* Was the question posed by Sièyes in his book, and the answer he gave was «all», «all the nation».[51] The privileged strata was excluded from the concept of the nation, confined then to the bourgeoisie.

The bourgeoisie, as stated by Sièyes, sought the «modest intention of having in the States General or Assembly an influence equal to that of the privileged»,[52] but the real situation, and particularly because of its economic power and the reaction against privileges, led the bourgeoisie to obtain power, through the French Revolution, with popular support.[53] The French a Revolution, therefore has been considered a Revolution of the bourgeoisie, for the bourgeoisie and by the bourgeoisie,[54] and was basically an instrument against privileges and discrimination and for seeking equality of all men in the enjoyment of their rights. Thus the Declaration of Rights of Man and of Citizen was qualified as being «the ideological expression of the triumph of the bourgeoisie».[55]

Anyway, sovereignty was in the Nation, as the Declaration of Rights expressly established:

> «The source of all sovereignty is essentially in the nation; no body, no individual can exercise authority that does not proceed from it in plain terms».[56]

Therefore, after the Revolution, the basis of public authority in France ceased to be the divine right of the personal monarch, and started to be the sovereignty of the nation (*souveraineté nationale*), that was not to be exercised directly by the nation, but through its representatives.[57]

Thus, the French constitution was also a representative constitution, since the nation exercised its power through representatives, and it is precisely in the structure of representation that the social significance of the Revolution was specifically reflected, because, in accordance with the system of suffrage which was established, a large number of citizens was excluded from electoral activity.[58]

---

50 BERTHELEMY-DUEZ, *Traité elémentaire de droit constitutionnel*, Paris 1933, p. 74, quoted by M. GARCÍA-PELAYO, *op. cit.*, p. 461.

51 E. SIÈYES, «*Quést-ce que le tièrs Etat?*» (Ed. R. ZAPPETI), Genève 1970, p. 121.

52 *Idem*, p. 135.

53 «The people -the not privileged- of course where the ones that supported the Third State, that is to say, the bourgeoisie, because they did not have other alternative, in the sense that they could not support the nobility or the clergy, who represented the privileges». G. DE RUGGIERO *The History of the European Liberalism*, Boston 1967, p. 74.

54 G. DE RUGGIERO, *op. cit.*, p. 75, 77.

55 J.L. ARANGUREN, *Ética y política*, Madrid 1963, p. 293, 297, quoted by E. DÍAZ, *Estado de derecho y sociedad democrática*, Madrid 1966, p. 80.

56 Art. 3.

57 Although ROUSSEAU considered representative regime incompatible with the principle of national sovereignty: «Sovereignty consists in the general will and the general will cannot be represented; deputies of the people are only commissioners; they can decide nothing definitely». *Contract Social*, 3, 15, quoted by J. BRISSAUD, *A History of French Public Law*, London 1915, p. 546.

58 Under the influence of Sièyes, the Constitution established two categories of citizens: active citizens and passive citizens. G. LEPOINTE, *Histoire des institutions du droit public français au XIX Siècle.1789-1914*, Paris 1953, p. 44.

Moreover, the French constitution established another principle of modern public law, which is particularly developed in France and which is summarized in the following statements: «There is no authority in France superior to that of the law»[59] and the law was considered to be «the expression of the general will».

This is an affirmation of the legal state and of the idea that it is not men who command, but laws. Hence the state bodies could demand obedience only insofar as they are an expression of the law, to the extent, said the constitution, that the king himself «only reigns by law, and it is only in the name of the law that he can demand obedience».[60]

The first constitution of France of 1791, despite of the Revolution, continued to establish a monarchical government: the exercise of the executive power and a share, though very limited, of the legislative power was conferred upon the king. But he was nothing more than the chief public functionary; he was considered a delegate of the nation, subject to the sovereignty of the law. Consequently, the monarch became a state body for the first time, and the ancient institution of divine right became a body of positive law. The king became king of the French people instead of king of France.[61]

Finally, the constitution also established a system of strict separation of powers, in accordance with what was stated in the Declaration of Rights of Man and the Citizen, in the sense that:

> «Any society in which the separation of power is not determined has no constitution at all».[62]

However, in the French system of separation of powers a clear predominance of the legislative power was shown. Thus, the king neither convened, nor suspended, or dissolved the assembly; he had the power of veto, but only for suspension, and could not take any initiative, although he could invite the legislative body to take something into account.

The assembly, for its part, had no control over the executive, since the king's person was sacred and inviolable; ministers were only subject to penal responsibility. However, the assembly had important executive attributions such as the appointment of principal officials, the surveillance of departmental administration, the declaration of war, the ratification of treaties, etc.[63]

In Europe, therefore, since the French Revolution in 1789 and the 1791 constitution, constitutions during last century were generally the result of Revolutions, establishing the fundamental scheme of the *État de droit* with fundamental rights and division of powers, and with an additional characteristic, namely that the state was organized from a negative standpoint vis-à-vis its own powers, that means keeping in mind the protection of the citizens against the abuse of state power. Consequently, the ways and means of control over the state were even more organized than the state itself.

---

59 «Il n'y a point en France d'autorite superieur a celle de la loi». M. GARCÍA-PELAYO, *op, cit.*, p. 465-466.
60 Art. 4, Chap II, Sec. 1.
61 G. LEPOINTE, *op. cit.*, p. 44.
62 Art. 16.
63 G. LEPOINTE, *op. cit.*, p. 45, 49.

In this process of constitutionalization of the *État de droit*, the principle of constitutional rigidity was also established, in the sense that the constitution was really fundamental. It was a fundamental law, which could not be modified by ordinary legislation, requiring special procedures for its amendment. This gave rise to the development of the theory of constituent power. In the French example, this presupposed that the people were an existential political entity. As a result of the Revolution, the people became the subject of constituent power, became aware of their political capacity of action and provided themselves with a constitution, based on the assumption, clearly stated, of their political unity and capacity of action.

The constitution was then the fundamental law of the state and was not to be modified easily. Thus, the distinction between the constituent power of the people and the legislative power was developed, and consequently the distinction between constitutional acts (*lois constitutionelles*) and ordinary laws. The Nation always retained the right to change its constitution, but this could only be done following the means, which had been prescribed in the constitution itself. Nevertheless, this did not prevent changes in the constitution and because of the revolutionary struggles, four constitutions were adopted in the eleven years between 1789 and 1800: that of 3-14 September 1791; 24th June 1793; 5 *Fructidor*, year III (1795); and that of 22nd *Frimaire*, year VIII (1800).

Anyway, the significance of the French Revolution lies in the fact that it led to the establishment of an *État de droit*, in the sense that it produced a constitution which limited and controlled the exercise of state power, thereby endowing the modern state with a new political character. In this system, the nation, as subject of the constituent power, confronted the absolute monarch, eliminated his absolutism and completely took his place, which actually led to an increase in the power of the state itself.

Naturally, the American model exerted considerable influence in this respect: the Declaration of Independence of 1776 and the American Constitution of 1787 itself, were also the result of the decision adopted by the people of the United States, although, in the case of the United States, it was not a matter of transforming a state already in existence, as was the case in France, but rather a question of the constitution of a new political formation, the act of providing a constitution to accompany the political foundation of a new state.

4. The Inspiration of France and America and the Latin American Constitutionalism

After the American and French revolutions aimed at creating a republican federal state in the American case or to transform an absolute monarchical state into a republican state in the French case, the constitutionalization of the legal state in their respective constitutions at the end of the eighteenth century was followed all over the world, mainly in Latin America and Europe during the nineteenth century.

In Europe, the French constitution of 1795 particularly inspired the Spanish constitution of Cadiz 1812 and the Norwegian constitution of 1814,[64] but in Latin

[64] J.A. HAWGOOD, *Modern Constitutions since 1787*, London 1939, p. 51.

American countries, being colonies of Spain and Portugal, the influence of the American and French revolutions and constitutionalism was immediate and definitive. We will refer only to one of the Latin American countries, Venezuela, not only because it is our own country, but also because it was the first Latin American country to gain independence from Spain, the third country in the world whose Declaration of Rights of the People was approved by an elected Congress, and where the first of the Latin American constitutions was sanctioned in 1811.

In effect, one of the first reactions against the Spanish monarchy inspired by the French Revolution, was the so-called *San Blas* conspiracy in Madrid, intended to take place on the 3rd February 1796. It ended before it began; the conspirators were detained the day before, went on trial and a few of them deported to the colonies for life imprisonment. The principal conspirators, including Juan Bautista Picornell, were sent to Venezuela, where they managed to get in touch with local conspirators, and in 1797 they developed what has been called the conspiracy of Gual y España, named after the two main participants: Manuel Gual and Jose María España.

Even though the conspiracy failed, it remained as the most serious attempt at liberation in all Latin America, and also produced one of the most important documents that inspired the subsequent constitutionalization process in our countries.

The conspirators published a booklet entitled Rights of Man and Citizens, in 1797 with an «address to the Americans», that in fact was a translation of the French Declaration of Rights of Man and the Citizen contained in the 1795 French Constitution.[65]

The importance of this document was that it inspired the Declaration of Rights of the People, approved by the first Venezuelan Congress four days before the Declaration of Independence was proclaimed on 5th July 1811, which at the same time was inspired by the American Declaration of Independence.

Therefore, Latin America received the direct influence of both revolutions, the American and the French and altogether at the beginning of its constitutionalization process, of the French Declaration of Rights of Man and Citizens and of the American Declaration of Independence. Subsequently, the first of the Latin-American Constitutions, the Federal Constitution of the States of Venezuela of 21st December 1811, followed not only all the general trends of the constitutionalization process of the *État de droit* existing at the time[66] but also the fundamental ideas of Hobbes, Bodin, Locke, Montesquieu and Rousseau, all reflected in the articles of the constitution.

In effect, the constitution firstly followed the formal shape of the French, containing 228 articles, much more than the few articles in the American constitution. It was also conceived in the way constitutions were afterwards developed, with both a dogmatic and an organic part. The dogmatic part contained a declaration of «The Rights of lean that are recognized and that are to be respected in the state» in 58 articles much more than the French model. The organic part established the fundamental framework of the state and its organs, in 140 articles.

Secondly, the constitution was adopted by the «people of the States of Venezuela, using our sovereignty», following the general trend of the American and

65 P. GRASES (ed.), *Derechos del hombre y del ciudadano*, Caracas 1959, p. 105-121.
66 See the texts in A.R. BREWER-CARÍAS, *Las Constituciones de Venezuela*, Madrid 1985.

French process in relation to the concept of national sovereignty and representation. The article 144 of the constitution, in this respect established:

> «144. The sovereignty of a country or supreme power to govern or direct community interests equitably essentially and originally lays in the general mass of its inhabitants, and is exercised by means of agents or representatives appointed and established in accordance with the Constitution».

Thus, continued article 145 and 146:

> «145. No individual, no family or portion or group of citizens, no particular corporation, no village, city or county can confer upon itself national sovereignty, which is inalienable and indivisible, in essence and origin. Neither may any individual exercise governmental public functions unless it has been obtained by the Constitution.
>
> 147. Magistrates and officials of Government, invested with any kind of authority whether in the Legislative, Executive or Judicial Departments, consequently, are simple agents and representatives of the people in their functions and are always responsible to the inhabitants for their public conduct through legal and constitutional means».

Thirdly, the constitution was conceived as a manifestation of the social contract according to Locke's and Rousseau's concepts, to protect the rights of the people once renounced to the natural condition of man. In this sense, the articles 141 and 142 stated:

> «141. Once men have set themselves up in a Society, they renounce that unlimited and licentious liberty in which their passions easily led them to indulge, passions characteristic only of the wild state. The establishment of a society presupposes the renouncement of those ill-fated rights, the acquisition of other sweeter and more pacific rights and subjection to certain mutual duties.
>
> 142. The social pact assures each individual the enjoyment and possession of his goods, without prejudice to the right of others to have theirs».

The articles 151 and 152 also stated:

> «151. The aim of society is the common happiness, and governments have been instituted to make man secure, protecting his physical and mental faculties, improving the sphere of his enjoyment and to produce the honest and equitable exercise of his rights.
>
> 152. These rights are liberty, equality, property and security».

Fourthly, the supremacy of law was formally declared in accordance with Rousseau's concept as the expression of the general will, and secured by sanctioning illegal acts as tyrannical. In this respect, the articles 149 and 150 stated:

> «149. The law is the free expression of the general will or of the majority of the citizens, indicated by the body of its representatives legally constituted. The law is founded on justice and on the common needs and must protect public and individual liberty against any oppression or violence.
>
> 150. Those acts committed against any person which do not fall within the cases and forms determined by the law, are iniquitous, and when they involve

the usurpation of constitutional authority or the liberty of the people, they shall be considered to be tyrannical».

Fifthly, the constitution adopted the principle of separation of powers in accordance with Montesquieu's thoughts.

In the preamble to the constitution, when establishing the basis of the federal pact, it was stated:

«The various functions of the authority entrusted to the Confederation shall never be performed together. The Sovereign Power must be divided into Legislative, Executive and Judicial power, and entrusted to different bodies, independent both reciprocally and in their respective faculties».

Furthermore, article 189 stressed that:

«The three essential government departments, namely the Legislature, the Executive and the Judiciary must be as separate and mutually independent as is required by the nature of a free government or as is in keeping with the links which bind together the system of the Constitution in indissoluble friendship and unity».

Finally, the Venezuelan Constitution of 1811 adopted the federal form of the state following the American model, as a mean to unite several former colonial provinces that were highly decentralized in the Spanish system of colonial government. The federal scheme adopted in the United States was then the ideal system to be adopted in the now independent state, in which the provinces, kept their «sovereignty, liberty and independence» in all matters not assigned by the Federal Pact to the general authority of the Confederation.

But in fact, the federal form adopted in the organisation, establishing a weakened power in the federal government, undoubtedly provoked the crisis of the First Republic and the beginning of a ten-year war of independence. The crisis was also provoked by the absence of a unipersonal executive, because originally our country had a collective triunviral executive.

Simon Bolivar, in whose honour the Simon Bolivar Chair of this University is named, criticised the adoption of the federal form of the state in the first constitution and attributed the absence of political stability and continuity, mainly facing the counter offensive of the Spanish Empire, to the weakened and powerless republic that resulted from it. In 1815, in effect, he said:

«In the same way that Venezuela has been the American Republic that has made most progress in its political institutions, it has also been the clearest example of the inefficiency of the federal-democratic form for our nascent states».[67]

Four years later, in 1819, on the same matter, he insisted:

The more I admire the excellencies of the Federal Constitution of Venezuela, the more I am persuaded of the impossibility of its application to our state and from my point of view it is a prodigy that whose model in the North part of America be still in force, so prosperily».[68]

---

[67] S. BOLÍVAR, «Carta de Jamaica» (1815), in *Escritos Fundamentales*, Caracas 1982, p. 97.
[68] S. BOLÍVAR, «Discurso de Angostura» (1819), in *Escritos Fundamentales, cit*, p. 120.

Bolívar qualified the North American federal constitution as the most perfect at the time, but blamed the 1811 Venezuelan legislators for being:

> «Seduced by the dazzling shine of happiness of the American people, thinking that the blessings they enjoy are the exclusive result of its form of government and not of the character and customs of its citizens. And in effect, the example of the United States because its prosperity, was too flattering so as not to be followed».[69]

He finished his argument against the federal form of the state, arguing that at the beginning of the republic, we were not yet prepared for a highly decentralized form of vertical division of power, and for adopting weak central government. He expressed conclusively, in relation to the copying of the North American federal system,

> «I think that it would be better for America to adopt the Koran, than the government of the United States even if it is the best in the world».[70]

But in spite of Bolivar's recommendations, federalism in particular, spread throughout Latin America. Venezuela has always had a federal system of government and it is still a Federal state. In the same way, all the other large states in Latin America have a federal form of government, as is the case of Argentina, Brazil and Mexico.

Anyway, American and French constitutionalism inspired the process, both of independence and constitution framing all the Latin American States during the first half of the last century, which adopted the general trends of the constitutionalization of the *État de Droit*. The same influence happened to develop in most European countries.

The constitutionalization process of North America and France soon brought about the development of constitutional an political studies, and perhaps the first of the constitutional thinkers of modern times was Alexis de Tocqueville. Tocqueville was a Frenchman who visited the United States in the 1830's to study the penitentiary system and finished by publishing one hundred and fifty years ago, one of the most important books in the history of constitutional law: *Democracy in America* (1835), followed a few years later by another very important book of his own, this time related to the French Revolution and its constitutionalization process: The *Ancient Regime and the Revolution* (1856).

These two books have undoubtedly influenced the process of constitutionalization and democracy all over the world since their publication. Their influence upon the conception of the *État de droit* was definitive.

We want to stress the impact of the American process of constitutionalization in modern constitutional law, but we want to do so through De Tocqueville's prism as a continental European constitutional and political thinker when he discovered for Europe the principles of democracy and constitutionalism that had occurred on the other side of the Atlantic. It is also a way of celebrating the one hundred and fiftieth anniversary of the publication of his *Democracy in America* in 1835.

II. GENERAL TRENDS OF CONTEMPORARY CONSTITUTIONALISM

In effect, one can say that the fundamental principles and institutions of modern constitutional law had their factual origin in the American Revolution. This event

---

69 *Idem.*

70 S. BOLÍVAR (letter to D.F. O'LEARY), in *Escritos Fundamentales, cit.*, p. 200, 201.

and the whole process of independence and constitutionalism in the United States radically transformed the constitutional trends of the time, and established the basis of contemporary constitutional law.

An exceptional witness to those processes was Alexis De Tocqueville, perhaps the first modern constitutional thinker of the last century, whose studies regarding the American and French Revolutions and their constitutional consequences were considered as masterpieces by his contemporaries in France and other European countries. Today, these books are still essential works for understanding the fundamental changes and trends that took place after the American and French Revolutions, as well as the causes of those processes.

Our intention, as we said, is to stress the fundamental contributions of the American Revolution to constitutional theory and Law, through De Tocqueville's prism, which we consider a fundamental one, since it was a European continental approach to the North American constitutional process, still unknown in this part of the world in the 1830's .[71]

De Tocqueville, for instance, stressed among the points of departure of the Anglo-Americans and its importance for the future, the situation of the English colonies in the seventeenth century and particularly that of New England.

He stated:

> «All the general principles on which modern constitutions rest, principles which most Europeans in the seventeenth century scarcely understood and whose dominance in Great Britain was then far from complete, are recognised and given authority by the laws of New England; the participation of the people in public affairs, the free voting of taxes, the responsibility of governments officials, individual freedom, and trial by jury - all these things were established without question and with practical effect».[72]

Those «general principles on which modern constitutions rest», as De Tocqueville called them, today and after the American independence, are the following:

First, the notion of constitution itself, as a written document, of permanent value, containing a fundamental or higher law, which form the basis of the constitutionalization process.

Second, the notion of democracy itself, the democratic regime or state, and the concept of sovereignty belonging to the people and not to state organs.

Third, the political centralization or decentralization of the state, as a basic element for its organization, and its reflections on the Federal form of the state and upon the development of local government.

Fourth, the principle of separation of powers, and the different forms of government, particularly presidential or parliamentary governments.

Fifth, the role of the Judicial power, the Supreme Court of Justice and the judicial control of the constitutionality of legislation, and in the sixth place, the establishing of an entrenched declaration of fundamental rights and liberties.

---

[71] J.P. MAYER, «Foreword», A. DE TOCQUEVILLE, *Democracy in America* (edited by J.P. Mayer and M. Lerner), London 1968, p. XIII-XXXIII.

[72] A. DE TOCQUEVILLE, *op. cit.*, p. 50.

All these six principles were, and still are, general principles on which modern and contemporary constitutions rested and still rest, and that identifies the modern *État de droit.* All those principles were analysed by De Tocqueville in relation to the American systems to which he dedicated his book even though in its Introduction of his book he said that he was:

> «Very far from believing that they (the Americans) have found the only form possible for democratic government»,[73]

and that he did

> «Not think that American Institutions are the only ones, or the best, that a democratic nation might adopt».[74]

Any way, he studied all of them and made fundamental and still valid reflections on them, which we want to comment upon.

1. Constitutionalism

The first of the principles of present constitutional law is constitutionalism, that is to say, the trust which men place in the power of words formally written down to keep a government in order.[75]

As we have said, written constitutions in the modern world, with the exception of Cromwell's *Instrument of Government* 1653, can be considered a North American political invention based on three elementary notions: that of a greater and higher law placed above government and individuals; that of fundamental rights of individuals, which must be guaranteed in regard to the state, and that of a charter, where the submission of the state to the law, limiting its powers, and individual rights were to be expressly written, with some sense of permanence.

This practice of written constitutions was initiated in the English colonies in America when they became independent states in 1776, giving rise to the rational-normative concept of the constitution, as a written and systematic document, referring to the political organization of society, establishing the powers of the different state bodies and generally preceded by a list of rights inherent in man. Thus, the general division of the contents of modern constitutions into an organic and a dogmatic part, the former comprising the concept of separation of power and supremacy of the law, and the latter the declaration of fundamental rights. As we have seen, after the Declaration of Rights and the Constitution of Virginia in 1776, the practice of written constitutions spread to Europe and Latin America.

The basic element in the process of constitutionalization or of constitutionalism, is, of course, the concept that the constitution is a supreme and fundamental law, placed above all state powers and individuals. In this respect De Tocqueville when comparing the constitutions of France, England and the United States, pointed out:

> «In France, the Constitution is, or is supposed to be, immutable. No authority can change anything in it; that is the accepted theory.
>
> In England, Parliament has the right to modify the Constitution. In England, therefore, the Constitution can change constantly, or rather it does not exist at all. Parliament being the legislative body, is also the constituent one».

---

73 *Idem*, p. 17.
74 *Ibid*, p. 285.
75 W.H. HAMILTON, «Constitutionalism», *Encyclopaedia of the Social Sciences*, Vol. III, IV, p. 255.

American political theories are simpler and more rational -he said-.

«The American Constitution is not immutable, as in France; it cannot be changed by the ordinary authority of society as in England. It is a thing apart; it represents the will of the whole people and binds the legislators as well as plain citizens, but it can be changed by the will of the people, in accordance with established forms».[76]

And he concluded:

«In America, the Constitution rules both legislators and simple citizens. It is therefore the primary law and cannot be modified by a law. Hence it is right that the courts should obey the Constitution rather than all the laws».[77]

From this came as a consequence, the concepts not only of written constitutions, but also of rigid ones, and above all, the notion of the supremacy of the constitution that by the time De Tocqueville visited the United States, had been developed by Chief Justice Marshall in the famous *Marbury v. Madison* case 1803 decided by the Supreme Court. In relation to this principle of Constitutional Supremacy, in that case it was stated:

«It is a proposition too plain to be contested, that the Constitution controls any legislative act repugnant to it; or, that the legislature may alter the Constitution by an ordinary act.

Between these alternatives there is no middle ground. The constitution is either a superior paramount law, unchangeable by ordinary means, or it is on a level with ordinary legislative acts, and, like other acts, is alterable when the legislature shall please to alter it».[78]

In the same case, Marshall then concluded with his formidable proposition related to written constitutions:

«Certainly, all those who have framed written constitutions contemplate them as forming the fundamental and paramount law of the nation, and consequently, the theory of every such government must be, that an act of the legislature, repugnant to the constitution, is void.

This theory is essentially attached to written constitutions, and is, consequently, to be considered by this court as one of the fundamental principles of our society».[79]

Constitutionalism through written, rigid and supreme constitutions is a principle developed as a general trend in modern and contemporary constitutional law and is followed in almost all countries in the world, except in the United Kingdom and a very few other countries. In any case, it has been the common trend in Latin-American constitutionalism ever since 1811.

2. Democracy and the People's Sovereignty

The second of the principles developed in constitutional and political practice in the modern world, influenced by American constitutionalism is that of democracy

---

[76] A. DE TOCQUEVILLE, *op. cit.*, p. 123.

[77] *Idem*, p. 124.

[78] *Marbury v. Madison*, 5 U.S. (1 Cranch) 137, 2L, Ed. 60 (1803). See text in R.A. ROSSUM and G. Alan TARR, *American Constitutional Law. Cases and Interpretation*, New York 1983, p. 70.

[79] *Idem*, p. 70.

as republicanism based on the concept of people's sovereignty. With the American Revolution, the traditional monarchical legitimacy of government was definitively substituted. The sovereign was no longer the monarch, but the people, and therefore the practice of democratic government was initiated in the modern world.

This was a fundamental concept in De Tocqueville's work, forming the very title to his book *Democracy in America*, in which he said:

> «Any discussion of the political laws of the United States must always begin with the dogma of the sovereignty of the people».[80]

> A principle that De Tocqueville considered to be «over the whole political system of the Anglo-Americans».[81]

> He added:

> «If there is one country in the world where one can hope to appreciate the true value of the dogma of the sovereignty of the people, study its application to the business of society, and judge both its dangers and its advantages: that country is America».[82]

> To that end he devoted his book, precisely to study democracy in America.

Of course, democracy developed in America long before independence, and De Tocqueville located its exercise «in the provincial assemblies, especially that of the township» where it «spread secretly»[83] during colonial rule. But once the American Revolution broke out:

> «The dogma of the sovereignty of the people came out from the township and took possession of the government; every class enlisted in its cause; the war was fought and victory obtained in its name; it became the law of laws».[84]

In accordance with this dogma of the sovereignty of the people, when it prevails in a nation, -he said-, «each individual forms an equal part of that sovereignty and shares equally the government of the state».[85] Thus he asserted that «America is the land of democracy.[86]

The title of the chapter one of the second part of his book said: «Why it can strictly be said that the people govern in the United States», and in its first paragraph De Tocqueville said:

> «In America the people appoint both those who make the laws and those who execute them; the people form the jury which punishes breaches of the law. The institutions are democratic not only in principle but also in all their developments; thus, the people *directly* nominate their representatives and generally choose them annually so as to hold them more completely dependent. So direction really comes from the people, and though the form of governments is representative, it is clear that the opinions prejudices, interests,

---

80 A. DE TOCQUEVILLE, *op. cit.*, Vol. 1, p. 68.
81 *Ibid*, p. 78.
82 *Ibid*, p. 68.
83 *Ibid*, p. 69.
84 *Ibid*, p. 69.
85 *Ibid*, p. 78-79.
86 *Ibid*, p. 216.

and even passions of the people can find no lasting obstacles preventing them from being manifest in the daily conduct of society».[87]

But one of the main aspects to which De Tocqueville referred in relation to democracy, was «the main causes tending to maintain a democratic republic in the United States».[88] He said:

«Three factors seem to contribute more than all others to the maintenance of a democratic republic in the New World.

The first is the federal form adopted by the Americans, which allows the Union to enjoy the power of a greater republic and the security of a small one.

The second are communal institutions which moderate the despotism of the majority and give the people both a taste fox freedom and the skill to be free.

The third is the way judicial power is organized. I have shown -he said- how the courts correct the aberrations of democracy and how, though they can never stop the movements of the majority, they do succeed in checking and directing them».[89]

Thus, he established the relation between democracy and decentralization, and he stated that the problems of the «omnipotence of the majority» and even the «tyranny of the majority»[90] was tempered by the almost non-existence of administrative centralization in North America,[91] and by the influence of the American legal profession.[92]

Democracy as a form of government, always attained or maintained, is the second general trend in modern and contemporary constitutionalism, inspired by the American constitutional process. All the constitutions in the world established it as a basic component of their political systems, and is the sign of our times, even though its maintenance has not always been secured.

3. The vertical distribution of State Powers: Federal State, Decentralisation and Local Government

In his study of the American constitution, one of the aspects to which De Tocqueville devoted much of his attention due to its importance to democracy, was that of political decentralisation or the vertical distribution of state powers among different political territorial units; the third main feature of modern constitutionalism.

He observed:

«In no country in the world are the pronouncements of the law more categorical than in America, and in no other country is the right to enforce it divided among so many hands».[93]

---

87 *Ibid*, p. 213.
88 Title of Charter IX of 2nd part, *op. cit.*, p. 342.
89 *Idem*, p. 354.
90 *Idem*, p. 304, 309.
91 *Idem*, p. 323.
92 *Idem*, p. 324.
93 *Ibid*, p. 87.

He stressed that «nothing strikes a European traveller in the United States more than the absence of what we call government or administration .... Functions (are) multiplied... (and) by sharing authority in this way its power becomes, it is true, both less irresistible and less dangerous, but it is far from being destroyed.[94]

He concluded his observation:

> «There is nothing centralized or hierarchical, in the constitution of American administrative power, and that is the reason why one is not at all conscious of it. The authority exists but one does not know where to find its representative».[95]

De Tocqueville observed that the distribution of powers in the vertical sense, in North America, was not produced by a process of decentralization but rather of centralization, in the sense that the township, the country and the States, first existed so that «The federal government was the last to take shape in the United States».[96]

In his own words:

> «In most European nations political existence started in the higher ranks of society and has been gradually but always incompletely, communicated to the various members of the body social.
>
> Contrariwise, in America one may say that the local community was organized before the county, the county before the States; and the state before the Union».[97]

Referring to New England, he stated that the local communities there had taken complete and definite shape as early as 1650, and he stressed:

> «Inside the locality there was a real active life which was completely democratic and republican. The colonies still recognised the mother country's supremacy; legally the state was a monarchy, but each locality was already a lively republic».[98]

Thus, from this historical approach, the importance that De Tocqueville assigned to local government as the source of democracy is classical. His famous words concerning local government are well known and always valid:

> «The strength of free peoples resides in the local community. Local institutions are to liberty what primary schools are to society; they put it within the people's reach; they teach people to appreciate its peaceful enjoyment and accustoms them to make use of it».[99]

And he added: 'In the townships, ... the people are the source of power, but nowhere else do they exercise their power so directly';[100] that is why, he insisted, local institutions «exercise immense influence over the whole of society»,[101] and concluded by saying that «political life was born in the very heart of the townships».[102]

---

94 *Ibid*, p. 86.
95 *Ibid*, p. 87.
96 *Ibid*, p. 72.
97 *Ibid*, p. 51.
98 *Ibid*, p. 51.
99 *Ibid*, p. 74.
100 *Ibid*, p. 75.
101 *Ibid*, p. 75.
102 *Ibid*, p. 79.

Regarding the federal form of the state, a product of the process of political centralization in a highly decentralized society, De Tocqueville said:

> «This constitution, which at first sight one is tempted to confuse with previous federal constitutions, in fact rests on an entirely new theory, a theory that should be hailed as one of the great discoveries of political science in our age.[103]

And in fact, one can say that the federal state came into being in history with the American constitution 1789, and even though the word «federal» or «federation» is not used in the constitution, it was in the United States that this form of political organisation was born.[104]

It did not respond to a previous scheme, but to practical need: the purpose was to seek a formula that made the existence of independent states compatible with a central power with enough attributions to act by itself at federal level.

This new institution, De Tocqueville said, cannot be compared to the confederations that existed in Europe well before the American constitution, mainly because the central power in the American constitution as he observed, «acts without intermediary on the governed, administering and judging them, as do national governments», adding:

> «Clearly here we have not a federal government but an incomplete national government. Hence a form of government has been found which is neither precisely national nor federal; but things have halted there, and the new word to express this new thing does not yet exist».[105]

This «new thing» is precisely what in constitutional law is known as federal state, and although De Tocqueville admired its novelty, he also pointed out its defects, and clearly observed that it was not a product for export.

He said,

> «The Constitution of the United States is like one of those beautiful creations of human diligence which give their inventors glory and riches but remains sterile in other hands».[106]

In this sense, in his book De Tocqueville referred to the case of Mexico in the 1830's with its imported federal system but his remarks can be applied to all Latin America. Tries Federal organization of the state was, precisely, one of the main features of American constitutionalism that was immediately followed by almost all large Latin-American countries.

In contrast to the centralized states of Europe, and the national concentration of political power, De Tocqueville pointed out that «the most fatal of all defects which I regard as inherent in the federal system is the comparative weakness of the government of the Union», adding that «a divided sovereignty must always be weaker than a complete one».[107]

As we have said, this weakness referred to the federal form of the state, once adopted in the Venezuelan constitution 1811, 6 months after the Declaration of

---

103 *Ibid*, p. 192.

104 *Cf.* M. GARCÍA PELAYO, *Derecho constitucional comparado*, Madrid 1957, p. 215, 341.

105 A. DE TOCQUEVILLE, *op. cit.*, p. 194.

106 *Ibid*, p. 203.

107 *Ibid*, p. 204.

Independence, and which was precisely one of the main causes of the failure of the First Republic the following year. Thus, of Simon Bolivar definitively asserted in a letter to the governor of one of the Venezuelan provinces, (Barinas), on 12 August 1813:

> «Never the division of power had established and perpetuated governments; only its concentration had infused respect for a nation».[108]

We mentioned before that Bolivar expressed all his life bitter criticism regarding the federal form of the state and its adoption in Venezuela, and always advocated a concentrated form of state power. In addition, for example, in his famous Manifesto of *Cartagena* of 1812, written the year following the sanctioning of the Constitution and after the failure of the First Republic, he expressed:

> «What make the government of Venezuela more weaken was the federal form it adopted, following the exaggerated expression of the rights of man that by allowing them to self-government, braked the social pacts, and leads nations to anarchy. That is the real situation of the Confederation. Each Province had an independent government; and in accordance with its example, each Township wanted equal powers and adopted the theory that Man and towns the prerogative of establishing, as they liked the government that best suited them... The federal system, if it is true that is the most perfect and oriented to provide human happiness in society, is nevertheless, the most opposed to the interests of our new-born States.[109]

Later, in his address to the Angostura Congress, in 1819, he persisted in the same idea:

> «The Venezuelans -he said- were not to get the magnificent federal system suddenly after the independence. We were not prepared for so much welfare; the good as well as the evil can kill when it is sudden and excessive».[110]

Finally, one year before his death, in a letter to his former aide-de-camp, Daniel Florencio O'Leary, he definitively qualified the federal system as a

> «Regularized anarchy, or better still, the law that establishes the implicit duty of disassociation and destruction of the state with all its individuals».[111]

But in spite of Bolivar's remarks and criticism of Federations, in Venezuela's case, since those days of independence and after the 1830 constitution, the form of our state has always been federal, and in the name of federation we had our bloodiest civil war and social revolution in the middle of last century: the Federal War of 1858-1863.

On the other hand, all the largest states of Latin America and of the world today have a federal form, to an extent that the federal system of government covers more than a half of the earths surface.

Anyway, although De Tocqueville was also a critic of the federal form of state, he conversely praised the beneficial effects of political decentralization and local government. He said:

---

108 S. BOLÍVAR, *Escritos Fundamentales*, Ed. 1982, p. 63.
109 *Idem*, p. 61-62.
110 *Idem*, p. 140.
111 *Idem*, p. 200, 201.

«The partisans of centralization in Europe maintain that the government administers localities better than they can themselves; that may be true when the central government is enlightened and the local authorities are not, when it is active and they are lethargic, when it is accustomed to command and they to obey...».

But when people are enlightened, awake to their own interests, and used to thinking for themselves, as he had seen in America, he said that he was:

«Persuaded that in that case the collective force of the citizens will always be better able to achieve social prosperity than the authority of the government».[112]

He finally declared that:

«The political advantages derived by the Americans from a system of decentralization would make me prefer that to the opposite system».[113]

4. Separation of Powers and Presidential System of Government

In the constitution of the United States of 1787, and previously, in the various constitutions of the former colonies, the fourth principle of modern constitutionalism, the principle of separation of power within the more orthodox doctrine at the time, was formally expressed for the first time.

For instance, the first of those constitutions, the one of Virginia in 1776, stated (Art. III):

«The Legislative, Executive and Judiciary departments, shall be separate and distinct, so that neither exercise the powers properly belonging to the other; nor shall any person exercise the powers of more than one of them at the same time».

The American constitution has no similar norm within its articles, but its main objective was precisely to organize the form of government, within the principles of the separation of powers, but allowing various interferences between them in a check and balance system. Particularly, regulating the powers of the executive in what was a new way, giving rise to presidentialism as opposed to parliamentarism, and to a particular shape of the judiciary, never previously known in constitutional practice.

De Tocqueville referred, in his book, to these two aspects of the principle.

Regarding the executive power, he immediately pointed out that in the United States, «maintenance of the republican form of government required that the representative of executive power should be subject to the national will»; thus, «the president is an elective magistrate... the one and only representative of the executive power of the nation».[114] But, he noted, «in exercising that power he is not completely independent».[115]

That was one of the particular consequences of the check and balance system of separation of powers adopted in the United States, but without making the

[112] A. DE TOCQUEVILLE, *Democracy in America, cit.*, p. 110.
[113] *Idem*, p. 113, 115.
[114] *Idem*, p. 148.
[115] *Idem*, p. 149.

executive dependent on parliament, as in parliamentary systems of government. That is why when comparing the European parliamentary system with the presidential system of the United States, De Tocqueville referred to the important part that the executive power played in America in contrast with the situation of a constitutional king in Europe.

A constitutional king, he observed, «cannot govern when opinion in the legislative chambers is not in accord with his».[116] In the presidential system, he said, conversely, the sincere aid of Congress to the president «is no doubt useful, but it is not necessary in order that the government should function».[117]

The separation of powers and the presidential system of government was followed very closely, sooner or later, in all Latin American republics after Independence or after the monarchical experience that a few countries had.

Thus, one can say that presidentialism is the sign of our constitutional system of government, and to such an extent, that parliamentarism has never developed in Latin America. This is rather a European form of government that Europe never managed to export to Latin America.

5. The role of the judiciary

But among the American born constitutional institutions, the one that perhaps has the most distinguished originality is the role assigned to the judicial power in the system of separation of powers. This is true even at the present time and was so when De Tocqueville visited North America. He devoted a separate chapter of his book to the powers of judges and to its great political importance, beginning with this assertion:

> «Confederations have existed in other countries besides America, and there are republics elsewhere than on the shores of the New World; the representative system of government has been adopted in several European States; but so far, I do not think that any other nation in the world has organized judicial power in the same way as the Americans.[118]

Three aspects of the organization and functioning of judicial power can be considered as a fundamental American contribution to constitutional law: the political role of judges; the institution of a Supreme Court; and judicial review of legislation. De Tocqueville noticed all three aspects.

The first thing he observed in the American institu-tions was the «immense political power»[119] attributed to judges, which he considered «the most important political power in the United States».[120] The reason for this immense power, said De Tocqueville:

> «Lies in this one fact: the Americans have given their judges the right to base their decisions on the Constitution rather than on the laws. In other words, they allow them not to apply laws which they consider unconstitutional».[121]

116 *Ibid*, p. 155.
117 *Ibid*, p. 156.
118 *Ibid*, p. 120.
119 *Ibid*, p. 122, 124.
120 *Ibid*, p. 120.
121 *Ibid*, p. 122.

Therefore, «there is hardly a political question in the United States which does not sooner or later turn into a judicial one»;[122] thus the fundamental changes in political and social life in the United States that have been led by the Supreme Court decisions in all American history.

The second fundamental aspect of the Judiciary in American institutions, De Tocqueville stressed, was the high standing of the Supreme Court among the great authorities in the state. De Tocqueville observed:

> «The Supreme Court has been given higher standing than any known tribunal, both by the nature of its rights and by the categories subject to its jurisdiction... a mightier judicial authority has never been constituted in any land».[123]

De Tocqueville explained these powers of the Supreme Court, in which he said, «the peace, prosperity, and very existence of the Union rest continually», by saying the following:

> «Without (the judges of the Supreme Court)... the Constitution would be a dead letter; it is to them that the executive appeals to resist the encroachments of the legislative body, the legislature to defend itself against the assaults of the executive, the union to make the states obey it, the states to rebuff the exaggerated pretensions of the Union, public interest against private interest, the spirit of conservation against democratic instability».[124]

Thus, the whole system of check and balance in the separation of powers, in the United States relied and still relies on the Supreme Court, and on the power of judges to control the constitutionality of legislation, precisely, the third main feature of the judiciary in North America.

In effect, in relation to the supremacy of the constitu-tion, De Tocqueville observed that it «touches the very essence of judicial power; it is in a way the natural right of a judge to choose among legal provisions that which binds him most strictly».[125] This led to the control of the constitutionality of law, a creation of American constitutionalism, referred to by De Tocqueville with these simple and logical words:

> «If anyone invokes in an American court a law which the judge considers contrary to the Constitution, he can refuse to apply it. That is the only power peculiar to an American judge, but great political influence derives from it.[126]

This was termed as being the «very essence of judicial duty» by John Marshall in the famous *Marbury v. Madison case* (1803), when referring to written constitutions and their fundamental and superior character, in relation to the other laws of society. This duty of the courts to consider acts of the legislature repugnant to the constitution void, was described in that famous case with the following logical arguments:

> «If an act of the legislature, repugnant to the Constitution, is void, does it, notwithstanding its invalidity, bind the courts, and oblige them to give it

122 *Ibid*, p. 184.
123 *Ibid*, p. 184.
124 *Ibid*, p. 185.
125 *Ibid*, p. 123.
126 *Ibid*, p. 124.

effect? Or, in other words, though it be not law, does it constitute a rule as operative as if it were a law? This would be to overthrow in fact what was established in theory, and would seem, at first view, an absurdity too gross to be insisted on. It shall, however, receive a more attentive consideration».

Then concluding:

«It is emphatically the province and duty of the judicial department to say what the law is. Those who apply the rule to particular cases must, of necessity, expound and interpret that rule. If two laws conflict with each other, the courts must decide on the operation of each.

So, if a law be in opposition to the Constitution; if both the law and the Constitution apply to a particular case, so that the court must either decide that case conformably to the law, disregarding the Constitution; or conformably to the Constitution, disregarding the law; the court must determine which of these conflicting rules governs the case. This is the very essence of judicial duty».[127]

This judicial duty, discovered by the North Americans, is another of the major contributions of American constitutionalism to contemporary constitutional law, and has been followed and developed all over the world judicial constitutional control, however, is essentially related to the federal form of the state as a mean to control unauthorized invasions and interferences between the decentralized powers of the state. That is why in all the Latin American countries with federal organizations, judicial review of legislation was immediately established under the American influence, a few decades before the first continental ever European experiences in the matter.

Today and ever since the last century, judicial review or control of constitutionality of laws is a general trend of Latin American legal systems, but in a much more original way than the North American system. Various Latin American countries, for instance, as is the case of Venezuela and Colombia since the last century, combine the North American system of judicial review that allows all courts to decide upon the applications of laws on constitutional grounds, with the power of the Supreme Court of Justice to declare a law void with general effects, when considered unconstitutional by means of a popular action granted to all citizens even without particular interest in the matter. This second control is an original Latin American mean of judicial review, developed only with approximate similarities after the twenties and in the forties in some continental European countries.

6. The entrenched Declaration of Fundamental Rights and Liberties

The sixth major contribution of North American constitutionalism to modern constitutional law has been the practice of establishing formal and entrenched declarations of fundamental rights and liberties. As we have said, the first modern declaration of this kind was adopted in the American colonies the same year of the Declaration of Independence, and in this sense the Declaration of Rights of Virginia 1776 is famous.

These declarations of the rights of man were new in history mainly because they were not based on common law or tradition, as the 1689 English Bill of Rights

---

[127] *Marbury v. Madison*, S.U.S. (1 Cranch), 137; 2 L. Ed. 60 (1803).

was, but on human nature. They were natural rights of people, declared politically by the new constituent powers of the colonies as a limit on state powers.

However, as we have also said, the American constitution, 1787, did not include a bill of rights in its articles, which aroused several objections during the convention. This led to the approval, two years later, of the first ten amendments that the American Bill of Rights contained.

Alexander Hamilton, justifying the absence of a Bill of Rights in the Constitution, said:

> «That bills of rights, in the sense and to the extent in which they are contended for, are not only unnecessary in the proposed Constitution, but would even be dangerous. They would contain various exceptions to powers not granted; and, on this very account, would afford a colourable pretext to claim more than were granted».

He finished his argument by asking:

> «For why declare that things shall not be done which there is no power to do?»[128]

This concept of rights as limitations of state powers was followed in the first ten amendments of the constitution but adding to it the concept of rights as natural rights of man established in the Declaration of Independence 1776. They both influenced all the formal and entrenched declarations of human rights that were adopted later, particularly the French Declaration of Rights of Man and the Citizen, (1789), and through the latter, the Latin American declarations, up to the present, where those declarations have been internationalised.

However, De Tocqueville did not devote particular comments in his book to the declaration of rights, undoubtedly, because by the time he visited America, the French Declaration of 1789 was already famous and unique. Nevertheless, he referred to specific rights, particularly important in North America like equality, freedom of press and political association,[129] and not always with complete acceptance. For instance, referring to freedom of press, he said:

> «I admit that I do not feel toward freedom of the press that complete and instantaneous love which one accords to things by their nature supremely good. I love it more from considering the evils it prevents than on account of the good it does».[130]

North American Independence (1776) and the North American constitution (1787) were the immediate results of a great revolution that gave birth to a new state; but at the same time they brought about an authentic revolution in the area of political and constitutional institutions in the world, giving rise to new forms of government and political acts. After the American Revolution, written constitutions, republicanism and sovereignty of the people, federal states, separation of powers in a system of check and balance, presidentialism and judicial review, were all new institutions that spread throughout the world. In the first place, they influenced definitively the shape of Latin American constitutionalism that began to develop twenty years afterwards.

---

[128] A. HAMILTON in *The Federalist* (ed. B.F. Wright), Cambridge, Mass 1961, Nº 84, p. 535.

[129] A. DE TOCQUEVILLE, *op. cit.*, Vol. 1, p. 222, 232.

[130] *Idem*, p. 222.

Alexis De Tocqueville was the first European raised in the European continental system of law to study the importance and impact of the American Revolution one hundred and fifty years ago and led the way to major transformations of constitutional institutions in Europe. That is why we consider that we can still say today the same as John Stuart Mill wrote in 1840 about De Tocqueville's Democracy in America, in the sense that it was not only «the first philosophical book ever written on democracy as it manifests itself in modern society», but it was also a book that marked «the beginning of a new era in the scientific study of politics».[131]

Its influence all over the world, therefore, has been outstanding not only because of the book itself, but also because its aim was to study the American institutions that contributed the most to the shaping of modern constitutionalism.[132]

III. THE *ÉTAT DE DROIT* AND JUDICIAL REVIEW

The *État de droit* or the state according to the rule of law, as we have seen, can be characterized by three main trends:

First, as a state in which powers are limited, as a guarantee of liberty, and that limitation is established through a system of distribution and separation of powers.

The *État de droit,* in this perspective, is the contrary of the absolute state, and this limitation of powers is expressed in three sorts of state power distribution: in the *first place,* by a distinction between the powers of the state themselves and an area of liberties, freedoms and rights of citizens that are beyond the sphere of state action. In the *second place,* by a distinction in the state between constituent power, attributed to the people as sovereign electorate, which demonstrate its activity normally through a written constitution and the constituted powers, represented by the organs of the state, comprising the legislature, all submitted to the constituent powers will. Finally, in the *third place,* by a separation of powers within the constituted organs, in a vertical and horizontal way. In the vertical way, the separation of powers leads to a system of political decentralization throughout state organs at various territorial levels, including the federal form of the state. In the horizontal way, the separation of powers leads to the classical division between the legislative, executive and judicial organs, with their respective powers in a check and balance system with established mutual interference and restraint.

The second main feature of the *État de droit* besides the distribution and separation of powers, is that the state is submitted to the rule of law, in the sense that all state organs are submitted to limits imposed by the law. Therefore, the only body not submitted to legal limitations is the sovereign, identified in most States with the electoral body. This is, as we have said, the constituent power whose actions are normally reflected in a written constitution.

In relation to the state organs, however, the rule of law or the principle of legality implies their necessary submission to the law, varying the scope or ambit of legality, in relation to the level that the particular acts of those state organs have in the graduated or hierarchical system of rules of law that, in general, can be

---

131 J.S. MILL, *The Edinburgh Review*, October 1840, N° CXLV, p. 3, quoted by J.P. MAYER, «Tocqueville's Democracy in America: Reception and Reputation», in A. DE TOCQUEVILLE, *op. cit.*, Vol. I, p. XIX.

132 See for example, the references to the influence of DE TOCQUEVILLE book regarding judicial review in México, in R.D. BAKER, *Judicial Review in México. A Study of the Amparo Suit*, Austin 1971, p. 15.

established in all legal systems. In this context, we have said that legality in relation to state organs, means» legal order» and not just an act of the legislative organ. Therefore, it could just mean «constitutionality», or submission to the constitution, if a particular act is issued in direct execution of the constitution; or «legality» in a broader sense, as submission to the legal order, if a state act is issued in indirect execution of the constitution. Regarding the administration, this is the traditional meaning of legality.

Finally, apart from the principles of distribution of powers and of the submission of the state to the rule of law, we have also referred to the third main feature of the modern *État de droit*, that of the establishment of an entrenched Bill of Rights, as a guarantee to individuals against state organs, normally in a written constitution.

These three main characteristics of the *État de droit*, in contemporary constitutional law, have been constitutionalized, in the sense that they have been formally established in a written and rigid constitution. Therefore, the *État de droit* implies that the principles of distribution and separation of powers, the subjection of the state organs to the rule of law, and the declaration of rights and liberties must all be embodied in a written constitution formulated in an entrenched way so as to be protected from changes introduced by the ordinary legislator.

However, all these principles of the *État de droit* and their establishment in a written and rigid constitution require some means of protection to guarantee the existence of the limits imposed on the state organs and on the enjoyment of individual rights. In this respect the argument of John Marshall in the famous *Marbury v. Madison case* decided by the United States Supreme Court was precise:

> «To what purpose are powers limited, and to what purpose is that limitation committed to writing, if these limits may, at any time, be passed by those intended to be restrained? The distinction between a government with limited and unlimited powers is abolished, if those limits do not confine the persons upon whom they are imposed, and if acts prohibited and acts allowed are of equal obligation».[133]

Moreover, along the same line of argument we can ask to what purpose are state powers limited, to what purpose is the principle of legality established, to what purpose are fundamental rights and liberties formally declared, and to what purpose are all those principles committed to writing in a constitution considered as fundamental law, if there is no mean of guaranteeing the existence and permanence of said limits, of the state organs submission to legality and of the effective enjoyment of the citizens, rights and liberties?

Therefore, the *État de droit* with all its characteristics, only exists if these means of protection of the Constitution and of legality are established, and if the judiciary is in charge of making those means of protection of the constitution effective.[134] Consequently, the courts in the *État de droit* must ensure the effectiveness of the limits imposed on the state organs, their submission to the rule of the constitution

---

[133] *Marbury v. Madison*, 5.U.S. (1 Cranch) 137; (1803); 2 L, Ed 60 (1803). See the text in R.A. ROSSUM and G. A. TARR, *American Constitutional Law. Cases and Interpretation*, New York 1983, p. 70.

[134] See in general, H. KELSEN, «La garantie juridictionnelle de la Constitution (La justice constitutionnelle)», *Revue du droit public et de la science politique en France et à l'étranger*, T. XLV, Paris 1928, p. 197-257.

and to the principle of legality, and the enjoyment of the fundamental rights and liberties of individuals.

Thus, there is no *État de droit*, if there is no power granted to the courts of the state to control the submission of the state organs to the rule of law.

Therefore, we can say that the basic element of the *État de droit* or state submitted to the rule of law or to the principle of legality is the existence of a system of judicial review, aimed at controlling that submission to the rule of law of all the state acts, particularly, of legislative, administrative and even judicial acts. The two fundamental objectives of this system of judicial review are obviously: one to ensure that all those acts of the state are adopted or issued in accordance to the law of the said state; two, to ensure that state acts respect the fundamental rights and liberties of citizens.

Thus, we can distinguish two main judicial review systems in the contemporary *État de droit*: On the one hand, a system which seeks to control the conformity of all state acts to the law; and on the other hand, a system which seeks to guarantee the fundamental rights and liberties of individuals; both giving individuals, precisely, a fundamental right to accede to justice by means of judicial actions aimed at obtaining such control.

1. Judicial control of the conformity of State acts with the rule of law

As we said, the first of these systems of judicial review or control, has the purpose of ensuring the effective submission of state acts to the rule of law or to the principle of legality. However, as we have seen, the sphere or confines of «legality» are certainly not the same for all state acts. In other words, «legality» does not mean the same for all acts of the state. Its meaning or the confines of legality for each of these acts, depends on the rank the specific act holds in the legal order, particularly in relation to the constitution or to the supreme law of the land.

So, one distinction above all can be traced in legal systems with written constitutions, namely that between state acts that are issued in direct execution of the constitution and acts that are issued in indirect execution of the constitution. This distinction between state acts, leads, of course, to a distinction between the systems of judicial review or control that are laid down.

In effect, as we have studied, there are some state acts that are adopted in direct execution of the constitution, in the sense that they are acts that have their origin in powers granted directly in the constitution and itself to the state organ that produces them, and to which they must be submitted. In relation to these acts, the system of judicial review has and can only have the purpose of ensuring that the said acts are issued or adopted in accordance to the constitution itself. In this case, as Hans Kelsen pointed out in 1928:

> «The guarantee of the constitution means guarantees of the regularity of the constitution's immediate subordinated rules, that is to say, essentially, guarantee of the constitutionality of laws».[135]

Therefore, regarding those acts of the state, «legality» as we already know, is equivalent to «constitutionality», and judicial review or control of legality is also equivalent to judicial control or review of the constitutionality of such acts.

[135] H. KELSEN, *loc.cit.*, p. 201.

Of course, this distinction between acts issued in direct execution of the constitution and acts issued in indirect execution of the constitution, and consequently, the distinction between judicial control of constitutionality and the judicial control of legality only exists in the strictest sense of the term, in those legal systems possessing a written constitution as a fundamental law constituting the superior source of the whole legal order. Therefore, in systems without a written constitution, and where acts of Parliament are the supreme law, the distinction cannot be made and a system of judicial review of constitutionality cannot exist.

On the contrary, this control of constitutionality in legal systems with written constitutions has been developed particularly in relation to legislative acts, that is to say, to normative acts of Parliament. Hence, one usually speaks of judicial control of the constitutionality, of legislation or simply of «judicial review of the constitutionality of legislation».[136]

In effect, if Parliament, Congress or the National Assembly as a representative of the sovereign people, is and must be the supreme interpreter of the law, and through the law, of the general will, it always does so in execution of constitutional rules, particularly in those cases where a written and rigid constitution exists, which cannot, therefore, be changed by the ordinary legislator. Consequently, the law as an act of Parliament is always submitted to the constitution, and when it exceeds the limits established by that constitution, the act of Parliament is unconstitutional and, therefore, liable to be annulled. As stated in the *Marbury* v. *Madison case* by the United States Supreme Court in 1803:

> «Certainly, all those who have framed written constitutions contemplated them as forming the fundamental and paramount law of the nation, and consequently, the theory of every such government must be, that an act of the legislature, repugnant to the Constitution, is void».[137]

Judicial control or review of constitutionality, therefore, affords the courts the possibility of determining the unconstitutionality of the laws, deciding not to apply them giving preference to what is stated in the constitution, and, in some cases, allowing some special courts to declare with general effect the nullity of the law considered unconstitutional.

But in legal systems with judicial review of constitutionality, all other acts of the legislature other than formal laws, which are also issued by Parliament in direct execution of the constitution, can also be submitted to judicial control of constitutionality likewise. This is the case, for example, of internal regulations for the functioning of legislative bodies, and of parliamentary acts of specific effect, issued for the purpose of authorising or approving some executive acts, like the appointment of some officials, or the adoption of some budget changes. All these acts, in written constitutional legal systems, are subject to and must be adopted according to the constitution, and therefore, can be judicially controlled to ensure their submission to the fundamental rules of the constitution.

Moreover, not only the acts of legislative bodies are subject to judicial control of constitutionality. In general, all acts of state bodies and organs issued in direct and immediate execution of the constitution are also subject to such control.

---

136 M. CAPPELLETTI, *Judicial Review in the Contemporary World*, Indianapolis 1971, p. VII.

137 *Marbury v. Madison*, 5.U.S. (1 Cranch), 137; (1803); 2 L, Ed. 60, (1803).

In particular, acts of government with or without the same force of formal law, issued by the head of state or by the government in direct execution of powers provided for directly in the constitution, and which due to the distribution of powers, cannot be regulated by Parliament, are also subject to judicial control of constitutionality.

In short, it is through this system of judicial review of the constitutionality of state acts that the effective submission of state organs to the constitution can be ensured when they execute it directly. Therefore, this is possible only in legal systems with written constitutions, where the courts have such powers of judicial review.

Consequently, when there is no written constitution, or when although this fundamental law exists, the courts do not have the power to control the constitutionality of legislative acts, the legal situation is very similar.

As Professor J.D.B. Mitchell pointed out:

> «The mere fact of there being a written Constitution does not by itself necessarily mean that courts play any greater role in protecting individual rights or policing the Constitution.
>
> Where there is such a Constitution, but courts do not possess the power to declare legislation unconstitutional, the only means by which the courts can protect the basic principles of that constitution from encroachment of erosions is by the restrictive interpretation of legislation. In such circumstances the position of the courts and the protection for fundamental constitutional principles do not differ materially from those which exist when there is no written Constitution».[138]

Therefore, the real difference between a legal system with a written constitution and one without a written constitution really lies in the powers granted to the courts to control the constitutionality of state acts. Professor Mitchell also mentioned this in relation to the British constitutional system:

> «The real contrast with our own system is afforded by a system under which there is not only a written constitution but also a recognised power in the courts to declare legislation invalid as being unconstitutional».[139]

In any case, the control of the constitutionality of formal laws, or of any other state act issued in direct execution of the constitution, is only possible in those constitutional systems possessing a written constitution and, furthermore, where the constitution is rigid, that is to say, it cannot be changed through the channel of ordinary legislation.

The rules established in this type of constitution are, of course, applied directly, and the constitution itself occupies a pre-eminent rank in the hierarchy of the legal order. In this respect, it is precisely in the countries where the courts have been granted the power to control the constitutionality of the laws that the juridical-normative nature of the constitutions, that is to say, their obligatory nature, is clearest. Likewise, it is in those countries that the principle of the hierarchical pre-eminence of the constitution in relation to the ordinary laws has its origin.

---

[138] J.D.B. MITCHELL, *Constitutional Law*, Edinburgh 1968, p. 13.

[139] *Idem*, p. 13.

This first system of judicial review of constitutionality, particularly of legislation is generally organized in two ways: by assigning the power to decide upon the unconstitutionality of laws to all the courts of the particular judicial order of a state, or by reserving that power to one judicial organ only, the Supreme Judicial Court of the country or to a special constitutional court or tribunal, giving rise to the distinction between the diffuse and concentrated systems of judicial review of constitutionality to whose study this book is devoted.

Apart from state acts adopted in direct execution of constitutional powers granted to state organs, in particular, legislative acts and acts of government, there are other state acts adopted in direct execution of the «legislation», that is to say, the first level of constitutional execution, whose legality not only means submission to the constitution but also to all the other rules of law comprised in the legal order. Therefore, in relation to those acts, particularly administrative and judicial acts, «legality» means submission to the legal order considered as a whole, and the *État de droit* must provide the means for judicial control or review to ensure the effective submission of the state organs to the rule of law when issuing such acts. This has led to the establishment of systems of judicial review of administrative actions and of judicial review of judicial decisions themselves in the modern *État de droit*.

Regarding the judicial review of administrative action, or judicial control of administration, one can say that it is more developed in modern constitutional and administrative law, particularly as a result of the submission of administration to the principle of legality. So important has this system of judicial review been, that one can even say that judicial review of administrative action has given rise to the development of administrative law itself, not only in continental European countries but also in common law countries. It is through the exercise by the courts of their inherent power to control the legality of administrative action, that the fundamental principles of administrative law have been developed, particularly during the present century.

Therefore, judicial review of administrative action is the power of the courts to decide upon the legality of the activities undertaken by the administrative organs of the state, in other words, to decide in relation to the submission of the activities of the executive organs of the state to the law or rather to the principle of legality. Law, understood in this context, means legal order, that is to say, not only the formal law, but also all the norms and rules that are comprised in the legal order, including, of course, the constitution itself.

There is a substantial difference regarding the organization of judicial review of administrative action, between the legal systems influenced by the European continental countries, mainly France, and the systems influenced by the Anglo-American common law countries. Judicial review in the Latin and German tradition is the power of special courts to decide on the legality of administrative action, when demanded through special judicial means, or actions granted to individuals with the necessary standing to bring an action to declare a particular administrative act void. This led to the development *of* the *contentieux administrative* recourses in continental Europe that are to be decided by special judicial-administrative courts. In some cases, these special courts were established completely separated from the ordinary courts, as is the case in France of the *jurisdiction contentieux administrative*. In other cases, the special judicial administrative courts are established within the ordinary judicial order, in the same manner as there are special courts in labour law, civil law or commercial law. In all these cases, not only are the remedies for judicial review special ones, but the courts that are to exercise the review power, are also special.

By contrast with this situation, the common law tradition on judicial review generally implies that the ordinary courts of justice are the ones that exercise the power of judicial review of administrative action through the ordinary remedies established in common law and also used in private law, although it is certain that in more recent times special remedies of public law have been developed.

Anyway, all over the world, the most traditional and popular judicial control of the submission of the state to the rule of law has been the judicial review of administrative action.

However, the term *État de droit* does not only imply the need for systems of judicial review of the constitutionality of legislation and acts of government, and the judicial review of administrative action, in other words, the judicial control of legislative and administrative action to ensure its conformity with the rule of law, but also the need for establishing a system of judicial control of judicial decisions themselves.

The courts are, in effect, typical «executive» bodies of the state. Consequently, all their activities in the application of the law must be submitted to the whole legal order, comprising the constitution, the formal laws and delegate legislation, and the regulations and other normative acts of the state organs. Consequently, in the *État de droit*, court decisions must be also subject to judicial control, which is normally implemented through two mechanisms.

On the one hand, the ordinary appeal systems that allow for control of the decisions of the inferior courts by the superior courts, within the hierarchy of the judicial system; and on the other, the system of control of the legality of judicial decisions through extraordinary remedies, as happens in continental law, for example with the *recours de cassation*, developed in the systems influenced by continental European procedural law.

By these means of control, Supreme Courts have the power to verify the legality of decisions made by inferior courts, and deciding upon them, considering the merits of the decision under appeal, or just controlling the legal aspects of the decision in the recourse of cassation. In this case, it is also a matter of control of the legality of state acts.

All these three systems of control of the submission of the state organs and acts to the rule of law, the control of the constitutionality of legislation, the judicial review of administrative action, and the judicial control of courts decisions, are basically a question of formal control, which seeks to determine the conformity of state decisions with the superior rules contained in the legal order, applicable to the concrete act. Of all three, the first one related to the control of the constitutionality of legislation, the protection of the constitution being its fundamental objective when its norms are executed directly by state organs, will be the subject in the subsequent parts of this course.

2. Judicial guarantees of Fundamental Rights

Apart from these judicial systems of control of state acts to ensure their submission to the principle of legality or to the rule of law, there is another system of control of state actions aimed specially at the protection of fundamental rights and liberties generally established in the constitution and which is normally established in the constitution as a guarantee for the effective fulfilment of such rights and liberties.

We have seen, in effect, that the principle of distribution of powers in the legal state, expresses itself in various ways, among them, in a system of distribution of powers between on the one hand, the sphere of the citizens and individuals which are granted by the constitution with various fundamental rights and liberties, that cannot be eliminated or restricted unless by the means established in the constitution; and on the other hand, the powers of the state organs. This distribution of powers is normally established in a written constitution or in an entrenched Bill of Rights, so that invasions of the sphere of fundamental rights and liberties by the state or even by other individuals, are subject to judicial control or protection.

This judicial protection of fundamental rights, in the end, is also a protection of the constitution itself because such rights and liberties are established in the constitution, and therefore, all violations or infringements upon such rights and liberties are at the same time, violations of the constitution.

The *État de droit* has developed mechanisms to assure the protection of these fundamental rights and liberties and to avoid their violation mainly by public bodies, either by actions brought before the ordinary courts through ordinary actions or remedies, or by special actions of protection brought before ordinary courts or before a special constitutional court.

As this course mainly deals with judicial review of the constitutionality of legislation, we will also refer to the judicial protection of these fundamental rights, particularly through special actions, when in order to protect them, the courts must also exercise their powers of judicial review of legislation.

As we can see, the concept of the *État de droit* is closely related to the judicial control of legality in a way that there is no state according to law if there is no judicial control of legality of state acts. Also, effective judicial control of legality of state acts cannot exist except within the frame of the *État de droit*.

The *État de droit*, as we have seen, implies the submission of all state organs and acts to the legal order, which the constitution has at its apex. This is the supreme law, to which all state acts must be submitted. Therefore, the control of the submission of state acts to the constitution, when exercised by the courts, is an essential aspect of the *État de droit* and is the one we are going to analyse in the four subsequent parts of this course, in which we will study the judicial control of constitutionality, mainly of legislation.

PART THREE

THE FOUNDATION OF JUDICIAL REVIEW OF THE CONSTITUTIONALITY OF LEGISLATION

I. THE LIMITED STATE ORGANS AND JUDICIAL REVIEW

Judicial review of constitutionality is the power of the courts to control the conformity with the constitution of acts of state, particularly of legislative acts, issued in direct execution of the constitution.

Therefore, in principle, judicial review can only exist in legal systems in which there is a written constitution, imposing limits on the state organs' activities and within such organs, on Parliament in particular. As a result, the power of the courts to control the constitutionality of state acts is not necessarily a consequence of the sole judicial power, but of the legal limitations imposed on state organs, particularly on Parliament and on the government, in a constitution established as a supreme law.

In this sense, judicial review of the constitutionality of state acts is the ultimate consequence of the consolidation of the *État de Droit* where the state organs are not sovereign, are subject to limits imposed by a constitution having the force of a superior law, and in particular, when the legislator is limited in his legislative action and there is judicial control over the «legality of laws».

Professor Paul Duez stressed the argument a few decades ago in an article published in the *Mélanges Hariou* when he wrote:

> «Modern Public Law establishes as an axiom that Governments are not sovereign and that in particular, the Parliament is limited in its legislative action by superior legal rules, that it could not infringe; Acts of Parliament are submitted to the law, and no Act of Parliament can be contrary to the law».[1]

This is the principle accepted today in France but certainly not the one accepted in that country sixty years ago when Professor Duez wrote his essay and when the principle of the sovereignty of the National Assembly was still in force. That is why this article is of historical importance in France. In effect, Professor Duez, by establishing the principle of the limitation of all state organs by a constitution as a superior rule, added:

---

[1] P. DUEZ, «Le contrôle juridictionnel de la constitutionalité des lois en France», *Mélanges Hauriou*, Paris 1929, p. 214.

> «But it is not sufficient to proclaim such a principle: it must be organized, and practical and effective measures, must be adopted to ensure it».[2]

Subsequently, he referred to the very important French system of judicial control related to public administration and to administrative action, through the *recours pour excès de pouvoir*; nevertheless, he said:

> «The spirit of legality requires that a similar control be established in relation to legislative action».[3]

And concluded by saying that,

> «There is not a real organized democracy, and a Legal state (*État de Droit*), except only where this control of legality of laws (Acts of Parliament) exists and functions».[4]

The logic of Professor Duez's statement in our perspective is certainly impeccable: No organ of the and state can be considered sovereign; and all state organs, particularly, the legislator in its actions are submitted to limit established in superior rules, embodied in a constitution.

Therefore, acts of Parliament must always be submitted to the law, and cannot be contrary to the law. Consequently, the spirit of legality imposes the existence and functioning not only of a control of legality of administrative acts, but also of a control of the legality of laws, as acts of Parliament. Only in countries where this control exists, are there truly organized democracies and *État de Droit*.

Therefore, this judicial control of the «legality of laws» is, precisely, the judicial control of the constitutionality of legislation and of other state acts issued in direct execution of the constitution, in relation to which legality means «constitutionality». Thus, there is the existence of judicial review of constitutionality that we are now going to study.

This judicial review of constitutionality is normally possible, of course, not only in those legal systems that have a *written* constitution as a supreme rule embodying the fundamental values of society, but when that superior rule is established in a rigid or entrenched way, in the sense that it cannot be modified by ordinary legislation. In principle, it is in a system of this kind that all the organs of the state are limited by and subject to the constitution and must therefore pursue their activities according to this supreme law.

This implies therefore, that not only are the traditional state organs for executing the law -the administration and the judges- subject to the law (Constitution and «legislation»), but that the organs which create the «legislation», particularly the legislative bodies, are also subject to the constitution.

Of course, a written and rigid constitution, situated at the apex of a legal system, not only demands that all the acts issued by state organs in direct execution thereof should not violate the constitution, but must also provide a guarantee to prevent or sanction such violations.[5] Thus, the judicial review of constitutionality

---

2 *Idem*, p. 214.

3 *Idem*, p. 215.

4 *Ibid*. p. 215.

5 *Cf.* H. KELSEN, «La garantie juridictionnelle de la Constitution (La Justice constitutionnelle)» *Revue du droit public et de la science politique en France et à l'étranger*, T. XLV, 1928, p.197-257.

as the power of the judiciary to control the submission of state organs to the superior rule of the country.

1. Execution of the Constitution and Control

Anyway, we have said a hierarchy of rules exists in all legal systems with written and rigid Constitutions.

Evidently, not all state acts have, therefore, the same level of derivation in creating legal rules. There are acts that directly and immediately execute the constitution, and that are subject to this superior rule alone; there are also state acts which execute the constitution in an indirect way, being at the same time acts issued in direct and immediate execution of «legislation», thus directly subject to it. Among the former are, basically, the formal laws and other acts of Parliament and acts of government issued in accordance with their constitutionally attributed powers; and among the latter, there are the administrative and the judicial acts.

In a *État de Droit* then, the guarantee of the rule of law must be established at the two mentioned levels of creation or derivation of legal rules by way of three judicial systems of control: first, the judicial review of constitutionality, established to control state acts issued in direct execution of the constitution; second, the judicial control of administrative action basically established regarding administrative acts; and concerning judicial acts issued by courts, the judicial control system is thirdly established by systems of appeal or cassation.

Moreover, in the *État de droit,* which implies that in the constitution fundamental rights and liberties are established, judicial mechanisms of control must also be provided to protect and guarantee such rights against any act by the state that may violate them, and even against acts by individuals which may so affect them.

Our objective, in the subsequent parts of this course is to analyze the first of these systems of judicial control previously mentioned, judicial review of constitutionality, which, we insist, fundamentally refers to the acts of the state constitutional organs, in which the rule of law becomes the «rule of the constitution»; since they are acts that execute the constitution itself, directly and immediately.

2. State Acts Submitted to Control

Therefore, one of the acts subject to judicial review of constitutionality are formal laws or acts of Parliament, and it is precisely because of this that judicial review of constitutionality is often identified with the judicial review of the constitutionality of legislation.[6] However, laws are not the only state acts issued in direct execution of the constitution, and as an expression of constitutional powers. So too are other acts of Parliament, such as internal parliamentary rules of procedure and even other parliamentary acts that do not have the form of law and that are not normative, such as those established in the constitution regarding the relations between the Congress or Assembly and the other constitutional organs of the state. All these acts adopted by Parliament are subject to the constitution because they are issued by virtue of powers attributed directly in that fundamental text. Thus, in a *État de droit* they must also be liable to judicial review of constitutionality.[7]

---

6 See, for example, M. CAPPELLETTI, *Judicial Review in Contemporary World*, Indianapolis 1971, p. VII.

7 *Cf.* H. KELSEN, *loc. cit.*, p. 228.

Apart from these acts of Parliament, however, the government, in a *État de droit,* also issues acts that directly execute the constitution, which have the same status as laws in the hierarchical legal system, and which, in some cases, even have the same force as formal law.

In fact, in contemporary constitutional law, the government issues acts with the same force as the formal laws in a variety of forms, either as delegate legislation or because of powers established in the constitution itself. In these cases, they are executive acts with legislative content, and with the same ranking, force and power of derogation as the formal law established in acts of Parliament. For this reason, such executive acts issued in direct execution of the constitution are not administrative acts, but acts of government with normative and legislative content. Thus, they are also liable to judicial review of constitutionality.[8]

But we have seen that the government also has powers established in the constitution to produce certain acts without any legislative interference, for instance when declaring a state of siege or the restriction of constitutional guarantees, when directing international relations or when vetoing an act of Parliament. All these acts, shaped by the continental European doctrine of administrative law, as «acts of government», are also subject to judicial review of constitutionality. It is true that in the traditional criteria of administrative law, such «acts of government» were developed to exclude them from judicial administrative control either because of their political content or motives or because they were issued by the government in its relations with other constitutional bodies, particularly with Parliament.[9] Nevertheless, as we have seen, these acts are also subject to the constitution, and they are also liable to be submitted to judicial review of constitutionality.[10]

Moreover, in contemporary legal systems and leaving aside problems arising from monist and dualist conceptions, international treaties and agreements are also subject to judicial review of constitutionality in the *État de droit*[11] whether this be directly, or by review of the acts of Parliament or government that introduce them into domestic law, also by virtue of constitutional powers granted to those state organs.

Therefore, all state acts issued in direct execution of the constitution in legal systems with written constitutions are subject to judicial review of constitutionality.

3. The Variety of Judicial Review

It is evident, however, that in comparative law no single system for judicial review of constitutionality exists, but rather a very varied range of systems in which not even all the state acts mentioned can be subject to judicial review.

In fact, different criteria can be adopted for classifying the various systems of constitutional justice or judicial review of the constitutionality of state acts, particularly of legislation,[12] but all are related to a basic criterion referring to the state organs that can carry out constitutional justice functions.

---

8 *Idem,* p. 229.

9 See the classical work of P. DUEZ, *Les actes de gouvernement,* Paris 1953.

10 *Cf.* H. KELSEN, *loc. cit.,* p. 230.

11 *Idem,* p. 231.

12 See in general M. CAPPELLETTI, *op .cit.,* p. 45 and M. CAPPELLETI and J.C. ADAMS, «Judicial Review of Legislation: European Antecedents and Adaptations», *Harvard Law Review,* 79, 6, April 1966, p. 1207.

In effect, judicial review of constitutionality can be exercised by all the courts of a given country or only by the Supreme Court of the country or by a court specially created for that purpose.

In the first case, all the courts of a given country are empowered to judge the constitutionality of laws. This is the case in the United States of America, thus this system has been identified as the 'American system', because it was first adopted in the United States particularly after the famous *Marbury* v. *Madison* case decided by the Supreme Court in 1803. This system is followed in many countries with or without a common law tradition. This is the case, for example, in Argentina, Mexico, Greece, Australia, Canada, India, Japan, Sweden, Norway and Denmark. This system is also qualified as a diffuse system of judicial review of constitutionality,[13] because judicial control belongs to all the courts from the lowest level up to the Supreme Court of the country.

By contrast, there is the concentrated system of judicial review, in which the power to control the constitutionality of legislation and other state organs issued in direct execution of the constitution is assigned to a single organ of the state, whether to its Supreme Court or to a special court created for that particular purpose. In the latter case, it is also called the Austrian system because it was first established in Austria, in 1920. This system also called the «European model» is followed, for instance, in Germany, Italy, and Spain. It is called a concentrated system of judicial review, as opposed to the diffuse system, because the power of control over the constitutionality of state acts is given only to one single constitutional body that can be the Supreme Court of a given country or as in the Austrian or European model, to a specially created constitutional court 'or tribunal, that even though it exercised judicial functions, in general, it is created by the constitution outside ordinary judicial power, as a constitutional organ different to the Supreme Court of the country.

Regarding the judicial organs that can exercise the power of controlling the constitutionality of laws, other countries have adopted a mixture of the above mentioned diffuse and concentrate systems, in the sense that allow for both types of control at the same time. Such is the case in Colombia and Venezuela where all courts are entitled to judge the constitutionality of laws and therefore decide autonomously upon their inapplicability in a given process, and the Supreme Court has the power to declare the unconstitutionality of laws in an objective process. One can say that these countries have a diffuse and concentrated parallel system of judicial review at one and the same time, perhaps the most complete in comparative law.

But regarding the so-called concentrated systems of judicial review, in which the power of control is given to the Supreme Court or to a constitutional court, other distinctions can be observed.

In the first place, in relation to the moment at which control of the constitutionality of laws is performed, it may be prior to the formal enactment of the particular law, as is the case in France, or the judicial control of the constitutionality of laws which can be exercised by the court after the law has come into effect, as is the case in Germany and Italy.

---

[13] M. CAPPELLETTI, «El control judicial de la constitucionalidad de las leyes en el derecho comparado», *Revista de la Facultad de Derecho de México*, 61, 1966, p. 28.

In this respect, other countries have established both possibilities as is the case Spain, Portugal and Venezuela. In the latter, a law sanctioned by Congress prior to its enactment, can be placed by the president of the republic before the Supreme Court to obtain a decision regarding its constitutionality, and also the Supreme Court can judge the constitutionality of the law after it has been published and has come into legal effect.

Moreover, in relation to the concentrated systems of judicial review, two other types of control can be distinguished regarding the manner in which review is required either incidentally or through an objective action. In the first place, the constitutional question is not considered justiciable unless it is closely and directly related to a particular process, in which the constitutionality of the concrete law is not normally necessary to the unique issue in the process. In this case, judicial control is incidental, and the Supreme Court or constitutional tribunal can only decide when it is required to do so by the ordinary court that has to decide the case. In this circumstance, it is basically the function of the ordinary courts, upon hearing a concrete case, to place the constitutional issue before the constitutional court.

Of course, the incidental nature of judicial review is essential to diffused control systems and, therefore, to all legal systems that follows the American model.

But in the field of the concentrated system of judicial review, the control granted to the constitutional court can also be exercised through direct action where the constitutionality of the particular law is the only issue in the process, without reference or relation to a particular process.

In this latter case, another distinction can be made, in relation to the *locus standing* to exercise the direct action of unconstitutionality: in most countries with a concentrated system of judicial review, only other organs of the state can place the direct action of constitutionality before the constitutional court, for instance, the head of government, or a number of representatives in Parliament.

Other systems of concentrated judicial review grant the action of constitutionality to individuals, whether requiring that the particular law affects a fundamental right of the individual, or by means of a popular action, in which any citizen can request the constitutional court or Supreme Court to decide upon his claim concerning the constitutionality of a given law, without particular requirement regarding his standing.

As we have seen, the basic division we can establish regarding the various systems of judicial review, depends in our opinion, upon the concentrated or centralized or diffuse or decentralized character of judicial control of constitutionality, that is to say, when the power of control is given to all the courts of a given country or to one special constitutional court or to the Supreme Court of that country. We have also said that some countries have even adopted both systems of judicial review that developed in parallel. Related to this main classification, as we said, other criteria can be adopted to identify the various systems of judicial control of the constitutionality of laws: the incidental and the principal or objective action systems.

But in relation to the main distinction between the diffuse and concentrated systems of judicial review, we can also distinguish other criteria for classifying the various systems, according to the legal effects given to the particular judicial decision of review.

Within this scope, we can distinguish decisions with *in casu et inter partes* or *erga omnes* effects, that is to say, when the judicial decision has effects only within the parties in a concrete process, or when it has general effects applicable to everyone.

For instance, in the diffused systems of judicial review, according to the American system, the decision of the courts in principle, only has effect relating to the parties of the process; effects that are closely related to the incidental character of judicial review.

Whereas in the concentrated system of judicial review, following the Austrian model, when the judicial decision is a consequence of the exercise of a objective action, the effects of such a decision are general, with *erga omnes* validity.

Thus, in the diffused systems of judicial review a law declared unconstitutional with *inter partes* effects, basically is considered null and void, with no effect whatsoever. Therefore, in this case the decision in principle is retroactive in the sense that has *ex tunc*, or *pro pretaerito* consequences; that is to say, the law declared unconstitutional is considered never to have existed or never to have been valid. Thus, this decision, in principle, has «declarative» effects, in the sense that it declares the pre-existing nullity of the unconstitutional law.

In the concentrated systems of judicial review, on the contrary, a law declared unconstitutional, with *erga omnes* effect, in principle is considered annullable. Therefore, in this case, the decision is prospective, in the sense that has *ex nunc*, *pro futuro* consequences, that is to say, the law declared unconstitutional is considered as having produced its effect until its annulation by the court, or until the moment determined by the court subsequent to the decision. In this case, therefore the decision has «constitutive» effects, in the sense that the law will become unconstitutional only after the decision has been made.

Nevertheless, this distinction related to the effects of the judicial decision regarding the unconstitutionality of a law is not absolute. On the one hand, if it is true that in the diffuse systems of judicial review, the decision has *inter partes* effects, when the decision is adopted by the Supreme Court, as a consequence of the *stare decisis* doctrine, the practical effects of the decision, in fact, are general, in the sense that it binds all the lower courts of the country. Therefore, as soon as the Supreme Court has declared a law unconstitutional, no other court can apply it.

On the other hand, in concentrated systems of judicial review, when a judicial decision is adopted on an incidental issue of constitutionality, some constitutional systems have established that the effects of that decision are only related in principle, to the particular process in which the constitutionality question was raised, and between the parties of that process, even though this is not the general rule.

In relation to the declarative or constitutive effects of the decision, or its retroactive or prospective effects, the absolute parallelism with the diffuse and concentrated systems has also disappeared.

In the diffuse systems of judicial review, even though the effects of the declarative decisions of unconstitutionality of the law, are *ex tunc, pro pretaerito,* in practice exceptions have been made in civil cases to allow for the invalidity of the law not to be retroactive: In the same manner, in the concentrated systems of judicial review, even though the effects of the constitutive judicial decisions of unconstitutionality of the law, are *ex nunc, pro futuro,* in practice exceptions were needed to be made in criminal cases to allow for the invalidity of the law to be retroactive, and benefit the accused.

Our purpose in the subsequent parts of the course is to study all these systems of judicial review of constitutionality of state acts, and particularly of legislation in comparative law. To that end we will analyze the most important legal systems in contemporary constitutional law, classifying them in accordance with the main distinctions we have made between the diffuse and the concentrated systems of judicial review.

Before doing so, however, we consider it necessary to examine the juridical foundations of the judicial review of constitutionality, in which we will recall various aspects previously mentioned but particularly, relating them to the judicial review of constitutionality in the *État de droit* bearing in mind that if it is true that judicial review appeared with the *État de droit* at the beginning of the last century in the American Constitution, it has been the most recent trend it adopted in contemporary legal systems.

In analyzing those foundations of the judicial review of constitutionality in comparative law, we will refer to what has been called the legitimacy of judicial review, which was one of the main subjects of the 1984 Colloquium of the International Association of Legal Sciences, held in Uppsala.[14]

4. The Controlled and Limited Legislator

Judicial Review, it has been said, is «the culmination of the building of the *État droit*[15] and is the direct consequence of its constitutionalization process, that is to say, of the adoption of a constitution as a higher law, in which the organization of state powers and their limits are established and to which the fundamental rights of individuals are declared and guaranteed.

In this sense, judicial review as the power of the courts -ordinary or special constitutional courts- to control the constitutionality of legislation is, without doubt, the ultimate triumph of the individual against the absolute power of state organs, and particularly, against the supremacy and sovereignty of Parliaments.

Even in its origin, in the same manner as American constitutionalism emerged as a reaction against the sovereignty of the English Parliament, judicial review in its original American conception, was also a reaction against the legislative body and its powers.[16] The Congress, like all state organs, was to be submitted to the Constitution and therefore, all the laws of Congress sanctioned in violation of the Constitution were to be considered null and void. On the contrary, the Constitution would be a dead letter, or as Alexander Hamilton said: «would amount to nothing».[17]

---

14 L. FAVOREU and J.A. JOLOWICZ (ed.), *Le contrôle juridictionnel des lois. Légitimité, effectivité et developments récents*, Paris 1986, p. 316.

15 P. Lucas MURILLO DE LA CUEVA «El examen de la constitucionalidad de las leyes y la soberanía parlamentaria», *Revista de estudios politicos*, 7, Madrid 1979, p. 200.

16 E.S. CORWIN, «*The 'Higher Law' Background of American Constitutional law*», NY 1955, p. 53 (Reprinted from *Harvard Law Review*, Vol. XLII, 1928-1929 (p. 149-185 and 365-409).

17 Alexander HAMILTON, *The Federalist* (ed. by B. F. Wright), Cambridge, Mass 1961, p. 491.

This conception is in the logic of the *État de droit,* and in this sense, Professor Jean Rivero, in his synthesis Report to the 2nd Colloquium held in Aix-en-Provence in 1981 on the subject «Cours Constitutionelles Européennes et Droits Fondamentaux» pointed out:

> «The logic of the *Rechstaat* places the Constitution at the summit of the pyramid of norms, from which all other norms draw their validity. But we must recognize that over a long century this logic was stopped... because of the myth of the supremacy of the law, and therefore, to attain the last stage of the building of the Legal state, the one in which the legislator itself is subject to a superior norm, (the concept of the law) ought then to be transformed».[18]

Therefore, judicial review is the direct consequence of the culmination of the building of the *État de droit,* as a state whose organs are limited in their actions by a Constitution, which additionally establishes the fundamental rights of individuals and its means of protection against those state organs, and particularly, against the legislator. This led Professor Rivero to affirm that:

> «The evolution of the *État de Droit* produced of course in relation to the French constitutional system, what Professor Rivero considered the extraordinary phenomenon of the acceptance of a superior authority to the legislator itself, in charge of imposing the respect of the Constitution on the legislator, possible».[19]

The constitutionalization of the *État de droit* therefore, is essentially linked to the idea of judicial review, and this is why Professor Mauro Cappelletti in one of his reports to the same Colloquium in Aix-en-Provence said that,

> «Constitutionalism, in its most advanced state, has needed a state organ or a group of state organs, sufficiently independent of «political powers -the legislative and the executive- in order to protect a superior and relatively permanent rule of law, against the inherent temptations of power».[20]

These independent organs are the courts, considered as being the politically «less dangerous» or the «weakest» of the three state powers in charge of controlling the submission of the Legislative and Executive powers to the Constitution.

Therefore, the subject of judicial review of constitutionality, is essentially related to all the fundamental aspects of the contemporary state as a *État de droit* and particularly those relating to constitutionalism; to the separation of powers and to the role of Parliament; to the form of the state and particularly, to Federalism and political decentralization; to the system of Government, and to the fundamental rights of the individual. All these elements of the *État de droit* have undoubtedly served as a means to justify the need to establish a system of judicial review of the constitutionality of legislation and other state acts and of its legitimacy. They have also served to justify arguments in some cases, against the emergence of such control. In studying the foundations of judicial review of constitutionality I will then consider some of their main arguments for and against, as have been developed in contemporary constitutional law.

---

18 J. RIVERO, «Rapport de Synthèse», in L. FAVOREU (ed.), *Cours constitutionnelles européennes et droit fondamentaux,* Aix-en-Provence 1982, p. 519.

19 *Idem.* p. 519.

20 M. CAPPELLETTI, «Necessité et légitimité de la justice constitutionnelle» in L. FAVOREU (ed.) *Cours constitutionnelles européennes et droit fondamentaux, cit,* p. 483. Also reproduced in *Revue internationale de droit compare,* 1981, (2), p. 647.

Anyway, we must admit that the possibility of a judicial control of the constitutionality of legislation and other state organs, only has its full juridical sense in a *État de droit* where the following principles derive from the submission of state organs to the rule of law: first, the principle of the organization of state powers in such a way as to eliminate all possibility of the unlimited exercise of power; secondly, the principle of a legal guarantee established against arbitrariness in the functioning of the state organs; thirdly, the establishment of the fundamental rights of individuals, as a limit upon the state itself; and fourthly, the formal expression of the afford mentioned principles in a fundamental law or Constitution, as a basic legal rule of state action.

II. THE CONSTITUTION AND ITS SUPREMACY

The *État de droit* is obviously closely related to the idea of a constitution as a fundamental norm and to the theory of a graduated or hierarchical system of the legal order, as Professor Manuel García Pelayo, former President of the Spanish Constitutional Tribunal said, it implies:

> «That the constitution as a fundamental positive norm, links all the public powers, including Parliament, and thus, consequently, the law cannot be contrary to constitutional precepts, to those principles which arise or are to be inferred from them, and to the values which it aspires to put into practice. This, -he concluded-, is the essence of the *Estado de Derecho*».[21]

Therefore, the fundamental rule in the *État de droit*, as we have seen, is the primacy of the rule of law in the sense that all state organs are subject to the rule of law. This fundamental rule shows itself, above all, in two ways: first, in the primacy of the constitution over acts of Parliament and over all other state acts, particularly those issued in direct execution of the constitution; and second, in the primacy of acts of Parliament over all other state acts regulated by it, and to which they must be submitted.

However, when we say that the first consequence of the constitutionalization process in the *État de droit* is the primacy of the constitution this does not mean, of course, that the only constitutional norms that have primacy are the sole formal written articles of the constitution, but also the entirely of the fundamental values that are the pillar of the constitution itself and that, at the same time, are to be inferred from its norms. The role of the judiciary in this aspect, as we will see, has been and is essential.

1. The Constitution as a Higher and Effective Law

The whole possibility of judicial review of constitutionality is not only the ultimate result of the consolidation of the *État de droit*, but also in particular, of the notion of the constitution as a higher and fundamental positive law itself with the characteristics of an effective law. That is to say, the constitution conceived «not as a mere guideline of a political, moral, or philosophical nature, but as a real law, itself a positive and binding law, although of a superior, more permanent nature than ordinary positive legislation».[22]

---

[21] M. GARCÍA PELAYO, «El Status del Tribunal Constitucional», *Revista española de derecho constitucional*, 1, Madrid 1981, p. 18.

[22] M. CAPPELLETTI, *Judicial Review of Legislation and its Legitimacy. Recent Development. General Report. International Association of Legal Sciences*, Uppsala 1984, (mineo), p. 20; also published as the «Rapport Général» in L. FAVOREU and J.A. JOLOWICZ (ed.). *Le contrôle juridictionnel des lois. Légitimité, effectivité et développement récents*, Paris 1986, pp. 285-300.

Therefore, one of the fundamental trends in modern constitutionalism is the concept of a constitution as a normative reality and not as an occasional political compromise of political groups, changeable at any moment when the equilibrium between them is modified. In this sense in the contemporary world, constitutions are effective juridical norms, which overrule the whole political process, the social and economic life of the country, and which give validity to the whole legal order.[23] In this sense, constitution, as a supreme real and effective norm, must contain rules applicable directly to state organs and to individuals.

In relation to the state, constitution today has the same fundamental character that it had in the origins of constitutionalism in North America, and that were later changed in Europe during the course of the last century.

The constitution was originally a fundamental law limiting state organs, and it declared the fundamental rights of individuals, as a political consensus given by the people themselves and, therefore, directly applicable for the courts. The adoption of this concept in continental Europe with the French Revolution was later modified by the monarchical principle, which turned the concept of the constitution into a formal and abstract code of the political system, given by the monarch, and not to be applied by the courts. The constitution in this context had no norm directly applicable to individuals who were only ruled by the formal laws, and even though it contained an organic part, the absence of means of judicial review brought about the loss of its normative character.

Nevertheless, in the European continental legal systems, the concept of the constitution has changed and is again closer to its original conception as a higher law with norms applicable to state organs and to individuals, judged by the courts. In this sense, we can consider as valid the terms of the American Supreme Court decision in *Trop.* v. *Dulles*, 1958, in which the following was stated in relation to the normative character of the constitution:

> «The provisions of the constitution are not time-worn adages ox hollow shibboleths. They are vital, living principles that authorise and limit governmental powers in our nation. They are rules of government. When the constitutionality of an act of Congress is challenged in this Court, we must apply those rules. If we do not, the words of the constitution become little more than good advice».[24]

Therefore, in contemporary legal systems, constitutions are not those simple pieces of «good advise» or «time-worn adages»; on the contrary, their contents are of a normative character, which rule both governments and individuals. This is in true even in France, where in the traditional constitutional system after the 1875 Constitutional Laws, due to the exclusion of the declaration of rights from the text of the constitution,[25] its provisions were considered not to be directly applicable to individuals.

However, after recent decisions of the Constitutional Council adopted in the seventies, the *bloc de la constitutionalité*[26] has been enlarged to include the Declaration

---

23 E. García de Enterría, *La Constitución como norma y el Tribunal Constitucional*, Madrid 1985, pp. 33, 39, 66, 71, 177, 187.

24 356 US 86 (1958).

25 J. Rivero, *Les libertes publiques*, Vol. 1, Paris 1973, p. 70.

26 L. Favoreu, «Le principe de constitutionalité. Essai de definition d'après la jurisprudence du Consel constitutionnel», in *Recueil d'etudes en 1'honneur de Charles Eisenmann*, Paris 1977, p. 33.

of Rights of Man and Citizens of 1789, the Preambles of the 1946 and 1958 Constitutions, and the fundamental principles recognised by the laws of the Republic.[27] This has led Professor Jean Rivero to say with regard to the creation of the law by the constitutional judge, that with the decisions of the Constitutional Council, based on «the constitution and particularly on its Preamble», a revolution has taken place. He wrote:

> «In a single blow, the 1789 Declaration, the 1946 Preamble, the fundamental principles recognised by the laws of the Republic, have been integrated into the French constitution, even if the Constituent did not want it. The French constitution, has doubled its volume through the single will of the Constitutional Council».[28]

This normative character of the constitution, relating to state organs and to individuals, and its enforcement by the Courts, has also brought about a change in the so-called «programmatic norms» of the constitution, which have been considered as norms directly applicable only to the legislator.[29]

In effect, it is current to find in modern constitutions, even in the context of social and economic rights, norms that are, in fact, formulated as a political guideline directed to the legislator. This has led to the consideration that those constitutional norms were not directly applicable to individuals until the legislator itself had adopted formal laws in accordance with the «program» established in the constitution. Therefore, only laws, issued for its legal development were to be applied by the courts.

The normative character of the constitution on the contrary, as a fundamental trend of contemporary constitutionalism, tends to overcome this programmatic character attributed to certain constitutional norms, and seek its enforcement by the courts as norms directly applicable to individuals, so as not to consider them as those pieces of «good advice» referred by Chief Justice Warren to in the *Trop v. Dulles case* (US. 1958). Therefore, those «programmatic norms» or provisions of state aims must be also enforceable by the courts as principles that must orientated the actions of the state.

Nevertheless, in contemporary constitutional law and in relation to judicial review, this judicial control of the constitution is essentially possible not only when a constitution exists as a real norm enforceable by the courts, but also when it has supremacy over the whole legal order, in the sense that it has primacy over all the rules of law contained in a given legal system. This supremacy of the constitution over the other rules of law, and particularly over acts of Parliament implies that the constitution is the supreme norm which establishes the supreme values of a legal order. From this position of supremacy, it can be taken as the parameter for the validity of the remaining legal rules of such a system.

---

27 L. FAVOREU, *Le contrôle juridictionnel des lois et sa légitimité. Développements récents en Europe Occidentale*, Association Internationale des Sciences Juridiques, Colloque d'Uppsala 1984, (mineo), p. 8; also published in L. FAVOREU and J.A. JOLOWICZ, *op. cit.*, pp. 17-68.

28 J. RIVERO, «Rapport de Synthèse» in L. FAVOREU (ed.), *Cours constitutionnelles europeenes et droit fondamentar*, Aix-en-Provence 1982, p. 520.

29 E. GARCÍA DE ENTERRÍA, *op. cit.*, p. 37, 69. *Cf.* P. BISCARETTI DI RUFFIA and S. ROZMARYN, *La Constitution comme loi fondamentale dans les Etats de l'Europe occidentale et dans les Etats socialistes*, Torino 1966, p. 39.

2. English Background of the Constitutional Supremacy and the American Constitutionalism

This concept of the constitution as a higher law is, undoubtedly, the great creation of American constitutionalism, and a contribution to the universal history of law, and it is the basis of the very notion of judicial review.

This concept, particularly in North America, as developed by Edward S. Corwin in his well known work *The 'Higher Law' background of American Constitutional Law*,[30] incorporates the tradition of natural law in the version of Locke and Coke as the «law of laws», the «immutable law», that is to say, *lex legum, lex aeterna* and *lex immutabile.* That law was given concrete form in the pacts and charters of the American colonies, and later formalized as a fundamental law in a solemn document, precisely that document which was to become known by the term «constitution».

The concept of the constitution as a supreme or fundamental law, derived in North America from the technique of judicial review, which developed that constitutional supremacy stemmed, in fact, from English *common law*, considered as a fundamental law.

Prior to the seventeenth century, in the English system, *common law* as non-legislated law, prevailed over statutes, considered as singular or exceptionally created norms in relation to the previously established common law.[31] This technique of the predominance of common law over statutes, or as Chief Justice Edward Coke stated, «the traditional supremacy of the common law over the authority of Parliament»[32] led to the famous *Bonham's case* 1610, in which Coke stated, that:

> «It appears in our books, that in many cases, the common law will control acts of Parliament, and sometimes adjudge them to be utterly void: for when an act of Parliament is against common right and reason, or repugnant, or impossible to be performed, the common law will control it and adjudge such act to be void».[33]

That «common right and reason» was, undoubtedly, something fundamental, something permanent; in short, a higher law, binding on Parliament and on ordinary courts.

One of these fundamental laws, according to Coke, was precisely the *Magna Carta* of which he said was called

> «Magna Charta, not for the length or largeness of it... but... in respect of the great weightiness and weighty, greatness of the matter contained in it; in a few words, being the fountain of all the fundamental laws of the realm».[34]

The Magna Charta was, therefore, considered a fundamental law and it is in this sense that it must be considered as the remote antecedent of modern constitutions.

---

30 E.S. CORWIN, *The 'Higher Law' Background of American Constitutional Law*, NY 1955; Reprinted from *Harvard Law Review*, Vol. XLII, 1928-1929, p. 149-185 and 365-409.

31 M. CAPPELLETTI, *Judicial Review in the. Contemporary World,* Indianapolis 1971, p. 36-37.

32 Quoted by E.S. CONWIN, *op. cit.*, p. 38. Regarding the inconsistance of Coke's views see W. HOLDSWORTH, *A History of English Law*, Vol. V, London 1966, p. 475.

33 See the quotation and its comments in Ch. H. MCILWAIN, *The High Court of Parliament and its Supremacy*, Yale 1910, p. 286-301. See the criticisms on Lord Coke's concepts in L.B. BOUDIN, *Government by Judiciary*, NY 1932, Vol. I, p. 485-517.

34 E.S. CORWIN, *op. cit.* p. 54-55

But, with regard to the concept of a higher law binding acts of Parliament, Corwin referred to another case *Day* v. *Savadge* 1614, where Chief Justice Hobart, even though without direct reference to Bonham's case, stated:

> «Even an act of Parliament, made against Natural Equity, as to make a Man Judge in his own cause, is void in itself; for *jura naturae sunt immutabilia* and they are *leges legume*».[35]

After the 1688-1689 Revolution, the principle of the supremacy of Parliament took place in English law and, therefore, the principle of general submission to legislative power. Even though, twelve years after the Revolution, Chief Justice Holt commented on Dr. *Bonham's* Case in the case City of *London v. Wood*, 1701 stating:

And what my Lord Coke says in Dr. Bonham's Case... is far from any extravagancy, for it is very reasonable and true saying, that if an act of Parliament should ordain that the same person should be party and judge, or which is the same thing, judge in his own cause, it would be a void act of Parliament; for it is impossible that one should be judge and party, for the judge is to determine between party and party.[36]

Nevertheless, Holt accepted the principle that,

> «An act of Parliament can do no wrong» thus the supremacy of Parliament was already accepted, even though he considered that if it was against the principles of natural law -today's natural justice- it would only look pretty odd».[37]

It must be said that this supremacy of Parliament had a paradoxical direct effect on the development of judicial review in North America in the sense that before the Declaration of Independence, laws passed by the colonial legislatures were in several cases, pronounced invalid as contrary to the laws of England or to the colonial charters.[38] Therefore, as Mauro Cappelletti has said,

> «Though the Glorious Revolution of 1688 marked the triumph of Legislative supremacy in England, the American colonies had nonetheless inherited both Coke's ideas regarding the subordination of Crown and Parliament to higher law and a judiciary accustomed to interpreting and at times ignoring legislative acts violating higher principles... Paradoxically the Glorious Revolution not only did not hinder, but rather it spurred the development of the new doctrine of judicial review».[39]

In his same book about *Judicial Review in the Contemporary World*, Cappelletti insisted on the same idea:

> «The principle of parliamentary supremacy - and hence the supremacy of positive law which was introduced in England following the Glorious Revolution of 1688, produced quite different results in America than in England. In England, the result was to remove every control over the validity of legislation from the judges, despite the early successes of Lord Coke's doctrine.

---

35 *Idem*, p. 52.

36 *Idem*, p. 52.

37 Ch. H. MCILWAIN, *op. cit.*, p. 307

38 C.P. PATTERSON, «The Development and Evaluation of Judicial Review», *Washington Law Review*, 13, 1938, p. 75, 171, 353.

39 M. CAPPELLETTI, *Judicial Review in the Contemporary World, cit.*, p.-38-39.

In America, on the contrary, the result was to empower the colonial judges to disregard local legislation not in conformity with the English law. Thus, the apparent paradox has been explained: how the English principle of the uncontrolled supremacy of the legislature helped, rather than hindered, the formation in America of an opposite system».[40]

In this way, if it is true that the dictum in *Dr. Bonham's case* after the final triumph of Parliament over the Crown had no place of importance in judicial decisions in England, it passed to America. As Professor E.S. Corwin said,

> «To join there the arsenal of weapons being accumulated against Parliament's claims to sovereignty».[41]

Thus, the North American colonist linked up directly with the tradition of Coke, regarding the subordination of Crown and Parliament to a higher law embodied to a great extent in a particular document, that were after the Declaration of Independence the constitutions adopted by the new states. That is why in a few states, particularly in Pennsylvania and Vermont, after 1776, the idea that state laws could not be repugnant to their basic laws was emphasized; and the courts of New Jersey started to put the idea of judicial review into practice in 1780.[42]

During the Constitutional Convention of 1787 the problem of judicial review was only considered incidentally, and the discussions on the matter were related more to the supremacy of the constitution over the state's legislation. Thus, the principle that the constitution is the supreme law of the land which should be applied by judges, notwithstanding any disposition to the contrary in the constitutions or laws of the member states appears incorporated in the 1787 constitution. It is what is known as the «Supremacy Clause».[43]

We must additionally stress that in Article I, Section 9, some limitations were imposed on Congress in the constitution[44] and in 1789 the first amendment of the constitution, with the other nine aimed at establishing a Bill of Rights, was conceived as a limit on Legislative Power, stating that

> «Congress shall make no law respecting an establishment of religion or prohibiting the free exercise thereof; or abridging the freedom of speech or of the press; or the right of the people peaceable to assemble, and to petition the Government for a redress of grievances».

The «supremacy clause», the constitutional limitations imposed on Congress by the constitution and the authority given to the Supreme Court to «extend to all causes, in law and equity, arising under this constitution» (Article III, section 2), together with the «higher law» background of the constitutional system, led to the formal adoption of the doctrine of constitutional supremacy and therefrom of judicial review.

---

40 *Idem*, p. 40.

41 E.S. CORWIN, *op. cit.*, p. 53.

42 W.J. WAGNER, *The Federal States and their Judiciary*, The Hague 1959, p. 87-88.

43 Article VI, paragraph 2nd of the constitution state: «This constitution, and the Laws of the United States which shall be made in pursance thereof; and all Treaties made, or which shall be made, under the Authority of the United States, shall be the Supreme Law of the Land; and the Judges in every State shall be bound thereby, anything in the constitution or Laws of any State to the contrary notwithstanding».

44 For instance: «The privilege of the Writ of Habeas Corpus shall not be suspended, unless when in cases of Rebellion or Invasion the public Safety may require it. No Bill of Attainder-or ex post facto law shall be passed».

The supremacy of the constitution considered as a higher and fundamental law was first developed in 1788 by Alexander Hamilton in *The Federalist*. When referring to the role of the courts as interpreters of the law; he stated:

> «A constitution is, in fact, and must be regarded by the judges, as a fundamental law. It therefore, belongs to them to ascertain its meaning, as well as the meaning of any particular act proceeding from the legislative body. If there should happen to be an irreconcilable variance between the two, that which has the superior obligation and validity ought, of course, to be preferred; or, in other words, the constitution ought to be preferred to the Statute, the intention of the people to the intention of their agents».

He added in response to the assertion that «the rights of the courts to pronounce legislative acts void, because contrary to the constitution» would «imply a superiority of the judiciary to the legislative powers», the following:

> «Nor does this conclusion -that the Courts must prefer the constitution over statutes- by any means supposes a superiority of the judicial to the legislative body. It only supposes that the power of the people is superior to both; and that where the will of the legislature, declared in its Statutes stands in opposition to that of the people declared in the constitution, the judges ought to be governed by the latter rather than the former. They ought to regulate their decisions by the fundamental laws, rather than by those which are not fundamental.

Thus, his conclusive assertion that:

> «No legislative act, therefore, contrary to the constitution, can be valid. To deny this, would be to affirm, that the deputy is greater than his principal; that the servant is above his master; that the representative of the people are superior to the peoples themselves; that men acting by virtue of powers, may do not only what their powers do not authorize, but what they forbid».

Thus, in *The Federalist*, Hamilton not only developed the doctrine of the supremacy of the constitution, but more importantly the doctrine of «the judges as guardians of the constitution», as the title of letter N° 78 reads, where Hamilton said, considering the constitution as a limit to state powers and particularly to the Legislative authority, that,

> «Limitations of this kind can be preserved in practice no other way than through the medium of courts of justice, whose duty it must be, to declare all acts contrary to the manifest tenor of the constitution, void. Without this, all the reservations of particular rights or privileges would amount to nothing».[45]

The First Congress, in the first judiciary act of 1789 contemplated the possibility of invalidating statutes «repugnant to the constitution, treaties or laws of the United States» by the courts. This led the Federal Circuit Court in 1795 (*Vanhorne's Lessee v. Dorrance*) and in 1800 (*Cooper v. Telfair*) to declare state laws void on the grounds that they were repugnant to the states and to the federal constitutions.[46]

In fact, the principle of the supremacy of the constitution was first developed in relation to the legislation of the Federal states, in *Vanhorne's Lessee v. Dorrance*

---

45 *The Federalist* (ed. by B.F. Wright), Cambridge, Mass 1961, p. 491 -493

46 W.J. WAGNER, *op. cit.*, p. 90-91.

(1795), a federal circuit court case in which Justice William Paterson declared a Pennsylvania Statute invalid. In his charge to the jury, comparing the system of England and America, he said:

> «Some of the judges in England, have had the boldness to assert, that an act of Parliament made against natural equity, is void; but this opinion contravenes the general position that the validity of an act of Parliament cannot be drawn into question by the judicial department; It cannot be disputed, and must be obeyed. The power of parliament is absolute and transcendent; it is omnipotent in the scale of political existence. Besides, in England there is no written constitution, no fundamental law, nothing visible, nothing real, nothing certain, by which a Statute can be tested. In America, the case is widely different: Every state in the Union has its constitution reduced to written exactitude and precision».

And he asked:

> «What is a constitution? It is the form of government, delineated by the mighty hand of the people, in which certain First principles of fundamental laws are established. The constitution is certain and fixed; it contains the permanent will of the people, and is the supreme law of the land; it is paramount to the power of the legislation, and can be revoked or altered only by the authority that made it».

Along the same line of thought, he also referred to legislation, by asking:

> «What are legislatures? Creatures of the constitution; they owe their existence to the constitution; they derive their powers from the constitution; it is their commission; and, therefore, all their acts must be conformable to it, or else they will be void. The constitution is the work or will of the people themselves, in their original, sovereign, and unlimited capacity. Law is the work or will of the legislature in their derivative and subordinate capacity. The one is the work of the Creator, and the other of the creature. The constitution fixes limits to the exercise of legislative authority and prescribes the orbit within which it must move».

Justice Paterson concluded his statement delivered in 1795 by saying to the jury

> «In short, gentlemen, the constitution is the sum of the political system, around which all legislature, executive and judicial bodies must revolve. Whatever may be the case in other countries, yet in this, there can be no doubt, that every act of the legislature, repugnant to the constitution, is absolutely void...».[47]

Following these trends, and despite the Framers of the constitution intending that judicial review be one of the fundamental principles of the American constitutional system or not, it was first established in relation to federal laws in the Case celebrated *Marbury v. Madison* Case 1803.[48] In it the principle of supremacy of the constitution was the basic argument for the exercise of that power of judicial review by the Supreme Court.

---

[47] 2. Dallas 304 (1795). See the text in S.I. KUTLER (ed.), *The Supreme Court and the Constitution. Readings in American Constitutional History*, NY 1964 , p. 7-13.

[48] 5.U.S. (1 Cranch), 137; 2 L. Ed 60 (1803). In relation to this case see in general E.S. CORWIN, *The Doctrine of Judicial Review. Its Legal and Historical Basis and other Essays*, Princeton 1914, p. 1-78.

In effect, Chief Justice Marshall aiming to determine whether the Supreme Court in accordance with the constitution, could exercise the authority given it by the Judiciary act 1789 to issue writs of mandamus to public officers, and considering that it «appears not to be warranted by the constitution», decided to «inquire whether a jurisdiction so conferred can be exercised», and to that end he developed the doctrine of the supremacy of the constitution based on the question «whether an act repugnant to the constitution can or cannot become the law of the land».

To answer this question, he followed a logical approach, establishing first the principle of the supremacy of the constitution. He started his argument by accepting the idea of an «original right» of the people to establish the principles regulating «their future government», as «the basis on which the whole American fabric had been erected». This original right to adopt those «fundamental» and «permanent» principles, he considered, was a very great exertion, so was not to be «frequently repeated».

This «original and supreme will», he said, «organizes the government... assigns to different departments their respective powers... (and) establishes certain limits not to be transcended by those departments». He considered that the government of the United States was of that kind, in which «the powers of the legislature are defined and limited», and it was precisely for the purpose «that those limits may not be mistaken, or forgotten», that a written constitution containing those fundamental and permanent principles was adopted.

He then asked:

«To what purpose are powers limited, and to what purpose is that limitation committed to writing, if these limits may, at any time, be passed by those intended to be restrained? The distinction between a government with limited and unlimited powers is abolished if those limits do not confine the person on whom they are imposed, and if acts prohibited and acts allowed are of equal obligation».

Thus, he stressed the alternative as:

«A proposition too plain to be contested that the constitution controls any legislative act repugnant to it; or, that the legislative may alter the constitution by an ordinary act; «

in relation to which, he stated:

«Between these alternatives there is no middle ground. The constitution is either a superior paramount law, unchangeable by ordinary means, or it is on a level with ordinary legislative acts, and, like other acts, is alterable when the legislature shall please to alter it.

If the former part of the alternative be true, then a legislative act contrary to the constitution is not law; if the latter part be true then written constitutions are absurd attempts on the part of the people to limit a power in its own nature illimitable».

Of course, his conclusion was that the constitution was the «fundamental and paramount law of the nation», a principle that he considered «as one of the fundamental principles of our society». Therefore, he accepted the principle that «an act of the legislature repugnant to the constitution is void», considering «the very essence of judicial duty» to determine the rules that govern the case when a law is in opposition to the constitution. In such cases, he concluded, «the constitution is superior to any ordinary act of the legislature, the constitution and not such ordinary acts, must govern the case to which they both apply». The contrary, -he stated-, would mean to give «to the legislature a practical and real omnipotence... would be the same as prescribing limits and declaring that those limits may be passed at pleasure all of which, -he concluded-, would «subvert the very foundation of all written constitutions».

After this case, the principle of the supremacy of the constitution in the sense that it overrides any other law inconsistent with it, became one of the main features of modern Constitutionalism, and of course, of the possibility itself, of judicial review of legislation.

Nevertheless, the supremacy of the constitution in modern times is not only a matter of implication according to the logic of the *Marbury v. Madison* case, but is a consequence, in many cases, of express declarations in that sense in the constitution itself, as was the classic case of the 1920 Czechoslovakian constitution, which stated in article I, 1:

> «All the laws contrary to the Constitutional Charter, to its parts and also to the Laws that modify or complement it, are invalid».

This sort of express declaration, considered by Hans Kelsen as one of the «objective guarantees» of the constitution,[49] can be as a common trend in contemporary constitutionalism, particularly, in the constitutions of Latin America[50] and Africa.[51] In the latter, as B.O. Nwabueze said:

> «When a court declares a statute invalid for unconstitutionality it is merely acting as a mouthpiece, an instrumentality, of the constitution».[52]

However, the concept of Constitutional supremacy, the constitution considered as a fundamental and higher law built up by American Constitutionalism, was not followed in Europe in the last century, and was only adopted in the 20th century. This European immunity regarding the supremacy of the constitution and judicial review, taking into account the historical process developed after the French Revolution, is explained by the development of the monarchical principle, as a consequence of the restoration of the monarchical idea that made the monarch a pre-constitutional source of power, all reducing the constitution to a simple formal code given by the monarch regarding the relation of the organs of the state, without any other outcome and in particular, without a dogmatic part related to fundamental rights and applicable to the citizen.[53] Additionally, both the principle of parliamentary sovereignty and the extreme interpretation of the separation of powers, the doctrine that gave the legislator immunity from the judicial power also contributed to the non-adoption of the principle of the supremacy of the constitution.

---

49 H. KELSEN, «La guarantie juridictionnelle de la constitution. La Justice constitutionnelle», *Revue du droit public et de la science politique en France et à l'étranger*, Paris 1928, p. 214.

50 The Venezuelan constitution 1961 for example in article 46 establishes: «Every act of the Public Power which violates or impairs the rights guaranteed by this constitution is void....»

51 Constitution of Uganda (Art. 1), Kenya (Art. 3), Nigeria (Art. 1), Swaziland (Art. 2). *Cf.* B.C. NWABUEZE, *Judicial Control of Legislative Action and its Legitimacy. Recent Development* (African Regional Report), International Association of Legal Science. Uppsala Colloquium 1984 (mineo), p. 2.

52 *Idem*, p. 2.

53 E. GARCÍA DE ENTERRÍA, *op. cit.*, p. 55-56

In Europe, the reception of the doctrine of supremacy of the constitution and of judicial review took place only after the First World War, mainly through the constitutional system designed by Hans Kelsen for his own country, Austria, and reflected in the 1920 Austrian constitution. It was also reflected in the constitution of Czechoslovakia in the same year.

Years later, after the Second World War, the Austrian system of constitutional supremacy and judicial review was adopted in Germany and Italy and through their influence, in other European constitutional systems.

As Professor Louis Favoreu recently pointed out, it has only been over the last decades that Europe has «rediscovered» the constitution as a superior law which establishes certain fundamental values of society out of reach of temporary or passing majorities, transferring the traditional sacred character of acts of Parliament to the constitution. Therefore, the constitution has been «rejuridicised» in the sense of now being considered as a fundamental law directly enforceable by the judges and applicable to individuals.[54]

3. Supremacy and Rigidity of the Constitution

We have said that judicial review of constitutionality, particularly of the constitutionality of legislation, translated into a judicial control of legislative action, firstly requires the existence of a written constitution, a product of a constituent sovereign power, the people, conceived as a fundamental and enforceable real law with direct effects on both state organs and individuals. We have also said that for the existence of judicial review, the constitution is also required to have a hierarchical pre-eminence, superiority or supremacy over all the constituted powers established by the constitution itself.

This supremacy of the constitution is, of course, closely related to its rigid character, which means that the norms of the constitution are immune to the powers of the ordinary legislator. This characteristic of the constitution is the general trend in constitutional law all over the world, with the exception of systems like those of the United Kingdom, New Zealand and Israel, which have unwritten constitutions, therefore flexible ones.[55]

In principle, judicial review is essentially related to rigid constitutions,[56] although not all the countries with this kind of constitution have a system of judicial review, and it has also been accepted that even in systems with flexible constitutions some kind of judicial review is possible. Nevertheless, as we have said, the judicial control of the constitutionality of legislation finds its complete sense and meaning, in constitutional systems, with written and rigid constitutions, in which the fundamental law is adopted in an entrenched way, implying that its amendments and reforms can only take place through special procedures and not through ordinary legislative processes.

In this sense, for instance, Professor Maurice Duverger considered conclusively that «the existence of a judicial control of the constitutionality of laws needs the

---

54 L. FAVOREU, *Le contrôle juridictionnel des lois et sa légitimité. Développements récents en Europe occidentale, doc. cit.*, p. 23.

55 J. BRYCE, *Flexible Constitutions and Rigid Constitutions*, Spanish edition: *Constituciones flexibles y constituciones rígidas*, Madrid 1962, p. 19.

56 See in contrary, G. TRUJILLO FERNÁNDEZ, *Dos Estudios sobre la constitucionalidad de las leyes*, La Laguna 1970, p. 11, 17.

constitution to be a rigid constitution and not a flexible constitution».[57] And in fact, it is in the framework of rigid constitutions that one may distinguish between constitutional and ordinary norms, and where the principle of constitutional supremacy is definitively accepted.

In rigid constitutional systems the principle of *lex superior derogat legi inferiori* is the one to be applied when judging the constitutionality of laws; whereas in flexible constitutional systems, in which the constitution does not have the character of supreme law, the conflict between legal norms is not that expressed by Chief Justice Marshall in the *Marbury v Madison* case, but between norms of equal rank. Therefore, in such cases, the traditional principles of interpretation: *lex posterior derogat legi priori* and *lex specialis derogat legi generali*[58] are in fact normally applicable. Consequently, judicial review is closely related to rigid constitutions, even though as we have said, not all the countries that have rigid constitutions, have a system of judicial review.

Nevertheless, if it is true that in flexible constitutional systems the absence of an entrenched constitutional text allows the ordinary legislator to reform or amend the constitution, and, therefore, prevent the development of an effective system of judicial review, it has been correctly pointed out that some distinction can be established between constitutional norms and ordinary legislative norms, not with regard to their formal aspects but in relation to their content. In rigid constitutions, the difference between these norms is especially a formal one, in the sense that constitutional norms are only amendable through special procedures, but the distinction also exists in flexible constitutions even though not in a formal sense, but in relation to the content of such norms.[59]

Thus, if it is true that in flexible constitutions, judicial review in the formal sense cannot exist, it is not impossible in the substantive sense regarding the content of the norms.[60]

In this respect we can also say that in systems with flexible constitutions, certain conditions over reforming some acts of Parliament, allowing the formal control of the «constitutionality» of legislation can be established. In some respects, it is Israel's case that we must stress, a country that we said, has a non-written constitution.

In effect, in the 1948 Declaration of the Establishment of the State of Israel adopted on the eve of the termination of the British Mandate over Palestine, some fundamental principles were proclaimed by the People's Council, among which it was stated that a constitution was «to be drawn up by the Constituent Assembly not later than the 1st of October, 1945».[61] The constitution was never drafted and instead the Knesset passed what is called the *Harari* Resolution, in which «the

57 M. DUVERGER, *Institutions politiques et droit constitutionnel,* Paris 1965, p. 222.

58 P. DE VEGA GARCÍA, «Jurisdicción constitucional y crisis de la Constitución», *Revista de estudios políticos,* 7, Madrid 1979 p. 94.

59 G. TRUJILLO FERNÁNDEZ, *op. cit.,* p. 17, 18.

60 P. Lucas MURILLO DE LA CUEVA, «El examen de la constitucionalidad de la leyes y la soberanía parlamentaria», *Revista de estudios políticos,* 7, Madrid 1979, p. 206.

61 A. SHAPIRA, *The Constitution and its Defense in Israel: Fundamentals, Guarantees Emergency Powers and Reform,* Internacional Congress on the constitution and its Defense, U.N.A.M. México 1982, (mimeo), p. 2-5. See also A. SHAPIRA, «Judicial Review without a Constitution: The Israeli Paradox», *Temple Law Quarterly,* 56, 1983, p. 405.

Constitutional Legislative and Judicial Committee» was charged «with the duty to prepare a draft constitution for the state», following these guidelines:

> «The constitution shall be composed of individual chapters in such a manner that each of them shall constitute a basic law in itself. The chapters shall be brought before the Knesset to the extent at which the Committee will terminate its work and all chapters together will form the state constitution».[62]

It has been considered that with this Resolution, the constituent powers inherent in the first Knesset have passed on to all successive Knessets, and in its «continuing constituent authority» the Knesset has approved various «basic laws» related to the Knesset itself, to Israeli lands, to the president of the state, to the government, to the state economy, to the Army, and to Jerusalem Capital of Israel.[63] Some of these «basic laws» have been passed in an entrenched way, in the sense that their repeal or amendments can be adopted only by «a majority of the members of the Knesset». Among these «basic laws» is the «Basic law: The Knesset» passed in 1958, in which the Knesset limited its own parliamentary supremacy.

In 1969, the problem of the reviewability of ordinary legislation that is inconsistent with the basic laws was placed before the Supreme Court and was decided upon in the case *Bergman v Minister of Finance*.[64] The facts were the following: the Knesset passed a law providing for the financing of the political parties' election costs, out of public funds, and the funds were to be distributed in proportion to the party's representation in the outgoing Knesset and not in strictly equal terms. Dr. Bergman, a Tel-Aviv lawyer, challenged this statute as being inconsistent with the «Basic law-The Knesset», which provided not for proportional participation in the election but «for general, national... equal... elections», and he challenged the Statute considering that it was passed by the Knesset by less than the required absolute majority of its total membership for its amendment. The Supreme Court, although it did not expressly decide upon the constitutional questions, by stating that it was «far from purporting to affect whosoever the sovereignty of the Knesset as the legislative authority», in fact opened the way to judicial review of legislation inconsistent with the Basic Laws.[65] The decision, in fact, offered the Knesset two possible courses of action: it could either re-enact the Financing law, tainted with inequality as it was, by the absolute majority needed under the Basic law: the Knesset; or it could rectify the legislative scheme of financing so as to remove there from the unacceptable element of inequality.

Reacting to the *Bergman* case, the Knesset took two steps to rectify its mistakes: first, it adopted an amendment to the Financing law which cured its original defect of inequality; second, the Knesset passed, by an absolute majority, the Election law, 1969, which provided that:

> «For the purpose of removing doubt it is hereby laid down that the provisions contained in the Knesset Election law are from the date of their coming into effect valid for ever legal proceeding and for every matter and purpose».[66]

---

62 A. SHAPIRA, *The Constitution ..., cit.*, p. 8.

63 *Idem*, p. 9.

64 23. P.D. (1) 693 (1969). See the references in J.D. WHYTE, *Judicial Review of Legislation and its Legitimacy: Developments in the Common Law World*, International Association of Legal Sciences, Uppsala Colloquium 1984, p. 57; A. SHAPIRA,*The Constitution... op. cit.*, p. 9-13.

65 J.D. WHYTE, *op. cit.*, p. 58.

66 A. SHAPIRA, *The Constitution..., cit.*, p. 10.

The *Bergman* decision is without doubt of particular importance and as Professor Amos Shapira has pointed out, it can lead the way to judicial review of constitutionality in a country like Israel, with an unwritten and flexible constitution. Of course, the Supreme Court did not invalidate the challenge law, but did not hesitate to investigate its validity by looking at the legislative journals to see if the Financial law had or had not been passed by an absolute majority. Furthermore, it did not declare the defective Financing law as unconstitutional and void but ordered the Minister of Finance not to give effect to the law; it recognized the sovereignty of the Knesset or Parliament but acknowledged the constituent power of the Knesset to bind itself and its successors through an entrenched clause of its Basic law. Finally, it was careful not to establish a precedent but really it revolutionized the Israeli legal system «by introducing *de facto* judicial supervision of the constitutionality of primary legislation».[67]

In conclusion, a principle of differentiation between higher law (Basic Laws) and ordinary law (regular Knesset legislation) can almost be established in Israel, even if it does not have a written constitution and the constitution is flexible; and after the *Bergman* decision a principle of judicial review can also be distinguished, even though it seems, it is only the beginning of a long ongoing process.

Of course, this special situation is exceptional and evidently not resolved definitively. What is admitted is that the supremacy of the constitution and judicial review of legislation is normally found in legal systems with written and rigid constitutions.

4. The Supremacy and the unwritten constitutional principles

Nevertheless, this assertion leads us to another problem related to written constitutions and to the possibility of judicial review. The problem concerning the scope of judicial review powers regarding the formal text of written constitutional rules and the admissibility of judicial review of legislation based on the unwritten principles and values of the written constitution. In other words, the question to determine is whether judicial control of the constitutionality of legislation must only be exercised in relation to norms contained in written articles of the constitution, or whether it can be exercised in relation to non written norms that result from deduction from the constitution and its spirit.[68]

The problem regarding the active role of the supreme Court has been widely discussed in North America particularly over the protection of fundamental rights and has produced two antagonistic alternatives concerning the role of judges in judicial review: the interpretative and the non-interpretative role.[69]

According to the interpretative method, constitutional judges are limited to the application of the concrete norms established in the written constitution itself

---

67 *Idem*, p. 11.

68 L. FAVOREU «Rapport général introductif» in L. FAVOREU (ed.), *Cours constitutionnelles... cit.*, p. 45

69 J.H. ELY, *Democracy and Distrust. A Theory of Judicial Review*, 1980, p. 1-2; T. GREYZ, «Do We Have an Unwritten Constitution», *Stanford Law Review*, 27 1975, p. 703; T. GREY «Origins of the Unwritten Constitution: Fundamental Law in American Revolutionary thought», *Stanford Law Review*, 30, 1978, p. 843-847; E. GARCÍA DE ENTERRÍA, *op. cit*, p. 210-221; M. CAPPELLETTI, «El formidable problema del control judicial y 1a contribución del análisis comparado», *Revista de estudios políticos*, 13, Madrid 1980, p. 68-69 («The Mighty Problem» of Judicial Review and the Contribution of Comparative Analysis, in *Southern California Law Review*, 1980, p. 409); B. CAINE, «Judicial Review: Democracy Versus Constitutionality», *Temple Law Quarterly*, 56, (2), 1973, p. 298.

or clearly implicit therein; this was the model originally followed by Hamilton and Chief Justice Marshall and according to which legislation can only be invalidated by a deduction, whose fundamental premise is clearly found in the constitution.

At the other extreme, the non-interpretative model wants judges to go beyond the literal references of the constitution and to execute the norms that are not to be found within the boundaries of the written document, but that form the permanent and fundamental values of a given society and its political system.

In Thomas Grey's opinion, the purest form of the non-interpretative model, which he considered almost dead in North America, recognizes the general principles of republican government and natural justice of human rights, establish limitations on legislative authority, the actual words of the written text of the constitution or even its existence not being important.[70] This non interpretative model was followed by the Warren Court in the decisions concerning the discrimination issues and the protection of minorities,[71] bearing in mind that the 1789 constitution and the 1791 amendments did not establish the principle of equality and that the XIV Amendment (1868) only established an equal protection clause.[72]

The question regarding the choice between the interpretative model and the non-interpretative model, has been, and almost certainly will continue to be, one of the most important issues of the role of constitutional justice and of judicial review of legislation. The adoption of one model or the other depends, in fact, on the content of the constitution itself and on the way the articles of the constitutional text are written, and when they were written. The fact is that when a constitution is two centuries old, like the American one, it is impossible to solidify the known intentions of the framers who lived in a patriarchal society, which vanished long ago, particularly in relation to the so-called open-ended or open clauses of the constitution.[73] Those must be determined and that is the role of the courts.

Of course, the situation is different in constitutional systems with modern and detailed constitutional codes, where the non-interpretative model is difficult to develop, and in any case, the adoption of one model or the other depends on the juridical tradition of the particular country.

For instance, in the sphere of fundamental rights, the Swiss federal tribunal has largely developed the non-interpretative model for the protection of fundamental rights. In effect, important fundamental rights like personal liberty, freedom of opinion, the right to a previous hearing are not in the text of the federal constitution but are recognized by the federal tribunal as non-written constitutional rights. In this respect, it has been said, the tribunal does not interpret the constitution but rather perfects it, because it considers it its duty as a constitutional judge to do so and justifies this attitude by the fact that its function is precisely to guarantee the foundations of the democratic, and federal state submitted to the law.[74]

---

70 T. GREY, «Origins...», *loc. cit.*, p. 844.

71 See particularly *Brown v. Board of Education of Topeka*, 347 U.S. 483 (1954). See the text in S.I. KUTLER (ed.) *op. cit.*, p. 548-552.

72 *Cf.* J.H. ELY, *op. cit*, p. 79-90; E. GARCÍA DE ENTERRÍA, *op. cit.*, p. 216-217. See also R. BERGER, *Government by Judiciary. The Transformation of the Fourteen Amendment*, 1977.

73 J.H. ELY, *op. cit*, p. 13; E. GARCÍA DE ENTERRÍA, *op. cit*, p. 211.

74 T. OHLINGER, «Object et portée de la protection des droits fondamentaux Cours constitutionnelle antrichienne», in L. FAVOREU (ed.), *Cours constitutionnelles ...*, p. 335-336.

But on the contrary, as Professor Theo Ohlinger pointed out, the Austrian constitutional court does not follow a similar method of law making and considers itself bound to the constitutional text even though it has to be interpreted. Nevertheless, this interpretation is considered as being of great importance in Austria because the most important norms of the constitution related to fundamental rights were written in the last century and have a formalistic and lapidarian style.

But even in those cases, the positivist orientation of the constitutional court is determinant and shows itself in a careful application of interpretative methods. Thus, when the constitutional court considers that the absence of a constitutional norm in a particular context is wrongful its role is to ask the constitutional legislator to fill the gap, considering itself incompetent to do so.[75]

In the sphere of the protection of fundamental rights, the role of the French Constitutional Council during the last decade as an example of the non-interpretative model must be stressed. It has been considered that the constitutional judges in France have not only surpassed the pure interpretative model, but have also reached the purest form of the non-interpretative judicial control model, when they have decided to control the conformity of executive legislation to «general principles» or undefined, vague and non-written «republican traditions», which have been «found» by the judges and defined as having a superior law rank.[76]

In this sense, the attitude of the French Constitutional Council radically changed in the 70's.After the important decision adopted on 16th July 1971[77] concerning the liberty of association, the following contrasting position resulted: in 1958, when the constitution was drafted, in the Consultative Constitutional Committee it was considered that the role of the Constitutional Council was not to ensure the respect of the provisions of the preamble to the constitution; on the contrary, in 1971, the Constitutional Council accepted the positive law value of the preamble to the 1958 constitution with all its consequences[78] regarding what Professor Favoreu called the *bloc de constitutionnalité*.[79]

In effect, the preamble to the 1958 French constitution says:

> «The French people, solemnly proclaim their subjection to the rights of Man and to the national sovereignty principles as have been defined by the Declaration of 1789, confirmed and completed by the Preamble to the constitution of 1946».

This preamble to the constitution was considered by the Constitutional Council itself, up to the 70's only as a principle for the orientation of constitutional interpretation, its competence being «strictly limited» by the constitutional text.[80]

Nevertheless, this attitude changed after the Constitutional Council decision of 16th July 1971, when it was decided that a proposed law establishing a procedure

---

75 *Idem*, p. 346.

76 M. CAPPELLETTI, «El formidable problema..., *loc. cit.*, note 20, p. 69.

77 See in L. FAVOREU and L. PHILIP, *Les grandes décisions du Conseil Constitutionnel»*, Paris 1984, p. 222-237.

78 L. FAVOREU, «Rapport général introductif», *loc. cit.*, p. 45-46.

79 L. FAVOREU, «Le principe de Constitutionalité. Essai de definition d'apres la jurisprudence du Conseil Constitutionnel», *Recueil d'etude en Hommaqe a Charles Eisenman*, Paris 1977, p. 34.

80 L. HAMON, «Contrôle de Constitutionalité et protection des droits individuels. Apropos de trois decisions récents du Conseil Constitutionnel», *Recueil Dalloz Sirey 1974*, Chronique XVI, p. 85.

to set up preliminary judicial controls for the acquisition of legal capacity by association was against the constitution. The proposed law was an amendment bill to a 1901 law relating to non-profit making associations submitted by the government to the National Assembly in 1970, which the Council considered unconstitutional,[81] using the following argument:

The 1958 constitution through the preamble to the 1946 constitution referred to the «fundamental principles recognized by the laws of the Republic» among which the principle of liberty of association must be listed.

In accordance with this principle, associations were to be constituted freely and could publicly develop their activities, the only condition being to make a previous declaration, - whose validity was not to be submitted to a previous intervention by either administrative or judicial authorities.

Thus, the Constitutional Council decided that the limits imposed on associations by the proposed bill establishing a prior judicial control of the said declaration were unconstitutional. In this way, Professor Rivero said,

> «The liberty of association, which is not expressly established either in the Declaration or by the particularly needed principles of our times, but which is only recognized by a Statute of 1 July 1901, has been recognized by the Constitutional Council decision, as having a constitutional character, not only as a principle, but in ´relation to the modalities of its exercise».[82]

The significance of this decision was summarized by Professor Barry Nicholas, in an article published in the *Public Law Journal* in 1978, by saying:

> «It made an unambiguous breach with the constitutional tradition of the supremacy of *loi*. It declared beyond any question that even within the area set aside for legislation by article 34 of the constitution there were fundamental principles, which Parliament could not alter or contravene. And above all, it declared that those fundamental principles were to be found not only in the constitution proper but also in its Preamble and via that Preamble, in the Preamble of 1946 (and presumably also in the Declaration of 1789)».[83]

The decision of 16th July 1971 on the liberty of association is an example of the creative will of fundamental rights by the Constitutional Council, even though for that purpose it has based its decision on the preamble to the constitution, and through it, in what the preamble to the 1946 constitution considered the «fundamental principles recognized by the laws of the Republic». In general, therefore, to establish a fundamental right or liberty as such a «fundamental principle», the Constitutional Council has based itself on a particular existing statute, as happened with the liberty of association which was recognized by the Statute of 1 July 1901.

---

81 See the Constitutional Council decision in L. FAVOREU and J. PHILIP, *Les grandes décisions du Conseil Constitutionnel*, *cit.*, p. 222. See the comments of the 16 July 1971 decisions in J. RIVERO, «Note», *L'Actualité Juridique. Droit Administratif*, 1971, p. 537; J. RIVERO, «Principes fondamentaux reconnus par les lois de la Republique; une nouvelle categorie constitutionnelle?», *Dalloz 1974*, Chroniques, p. 265; and J.E. BARDSLEY, «The Constitutional Council and Constitutional Liberties in France», *The American Journal of Comparative Law*, 20, (3), 1972, p. 43; B. NICHOLAS, «Fundamental Rights and Judicial Review in France», *Public Law*, 1978, p. 83.

82 J. RIVERO, «Les garanties constitutionnelles des droits de l'homme en droit français», *IX Journees Juridiques Franco-Latino Americaines*, Bayonne 21-23 mai 1976, (mimeo), p. 11.

83 B. NICHOLAS, *loc. cit.*, p. 89.

But in other cases,[84] as has happened with the right to self defense, the Constitutional Council has not based itself in a particular Statute for deducing a liberty based on «the fundamental principles recognized by the laws of the Republic». In effect, in a decision dated 19th-20th January 1981[85] the Constitutional Council radically changed the previous situation regarding the right to one's own defense, which was considered by the *Conseil d'État* simply as a general principle of law.[86] Conversely, after the 1981 decision, the Constitutional Council recognized it as part of the «principles and rules of constitutional value», an expression used by the Constitutional Council,

> «To designate in a generic manner all the norms that, without being contained in the text of the constitution itself, have Constitutional rank».[87]

Therefore, in France, «conformity with the constitution» as a consequence of the principle of constitutionality, is not understood today strictly as conformity with an express disposition of the constitution. On the contrary, since the 1970's, the notion of constitutional norms that could serve as reference norms to control the constitutionality of legislation is progressively understood in a wider sense, comprising dispositions or principles outside the constitutional text, and in particular, the Declaration of 1789, the preambles to the 1946 and 1958 constitutions, the fundamental principles recognized by the laws of the Republic, and the general principles of constitutional value.[88] All these sources of the principle of constitutionality enjoy the same supremacy character as the written articles of the constitution.

Anyway, the discussion concerning the need of a written or unwritten norm of reference to allow for the judicial control of the constitutionality of legislation is a permanent one, with different solutions in the various systems of judicial review,[89] even though a clear tendency to allow the non-interpretative method of judicial review and the active role of the constitutional judge can be observed.

5. The adaptation of the Constitution and its interpretation

Nevertheless, it is obvious that the normal and customary type of judicial control of constitutionality that has developed in all constitutional systems, where the principle of the supremacy of the constitution is established, is based on the existence of written rules in the constitution, to which all state organs, particularly the legislator, must conform. In this case, of course, the basic problem regarding

---

84 Decisions of 8 Nov 1976; 2 Dec 1976; 20 July 77, 19 January 1981; 20 January 1981, *Cf.* the quotations in F. LUCHAIRE, «Procedures et techniques de protection des droits fondamentaux. Conceil Constitutional français», in L. FAVOREU (ed.), *Cours constitutionnelles europeenes ..., cit.*, p. 69, 70, 83.

85 L. FAVOREU et L. PHILIP., *Les grandes décisions..., cit.*, pp. 490, 517.

86 *Cf.* D.G. LAVROFF, «El Consejo Constitutional francés y la garantía de las libertades públicas», *Revista española de derecho constitucional*, 1 (3), 1981, pp. 54-55; L. FAVOREU et L. PHILIP, *Les grandes décisions..., cit.*, p. 213.

87 L. FAVOREU «Les décisions du Conseil Constitutiornel dans l'affaire des nationalisations», *Revue du droit public et de la science politique en France et à l'étranger*, T. XCVIII, N° 2, Paris 1982, p. 401.

88 L. FAVOREU, «L'application directe et l'effect indirect des normes constitutionnelles», *French Report to the XI International Congress of Comparative Law*, Caracas 1982, (mineo), p. 4

89 See E. SMITH, «Contrôle juridictionnel de la législation et sa légitimite. Dévelopment récents dans les cinq pays scandinaves», *Rapport au Symposium de l'Association Internationale des Sciences Juridique*, Uppsala 1984, (mimeo), p. 61. Also published in L. FAVOREU and J.A. JOLOWICZ (ed.), *Le contrôle juridictionnel des lois..., cit.*, pp. 225-282.

judicial review of constitutionality, based on the interpretative model, refers to the degree of clarity of the particular constitutional text and, consequently, to the possibility of judicial review of legislation in relation to vague, imprecise or undetermined notions contained in constitutional articles and to the need for the constitutional judge to adapt the text of the constitution to ensure its effectiveness and supremacy.

As mentioned, the situation varies depending on the modernity or antiquity of the constitution, on the numerous or few provisions or regulations of the constitutional text, and on the preciseness or vagueness of the articles of the constitution.

But even modern constitutions, particularly concerning fundamental rights are written down in a synthetic, vague and elusive way, and their norms are generally expressed in ambiguous terms, full of worthy characteristics, like liberty, democracy, justice, dignity, equality, social function, public interests,[90] all of which lead to the need for an active role by judges, when interpreting what have been called, the «precious ambiguities»,[91] in which constitutions are written down.

Anyway, these vague and ambiguous phrases of constitutions, always express certain concepts or values related to the general foundations of the given society and its political system, and it is in relation to these that the constitutional judge must play his creative role determining the exact meaning of the concept.

They are what in the continental European legal systems are called the «undetermined legal concepts» or «imprecise juridical notions»[92] that are of course, also included in the constitution, more than anything because of its general character. The constitutional judge must fill in these concepts, pinpoint and determine their boundaries through an interpretative process, bearing in mind basically, the superior values followed by the constitution, and generally established in the preamble or in its first articles.

The position of the judge facing the constitution, therefore, is not different from the position he normally has facing all other laws, which must be interpreted, and if it is true that the judges must not substitute the legislator in deducing concepts which could be against what is written in the law, neither must they interpret the constitution in a way so as to arrive at concepts that could be contrary to the constitutional text and its fundamental values.[93]

But the constitutional judge always has an additional duty compared to the ordinary judge: he must defend the constitution and particularly, the values that are at its foundation at a given time. That is why the constitutional judge in his

---

90 M. CAPPELLETTI, «Necessité et légitimité de la justice constitutionelle» in L. FAVOREU (ed.), *Cours constitutionelle européenes et droit fundamentaux,* Paris 1982, p. 474

91 «If it is true that precision have a place of honor in the writting of a governmental decision, it is mortal when it refers to a constitution which wants to be a lively body». S.M. HUFSTEDLES, «In the Name of Justice», *Stanford Lawyers,* 14, (1), 1979, p. 3-4 quoted by M. CAPPELLETTI, «Nécessité et légitimité ...», *loc. cit,* p. 474. See the references in E. GARCÍA DE ENTERRÍA, *op, cit,* p. 229; L. FAVOREU, *Le contrôle juridictionnel des lois et sa légitimité..., cit.,* p. 32.

92 F. SAINZ MORENO, *Conceptos jurídicos, interpretación y discrecionalidad administrativa,* Madrid 1976; E. GARCÍA DE ENTERRÍA, *La lucha contra las inmunidades de poder en el derecho administrativo,* Madrid 1980, p. 32.

93 F. LUCHAIRE, «Procedures et techniques ...», *loc. cit.,* p. 83.

interpretative process must adapt the constitution to the current values of society, and of the political system, in order precisely, «to keep the constitution alive».[94] To that end, undoubtedly, the constitutional judge must develop a creative activity so as to allow the current and effective application of constitutions written, for instance, in the 19th century, to control the constitutionality of legislation.

In this respect, the constitution cannot be seen as a static document. On the contrary, it must be adapted to the evolution of social needs and institutions. The role of the constitutional judge in this process of adaptation of the constitution has been crucial, as the role of the North American Supreme Court has demonstrated. In this respect, it suffices to recall the important decisions of the Supreme Court in the matter of discrimination in the educational system.

When referring to the XIV Amendment, for example, Chief Justice Warren said in *Brown v. Board of Education of Topeka* in 1954:

> «In approaching this problem, we cannot turn the clock back to 1868 when the Amendment was adopted, or even to 1896 when *Plessy v. Ferguson* was written. We must consider public education in the light of its full development and its present place in American life throughout the Nation. Only in this way can it be determined if segregation in public schools deprives these plaintiffs of the equal protection of the laws».

This assertion led Chief Justice Warren to conclude then,

> «That in the field of public education the doctrine of «separate but equal» has no place. Separate educational facilities are inherently unequal. Therefore, we hold that the plaintiffs, and others similarly situated from whom the actions have been brought are by reason of the segregation complained of, deprived of the equal protection of the laws guaranteed by the Fourteenth Amendment».[95]

In the same sense, this adaptation of the constitution by the constitutional judge has recently been demonstrated in France by the Constitutional Council in the well-known Nationalization case in 1982 in which the article concerning the right of property in the Declaration of the Rights of Man and Citizen of 1789 was applied, and the right to property itself was then declared as having constitutional force. In its decision of 16 January 1982,[96] even though the article of the Declaration concerning property rights was considered obsolete and that its interpretation could not be given other than in a completely different sense to that which applied in 1789,[97] the Constitutional Council stated that:

> «Taking into account that if it is true that after 1789 and up to the present, the aims and conditions of the exercise of the right to property have undergone an evolution characterized both, by a notable extension of its application to new individual fields and by limits imposed by general interests, the principles themselves expressed in the Declaration of Rights of Man have complete constitutional value, particularly regarding the fundamental character of the right to property, the conservation of which constitutes one of the aims of

---

94 M. CAPPELLETTI, «El formidable problema ...», *loc. cit.*, p. 78.

95 347 U.S. 483 (1954). See the text in S.I. KUTLER (ed.) *op.cit.*, p. 550.

96 See in L. FAVOREU et L. PHILIP, *Les grandes décisions ..., cit.*, p. 525-562.

97 L. FAVOREU, *Le contrôle juridictionnel des lois et sa légitimité..., cit.*, p. 32.

political society, and located on the same rank as liberty, security and resistance to oppression, and also regarding the guarantees given to the holders of that right and the prerogatives of public power».[98]

In this way, the Constitutional Council not only created constitutional right by giving the 1789 Declaration constitutional rank and value, but also adapted the «sacred» right to property established two hundred years ago, to the limitable right of our times, although its conservation led to the declaration by the Constitutional Council of certain articles in the Nationalization act, as unconstitutional.

Anyway, what is certain today is that in all constitutional systems with written constitutions, the principle of constitutional supremacy exists so that constitutions are supreme laws, whose norms prevail over all others in a given legal order; and as we have said, this principle of the supremacy of the constitution applies not only to its written articles, but also to non-written norms that can be deduced from the constitution by constitutional judges, as forming the superior values that lay at the foundation of a given society and of its political system.

Of course, the principle of the supremacy of the constitution would be a dead letter if the constitutional system did not provide for a whole set of constitutional guarantees to give effectiveness to the said constitutional supremacy. One of these guarantees is precisely, judicial review, that is to say, the powers given to judges - ordinary judges or special constitutional courts- to control the constitutionality of legislation and of all other state acts.

III. THE JUDICIAL GUARANTEE OF THE CONSTITUTION

One of the basic elements of the state submitted to law in systems with written constitutions is the principle of the supremacy of the constitution over all other norms in the legal order and over all state acts. Therefore, the supremacy of the constitution itself, being the foundation of the state and the basis of the whole legal order, implies that acts of Parliament and of the other organs of the state, cannot be contrary to the rules embodied in the constitution.

However, this supremacy also implies not only submission to the procedural and organic rules established in the constitution, but also the respect of the fundamental rights of individuals contained therein. As we have seen, modern constitutions contain both an organic and a dogmatic part. The former refers to the organization of the state, the distribution and separation of powers and the procedural rules for its functioning. The latter refers to the fundamental rights of individuals and to the limits imposed on state organs regarding such rights. This implies, for instance, in relation to the legislative organ, not only the need to respect the rules of distribution of power, so as not to invade the powers assigned to the executive or judicial organs, but also to act in accordance with the procedural rules established in the constitution for the sanctioning of statutes. But it also implies that the legislator, when approving any statute, cannot in any way violate the fundamental rights guaranteed in the constitution.

Therefore, regarding its supremacy, the constitution must not only be seen as an organic and procedural rule, but also as a substantive rule. Therefore, for instance,

---

[98] L. FAVOREU et L. PHILIP, *Les grandes décisions...*, p. 526. *Cf.* L. FAVOREU, «Les décisions du Conseil Constitutionnel dans l'affaire des nationalisations», *loc. cit.*, p. 406.

a statute could be unconstitutional not only because procedural irregularities have taken place during its formation, but also when its contents are contrary to the principles established in the constitution regarding the rights of individuals. Then unconstitutionality could be not only formal, but also substantive.[99]

But the supremacy of the constitution in itself would be juridically imperfect if there were no specially established guarantees to protect the constitution against unconstitutional acts of the state or against any breach in the constitutional order. Constitutional supremacy would mean nothing if there were no particular means of protection of the constitution, established namely in the organic and procedural rules contained in its norms and in the fundamental rights enumerated in its dogmatic part.

1. Judicial Review and the End of Parliamentary Absolutism

Two types of guarantees of the supremacy of the constitution can be distinguished: the political and the judicial guarantee. In general, the political guarantee of the constitution is exercised by the supreme representative political organ of the state and is commonly adopted in legal systems where an extreme interpretation of the principle of the separation of powers or at the other extreme the principle of the unity of state powers prevails. This was the traditional solution in France up to the establishment of the Constitutional Council in the 1958 constitution, where the National Assembly was the only state power that could control the constitutionality of legislation; and it is the solution in almost all socialist countries, where the supreme representative political organ is the only one that can control the constitutionality of legislation.

Obviously, this system identifies the controlled organs with the organs of control,[100] and has been criticized in the socialist world, as being an inconvenient system for the protection of the constitution, or at least a system with an «insufficient suitability».[101]

As we mentioned, the argument in favor of this kind of means for the protection of the constitution is based on the principle of the unity of state power and on the rejection of the principle of separation of powers that characterizes the public law system in socialist countries, which implies the supremacy power of the representative political organ of the state. Therefore, the logical consequence of this supremacy is the exclusion of the possibility of giving the power to control the constitutionality of laws to any other organ, and to consider any control that could be exercised by any other organ of the state different to the representative supreme one, illegitimate including the judicial organ.[102]

Nevertheless, three of the socialist countries, Yugoslavia, Czechoslovakia and Poland, have established a judicial guarantee of the constitution, assigning the power

---

99 H. KELSEN, «La garantie juridictionelle de la constitution (La Justice constitutionnelle)», *Revue du droit public et de la science polotique an France et à l'étranger*, J. XLV, Paris 1928, p. 206.

100 P. BISCARETTI DI RUFFIA, «Les Constitutions européenes: notions introductives» in P. Biscaretti di Ruffia and S. ROZMARYN, *La constitution comme loi fondamentale dans les Etats de l'Europe occidentale et dans les Etats socialistes*, Torino 1966, p. 70.

101 P. NIKOLIC, *Le contrôle juridictionnel des lois et sa légitimité. (Developnements récents dans les pays socialistes)*, Rapport, Association Internationale des Sciences Juridiques, Uppsala 1984 (mineo), p. 14. Also published in L. FAVOREU and J.A. JOLOWICZ (ed.), *Le contrôle juridictionnel des lois. Légitimité, effectivité et développements récents*, Paris 1986, p. 71-115.

102 *Idem.*, p. 17.

of control of the constitutionality of legislation to special constitutional courts, based on the principle of the supremacy of the constitution and accepting, undoubtedly, a principle of separation of state powers.[103]

On the other hand, in systems with an extreme interpretation of the separation of powers or where the principle of the supremacy of Parliament still prevails, no system of judicial control of the constitutionality of legislation can, of course, be accepted. As we mentioned before, that was the situation in continental Europe, after the French Revolution and up to recent years, and is still the situation in the United Kingdom. In Europe, the monarchical regime and the principle of representation developed through the elected legislator, led to the adoption of the principle of the supremacy of Parliament over other state powers and, consequently, to the principle of the primacy of laws or acts of Parliament over other legal rules.

During the last century, in effect, it was inconceivable to the concept of liberalism, that there could be any deviation from the principle of the supremacy of the law as the expression of the general will; and this principle made it simply unthinkable, that Parliament could ever commit an error with respect to the constitution. The enemy of the constitution, in the liberal framework of the last century, was really the executive -the monarch- who was tempted to put his individual will before that of the people, as expressed in Parliament. Thus, the possibility that Parliament could be in error or act mistakenly was not conceivable.

This myth of the assembly as the absolute expression of the general will of the people, in which the certain and infallible collective spirit reposes, was without doubt, a historical product of French Jacobinism.

In effect it was Jacobinism, based on the absolute representative principle of the general will, which led to the dogma of parliamentary sovereignty in France. According to this principle, all power over the Assembly was resolutely proscribed and, of course, the judiciary power was a simple executive instrument of the laws passed by the Assembly, with absolutely no liberty even to interpret the laws. Thus, the well-known figure of the *référé législatif* according to which judges were obliged to consult the National Assembly when they had doubts about the interpretation of a Statute.[104]

This limitation was based on the purest tradition of the thoughts of Montesquieu, who considered the national judges, «... as no more than the mouth that pronounces the words of the law, mere passive beings, incapable of moderating either its force or rigor»;[105] and was expressly established in the well known Statute of 16-24 August 1790 referred to the judiciary organization. Article 10 of this law regulated the separation between Legislative and judicial power, by saying that, «the courts could not take part directly or indirectly in the exercise of legislative power, neither prevent nor suspend the execution of acts of the legislative body...»

---

103 P. NIKOLIC said in its Raport to the Uppsala Coloquium that the introduction of this judicial control of the constitutionality of legislation in some socialist countries does not mean the introduction of important elements of the separation of powers in the assambly's government system (*doc. cit.*, p. 19), but in explaining the suitables of that judicial control he said that it is exercise by an authority known and recognised *separately* and *different* from the legislative power, because it is precisely its legislative activity the one that it must control and evaluate (*doc.cit.*, p. 21).

104 E. GARCÍA DE ENTERRÍA, *La Constitución como norma y el Tribunal Constitucional*, Madrid 1981, p. 164.

105 Quoted by Ch. H. MCILWAIN, *The High Court of Parliament and its Supremacy*, Yale 1910, p. 323.

adding in article 12 that the Courts «could not make regulations, but they must always address themselves to the legislative body when they think it necessary to interpret a Statute or to make a new one».[106] The *référé législatif* then was the instrument of the legislative body for interpreting the laws, which could not even be done by the judges.

Therefore, it was precisely this Jacobin principle of the assembly, a product of the French Revolution, which maintained the negation of the legitimacy of the courts to be able to annul the normative products of the assembly for a long time; and in the United Kingdom it is precisely the same principle of the sovereignty of Parliament a product of the glorious Revolution of 1688, which actually prevents the courts from controlling the constitutionality of legislation. The judges, in accordance with this principle must apply laws and of course, interpret them, but they are not to control them because acts of the legislative body are the expression of the sovereign will of the people.

In this traditional framework of the separation of powers, a system of judicial review of the constitutionality of laws was considered a violation of the principle of parliamentary sovereignty, based on the pre-eminence of the legislative power over other state powers. This was because Parliament was constituted by the representatives of the people who, as such, in the representative democratic state represented the sovereign. Through this approach, any intervention by a constitutional body to limit the autonomy of the supreme representative organ of the state was considered inadmissible, and therefore, legislation could only be controlled by that supreme representative organ.

In any case, it is clear that this principle of popular sovereignty expressed in modern constitutions today as the basic dogma of the democratic *État de droit* is a political principle which refers to the constituent power of the state, represented in all the constituted bodies of the state, and not to the power of one or other of the constituted bodies which exercise public power. It thus cannot lead to a discussion about the relative sovereignty of the constituted state bodies, since all the bodies of the state are the product of the sovereign, and are its representatives. Thus, it makes no sense today to preach the sovereignty of Parliament, to reject a mechanism, which guarantees the constitution to which Parliament is also subject.

To reinforce the argument in another way, it should not be forgotten that in presidential and Parliamentary democratic systems, the president of the republic or the head of government are designated by popular election and are thus also a product of the sovereignty of the people, just as Parliament is. From the moment the constitution attributes sovereignty to the people, it is definitely clear that this quality cannot be affirmed in one body of the state with respect to another; therefore, all the powers of state and all the bodies which carry them out find their legitimacy in the people. Thus, no constitutional body is or can be really sovereign, not even the Chambers of Parliament,[107] and all of them must be submitted to the constitution.

Furthermore, it should not be forgotten that in contemporary democracies, political and social forces produce a greater relativity in the constitutional functions of the state bodies, converting Parliament into a forum for the political parties and

---

106 Quoted by E. García de Enterría, *op. cit.*, p. 164, note 88.

107 P. Lucas Murillo de la Cueva, «El examen de la constitucionalidad de las leyes y la soberanía parlamentaria», *Revista de estudios políticos*, 7, Madrid 1979, p. 212.

subjecting the government to necessary negotiations with them and with trade unions and pressure groups. On many occasions, this primacy of the parties has erased the principle of the separation of powers and has conversely led to its factual concentration in the hands of the government and or those of the parties themselves. Thus, there can be no doubt about the need to adopt measures which serve to guide the activities of state bodies and those of the parties themselves, within constitutional channels.[108]

In any case, exception being made of the United Kingdom, this very myth of parliamentary sovereignty was broken in Europe. Review of constitutionality really appeared in Europe after the great crisis brought about by the First World War and by the tragedies that political irrationality caused throughout Europe. This led both to the transformation of the constitution into a normative code that could be directly applicable and enforceable, and to the establishment of a constitutional body for constitutional justice, which would ensure the supremacy of the constitution not only over the executive power which, apart from this, was controlled by another type of tribunal -but basically over Parliament; that is to say, over legislative acts, and particularly, the laws. Consequently, the sovereignty of Parliament ceased to be above justice, and judicial review of constitutionality was to become the instrument governing the subjection of Parliament to the constitution when, as a result of occasional majorities, the balance was upset among state powers, or in the rationality of political and social relations themselves. In fact, the terrible lessons learnt from the abuses of the Nazi and Fascist regimes in Europe, doubtlessly brought about a complete change in the existing myths and theories in Europe regarding the infallibility of the law. Thus, as Professor Favoreu pointed out, the Rousseaunian myth of the infallibility of the law and, thus, of Parliament which expresses the general will, began to collapse, and the celebrated formula, according to which the legislator could do no wrong, began to be re-examined.[109]

This European experience generated a skeptical wisdom regarding Parliaments and representativeness, and as Professor Mauro Cappelletti said, «it was realized that there was too much illusion in the Liberal democratic theory» in the sense that most often the reality was far from the myth of the supremacy of the peoples will and that «Parliaments and their legislation, too, would become instruments of despotic regimes; and that majorities could themselves be brutally oppressive».[110] In fact, the legislators of Weimar Germany and Mussolini's Italy failed as guarantors of freedom. On the contrary, they became the instruments of circumstantial majorities for consolidating totalitarian regimes. Consequently, these two countries learnt from experience and in their new post-war constitutions they not only established entrenched fundamental values, freedoms and rights out of the reach of Parliament, but adopted the principle of the judicial review of constitutionality of laws, as it was previously established in the Austrian system in the 1920's.

---

108 *Idem*, p. 212.

109 L. FAVOREU, *Le contrôle juridictionnel des lois et sa légitimité. Développements récents en Europe occidentale*. Association Internationale des Sciences Juridiques. Colloque d'Uppsala 1984 (mineo), p. 22. Published as «Actualité et légitimité du contrôle juridictionnel des lois en Europe Occidentale», in *Revue du droit public et de la science politique en France et à l'étranger*, Paris 1984 (5), p. 1147 and 1201. Also published in L. FAVOREU and J.A. JOLOWICZ (ed.), *Le contrôle juridictionel des lois. Légitimité, effectivité et developments récents*, Paris 1986, p. 17-68.

110 M. CAPPELLETTI, *Judicial Review of Legislation and its Legitimacy. Recent Developments*, General Report. International Association of Legal Science Colloquium, Uppsala 1982, (mimeo), p. 19. Also published in L. FAVOREU and J.A. JOLOWICZ (ed.), *Le contrôle juridictionnel des lois... cit.*, p. 285-300.

In this way, the awareness that it was necessary to protect liberties not only from the executive, but also from the legislative grew. As Professor Jean Rivero described,

> «The old idea that marked the liberal 19th century, that of the protection of liberty *by the law*, tended to be substituted by the experimental idea of the need of protection of liberties *against the law*. This evolution made the extraordinary phenomenon of the acceptance of a superior authority to the Legislator itself, of an authority in charge to impose upon the Legislator the respect of the constitution possible».[111]

Thus, European continental countries adopted the review of the constitutionality of laws following a different path from that of the North American system, adopting the principle of judicial review for other reasons. According to what Professor Louis Favoreu said, the European phenomenon was less in response to a problem of legal logic -that is, in the *Marbury v. Madison* tradition, that a law contrary to the constitution could not be applied- than to a political logic. It was the fear of oppression by a parliamentary majority, which was decisive in the change in the position of the continental European countries regarding the review of the constitutionality of laws.[112]

This political logic of judicial review can also be found in the fact that the myth of representativeness of the general will as expressed by those elected, has broken down in many countries, particularly because the legislative body is frequently made up of men chosen by the political parties, and who definitely represent these parties, not being really, in fact, representatives of the general will.

Anyway, the idea that certain number of fundamental values should be established beyond the reach of a circumstantial or temporary majority, is what led, in-one way or another, to the transfer of the traditional sacredness of the law to the constitution.

Thus, it was, after the Second World War, that the European continental countries «rediscovered the constitution as a text of juridical character»[113] or rather, when they discovered the true fundamental nature of the constitution as a higher and supreme law, applicable to all state organs and enforceable by the courts. In the words of Professor Mauro Cappelletti, what is really new in modern constitutionalism.

> «Is the serious attempt to conceive the constitution not as a mere guideline of a political, moral, or philosophical nature, but as a real law, itself a positive and binding law although of a superior, more permanent nature than ordinary positive legislation».[114]

And of course, this positive and superior law was to be applied to the legislator as well as to all the state organs. The Constitutional Council in France expressly declared that in the well-known Nationalization decision of 16 January 1982, which stated that:

---

[111] J. RIVERO, «Rapport de Synthese» in L. FAVOREU (ed.), *Cours constitutionnelles européenes et droit fondamentaux*, Aix-en-Provence 1982, p. 519.

[112] L. FAVOREU, *Le contrôle juridictionnel..., doc. cit.*, p. 22.

[113] L. FAVOREU, *Le contrôle juridictionnel..., doc.cit.*, p. 23.

[114] M. CAPPELLETTI, *doc. cit.*, p. 20.

«Considering that if article 34 of the constitution places «the nationalisation of companies and its transfer from .the public to the private sector», in the sphere of the statute, that disposition as well as the one that assigns the role of determining the fundamental principles of the right to property, to the statute, does not excuse the legislator, when exercising its powers, from the respect of the principles and rules of constitutional value that are imposed upon all state organs».[115]

Professor Louis Favoreu, when referring to this decision of the Constitutional Council qualified it as a «fundamental affirmation of the complete realization of the *État de droit* in France» comparing it to the previous situation in which the legislator «in fact escaped, if not legally, from the submission to a superior rule».[116]

Therefore, the supremacy of the constitution over Parliament marked the end of Parliamentary absolutism,[117] transformed the old concept of parliamentary sovereignty and led the way to constitutional review in France through the Constitutional Council, even though in a limited way and previously in a more complete way in other countries in continental Europe like Austria, Germany and Italy.

Another factor that contributed to the appearance of mechanisms for judicial review of the constitutionality of laws was the transformation of the very notion of «law» in the sense of an act of Parliament or statute. In fact, statutes -the work of the legislator, once the expression of the general will in the tradition of the XIX century- came to be seen, with the evolution of parliamentary systems, as acts adopted by both the parliamentary majority and the government, through a system of connecting vessels, through the political parties. In this form, the statutes are not necessarily the expression of the general will, approved by a solid and mythical majority, but as Professor Jean Rivero said, they are «no more than the expression of the governmental will approved by a solidarian majority».[118] Moreover, with the evolution of the tasks of the state, the law has tended to become a more technical product, whose content as a result, frequently even escapes the effective control of Parliament, since it is the technocrats within the administration, who draw it up and settle its real content, without effective participation of members of Parliament. Therefore, judicial review is an effective tool to control the constitutionality of such acts of Parliament or statutes that are the expression of governmental will, rather than the expression of the general will.

Anyway, the supremacy of the constitution and its enforceable character over the legislative body has led to the adoption of judicial rather than political guarantees of the constitution, the latter being proven ineffective as the French example of the Conservative Senates (*Sénat Conservateur*) of the 1799 and 1852 constitution showed. Constitutions commonly established a distribution of state powers among the various state organs, and basically, assigned fundamental powers to the legislative body, which used to be considered unable to do wrong, as the expression of the general will. Therefore, politically speaking, its self control is really an illusion.

---

[115] See in L. FAVOREU and L. PHILIP, *Les grandes décisions du Conseil Constitutionnel*, Paris 1984, p. 527. See also L. FAVOREU, «Les decision du Conceil Constitutionnel dans l'affaire des nationalisations», *Revue du droit public et de la science politique en France et à l'étranger*, 1962, p. 400.

[116] L. FAVOREU, «Les decisions du Conceil Constitutionnel...», *doc. cit.*, p. 400.

[117] J. RIVERO «Fin d'un absolutism», *Pouvoirs*, 13, Paris.1980, pp. 5-15.

[118] J. RIVERO «Rapport de synthesè», *doc. cit*, p. 519.

But constitutions also establish fundamental rights of individuals and minorities even against majoritarian will; hence, as Professor Cappelletti correctly said, «no effective system of review can be entrusted to the electorate or to persons and organs dependent on and strictly accountable to, the majority's will»[119] that is to say to the representative legislator itself.

Therefore, contrary to the political systems of review of the constitutionality of legislation, the common trend of contemporary constitutionalism in constitutional systems with written constitutions is the existence of judicial means of protection of the constitution, through the assignment of effective powers of judicial control of the constitutionality of legislation to the courts, either ordinary or special constitutional courts.

2. Judicial review and its legitimacy

Thus one of the traditional powers of the state, the judicial power, considered the «least dangerous» of all state powers[120] and in fact, being the politically less dangerous of the state organs, has been given the power to defend the constitution and to control the constitutionality of legislation. This has, of course, led to the endless discussion of what Professor Cappelletti called «the mighty problem of judicial review», that is to say, the discussion related to the legitimate or illegitimate power given to state organs that are not responsible to the people, to control the acts of those who, on the contrary, are politically responsible,[121] or from another angle, the democratic or non-democratic character of judicial review.[122]

Of course, the discussions have been developed either to justify the absence of judicial review in systems in which the sovereignty of Parliament prevails, or to criticized judicial review when judges have shown an outstanding activism in the adaptation of the constitution, in creating non-written constitutional rules or in attributing constitutional character to certain rules. In this context, judicial review has been considered illegitimate because it is believed that non-elected bodies must not control elected bodies of the state, and that non-elected state bodies must not determine which norm of the state is law, that is to say, which is constitutional or unconstitutional.

We think that this really is an abstract and Byzantine discussion, and that it will remain endless, mainly because it is orientated as if there were a problem of abstract legitimacy of judicial review that could be resolved in an abstract way, identifying democracy with sole representativeness. The problems of judicial review or of the powers assigned to judges to control the constitutionality of legislation cannot be explained or criticized on the grounds of legitimacy or illegitimacy considering the democratic principle as sole representativeness. Democracy does not exhaust itself in representativeness because it is as well, above all, a way of living, in which individual liberty and fundamental human rights are to be respected to a point that we can say that no effective judicial review of constitutionality is

---

[119] M. CAPPELLETTI, *doc. cit*, p. 23.

[120] A. BICKEL, *The Least Dangerous Branch. The Supreme Court at the Bar of Politics*, Indianapolis 1962.

[121] M. CAPPELLETTI, «El formidable problema del control judicial y la contribución del análisis comparado», *Revista de estudios políticos*, 13, Madrid 1980, p. 61-103 ('The Mighty Problem' of Judicial Review and the contribution of comparative analysis», *Southern California Law Review*, 1980, p. 409).

[122] M. CAPPELLETTI, *Judicial Review of Legislation and its Legitimacy...*, *doc. cit*, pp. 24-32.

possible in undemocratic regimes,[123] particularly because in such regimes there cannot be effective independence of judges; and «it is clear that judicial review cannot be practiced efficiently where the Judiciary has no guarantee of its independence».[124]

That is also why in most European countries it has been noted that after periods of dictatorship, systems of judicial review of constitutionality have been established, as was the case of Germany, Italy, Spain and Portugal.[125]

Therefore, in a representative and democratic regime, the power attributed to judges to control the deviations of the legislative body and the infringements by the representative body of fundamental rights is absolutely democratic and legitimate.[126] As Professor Jean Rivero stated in his final report to the 1981 International Colloquium of Aix-en-Provence on the protection of fundamental rights by constitutional courts in Europe:

> «I think that the (judicial constitutional) control marks progress, in the sense that democracy is not only a way of attribution of power, but also a way of exercising it. And I think that all that reinforces the fundamental liberties of citizens goes along with the democratic sense».[127]

Along this same line of thought, Professor Eduardo García de Enterría referring to constitutional liberties and fundamental rights as limits imposed on state powers, stated:

> «If the constitution established them, it is obvious that an occasional parliamentary majority who ignore or infringe them, is very far from being legitimate to do so based on the majoritarian argument, and is rather revealing its abuse of power and its possible attempts at exclusion of minorities. The protective function of the Constitutional Tribunal confronting that abuse, annulling the legislative acts which make an attempt on the liberty of a few or all citizens, is the only effective instrument against infringement; there is no other possible alternative if one prefers to have an effective guarantee of liberty, that could make it more than simply rhetoric in a constitutional document».[128]

This was also the main argument put forward by Hans Kelsen in his very important article published in the French *Revue du Droit Public et de la Science Politique en France et a l'étrangèr* in 1928, when arguing against the majoritarian argument. He said:

---

123 «An efficient system of judicial review is totally incompatible with any antilibertarian, absolute, dictatorial regime, as is ample proven by historical experience and comparative study» M. CAPPELLETTI, *Judicial Review of Legislation and its legitimacy..., loc. cit.*, p. 11.

124 J. CARPIZO and H. FIX-ZAMUDIO, *The Necessity for and the Legitimacy of the Judicial Review of the Constitutionality of the Laws in Latin America, Recent Development*, International Association of Legal Sciences. Uppsala Colloquium 1984 (mimeo), p. 22. Published in spanish «La necesidad y la legitimidad de la revisión judicial en América Latina. Desarrollo reciente», *Boletín mexicano de derecho comparado*, 52, 1985, pp. 31-64. Also published in L. FAVOREU and J.A. JOLOWICZ (ed.), *Le contrôle juridictionnel des lois..., cit.*, pp. 119-151.

125 L. FAVOREU, *Le contrôle juridictionnel des lois et sa légitimité..., doc. cit.*, p. 24. *Cf.* P. DE VEGA GARCÍA, «Jurisdicción Constitucional y Crisis de la Constitución», *Revista de estudios políticos*, 7, Madrid 1979, p. 108.

126 E.V. ROSTOW «The Democratic Character of Judicial Review», *Harvard Law Review*, 193, 1952.

127 J. RIVERO «Rapport de Synthese», *loc. cit.*, p. 525-526. *Cf.* M. CAPPELLETTI, *Judicial Review of Legislation and its Legitimacy..., doc. cit*, p. 32.

128 E. GARCÍA DE ENTERRÍA, *op. cit.*, p. 190.

«If one sees the essence of democracy, not in the all-powerful majority, but in the constant compromises between the groups represented in Parliament by the majority and the minority, and consequently in the social peace, constitutional justice appears as a means particularly proper for the achievement of this idea. The simple threat of an action to be brought before the Constitutional Court can be an adequate instrument in the hands of the minorities for preventing unconstitutional violations of juridically protected interests by the majority, and consequently being able to oppose the majority dictatorship, which is not less dangerous to social peace than the minority one».[129]

But democratic legitimacy of judicial review does not arise only through judicial protection of fundamental rights, but also through the protection of the organic part of the constitution, that is to say, through the control of the systems of distribution of powers adopted in the constitution.

In this respect, we must point out that the problem of legitimacy has never been posed regarding the vertical distribution of state powers in the politically decentralized or federal systems; on the contrary, judicial review is essentially and closely related to federalism.[130]

That is why the form of the state, and particularly federalism, as a vertical form of distribution of power, is among the most important political principles that have led to the establishment of judicial review of legislation and upheld its justification in contemporary constitutional law.

Federalism requires the affirmation of certain degree of supremacy for federal laws with regard to local, regional or state laws; and similarly, with regard to the sphere of powers attributed to them, according to the system adopted for the vertical distribution of power. Thus, it is not by chance that those countries with federal form of state and with politically decentralized state organization were among the first to establish judicial review of the constitutionality of legislation. This happened in the United States of America and in all the federal states of Latin America in the last century. It also happened in Europe, in Germany, which has a federal form of state, and in the decentralized forms of the Italian regional state and the Spanish Autonomous Communities state.

In all these cases, it is evident that the need for judicial review or the establishment of a constitutional court is justified by the demand for a constitutional body, which could settle conflicts of powers between the national and regional bodies. One of the fundamental tasks of the constitutional courts in Austria, Germany, Italy and Spain, for example, is precisely the resolution of conflicts between the levels of the national state and the member states of the Federation, or the political regions, or the Autonomous Communities, according to the country, and similarly, conflicts that may arise between the regions or states themselves, or between them and the national level. Thus, it is political decentralization, both in the federal states and in the so-called regional state that has encouraged the appearance and consolidation of constitutional tribunals responsible precisely for the function of constitutional review of legislation to guarantee the constitutional balance of the state and the territorial bodies. That is why, in federal states, or in politically

[129] H. Kelsen, *loc. cit.*, p. 253.
[130] W.J. Wagner, *The Federal States and their Judiciary*, The Hague 1959, p. 85.

decentralized states there are no doubts about the legitimacy of judicial review of constitutionality, and no debate has arisen on the matter, except to justify its existence and necessity.[131]

Therefore, the problems of legitimacy of judicial review of constitutionality are not referred to the guarantee of the constitution concerning federalism or political decentralization or to the guarantee of the fundamental rights of the individual. These constitute limitations on legislative power in reference to which judicial control is exercised without discussion.[132]

Nevertheless, the same cannot be said about the horizontal distribution or separation of powers. Even though it also imposes limitations on the legislative power, the acceptance of judicial review of the constitutionality of legislation has here prompted discussions over its legitimacy, based, particularly, on the notion of supremacy of Parliament over the other state powers. But on the other hand, it has given fundamental arguments in favor of judicial review, precisely, as the counter-weight's essential element, which should be established among the various state powers to guarantee the constitution.

In effect, the separation of powers as a consequence of the horizontal distribution of state powers among the state organs essentially requires an independent mechanism to guarantee the organic part of the constitution. This system of control is essential to the distribution of power particularly between the legislative and the executive power. Between them it is necessary to establish a third counterweight system so as to maintain the equilibrium that the constitution lays down. Thus, the powers granted to the judicial organs to control the constitutionality and legality of administrative actions, accepted without debate has been essentially related to the *État de droit*, as well as to control the constitutionality of legislation.

However, the tradition of the principles of Parliamentary supremacy on the one hand, and of separation of powers on the other, have been so powerful in Europe, that these have led to impeding ordinary judicial bodies from any possibility of judging the constitutionality of legislation, even though judicial review of legislation has been developed, but assigned to new constitutional organs. In this manner, the need for judicial review of legislation as a guarantee of the constitution has been adjusted to the principle of separation of powers that has traditionally considered any attempt to control the constitutionality of legislation an inadmissible intrusion by the judicial body in the sphere of the legislator.

It has been this confrontation between the need for constitutional judicial review as a guarantee or means of protection of the constitution and the principle of separation of powers that in continental Europe led to the creation of special constitutional bodies with the particular and special jurisdictional task of controlling

---

131 In this sense, Hans KELSEN said in 1928 that «it is in Federal States where the constitutional justice aquiered the most considerable importance. It is not excesive to affirm that the political idea of the Federal State is not entirily realized without the institution of a constitutional Tribunal», *loc. cit.*, p. 24. *Cf.* L. FAVOREU, *Le contrôle juridistionnel des lois et sa légitimité...*, *doc. cit.*, p. 35.

132 *Cf.* B.O. NWABUEZE, *Judicial Control of Legislative Action and its Legitimacy-Recent Developments*. African Regional Report. International Association of Legal Sciences. Uppsala Colloquium, 1984, (mimeo) p. 23. Also published in L. FAVOREU and J.A. JOLOWICZ (ed.), *Le contrôle juridictionnel des lois...*, *cit.*, p. 193-222.

the constitutionality of legislation, although not being part of the traditional structure of the Judiciary. Therefore, the solution to said confrontation has been resolved by creating new constitutional bodies above the traditional horizontal separation of powers, -equally above the legislator, the executive and the courts- to ensure the supremacy of the constitution with respect to them all.

The «Austrian System» of judicial review or the «European model» as it has also been qualified[133] is characterized by the fact that constitutional justice has been attributed to a constitutional body organized outside ordinary judicial organization, that is to say, outside the ordinary courts, and thus not integrated within the general structure of the Judiciary. The members of the constitutional tribunal, court or council do not become so by way of a judicial career, but rather are appointed, basically by political bodies, and in particular, by the Parliament and the executive. This system has given rise to a special constitutional organ, which, despite it's not being integrated within the Judiciary, resolves legal controversies according to the law, and thus pursues a proper jurisdictional activity.

These constitutional courts, councils or tribunals have been considered the «supreme interpreters of the constitution» as the Spanish Constitutional Tribunal Organic law qualified it[134] or as the «custodian of the constitution».[135] Professor Eduardo García de Enterría, currently (1985) judge in the European Court of Human Rights, referring to the Spanish Constitutional Tribunal, qualified it as a «commissioner of the Constituent power to sustain the constitution and to maintain all the constitutional organ in their strict quality of constituted powers»,[136] and the former president of the same Spanish Constitutional Tribunal Professor Manuel García Pelayo considered it «as a constitutional organ, established and structured directly in the constitution», and that:

> «As regulator of the constitutionality, of the state action, it is the one called upon to give full existence to the *Estado de derecho* and to ensure the validity of the distribution of powers established in the constitution, both essential components in our times of the true Constitutional state».[137]

In this sense and established as constitutional organs separately regarding the traditional legislative, executive and judicial organs, the European constitutional courts are conceived as being the supreme guarantor of the distribution of power in its various senses we have referred to.[138]

First of all, there is the distribution of the sphere of state power and the sphere of society; that is to say, between the powers of the state and the rights and liberties of individuals and groups. This principle of distribution of powers, expressly established in constitutions when they guarantee the rights and liberties of citizens must, moreover, be jurisdictionally guaranteed. This power of guaranteeing fundamental rights is frequently a power given to ordinary tribunals as well as to constitutional courts by means of «writs for protection» (*amparo*). In such cases, the

---

133 M. CAPPELLETTI, *Judicial Review of Legislation and its Legitimacy...*, p. 26; L. FAVOREU, «Actualité et légitimité du contrôle juridictionnel des lois en Europe occidental», *loc. cit.*, p. 1149.

134 Art. 1. Ley Orgánica del Tribunal Constitucional, Oct. 1979, *Boletín Oficial del Estado*, Nº 239.

135 G. LEIBHOLZ, *Problemas fundamentales de la democracia*, Madrid 1971, p. 148.

136 E. GARCÍA DE ENTERRÍA, *op. cit.*, p. 198.

137 E. GARCÍA PELAYO, «El Status del Tribunal Constitucional», in *Revista española de derecho constitucional*, 1, Madrid 1981, p. 15.

138 *Cf.* M. GARCÍA PELAYO, *loc. cit*, p. 20.

courts are the guardians of the limits on the power of the state imposed by the constitution in relation to the respect for fundamental individual rights and liberties.

In the second place, there is the distinction between the constituent power and the constituted power. The effectiveness of this division is not limited to the moment only when the constitution is adopted, but should be demonstrated throughout its validity, as a result of its very existence. The function of constitutional justice is precisely that of guaranteeing that the constituted powers act within limits established by the constituent power, as set down in the constitution. It is thus the aim of the constitutional court to be the custodian of the primacy of the constituent power over the constituted power. Thus, even in cases of preventive review of constitutionality, when a collision arises between a norm and the constitution, either the norm is not to be sanctioned, or a constitutional reform must take place.

The third system of distribution of power is the horizontal division, that is to say, its distribution among constitutional bodies of the same constitutional rank. This division is also guaranteed by the constitutional courts, both at the level of the central powers of the state, and at other territorial levels. In this respect, at the level of the constitutional bodies of the state, for example, it is the constitutional court that is called upon to resolve conflicts of powers between, for example, the Government and Congress, or between the Chamber of Deputies and the Senate, or between other bodies of constitutional rank. In the horizontal distribution of power at lower territorial levels, the constitutional tribunal must also resolve conflicts that arise between the authorities at those levels.

The fourth aspect of the division of power is the vertical division, which consists in the distribution of powers among the various political decentralized levels of the state: the powers of the national state; those at intermediate level, whether these be federal member states or autonomous regions or communities of the regional states; and thirdly, those at the municipal or local level. In these cases, the state structured by a system of vertical distribution of powers must ensure that the various legislative provisions at the different levels do not invade the sphere of power of other levels. For example, there should be no invasion of the powers of the communities or regions by the national level or of those of the member states of a federation, and vice-versa. The same holds good for the municipal level: the constitutional court is precisely the body that must ensure that the municipal powers that are normally guaranteed in the constitutions or by acts issued at national or intermediate levels are not to be invaded.

Thus, the fundamental reason for justifying the establishment of constitutional court in continental Europe relates to the solution of conflicts between state bodies, since within the constitutional organization, the constitutional court is the body in a position to prevent the invasion of the powers of others by one constitutional power, and objectively to ensure the maintenance of the balance that the constitution has established in the separation of powers.

In this way, the sharing of power among the national powers -for example, between Parliament and Government- and also the system of the distribution of powers among the powers in a vertical sense by the process of political decentralization -whether this be federalism, or regionalism or purely and simply, any system of local political decentralization- all these demand that there be a body to maintain a balance between these various powers, and this, without doubt, should be either a constitutional court or the supreme court of a given country.

But in the case of constitutional courts even though created as constitutional organs, independent and separate from the traditional legislative, executive and judicial organs of the state, and particularly, not within the organization of the Judiciary, they always decide upon constitutional conflict by means of a jurisdictional action. Therefore, constitutional courts, as is the case of ordinary courts on the American judicial the review model or the supreme judicial court on the Latin American model, exercise constitutional justice and have a jurisdictional function.

Therefore, constitutional courts cannot be considered the «negative legislator» as Hans Kelsen considered,[139] but rather as constitutional organs with a jurisdictional function.

In effect, in order to refute the objection to constitutional justice based on the principle of separation of power, Hans Kelsen argued that the constitutional tribunal when annulling an act of Parliament, did not exercise jurisdictional activity but a negative legislative activity. He said:

> «To annul a Statute, is to establish a general norm, because the annulment of a Statute has the same general character of its adoption, being, we can say, the same adoption but with a negative sign, and consequently in itself, a legislative function».[140]

In reality, the constitutional court when annulling a statute does not repeal it, and the annulment it can pronounce is not made based on discretionary powers but on legal criteria, applying a superior rule, the constitution, thus in no way does it exercise a legislative function.[141]

Its function is jurisdictional as is that assigned to the ordinary court[142] but characterized as being a guarantee of the constitution. And, if it is true that constitutional judges in many cases decide political issues when considering the constitutionality of legislative acts, they do so by legal methods and criteria, in a process initiated by a party with the required standing. And even in cases in which constitutional justice allows the possibility of exercising a popular action[143] to obtain a decision upon the unconstitutionality of a law by the Supreme Court, as is the case in Venezuela and Colombia, the judicial activity is developed by a process in which the Supreme Court decides a judicial controversy, although there are no proper parties in the traditional procedural law sense.

Nevertheless, the court must only act on the formal instance of or at the request of a person whose rights or interests are infringed by the particular law and cannot decide on its own initiative. Therefore, the role of a constitutional judge can in no way be considered a legislative function, but rather jurisdictional.

Anyway, as we have said, judicial review of constitutionality both on the American or European models, is conceived as being a constitutional guarantee of the distribution and limitation of state powers established in the constitution, exercised by independent bodies either the ordinary or special constitutional judges.

---

139 H. KELSEN, *loc. cit.*, p. 226.

140 *Idem*, p. 224.

141 A. PÉREZ GORDO, *El Tribunal Constitucional y sus funciones*, Barcelona 1982, p. 41.

142 H. KELSEN, eventually, accepted this view, *loc. cit.*, p. 226.

143 *Cf.* the argument in a contrary sense of B.O. NWABUEZE, *Judicial Control of Legislative Action ..., loc. cit.*, p. 3.

Furthermore, constitutional judges are also the guarantee of the functioning of the particular system of government resulting from the way state powers are distributed, and of democracy itself. Its legitimacy lies in there.

In effect, judicial review can be considered one of the tools for ensuring the solution of political and social conflict, and therefore, for contributing to the peaceful development of democratic political activity, in resolving conflicts of a political nature. In Professor E. García de Enterría's words, judicial review is a «formidable instrument of political and social integration of society»[144] and this has proven to be so in resolving political conflicts between government and minorities, which the electorate cannot assist in resolving. As Professor L. Favoreu pointed out:

> «When the majority and the opposition conflict on important issues without having recourse to an electoral decision, it is evident that recourse to a constitutional judge to decide upon the law adopted by the majority, has the virtue of calming the debate and transforming it more serenely. In many cases, when the decision of the constitutional judge has been adopted, the controversy is extinguished».[145]

In this respect, and as an illustration of this legitimacy of judicial review, Professor Favoreu in his comparative analysis of recent development of judicial review in continental Europe stressed the political conflict that arose from the sanctioning of laws in referring to abortion. The controversy raged in every country, both in Parliament and in public, but once decisions were made on the issue by the constitutional judge, the conflict died down.[146] The same happened in France over the most important aspects of the socialist government's program once executed in the early eighties, particularly in relation to nationalization and to decentralization processes and which subsequently died down after the Constitutional Council adopted its corresponding decisions in 1982.[147]

The same happened, for example, in Spain, with the law for the Harmonisation of the Autonomous Communities. Once the constitutional tribunal resolved the conflict over the powers of the state and the Autonomous Communities in 1983, the debate declined in its intensity. [148]

Judicial review has also been a guarantee of the constitution when working as an instrument for the maintenance of political stability and continuity in democratic societies and, particularly, in parliamentary systems of government.

In fact, parliamentary systems of government are generally linked with judicial review, and in continental Europe, we can observe that in all the countries with a system of judicial review of constitutionality of legislation, a parliamentary or quasi-parliamentary regime exists. In the case of Germany, Italy and Spain in the classical way and also in the cases of France, Austria and Portugal where even though a government responsible to Parliament exists, a president elected by the people also exists. Anyway, the counterweight of the opposition to a

144 E. GARCÍA DE ENTERRÍA, *op. cit.*, p. 192.

145 L. FAVOREU, *Le contrôle juridictionnel des lois et sa légitimité, cit.*, p. 6.

146 *Idem*, p. 36.

147 L. FAVOREU, «Les decisions du Consel Constitutionnel dans l'affaire des nationalisations», *loc. cit.*, p. 377; «Décentralisation et constitution», *Revue du droit public et de la science politique en France et à l'étranger*, Paris 1982, p. 1259-1295; and L. FAVOREU (ed.), *Nationalisations et constitution*, 1982.

148 P. BON, F. MODERNE and Y. RODRÍGUEZ, *La justice constitutionnelle en Espagne*, 1984, p. 168.

strong government supported by a parliamentary majority is judicial review. As Professor Favoreu said:

«There is a certain institutional logic in the political functioning of parliamentary systems of government, to encourage the development of mechanisms of judicial review of constitutionality as a reaction against the great power of the government block».[149]

Judicial review as a guarantee of political stability and continuity in parliamentary regimes has a shown itself to be a very important instrument when lessening the effects of political changes resulting from the alternation in power, particularly when a change in the majority in Parliament and in the government happens after a few years of leadership of one political force or party. This alternation of contrasting policies has occurred in almost all countries in continental Europe over recent decades, and was of particular importance in France in the early eighties.

In a recent article concerning «The Constitutional Council and the alternance», Professor Louis Favoreu demonstrated how the French Constitutional Council, instead of being a restraint upon or an obstacle to political alternance, has been «the guarantor of the alternance»:

«The Constitutional Council has first of all, permitted the alternance through the canalization of the stream of change, ensuring its regulation; and furthermore, with its decisions has given a regularized authentic certification to the measures taken by the new majority. In the end, the legislation of the new majority has passed through some kind of filter, but once the dispositions have been filtered and sifted, its promulgation gave a definitive juridical force to the dispositions, and it is no longer possible to attack them (at least on the grounds of its conformity with the constitution».[150]

This happened in France for example, with the laws concerning nationalization, decentralization, university teaching and municipal officials, between 1982 and 1984.[151] It also happened in Spain in the early eighties, and the example of the laws concerning the decentralization process through the harmonization of the Autonomous Communities, the *Rumasa* nationalization and university teaching is clear.[152]

In such situations, the existence of constitutional review of legislation has precisely had the effect of avoiding any rapid breakdown in the constitutional balance, since the laws and reforms approved by the new majority were submitted to review by the constitutional judges, to determine which could be enacted according to the constitution, and which laws and reforms require constitutional review. Of course, as Professor Favoreu pointed out, in these cases, constitutional review may mean a restraint on the possibilities for action open to the majority with respect to the proposed reforms. On the other hand, if these reforms are brought into question before a constitutional Judge, and his verdict declares them

[149] L. FAVOREU, *Le contrôle juridictionnel des lois et sa légitimité, doc. cit.*, p. 25.

[150] L. FAVOREU, «Le Conseil Constitutionnel et l'alternance», *Revue française de science politique (La constitution de la Cinquienne Republique*, 34, (4-5), Paris 1984, pp. 1005-1114.

[151] L. FAVOREU, «Libertes locales et libertes universitaires. Les décisions du Conseil Constitutionnel du 20 janvier 1984», *Revue du droit public et de la science politique en France et à l'étranger*, 1984, pp. 687-730.

[152] P. BON, F. MODERNE and Y. RODRÍGUEZ, *op. cit.*, p. 168, 217.

to be in accordance with the constitution, in a certain way it authenticates them and they enjoy a supplementary authority.[153]

However, the defense of the constitution is not only an essential role of constitutional justice in order to guarantee the various systems of distribution of powers between the constituted organs of the state, and to ensure political stability and continuity, even in situations of political alternance of majorities, but also, as we mentioned, to guarantee the fundamental rights and liberties of individuals. This is, as we said, an essential part of the *État de droit* and one of the basic arguments used to defend the legitimacy of judicial review.

In effect, constitutional justice and judicial review of the constitutionality of legislation are bound up with the effective establishment of fundamental rights. Therefore, the need for the establishment of a system of judicial review also arises when there are entrenched declarations of fundamental rights and liberties linked with the constitutional values of a given society.

Nevertheless, even though the idea of fundamental rights established in a constitution, as a superior and effective rule of law in an entrenched way, has historical antecedents, it did not appear in Europe until after the Second World War. Therefore, the problem of establishing a system of judicial review, exception made to the Austrian and Czechoslovakian systems in the 1920's only arose in Europe after the Second World War, as a mean for defending the rights of man, precisely because these suffered the greatest violations in Europe. Here, once again, it is not by chance that it was in Italy and Germany when, for the first time in their constitutional texts, the validity of the rights of man and the need to organize mechanisms for their defense was affirmed, and among which, was the review of constitutionality of legislation.

At the other extreme, the absence of entrenched fundamental rights of individuals with constitutional rank, as a limit upon the legislator, is one of the main reasons for the absence of a system of judicial review of constitutionality, as happened in the United Kingdom. That is why Professor D.G.T. Williams correctly pointed «out:

> «The underlying problem either of an entrenched bill of Rights or of an entrenched federal structure for the United Kingdom is judicial review», because «the adoption of a Bill of Rights would, of course, involve the exercise of judicial review by the English Courts» that is to say, the power of domestic courts, «to protect certain fundamental freedoms even against the legislative itself».[154]

Anyway, what is definitely true in constitutional systems with written constitutions is that if the constitution pretends to be a supreme, obligatory and enforceable law, the constitutional system must establish means for its defense and guarantee. On the contrary, as Hans Kelsen used to say:

> «A constitution without guarantees against unconstitutional acts, is not completely obligatory in its technical sense... A constitution in which

[153] L. FAVOREU, *Le contrôle juridictionnel des lois et sa légitimité, doc. cit.*, p. 37.

[154] D.G.T. WILLIAMS, «The Constitution of the United Kingdom», *Cambridge Law Journal*, 31, 1972, pp. 278–279.

unconstitutional acts and particularly, unconstitutional laws, remains valid because its unconstitutionality cannot lead to its annulment, is more or less, equivalent from a juridical point of view, to a desire without obligatory force».[155]

The judicial guarantees of the constitution, that is to say, the power given to judges -ordinary judges or special constitutional courts- to declare the unconstitutionality of state acts issued in violation of the constitution, or to annul those acts with general effects is, therefore, an essential part of the *État de droit.* It is a power to ensure precisely, that all state organs are submitted to the rule of law and, therefore, that they will respect the limits imposed upon them by the constitution, according to the system[156] of distribution of state powers adopted and that they will also respect the fundamental rights and liberties declared in the constitution itself.

Of course, there is no unique and uniform system of constitutional justice to guarantee and defend the constitution, nor is there one ideal system, which can be applicable to all countries. In contemporary constitutional law each country has developed its own system and precisely, it is to study their fundamental trends in comparative law that we will devote the following three parts, in which we will analyse separately the diffuse system of judicial review, the concentrated system of judicial review, and the mixed system of judicial review, which correspond, in broad terms, to three different models: the American, the European and the Latin American.

---

155 H. KELSEN, *doc. cit.*, p. 250.

156 As M. HIDEN said, «probably there are as many methods of securing the constitutionality of laws and regulations as there are countries with a written constitution», in «Constitutional Rights in the Legislative Process: the Finnish System of Advance Control of Legislation», in *Scandinavian Studies in Law*, 17, Stockholm 1973, p. 97.

PART FOUR

THE DIFFUSE SYSTEM OF JUDICIAL REVIEW

I. GENERAL FEATURES

The diffuse system of judicial review empowers all the judges and courts of a given country to act as a constitutional judge, in the sense that when applying the law, they are allowed to judge its constitutionality and therefore, not to apply a law in the concrete process when they consider it unconstitutional and void, giving priority to the constitution.

1. The Logic of the System

From a logical and rational point of view, this general power of all judges and courts to act as constitutional judges is the obvious consequence of the principle of the supremacy of the constitution. If the constitution is the supreme law of the land, in cases of conflict between a law and the constitution, the latter must prevail, and it is the duty of the judiciary to say which law is applicable in a particular case. As Justice William Paterson stated in *Vanhorne's Lessee* v. *Dorrance* (1795) almost two hundred years ago:

> «If a legislative act oppugns a constitutional principle the former must give way and be rejected on the score of repugnance. I hold it to a position equally clear and sound, that, in such case, it will be the duty of the court to adhere to the constitution, and to declare the act null and void».[1]

Or as it was definitively stated by Chief Justice Marshall in *Marbury* v. *Madison* (1803):

> «Those who apply the rule to particular cases, must of necessity expound and interpret that rule... so, if a law be in opposition to the constitution... the court must determine which of these conflicting rules governs the case: This is the very essence of judicial duty. If then, the courts are to regard the constitution, and the constitution is superior to any ordinary act of the legislature, the constitution, and not such ordinary act, must govern the case to which they both apply».[2]

Thus, supremacy of the constitution and judicial review as the power of all judges to defend the constitution and to control the constitutionality of legislation are essentially linked. That is why regarding the constitutions and laws of the

---

1 *Vanhorne's Lessec v. Dorrance*, 2 Dallas 304 (1795). See the text in S.I. KUTLER (ed.), *The Supreme Court and the Constitution. Readings in American Constitutional History*, NY 1984, p. 8.

2 *Marbury* v. *Madison*, 1 Cranch 137 (1803). See the text in S.I. KUTLER (ed.), *op. cit.*, p. 29.

federal states it was expressly established in the well-known «supremacy clause» of Article VI, Section 2, of the American constitution, which states:

> «This constitution, and the laws of the United states which shall be made in Pursuance thereof; and all Treaties made, or which shall be made, under the Authority of the United States, shall be the supreme law of the land; and the Judges in every state shall be bound thereby, anything in the constitution or laws of the state to the contrary notwithstanding».

This supremacy clause was extended to federal laws in *Marbury* v. *Madison* through a logical and rational interpretation and application of the principle of the supremacy of the constitution, and has been expressly established in a general sense, as a positive rule in other countries.

In this sense, for instance, since 1910 Article 215 of the Colombian constitution established:

> «In all cases of incompatibility between the constitution and the law, the constitutional dispositions will preferably be applied».[3]

In a similar sense, since 1897 the Venezuelan Civil Procedural Cod has also established in Article 20 that:

> «When a law in force whose application is required, collides with any constitutional disposition, the courts will preferably apply the latter».[4]

2. The Compatibility of the System with all Legal Systems

Therefore, the diffuse system of judicial review of constitutionality of legislation is not a system peculiar to the common law system of law, incompatible with the civil or Roman law tradition, at all. On the contrary, it has existed since the last century in most Latin American countries, all of them being part of the Roman law family of legal systems.

This is the case of Mexico, Argentina and Brazil, which followed the American model and is also the case of Colombia and Venezuela, in which a mixed system of judicial review is followed.

It has also existed in Europe in countries with a Civil law tradition, like Switzerland and Greece. In Switzerland, the diffuse system of judicial review was first established in the 1874 constitution, even though in a limited way. Also in a limited manner, the Swiss system currently allows the courts to decide on constitutional grounds, upon the applicability of legislative acts of the cantons but not of federal laws.[5] In Greece, where a mixed system is also adopted, the 1975 constitution entrusts all courts with the power to apply no legal dispositions whose contents they consider to be contrary to the constitution.[6] In particular, Article 95 establishes:

---

3 See in J. ORTEGA TORRES (ed.), *Constitución Política de Colombia*, Bogotá 1985, p. 130. The origin of this norm can be traced up to the Legislative act, N° 3, Art. 40, 1910.

4 The text is the one of the 1985 Civil Procedural Code. With similar words it was adopted in article 10 of the 1897 and 1904 Codes, and article 7 of the 1916 Code.

5 H. FIX-ZAMUDIO, *Los tribunales constitucionales y los derechos humanos*, México 1980, pp. 17, 84; A. JIMÉNEZ BLANCO, «El Tribunal Federal suizo», *Boletín de Jurisprudencia Constitucional*, Cortes Generales, 6 Madrid 1981, p. 477.

6 Art. 93, H. FIX-ZAMUDIO, *op. cit.*, p. 162; L. FAVOREU, *Le contrôle juridictionnel des lois et sa légitimité, Développements récents en Europe occidentale*. Association Internationale des Sciences Juridiques, Colloque d'Uppsala, 1984 (mimeo), p. 14. Also published in L. FAVOREU and J.A. JOLOWICZ (ed.), *Le contrôle juridictionnel des lois. Légitimité, effectivité et développements récents*, Paris 1986, pp. 17-68.

«Art. 95. The courts shall be bound not to apply laws, the contents of which are contrary to the constitution».

Therefore, the diffuse system of judicial review exists and has functioned in legal systems with a common law tradition as well as those with a Roman law tradition. Thus, we do not agree with what Professors Mauro Cappelletti and John Clarke Adams said, in the sense that a fundamental incompatibility exists between the diffuse system of judicial review and the legal systems based on Roman law[7] or as Professor Cappelletti said elsewhere, when referring to the sole experience of Italy and West Germany prior to the creation of constitutional court, in the sense that those countries «fully revealed the unsuitability of the decentralized method for civil law countries».[8]

In our opinion the arguments in favor of the concentrated system of judicial review cannot be settled on the grounds of unsuitability or suitability with a particular system of law, but with the particular constitutional system adopted regarding the supremacy of the constitution. If the principle of constitutional supremacy is adopted, the logical and necessary consequence is the powers of the courts to decide which norm is to be applied when a contradiction exists between a particular law and the constitution, being obliged to give priority to the constitution as their very duty, regardless of the particular common law or Roman law system of the given country.

Another question relates to the practical legal effects of the adoption of a diffuse system of judicial review. In the absence of any kind of judicial review system in Europe before the 1920's and with the traditional framework of separation of power based on the sovereignty of the legislator and of the law, and the distrust of the courts to control legislative action, the criticisms of the diffuse systems of judicial review from the European side of the Atlantic are as old as the existence of the European model itself. For example, Hans Kelsen, the creator of the Austrian model in Europe referred to the problems raised by the diffuse system for justifying the «centralization of the power to examine the regularity of general norms», stressing «the absence of unity in the solutions» and «the legal uncertainty « that results when a «court abstains from applying a regulation and even a law as irregular, while another court does the contrary».[9] In this same sense, Professors Mauro Cappelletti and John Clarke Adams stressed that the diffuse systems of judicial review «can lead to grave uncertainty and confusion, as one court may decide to enforce a Statute that another court will find invalid».[10]

But these problems exist in both common law and Roman law systems that followed the diffuse system of judicial review, and are not essentially peculiar to the countries with Roman law systems that have adopted it, as Professors Cappelletti and Adams seemed to demonstrate, basing their arguments on the corrective effects that

---

7 M. CAPPELLETTI and J.C. ADAMS, «Judicial Review of Legislation: European Antecedents and Adaptations», *Harvard Law Review*, 79 (6), 1966, p. 1215.

8 M. CAPPELLETTI, *Judicial Review in the Contemporary World*, Indiannapolis 1971, p. 59. In similar sense M. FROMONT considered that it is «difficult to admit» the diffuse system of judicial revue in countries with a roman law tradition. See «Preface» in J.C. BÉGUIN, *Le contrôle de la constitutionalité des lois en Republique Federale d'Allemagne*, Paris 1982, p. 218.

9 H. KELSEN, «La guarantie juridictionnelle de la constitution (La Justice constitutionnelle)», *Revue du droit public et de la science politique en France et à l'étranger*, 1928, p. 218.

10 *Loc. cit.*, p. 1215.

regarding those problems have the doctrine of *stare decisis*, peculiar to the common law systems of law and alien to the Roman law systems. Their argument is as follows:

> «Under the Anglo-American doctrine of *stare decisis*, a decision by the highest court in any jurisdiction is binding on all lower courts in the same jurisdiction, and thus as soon as the court has declared a law unconstitutional, no other court can apply it. The court does not need a specific grant of the power to declare a law invalid, nor must it decide anything beyond the applicability of the law in question to the concrete case; *stare decisis* does the rest by requiring other courts to follow the precedent in all succeeding cases. Thus, although the unconstitutional statute may remain on the book, it is a dead law».

Thus they finished their argument by saying that:

> «*Stare decisis*, however, is not normally part of the Roman law systems, and thus in these systems, the courts are not generally bound even by the decisions of the highest court».[11]

Professor Cappelletti later developed the argument in his book *Judicial Review in the contemporary world*, when he said:

> «Since the principle of *stare decisis* is foreign to civil law judges, a system which allowed each judge to decide on the constitutionality of statues could result in a law being disregarded as unconstitutional by some judges, while being held constitutional and applied by others. Furthermore the same judicial organ, which had one day disregarded a given law, might uphold it the next day, having changed its mind about the law's constitutional legitimacy. Differences could arise between judicial bodies of a different type or degree, for example, between ordinary courts and administrative tribunals or between the younger, more radical judges of the inferior courts and the older, more tradition conscious judges of the higher courts... The extremely dangerous results could be a serious conflict between the judicial organs and grave uncertainty as to the law».[12]

We insist that those problems deriving from the very principle of supremacy of the constitution exist in countries with both Common and Roman law systems of law, and if it is true that the doctrine of *stare decisis* is a correction of the problems, it is not absolute, because, as we know, not all cases in which constitutional matters are decided upon by lower courts can go before the United States Supreme Court which is the one that decides in a discretional way, which cases are to be considered by it.[13]

On the other hand, and even though the doctrine of *stare decisis* as known in Common law countries does not apply in those with a Roman law tradition, those who have adopted a diffuse system of judicial review have normally developed, in parallel, their own corrections to the problems posed with similar effect. For instance, in the Mexican system of *amparo*, the constitution established the principle that the particular law of *amparo* should establish the cases in which the *jurisprudencia* namely, the precedents derived from previous decisions of the federal courts, were to be considered obligatory.[14] Thus, the *Amparo law* has established the cases in which the supreme court and also other collegial circuit court decisions are to be considered

---

11 *Idem*, p. 1215.

12 M. CAPPELLETTI, *op. cit.*, p. 58.

13 28 U.S. Code, Secc. 1254, 1255, 1256, 1257. See also Rule N° 17 of the Supreme Court.

14 Art. 107, Section XIII, paragraph 1 of the Constitution (ammendment of 1950-1951).

as obligatory precedents, which happens only after five consecutive decisions to the same effect, uninterrupted by any incompatible ruling, have been rendered. The effects of the *jurisprudencia* even partially, have been considered equivalent to those resulting from the rule of *stare decisis*.

Furthermore, in the Mexican system of *Amparo*, the so called «*amparo* against laws» has also been developed as an extraordinary action of unconstitutionality of self-executing laws which could directly affect the rights of an individual, and that can be brought before the federal courts, allowing these courts to judge the unconstitutionality of a law without any relation to a particular process.[15]

Along the same line of facts, in Argentina and Brazil, countries that also closely followed the American model in the sense of the power granted to all the courts to decide upon the inapplicability of a law based on constitutional considerations, an institution called the «extraordinary recourse of unconstitutionality» has been developed, which can be brought before the supreme court against judicial decisions adopted at the last instance, when a federal law is considered as unconstitutional and inapplicable by a court.[16] In these cases, the decision adopted by the Supreme Court has *in casu et inter partes* effects, but being adopted by the highest court has factual binding effects upon the inferior court.[17] In the same sense, in some European countries with a Roman law tradition which have adopted the diffuse system of judicial review, special judicial mechanisms have been established to overcome the problems deriving from contradictory decisions of different courts on constitutional issues. It is the case in Greece in which the 1975 constitution regulates a special highest court with powers to decide upon the unconstitutionality of laws, when contradictory decisions on the matter have been adopted by the state Council, the court of cassation or the auditory court. In such cases, the decisions of the special highest court have absolute and general effect regarding the constitutionality of laws.[18]

Finally, in the other mentioned countries with a Roman law tradition where the diffuse system of judicial review has been adopted, the correction to the problems of uncertainty and conflictiveness have been established by adopting a mixed model of judicial review, that is to say, by having the diffuse and concentrated systems operate in parallel. In Latin America it is the case in Guatemala,[19] Colombia and Venezuela. Particularly in the last two in parallel with the diffuse systems of judicial review legally established in positive law, the concentrated system of judicial review also exists; and through it, the supreme court is empowered to formally annul a law on the grounds of unconstitutionality with *erga omnes* effects, as required through a *popular action* that can be brought before the Supreme Court by any inhabitant of the country whosoever.

---

15 R.D. BAKER, *Judicial Review in México. A Study of the Amparo Suit*, Austin 1971, pp. 164, 250-251, 256, 259.

16 H. FIX-ZAMUDIO, *Veinticinco años de evolución de la justicia constitucional 1940-1965*, México 1968, pp. 26, 36; J. CARPIZO and H. FIX-ZAMUDIO, «La necesidad y la legitimidad de la revisión judicial en América latina. Desarrollo reciente», *Boletín mexicano de derecho comparado*, 52, 1985, p. 33. Also published in L. FAVOREU and J.A. JOLOWICZ (ed.), *Le contrôle juridictionnel des lois. Légitimité, effectivité et développements récents*, Paris 1986, pp. 119-151.

17 J.R. VANOSSI and P.E. UBERTONE, *Instituciones de defensa de la Constitución en la Argentina*, UNAM, Congreso Internacional sobre la Constitución y su Defensa, México 1982 (mimeo), p. 32.

18 E. SPILIOPOULOS, «Judicial Review of Legislative Acts in Greece», *Temple Law Quarterly*, 56, (2), Philadelphia 1983, pp. 496-500.

19 J.M. GARCÍA LAGUARDIA, *La defensa de la Constitución*, México 1983, p. 52.

Therefore, in parallel with the powers of every court to decide the inapplicability of a law considered unconstitutional in a concrete case, the Supreme Court has the power to annul with general effect the laws contested as being unconstitutional.[20]

In the same sense, other European countries with a Roman law tradition which have adopted the diffuse system of judicial review, have also adopted the features of the concentrated systems in parallel giving the supreme court of the country the power to annul unconstitutional laws. It is the case in Switzerland where even though no constitutional judicial control is allowed regarding federal laws, the federal court has the power to declare the unconstitutionality of canton laws, with *erga omnes* effects when required by a special public law recourse in cases of violations of fundamental rights.[21]

Therefore, in the same sense of the development of the doctrine of *stare decisis* in the common law system countries, to resolve the problems of uncertainty and the possible conflictive character of judicial decisions made by different courts upon the unconstitutionality of laws which the diffuse system of judicial review could bring about, the countries with a Roman law tradition that have adopted the same diffuse system of judicial review have also developed various particular legal mechanisms to prevent the evil effect of those problems, either by giving obligatory character to precedents or by granting the necessary powers to declare the unconstitutionality of statutes to the supreme court of the country in some cases even with general and binding effects.

The eventual problems posed by the diffuse control of constitutionality of legislation, therefore, are common to countries with either common or Roman law systems of law, and cannot lead by themselves to consider the diffuse system of judicial review «incompatible» with the civil or Roman law system of law of a given country by the fact that in the latter the rule of *stare decisis* does not exist.

As we said, the only fact of compatibility that is absolute in this respect is that when the principle of the supremacy of the constitution exists, the logical consequence is the power of all judges, which are charged with applying the law, to decide upon the inapplicability of legislation when it contradicts the constitution, giving preference to the constitution itself. This was the original system of judicial review after the triumph of the constitution over the legislator.

Nevertheless in the European countries with a Roman law system of law, the traditional distrust of judicial power has led the way to the establishment of the concentrated system of judicial review, which has brought about the rediscovery of constitutional supremacy by other means. But this cannot lead us to consider the diffuse control of the constitutionality of legislation as being incompatible with civil or Roman law legal systems.

3. The Rationality of the System

As we have said, the essence of the diffuse system of judicial review is the very notion of constitutional supremacy: if the constitution is the supreme law of

---

20 A. R. BREWER-CARÍAS, *El control de la constitucionalidad de los actos estatales*, Caracas 1977; L.C. SACHICA, *El control de la constitucionalidad y sus mecanismos*, Bogotá 1980.

21 E. ZELLWEGER, «El Tribunal Federal suizo en calidad de Tribunal Constitucional», *Revista de la Comisión Internacional de Juristas*, Vol. VII (1), 1966, p. 119; H. FIX-ZAMUDIO, *Los Tribunales constitucionales ..., cit.*, p. 84.

the land prevailing over all other laws, no state act contrary to the constitution can be an effective law, on the contrary, it must be considered as null and void. In the words of Chief Justice Marshall, if the constitution is «the fundamental and paramount law of the nation... an act of the legislature, repugnant to the constitution, is void».[22] In this respect, the effective guarantee of the supremacy of the constitution is that acts repugnant to it are in fact null and void, and as such have to be considered by the courts that are the state organs called upon to apply the laws.

A. *The Nullity of the Unconstitutional State Act*

The first aspect that shows the rationality of the diffuse system is the principle of the nullity of state acts and particularly of legislation repugnant to the constitution.

In principle, the nullity of a state act means that an act that pretends to be a juridical state act, objectively is not, because it is irregular in the sense that it does not correspond to the conditions established for its enactment by a norm of a superior rank. This was what Hans Kelsen called an «objective guarantee» of the constitution,[23] and it means that a state act that is null and void cannot produce any effect, and does not need another state act to be produced to withdraw its usurped quality of state act. On the contrary, if such another state act were needed, then the guarantee would not be the nullity of the state act, but its annullability.

Thus, in strict logic, the supremacy of the constitution means that all state acts that violate the constitution are null and void; and therefore, theoretically, all public authorities and even individuals could be entitled to inspect its irregularity, to declared its existence and to consider the act neither valid nor obligatory. Of course, this could lead to juridical anarchy and, therefore, positive law normally establishes limits upon this power to examine the regularity of state acts, and reserves this power to the judges. Therefore, a state act that violates the constitution and is, therefore, null and void can only be examined by the courts and only the courts have the power to consider it as null and void.

However, even though the limits imposed by positive law on the examination power of the nullity of state acts exists, this fact does not mean that the guarantee of the constitution ceases to be the nullity of the state act and is converted into annullability. On the contrary, the nullity of the unconstitutional state act persists, but with the limitation deriving from the legal reserve granted to the judges to declare, in exclusivity, its nullity.

Thus, up to that moment, the irregular state act must be considered by other public authorities, particularly administrative authorities and by individuals, as being effective and obligatory; but once a judge declares it unconstitutional in relation to a particular process, then the act becomes null and void regarding that process.

In conclusion, in the diffuse systems of judicial review, the duty of all judges and courts is to examine the constitutionality of laws, and to declare, when necessary, that a particular law or statute should not be applicable to a particular process which the judge or the court is considering, because it is unconstitutional and therefore must be considered null and void.

---

[22] *Marbury v Madison* 5 US (1 Cranch), 137. (1803). See the text in S.I. KUTLER (ed.), *op. cit.*, p. 29.

[23] H. KELSEN, *loc. cit.*, p. 214.

B. *The Power of All Courts*

This leads us to the second aspect of the rationality of the diffuse system of judicial review, which is that the power to declare the unconstitutionality of legislation is assigned to all the judges in a given country.

In effect, if the constitution is the supreme law of the land, and the principle of supremacy is accepted, then the constitution overrides any other law inconsistent with it, whether this is expressly established in the written text of the constitution or is an implicit consequence of its supremacy. Consequently, the laws that violate the constitution or in any way are contrary to its norms, principles and values are, as we have said, null and void, and cannot be applied by the courts, which must give preference to the constitution.

Then all courts must decide the concrete cases they are considering, as Chief Justice Marshall said, «conformably to the constitution, disregarding the unconstitutional law» this being «of the very essence of judicial duty».[24] Therefore, this role in the diffuse system of judicial review must correspond to all courts and not only to one particular court or tribunal, and must not be seen only in terms of power conferred upon the courts, but of the courts duty[25] to decide in conformity with the rule of the constitution, disregarding the laws contrary to its norms.

C. *The Incidental Character of the system*

This duty of all courts to give preference to the constitution and, therefore, not to apply laws which they consider unconstitutional and consequently null and void, leads us to the third aspect that shows the rationality of the diffuse system of judicial review of the constitutionality of legislation, which is that this duty of the courts can only be accomplished *incidenter tantum*, through a particular process that has been brought before them, and where the unconstitutionality of a particular law is neither «the issue» nor the principal issue in the process.

Therefore, a process must be initiated before a court on any matter or subject whatsoever, the diffuse system of judicial review of constitutionality being, consequently, always an incidental system of review. In it, the question of the unconstitutionality of a law and of its inapplicability is raised in a concrete case or process whatever its nature and in which the applicability or not of the concrete law is considered by the judge relevant to the decision of the case.

Hence, in the diffuse system of judicial review the main purpose of the process and of the court decision is not the abstract constitutionality or unconstitutionality of a law, or its applicability or inapplicability but rather the resolution of the concrete civil, criminal, administrative, commercial, or labor case.

The question of constitutionality thus is only an incidental aspect of a process, which must be considered by the judge only to resolve the applicability or not of a law to the decision of the concrete case, when there are questions concerning its unconstitutionality.

---

[24] *Marbury v. Madison*, 5 US (1 Cranch), 137, (1803).

[25] Confront B.C. NWABUEZE, *Judicial Control of Legislative Action and its Legitimacy. Recent Development.* African regional report. International Association of Legal Sciences. Uppsala Colloquium, 1984 (mimeo), pp. 2-3. Also published in L. FAVOREU and J.A. JOLOWICZ (ed.), *Le contrôle juridictionnel des lois. Légitimité, effectivité et développements récents*, Paris 1986, p. 193-222.

D. *The Initiative Power of the Courts*

Now, if it is a duty of the judges to apply the constitution in a concrete decision and not to apply a law considered unconstitutional to the resolution of the case, it must be said that in principle the fourth aspect of the rationality of the diffuse system must allow the judge to consider the constitutional question even on his own initiative, and therefore, even when none of the parties in the particular process have raised the question of the constitutionality of the law before the judge.

In fact, this is the direct consequence of the guarantee of the constitution, established as an objective guarantee which means the nullity of laws contrary to its norms, and is also the consequence of the reserve granted to the judges to declare the nullity and, consequently, the inapplicability of the unconstitutional law in a particular case.

Within this framework, the unconstitutionality of a law in relation to a particular process, cannot be left to the sole instance of one of the parties, and on the contrary, even if the parties do not raise the question of unconstitutionality before the judge, he has the duty of considering it and on his own initiative decide upon the unconstitutionality of a law.

Even though this aspect of the rationality of the diffuse system of judicial review is followed in many countries as in the case of Venezuela and Greece,[26] we must admit that, in general, procedural rules in most countries forbid courts to consider any questions on their own initiative, even questions of the constitutionality of laws, when deciding concrete cases.[27]

In any case, the common trend in this aspect of the rationality of this system of judicial review, is that the question of constitutionality can only be incidental through a particular process, always of course initiated by a party.

E. *The inter partes effects of the Court decision*

The fifth and final aspect of the rationality of the diffuse system of judicial review concerns the effects of the decision adopted by the court regarding the constitutionality or applicability of the law in the concrete process; and this aspect of the effect of the judicial decision refers to two questions: first, who does the decision affect? And second when do the effects of the decision begin?

In relation to the first question, the rationality of the diffuse system of judicial review is that the decision adopted by the court only has effects regarding the concrete parties, in the concrete process in which the decision is adopted. That is to say, in the diffuse system of control of the constitutionality of legislation, the decision adopted upon the unconstitutionality and inapplicability of a law in a case only has

---

[26] L. SPILIOTOPOULOS, «Judicial Review of Legislative Acts in Greece», *loc. cit.*, p. 479.

[27] As B.C. NWABUEZE has said: «The fact that the duty is, and can only be performed at the instance of a person aggrieved by a violation of the law of the constitution by government reinforce the legitimacy of the function. What this means is that, given a justiciable violation of the constitution by the legislature, however flaGRANT, the court cannot, on its own initiative, intervene. It must wait until moved by someone», *doc. cit.*, p. 3. See the discussion on the matter, and the opinion in contrary sense in J.R. VANOSSI and P.E. UBERTONE, *op. cit.*, p. 24; in G. BIDART CAMPOS, *El derecho constitucional del poder*, Vol. II, Chap. XXIX; and in J.R. VANOSSI, *Teoría constitucional*, Vol. II, Buenos Aires 1976, pp. 318-319.

in casu et inter partes effects related to the concrete case and exclusively to the parties who have participated in the process, and therefore, it cannot be applied to other individuals. This is a direct consequence of the aspect previously mentioned regarding the incidental character of the diffuse system of review as raised in a concrete process.

In effect, if the court's decision upon the constitutionality and applicability of a law on the grounds of constitutionality can only be adopted in a particular process developed between concrete parties, the logic of the system is that the decision only applies to that particular process and to those concrete parties and, hence, can neither benefit nor prejudice any other individual or any other process.

Thus, if a law is considered unconstitutional in a judicial case decision, this does not mean that the law has been invalidated and that it is not enforceable and applicable elsewhere. It only means that concerning the particular process and parties in which the inapplicability of the law has been decided by the court, the law must be considered unconstitutional, null and void, with no effect regarding other cases, other judges or other individuals.

Nevertheless, to avoid the uncertainty of the legal order and of contradictions in relation to the value of the laws, corrections have been made to these *inter partes* effects through the *stare decisis* doctrine or through positive law, when the decision is adopted by the Supreme Court of a given country.

F. *The Declarative Effects of the Court Decision*

These *inter partes* effects of the judicial decision in the diffuse system of judicial review are closely related to the other question concerning the effects of the decision in time, namely to when the declaration of unconstitutionality is to be effective, and also, of course, to the already mentioned aspect of the nullity as a guarantee of the constitution.

In effect, we have said that the first and foremost fundamental aspect of the rationality of the diffuse system of judicial review is that of the supremacy of the constitution over all state acts that leads to the consideration that laws contrary to the constitution are null and void, the most important guarantee of the constitution. Consequently, when a court decides upon the constitutionality of a law and declares it unconstitutional and inapplicable in a concrete case, it is because it considers the law null and void, as if it had never existed.

Therefore, the decision has *declarative* effects: it declares that a law is unconstitutional and consequently, that it has been unconstitutional ever since its enactment. Thus, the law whose inapplicability is decided upon, is considered by the court as never having been valid and as always having been null and void. That is why it is said that the decision of the court, as it is a declarative one, has *ex tunc, pro-pretaerito* or retroactive effects in the sense that they go back to the moment of the enactment of the statute considered unconstitutional preventing it from having any effect, of course, only concerning the concrete case decided by the court and regarding the intervening parties. The legislative act declared unconstitutional by a court in the diffuse system of judicial review, as a result, is considered as being null and void *ab initio*, and consequently is not annulled by the court who only declare its pre-existing nullity.

4. Conclusion

In conclusion, we can say that as a matter of fact, the principle the rationality of the diffuse system of judicial review works as follows:

The constitution has a supreme character over the whole legal order; thus, acts contrary to the constitution cannot have any effects, and are considered null and void.

All Courts have the power and duty of applying the constitution and the laws and, therefore, to give preference to the constitution over statutes, which violate it, and to declare them unconstitutional and inapplicable to the concrete process developed before the court.

The power and duty of the courts to consider a statute unconstitutional giving preference to the constitution can only be exercised in a particular process initiated by a party, where the constitutional question is only an incidental matter, and when its consideration is necessary to resolve the case.

This court judgment regarding the unconstitutionality and inapplicability of a statute in a particular process can be taken by the judge on his own initiative, because it is his duty to apply and respect the supremacy of the constitution.

The decision adopted by the court concerning the unconstitutionality and inapplicability of a law only has *inter partes* effects regarding the concrete case in which it is made; and it is of a declarative effect in the sense that it only declares the *ab initio* nullity of the statute. Thus, when declaring the statute unconstitutional and inapplicable, in fact, the decision has *ex-tunc*, and *pro pretaerito* effects in the sense that they are retroactive to the moment of the enactment of the statute, considered as not having produced any effect regarding the concrete process and parties.

Of course, this logic of the diffuse system of judicial review is not always absolute, and each legal system has developed corrections to the possible deviation that each one of the aspects of the rationality of the system may produce, concerning the nullity or annullability of the unconstitutional act; the power assigned to all or a limited number of courts to review constitutionality; the incidental character of the system; the initiative of judges or the need of a party requirement of the constitutional question; the *inter partes* or *erga omnes* effect of the decision and its declarative or constitutive character.

In analyzing the most important diffuse systems of judicial review of the constitutionality of legislation we will refer to all those aspects of the rationality of the system and its special modifications.

II. THE AMERICAN SYSTEM OF JUDICIAL REVIEW

The most important example of the diffuse system of judicial review is, without doubt, the one developed in the United States of America since the beginning of the last century. The diffuse system of judicial review, therefore, can be considered as a North American constitutional product in origin. That is why this system of judicial review is also known in comparative law, as the «American system» [28]1), particularly, when opposed to one of the types of the concentrated system of judi-

[28] M. CAPPELLETTI, *Judicial Review in the Contemporary World*, Indianapolis 1971, p. 46.

cial review, known as the «Austrian system» also because its origins are in the 1920 Austrian constitution. Judicial review is, consequently, not only the most distinctive feature of the American Constitutional system, but also one of the main contributions of American Constitutionalism to the theory and practice of constitutional law.

1. Judicial review and judicial supremacy

When Alexis De Tocqueville visited America more than a hundred and fifty years ago, and described the political system of the United States, he stressed, in particular, the way Americans had organized their judicial power, which he considered unique in the world.[29] His observations about the powers of the courts, which he believed, «the most important power» of the country,[30] were directly referred to the powers for judicial review, whose basic trends can still be elaborated from them. He specifically pointed out that «that immense political power»[31] of the American courts, «lies in this one fact» -he said -:

> «The Americans have given their judges the right to base their decisions on the constitution rather than on the laws. In other words, they allow them not to apply laws which they consider unconstitutional».[32]

Following the same idea, he said:

> «If anyone invokes in an American Court a law which the judge considers contrary to the constitution, he can refuse to apply it».[33]

This power of American judges, De Tocqueville stressed, was «the only power peculiar to an American judge»;[34] today, it must be said, it is the power common to all judges in legal systems with a diffuse system of judicial review.

Nevertheless, what was peculiar to the American system was that the power of all courts to «pass upon the constitutionality of legislative acts which fall within their normal jurisdiction to enforce and.... to refuse to enforce such as they find to be unconstitutional and hence void»,[35] was not expressly established in the constitution. It was deduced from the whole constitutional system by the Supreme Court, particularly by Chief Justice John Marshall in the famous *Marbury* v. *Madison* case 1803,[36] based on two main arguments, first, the supremacy of the constitution, as a fundamental law, to which all other laws must be submitted; and second, the power and duty of the courts to interpret the laws, and not to apply laws repugnant to the constitution, which ought to be considered null and void.[37]

This fundamental duty of the American courts has been clearly summarised by the Supreme Court in the United *States* v. *Butler* case in 1936, with the following words:

---

29 Alexis DE TOCQUEVILLE, *Democracy in America* (ed. by J.P. MAYER and M. LERNER), The Fontana Library, London 1968, Vol. 1, p. 120.

30 *Idem*, p. 122

31 *Ibid*, pp. 122, 124.

32 *Ibid*, p. 122.

33 *Ibid*, p. 124.

34 *Ibid*, p. 124.

35 E.S. CORWIN, «Judicial Review» *Encyclopedia of the Social Sciences*, Vols. VII–VIII, p. 457.

36 «... the responsability for introducing the practice (of judicial review of legislative acts) as a rule for the federal courts is placed primarily on the great chief justice». Ch. G. HAINES, *The American Doctrine of judicial supremacy*, Berkeley 1932, p. 122.

37 E.S. CORWIN, «*Marbury v. Madison* and the Doctrine of Judicial Review», *Michigan Law Review*, 12, 1914, p. 538.

«The constitution is the supreme law of the land ordained and established by the people. All legislation must conform to the principles it lays down. When an act of Congress is appropriately challenged in the Courts as not conforming to the constitutional mandate the judicial branch of the Government has only one duty, -to lay the article of the constitution which is invoked beside the Statute which is challenged and to decide whether the latter squares with the former.

All the Court does, or can do, is to announce its considered judgment upon the question. The only power it has, if such it may be called, is the power of judgment. This Court neither approves nor condemns any legislative policy. Its delicate and difficult office is to ascertain and declare whether the legislation is in accordance with, or in contravention of, the provisions of the constitution; and, having done that, its duty ends».[38]

According to this doctrine, the courts in the American system of judicial review are considered the special custodians or guardians of the terms of the written constitution,[39] not only of the «national» constitution but also of the constitutions of the various states.

According to the federal system, three branches of judicial review have been distinguished in the United States: a «national» judicial review, referring to the power of all courts to pass judgment upon the validity of acts of Congress under the United States Constitution; a «federal» judicial review, referring to the power and duty of all courts to prefer the United States Constitution over all conflicting state constitution provisions and statutes; and a «state» judicial review, referring to the power of state courts to pass judgment upon the validity of acts of the state legislatures under the respective state Constitutions.[40]

The «national» judicial review branch was the only one not expressly established in the constitution and was deduced from the constitutional system by the Supreme Court. Whereas the «federal» judicial review branch was expressly established in what has been considered to be the «supremacy clause» of the constitution;[41] and the «state» judicial review branch is generally regulated in the constitutions of the states. Due to its importance, we will refer our comments on the general trends of the diffuse American system of judicial review, mainly to the «national» judicial review branch and the role of the Supreme Court.

However, before doing so, it must be pointed out that the power of judicial review in the American system derived from the concept of judicial supremacy can be exercised over all state acts, and not only over legislative acts. Therefore, all acts of Congress, constitutions and statuses of the states, all acts of the government and administration and even judicial acts are submitted to judicial review of constitutionality[42] and even though no treaty has ever been held to be unconstitutional by the courts,[43] in the leading *Missouri* v. *Holland* case (1920) it was clearly expressed

---

38 297 US. (1936).

39 Ch. G. HAINES, *op. cit.*, pp. 23, 221, 222.

40 E.S. CORWIN, «Judicial Review», *loc. cit.*, p. 457

41 Article VI, 2. See the comments of R. BERGER, *Congress v. The Supreme Court*, Cambridge, Mass 1969, pp. 223-284.

42 *Cf.* A. TUNC and S. TUNC, *Le système constitutionnel des Etats Unis d'Amerique*, Paris 1954, Vol. II, p. 272

43 P.G. KAUPER, «Judicial Review of Constitutional Issues in the United States» in H. MOSLER (ed.), Max-Planck-Institut für Ausländisches öffentliches recht und Völkerrecht, *Verfassungsgerichtsbarkeit in der Gegenwart* (Constitutional Review in the World Today) Internationalen Kolloquium, Heildelberg 1961), Köln-Berlin, 1962, p. 628.

that the constitutional validity of treaties and legislation resting on treaties may appropriately be the subject of judicial inquiry.[44]

Anyway, because of the importance of the subject to comparative analysis, we will basically refer to judicial review of legislative acts.

2. Judicial Review as a Power of All Courts

First of all, it must be said that judicial review as the power to control the constitutionality of legislation is a faculty conferred upon all courts and judges in the United States. Therefore, in the United States there is no special judicial body empowered to decide upon the constitutionality of state acts, particularly of legislation. Thus, all the courts, state courts, federal courts and the Supreme Court have the power of judicial review of constitutionality, and none of them have their jurisdiction limited in any special way at all, over the decision of constitutional questions.

Consequently, courts always decide upon constitutional matters or issues when they arise in the course of a concrete case and are necessary to the decision of the case brought before the court within its ordinary jurisdiction.

In general, and restricting our comments to the federal judicial system, courts, organized in the pyramidal format usual in contemporary legal systems, have either original or appellate jurisdiction. General original jurisdiction in the federal judicial system in the United States is vested in the «district courts» which are a large number of tribunals of territorial competence located throughout the country, generally coinciding with the territories of the states. The jurisdiction of these «district courts» extends to numerous types of controversies, particularly, civil and criminal cases arising out of the laws of the United States, controversies between citizens of different states, cases in which the United States is a plaintiff or defendant, *habeas corpus* proceedings, and cases arising out of federal civil rights litigation originating from violations by state officers of the constitutional rights of the plaintiff seeking damages or other relief.[45] It is in the course of these controversies that constitutional issues may be raised.

Over district courts, in the federal judicial system, there are the United States «courts of appeal». Federal judicial districts are organized into larger judicial units known as «circuits» and in each of these there is one court of appeal. These courts of appeal in the American system do not have original jurisdiction and are strictly appellate tribunals, with very extensive jurisdiction derived from the fact that all the final decisions of the district courts may be appealed against, at them. The work of these courts of appeals in the federal judicial system is very important due to the fact that they perform the function of ultimate appellate courts, bearing in mind that only the most important cases can be taken from a court of appeal to the Supreme Court.

Additionally, it must be pointed out that if it is true that in general the jurisdiction of the courts of appeal is directed to the review of the decisions of a federal district court, by statute they have been given appellate jurisdiction to review

---

44 *Missouri v. Holland,* 252 US 346 (1920) where the Court found that a «treaty in question does not contravene any prohibitory words to be found in the constitution» concluding that «we are of opinion that the treaty and statute must be upheld...».

45 28 US Code sec. 1331, 1332, 1345, 1346, 2241, 1343.

the decisions of some important federal administrative agencies (e.g. National Labor Relations Board, Federal Power Commission), and special federal courts, like tax courts, in which constitutional issues frequently arise.

In other federal matters, there are specialized courts with original and appellate jurisdiction separate from the general system of the district and circuit courts, as in the case of the Court of Customs and Patent Appeals, the Court of Military Appeals and the Court of Claims.[46]

At the apex of the federal judicial system is the United States Supreme Court, which has not only an appellate jurisdiction, but also an original jurisdiction established in the constitution that cannot be enlarged upon by Congress.[47] The original jurisdiction refers to «cases affecting ambassadors, other public ministers and Consuls, and those in which a state shall be party»[48] and it is classified by the United States Code, in Sec. 1251, title 28, as exclusive and non-exclusive jurisdiction. It states as follows: The original and exclusive jurisdiction refers to all controversies between two or more states; and the original but not exclusive jurisdiction refers to all actions or proceedings brought by ambassadors or other public ministers of foreign states or to which consuls or vice consuls of foreign states are parties; all controversies between the United States and a state; and all actions or proceedings by a state against the citizen of another state or against aliens.

To summarize, the original jurisdiction of the Supreme Court refers to cases that may be brought directly before the court, which includes cases to which a state is a party and cases involving ambassadors. Disputes between two states commonly referring to conflicts regarding boundaries, water or mineral rights can be heard only by the Supreme Court, but other cases under the original nonexclusive jurisdiction of the court can be heard alternatively by a district court.[49]

Consequently, because of the limited and less important nature of the original jurisdiction of the Supreme Court, it is evident that its most important activity as interpreter of the constitution and the laws and treaties of the United States is developed through its appellate jurisdiction, in which it operates as the court of last resort.

In this respect, particularly in the field of constitutional matters, the Supreme Court appears as «the most important tribunal in the American system»[50] with a very broad appellate jurisdiction regulated by Congress, to ensure a final, authoritative, and uniform interpretation of the constitution and the laws and treaties of the United States.

Thus, the Supreme Court is authorized to review all decisions of the United States Courts of Appeal,[51] which, as we have seen, have the power to review the decisions of all the district courts so that in general the appellate jurisdiction of the Supreme Court can be extended to all cases originating in the federal court system.

---

46 *Cf.* L. BAUM, *The Supreme Court*, Washington 1981, p. 10.

47 *Cf. Marbury v. Madison*, 5 US (1Cranch) 137 (1803); *Muskrat v. United States*, 219 US, 346, (1911).

48 Art. III, section 2 of the constitution.

49 *Cf.* L. BAUM, *op. cit.* p. 11.

50 B. SCHWARTZ, *American Constitutional Law*, Cambridge 1955, p. 129.

51 28, US Code 1254 which referes to the methods through which cases in the court of appeals may be reviewed by the Supreme Court.

In addition, the Supreme Court has appellate jurisdiction to review the decisions of the highest court of the various states, in all cases of federal laws, that is to say, cases that draw into question the validity of a federal statute or treaty or the validity o a state statute or where otherwise a claim of right under the constitution, treaties or laws of the United States is involved.[52] Finally, the Supreme Court also has appellate jurisdiction to review the decisions of specialized federal Courts, like the Court of Claims, the Court of Customs and Patent Appeals and the Court of Military Appeals.[53]

However, apart from the appellate jurisdiction following the hierarchical pattern of the judicial system, there are also cases in which the Supreme Court can act as an appellate court of last resort to review decisions of the federal district courts brought directly to the Supreme Court by means of an appeal. In this respect, the US Code establishes a right to appeal to the Supreme Court from the decision of any federal court, including federal district courts, «holding an act of Congress unconstitutional in any civil action, suit, or proceeding to which the United States or any of its agencies, or any officer or employee thereof, as such officer or employee, is a party».[54] Likewise the United States may appeal directly to the Supreme Court against any decision of a federal district court dismissing a criminal proceeding or setting aside a criminal conviction on the grounds of unconstitutionality of the federal criminal statute.[55] Finally, the US Code also allows any party to appeal directly «to the Supreme Court from an order granting or denying, after notice and hearing, an interlocutory or permanent injunction in any civil action, suit or proceeding required by any act of Congress to be heard and determined by a district court of three judges»,[56] which is needed when either a federal or state statute is questioned on the grounds of its constitutionality.

3. The Mandatory or Discretionary Power of the Supreme Court for Judicial Review

As we can realize, the appellate jurisdiction of the Supreme Court is enormous so that the right to appeal to the highest tribunal has been restricted. Moreover, the Supreme Court has been progressively made the judge as to whether or not it would receive an appeal to it, being allowed to refuse to hear a case when it feels that the question involved is not one of sufficient importance.

The appellate jurisdiction of the Supreme Court, therefore, is twofold: mandatory and discretionary, the latter being the most important in the number of cases reviewed.

The main reform in this respect was taken by the 1925 Judiciary act[57] through which the discretionary appellate jurisdiction was widened, bearing in mind the public interest. This discretionary power to determine the cases to be heard by the court has changed the character of the Supreme Court as an ultimate appellate tribunal or an ordinary judicial body. As Professor B. Schwartz pointed out, it has resulted that today, the Supreme Court:

---

52 28. US Code, 1257.
53 28. US Code, 1255, 1256.
54 28. US Code, 1252.
55 18. US Code, 3731.
56 28. US Code 1253, 2281, 2282, 2284.
57 See TAFT, «The Jurisdiction of the Supreme Court under the Act of February 13, 1925», *Yale Law Review*, 35, 1925, p. 2.

«Is a Court of Special Resort for the settlement only of such question as it deems to involve a substantial public concern, rather than the concerns only of private persons as such».[58]

The distinction between the mandatory and the discretionary appellate jurisdiction of the Supreme Court depends on the methods established in the US Code through which three cases may be reviewed by the Supreme Court. These three methods are the appeals, the petitions for writ of certiorari and the certifications.

A. *Right to Appeal and Mandatory Appellate Jurisdiction*

Obligatory or mandatory appellate jurisdiction exists when a right of appeal is granted to a party to bring a case before the Supreme Court, and this is restricted to the following cases, all related to constitutional justice:

a. Cases in which a federal court, even district courts, has held an act of Congress to be unconstitutional, if the federal government is a party.[59]

b. Cases in which a federal court of appeal has held a state statute to be invalid as repugnant to the constitution, treaties or laws of the United States.[60]

c. Cases in which a state supreme court has drawn into question the validity of a treaty or statute of the United States (act of Congress) and the decision is against its validity.[61]

d. Cases in which a state supreme court has drawn into question the validity of a statute of any state on the grounds of its being repugnant to the constitution treaties or laws of the United States, and the decision is in favor of its validity.[62]

e. Cases decided by special three-judge federal district courts, bearing in mind that a special three judge federal court must be set up through the enlargement of the federal district court where normally only one judge sits to hear the case when a proceeding is initiated to enjoin either a federal or state statute on the grounds of its constitutionality.[63]

As can generally be seen, the right to appeal and the mandatory appellate jurisdiction of the Supreme Court are established when important constitutional issues are in question, and particularly, when an act of Congress is considered to be unconstitutional by a federal court or a state supreme court, or when a state statute has been considered to be unconstitutional by a federal court of appeal, or its constitutionality has been questioned before a state supreme court.

B. *The Discretionary Appellate Jurisdiction and the Writ of Certiorari*

In all other cases, whether or not they involve constitutional issues, the United States Supreme Court is authorized to review all the decisions of the federal courts

---

58 B. SCHWARTZ, *op. cit.*, p. 139.

59 28 US Code, 1252.

60 28 US Code, 1254, 2.

61 28 US Code, 1257, 1 (Cases in which a State Supreme Court has ruled an act of Congress unconstitutional).

62 28 US Code 1257, 2 (Cases in which a State Supreme Court has upheld a State law against a claim that it conflicts with the constitution or a federal law).

63 28 US Code 1253, 2281, 2282, 2284.

of appeals, and of the specialized federal courts, and all the decisions of the supreme courts of the states involving issues of federal law, but on a discretionary basis, when considering a petition for a writ of certiorari.

In effect, in all such cases in which there is no right of appeal established and where the mandatory appellate jurisdiction of the Supreme Court is not established, they can reach the Supreme Court as petitions for certiorari, where a litigant who has lost in a lower court, petitions the Supreme Court to review the case, setting out the reasons why review should be granted.[64] This method of seeking review by the Supreme Court is expressly established in the following cases:

a. Cases decided by the federal court of appeals, granted upon the petition of any party to any civil or criminal case, before or after rendition of judgment or decree.[65]

b. Cases decided in the Court of Claim granted on petition of the United States or the claimant.[66]

c. Cases decided in the Court of Customs and Patent Appeals.[67]

d. Cases decided by the supreme courts of the states where the validity of a treaty or statute of the United States is drawn into question or where the validity of a state statute is drawn into question on the grounds of its being repugnant to the constitution, treaties or laws of the United States, or where any title, right, privilege or immunity is specially set up or claimed under the constitution, treaties or statues of, or commission held or authority exercised under the United States.[68]

In all these cases, as the Supreme Court's Rule N° 17 establishes when referring to the «considerations governing review on certiorari»:

> A review on writ of certiorari is not a matter of right, but of judicial discretion, and will be granted only when there are special and important reasons therefore.[69]

The same Rule N° 17 adopted by the Supreme Court, listed the factors that might prompt the court to grant certiorari even though without «controlling nor fully measuring the court's discretion», as follows:

«a. When a federal court of appeal has rendered a decision in conflict with the decision of another federal court of appeal on the same matter; or has decided a federal question in a way in conflict with a state court of last resort; or has so far departed from the accepted and usual course of judicial proceedings, ox has so far sanctioned such a departure by a lower court, as to call for an exercise of this Court's power of supervision;

b. When a state court of last resort has decided a federal question in a way in conflict with the decision of another state court of last resort or of federal court of appeal;

[64] L. BAUM, *op. cit.*, p. 81.
[65] 28 US Code, 1254, 1.
[66] 28 US Code, 1255, 1.
[67] 28 US Code, 1256.
[68] 28 US Code, 1257, 3.
[69] Section 1. see in L. BAUM, *op. cit.*, p. 86.

c. When a state court or a federal court of appeal has decided an important question of federal law which has not been, but should be, settled by this Court, or has decided a federal question in a way in conflict with applicable decisions of this Court».[70]

According to this Rule, consequently, in order to promote uniformity and consistency in federal law, the following factors might prompt the Supreme Court to grant certiorari: 1. Important questions of federal law on which the court has not previously ruled; 2. Conflicting interpretations of federal law by lower courts; 3. Lower courts decisions that conflict with previous Supreme Court decisions; and 4. Lower court departures from the accepted and usual course of judicial proceedings.[71]

Of course, review may be granted on the basis of other factors or denied even if one or more of the above-mentioned factors is present. The discretion of the Supreme Court is not limited, and it is the importance of the issue and the public interest viewed by the Court in a particular case, which leads the Court to grant certiorari and to review some cases.

C. *The Jurisdiction of the Supreme Court in Cases of Certification*

Apart from the appeals and the petition for writ of certiorari, the appellate jurisdiction of the Supreme Court can be exercised through the request of certification by a federal court of appeal or by the Court of Claims, although it is very rarely employed.

In effect, the US Code establishes in section 1254, as one of the methods through which the decisions of the courts of appeals may be reviewed by the Supreme Court, the following:

> «By certification at any time by a court of appeal of any question of law in any civil or criminal case as to which instructions are desired, and upon such certification the Supreme Court may give instructions or require the entire record to be sent up for decision of the entire matter in controversy».[72]

As a result, certification is the procedure whereby a lower federal court requests instruction from the Supreme Court on a point of law, relevant to the case under consideration. In these cases of certified questions, the Supreme Court is obliged to consider and answer the questions put to it.[73] In this situation, the Supreme Court does not normally deal with the whole case, but sends its instructions back to the court of appeal, even though the Court is authorized to require the entire case to be brought before it.

4. The Incidental Character of Judicial Review

A. *Cases and Controversies*

Judicial review of legislation, whether exercised by lower courts or by the Supreme Court in its original or appellate jurisdiction, is always a power that can only be exercised by the courts within the context of a concrete adversary litigation,

---

70 *Idem.*
71 *Cf.* R.A. ROSSUM and G.A. TARR, *American Constitutional Law*, New York 1983, p. 28.
72 28 US Code, 1254, 3.
73 P.G. KAUPER, p. 579, 608.

when the constitutional issue becomes relevant and necessary to be resolved in the decision of the case.

In this respect, as we said, there is no special type of proceeding required for raising constitutional issues in the courts. As Professor Paul G. Kauper pointed out in his study on judicial review of constitutional issues in the United States:

> «The constitutional question, if relevant to the disposition of the case and if asserted by a proper party in interest in an adversary proceeding, may be raised regardless of the nature of the proceeding. Thus it may be raised in the course of a civil proceeding between private parties where damages or other relief are sought; as a defense in a criminal proceeding under the criminal laws of the United States, as the basis for an injunction sought by a party in a proceeding directed either against public authorities or private persons to restrain the enforcement of a statute or an administrative order or other administrative action, in a mandamus proceeding to compel the performance of a public duty, in a damage action brought against the United States to collect taxes or to enforce a federal administrative order or in a declaratory judgment proceeding designed to obtain a judicial declaration of rights between opposing parties».[74]

Thus, the incidental character of judicial review, essential to the diffuse system, is the main trend of the American system, and has been developed by the Supreme Court by interpreting the expressions «cases» and «controversies» used in Article III, Section 2 of the constitution.

Therefore, no abstract judicial review of the validity of legislation is authorized in the United States[75] and judicial review by the courts can only be exercised within the limits of a concrete case or controversy, at the request of a party. In this respect, Justice Sutherland in *Frothinaham* v. *Mellon* (1923) was definitively conclusive:

> «We have no power per se to review and annul acts of Congress on the grounds that they are unconstitutional. The question may be considered only when the justification for some direct injury suffered or threatened, presenting a justiciable issue, is made to rest upon such an act. Then, the power exercises is that of ascertaining and declaring the law applicable to the controversy».[76]

And in this same respect, it was stated in *Muskrat* v. *United States* (1911),

> «By cases and controversies are intended the claims of litigants brought before the courts for determination by such regular proceedings as are established by law or customs for the protection or enforcement of rights, or the prevention, redress, or punishment of wrongs. Whenever the claim of a party under the constitution, laws, or treaties of the United States takes such a form that the judicial power is capable of acting upon it, then it has become a case.

---

[74] P.G. KAUPER, *loc. cit.*, pp. 586-587. *Cf.* J.A.C. GRANT «El control jurisdiccional de la constitucionalidad de las leyes: una contribución de las Américas a la ciencia política», *Revista de la Facultad de Derecho de México*, 45, México 1962, pp. 425-429.

[75] In words of Chief Justice Stone, the Court has «considered practice not to decide abstract, hypothetical or contingent questions» *Alabama Federation of Labor v. Mc. Adory*, 325 US, 450 (1945), p. 461.

[76] *Frothingham v. Mellon*, 262, US 447 (1923).

The term implies the existence of present or possible adverse parties whose contentions are submitted to the court for adjudication».[77]

Therefore, judicial review of constitutionality has only an incidental character in the United States, as an issue brought before the court in a concrete case or controversy. That is why Justice Brandeis in his concurring opinion to *Ashwander* v. *Tennessee Valley Authority* (1936), said that:

> «The Court will not pass upon the constitutionality of legislation in a friendly, non-adversary, proceeding, declining because to decide such questions is legitimate only in the last resort, and as a necessity in the determination of real, earnest and vital controversy between individuals».[78]

Consequently, the courts must not decide constitutional questions when they are convinced that the parties are acting in accord. «It never was thought -added Justice Brandeis in his concurrent opinion already mentioned- that, by means of a friendly suit, a party beaten in the legislature could transfer to the courts an. inquiry as to the constitutionality of the legislative act».[79]

Nevertheless, the need for cases or controversies to seek judicial review of the constitutionality of legislation does not prevent the possible questions of constitutionality from being raised in a declaratory judgment.

Even though discussed by the courts in applying state legislation, after the 1934 Federal Declaratory Judgment Act, it has been definitively accepted that, provided all other jurisdictional requirements are satisfied, federal courts are authorized to declare the rights of the parties in a case before them, although a specific form of remedy, such as a judgment for damages or an equitable decree, is not sought by the petitioner.[80]

In any case, it has been pointed out that even though of declaratory character, these judgments are not mere advisory opinions, in the sense that to be accepted a genuinely adversary proceeding between parties asserting appropriate interests must exist.[81] Thus, declaratory judgments are considered cases or controversies, and can be used to obtain a judicial decision upon constitutional issues.[82]

On the other hand, we must point out that judicial review being a power conferred on all courts to review the constitutionality of legislation in cases and controversies, the United States is not always necessarily a party in the proceedings,

---

77 *Muskrat v. United States*, 219 US, 346, (1911) In this case Justice Day, commenting *Marbury v. Madison* (1803), said: «In that case, Chief Justice MARSHALL, who spoke for the Court, was careful to point out that the right to declare an act of Congress unconstitutional could only be exercised when a proper case between opposing parties was submitted for judicial determination; that there was no general veto power in the Court upon the legislation of Congress; and that the authority to declare an act unconstitutional sprung from the requirement that the courts in administering the law and pronouncing judgement between parties to a case, and choosing between the requirements of the fundamental law established by the people and embodied in the constitution and an act of the agents of the people, acting under authority of the constitution should enforce the constitution as the Supreme Law of the land».

78 *Ashwander v. Tennessy Valley Authority* 297 US 288 (1936), p.345.

79 *Idem.*

80 28. US Code, secc 2201.

81 *Maryland Casualty Co. v. Pacific Coal and Oil Co.*, 312, US. 270 (1941).

82 *Nashville, C. and St. L. Ry. Co v. Wallace*, 288 US, 249 1933.

because, as we have seen, the constitutional question can be raised in any type of proceeding even when it is developed between private parties. Nevertheless, in all cases when the United States or any agency officer or employee thereof is not a party, and wherein the constitutionality of any act of Congress affecting the public interest is drawn into question, the court shall certify such facts to the attorney general and shall permit the United States to intervene for presentation of evidence and for argument on the question of constitutionality. In such cases, the United States shall have all the rights of a party.[83]

Even if the consideration of constitutional issues must be confined to cases or controversies, the invalidity of the legislation must be raised by a party with sufficient standing and its resolution being necessary and indispensable for the decision of the case. In this respect, the Supreme Court has developed a few rules that have been considered as «self-restraint»[84] over its judicial review powers, particularly in three aspects specifically related to the incidental character of judicial review. The standing requirement and the evident and indispensable character of the constitutional question.

B. *The Personal Interest and the Constitutional Question.*

First of all, within a case or controversy, the court has developed the principle of the need of the constitutional issue to be alleged by a party and particularly, by a party that must show that it is the proper party with personal interest. As we have mentioned in *Frothinqham* v. *Mellon* (1923) the court expressly established that the constitutional questions:

> «May be considered only when the justification for some direct injury suffered or threatened, presenting a justiciable suit is made to rest upon such an act...»[85]

Along the same lines of thought Justice Brandeis said in the case *Ashwander* v. *Tennessee Valley Authority*, «the Court will not pass upon the validity of a statute upon complaint of one who fails to show that he is injured by its operation».[86] Therefore, to raise an issue of validity of a statute, the necessary standing to sue is required and to have such standing the party involving the invalidity of a statute must show, as was stated in *Frothingham* v. *Mellon* (1923):

> «Not only that the statute is invalid, but that he has sustained or is immediately in danger of sustaining some direct injury as the result of its enforcement, and not merely that he suffers in some indefinite way in common with people generally».[87]

---

[83] 28 US Code, secc 2403.

[84] See H.J. ABRAHAM, *The Judicial Process*, NY 1980, p. 373. These self-restrain has been summarized by Justice Rutledge as followed: «... Constitutional issues affecting legislation will not be determined in friendly, nonadversary proceedings; in advance of the necessity of deciding then; in broader terms than required by the precise facts to which the ruling is to be applied; if the record presents some other ground upon which the case may be disposed of; at the instance of one who fails to show that he is injured by the statute's operation, or who has availed himself of its benefits; or if a construction of the statute is fairly possible by which the question may be avoided», *Rescue Army v. Municipal Court of Los Angeles*, 331 US 549, (1947) p. 569.

[85] *Frothingham v. Mellon*, 262 US 447 (1923).

[86] *Ashwander v. Tennessy Valley Authority*, 297 US 288 (1936), p. 346.

[87] *Frothingham v. Mellon*, 262 US 447, (1923), p. 488.

In this respect, and when considering the due standing of taxpayers to question the budget decisions of Congress[88] Chief Justice Burger in *United States* v. *Richardson* (1974), refereed to the always valid:

> «Basic principle that to invoke judicial power the claimant must have a «personal stake in the outcome»... or a «particular concrete injury»...»that he has sustained... a direct injury»... in short, something more than generalized grievances».[89]

Therefore, not only is a case or a controversy needed for judicial review, but also that the constitutional issue should be alleged by a party with the necessary standing, that is to say, based on «his own legal rights and interests» affected by the act whose validity is questioned».[90] Moreover, even in cases in which the Supreme Court allows persons or organizations or public authorities not party to a case before it, to file a brief as *amicus curae,* this only happens when they have a special interest in the matter, have applied for it to the Court or acted with the consent of the parties, their briefs being intended to support or supplement the arguments of the parties.[91]

Anyway, without the limitations imposed on the parties regarding standing to raise constitutional questions as stated by Justice Powell in *Wart* v. *Seldin* (1975) it would mean that:

> «The courts would be called upon to decide abstract questions of wide public significance even though other governmental institutions may be more competent to address the questions and even though judicial intervention may be unnecessary to protect individual rights...».[92]

The action to review the constitutionality of a law in the federal courts, therefore, is clearly not the *actio popularis* that exists in some concentrated and mixed systems of judicial review. On the contrary, in the United States, as Professor B. Schwartz pointed out:

> «Citizens cannot bring it in the interest of the community as a whole, to see that the rule of law is respected by the legislative and executive branches. Unless the action is brought by one who has a direct personal interest, he does not have the standing required to bring the suit».[93]

But the requirement of standing to sue and to raise the constitutional question is not sufficient to be considered by the court; the party that alleges the invalidity of a statute must demonstrate its invalidity. The Supreme Court has, in this sense, established that there is a presumption of constitutionality and validity in the statutes approved by Congress, unless the opposite is clearly demonstrated.[94]

---

88 See *Flast v. Cohen* 392 US. 83 (1968).

89 *United States v. Richardson*, 418, US. 966 (1974). *Cf. De Funis v. Odegaard*, 416, US 312 (1974).

90 *Warth v. Seldin*, 422 US 490 (1975).

91 *Cf.* L. BAUM, *op. cit.*, pp. 74, 80, 91.

92 *Warth v. Seldin*, 422 US 490 (1975).

93 B. SCHWARTZ, *op. cit.*, p. 151.

94 *Ogden v. Saunders*, 12 Wheaton, 213 (1827) Justice Washington said: 'It is but a decent respect due to the wisdom, integrity and patriotism of the legislative body, by which any law is passed, to presume in favour of its validity' . Also in *Cooper v. Telfair*, 4 Dallas (4.US) 14 (1800) Justice Washington said: 'The presumption indeed, must always be in favour of the validity of laws, if the contrary is not clearly demonstrated'.

C. *The Evident and Indispensable Unconstitutionality*

This presumption of validity and constitutionality of the statutes lead us to the second of the self-restraints developed by the Supreme Court regarding its powers of judicial review. It is that the Court should declare an act of Congress unconstitutional, only when its invalidity is clear and undoubtedly established and demonstrated. The principle was established by Chief Justice Marshall in *Fletcher* v. *Peck* (1810), saying:

> «The question whether a law be void for its repugnance to the constitution, is, at all times, a question of much delicacy, which ought seldom, if ever, to be decided in the affirmative, in a doubtful case... But it is not on slight implication and vague conjecture that the legislature is to be pronounced to have transcended its powers, and its acts to be considered as void. The opposition between the constitution and the law should be such that the judge feels a clear and strong conviction of their incompatibility with each other».[95]

Therefore, even though adopted by a majority of votes, the decision of the Supreme Court upon the unconstitutionality of an act of Congress must be based on clear, evident and conclusive reasons for its invalidity.

The third self-restraint developed by the Supreme Court upon its judicial review powers, also closely related to the need for a case or controversy where the constitutional issue is to be raised, is that the invalidity of a statute must only be resolved by the court when the decision upon the constitutionality or unconstitutionality of an act of congress is «absolutely necessary to the decision of the case».[96] Consequently, the courts must not decide upon the unconstitutionality of a statute, when it would not necessarily change its definitive decision over the rights of the parties; for example, when the question has insufficient relation with the controversy or when there are other ways of satisfying the claim of a party, without referring to the constitutional issue raised.

Chief Justice Marshall in *Ex parte Randolph* (1833) enunciated the rule, when saying:

> «No questions can be brought before a judicial tribunal of greater delicacy than those which involve the constitutionality of a legislative act. If they become indispensably necessary to the case, the Court must meet and decide them; but if the case may be determined on other points, a just respect for the legislative requires that the obligation of its laws should not be unnecessarily and wantonly assailed».[97]

In this respect, Justice Brandeis, in his concurring opinion to *Ashwander* v. *Tennessee Valley Authority* (1936) insisted on one of the rules under which the Supreme Court has avoided passing upon a large part of the en»tire constitutional question by stating:

> The Court will not pass upon a constitutional question, although properly presented by the record, if there is also some other ground upon which the

---

[95] *Fletcher v. Peck*, 6 Cranch 87 (1810).

[96] *Burton v. United States*, 196, US. 283, 295 quoted in *Ashwander v. Tennessy Valley Authority*, 297 US 288 (1936).

[97] *Ex parte Randolph*, 20 Fed. Cas. 242 (1833) quoted by W.J. WAGNER, *The Federal States and their Judiciary*, The Hague 1959, p. 97.

case may be disposed of.... thus, if a case can be decided on either of two grounds, one involving a constitutional question, the other a question of statutory construction or general law, the court will decide only the latter».[98]

Along the same lines, in *Crowell* v. *Benson* (1932), it was stated:

«When the validity of an act of the Congress is drawn in question, and even if a serious doubt of constitutionality is raised, it is a cardinal principle that this Court will first ascertain whether a construction of the statute is fairly possible by which the question may be avoided».[99]

Therefore, the decision upon the validity or invalidity of a statute must be indispensable and unavoidable in the resolution of the case; thus, if there are other ways of resolving the controversy avoiding the constitutional question, the court must follow that path. This leads to the criteria developed by the Supreme Court in the sense that statutes must be constructed, and interpreted, if possible, so as to avoid constitutional issues, and that the courts must draw interpretations in order to achieve this result.[100]

D. *The Exception: Political Questions*

Even when a constitutional issue is raised in a case or controversy by a party with the required standing, and the resolution of the invalidity of a statute being indispensable for the resolution of the case, the Court has considered as non-justifiable certain «political questions» mainly related to the «separation of powers» and particularly with «the relationship between the judiciary and the co-ordinate branches of the Federal Government».[101]

The main source of questions considered as political and thus non justiciable by the Supreme Court are related to foreign affairs which involves as the Supreme Court stated in *Ware* v. *Hylton* (1796) «considerations of policy, considerations of extreme magnitude, and certainly entirely incompetent to the examination and decision of a Court of Justice».[102] Decisions concerning foreign relation therefore, as stated by Justice Jackson in *Chicago and Southern Air Lines* v. *Waterman Steamship Co.* (1948):

«Are wholly confined by our constitution to the political departments of the government. ... They are decisions of a kind for which the Judiciary has neither aptitude, facilities nor responsibility and which has long been held to belong in the domain of political power not subject to judicial intrusion or inquiry».[103]

Even though developed mainly in the foreign affairs sphere, the Supreme Court has also considered certain matters relating to the government of internal affairs, a political question, and thus non justiciable; like the decision as to whether a state must have a republican form of government, which in *Luther* v. *Borden* (1849) was considered a «decision binding on every other department of the government, and could not be questioned in a judicial tribunal».[104]

---

98 *Ashwander v. Tennessy Valley Authority*, 297, US. 288 (1936).

99 *Crowell v. Benson*, 285 US 22 (1932), quoted in *Ashwander v. Tennessy Valley Authority*, 297, US. 288 (1936).

100 *United States v. Congress of Industrial Organization* 335 US 106 (1948).

101 *Baker v. Carr*, 369 US 186 (1962).

102 *Ware v. Hylton*, 3 Dallas, 199 (1796)

103 *Chicago and Southern Air Lines v. Waterman Steamship Co.*, 333 US 103 (1948) p. 111.

104 *Luther v. Borden*, 48 US (7 Howard), 1 (1849).

Any way and even though that through the decisions of the Supreme Court, a list of «political questions» that the Court has considered as non justifiable can be elaborated, the ultimate responsibility in determining them corresponds to the Supreme Court.

As the Court said in *Baker* v. *Carr* (1962):

> «Deciding whether a matter has in any measure been committed by the constitution to another branch of government, or whether the action of that branch exceeds whatever authority has been committed, -said the Court- is itself a delicate exercise in constitutional interpretation, and is a responsibility of this Court as ultimate interpreter of the constitution».[105]

5. The Decision Upon the Constitutionality of the Statutes

Setting apart the problems related to political questions, considered by Professor Schwartz as a possible and undesirable exception to the principle of legality,[106] once a judicial decision is adopted by the courts on a constitutional issue, the classic problem of the effects of the judicial decision must be resolved.

The general «principle», in this matter, is that a judicial decision in matters of control of constitutionality in a diffuse system of judicial review, has *in casu et, inter partes* and *ex tunc* retroactive effects, that is to say, as a consequence of the decision the act considered unconstitutional must be understood for the parties in the case, to be null and void and as never having existed. This principle, however, has been tempered in its concrete application due to the requirements of legal reliability and justice.

A. The inter partes effect and the stare decisis doctrine

In effect, the decision adopted by an American court concerning a constitutional question in principle has relevancy only for the parties to the case. Thus, the decision has no *per se* general effects and these effects do not apply *erga omnes*. The statute declared unconstitutional is not annulled by the court nor repealed by it, the legislature which enacted a statute being the only one who has the power to do so. Consequently, the statute declared null and void by a court continues on the books notwithstanding the adverse decision on its validity.

Nevertheless, when the decision upon the unconstitutionality of a statute is adopted by the Supreme Court, as far as the inferior courts are concerned the rule *stare decisis et non quieta movere* (let the decision stand) applies and the inferior courts are bound by the decision of the Supreme Court. In practice, the statute may be considered as no longer enforceable since it may be supposed that after the Supreme Court decision, if any other proceedings are brought under the same statute, they too will result in dismissal, because it may be anticipated that the Supreme Court which held the statute to be unenforceable in one case will find it equally unenforceable in the next case arising under it.[107]

On the other hand, it must be borne in mind that the Supreme Court, when ruling upon the constitutionality of a statute, interprets the constitution declaring

105 *Baker v. Carr*, 369 US 186 (1962).
106 B. SCHWARTZ, *op. cit.*, p. 157
107 *Cf.* P.G. KAUPER, *loc. cit.*, p. 611.

at the same time which is the supreme law of the land. This declaration has binding effects on all state bodies though, including, as we said, the judiciary. This was expressly resolved by the Supreme Court in the *Cooper* v. *Aaron* case (1958) in which the Court reaffirmed the binding effects of its previous decision in the *Brown* v. *Board of Education of Topeka* case (1954)[108] on segregation practices in education over all state bodies whether executive, legislative or judiciary.

In *Cooper* v. *Aaron,* the Court said:

> «Article VI of the constitution makes the constitution the Supreme law of the land. In 1803, chief Justice Marshall, speaking for a unanimous Court, referring to the constitution as the fundamental and paramount law of the nation, declared in the notable *Marbury v. Madison* case... that «It is emphatically the province and duty of the judicial department to say what the law is». This decision declared the basic principle that the federal judiciary is supreme in the exposition of the laws of the constitution, and that principle has ever since been respected by this Court and the Country as a permanent and indispensable feature of our constitutional system. It follows that the interpretation of the Fourteenth Amendment enunciated by this Court in the Brown case is the supreme law of the land, and Art. VI of the constitution makes it of binding effect on the states anything in the constitution or laws of any state to the contrary notwithstanding».[109]

Therefore, we can say that the principle of *stare decisis* applies in the United States regarding the binding effects of the decisions of the Supreme Court over inferior courts, contributing to the uniformity of the interpretation of the constitution and tending to avoid contradictory decisions on constitutional issues by the Courts.

However, the *stare decisis* rule is not absolute, and in the United States it has less rigidity than in the British legal system,[110] particularly regarding the Supreme Court itself. As Justice Brandeis said in *Burnet* v. *Coronado Oil and Gas Co. (1972) stare decisis:*

> «Is usually the wise policy, because in most matters it is more important that the applicable rule of law be settled than that it be settled right ... But in cases involving the Federal constitution, where corrections, through legislative action are practically impossible, this Court has often overruled its earlier decisions. The Court bows to the lessons of experience and the force of better reasoning, recognizing that the process of trial and error, so fruitful in the physical sciences, is appropriate also in the judicial function».[111]

> «If adherence to precedent were the only judicial virtue -said Professor Bernard Schwartz-, it could hardly be gain said that the Supreme Court since 1937 has been among the least virtuous of modern judicial tribunals».[112]

In fact, over the last fifty years, one of the outstanding features of the Supreme Court of the United States has been the frequency with which it has repudiated its

---

108 347 US 483 (1954).

109 *Cooper v. Aaron,* 358 US 1 (1958).

110 *Cf.* A. TUNC and S. TUNC, *Le droit des Etats Unies d'Amérique. Sources et techniques,* Paris 1955, p. 174; B. SCHWARTZ, *op. cit.,* p. 159.

111 *Burnet v. Coronado Oil and Gas Co.* 285 US 393 (1932), p. 406.

112 B. SCHWARTZ, *The Supreme Court. Constitutional Revolution in Retrospect,* New York 1957, p. 345.

earlier attitude toward questions of constitutionality, not following decisions handed down by its predecessors and overruling many of its earlier decisions, «some of which had been regarded as settled in American law for the better part of a century».[113] This attitude of the Supreme Court has been explained by Justice Reed delivering the opinion of the Court in *Smith* v. *Allwright* (1944), in which a previous constitutional interpretation was overruled, with the following words:

> «In reaching this conclusion we are not unmindful of the desirability of continuity of decisions in constitutional questions. However, when convinced of former error, this Court has never felt constrained to follow precedent. In constitutional questions, where corrections depend upon amendments and not upon legislative action, this Court throughout its history has freely exercised its power to re-examine the basis of its constitutional decisions. This has long been accepted practice, and this practice has continued to this day. This is particularly true when the decision believed erroneous is the application of a constitutional principle rather than an interpretation of the constitution to extract the principle itself».[114]

Nevertheless, even in its application to the lower courts, the *stare decisis* principle concerning Supreme Court decisions has different scope depending on the contents of the decision. For instance, in some situations a statute may be held to be invalid, only in its application to the situation before the court and not invalid on its face, in which case the statute may continue to have validity in its application to other situations.[115] The binding effect of a Supreme Court decision, therefore, will depend upon the nature of the attack on the statute, whether on its validity or only on its application to the party by reference to facts peculiar to it.

B. *The Nullity of Unconstitutional Acts and the Retroactive Effects of the Courts Decisions*

As far as the effects of the judicial decision on constitutional issues is concern, additional to the problems posed by the *inter partes* effect and the *stare decisis* doctrine concerning Supreme Court decisions, in a diffuse system of judicial review like the American one, the courts do not annul the statute considered unconstitutional, but only declare its nullity and invalidity, considering the unconstitutional act void and null *ab initio*. This was the general principle applied to the American system during the last century, which implied that the decisions of the Court on matters of constitutionality had *ex-tunc* and retroactive effects. This was the doctrine defined in the circuit Court *Vanhorne's Lessee* v. *Dorrance* case (1795) in which it was considered that a void act

> «Never had constitutional existence; it is a dead letter, and of no more virtue or avail, than if it never had. been made...»[116]

A hundred years later, (in *United States* v. *Realty* (1895) the Supreme Court expressed the same principle in more conclusive way, by saying that an:

> «Unconstitutional act of Congress is the same as if there were no act».[117]

---

113 B. SCHWARTZ, *American Constitutional Law, cit.*, p. 159.
114 *Smith v. Allwright*, 321 US 649 (1944).
115 *Cf.* P.G. KAUPER, *loc. cit.*, pp. 611, 617.
116 *Venhorn's Lessee v. Dorrance*, 2 Dallas, 304 (1795).
117 *United States v. Realty Co.*, 163 US 427 (1895), p. 439.

Previously, in *Norton* v. *Selby County* (1886) the court had also said, that an

> «Unconstitutional act is not a law; it confers no rights; it imposes no duties; it affords no protection; it creates no office; it is, in legal contemplation, as inoperative as though it had never been passed».[118]

Thus, the traditional principle of the nullity of the unconstitutional act, and therefore, the declarative effects of the judicial decision that considers a statute void and null, as if «it had never been passed» or if it «never had been made» was also applied in the United States. Consequently, judicial decisions on constitutional questions were considered to have *ex tunc* effects, thus, having retroactive effects.

Nevertheless, the rigidity of this doctrine led to a change in its application, and to establishing whether or not the retroactive effects of the decisions regarding each case in particular would apply, particularly because of the negative or unjust effects that could be produced by the possible decisions of the court regarding the effects already factualy produced by the statute considered invalid, and because of the binding effect of the Supreme Court decisions upon the lower court,. This was expressly stated by Justice Clark in *Linkletter* v. *Walker* (1965), in which the Supreme Court applied new constitutional rules to cases finalized before the promulgation of other rulers. The Court said:

> «Petitioner contends that our method of resolving those prior cases demonstrates that an absolute rule of retroaction prevails in the area of constitutional adjudication. However, we believe that the constitution neither prohibits nor requires retrospective effect. As Justice Cardozo said, we think the federal constitution has no voice upon the subject. Once the premise is accepted that we -are neither required to apply, nor prohibited from applying a decision retrospectively, we must then weigh the merits and demerits in each case by looking to the prior history of the rule in question, its purpose and effect, and whether retrospective operation will further or retard its operation...»[119]

Therefore, considering that «the past cannot always be erased by a new judicial decision»,[120] the retroactive effects of the Supreme Court decisions in constitutional issues has been applied in a relative way. «The questions -said the Supreme Court in *Chicot County Drainage District* v. *Baxter State Bank* (1940)-, are among the most difficult of those that have engaged the attention of courts, state and federal, and it is manifest from numerous decisions that an all-inclusive statement of a principle of absolute retroactive invalidity cannot be justified».[121]

In this sense, Professor J.A.C. Grant said in his classical study on «The legal Effects of a Ruling that a Statute is Unconstitutional», contrary to what the Supreme Court said in *Norton* v. *Selby County* in 1886, «An unconstitutional act may give rise to rights. It may impose duties. It may afford protection. It may even create an office. In short, it may not be as inoperative as though it had never been passed».[122]

---

118 *Norton v. Selby County*, 118 US 425 (1886), p. 442.

119 *Linkletter v. Walker*, 381 US 618 (1965).

120 *Chicot County Drainage District v. Baxter State Bank*, 308 US 371 (1940), p. 374.

121 *Idem*.

122 J.A.C. GRANT, «The Legal Effect of a Ruling that a Statute is Unconstitutional', *Detroit College of Law Review*, 1978, (2), p. 207.

Therefore, the Supreme Court has recognized its authority to give or to deny retroactive effects to its ruling on constitutional issues, and the Supreme Courts of the states have done the same during recent decades.

For instance, in criminal matters, the Courts has given full retroactive effects to its rules when they benefit the prosecuted. In particular it has given retroactive effects to decisions in the field of criminal liability, permitting prisoners on application for *habeas corpus* to secure their release on the grounds that they are being held under authority of a statute which subsequent to their conviction was held to be unconstitutional.[123] The Court has also given retroactive effects to its decisions on constitutional matters, as referred to by Professor J.A.C. Grant, when it considers the rules essential to safeguard against convicting innocent persons, such as the requirement that counsel be furnished at the trial (*Gideon* v. *Wainwright*, 327 US, 335, 1963), or when the accused is asked to plead (*Arsenault* v. *Massachusetts*, 393 US 5, 1968), or when it is sought to revoke the probation status of a convicted criminal because of his subsequent conduct (*McConnell* v. *Rhay*, 393, US, 2, 1968), as well as the rule requiring proof beyond a reasonable doubt (*Ivan* v. *City of New York*, 407 US, 203, 1972). Its ruling concerning the death penalty has also been made fully retroactive (*Witherspoon* v. *Illinois*, 391, US, 510, 1968).[124]

In other criminal cases, the position of the Court has been to give no retroactive effects to its rulings on constitutional issues when it also benefits the prosecuted. As Professor Grant says, in 1977 the Supreme Court held that any change in the interpretation of the constitution that has the effect of punishing acts which were not penalized under the earlier interpretation cannot be applied retroactively, since as it stated in *Marks* v. *United States* (1977), «the notion that persons have a right to fair warning of that conduct which will give rise to criminal penalties, is fundamental to our concept of constitutional liberty».[125]

Therefore, the rule of retro activeness on prospectiveness of the effects of the Courts decisions in criminal cases is not absolute, and has been applied by the Court considering the justice of its application in each case. Consequently, when the decision has not for instance affected the «fairness of a trial» but only the rights to privacy of a person, the Court has denied the retroactive effects of its ruling. Such was the case in *Linkletter* v. *Walker*, (1965) where Justice Clarke delivering the opinion of the Court stated:

> «In ... the ... areas in which we have applied our rule retrospectively the principle that we applied went to the fairness of the trial, the very integrity of the fact-finding process. Here ... the fairness of the trial is not under attack. All that petitioner attacks is the admissibility of evidence (illegally seized), the reliability and relevancy of which is not questioned, and which may well have had no effect on the outcome...».[126]

Therefore, as Professor Grant reported, when the purpose is merely to protect the privacy of the individual or to improve police standards, as in the case of new rules as to searches through electronic surveillance (*Desist* v. *United States*, 394, US, 244, 1969), or in connection with a lawful arrest (*Hill* v. *California*, 401, US, 797, 1971),

123 *Ex parte Siebold*, 100 US 371, (1880).
124 J.A.C. GRANT, *loc.cit.*, p. 237.
125 *Marks v. United States*, 430 US 188 (1977), p. 191; J.A.C. GRANT, *loc.cit.*, 238.
126 *Linkletter v Walker*, 381, US, 618 (1965).

police questioning, leading to confessions (*McMann* v. *Richardson*, 397, US, 759, 1970) or the use of incriminating reports filed by the accused (*Mackey* v. *United States*, 401 US, 667, 1971), the doctrine of non retro activeness adopted in *Stovall* v. *Denno*[127] has been applied.[128]

It must also be mentioned that even in cases of rules related to the idea of the type of trial necessary to guard against convicting the innocent, the rules established by the Supreme Court have been made wholly prospective when to give them retroactive effect would impose what the Court considers unreasonable burdens upon the government brought about at least in part by its reliance upon previous rulings of the Supreme Court. This happened in *De Stefano* v. *Woods* (1968), which established that state criminal trials must be by jury[129] and in *Adam* v. *Illinois* (1972), established the right to counsel at the preliminary hearing whose retroactivity the Court said, «could seriously disrupt the administration of our criminal laws».[130]

On the other hand, in civil cases, it has been considered that the new rule established in a court decision on constitutional matters, cannot disturb property rights or contracts previously made. In this respect, the Supreme Court in *Gelpcke* v. *Dubuque* (1864) considered that a decision of the Supreme Court of Iowa, was to be given prospective effect only, by stating:

> «The sound and true rule is, that if the contract, when made, was valid by the laws of the state as then expounded... and administered in its courts of justice, its validity and. obligation cannot be impaired by any subsequent action of legislation, or decision of its courts altering the construction of the law».[131]

This doctrine of prospectiveness was also developed and applied by state supreme courts regarding liability for acts of dependents. For instance, the Supreme Court of Illinois in 1958 considered «unjust, unsupported by any valid reason, and (without) ... rightful place in modern day society» the rule previously established by the same Court (1898), that held that a school district cannot be held liable for the careless acts of the drivers of its school buses. In principle, the overruling of the 1898 decision could have led to its application retroactively; nevertheless, bearing in mind that its full retroactivity might endanger the fiscal integrity of many small school districts, the Court stated:

> «Retrospective application of our decision may result in great hardship to school districts, which have relied on prior decisions upholding the doctrine of tort immunity of school districts. For this reason we feel justice best be served by holding that, except as to the plaintiff in the instant case, the rule herein established shall apply only to cases arising out of future occurrence».[132]

Finally, it must also be stated that in administrative cages, the doctrine of *de facto* officers has lead to the adoption of the prospective rule effects of the decisions on judicial review. In this respect, in *State* v. *Carroll* (1871) the Supreme Court of Connecticut stated that a statute «... which creates an office and provides an officer

---

127 *Stovall v. Denno*, 388, US, 293, (1967).
128 J.A.C. GRANT, *loc.cit.*, 237.
129 *De Stefano v. Woods*, 392, US, 631 (1968).
130 *Adams v. Illinois*, 405, US, 278 (1972).
131 68 US (1 Wall) 175 (1864).
132 *Molitor v. Kaneland Community Unit Dist. N° 302*, 18 III. 2d at 25, 162 N.E. 2d at 96. quoted by J.A.C. GRANT, *loc. cit.*, p. 220.

to perform its duties, must have the force of law until set aside as unconstitutional by the courts»,[133] thus the invalidity of the office could not affect the acts accomplished by the *de facto* officer.

C. *The Practical Effects of the Decision on Judicial Review*

As we have said, there are no special types of proceeding required for the raising of constitutional issues in the courts; therefore, the constitutional question car be raised incidentally in any type of proceeding. Nevertheless, in the United States, particular types of proceedings and remedies that are usually used for raising constitutional issues have been traditionally identified. These are apart from the declaratory judgment proceeding, the request for an injunction, for a writ of mandamus or for a writ of habeas corpus[134] which result in having concrete and particular effects, referred to constitutional justice.

For instance, the injunction against enforcement of a statute by a prosecutor or by public agencies is the most drastic remedy available in a case raising constitutional issues. It is equity proceeding of preventive and negative effects. It consists in the prohibition established regarding a subject to enforce certain acts that could be prejudicial to other subjects. Therefore, it is a preventive and protective proceeding, and its effects would depend on whether the decision holding a statute invalid considered the statute void in its face or invalid only in its application to factual circumstances peculiar to the person raising the issue. In this respect, Professor P.G. Kauper said, if an injunction is sought against the enforcement of a statute on the grounds that it is void on its face as an impairment of constitutional rights, the court's decree may be broad enough to prevent further enforcement of the statute against any other person, with the practical effect of making the statute completely unenforceable.[135]

Another remedy commonly used for controlling the constitutionality of statutes is the request for a writ of *mandamus*, which consists in a judicial order directed to a public officer, commanding him to perform certain acts regarding the petitioner which he is obliged to perform.[136]

Finally, another remedy that is also used to test the constitutionality of a statute is the request for a writ of *habeas corpus* through which a person, who is being held in custody on a charge of violating a criminal statute, alleges its invalidity. If the claim in this proceeding is sustained, the court orders the release of the petitioner from official custody.

III. THE DIFFUSE SYSTEM OF JUDICIAL REVIEW IN LATIN AMERICA

In the middle of the 19th century, the American system of judicial review influenced most of the Latin-American systems, which we can say, generally adopted in one way or another, the diffuse system of judicial review. Alexis De Tocqueville's

---

133 *State v. Canoll*, 38 Conn. 449, (1871), quoted by J.A.C. GRANT, *loc. cit.*, p. 232.

134 G.H. JAFFIN, «Les modes d'introduction du contrôle judiciaire de la constitutionalité des lois aux Etats-Unis», in *Introduction a l'etude du droit comparé, Recueil d'etudes en l'honneur d'Eduard Lambert*, Paris 1938, Vol. II, p. 256.

135 P.G. KAUPER, *loc. cit.*, p. 620.

136 28 US Code 1361.

influential book, *Democracy in America*,[137] has been considered as having played a fundamental role in the adoption of the system, particularly regarding the Latin American countries with a federal form of state all of whom adopted a form of constitutional justice, as was the case in Argentina (1860), Mexico (1857), Venezuela (1858) and Brazil (1890). The system was also adopted in other countries like Colombia (1850) which had a brief federal experience, and even without connection with the federal form of state, in the Dominican Republic (1844) where it is still in force.[138]

Most of the Latin American systems of judicial review moved from the original diffuse system towards a mixed system, by adding concentrated aspects of judicial review, or adopting the mixed system from the beginning, but the Argentinean system remained the most similar to the American model,[139] though with its own natural characteristics. The Mexican system also remained as a diffuse system but with the peculiarities of the *juicio de amparo* (trial for constitutional protection), which has produced a unique and complex institution.

That is why when considering the diffuse system of judicial review in Latin America, we will now refer to the Argentinean and Mexican systems, leaving the analysis of the Brazilian, Colombian and Venezuelan systems to when we study the mixed systems of judicial review.

1. The Argentinean System

A. *Judicial Control of the Constitutionality as a Power of All Courts*

The constitution of the Republic of Argentina of 1860 established in articles 31 and 100, in terms very similar to those of the American constitution, the principles of constitutional supremacy and the role of the judiciary.

Article 31, in similar terms to the «supremacy clause» of the American constitution, established:

> «This constitution, the laws of the Nation that the Congress consequently approves and the treaties with foreign powers, are the supreme law of the Nation, and the authorities of each Province are obliged to conform to it, notwithstanding any contrary disposition which the provincial laws or Constitutions might contain».

---

137 The first edition in Spanish of the book was issued in 1836, one year after the French and English edition. On the influence of the DE TOCQUEVILLE book on the matter, see J. CARPIZO and H. FIX-ZAMUDIO, «La necesidad y la legitimidad de la revisión judicial en América Latina. Desarrollo reciente», in *Boletín Mexicano de Derecho Comparado*, 52, 1985, p. 33; R.D. BAKER, *Judicial Review in México. A Study of the Amparo Suit*, Austin 1971, pp. 15, 33.

138 The 1844 constitution, as well as the 1966 constitution (Art. 46) established that 'are null and void all Laws, Decrees, Resolutions, Regulations or Acts contrary to the constitution'. Consequently, all the Courts can declare an act unconstitutional and not applicable to the concrete case. *Cf.* M BERGES CHUPANI, «Report» in *Memoria de la Reunión de Cortes Superiores de Justicia de Ibero-America, El Caribe, España y Portugal*, Caracas 1983, p. 380.

139 A. E. GHIGLIANI, *Del control jurisdiccional de constitucionalidad*, Buenos Aires 1952, who speaks about «Northamerican filiation» of the judicial control of constitutionality in Argentinian law, p. 6, 55, 115. *Cf.* R. BIELSA, *La protección constitucional y el recurso extraordinario. Jurisdicción de la Corte Suprema*, Buenos Aires 1958, p. 116; J.A.C. GRANT, «El control jurisdiccional de la constitucionalidad de las Leyes: una contribución de las Américas a la ciencia política», *Revista de la Facultad de Derecho de México*, UNAM, T. XII, 45, 1962, p. 652; C.J. FRIEDRICH, *The Impact of American Constitutionalism Abroad*, Boston 1967, p. 83.

On the other hand, article 100 referring to judicial power, established:

> «The Supreme Court and the inferior Court of the Nation are competent to try and decide all cases related to aspects ruled by the constitution, by the laws of the Nation and by the Treaties with foreign nations».

Therefore, in similar terms to the American constitution, the 1860 Argentinean constitution established no norm expressly conferring no judicial review power upon the Supreme Court or the other courts. Thus, in a similar way to the American process, judicial review in Argentina was also a creation of the Supreme Court, based on the principles of supremacy of the constitution and judicial duty when applying the law; and the first case in which it was exercised regarding a federal statute was the *Sojo* case, (1887), also concerning the unconstitutionality of a law that tried to enlarge the original jurisdiction of the Supreme Court[140] as was the *Marbury* v. *Madison* case.

Nevertheless, the question of the powers of the judiciary to control the constitutionality of legislation was a matter of discussion in the Panama Constitutional Convention in 1857-1858, where the predominant opinion on the subject was: first, the character of the constitution as a supreme law and the power of the courts to maintain that supremacy over the laws which infringed upon it; second, the limits imposed over the constituted powers by popular sovereignty, so that laws contrary to the principles embodied in the constitution, could not be binding on the courts; and third, that the judiciary was precisely the branch of the state organs which ought to have enough power to interpret the constitution regarding the other state powers.[141]

Therefore, through the work of the courts, the Argentinean system of judicial review has been developed over the last century as a diffuse system[142] in which all the courts have the power to declare the unconstitutionality of legislative acts, treaties,[143] executive and administrative acts and judicial decisions, whether at national or provincial levels.[144] This power of judicial review is, of course, reserved to the courts and the executive cannot decide not to apply a statute on unconstitutional grounds.

Therefore, in Argentina, the power to control the constitutionality of state acts is not reserved to one single judicial body or a group of them; it concerns all courts, of course, within the scope of the jurisdiction that each of them has.

---

140 *Cf.* A.E. GHIGLIANI, *op. cit.*, p. 5; R. BIELSA, *op. cit.* p. 41, 43, 179 who speaks about a «pretorian creation» of judicial review by the Supreme Court, *op. cit.*, p. 179. *Cf.* J.R. VANOSSI and P.F. UBERTONE, *Instituciones de defensa de la Constitución en la Argentina*, UNAM, Congreso Internacional sobre la Constitución y su defensa, México 1982, (mimeo), p. 4; H. QUIROGA LAVIE, *Derecho constitucional*, Buenos Aires 1978, p. 481. Previously in 1863 the firsts Supreme Court decisions where adopted in constitutional matters but referred to provincial and executive acts. *Cf.* A.E. GHIGLIANI, *op. cit.*, p. 58.

141 *Cf.* A.E. GHIGLIANI, *op. cit.*, p. 58.

142 N.P. SAGÜES, *Recurso Extraordinario*, Buenos Aires 1984, Vol. I, p. 91. J.R. VANOSSI and P.F. UBERTONE, *op. cit.* p. 2, 14. See also J.R. VANOSSI, *Teoría constitucional*, Buenos Aires, Vol. II, *Supremacía y control de constitucionalidad*, Buenos Aires 1976, p. 155.

143 In particular, regarding the unconstitutionality of Treaties and the posibility of the Courts to control them, A.G. GHIGLIANI, *op. cit.*, p. 62; J.R. VANOSSI, *Aspectos del recurso extraordinario de inconstitucionalidad*, Buenos Aires 1966, p. 91, and *Teoría constitucional*, *op. cit.*, Vol. II, p. 277.

144 *Cf.* R. BIELSA, *op. cit.*, pp. 120-148. J.R. VANOSSI and P.F. UBERTONE, *doc. cit.*, p. 6.

In Argentina, being a federal state, the organization of the judiciary led to two court systems established from their origin following the American model:[145] National and provincial courts. The provincial courts have jurisdiction over all matters of «ordinary law», (*derecho común*) like civil, commercial, criminal, labour, social security, and mining law and public provincial law (constitutional and administrative provincial law). In each Province there are courts of first and second instances, and at their apex a Superior Provincial Court.

At the national level, the national courts have jurisdiction over all matters regulated by «federal law»; particularly concerning constitutional and administrative law cases and in all cases in which the nation is a party or foreign diplomatic agent are involved. The organization of the national courts is as follows: National courts with territorial jurisdiction in the first instance; national chambers of appeals, in the second instance, and at the apex the Supreme Court of Justice, that also acts as a third instance.[146]

The Supreme Court of Justice, the only judicial body created in the constitution and considering itself «final interpreter of the constitution» or as the defendant of the constitution»,[147] has two sorts of jurisdiction: original and appellate. The original jurisdiction is established in the constitution and, therefore, is not enlargeable by statute, and concerns all matters related to ambassadors, ministers and foreign consuls and to which the Provinces are party.[148]

In its appellate jurisdiction, the Supreme Court has jurisdiction through two sorts of appeals: ordinary and extraordinary. In its appellate jurisdiction through ordinary appeals, the Supreme Court has the power of reviewing the decisions of the national chambers of appeal in the following cases:

1. Cases in which the nation is a party according to an amount fixed periodically;
2. Cases concerning extradition of criminals sought by foreign countries.
3. Cases concerning the seizure of ships in time of war and other cases concerning maritime law.[149]

In these cases of appellate jurisdiction through ordinary appeal, the Supreme Court acts as a court of third instance and last resort reviewing the whole case decided by the national chambers of appeals.

However, as we have said, the appellate jurisdiction of the Supreme Court of Justice can also be exercised through what has been called an «extraordinary appeal» that is in fact an «extraordinary recourse» that the party in a case decided by the national chambers of appeals and by the Superior Courts of the Provinces can bring before the supreme Court, in particular cases related to constitutional issues and with special conditions. This is, undoubtedly, the mean through which the Supreme Court normally decides upon the final interpretation of the constitution when reviewing the constitutionality of state acts, and consequently it is the most important mean for judicial review.

---

145 *Cf.* R. BIELSA, *op. cit.*, p. 57; A.E. GHIGLIANI, *op. cit.*, p. 55.
146 *Cf.* J.R. VANOSSI and P.F. UBERTONE, *doc. cit.*, p. 14-18; A.E. GHIGLIANI, *op. cit.*, p. 76.
147 R. BIELSA, *op. cit.*, p. 270; J.R. VANOSSI and P.F. UBERTONE, *doc. cit.*, p. 18.
148 Art. 101.
149 *Cf.* R. BIELSA, *op. cit.*, p. 60-61; J.R. VANOSSI and P.F. UBERTONE, *doc. cit.*, p. 19.

Before studying this «extraordinary recourse» we will refer to the general trends of the incidental character of the Argentinean diffuse system and its consequences.

B. *The Incidental Character of Judicial Review*

In effect, as a diffuse system of judicial review, the Argentinean system is essentially an incidental one, in which the question of constitutionality is not the principal object of a process; thus the constitutional issue can be at any moment and at any stage of any proceeding. This incidental character has led to considering the Argentinean System of judicial review, as an «indirect» control system,[150] because the constitutional issue can only be raised in a judicial controversy, case or process, normally through an exception, at any moment before the decision is adopted by the court, and therefore not necessarily in the *litis contestatio* of the proceeding.[151]

The principal condition for raising constitutional questions is that they can only be raised in a «judicial case» or litigation between parties;[152] therefore, they cannot be raised as an abstract question before a court, and the courts cannot render declarative decisions upon unconstitutional matters.[153]

Nevertheless, the existence of a case or controversy in which the constitutional question could be raised is not only necessary, it is also indispensable that the question be raised by a party in the process with due interest in the matter, that is to say, which alleges a particular injury in his own right caused by the statute considered invalid.[154]

Consequently, the court on its own cannot raise constitutional issues in the Argentinean system. Thus, even if the court is convinced of the unconstitutionality of a statute, if a party has not raised the question, the Court is bound to apply the Statute to the decision of the case.[155] In this respect, it must be stressed that even though this has been the judicial doctrine invariably applied by courts, some authors have considered that the constitutional questions can be decided by courts without being raised by a party, based on the principle of constitutional supremacy and the notion of «public order».[156]

Nevertheless, an exemption to the need for party intervention when raising the constitutional issue has been established by the Supreme Court, allowing that the court can consider constitutional questions on its own, only in matters concerning the jurisdiction of the courts themselves and their functional autonomy. Consequently, the Supreme Court decided upon the unconstitutionality of a statute that enlarged its original jurisdiction of the supreme Court of Justice established in the constitution, although not being raised by a party.[157]

---

150 A.E. GHIGLIANI, *op. cit.*, p. 75.

151 A.E. GHIGLIANI, *op. cit.*, p. 76.

152 Art. 100 of the constitution; *Cf.* R. BIELSA, *op. cit.*, p. 213, 214; A.E. GHIGLIANI, *op. cit.*, p. 75; J.R. VANOSSI and P.F. UBERTONE, *doc. cit.*, p. 23.

153 *Cf.* R. BIELSA, *op. cit.*, p. 213, 214; A.E. GHIGLIANI, *op. cit.*, p. 80; S.M. LOZADA, *Derecho Constitucional Argentino*, Buenos Aires 1972, Vol. I, p. 342.

154 S.M. LOZADA, *op. cit.*, p. 342; A.E. GHIGLIANI, *op.cit.*, p. 82; J.R. VANOSSI and P.E. UBERTONE, *doc. cit.*, p. 23.

155 R. BIELSA, *op. cit.*, p. 198, 214; H. QUIROGA LAVIE, *op. cit.*, p. 479.

156 G. BIDART CAMPOS, *El derecho constitucional del poder*, Vol. II, Chap. XXIX; J.R. VANOSSI, *Teoría constitucional*, *op. cit.*, Vol. II, p. 318, 319.

157 *Cf.* J.R. VANOSSI and P.E. UBERTONE, *doc. cit.*, 25; .R. BIELSA, *op. cit.*, 255; H. QUIROGA LAVIE, *op. cit.*, p. 479.

Furthermore and related to the incidental or indirect character of judicial review in the Argentinean system, the constitutional question raised in a case particularly due to the presumption of constitutionality of all statutes,[158] must be of an unavoiding character, in the sense that its decision must be essential to the resolution of the case which depends on it.[159] Moreover, the constitutional question must be clear and undoubted. Therefore, the declaration of unconstitutionality being considered an act of extreme gravity and the last ratio of the legal order, the court must abstain its consideration when there are doubts about the issue.[160] Thus when an interpretation of the statute avoiding the consideration of the constitutional question is possible the court must follow this path.[161]

Finally, it must be said that in the Argentinean system, the Supreme Court of Justice has developed the same exception to judicial review established in the American system, concerning political questions, even though the constitution does not expressly establish anything on the matter.[162] These political questions are related to the «acts of government» of «political acts» doctrine developed in continental European law, and within which we can mention the following: the declaration of state of siege; the declaration of federal intervention in the provinces; the declaration of «public use» for means of expropriation; the declaration of war; the declaration of emergency to approve certain direct tax contributions; acts concerning foreign relations; the recognition of new foreign states or new foreign state governments; the expulsion of aliens, etc., In general, within these political questions there are acts exercised by the political powers of the state in accordance with powers exclusively and directly attributed to them in the constitution,[163] which can be considered the key element for their identification.

C. *The «Extraordinary Recourse» before the Supreme Court of Justice and Judicial Review*

We have said that the Supreme Court of Justice is vested in the Argentinean system, like it is in the United States, with two sorts of jurisdiction: original and appellate jurisdiction, and in the latter two other sorts can be distinguished: ordinary appellate jurisdiction and «extraordinary appellate jurisdiction» that can be exercised by the Supreme Court through the so called «extraordinary recourse», which accomplishes a similar result to the request for writ of *certiorari* in the United States Supreme Court activities.

But of course, the «extraordinary recourse» is quite different to the American request for writ of *certiorari,* in the sense that the Supreme Court of Justice does not have discretionary powers in accepting extraordinary recourses. Thus, in the Argentinean system, all the appellate jurisdiction of the Supreme Court, whether ordinary or extraordinary, is a mandatory jurisdiction, exercised as a consequence of a right the parties have, whether to appeal or to introduce the extraordinary recourse.

---

158 A.E. GHIGLIANI, *op. cit.*, p. 89, 90.
159 A.E. GHIGLIANI, *op. cit.*, p. 89; S.M. LOSADA, *op. cit*, p. 341.
160 H. QUIROGA LAVIE, *op. cit.*, p. 480.
161 A.E. GHIGLIANI, *op. cit.*, p. 91.
162 J.R. VANOSSI and P.E. UBERTONE, *doc. cit.*, p. 11.
163 *Cf.* A.E. GHIGLIANI, *op. cit.*, p. 85; H. QUIROGA LAVIE, *op. cit.*, p. 482; S.M. LOSADA, *op. cit.*, p. 343; J.R. VANOSSI and P.E. UBERTONE, *doc. cit.*, p. 11, 12.

Nevertheless, the difference between the ordinary appeal and the extraordinary recourse is that although called «extraordinary appeal» this recourse is not properly an appeal: it is rather an autonomous recourse. When it is exercised, the Supreme Court does not act as a mere third instance court,[164] particularly because the Court does not review the motives of the judicial decision under consideration, regarding the facts; its power of review being concentrated only in aspects of law regarding constitutional questions. That is why it has been said that the Supreme Court as a consequence of an extraordinary recourse, «does not act *jure litigatoris*» but *jure constitutionis*, does not judge a *questio facti*, but a *questio juris*».[165]

This substantive difference between the function of the Supreme Court as a consequence of the exercise of an appeal or an extraordinary recourse is followed by another formal difference, particularly, that contrary to the appeal, the extraordinary recourse must be motivated and founded on constitutional reasons.[166]

Even though it is called «extraordinary» it must be said that the ordinary appeal being reduced to the review of very few decisions of the National Chambers of Appeals, the «extraordinary recourse» is the judicial means through which the parties can most commonly reach the Supreme Court of Justice in order to obtain judicial review of constitutionality of state acts.[167] Particularly because, as we have mentioned, not only the definitive decisions of the National Chambers of Appeals can be the object of an extraordinary recourse but also the definitive decisions of the Superior Courts of the Provinces where the generality of ordinary law cases reach.

Now, the exercise of this extraordinary recourse is submitted to various particular rules, which must be stressed:

First of all, the extraordinary recourse can only be exercised in connection with constitutional matters, thus its importance regarding judicial review. In this respect, the extraordinary recourse can be exercised in three cases:

a. When in a case the question of validity of a treaty, an act of Congress or of another authority exercised in the Nation's name has been raised, and the judicial decision has been against the validity of the particular act;

b. When the validity of an act or decree of the Provincial authorities has been questioned on the grounds of its repugnance to the constitution, treaties or acts of Congress, and the judicial decision has been in favor of the validity of the particular act.

c. When the interpretation of a clause of the constitution, of a treaty or of an act of Congress or other national act has been questioned, and the judicial decision has been against the validity of a title, right, privilege or exemption founded in the said clause which has been a matter of the case.[168]

As a creation of the Supreme Court of Justice doctrine, the extraordinary recourse against «arbitrary judicial decisions» has also been accepted, being considered arbitrary judicial decisions those in which the right to defend one self in

164 *Cf.* N. P. SAGÜES, *op. cit.*, p. 270; pp. 185, 221, 228, 275.

165 R. BIELSA, *op. cit.*, p. 222

166 *Cf.* R. BIELSA, *op. cit.*, pp. 245, 252.

167 *Cf.* J.R. VANOSSI and P.E. UBERTONE, *doc. cit.*, p. 19.

168 Statute 48, Art. 14. *Cf.* J.R. VANOSSI and P.E. UBERTONE, *cit.* p. 20; R. BIELSA, *op. cit.*, p. 210, 211; N.P. SAGÜES, *op. cit.*, p. 272.

a proceeding is said to have been violated. It has also been accepted in cases of so called «institutional gravity», when the Supreme Court can be reached even though the extraordinary recourse would be normally inadmissible; and in cases when an «effective deprivation of justice» has been committed.[169]

The second rule referred to the admissibility of the extraordinary recourse states that the constitutional question must have been discussed in the proceeding in the lower courts, and considered in its decision, before it can be brought before the Supreme Court through the extraordinary recourse.[170] Therefore, the Supreme Court has rejected the recourse when the constitutional issue has not been discussed in the lower courts and has not been considered in the decision.[171] Furthermore, the constitutional issue must have been maintained in the various judicial instances in the lower courts and not abandoned by the interested party. On the contrary, the Supreme Court would reject the extraordinary. Recourse.[172]

In the third place, all the other aspects of the incidental character of judicial review already mentioned apply, of course, to the admissibility of the extraordinary recourse, and particularly the fact that it must be exercised by a party with direct interests in the matter, whose rights are affected by the decision regarding the invalidity of a statute, and that the solution of the constitutional question must be unavoidable and indispensable for the decision of the case. Regarding standing, it must be pointed out that in the Argentinean system, it is expressly accepted that public bodies whose acts have been questioned on the grounds of unconstitutionality and also the Public Prosecutor, have the quality of party regarding the exercise of the extraordinary recourse.[173]

D. *The Effects of the Decision on Judicial Review*

Finally, in the Argentinean system of judicial review, as a pure diffuse system, we must refer to the effects of the decision adopted by the courts when exercising their powers of judicial review of constitutionality.

First of all, it must be said that judicial decisions adopted on matters of constitutionality, whether adopted by inferior courts or by the Supreme Court when they consider a law to be unconstitutional, simply do not apply the invalid statute by giving preference to the constitution, but do not annul it. The courts in Argentina do not have the power to annul or repeal a law. That power is reserved to the legislator, and the only thing they can do is to refuse its application to the concrete case when they consider it unconstitutional.[174] The statute, therefore, when considered unconstitutional and non-applicable by the judge, is considered null and void, with no effect whatsoever[175] in the particular case. This leads to the consideration of the retroactive effect of the decision, bearing in mind its declarative character, thus *ex tunc, pro praeterito.* We insist, however, that the statute remains valid and generally applicable and even the same court can change its criteria about its unconstitutionality and apply it in the future.[176]

[169] *Cf.* J.R. VANOSSI and P.E. UBERTONE, *doc. cit.*, p. 20.
[170] *Cf.* R. BIELSA, *op. cit.*, pp. 190, 202, 203, 205, 209.
[171] *Cf.* R. BIELSA, *op. cit.*, p. 204.
[172] *Cf.* R. BIELSA, *op. cit.*, p. 260.
[173] *Cf.* R. BIELSA, *op. cit.*, pp. 237, 238.
[174] *Cf.* R. BIELSA, *op. cit.*, pp. 197, 198, 345; N.P. SAGÜES, *op. cit.*, p. 156.
[175] *Cf.* A.E. GHIGLIANI, *op. cit.*, p. 95.
[176] *Cf.* R. BIELSA, *op. cit.*, p. 196; A.E. GHIGLIANI, *op. cit.*, p. 92, 97; N. P. SAGÜES, *op. cit.*, p. 177.

That is why these effects of the judicial decision on constitutional matters, in the Argentinean system are strictly *inter partes* effect, a consequence of the diffuse character of the system. Thus the decision considering the nullity of a statute has effect only in connection with the particular process where the question has been raised and between the parties which have intervened in it and, therefore, has no *erga omnes* effects at all.[177]

On the other hand, in the Argentinean system, the decision on judicial review, even the decisions of the Supreme Court on constitutional issues are not obligatory for the other courts or the inferior courts.[178] Moreover, even though in the 1949 constitutional reform it was expressly established that the interpretation adopted by the Supreme Court of Justice upon the articles of the constitution would be considered binding on the national and provincial courts,[179] this article of the constitution was later repealed and the situation today is the absolute power of all courts to render their judgment autonomously with their own constitutional interpretation.

Nevertheless, it is certain that the Supreme Court of Justice being the highest court in the country with wide appellate jurisdiction, particularly through the extraordinary recourse, its decisions have a definitive influence upon all the inferior courts particularly when a doctrine has been clearly and reiterated established by the Court.[180]

E. *The recourse for amparo and judicial review*

Finally, regarding the Argentinean system, discussions have arisen concerning the possibility of the exercise of the diffuse system of judicial review, by the courts, when deciding recourse for *amparo* (constitutional protection) brought before them for the protection of fundamental rights. These recourses for constitutional protection can also be considered a creation of the courts,[181] particularly of the Supreme Court, beginning with the well-known *Angel Siri* case decision of 27 December 1957,[182] in which the competence of ordinary courts to protect the fundamental rights of citizens, against violation from public authorities actions or from individuals was definitively accepted,[183] through a special judicial means known as the *recurso de amparo*.

Now since its acceptance and despite the diffuse system of judicial review followed in Argentina, the Supreme Court established the criteria of the incompetence of the *amparo* judge to review the constitutionality of legislation, reducing the powers of the judge of *amparo* to decide only on acts or facts that could violate fundamental rights. Thus, it was established that the *amparo* could not be granted when the complaint contained the allegation of unconstitutionality of a law on which the said acts or facts were based. Thus, the Supreme Court considered

177 *Cf.* H. QUIROGA LAVIE, *op. cit.*, p. 479.
178 *Cf.* R. BIELSA, *op. cit.*, pp. 49, 198, 267; A.E. GHIGLIANI, *op. cit.*, pp. 97, 98.
179 Art. 95 of the 1949 Constitution. *Cf.* C.A. AYANAGARAY, *Efectos de la declaración de inconstitucionalidad*, Buenos Aires 1955, p. 11; R. BIELSA, *op. cit.*, p. 268.
180 *Cf.* J.R. VANOSSI and P.E. UBERTONE, *doc. cit.*, p. 32.
181 *Cf.* G. R. CARRIO, *Algunos aspectos del recurso de amparo*, Buenos Aires 1959, p. 9; J. R. VANOSSI, *Teoría constitucional, cit.*, Vol. II, p.277.
182 See G. R. CARRIO, *op. cit.*, p.10.
183 See the Samuel Kot Ltd. case of 5 September, 1958, S.V. LINARES QUINTANA, *Acción de amparo*, Buenos Aires 1960, p. 25.

that the judicial decision in cases of recourse for *amparo* could not have declarative effects regarding the unconstitutionality of laws, due to the summarized nature of its proceeding.[184] This doctrine was followed later by law 16.986 of 18 October 1966 about the recourse for *amparo*, in which it was expressly established that the «action for constitutional protection (*amparo*) will not be admissible when the decision upon the invalidity of the act will require.... the declaration of the unconstitutionality of laws, decrees or ordinances».[185]

Nevertheless, and more recently in 1967, the Supreme Court, without declaring the unconstitutionality of the above-mentioned disposition of law 16.986 in the *Outon* case,[186] in an implicit way, decided its inapplicability and accepted the criteria that when considering *amparo* cases, the courts have the power to review the unconstitutionality of legislation, which has been supported by the leading constitutional law authors of the country.[187]

Anyway, the acceptance of this means of judicial review of legislation, through the action for protection (*amparo*), could lead to a direct action of unconstitutionality, although of a diffuse character, which differs from the incidental normal character of the constitutional review system, which is commonly exercised as a consequence of an exception raised by a party in a concrete process, whose main objective is not the constitutional question.

On the contrary, in the action of *amparo* when founded on reasons of unconstitutionality of a law on which the concrete act that violates the fundamental right that the petitioners seek to be protected is based the unconstitutionality of the laws becomes a direct issue of the action itself. That is why it has been said that by accepting this feature of the action for protection, the Supreme Court has opened the way to a new direct means of judicial review of constitutionality of legislation.[188]

2. The Mexican System of Judicial Review of the Constitutionality of Legislation

Also, under the influence of the North American system of judicial review, as described by Alexis De Tocqueville,[189] a diffuse system of judicial review was adopted in the Mexican 1847 constitution,[190] by assigning to the federal courts the duty to «protect» the rights and freedoms established in the constitution, against any attack from the Legislative and Executive powers either of the Federation or of the states.

Article 25 of the Acts of Reforms of 1847, established:

> «The courts of the federation will protect (*ampararán*) any inhabitant of the Republic in the exercise and conservation of the rights granted to him in the constitution and the constitutional laws, against any attack by the Legislative

---

184 See the *Aserradero Clipper SRL* case 1961), J. R. VANOSSI, *Teoría constitucional, cit.*, Vol. II, p. 286.

185 Art. 2,d.

186 Outon case of 29 March 1967. J. R. VANOSSI, *Teoría constitucional, cit.*, Vol. II, p. 288.

187 G. J. BIDART CAMPOS, *Régimen legal del amparo*, 1969; G. J. BIDART CAMPOS, «El control de constitucionalidad en el juicio de amparo y la arbitrariedad o ilegalidad del acto lesivo», *Jurisprudencia argentina*, 23-4-1969; N. P. SAGÜES, «El juicio de amparo y el planteo de inconstitucionalidad», *Jurisprudencia argentina*, 20-7-1973; J. R. VANOSSI, *Teoría constitucional, cit.*, Vol. II, pp.288-292.

188 J. R. VANOSSI, *Teoría constitucional, cit.*, Vol. II, p.291.

189 *Cf.* R.D. BAKER, *Judicial Review in México. A Study of the Amparo Suit*, Texas 1971, p. 15, 33.

190 The Constitution of Yucatan of 1841 adopted the institution of *amparo* only in relation to that State. *Cf.* R.D. BAKER, *op. cit.*, p. 17.

or Executive powers, whether of the Federation or of the states; the said courts being limited to give protection in the particular case to which the process refers, without making any general declaration regarding the statute or the act which brings it about».[191]

A similar article was definitively adopted later in the 1857 constitution, which produced, through a very important and special process, a unique jurisdictional institution, known as the *juicio de amparo*, («trial for protection»), based today on the provisions of the constitutional text published in 1982, following the lines established in the 1917 constitution.

This «trial for protection» although it is the only judicial means which can be used for judicial review of the constitutionality of legislation, does not only have that purpose being a very complex institution which comprises at least five different judicial actions and proceedings which are generally differentiated between in countries with a civil law tradition. That is why before referring to the so called *amparo* against laws, a modality of the trial for protection which could be considered as a particular means of judicial review of the constitutionality of legislation, we will refer to the various aspects comprised in the trial for protection (*amparo*) and its relation to judicial review.

A. The trial of amparo and the diffuse system of judicial review

The present bases of the trial for *amparo* are established directly in the constitution, which first of all, reserves the proceeding to the jurisdiction of the federal courts. In this respect, article 103 of the constitution states:

«Art. 103. The federal courts shall decide all controversies that arise:

i. Out of law or acts of the authorities that violate individual guarantees;

ii. Because of laws or acts of the federal authority restricting or encroaching on the sovereignty of the states;

iii. Because of laws or acts of State authorities that invade the sphere of federal authority».

Therefore, only the federal courts have the power of judicial review and the trial for *amparo* can only be brought before them.[192]

The basic constitutional provisions related to this trial for *amparo* are established at the beginning of article 107 of the constitution:

A trial for *amparo* shall always be held at the instance of the injured party.

«II. The judgment shall always be such that it affects only private individuals being limited to affording them shelter (*ampararlos*) and protection in the special cases to which the complaint refers, without making any general declaration as to the law or act on which the complaint is based».

---

191 See the text in J. CARPIZO, *La Constitución Mexicana de 1917*, México 1979, p. 271; R.D. BAKER, *op. cit.*, p. 23; and H. FIX-ZAMUDIO, «Algunos aspectos comparativos del derecho de amparo en México y Venezuela», *Libro Homenaje a la Memoria de Lorenzo Herrera Mendoza*, Caracas 1970, Vol. II, p. 336. See also H. FIX-ZAMUDIO «A Brief Introduction to the Mexican Writ of Amparo», *California Western International Law Journal*, San Diego 1977, p. 313.

192 *Cf.* R.D. BAKER, *op. cit.*, p. 91; J.A.C. GRANT, «El control jurisdiccional de la constitucionalidad de las leyes: una contribución de las Americas a la ciencia politica», *Revista de la Facultad de Derecho de México*, Vol. XII, 45, 1962, p. 657.

In accordance with the entire provisions of this article 107 of the constitution, and of the regulations of the *Amparo* Law, the trial for *amparo* originally sought as a proceeding for the protection of constitutional rights and freedoms, today comprises five different aspects which in most civil law countries correspond to five different judicial proceedings. These five different aspects of the trial for *amparo*, have been systematized by Professor Héctor Fix-Zamudio,[193] as follows:

The first aspect of the trial for *amparo* is the so called *amparo de la libertad* (protection of liberty) in which the *amparo* proceeding functions as a judicial means for the protection of fundamental rights established in the constitution. In this respect the trial for *amparo* could be equivalent to the request for a writ of *habeas corpus* when it seeks the protection of personal liberty, but can also serve as the protection of all other fundamental rights established in articles 1 to 29 when violated by an act of an authority.[194]

The second aspect of the trial of *amparo* is that it also proceeds against judicial decisions[195] when it is alleged that they have incorrectly applied legal provisions, which results in the so called *amparo judicial* or *amparo casación*, that is to say, in a judicial recourse very similar to the recourse of cassation that exists in civil and criminal procedural law in the civil law countries, to control the legality of judicial decisions.

The third aspect of the trial for *amparo* is the so called *amparo administrativo* through which it is possible to impugn administrative acts that violate the constitution or the statutes.[196] This aspect of the trial for *amparo* results in a means for judicial review of administrative action, equivalent to the French born *contentieux administratif* extended to almost all civil law countries.

The fourth aspect of the trial for *amparo* is the so called *amparo agrario* which is set up for the protection of peasants against acts of the agrarian authorities which could affect their agrarian rights, regulated by the agrarian reform provisions particularly referred to collective rural property.[197]

Finally, the fifth aspect of the trial for *amparo*, is the so called *amparo contra leyes* (*amparo* against laws), which can be used to impugn statutes that violate the constitution, which results in a means of judicial review of the constitutionality of legislation, exercised in a direct way in the absence of any administrative act of enforcement or judicial act of application of the statute considered unconstitutional. This aspect of the trial for *amparo* has been considered as the most specific in constitutional justice aspects.[198]

In all these five aspects of the trial for *amparo*, this particular means of constitutional judicial protection can be used as a means of judicial review of the

---

193 H. FIX-ZAMUDIO, *El juicio de amparo*, México 1964, p. 243, 377; H. FIX-ZAMUDIO, «Reflexiones sobre la naturaleza procesal del amparo», *Revista de la Facultad de Derecho de México*, 56, 1964, p. 980. H. FIX-ZAMUDIO, «Algunos aspectos comparativos del derecho de amparo en México y Venezuela», *loc. cit.*, p. 345; H. FIX-ZAMUDIO, «Lineamientos fundamentales del proceso social agrario en el derecho mexicano» in *Atti della Seconda Assemblea. Istituto di Dirito Agrario Internazionale a Comparato*, Vol I, Milán 1964, p. 402.

194 *Cf.* R.D. BAKER, *op. cit.*, p. 92.

195 Art. 107, III, V.

196 Art. 107, IV.

197 Art. 107, II.

198 H. FIX-ZAMUDIO, «Algunos problemas que plantea el amparo contra leyes», *Boletín del Instituto de Derecho Comparado de México*, UNAM, 37, 1960, 15, 20.

constitutionality of legislative acts, in which cases they have the common trends of the diffuse system of judicial review, the fifth aspect of the *amparo* against laws, having additional peculiarities.

In effect, all the four first mentioned aspects of the trial for *amparo* can be used as a means for judicial review of legislation when a constitutional question, having been raised in a particular proceeding, the courts decide the case, based on a statute considered to be unconstitutional. In such cases, the party which alleges being injured in its private rights or interests by the decision, can exercise a recourse of *amparo* against the judicial decision, seeking judicial review of legislation.[199] In these cases, the recourse of *amparo*, being a review of a judicial decision, must be brought before a Collegiate Circuit Court or the Supreme Court of Justice, according to their respective jurisdictions.[200]

In cases of this direct *amparo* brought before the Collegiate Circuit Courts, the constitution confers the power of reviewing them, only when constitutional issues are involved, to the Supreme Court. In particular, the constitution states:

> «Decisions, in direct *amparo* rendered by a Collegiate Circuit Court are not revisable unless the decision involves the unconstitutionality of a law or establishes a direct interpretation of a provision of the constitution, in which case it may be taken to the Supreme Court of Justice, limited exclusively to the decision of actual constitutional questions».[201]

Nevertheless, the same constitutional provision states, the Collegiate Circuit Courts decisions in direct *amparo* are not revisable if they are based «on a precedent established by the Supreme Court of Justice as to the constitutionality of a law or the direct interpretation of a provision of the constitution».

Anyway, in all these cases of *amparo*, judicial review of legislation has an incidental character regarding a concrete judicial proceeding in which the constitutional question is raised and which brings about the use of the «recourse» of *amparo*, against the judicial decision which applied the unconstitutional statute.

Judicial review of legislation through the trial for *amparo*, therefore, has the general trends of the diffuse systems of judicial review according to the North American model,[202] even though with a few very important particular features which result from this unique judicial proceeding.

First of all, as we mentioned, the jurisdiction for a trial for *amparo* being reserved to the federal courts, judicial review of the constitutionality of legislation in Mexico is not a power of all courts but attributed only to the federal courts.

Secondly, the *amparo* trial being initiated either through a recourse of *amparo* in its first four aspects or through an action in the fifth aspect of the *amparo* against laws, is always developed against a «public authority», whether it be the judge who has dictated the judicial decision or the administrative authority that has produced the administrative act which are both the object of the recourse of *amparo*; or the

---

199 H. FIX-ZAMUDIO, «Aspectos comparativos del derecho de amparo...» *loc. cit.* p. 358, 359; «Algunos problemas que plantea el amparo...», *loc. cit.*, p. 22, 23.

200 Art. 107, V,VI. *Cf.* H. FIX-ZAMUDIO, «Algunos problemas que plantea el amparo...», *loc. cit.*, p. 22

201 Art. 107, IX.

202 J.A.C. GRANT, *loc. cit.*, p. 657.

legislative authorities that have approved the statute which is the object of the *amparo* against laws action. This aspect reveals another substantial difference between the Mexican system and the general diffuse system, in which the parties in the process in which a constitutional question is raised, continue to be the same.[203]

As we have said, in the first four aspects of the trial for *amparo,* the proceedings are initiated through a recourse of *amparo* normally exercised against a judicial decision, the situation being different in the fifth aspect of the trial for *amparo,* so called *amparo* against laws, in which judicial review of constitutionality of legislation is sought through an «action of unconstitutionality», rather than through a recourse, which action is exercised against the legislative bodies that approved the challenged statute.

B. *The amparo against Laws*

In effect, as we have said, one of the five aspects of the trial for *amparo* is the so called «*amparo* against laws», whose peculiarity regarding the other aspects of the trial for *amparo* consists in the fact that in this case, it is a proceeding initiated through a direct action brought before a federal district court[204] by a plaintiff, against a particular statute, the defendants, being the supreme organs of «the state» which intervened in the process of formation of the statute, namely, the Congress of the Union, or the state Legislatures which produced it; the President of the Republic or the Governors of the states which enacted it, and the Secretaries of state which countersigned it and ordered its publication.[205] In these cases, the federal district courts decisions are revisable by the Supreme Court of Justice.[206]

The *amparo* against laws, therefore, is a direct action against a statute, the existence of a concrete administrative act or judicial decision for its enactment or its application not being necessary to its exercise.[207] Nevertheless, the constitutional question involved in this action is not an abstract one, and that is why only the statutes that inflict a direct injury on the plaintiff, without the necessity of any other intermediate or subsequent state act, can be the object of this action.[208] Therefore, the object of this action is self-executing statutes, that is to say, statutes that with their sole enactment, cause personal and direct prejudice to the plaintiff. That is why, in principle, the action seeking the *amparo* against laws must be brought before the court within 30 days after their enactment. Nevertheless, the action can also be brought before the Court within 15 days after the first act of enactment of the said statute so as to protect the plaintiff's rights to sue.[209]

C. *The effects of the decision on judicial review*

Regarding the effects of the judicial decision on any of the aspects of the trial for *amparo,* in which judicial review of constitutionality is sought whether in a pure

---

203 *Idem,* p. 657-661.
204 Art. 107, XII.
205 H. FIX-ZAMUDIO, «Algunos problemas que plantea el amparo...», *loc. cit.,* p. 21.
206 Art. 107, VIII,a.
207 *Cf.* R.D. BAKER, *op. cit.,* p. 164.
208 Self-executed Statutes (auto-aplicativas). *Cf.* R.D. BAKER, *op. cit.* p. 167; H. FIX-ZAMUDIO, «Algunos problemas que plantea el amparo...», *loc. cit.* p. 24.
209 Art. 21. Amparo Law. *Cf.* H. FIX-ZAMUDIO, «Algunos problemas que plantea el amparo...», *loc. cit.,* p. 32. *Cf.* R.D. BAKER, *op. cit.* p. 171.

incidental way or through the action to request an «*amparo* against laws», since the institution of the trial for *amparo* in the middle of the last century, the constitution has expressly established that the courts cannot «make any general declaration as to the law or act on which the complaint is based», the judgment affecting «only private individuals» and limited to affording them shelter and protection in a special case to which the complaint refers».[210] Therefore, a decision in a «trial for *amparo*» in which judicial review of legislation is accomplished, can only have *inter partes* effects, and can never consist of general declarations with *erga omnes* effects.

Therefore, the courts in their decisions regarding the unconstitutionality of a statute do not annul or repeal it; therefore, the statute remains in the books and can be applied by the courts, the only effect of the declaration of its unconstitutionality being directed to the parties in a concrete process.

On the other hand, it must be said that the decisions of the trials for *amparo*, whether or not referred to judicial review, do not have general binding effects even regarding other courts, and are only obligatory to other courts in cases of established *jurisprudencia,* that is to say, of obligatory precedent. The constitution does not expressly establish when an obligatory precedent exists and refers to the special Organic law of the Constitutional Trial to specify «the terms and cases in which the *jurisprudencia* of the courts of the federal judicial power is binding, as well as the requirements for modifying it».[211] According to that Organic law *jurisprudencia* is established by the Supreme Court of Justice or by the Collegiate Circuit Courts when five consecutive decisions to the same effect, uninterrupted by any incompatible rulings are rendered,[212] but it can be modified when the respective Court pronounces a contradictory judgment with a qualified majority of votes of its members.[213]

Nevertheless, as *jurisprudencia* can be established by the federal Collegiate Circuit Courts and by the Supreme Court, contradictory interpretations of the constitution can exist, having binding effects upon the lower courts. In order to resolve these conflicts, the constitution establishes the power of the Supreme Court or of the Collegiate Circuit Court to resolve the conflict, when the contradiction is denounced by the Chambers of the Supreme Court or another Collegiate Circuit Court; by the Attorney General or by any of the parties to the cases in which the *jurisprudencia* was established.[214] Anyway the resolution of the contradiction between judicial doctrines, has the sole purpose of determining one single *jurisprudencia* on the matter, and does not affect concrete juridical situations, derived from the contradictory judicial decisions adopted in the respective trials.[215]

Finally, regarding the practical effects of the trial for *amparo*, it must be stressed that the constitution establishes a particular preliminary remedy during the trial for *amparo*, which consists of the possible suspension of the application of the

---

[210] Art. 107, II, The principle is named the «Otero formula» due to its inclusion in the 1857 constitution under the influence of Mariano Otero. *Cf.* H, FIX-ZAMUDIO, «Algunos aspectos comparativos del derecho de amparo...» *loc. cit,.* p. 360; and H. FIX-ZAMUDIO, «Algunos problemas que plantea el amparo...», *loc. cit.*, p. 33, 37.

[211] Art. 107, XIII, 1.

[212] Art. 192, 193. See the quotations in R.D. BAKER, *op. cit.*, pp. 256, 257.

[213] Art. 194. See the quotations in R.D. BAKER, *op. cit.* p. 263.

[214] Art. 107, XIII. See the comments, in R.D. BAKER, *op. cit.*, p. 264.

[215] Art. 107, XIII. See the comments in J.A.C. GRANT, *loc. cit.* p. 662.

contested state act, which in certain aspects is similar to the injunction in the North American system but reduced to an *injunction pendente litis*.[216] In this respect, article 107 of the constitution established that:

> «Contested acts may be subject to suspension in those cases and under conditions and guarantees specified by law, with respect to which account shall be taken of the nature of the alleged violation, the difficulty or remedying the damages that might be incurred by the aggrieved party by its performance, and the damages that the suspension might cause to third parties and the public interest».[217]

As we can see, although having peculiarities that can not be reproduced in any other legal system, the trial for *amparo* remains within its own particular trends, a means for judicial review that follows the features of the diffuse system of judicial review.

IV. THE DIFFUSE SYSTEM OF JUDICIAL REVIEW IN EUROPE AND IN OTHER CIVIL LAW COUNTRIES

The diffuse system of judicial review, apart from the Latin American experiences, has also been followed in other civil law countries, particularly in Europe (in Greece and in some Scandinavian countries) and in Japan. Other European countries with a civil law tradition have also adopted the diffuse system of judicial review but mixing its features with elements of the concentrated systems, as is the case of Portugal and Switzerland, which we will analyze when studying the mixed systems of judicial review.

1. The Diffuse System of Judicial Review in Greece

In effect, after its establishment in the United States, and additional to the Latin American experiences, the diffuse system of judicial review was also followed in Greece, whose system has been considered to be «very similar to the United States' system of judicial review».[218]

A. General Trends

Based on the principle of the supremacy of the constitution, and on the rigid character of the 1844 and 1864 constitutions, the notion of judicial review was originally formulated by the Supreme Court of Greece in 1847, with limited scope, as the power of all courts to examine in a concrete litigation between parties, whether legislative act «bears all the forms that are necessary, according to the constitution, for the establishment of a legislative decision»,[219] thus reduced to the formal constitutionality of statutes. In the same decision, the Court excluded the courts' judicial review power to examine the substantive constitutionality of statutes by stating that its jurisdiction did not include the examination of «the contents of the legislative decision, because it cannot be assumed that the Power, which represents the sovereignty of the state, is acting unlawfully».[220] Later, in 1871 and

---

[216] J.A.C. GRANT, *loc. cit.*, p. 652, note 33.

[217] Art. 107, X.

[218] E. SPILIOTOPOULOS, «Judicial Review of Legislative Acts in Greece», *Temple Law Quarterly*, 56 (2), Philadelphia 1983, p. 57.

[219] Judgment N° 198 (1847), quoted in E. SPILIOTOPOULOS, *loc. cit.*, p. 471.

[220] *Idem*, p. 471.

1879, the Supreme Court reversed its opinion regarding the limited scope of judicial review and considered that judicial review could refer to a statute when it «is in evident contradiction with a superior provision of the constitution» in which case «the court has the power not to apply it in the case that the court is hearing».[221]

The first constitution which expressly established judicial review powers of all courts was the 1927 constitution, in which article 5 was amended to include an interpretative clause, which in the Greek constitutional system has the same legal force as constitutional provisions, in which it was stated that «the true sense» of the provision which declares that the «judicial Power is vested in independent courts subject only to the law».[222]

> «Is that the courts have the duty not to apply statutes, the contents of which are contrary to the constitution».[223]

This express constitutional norm concerning judicial review, even though eliminated from the constitution after 1935, and in accordance with the previous judge-made principle continued to be applied by the Supreme Court and the Council of state as a matter of «supplementary custom» of the constitution.[224] As Professor Epaminondas Spiliotopoulos said:

> «On the basis of this judge-made law, and in the absence of the express constitutional provisions that had previously existed in the 1927 constitution, scholars of public law supported the theory that the power of the courts to review the constitutionality of statutes and to deny applications of those statutory provisions they considered unconstitutional derived from a supplementary custom of the constitution».[225]

The constitution of 29 September 1968, published by the military dictatorship, and even though without real enforcement particularly on the grounds of judicial review, re-established its constitutional basis by stating in article 118, that

> «The courts have the duty not to apply provisions of statutes, legislative decrees and rules, which have been enacted in breach of the constitution or are contrary to its contents».[226]

This principle was also established later in the present 1975 constitution, in which it is stated that «The courts shall be bound not to apply laws, the contents of which are contrary to the constitution».[227] Along the same line of principles, article 87 of the constitution states:

> «Judges shall in the discharge of their duties be subject only to the constitution and the laws; in no case whatsoever shall they be obliged to comply with provisions enacted in abolition of the constitution».[228]

Thus, judicial review of legislation in the Greek constitutional system is an express constitutional duty and power of all judges, that can be exercised as in all

---

221 Judgments Nº 18 (1871) and Nº 23 (1897), quoted by E. SPILIOTOPOULOS, *loc. cit.*, p. 472.
222 Art. 5.
223 See in E. SPILIOTOPOULOS, *loc. cit.*, p. 472, note 43.
224 *Cf. Idem*, 470, note 30 and p. 474.
225 *Idem*, p. 475.
226 See in *Información Jurídica*, 300, Madrid 1969, p. 103.
227 Art. 93, 4.
228 Art. 87, 3.

the diffuse systems of judicial review, only when the courts decide upon a concrete case in which the challenged statute applies.

Nevertheless, contrary to the general rule in the common law countries, in which the constitutional question must always be raised by a party in the proceeding, in the Greek system, judicial review is a real duty and the courts can on their own and without party requirements, review the constitutionality of legislation. In this respect, as we have seen, the Greek system of judicial review follows the strict logic of the diffuse system, as is the case in Venezuela, but not the general pattern of the common law world.[229] Therefore, in Greece, the courts can proceed with the review *ex officio*, without a specific request being submitted by the litigants challenging the constitutionality of a statute. Of course, if such a request is presented, and this can only be by a party with personal interests in the matter, the court must examine the constitutional issue. But Professor Spiliotopoulos has said,

> «In the absence of a specific request, the court may itself raise the questions when a doubt regarding the constitutionality of such a statute or provision arises during the adjudication of the case».[230]

Finally it must be said that in accordance with the general trends of the diffuse system of judicial review, the contents of the decisions of the courts according to the constitution is not to apply the unconstitutional statue, which is considered as null and void, hence, with no effect whatsoever regarding the concrete case. That is why, for instance, if the act held unconstitutional had abrogated or amended a previous statutory provisions, the Council of state has considered that the abrogation or amendment never took place, and has applied the previous provision as if it were effective and unammended.[231]

Therefore, the unconstitutional statute is not annulled by the courts, but only declared null and void, the decision having only *inter partes* effects. Furthermore, the courts' decisions upon constitutional questions are not binding regarding the same or another court in other cases where the same statutory provision may be challenged. Thus, the *stare decisis* doctrine does not apply in the Greek system, and if the decisions of the Supreme Court or of the Council of state are followed by the inferior courts of the judiciary, it is due to practical reasons derived from the factual influence of the Supreme courts.[232]

B. *Constitutional Justice and Conflicting Judicial Review Adjudications: the Special Highest Court*

The diffuse system of judicial review in Greece, though very similar to the one developed in the United States of America, has a substantial differential element within it, derived from the particular organisation of the Greek judiciary.

In effect, the basic judicial bodies in Greece are organized in two fundamental and separate branches, with some similarities to the French model: a civil and

[229] *Cf.* B.O. NWABUEZE, *Judicial Control of Legislative Action and its Legitimacy. Recent Developments*. IALS, Uppsala Colloquium, 1984, (mimeo), p. 3; also published in L. FAVOREU and J.A. JOLOWICZ, *Le contrôle juridictionnel des lois. Légitimité, effectivité et développements récents*, Paris 1986, pp. 193-222.

[230] E. SPILIOTOPOULOS, *loc. cit*, p. 479.

[231] See judgment N° 2241 (1953), quoted by E. SPILIOTOPOULOS, *loc. cit.*, pp. 485, 123.

[232] *Cf.* E. SPILIOTOPOULOS, *loc. cit.*, p. 486.

criminal judiciary with a Supreme Court at its apex, and an administrative judiciary with a council of state at its apex.[233] Therefore there are two supreme judicial bodies with final appellate jurisdiction in the ordinary civil and criminal jurisdiction or in the administrative jurisdiction. Additionally the constitution establishes a third separate branch of the judicial power attributed to the Comptrollers Council, mainly concerned with public audit and financial matters.[234]

All the courts of the three branches of the judicial powers have the power of judicial review, and therefore, it can happen that the Supreme Court, in civil or criminal case, the Council of state, in administrative cases, or the Comptrollers Council, in audit matters, may render contradictory and conflicting judgments on constitutional issues, which could produce legal uncertainty.

To resolve possible conflicting decisions on constitutional matters between these judicial organisations, the 1968 constitution established a Constitutional Court,[235] which the 1975 constitution transformed into a Special Highest Court. The jurisdiction of this Special Highest Court has approximated the Greek system of judicial review to the mixed systems[236] but owing to its peculiar character due to the existence of three separate judicial organizations, its functions are rather a corrective effort regarding the inconsistencies that the diffuse system may cause in the three branches of the judiciary.

This Special Highest Court, according to article 100, has jurisdiction not only over constitutional aspects, bur also over electoral matters and the settlement of controversies related to the designation of rules on international law.[237] Furthermore, it acts as a jurisdictional conflict court like the French Tribunal of Conflicts;[238] but basically it acts as the final resort court for the settlement of controversies on constitutional matters between the supreme courts of the Judicial Power. In this respect, the constitution gives jurisdiction to this Special Highest Court, for the

> «Settlement of controversies on whether a law enacted by Parliament is fundamentally unconstitutional, or on the interpretation of provisions of such law when conflicting judgments have been pronounced by the Council of State, the Supreme Court of the Comptrollers Council».[239]

This Special Highest Court is composed of the president of the Council of state, the president of the Supreme Court and the President of the Comptrollers Council, four Councilors of state and four members of the Supreme Court and when acting in the settlement of controversy on constitutional matters, its composition shall be expanded to include two ordinary law professors of the law schools of the country.[240]

---

[233] Art. 93-97, 1975 constitution. *Cf.* E. SPILIOTOPOULOS, *loc. cit.*, pp. 475-477, The Council of State although originally created in 1835, it initiated its functioning in 1929. *Cf.* E. SPILIOTOPOULOS, *loc. cit.*, p. 472, note 45.

[234] Art. 98-99.

[235] Art. 106. See in *Información Jurídica, cit.* p. 99-100. *Cf.* the comments regarding this Tribunal in H. FIX-ZAMUDIO, *Los Tribunales constitucionales y los derechos humanos*, UNAM, México 1980, pp. 160-161.

[236] *Cf.* H. FIX-ZAMUDIO, *op. cit.*, p. 162.

[237] Art. 100, 1, a,b,c,f.

[238] Art. 100,1,d.

[239] Art. 100,1,e.

[240] Art. 100,2.

According to the special law or statute no. 345 of 1978, which regulates the procedure to be followed by the Special Highest Court to settle controversies, a «controversy» arises when one of the supreme courts, when examining the constitutionality of a statute involved in the case, forms an opinion contrary to an opinion already expressed by another supreme court covering the same statute.[241] In that case, the controversy may be submitted to the Special Highest Court, in two ways incidental or principal.

The first means of an incidental character allows the supreme court whose opinion created the controversy to refer a preliminary judgment concerning the question of constitutionality, directly to the Special Highest Court, the final adjudication of the case being postponed. The second means of a principal character can be exercised when the Supreme Court concerned does not postpone its final adjudication and renders it, and the question can be brought before the Special Highest Court through a petition by the Minister of Justice, the Public Prosecutor of the Supreme Court, the state Commissioner to the Comptroller's Council, and the state Commissioner to the Administrative Justice; and also, by any person who has a legally protected interest including the party who has lost the case.[242]

The Special Highest Court examines only the question of constitutionality referred or submitted to it, and the decision rendered on the matter has *erga omnes* effects.[243] According to Article 100, of the constitution, «provisions of law declared unconstitutional shall be invalid as of the date of publication of the respective judgment, or as of the date specified by the ruling». Therefore, the decision of the Special Highest Court in principle, annuls the unconstitutional act, with *ex nunc*, prospective effects, but the Special Highest Court can give its decision retroactive effects.[244]

Consequently, if after the Special Highest Court decision, a lower court renders a decision with respect to the constitutionality of a statute contrary to the opinion of the Special Highest Court, the litigants have the right to make an appeal, and if the said decision is adopted by one of the Supreme Courts, the parties have the right to submit a petition for a new hearing.[245]

However concerning the case in which the constitutional question was raised, the immediate effects of the Special Highest Court decision are different regarding the incidental or principal characters of the proceeding. If the proceeding was an incidental one and the final adjudication was postponed in a supreme court, after the judgment of the Special Highest Court is pronounced, the Supreme Court must continue its proceeding consistent with the Special Highest Court ruling.

But if the proceeding before the Special Highest Court was a principal one, and the supreme court concerned pronounced a final judgment prior to the Special Highest Court decision, instead of postponing it, that decision does not automatically have effect upon the Supreme Court final adjudication. Its results are that the litigants have the right within ninety days from the date on which the judgment of the Special Highest Court is pronounced to submit a special petition and demand a

---

241 Art. 48, 2 quoted in E. SPILIOTOPOULOS, *loc. cit.*, p. 497.
242 *Cf.* E. SPILIOTOPOULOS, *loc. cit.*, p. 497.
243 Art. 51, Statute 345. quoted in E. SPILIOTOPOULOS, *loc. cit.*, p. 498, note 199.
244 E. SPILIOTOPOULOS, *loc. cit.*, p. 500.
245 Art. 51, statute 345. quoted in E. SPILIOTOPOULOS, *loc. cit.*, p. 499.

new hearing of the case by the Supreme Court, which then must apply the Special Highest Court ruling.[246]

Thus, in spite of the existence of this Special Highest Court to settle conflicting decisions on constitutional issues, and of the effects of its decision, it can be, considered that the general trends of the diffuse system of judicial review continue to prevail in the Greek system.

2. Judicial review in some of the Scandinavian Countries

The other European countries with a diffuse system of judicial review are some of the Nordic or Scandinavian Countries, all of which have a parliamentary system of government and a unitarian form of the state. In particular in Sweden, Norway, Denmark and Iceland, a diffuse system of judicial review of legislation can be identified,[247] with the general trends of the North American model.[248]

In Finland, even though the general legal opinion is that no judicial review of legislation is accepted, and that there are no cases in which a court has questioned the constitutionality of an act of Parliament, the constitutional basis for judicial review is established although not regarding acts of Parliament, but inferior regulations.

According to Art. 92 of the Finnish constitution act of 1919, «if a provision in a decree is contrary to a constitutional or other law, it shall not be applied by a judge or other official».[249] Commenting on this article, Mikael Hiden, said: «any official or authority is empowered, and is duty bound, not to apply any legal pro-vision below the level of acts of Parliament if he or it deems the provision to be contrary to the constitution or any act of Parliament».[250] Nevertheless, Hiden said, according to predominant legal opinion and due to the absence of courts decisions, it can be accepted that «the Finnish system does not recognise the judicial review of legislation in the most significant meaning of that expression, i.e. as exercised by courts in applying the law in a litigation»;[251] instead, a system of control of legislation only exists prior to its enactment, during the legislative process, in which judicial bodies can intervene. In effect, the President of the Republic can request opinion on a bill before presenting it to Parliament, either from the Supreme Court or the Supreme Administrative Court or from both.[252] In fact, this is a form of «pre-Parliamentary» control, and the decision of the courts in these cases is merely an «advisory opinion». Nevertheless, this form of preventive control of the constitutionality of legislation, added to the political control developed over bills in Parliament, seems to occupy an important place in the system.[253]

It must also be stressed that in Sweden there is also a preventive system of judicial review of bills. In this respect Article 8:18 of the constitution creates a

---

246 *Idem*.

247 *Cf.* E. SMITH, *Contrôle juridictionnel de la législation et sa légitimité. Développements récents dans les cinq pays scandinaves*, AISJ, Colloque Uppsala, 1984, (mimeo), pp. 2, 3, 4, 7, 50, 74. Also published in L. FAVOREU and J.A. JOLOWICZ, (ed.), *Le contrôle juridictionnel des lois..., cit.*, pp. 225-282.

248 *Idem, doc. cit.*, p. 12.

249 See in M. HIDEN, «Constitutional Rights in the Legislative Process: the Finnish System of Advance Control of Legislation» *Scandinavian Studies in Law*, 17, Stockholm 1973, p. 97.

250 *Idem*, p. 97, 98.

251 *Ibidem*, p. 98. *Cf.* E. SMITH, *doc.cit.*, p. 12.

252 M. HIDEN, *loc. cit.*, p. 106.

253 E. SMITH, *doc. cit.*, p. 12.

«Council of the Laws» which is formed by members of the two highest courts of the Country (Supreme Court and Supreme Administrative Court), which is in charge of giving advice, among other things, on the relations between a bill and the Constitutional text, at the request of the Government and of Parliament.[254] This control, it must be said, only refers to bills drafted by the Government, and consequently cannot be exercised regarding the laws finally adopted by Parliament, and in no case is the advisory opinion of the Council obligatory either fox the Government or for Parliament.[255] That is why it has not been considered in the strictest sense as a judicial review control.[256]

Now, excluding Finland, in the other Scandinavian countries, as we have said, a system of judicial control of the constitutionality of legislation is accepted, even though with a very different longevity, beginning with Norway from 1890; and finishing with Sweden from 1960.[257]

The common fundamental trends of the judicial control of the constitutionality of legislation in the four Nordic countries, following the general features of the North American system of judicial review, have been summarized by Professor Eivind Smith, as follows:

> «First, the power of judicial review is attributed to all judges. Thus, there are not specialised judicial organs in charge of this control.
>
> Second, constitutional questions must be raised in cases or controversies in ordinary civil criminal or administrative litigation, by a party having personal interests to do so.
>
> Third, the constitutional issue raised in a particular process must only be decided upon if it is unavoidable for the resolution of the concrete case, and the judge has a certain criteria concerning the unconstitutionality of the act, which would depend on the degree of precision of the constitution.
>
> Fourth, because constitutional questions must be considered in accordance with the normal procedural rules, the effects of the judicial decision on the matter, only applies to the parties in the process. The judges do not annul the laws but only limit their decisions to not applying the unconstitutional act to the concrete case, without *erga omes* effects».[258]

It has been in Sweden where the power of the courts to control the constitutionality of legislation, has been more recently recognized in the 1974 constitution.

In article 11:14 it states:

> «When a (judicial or administrative) court finds a (legislative or executive) disposition contrary to the constitution or to other superior rules, or when it finds that the proceeding rules have not been observed in an essential point during the process of elaboration of the above mentioned disposition, it will be inapplicable».[259]

254 See in E. SMITH, *op. cit.*, pp. 12, 20.
255 E. SMITH, *doc. cit.*, p. 20.
256 *Idem*, p. 20.
257 *Idem*, pp. 7-8.
258 *Idem*, p. 10-12, 62, 67, 74.
259 See in E. SMITH, *doc. cit.*, p. 16.

Even though this article, as written down could lead to the admissibility of *ex officio* powers of the courts to declare an unconstitutional statute inapplicable, in practice, the incidental character of the system where only a party can raise the constitutional issue in a particular process, is accepted.[260]

Anyway, although article 11:14 establishes a very broad system for judicial review, it must be stressed that the same article establishes a substantial restriction to the power conferred upon the judges to control the unconstitutionality of Acts of Parliament, when establishing that when the disposition whose unconstitutionality has been raised is adopted by Parliament or by the Government, the inapplicability can only be pronounced when the on record error is a «manifest» one.[261] Thus the determination of the manifest errors by the courts is an important restraint upon their control power vis-à-vis the political organs of the state.

Finally, we must also say that in Norway, where Professor Cappelletti and Adams found «at least in theory the most comprehensive power of judicial review found anywhere»,[262] additional to the power of all courts to declare incidentally on the settlement of a specific case, the invalidity of statutes contrary to the constitution, the Supreme Court of the country can also be requested by Parliament to give advisory opinions on the constitutionality of Statutes.

3. The Diffuse System of Judicial Review in Japan

But outside the European and Latin American continents, a diffuse system of judicial review can also be identified in the Japanese Constitutional system. In effect, contrary to the tradition of the legal system of the country,[263] the 1946 constitution of Japan, drafted under overwhelming American influence,[264] established the basis of the diffuse system of judicial review in the country, regulated in only one Constitutional article, which states the following:

> «Art. 81: The Supreme Court is the court of last resort with power to determine the constitutionality of any law, order, regulation or official act».[265]

In spite of the ambiguity of the text, and of the absence of any statutory regulation regarding its content[266] the Supreme Court has considered that the courts review power provided for in the constitution, «has been developed through interpretation of the American constitution».[267] Thus the system has developed as a

---

260 E. SMITH, *doc.cit.*, p. 18.

261 See in E. SMITH, *doc.cit.*, pp. 17, 22.

262 M. CAPPELLETTI and J.C. ADAMS, «Judicial Review of Legislation: European Antecedents and Adaptations», *Harvard Law Review*, 79, (6), 1966, p. 1217

263 *Cf.* Y. TANIGUCHI, *Judicial Control of Legislation and its Legitimacy in Japan*, IALS, Uppsala Colloquium 1984 (mimeo), p. 2. Also published in L. FAVOREU and J.A. JOLOWICZ (ed.), *Le contrôle juridictionnel des lois..., cit.*, pp. 175-190.

264 *Cf.* Y TANIGUCHI, *doc. cit.*, p. 7,3; Y. HIGUCHI, «Evolution récente du contrôle de la constituionnalité sous la Constitution japonaise de 1946», *Revue internationale de droit comparé*, 31, (1), Paris 1979, p. 22; T. FUKASE and Y. HIGUCHI, *Le constitutionnalisme et ses problèmes ou Japon. Une approche comparative*, Paris 1984, p. 28; J.D. WHYTE, *Judicial Review of Legislation and its Legitimacy: Developments in the Common Law* World, IALS, Uppsala Colloquium 1984 (mimeo), p. 61. Also published in L. FAVOREU and J.A. JOLOWICZ, *Le contrôle juridictionnel des lois..., cit.*, pp. 155-174.

265 See in Y. TANIGUCHI, *doc.cit.*, p. 2; J.D. WHYTE, *doc. cit.*, p. 62.

266 T. FUKASE and Y. HIGUCHI, *op.cit.*, p. 298.

267 Grand Bench, July 8, 1948: Keishu 2-8-801 quoted by Y. TANIGUCHI, *doc.cit.*, p. 2, note 3.

diffuse judicial review system, in which no direct or abstract action can be brought before the Supreme Court to challenge a statute. This was expressly resolved by the Supreme Court in a 1952 decision involving an action brought directly before the Court by the Chairman of one of the main political parties for the declaration of unconstitutionality of a National Police Force. The Court dismissed the action and held that the judicial review power is part of the ordinary judicial power and its exercise is conditioned by the existence of a concrete case of litigation that must be started in an appropriate lower court.[268]

Therefore, the Japanese judicial review system follows the theory of the diffuse system of judicial review as developed in the United States of America. Hence, judicial review is a power of all courts exercised within their own jurisdiction, the Supreme Court being at the apex of the judiciary.

The constitutional questions, therefore, can only be raised in a particular case or controversy between actual parties, in which the challenged state act directly affects the legal relationship between those parties.[269] The object of control can be «any law, order, regulation or official act», which includes of course, any normative state act. Discussions have been held regarding the reviewability of international treaties and although there has not been any decision by the Supreme Court considering the unconstitutionality of a treaty, the court has not excluded, in principle, its power to declare its unconstitutionality. In the *Sunagawa* case (1959), when dealing with the Japan-US Security Treaty it is understood that the Court took the position that Treaties are also subject to judicial review, although the Court abstained from deciding upon the unconstitutionality of that Treaty, on the grounds of considering the issue «highly political» and in which «the unconstitutionality did not reveal itself in a clear and evident way».[270]

This position of the Courts leads not only to the «political questions» doctrine/ but to the rule of the presumption of constitutionality of Statutes, which means that a Constitutional issue must only be decided when unavoidable for the resolution of the case, and when there is no other way of interpreting the Statute to avoid its unconstitutionality.[271]

Regarding the effects of the decisions adopted in judicial review, the principle of the nullity of unconstitutional state acts is accepted. Consequently, the Courts decisions do not annul the unconstitutional act, only declare its inapplicability to the concrete case, and with *inter partes* effects.[272] Discussions have taken place regarding the retroactive effects of the decision,[273] but bearing in mind the wide acceptance by the Supreme Court of deciding upon the unconstitutionality of statutory provisions no longer in force,[274] the retroactive effects of the decision, in principle, are evident.

The role of the Supreme Court of Japan regarding judicial review, contrary to the American Supreme Court, has been considered as passive, in the sense that in

---

268 Y. TANIGUCHI, *doc. cit.*, p. 3.
269 J.D. WHYTE, *doc.cit.*, p. 64
270 T. FUKASE and Y. HIGUCHI, *op. cit.*, p. 299; Y. TANIGUCHI, *doc. cit.*, p. 9.
271 Y. TANIGUCHI, *doc. cit.*, p. 14; T. FUKASE and Y. HIGUCHI, *op. cit.*, p. 299.
272 Y. TANIGUCHI, *doc. cit.*, p. 16; T. FUKASE and Y. HIGUCHI, *op. cit.*, p. 299.
273 Y. TANIGUCHI, *doc. cit.*, pp. 16-17.
274 Y. TANIGUCHI, *doc. cit.*, p. 11.

the 40 years of enforcement of the constitution, the Supreme Court has only held statutes unconstitutional in three cases, decided between 1933 and 1976.[275] Before 1973, the active character of judicial review referred mainly to statutory provisions no longer in force [276] or to the affirmation of the constitutionality of challenged statutes,[277] and it was only after 1973 that the Supreme Court declared the unconstitutionality of a few statutory provisions. First, of an article of the Penal code concerning parricide which prescribed a more severe penalty for murder of a close relative than for ordinary homicide as violating the equality under the law clause.[278] Later, in 1975, the Supreme Court declared the unconstitutionality of a provision of the pharmaceutical affairs act which prescribed that a newly opened pharmacy had to be not less than a certain distance from an existing one, as violating the freedom to choose one's occupation.[279] Finally, in 1976, the Supreme Court declared unconstitutional a provision of the Public Office Election Law fixing the electorate for each election district, as violating the equality under the law clause as a consequence of the inequalities derived from the movement of population into the cities.[280]

After this judicial activism of the Supreme Court, developed between 1973 and 1976, over recent years there have been no new decisions by the Court declaring the unconstitutionality of Statues. This has been interpreted as a return to the previous doctrine of the «interpretation of laws according with the constitution» developed in the sixties.[281]

Finally, it must be said that the doctrine of *stare decisis* is not accepted in Japan.[282] Thus the inferior courts are not legally bound by the decisions of higher courts, particularly by the decisions of the Supreme Court which refers only to the concrete case in which they are pronounced. Nevertheless, the authority of the Supreme Court produces de facto binding effects of its decisions upon the inferior courts.[283]

On the other hand, the Supreme Court is not bound by its own decisions, and has the power to override its previous decisions even on constitutional matters. This happened precisely in the Patricide case (1933) in which the Court overrode a previous 1950 decision in which it considered the constitutionality of Article 200 of the Penal Code which established the aggravation of the penalty for the parricide.[284]

---

275 *Cf.* Y. HIGUCHI, *loc. cit.*, pp. 22, 31; T. FUKASE and Y. HIGUCHI, *op. cit.*, pp. 300, 307; Y. TANIGUCHI, *doc. cit.*, p. 17; J.D. WHITE, *doc. cit.*, p. 64.

276 Y. TANIGUCHI, *doc. cit.*, p. 11.

277 Y. TANIGUCHI, *doc. cit.*, p. 14; T. FUKASE and Y. HIGUCHI, *doc. cit.*, p. 301

278 *Aizawa v. Japan* 27 Sai-han Keishu 256 (1973); Grand Bench, April 4, 1973, Keishu 27-3-265 quoted in J.D. WHYTE, *doc. cit.*, p. 64; Y. TANIGUCHI, *doc. cit.*, p. 10, note 16; Y. HIGUCHI, *loc. cit.*, p. 31.32; T. FUKASE and Y. HIGUCHI, *op. cit.*, p. 308.

279 *K.K. Sumiyoshi v. Governor of Hiroshima Prefecture*, 665 Saibansho Jiho 1 (1975); Grand Bench, April 30, 1975 Minshu 29-4-572 quoted in J.D. WHYTE, *doc. cit.*, p. 65; Y. TANIGUCHI, *doc. cit.*, p. 10, note 17; Y. HIGUCHI, *loc. cit.*, p. 32; T. FUKASE and Y. HIGUCHI, *op. cit.*, pp. 308-309.

280 *Kurokawa v. Chiba Prefecture Election Commission*, 30, Sai-han Minshu 223 (1976), Grand Bench, April 14, 1976, Minshu 30-3-223, quoted in J.D. WHYTE, *doc. cit.*, p. 65; Y. TANIGUCHI, *doc. cit*, p. 11 note 19; Y. HIGUCHI, *loc. cit.*, pp. 32-33; T. FUKASE and Y. HIGUCHI, *op. cit.*, pp. 309-310.

281 Y. HIGUCHI, *loc. cit.*, p. 33; T. FUKASE and Y. HIGUCHI, *op. cit.*, p. 310.

282 J.D. WHYTEP, *doc. cit* p. 63.

283 T. FUKASE and Y. HIGUCHI, *op. cit.*, 299.

284 Y. HIGUCHI, *loc. cit.*, pp. 31-32.

V. SOME ASPECTS OF THE DIFFUSE SYSTEM OF JUDICIAL REVIEW IN COMMONWEALTH COUNTRIES.

Even though followed in various civil law countries as we have seen, the diffuse system of judicial review of the constitutionality of legislation can nevertheless be considered a common trend in common law countries with written constitutions, which are the overwhelming majority. As we have seen, in civil law countries, the diffuse system of judicial review, in its classical features, is a rare institution to be found only in a few countries in Latin America and in Europe, and in other civil law countries like Japan. In most of the civil law countries, which have adopted the diffuse system of judicial review, in fact, it has not remained in its pure and classical form but has normally been mixed with trends of the concentrated system of judicial review. Therefore, it is in the common law world in which the diffuse system of judicial review has expanded.

In particular, and contrary to the situation of the United Kingdom constitutional system, the diffuse system of judicial review, is a common constitutional trend in almost all the commonwealth countries, formerly part of the British Empire. Thus, the majority of these countries have adopted a radically different principle for their constitutional system to the one, which prevails in the United Kingdom, where no judicial review of legislation is accepted.

In the establishment of this different constitutional system in the commonwealth countries, although due to various factors, the United Kingdom has nevertheless played, paradoxically, an important role.

In effect, it must firstly be said that all the commonwealth countries, with the single exception of New Zealand[285] have written constitutions and, in general, entrenched declarations of fundamental rights. Particularly during the processes of independence of the commonwealth countries developed during this century, or in the process of reshaping its constitutional system, as was the case of Canada in 1982, it is evident that the Westminster Parliament played a fundamental role in the drafting or establishing of the respective constitutional rules of the countries and in promoting the formal and entrenched declarations of fundamental rights.[286] Thus, written constitutions, considered as the supreme law of the land in each of the commonwealth countries, with entrenched declarations of fundamental rights, presupposed the establishment of limits upon state powers, and particularly, upon legislative power.

Consequently, the principle of the sovereignty of Parliament, considered as a constitutional law «curiosity»[287] peculiar to the British constitutional systems, is not followed in most commonwealth countries,[288] in which Parliament is submitted to

---

285 *Cf.* J.D. WHYTE, *Judicial Review of Legislation and its Legitimacy: Developments in the Common Law World,* International Association of Legal Sciences, Uppsala Colloquium 1984, (mimeo), p. 89; Also published in L. FAVOREU and J.A. JOLOWICZ (ed.), *Le contrôle juridictionnel des lois. Légitimité, effectivité et developments récents,* Paris 1986, pp. 155-174. M. ZANDER, *A Bill of Rights?,* London 1985, p. 30.

286 A. LESTER, «Fundamental Rights: the United Kingdom Isolated?», *Public Law,* 1984, pp. 56-57; J.D. WHYTE, *doc. cit.,* pp. 96-97.

287 S.O. GYANDOH Jr., «Interaction of the Judicial and Legislative Process in Ghana since Independence», *Temple Law Quaterly,* 56, 2, Philadelphia 1983, p. 354.

288 *Cf.* A.R. CARNEGIE, «Judicial Review of Legislation in the West Indian Constitutions», *Public Law,* London 1971, p. 276; Ch. OKPALUBA, «Challenging the Constitutionality of Legislative Enactment in Nigeria: the Factor of Locus Standi», *Public Law,* London 1982, p. 110; S.A. GYANDOH, Jr., *loc. cit.,* 351; E. MCWHINNEY, *Judicial Review,* Toronto 1969, p. 7.

constitutional restraint as are all other state powers. The constitution, therefore, is considered the supreme law of the land, and consequently, any state act contrary to its dispositions, is considered null and void. For instance, this is expressly stated in the constitutions of the West Indian countries,[289] and of Nigeria in which it is declared that «if any law is inconsistent with the provisions of this constitution, this constitution shall prevail and that other law shall, to the extent of the inconsistency be Void».[290] Also, concerning fundamental rights, the Indian constitution states that «the state shall not make any law which takes away or abridges the rights conferred by this Part (Part III, Fundamental Rights) and any law made in contravention of this clause shall, to the extent of the contravention, be void».[291] Thus the doctrine of parliamentary sovereignty has been substituted in the commonwealth countries by the principle of constitutional supremacy, even though discussions have arisen in some countries regarding the British model. For instance, S.N. Ray, said of the Indian constitutional system,

> «The framers of the Indian constitution were inclined in favor of the British principle of Parliamentary supremacy, but although they adopted the English model of Parliamentary government and made Parliament the focus of political power in the county and the dominant machinery to realise the goal of social revolution, they did not make it a sovereign legislature in the same sense and to the same extent as the British Parliament was sovereign. They placed as much supremacy in the hands of the legislature as was possible within the bounds of a written constitution with a federal distribution of powers and a bill of rights. In its turn, the judiciary has been assigned a superior position in relation to the legislature but only in certain respects. The constitution endows the judiciary with the power of declaring a law as unconstitutional if that is beyond the competence of the legislature according to the distribution of powers provided by the constitution, or if that is in contravention of the Fundamental Rights guaranteed by the constitution».[292]

This Indian dilemma between Parliamentary Supremacy and judicial review was explained in an adequate way in the well-known *A.K. Goplan v. State of Madras* case (1950) in which it was stated:

> «In India the position of the judiciary is somewhere in between the Courts in England and the United States. While in the main leaving our Parliament and the state Legislatures supreme in their respective legislative fields, our constitution has, by some of the articles put upon the Legislature certain specified limitations.... in so far as there is any limitation on the legislative power, the Court must on a complaint being made to it, scrutinize and a ascertain whether such limitation has been transgressed and if there has been any transgression the Court will courageously declare the law unconstitutional, for the Court is bound by its oath to uphold the constitution.... Our constitution, unlike the English constitution, recognizes the Courts supremacy over the legislative authority ... confined to the field where the legislative power is circumscribed by limitations put upon it by the constitution itself... But our constitution, unlike the American constitution, does not recognize the absolute

---

[289] A.R. CARNEGIE, *loc. cit.*, p. 276; J.D. WHYTE, *doc. cit.*, p. 32

[290] Ch. OKPALUBA, *loc .cit.*, p. 110.

[291] See in S.N. RAY, *Judicial Review and Fundamental Rights*, Calcuta 1974, p. 270.

[292] *Idem*, pp. 69-70.

supremacy of the Court over the legislative authority in all respects, for outside the restricted field of constitutional limitations our Parliament and the state Legislatures are supreme in their respective legislative fields and in that wider field there is no scope for the Court in India to play the role of the Supreme Court of the United States».[293]

Anyway, what is definitive in the Commonwealth Countries is that written Constitutions impose certain limits upon the legislature, particularly in relation to fundamental rights and to the vertical distribution of state powers, especially through the federal form of state which has contributed to the adoption of judicial review.[294]

However, even within the principle of parliamentary supremacy in the constitutional system of the United Kingdom, it must be also noted that the practice of judicial review regarding the former colonies and some commonwealth countries has also been a legacy of the United Kingdom constitutional system, because of the role played by the Privy Council as the final appellate Tribunal for the overseas Empire, particularly when exercising judicial review of the Constitutions of the self governing members of the Commonwealth and the concomitant power to strike down as invalid, those laws passed by the Parliament, of those countries contrary to the rules of the Imperial Parliament.[295] As Edward McWhinney pointed out:

> «The Privy Council was the highest appellate tribunal of the old British Colonial Empire, and it exercised the right to scrutinize colonial legislation and ordinances and the administration thereof to ensure their conformance to the provisions of the Imperially granted constitution or charter of the colony concerned and ultimately to ensure their conformance to the principles of Imperial constitutional law as a whole».[296]

It must be said that this jurisdiction of the Privy Council remained in force until as late as 1949, when it was generally swept away by legislation of the individual commonwealth countries with a few exceptions (i.e. Australia, Trinidad and Tobago and New Zealand), in favor of the jurisdiction of the Supreme Courts of those countries. Thus, the Supreme Courts of the Commonwealth countries can be seen as the «lineal successors to the Privy Council»,[297] and that is why it has been said regarding Canada that «after the abolition of the appeal to the Privy Council, the Canadian Supreme Court, for example, continues to exercise the power of judicial review in relation to legislation passed by the Canadian Parliament».[298] In a similar way, the High Court of Australia assumed the power to invalidate, on the grounds of unconstitutionality, legislation passed by the Australian Parliament on certain matters established on the Australian constitution, and in respect to which, therefore, «any appeal to the Privy Council was prohibited by the constitution».[299]

---

293 AIR 1950 SC 27; 1950 SCR 88 at 286-87, 288-90, quoted in S.N. RAY, *op. cit.*, p. 72-73. See the comments in pp. 259-268.

294 See particularly in relation to federalism and judicial review Ch. OKPALUBA, *loc. cit.* p. 111; E. MCWHINNEY, *op. cit.*, p. 14; and in relation to fundamental rights and judicial review, J.D. WHYTE, *doc. cit.*, p. 38.

295 E. MCWHINNEY, *op. cit.*, p. 49, 57; S.O. GYANDOH Jr., *loc. cit.*, p. 355

296 E. MCWHINNEY, «Constitutional Review in the Commonwealth», in H. MOSLER (ed.), Max-Planck-Institut für Ansländisches öffentliches recht and Völkerrecht, *Ve Verfassungsgerichtsbarkeit, in der Gegenwart*, Internationalen Kolloquium, Heidelberg 1961, Köln Berlin 1962, pp. 77-78.

297 E. MC WHINNEY, «Constitutional review ...», *loc. cit.*, p. 78.

298 E. MC WHINNEY, *Judicial Review, cit.*, pp. 58-59.

299 *Idem*.

Apart from all those British antecedents, it is also accepted that judicial review of the Constitutionality of legislation, even though not always expressly established in the Constitutions of the commonwealth countries, was also widely developed in these countries under the influence of the American system of judicial review whose fundamental trends were received particularly during recent decades.[300] That is why, it can be said that in general terms, the system of judicial review in the commonwealth countries, follows the general trends of the diffuse system of judicial review, but with the particular feature that in all matters related to general law and of course, constitutional questions, the Supreme Courts of the Commonwealth Countries, following the British pattern have the final appeal jurisdiction.[301]

On the other hand some Commonwealth Countries have expressly established in their constitution, the jurisdiction of the Courts to judge upon constitutional questions regarding legislation, and in particular, they have established the jurisdiction of the Supreme Court on the matter.

For instance, the constitution of the Republic of Ireland provides that the jurisdiction of the High. Court, and, on appeal, of the Supreme Court, shall extend «to the question of the validity of any law having regard to the provisions of the constitution».[302]

A similar system exists in Trinidad and Tobago. The High Court of Justice has wide ranging jurisdiction, including interpretation of the constitution. The Appellate Division of the Supreme Court is vested in the Court of Appeal, and there is an appeal as of right to it from decisions of the High Court on constitutional questions and fundamental rights. The peculiar regulation concerning Trinidad and Tobago, is that when the question is one of interpretation of the constitution from the Court of Appeal, there is an appeal to the Judicial Committee of the Privy Council.[303] Nevertheless, as Chief Justice C.A. Kelsick said:

> «The Supreme Court of Trinidad and Tobago) as guardian of the constitution has the power to declare null and void Acts of Parliament which violate the provisions of chapter 1 or other entrenched provisions of the constitution where the act is not passed in the prescribed manner with the requisite majority for an alteration of those provisions».[304]

The constitution of India distinguishes between an original and appellate jurisdiction of the Supreme Court. The original and exclusive jurisdiction of the Supreme Court extends to:

> «Any dispute between the Government of India and one car more states; or between the Government of India and any state or states on one side and one or more other states on the other; or between two or more states, if and in so far as the dispute involves any question on which the existence or extend of a legal right depends».[305]

---

300 *Cf.* E. MC WHINNEY, *Judicial Review, cit.*, pp. 236, 237; E. MC WHINNEY, «Constitutional Review», *loc. cit.*, pp. 79, 83, 87. Regarding India, *Cf.* S.N. RAY, *op. cit.*, p. 4, 72.

301 *Cf.* J.D. WHYTE, *doc. cit.*, p. 11; E. MC WHINNEY, «Constitutional review...» *loc. cit.*, p. 83.

302 *Cf.* B. CHUBB, *The Constitution of Ireland*, Dublin 1966, p. 31; *Cf.* K.C. WHEARE, *Modern Constitutions*, Oxford 1966, p. 101; J.D. WHYTE, *doc. cit.*, 72

303 C.A. KELSICK, «Report», in *Memoria de la reunión de Presidentes de Cortes Supremas de Justicia de Iberoamérica, el Caribe, España y Portugal*, Caracas 1983, p. 419.

304 *Idem*, p. 686

305 Art. 131. See in S.N. RAY, *op. cit.*, p. 290

The appellate jurisdiction of the Supreme Court in appeals from High Court an constitutional matters, is established as follows:

> «An appeal shall lie to the Supreme Court from any judgment, decree or final order of a High Court in the territory of India, whether in a civil, criminal or other proceeding, if the High Court certifies that the case involves a substantial question of law as to the interpretation of this constitution».[306]

Nevertheless, the constitution states that the Supreme Court may grant special leave to appeal when «the High Court has refused to give such a certificate» and «it is satisfied that the case involves a substantial question of law as to the interpretation of this constitution».[307]

Other Commonwealth countries have established an exclusive jurisdiction of the Supreme Court on Constitutional issues, which leads to the adoption of a concentrated system of judicial review although it has been considered as being generally «intolerant» with the common law legal systems.[308] As we will see, such is the case in Papua New Guinea whose constitution gives the Supreme Court exclusive jurisdiction over questions of interpretation and application of Constitutional law, subject to the constitution. Consequently, when such a question arises in any Court or tribunal it shall be referred to the Supreme Court.[309] Special jurisdiction is also given to the Supreme Court to enforce the fundamental Rights provisions of the constitution as well as to the National Court.[310]

As we mentioned, in general terms, the judicial review system followed in the commonwealth countries, is the diffuse system of judicial review, in accordance with the American model. Thus, it is traditional in these countries that courts *per se* and in an abstract way do not initiate actions, and that constitutional issues must be raised in a case or controversies, by a litigant with personal interest in the matter.[311] Nevertheless, a few exceptions to this principle could be found in the Commonwealth Countries Constitutional systems.

For instance, the constitution of Canada establishes the power of the Supreme Court to deliver «advisory opinions» ruling on an abstract constitutional issue referred to it by the federal government.[312] In a similar way, the constitution of India empowers the president to refer questions of laws or fact of particular nature or importance, to the Supreme Court to obtain opinion upon them–and the Court may, after such hearing as it thinks fit, report to the President its opinion there on.[313]

It must also be stressed that the constitution of the Republic of Ireland gives the President of the Republic the power to refer bills to the Supreme Court for an opinion as to whether the bill or any of its provisions is repugnant to the constitution.[314]

---

306 Art. 132,1.

307 Art. 132,2

308 E. Mc Whinney, «Constitutional Review ...», *loc.cit.*, p. 80

309 Art. 18, 19. See in J.D. Whyte, *doc. cit.*, p. 25. *Cf.* in relation to Uganda, T.M. Franck, *Comparative Constitutional Process*, London 1968, p. 75.

310 Art. 57, 1. See in J.D. Whyte, *doc. cit.*, p. 25.

311 *Cf.* S.N. Ray, *op. cit.*, pp. 77-89; Ch. Okpaluba, *loc. cit.*, p. 112; E. Mc Whinney, «Constitutional Review...», *loc.cit.*, pp. 83, 84

312 E. Mc Whinney, «Constitutional Review «, *loc. cit.*, p. 83.

313 Art. 143. See in S.N.Ray, *op. cit.*, p. 294.

314 B. Chubb, *op. cit.*, p. 22, 31; J.D. Whyte, *doc. cit.*, p. 72.

Finally, it must be said that due to the influence of the functioning of the British judicial organization,[315] the *stare decisis* principle generally applies in the Commonwealth Countries, thus the decisions on Constitutional questions adopted by the Supreme Court even though of *inter partes* effects, have binding effects on the inferior courts. That is expressly stated in the constitution of India, where article 141 establishes that «the law declared by the Supreme Court shall be binding on all courts within the territory of India».[316] Nevertheless, regarding the Supreme Courts own decisions, the principle has been interpreted in a flexible way. The *stare decisis* doctrine, the Supreme Court has pointed out, is not an inflexible rule of law and cannot be allowed to perpetuate errors of the Supreme Court to the detriment of the general welfare of the people.[317]

---

315 J.D. WHYTE, *doc. cit.*, p. 11; E. MCWHINNEY, Judicial Review, *op. cit.*, p. 17.

316 See in S.N. RAY, *op. cit.*, p. 293

317 *Bengal Immunity v. State of Bihar*, AIR 1955 SC 661; (1955), 2 SCR 603, quoted by S.N. RAY, *op. cit.*, p. 85. *Cf.* P. TRIKAMDAS, «El Tribunal Supremo de la India», *Revista de la Comisión Internacional de Juristas*, Vol. VIII, Nº 1, 1967, p. 106.

PART FIVE

CONCENTRATED SYSTEMS OF JUDICIAL REVIEW

I. GENERAL FEATURES

The concentrated system of judicial review, contrary to the diffuse system, is basically characterised by the fact that the constitutional system empowers one single state organ of a given country to act as a constitutional judge, in the sense of being the only state organ to decide upon constitutional matters regarding legislative acts and other state acts with similar rank or value, in a jurisdictional way.

This state body with the monopoly of acting as a constitutional judge, can either be the Supreme Court of Justice of the country, in its character as the highest court in the judicial hierarchy or it can also be a special Constitutional Court, Council or Tribunal, specially created by the Constitution to act as the only constitutional judge, and organised outside the ordinary judicial hierarchy. In both cases, the common trend regarding the activity of those bodies is that as constitutional judges they exercise a jurisdictional activity.

Therefore, the concentrated system of judicial review of the constitutionality of legislation, even though generally identified with the «European model» of special constitutional courts,[1] does not necessarily imply the existence of a special Constitutional Court, constitutionally organised separate from the ordinary judiciary. It only implies the assignment to a single state organ, which exercises jurisdictional activity, of the duty and power to act as a constitutional judge. This is the essence of the concentrated character of the system, contrasted with the diffuse system, whether the organ with constitutional justice power is the highest court of the judiciary or is a special constitutional body created outside the ordinary judicial organisation, not being essential to the distinction.

1. Logic of the System

From a logical and rational point of view, it can also be said that this power assigned to one state organ with jurisdictional activity to act as constitutional judge, is a consequence of the principle of the supremacy of the Constitution. In these systems of concentrated constitutional justice, the Constitution being the supreme law of the land, in cases of conflict between a state act and the Constitution, it is obvious that the latter must also prevail. But the constitutional system, in these

---

[1] M. Cappelletti, *Judicial Review in the Contemporary World*, Indianapolis 1971, pp. 50–53.

cases, does not always empower all courts to act as constitutional judges, and in certain cases, it reserves the power to act as a constitutional judge to the Supreme Court of Justice or to a special constitutional court particularly regarding certain acts of the state, which in cases of contradicting the Constitution, only the supreme court or the constitutional court has the power to annul it.

Therefore, it can be said that, in general terms, the logic of the system is also the supremacy of the constitution and the duty of the courts to say which law is applicable in a particular case,[2] but with a concrete limitation: the power to judge the unconstitutionality of legislative acts and other state acts of similar rank or value is reserved to the Supreme Court of Justice or to a Constitutional Court or Tribunal. Thus, in the concentrated system of judicial review, all courts only have the power to act as a constitutional judge and to decide upon the constitutionality of the other norms applicable to the case, other than statutes or acts adopted in direct execution of the Constitution.[3]

Consequently, the concentrated system of judicial review, based on the same principle of the supremacy of the Constitution, when reserving constitutional justice functions regarding certain state acts, to the Supreme Court or to a special Constitutional Court, cannot be developed by deduction through the work of the Supreme Court decisions, like it happened in the diffuse system of judicial review, as was the case for example, of the United States of America, the Republic of Argentina and some Commonwealth countries.

On the contrary, of course, due to the limits that the system imposes on the duty and power of all judges to say which law is applicable in the cases they are to decide, only when prescribed *expressis verbis* through constitutional regulations is it possible to establish the concentrated system of judicial review. It is the constitution, as the supreme law of the land, the only text that can establish limits upon the general power and duty of all courts to say which is the law applicable in a particular case and assign that power and duty in certain cases regarding certain state acts, to a specific constitutional body, whether it be the Supreme Court of Justice or a constitutional court or tribunal.

Therefore, the concentrated system of judicial review can only be a jurisdictional system established and regulated expressly in the constitution, and the state organs to which the constitution reserves the power to act as constitutional judges regarding certain state acts, are always constitutional bodies, that is to say, state organs expressly created and regulated in the constitution whether they be the Supreme Court of Justice of a given country or a specially created constitutional court, tribunal or council.

2. Compatibility of the System with all Legal Systems

Consequently, the concentrated system of judicial review of the constitutionality of legislation is not a system that can be considered peculiar to the

2 *Cf.* W.K. GECK «Judicial Review of Statutes: A Comparative Survey of present Institutions and Practices», *Cornell Law Quarterly*, 51, 1966, p. 278.

3 *Cf.* M. GARCÍA PELAYO, «El 'Status' del Tribunal Constitucional», *Revista española de derecho constitucional*, 1, Madrid 1981, p. 19; E. GARCÍA DE ENTERRÍA, *La Constitución como norma y el Tribunal Constitucional*, Madrid 1981, p. 65. In particular, in concentrated system of judicial review, the tribunals or courts empowered with administrative justice functions have always the power of acting as constitutional judge regarding administrative acts. See C. FRANK, *Les functions juridictionnelles du Conseil d'État dans 1'ordre constitutionnel*, Paris 1974.

civil law system of law, and incompatible with the common law tradition. It is only a system that must be expressly established and regulated in a written Constitution and it can therefore indifferently exist in systems with a common law tradition or with a civil law basis, though it is most commonly followed in civil law countries.

For instance, in Papua New Guinea, a country that gained its independence from Australia in 1975 and, therefore, with a common law tradition, the Constitution gives the Supreme Court exclusive jurisdiction over questions of interpretation and application of constitutional law, subject to the Constitution. Therefore, when such a question arises in any court or tribunal, it shall be referred to the Supreme Court.[4] In a similar sense, the 1966 Constitution of Uganda also established an exclusive jurisdiction of the High Court on constitutional matters. In this respect, article 95 stated that:

> «Where any question as to the interpretation of this Constitution arises in any proceedings in any court of law, other than a court-martial, and the court is of the opinion that the question involves a substantial question of law, the court may, and shall if any party to the proceedings so request, refer the question to the High Court consisting of a bench of no less than three judges of the High Court».

The same article added:

> «Where any question is referred to the High Court in pursuance of this article, the High Court shall give its decision upon the question and the court in which the question arose, shall dispose of the case in accordance with that decision».[5]

We must also refer to the system established in Ghana in the 1960, 1969 and 1979 Constitutions, which vested the Supreme Court with original and exclusive jurisdiction to exercise the power of judicial review. In effect, article 42 of the 1960 Constitution and article 106 of the 1969 Constitution stated:

> «The Supreme Court shall have original jurisdiction in all matters where a question arises whether an enactment was made in excess of the powers conferred on Parliament by or under the Constitution, and if any such question arises in the High Court or an inferior court, the hearing shall be adjourned and the question referred to the Supreme Court for decision».[6]

Additionally, article 2 of the 1969 Constitution established a direct action that could be brought before the Supreme Court to seek judicial review, as follows:

> «A person who alleges that an enactment or anything contained in or done under the authority of that or any other enactment is inconsistent with, or in contravention of, any provision of this Constitution, may bring an action in the Supreme Court for a declaration to that effect».[7]

---

4 Art. 18 and 19 of the Constitution. See in J.D. WHYTE, *Judicial Review of Legislation and its Legitimacy:Developments in the Common Law World*, IALS, Uppsala, Colloquium 1984, (mimeo), p. 25.

5 See in T.M. FRANCK, *Comparative Constitutional Process. Cases and Materials*, London 1968, pp. 75-76.

6 See in S.O. GYANDOH Jr., «Interaction of the Judicial and Legislative Processes in Ghana since Independence», *Temple Law Quarterly*, 56, 2, Philadelphia 1983, pp. 365-366, 370.

7 *Idem*, p. 370.

For the purpose of that declaration, added the Constitution, the Supreme Court shall «make such orders and give such directions as it may consider appropriate for giving effect to or enabling effect to be given to the declarations so made».[8] Those provisions regarding judicial review were also adopted in the 1979 Constitution,[9] but since 1971, they were interpreted by the Supreme Court to reduce the referral of proceeding cases to the Supreme Court, and to avoid referrals of frivolous submissions.[10]

Anyway, even though it is certain that the system of judicial review has not always functioned in some Commonwealth countries because of democratic instability,[11] what is certain is that the concentrated system of judicial review exists and has functioned in legal systems, with a common law tradition. Thus, there is the expression of Professor Edward McWhinney in the sense that common law «practice has always been intolerant of the notion of specialised, expert, tribunals on the continental model»[12] must be understood as referring to the specialised constitutional court, tribunal or council European system, but not, as he said, to a system «where jurisdiction is determined and limited in terms of subject matters»,[13] which refers to the very concept of the concentrated system of judicial review, when, for instance, assigned to a Supreme Court of Justice of a given country and not to a special non-judicial constitutional organ.

The concentrated system of judicial review cannot be reduced to the constitutional systems in which a constitutional court, tribunal or council exists; having produced a distortion of the approach to the system the misleading identification of the concentrated system with the European model of specialised constitutional courts, council or tribunal.

In effect, though the concentrated system of judicial review is also known as the «Austrian system»[14] or as the «European model»,[15] based on the existence of a specialised constitutional court, tribunal or council created, in the constitution, with the power to act as a constitutional judge although organised outside the ordinary judiciary, we must insist that the feature that characterises the system is not the existence of such a special constitutional court, tribunal or council at all, but the exclusive attribution to a single constitutional state body of the power to act as a constitutional judge regarding certain state acts, whether that body be the existing Supreme Court of Justice of the country or a specially created constitutional court, council or tribunal.

---

8 Art. 2, *Idem*, p. 370.

9 *Idem*, p. 384.

10 *Republic v. Maikankan* (1971) 2 G.L.R., 473 quoted by S.O. GYANDOH Jr., *loc. cit.*, p. 386.

11 See in relation to Ghana the comments of S.O. GYANDOH Jr., *loc. cit.*, p. 395.

12 E. MCWHINNEY, «Constitutional Review in the Commonwealth», in H. MOSLER (ed.), Max-Plank-Institut für Ausländisches öffentliches recht and völkerrecht, *Verfassungs gerichtsbarkeit in der Gegenwart*, Internationales Kolloquium, Heidelberg, 1961, Köln-Berlin 1962, p. 80

13 *Idem*, p. 80.

14 M. CAPPELLETTI, *op. cit.*, p. 50; J. CARPIZO and H. FIX-ZAMUDIO, «La necesidad y la legitimidad de la revisión judicial en América latina. Desarrollo reciente», *Boletín Mexicano de Derecho Comparado*, 52, 1985, p. 36.

15 L. FAVOREU, «Actualité et légitimité du contrôl juridictionnel des lois en Europe occidentale», *Revue du droit public et de la science politique en France et à 1'étranger*, Paris 1985 (5), p. 1149. Also published in L. FAVOREU and J.A. JOLOWICZ (ed.), *Le contrôle juridictionnel des lois, Légitimité, effectivité et développments récents*, Paris 1986, pp. 17-68.

The adoption of the system is always a constitutional option and decision according to the concrete circumstances of each country, but it does not necessarily imply the creation of special constitutional courts or bodies to ensure constitutional justice. In Europe, for instance, the flourishing of constitutional courts, tribunals or councils for the exercise of the concentrated system of judicial review, can only be seen as a concrete consequence of a peculiar constitutional tradition regarding the principles of the supremacy of the law, the separation of powers and the traditional fear of the judges to control legislative acts[16] and cannot lead to considering that «the» model of the concentrated system of judicial review consists in the creation of a constitutional body outside the ordinary judiciary to act as constitutional judge. Well before the European «discovery» of constitutional justice by creating those special constitutional courts or tribunals after the First World War, ever since the middle of the last century (19th century), other countries with a civil law tradition have developed concentrated systems of judicial review by attributing the original and exclusive jurisdiction to annul statutes and other state acts with similar rank and effects to their Supreme Courts of Justice when contrary to the constitution. This has been the common trend of the Latin American constitutional system, even though mixing the concentrated with the diffuse system of judicial review.

Therefore, from what we have said, three conclusions can be drawn: First, the concentrated system of judicial review can only exist when it is established *expressis verbis* in the constitution, therefore, it cannot be developed by interpretation of the principle of the supremacy of the constitution. Second, the concentrated system of judicial review characterised by the granting to one single constitutional body of the functions of constitutional justice, is compatible to any legal system, whether common law or roman law legal systems, even though it has widely developed in the civil law countries. Third, the concentrated system of judicial review does not only imply the attribution of the functions of constitutional justice to a special constitutional court, tribunal or council created separate to the ordinary judicial organisation. It also exists when constitutional justice functions are attributed to the existing Supreme Court of Justice of the country, even though in the latter case the system generally tends to mix its trends with elements of the diffuse system of judicial review.

3. Rationality of the System

As we have said, in a similar way as in the diffuse system of judicial review, the essence of the concentrated system of judicial review is also the very notion of the supremacy of the constitution: if the constitution is the supreme law of the land prevailing over all other laws, no state act contrary to it can be an effective law; on the contrary, it must be considered as null and void. Thus the main element that leads to the differentiation between both systems of judicial review is not, of course, a possible different notion of the constitution and its supremacy, but the type of guarantee adopted in the constitutional system to maintain that supremacy. As Hans Kelsen pointed out in 1928, these «objective guarantees» are the nullity or the annullability of the unconstitutional act. Nullity means -as he explained- the unconstitutional state act cannot be considered objectively as a juridical act, therefore in principle it is not necessary to take away its quality of usurped juridical act, by

---

[16] *Cf.* M. CAPPELLETTI, *op. cit.*, p. 54; M. CAPPELLETTI and J.C. ADAMS, «Judicial Review of Legislation: European Antecedents and Adaptation», *Harvard Law Review*, Vol 79, (6), 1966, p. 1211.

means of another juridical act. In this case, theoretically, everybody, public authorities or individuals would have the right to examine the regularity of the acts considered null and void, to declare the irregularity and to consider such acts as non-valid and non-obligatory. On the contrary, if another juridical act is necessary to establish the nullity of the unconstitutional act, the guarantee of the constitution would not be of nullity but of annullability.[17]

As we have seen, the nullity of unconstitutional state acts is the guarantee of the constitution that leads to the diffuse system of judicial review, even though as Kelsen pointed out, positive law normally restricts this power that anybody has of considering irregular acts as null and void,[18] and tends to attribute it exclusively to the courts, which is the general situation today due to the need for legal reliability.

On the other hand, it is precisely the other guarantee of the constitution, the annulability of the unconstitutional state acts, which leads to the concentrated system of judicial review.

A. Annullability of Certain Unconstitutional State Acts

In effect, the first aspect that shows the rationality of the concentrated system of judicial review is the principle of the annullability of certain state acts, particularly statutes and other acts issued in direct execution of the Constitution, when they are considered to be contrary to the constitution.

This annullability of a state acts as an objective guarantee of the constitution, and contrary to the situation concerning the nullity of such acts, means that a state act, even if it is irregular or unconstitutional, once issued by a public body it must be considered as such a state act, and therefore, valid and effective, until it is repealed by the same organ which produced it or until it is annulled by another state organ with constitutional powers to do so. It is precisely in the concentrated systems of judicial review, in which the constitution assigns the power to annul certain state acts when considered unconstitutional, to only one state organ, whether it be to the existing supreme court of justice or to a special constitutional body created separate from the ordinary judiciary, but with jurisdictional functions to act as a constitutional judge.

In fact, we must bear in mind that in the concentrated systems of judicial review, the annullability of state acts is not really the only guarantee of the constitution and is always accompanied by the nullity. In a certain way it is a restriction to the nullity rule resulting from the violation of the constitution.

We have said, in effect, that in the case of the nullity of unconstitutional state acts that exist in the diffuse system of judicial review, in order to avoid juridical anarchy, positive law limits the theoretical general power that public authorities and individuals have to declare the inexistence of an unconstitutional state act and to consider it invalid and reserves this power to the judges. This means that in fact, the unconstitutional state act can only be examined by the courts and only the courts have the power to consider it null and void, which means that up to that moment, the irregular act must be considered by other public authorities and

---

[17] H. KELSEN, «La guarantie juridictionelle de la Constitution. La Justice constitutionnelle», *Revue du droit public et de la science politique en France et à l'étranger*, Paris 1928, p. 214.

[18] *Idem*, p. 215.

individuals as being effective and obligatory. In the diffuse system of judicial review, once the court declares the invalidity of the unconstitutional act in relation to a particular process, then the act becomes null and void regarding that process.

It can be said that, in principle, this same situation exists even in constitutional systems with a concentrated system of judicial review regarding all other state acts different to those which can only be annulled by the Constitutional or the Supreme Courts. In effect, as we have said, regarding state acts of lower levels in the hierarchy of norms, for instance, administrative acts with normative effects, all judges in a concentrated system of judicial review normally have the power to consider them null and void when unconstitutional, with respect to the particular process in which they are questioned. In such cases, the guarantee of the constitution is the nullity of the unconstitutional state act, even though only the courts can assume it.

Therefore, what is peculiar to the concentrated system of judicial review is that constitutional positive law establishes an additional limitation concerning the effects of the unconstitutionality of state acts, in the sense that concerning certain acts, the power to declare their unconstitutionality and invalidity and therefore, to consider them to be without effect, has been exclusively reserved to one constitutional organ: the existing supreme court of justice or a special constitutional court, tribunal or council. In those cases, and regarding such certain acts, normally being legislative acts and other state acts of similar rank or effect in the sense of being issued in direct execution of the constitution, the guarantee of the constitution has been reduced to the annullability of the state act considered unconstitutional.

In conclusion, in constitutional systems with a concentrated system of judicial review, the duty of all judges and courts is also to examine the constitutionality of statutes and other state acts. Nevertheless when the state act questioned on the grounds of unconstitutionality is a statute or other state act issued in direct execution of the constitution, the ordinary courts cannot judge its unconstitutionality, That power is reserved to a special constitutional court or to the supreme court of a given country, which can annul the act. In this case the guarantee of the constitution is the annullability, in which case, the act is annulled with general effects, and not only considered or declared null and void in a particular case.

Leaving aside this particular reserve -which is the feature of the concentrated system of judicial review- all other courts, regarding the normative state acts not included in the reserve, have the power to examine their unconstitutionality. Moreover, when necessary the courts have the power to establish their inapplicability to a particular process that the court is considering, because it is unconstitutional and therefore must be considered null and void. In those other cases, the guarantee of the constitution certainly is the nullity.

B. Power of a Special Constitutional Body Regarding the Annulment of Certain State Acts on the Grounds of Unconstitutionality

This leads to the second aspect of the rationality of the concentrated system of judicial review, which is that the power to declare the nullity of legislation is assigned to one single constitutional organ with jurisdictional functions, whether it be the existing supreme court of a country or a specially created constitutional court, tribunal or council. Therefore, the concentrated system has a double particularity: first that the power to annul unconstitutional acts is assigned to a single constitutional organ with jurisdictional functions. Second, that the reserve assigned to that constitutional body to judge the unconstitutionality and declare the nullity of state acts concerns not all state acts, but rather a limited number of them normally identified with statutes (legislation) and other acts of Parliament or of the government issued in direct execution of the constitution, thus being subject to the sole rule of the constitution.

We have said that the concentrated system of judicial review does not necessarily imply the assignment of the power to annul statutes to a specially created constitutional court, tribunal or council in the European fashion, and that power can be assigned to the existing Supreme Court of Justice of a given country, as happened well before the constitutional court fashion developed after the 1920's in continental Europe.

In effect, since the middle of the last century (19th century), many Latin American countries have adopted a concentrated system of judicial review by assigning the supreme court of the country with the power to declare the nullity of legislation. This was the case in Colombia and Venezuela in which an authentic concentrated system of judicial review has existed since 1850 and in which the supreme courts have the monopoly of annulling statutes. It is true that normally the concentrated systems of judicial review in Latin America developed in the last hundred and thirty years have moved towards a mixed system of judicial review in which the diffuse and the concentrated systems of judicial review coexist. That is the system that currently exists, for instance in Colombia, Venezuela and Guatemala, which we will analyse further on in our course. Yet, some Latin American systems have remained concentrated ones, as is the case in Uruguay and Paraguay, in which countries the Supreme Court of Justice has exclusive and original jurisdiction to declare the unconstitutionality of statutes.[19]

Of course, the modality of the concentrated system of judicial review that consists in establishing a special constitutional body, whether court, tribunal or council to act as a constitutional judge vested with original and exclusive power to annul statutes and other similar acts in rank or effects, because of its novelty, has marked the development of constitutional, justice during the recent decades, since the first constitutional courts were established in Austria and Czechoslovakia in 1920. The system was later adopted in Germany and Italy, after the Second World War, and more recently in Spain and Portugal. It has also been adopted in some socialist countries (Yugoslavia, Czechoslovakia and Poland) and has been developed with particular trends, in France. Under the influence of the European model, but in an incomplete way the system was adopted in the early seventies in Chile, where a Constitutional Tribunal was established, and more recently in Ecuador and Peru, where Constitutional Guarantees Tribunals have been created.

We will refer to all these experiences, but firstly we will concentrate our comments on the European model and in particular, on the analysis of the various Constitutional Courts experiences.

As we have said, even though constitutionalism developed in the theory and practice of constitutional law since the beginning of the last century (19th century), mainly as a contribution of the North American experience, it must be admitted that

---

[19] H. GROS ESPIELL, *La Constitución y su Defensa*. Uruguay, UNAM, Congreso Internacional sobre la Constitución y su defensa México, 1982, (mimeo) p. 7; J.P. GATTO DE SOUZA, «El control constitucional de los actos del poder público», *Memoria de la reunión de Presidentes de Cortes Supremas de Justicia de Iberoamérica, el Caribe, España y Portugal*, Caracas 1983, p. 661; L.M. ANGAÑA, «Ponencia» (Paraguay), *idem*, p. 551.

continental European constitutionalism remained on the fringes of the American conceptions, and a system of constitutional justice was not accepted in Europe until after the First World War and took place through two paths. One concluded in the *Weimar* Constitution (1919), whereby Germany established a Tribunal entrusted with jurisdiction to settle disputes between the state constitutional powers, and more specifically, between the different territorial powers, vertically distributed as a result of the federal organisation of the state. The second was the Austrian system, the personal masterpiece of Professor Hans Kelsen, who conceived a system first expressed in the 1920 Austrian constitution and perfected by the 1929 constitutional reform.

In any case, it can be considered that the incorporation of a system of constitutional justice in Europe was due to the influence of Hans Kelsen's pure theory of law. This theory, as we have mentioned, conceived the constitutional norm as the grounds for the validity of all the norms of a given legal order, with a fundamental corollary: the need for a state body to guarantee the constitution, that is to say, to settle disputes over the consistency of all legal norms, both specific and general, with the superior hierarchy on which they are based, and in the last instance, with the constitution.[20]

Kelsen himself established quite clearly that constitutional justice was in itself a special case of a more general issue, which consisted of the guarantee of the consistency of an inferior norm to a superior norm from whence it arose, and its contents were determined. In the end constitutional justice was a guarantee of the constitution resulting from the «juridical pyramid» of the legal order whereby the unity and hierarchy of its different norms were established.

However, it should be noted that in addition to Austria, and also under the influence of Kelsen, Czechoslovakia was the first European country to adopt a system of constitutional control in the constitution of 29 February 1920.[21] The grounds for the establishment of the Czechoslovakian concentrated system of constitutional control are to be found, to be sure, in the existence of a constitutional norm, which explicitly sets forth the supremacy of the constitution over the rest of the legal order, by stating that, «All laws contrary to the Constitutional Charter and any part thereof, as well as laws that modify and complement it, are considered null and void»;[22] and by explicitly prohibiting the courts from the possibility of exercising diffuse control over the constitutionality of laws.[23] In addition, the constitution established the obligation for all courts to consult with the Constitutional Tribunal, in cases of the enforcement of a law deemed to be in violation of the constitution. Those elements led to the concentration of constitutional jurisdiction to judge the constitutionality of laws in a single body, the Constitutional Tribunal, which continued to exist until 1938.[24]

---

20 H. KELSEN, *loc. cit.*, pp. 201-223.

21 Art. I.1. See in P. CRUZ VILLALON, «Dos modos de regulación del control de constitucionalidad: Checoslovaquia (1920-1938) y España (1931-1936)», *Revista española de derecho constitucional*, 5, Madrid 1982, p. 119.

22 Art. I.1., *idem*.

23 Art. 102 established «The courts can verify the validity of executive regulations, when deciding upon a specific question of laws; concerning statutes they can only verify if they have been correctly published», see in P. CRUZ VILLALON, *loc. cit.*, p. 135.

24 It also should be noted that the Rumanian constitutional regime also established a system of judicial review of laws, in Article 103 of the Fundamental Charter of 29 March 1923. However, it was conferred only on the Court of Cassation, and later on it was eliminated by the People's Republic, under Soviet influence, from the terms of the Fundamental Law of 1948.

Kelsen's conception of the concentrated system of judicial review, contrary to the diffuse system which, as we have seen, implies that all judges are entitled to abstain from enforcing laws they deem contrary to the Constitution, therefore results in the attribution of the exclusive power to declare the unconstitutionality of a law, and annul it, to a single state body, the constitutional tribunal, to which all courts must refer when they are in the situation of having to enforce a law of doubtful constitutionality. Consequently, in this system, ordinary courts lack the power to refrain from enforcing unconstitutional laws on their own.

In its original theoretical conception, this concentrated system of judicial control of constitutionality attributed to a special court, was not conceived by Kelsen as being the exercise of a jurisdictional function but rather as «a system of negative legislation».[25] In fact, a constitutional court does not specifically decide upon the unconstitutionality of statutes on any assumption of a single fact; this is reserved for the *a quo* court raising the question of constitutionality. Its competence is normally limited to the purely abstract issue of the logical compatibility, which must exist between the statute and the constitution. Therefore, in this purely logical judgement, as there is no real enforcement of the law in any specific case, it was considered that it was not the case of jurisdictional activity which implied a concrete decision. This led Kelsen to maintain that when the constitutional tribunal declares a statute unconstitutional, the decision having *erga omnes* effects was a typical legislative action, hence the common assumption that the constitutional tribunal's decision has the force of law. That is also why it is considered that until that decision is adopted, the statute is valid and that explains why judges of ordinary courts are obliged to enforce it.[26]

Kelsen developed this conception as an answer to the possible objections that the jurisdictional control of legislative action could produce, based on the concept of the supremacy of Parliament so embodied in European constitutional law. Thus, by forbidding ordinary judges to abstain from enforcing the laws and granting the power to declare a statute unconstitutional with *erga omnes* effect to the constitutional court, the judiciary was subject to the laws adopted by parliament. At the same time, the primacy of the constitution over Parliament could be maintained. In this way, it was considered that the constitutional tribunal instead of competing with parliament became its logical complement. Its function was reduced to judging the validity of a statute with simple and rational logic, completely separate from the need to settle disputes in specific cases, and acting as a negative legislator, albeit a legislator which does not act spontaneously but at the request of the parties involved. In this way, legislative power was for Kelsen divided into two bodies: the first, parliament, the holder of political initiative, the positive legislator; and the second, the constitutional tribunal, entrusted with the power to annul laws which violate the constitution.[27]

Under this conception, of course, the constitutional court needed to be a constitutional body separate from all traditional state powers: thus, it was not a judicial body.[28]

---

25 H. KELSEN, *loc. cit.*, pp. 224-226. See the comments of E. GARCÍA DE ENTERRÍA, *op. cit.*, pp. 57-132.

26 H. KELSEN, *loc. cit*, pp. 224-225.

27 See the comments on KELSEN's thought in E. GARCÍA DE ENTERRÍA, *op. cit.*, pp. 57, 58, 59, 131, and 132-133.

28 H. KELSEN, *loc. cit.*, p. 223.

Anyway, today, even though the jurisdictional character -non legislative- of the activity developed by these special constitutional bodies rejecting its supposed negative legislator character[29] is accepted without discussion, the conception of attributing constitutional justice functions to a specially created constitutional body (constitutional court, tribunal or council) generally not located within the judiciary organisation has prevailed in continental Europe, and has given way to the «European model» of judicial review. This model developed in a certain way as the result of a compromise between the need of a system of constitutional justice derived from the notion of constitutional supremacy, and the traditional European conception of the separation of powers which denied the power to invalidate statutes to all judicial organs.[30]

Nevertheless, as we have said, it is improper to identify the concentrated system of judicial review with this «European model», because it is also a concentrated system, one in which the exclusive and original jurisdiction to annul statutes and other state acts is conferred upon the existing Supreme Court of Justice of a given country and located at the apex of the judiciary organisation. Thus, the second aspect which shows the rationality of the concentrated system of judicial review is the assignment of the role of constitutional judge to annul statutes with *erga omnes* effects, to one single constitutional organ whether it be the supreme court of justice of a given country or a specially created constitutional court, tribunal or council.

C. *Principal and incidental character of the system*

Contrary to the diffuse system of judicial review, which is always of an incidental character, the concentrated system of judicial review can have either a principal or incidental character, in the sense that constitutional questions regarding statutes may reach the supreme court or the constitutional court, by virtue of a direct action or request brought before the court or by reference of the question to the court, from a lower court, where the constitutional question has been raised in a concrete proceeding, either *ex-officio* or through the initiative of a party.

Therefore, the third aspect that shows the rationality of the concentrated system of judicial review of the constitutionality of legislation, in which the power to annul statutes is attributed to a single court, is that the constitutional question can either reach the supreme court or the constitutional court, in a direct or principal form, through the exercise before the court of an action against the statute; or in an incidental form, when the constitutional issue is raised in a particular process in a lower court in which case the judge must refer his decision to the supreme court or the constitutional court, in order to subsequently render his final resolution of the case in accordance with the Supreme Court or Constitutional Court adjudication.

In both cases, the control of the constitutionality of legislation is a concentrated one, because one single organ is authorised to pass judgement upon the constitutionality of a statute, but this essential feature does not imply that the constitutional question must only be raised either in a principal or in an incidental way. It can be either one form or the other, or through both in parallel, depending on the concrete positive law regulations. Therefore, in our opinion, there is no

---

29 M. CAPPELLETTI and J.C. ADAMS, *loc. cit.*, pp. 1218-1219.
30 M. CAPPELLETTI, *op. cit.*, p. 67.

evidence in comparative law, to identify the concentrated system of judicial review with the principal character of the method of reviewing the constitutional question, in which such a question is entirely disassociated from a concrete case. If this was true in the original Austrian system established in 1920, it is no longer true in contemporary constitutional law,[31] where the concentrated system of judicial review can result from both methods, principal or incidental. In the principal method, the constitutional issue regarding a statute is the only and principal question of the process initiated through the exercise of a direct action that can be brought before the supreme court or the constitutional court, either by someone through an *actio popularis* or within some *locus standing* rules or by specific public officials and authorities. In the incidental method the constitutional issue is raised before an ordinary court as an incidental question aspect of a process, or the court can raise it *ex-officio*. This court is the one which must refer the constitutional question to the decision by the supreme court or by the constitutional court, the suspension of the decision of the concrete case being necessary until the constitutional issue is resolved by the supreme court or the constitutional court.

D. *Initiative Power on Judicial Review*

The constitutional question relating to the validity of a statute, as we have seen, is normally raised in the supreme court or in the constitutional court through an action or through reference by a lower court and in both cases, the constitutional judge must decide the issue on the basis of the law and without considering the facts.

In both cases, as we said, the constitutional question must be raised before the Supreme Court or the constitutional court, which does not have self initiative to act as a constitutional judge.[32] Thus the principle *nemo iudex sine actore* applies. But once a constitutional question has reached the court as a result of an action or of a lower court referral, the principle *ne iudex iudicet ultra petitum partis* does not apply. That is to say, the constitutional court as constitutional judge, once required by a party or through incidental means, has *ex-officio* powers to consider other questions of constitutionality, other than those already submitted.

However, if it is true that the supreme court or the constitutional court does not have its own initiative to initiate the constitutional justice proceeding regarding legislation, on the other hand it must be said that in the incidental method of concentrated judicial review, the lower courts that must refer the decision of the constitutional issue to the constitutional judge, can have the initiative in raising the issue for referral to the supreme court or to the constitutional court. That is to say, the ordinary courts when raising constitutional issues in the incidental method are not always bound by the requirements of the parties or of the public prosecutor, and when considering the particular case, they can raise the constitutional question *ex-officio* and refer it to the Supreme Court or the constitutional court for decision.

This is the consequence of the principle of the supremacy of the constitution and of the duty of all judges to apply the law. Moreover, if it is true that in the

---

31 *Cf.* M. CAPPELLETTI, *op. cit*, pp. 69-72.

32 Exceptionally, the Federal Constitutional Tribunal of Yugoslavia has *ex officio* powers to initiate a proceeding of judicial review of legislation. See Art. 4, Law of the Constitutional Court of Yugoslavia. 31-12-1963, in B.T. BLAGOJEVIC (ed.), *Constitutional Judicature*, Beograd 1965, p. 16.

concentrated system of judicial review, the constitution has forbidden the ordinary courts to act as constitutional judges, this could not mean that if they consider a statute applicable to the decision of a concrete case unconstitutional, they do not have the power to raise the constitutional question and cannot refer it to the constitutional judge. The contrary would mean a break in the principle of constitutional supremacy and in the role of the judiciary when applying the law.

E. *Erga omnes effects of the Court decision*

The fifth and final aspect of the rationality of the concentrated system of judicial review as in the diffuse system, also concerns the effects of the decisions adopted by the supreme court or the constitutional court regarding the constitutionality of the statute, according to the constitutional question posed in the action or in the lower court referral. This aspect of the effects of the judicial decision also refers in such cases, to two questions: first, whom the decision affects; and second, when do the effects of the decision begin.

In relation to the first question, the rationality of the concentrated system of judicial review is that the decision adopted by the constitutional court or the supreme court acting as a constitutional judge, has general effects, thus it applies *erga omnes*. This is particularly exact when judicial review is sought by a direct action brought before the constitutional court or the supreme court, in which there is no concrete case between parties whatsoever and in which proceeding there are no real parties in the strictest sense. When a direct action is brought before the constitutional judge, the process relation is not between a plaintiff and a defendant but basically between a petitioner and a statute whose constitutionality is challenged. In this case, the process is considered an objective process; consequently, the object of the decision upon the unconstitutionality of the statute being its annulment, its effects necessarily must be *erga omnes* and cannot be *inter partes* basically because of the absence of the said proper parties.

Nevertheless, in the concentrated system of judicial review even when sought by incidental methods, when a constitutional issue regarding a statute is raised in a concrete proceeding and the lower court refers it to decision by the supreme court or the constitutional court, its decision being concentrated on aspects regarding law only and not facts, also has *erga omnes* effects, that is to say, they are not limited to the concrete process and parties in which the constitutional question was originally raised.

In effect, in both cases of concentrated systems of judicial review, sought by principal or incidental methods, the supreme court or the constitutional court decides in abstract a question of constitutionality of a statute, without any reference to facts or to the concrete process in which the constitutional issue may be raised, if it be so. Therefore, the constitutional judge in the concentrated system is not deciding a constitutional issue only to decide a concrete case between parties. The constitutional judge, as we said, in these cases does not decide a concrete case, but only a question of constitutionality of a statute, therefore, the logic of the system is that the decision must apply in general, to everybody and to all state organs, thus the *erga omnes* effects.

Thus, if a law is considered unconstitutional by the Constitutional Court or by the supreme court acting as constitutional judge, this means that the law thereof is annulled and cannot be enforceable and applicable not only to the resolution of a particular case, but elsewhere.

F. *Constitutive effects of the Supreme Court or Constitutional Court decision*

These *erga omnes* effects of the judicial decision in the concentrated system of judicial review are closely related to the other question concerning the effects of the decision in time, namely as to when the declaration of unconstitutionality is to be effective, and of course, as to the already mentioned aspect of the annulability of certain state acts, as a guarantee of the constitution.

In effect, we have said that the first and foremost fundamental aspect of the rationality of the concentrated system of judicial review, as it is in the diffuse system, is that of the supremacy of the constitution over all state acts which leads to the consideration that the laws contrary to the constitution must be null and void. We have also said that, even if the guarantee of the constitution in the concentrated systems of judicial review in principle is also the nullity of the unconstitutional state acts, regarding certain state acts, like the legislative ones, the constitution has restricted its own guarantee by reserving the appreciation and declaration of its nullity to only one single constitutional organ: the supreme court or a specially created constitutional court, tribunal or council, to which the exclusive power of declaring the nullity of the said state acts has been granted.

Consequently, when a constitutional judge decides upon the unconstitutionality of a law and establishes it, the decision has a *constitutive* effect: it declares the nullity of a law because it is unconstitutional, the law having produced effects up to the moment in which its nullity is established. Thus the law, whose nullity is declared and established, is considered in principle by the court as having been valid up to that moment.

That is why it is said that the decision of the court, as it is a constitutive one, has *ex-nunc, pro futuro* or prospective effects, in the sense that, in principle, they do not go back to the moment of the enactment of the statute considered thereon unconstitutional, the effects produced by the annulled statute until that annulment being considered valid.

The legislative act declared unconstitutional by a constitutional judge in the concentrated system of judicial review, therefore, is considered as a valid act until its annulment by the court, having produced complete effects until the moment, when the court annuls it.

Nevertheless, this element of the logic of the concentrated system of judicial review is normally tempered by the constitutional system itself, when a distinction is established between the unconstitutionality errors, or defects that can affect statutes, whether they produce its absolute or relative nullity. Therefore, in cases when constitutional errors that may affect a statute produce an absolute nullity, when the annulment of the statute is decided upon by the constitutional judge, it evidently produces as an outcome *ex-tunc* effects of the decision, because a statute considered null and void in an absolute form is not capable of producing any effect. Thus, in those cases, the annulment of the statute has *pro-pretaerito* or retroactive effects, being considered null and void *ab initio*. On the contrary, if the constitutional errors or defects of the statute, which lead to its annulment by the constitutional judge, are not so grave as to produce its absolute nullity but only its relative nullity, the effects of the annulment of the statute are only *ex-nunc, pro futuro*.

4. Conclusion

In conclusion we can say that as a matter of principle, the rationality of the diffuse system of judicial review works as follows:

The Constitution has a supreme character over the whole legal order; thus, acts contrary to the Constitution cannot have any effects, and are considered null and void.

In principle and concerning state acts of a lower rank in the legal order, all courts have the power and the duty to apply the constitution and the laws, and therefore, to give preference to the constitution and statutes over those state acts which violate them, and to declare them unconstitutional and inapplicable to the concrete process developed before the courts. Nevertheless, regarding certain state acts, normally statutes (laws) and other acts issued in direct execution of the constitution, this fundamental text expressly reserves the power to examine and declare the unconstitutionality of such acts, and to annul them to one single constitutional organ, whether it be the supreme court of a given country or a specially created constitutional court, tribunal or council.

This power of the particular constitutional judge to declare the nullity of certain state acts, can only be exercised when required whether by means of a direct action brought before it against the unconstitutional statute, to be examined in an abstract way, or when a lower court refers a constitutional question that has been raised in a concrete process to the constitutional judge. In the latter case, the incidental character of the issue has suspensive effects, and the case before the ordinary court will only be decided after the constitutional judge has rendered his decision on the constitutionality of the statute, also in an abstract way without referring to the facts of the concrete process.

The judgement of the Constitutional Court must then be taken when required through a principal or incidental method, regarding the constitutionality of legislation, it not being possible to raise the constitutional question *motu proprio* or *ex-officio* by the constitutional judge. Nevertheless, when the constitutional question is brought before the constitutional judge it has *ex-officio* power to consider other constitutional issues; and in cases of incidental means the lower court that raised the issue has *ex-officio* powers to do so and is not limited to the parties' initiative.

The decision adopted by the court concerning the unconstitutionality of a law, has *erga omnes* effects regarding all state organs and individuals; and it is of a constitutive effect in the sense that it pronounces the nullity of the statute, thus, it annuls it. When declaring the nullity of the statute, therefore, the decision has *ex-nunc*, and *pro futuro* effects in the sense that they are not retroactive. In that case the annulled act must be considered as having produced its effects as a valid act prior to its annulment, unless when it is considered that it is affected by an absolute nullity.

Of course, in the concentrated systems of judicial review, this logic is not always absolute, and each legal system has also developed corrections to the possible deviation that each one of the aspects of the rationality of the system may produce concerning the nullity or annullability of the unconstitutional act; the initiative of the court; the *inter partes* or *erga omnes* effects of the decision and its declarative or constitutive character.

In analysing the most important concentrated systems of judicial review of the constitutionality of legislation particularly to those that follow the European model, we will refer to all the aspects of the rationality of the system and its special modifications.

II. ORIGIN OF THE «EUROPEAN MODEL» OF JUDICIAL REVIEW AND THE AUSTRIAN SYSTEM OF THE CONSTITUTIONAL TRIBUNAL

1. European Antecedents

The concentrated system of judicial review based on the assignment of the exclusive power to control the constitutionality of legislation to a single constitutional state body, specially created outside the normal organisation of the judicial power, is basically a European institution: it was originated in Europe, where it was developed particularly after the two World Wars, and has remained in Europe[33] giving rise to the so called «European model» of judicial review[34] also qualified as the «Austrian system».[35] It is not, of course, the only expression of the concentrated system of judicial review, because as we have mentioned, its essence is not the existence of a constitutional court or tribunal established separate from the ordinary judicial power, but the concentration of powers of judicial review of the constitutionality of legislation in one single organ, that can perfectly be the existing supreme court of a country situated at the apex of judicial power.[36] Therefore, the concentrated system of judicial review is not equivalent to the «European model», which is only one of its expressions, although the most notable one.

The «Austrian system» was originated in Europe after the First World War under the influence of the ideas and direct work of Hans Kelsen, particularly regarding the concept of the supremacy of the constitution and the need for a jurisdictional guarantee of that supremacy;[37] but it was also a direct result of the absence of a diffuse system of judicial review of the constitutionality of legislation whose exclusion was expressly or indirectly established in the Constitution.

In this respect, the Austrian Constitution has traditionally established a prohibition directed towards ordinary judges, to «examine the validity of laws, decrees or international treaties duly enacted»;[38] and the Czechoslovakian

---

33 Exceptionally and without doubt, under the European influence, some Latin American Countries have established Constitutional Tribunals. Is the case of Chile, Guatemala, Ecuador and Peru, with various and different control power that except in the case of Guatemala (J.M. GARCÍA LAGUARDIA, *La Defensa de la Constitución*, UNAM, México, 1983, p. 52) lead to the conclusion that the similarities with the European model are more a matter of names or denominations, than of power of control. See in general, H. FIX-ZAMUDIO, *Los tribunales constitucionales y los derechos humanos*, UNAM, México, 1980; H. FIX-ZAMUDIO, Veinticinco años de evolución de la justicia constitucional 1940-1965, UNAM, México, 1968.

34 L. FAVOREU, «Actualité et légitimité en contrôle juridictionnel des lois en Europe occidental», *Revue du droit public et de la science politique en France et à l'étranger*, Paris 1984 (5), p. 1149. Also published in L. FAVOREU and J.A. JOLOWICZ (ed.), *Le contrôle juridictionnel des lois. Légitimité, effectivité et développments récents*, Paris 1986, pp. 17-68.

35 M. CAPPELLETTI, *Judicial Review in the Contemporary World*, Indianapolis 1975, p. 46.

36 In the system followed, for instance in Uruguay, Panama, and Paraguay, and in the Latin American Countries that follows a mixed system (Venezuela and Colombia i.e.)

37 H. KELSEN, «La garantie juridictionnelle de la Constitution (La Justice constitutionnelle)», *Revue du droit public et de la science politique en France et à l'étranger*, Paris 1928, pp. 197-257.

38 Art. 89.1 See. E. ALONSO GARCÍA, «E1 Tribunal Constitucional austriaco» in *El Tribunal Constitucional*, Instituto de Estudios Fiscales, Madrid 1981, Vol I, p. 414; M. CAPPELLETTI, *op. cit.*, p. 72.

Constitution of 1920 indirectly led to the same principle when reducing the powers of ordinary judges regarding laws, to only «verify if they have been correctly published».[39]

Therefore, if the diffuse system of judicial review was prohibited, and reticence regarding judges to control legislation was still a main pillar of the doctrine of separation of power, the only means through which the supremacy of the constitution could be guaranteed was by creating a constitutional organ, not being part of the Judicial power, and originally even without jurisdictional powers, in charge of controlling the constitutionality of legislation, but as a «negative legislator».[40]

According to these fundamental conditioning ideas, the first constitutional tribunals were established in Czechoslovakia and Austria, in their respective Constitutions of the 29 February and 1st October 1920. The Czechoslovakian Tribunal during its existence did not develop an effective control of constitutionality, it disappeared in 1938[41] and was only re-established under the socialist system in 1968.[42] Nevertheless, its original regulations can be considered as the first antecedents of the European model of judicial review.

The general trends of that Czechoslovakian system, were the following:

The Constitution expressly established the principle of its supremacy, considering «invalid» statutes contrary to its regulations and to the constitutional laws,[43] but, as we said, reduced the role of the courts regarding the statutes, to only «verify if they have been correctly published».[44] Thus the monopoly for the appreciation of the unconstitutionality of statutes whether of the national Parliament or of the legislatures of the autonomous territorial units, was attributed to a Constitutional Tribunal created in the Constitution [45] and regulated by a special law enacted immediately after the enactment of the Constitution.[46] This constitutional body had only constitutional justice power with no other kind of attribution.[47]

The question of the unconstitutionality or invalidity of statutes could only be brought before the Constitutional Tribunal in an abstract way through a «recourse of unconstitutionality of statutes»,[48] without any relation to a particular case. Thus the method for seeking judicial review was a direct one through a direct action exercised only by some legislative and judicial state organs: the Chambers of the National Assembly, the Supreme Court, the Supreme Administrative Court and the Electoral Tribunal.[49]

---

39 Art. 102. See P. CRUZ VILLALON, «Dos modos de regulación del control de constitucionalidad: Checoslovaquia (1920-1938) y España (1931-1936), *Revista española de derecho constitucional*, 5, 1982, p. 135.

40 H. KELSEN, *loc. cit*, pp. 223, 224 and 226.

41 P. CRUZ VILLALON, *loc. cit.*, pp. 129-139.

42 P. NIKOLIC, *Le contrôle juridictionnel du lois et sa légitimité*, IALS, Uppsala Colloquium 1984, (mimeo), p. 46. Also published in L. FAVOREU and J.A. JOLOWICZ (ed.) in *Le contrôle juridictionnel des lois... cit.*, pp. 72-112.

43 Art. I, 1 of the Introductory Law to the Constitution.

44 Art. 102.

45 Art. III, 2 of the Introductory Law to the Constitution

46 Law of the Constitutional Tribunal of 9 March 1920.

47 *Cf.* P. CRUZ VILLALON, *loc. cit.*, p. 135.

48 Art. 121, a) of the Constitution.

49 Art. 9, Law of the Constitutional Tribunal.

The Constitutional Tribunal did not have *ex-officio* powers on constitutional issues [50]18) and the action could only be brought before the Tribunal within a period of 3 years following the publication of the statute.[51]

Finally, the effects of the decision of the Constitutional Tribunal were *erga omnes* and *ex-nunc, pro-futuro,* from the day of the publication of the decision.[52]

Due to its permanence and its reestablishment in 1945 the Austrian Constitutional Tribunal, created in the 1920 Constitution, was to be the leading institution of the «European» concentrated system of judicial review. Hans Kelsen, a member himself of the Constitutional Tribunal until 1929, formulated the original general trends of the institution, very similar to the Czechoslovakian one. They were reviewed by the constitutional amendments of 1925 and 1929, the latter being a fundamental one which gave the Tribunal its actual shape embodied in the 1945 Constitutional Law which has also been amended many times.[53]

2. The Austrian Constitutional Tribunal

The Austrian Constitutional Tribunal is regulated in the 1945 Constitution[54] as a constitutional organ established separate from the Judicial Power. Its basic regulations are established in the special Federal Law of the Constitutional Tribunal of 1953 modified on various occasions[55] and in the Interior Rules of the Tribunal enacted by itself[56] in accordance with its auto-regulatory power, which confirms its independence in the political system.

It is conceived as a constitutional organ independent of the other organs of the state, although its members are appointed by the executive power with participation of the legislative power.[57] In accordance with article 147 of the Constitution, the Tribunal is composed of a President, a Vice-President, twelve members and six alternate members. The President, the Vice-President, six members and three alternate members are appointed by the President of the Republic following a proposal from the Federal Government, and they must be chosen from among magistrates, public officers and University Law professors. The other six members and the other three alternate members are appointed by the President of the Republic following a proposal formulated by the National Council and the Federal Council, which are the legislative organs.

Consequently, the appointment of the members of the Tribunal follows the normal political rules of the country and the normal influence of the political parties,[58] which was clearly envisaged by Kelsen in 1928, when referring to the danger of political influence over the activities of the Tribunal. He said:

---

50 *Cf.* P. CRUZ VILLALON, *loc. cit.*, p. 138.

51 Art. 12. Law of the Constitutional Tribunal.

52 Art. 20. Law of the Constitutional Tribunal.

53 *Cf.* E.A. GARCÍA, *loc. cit.*, p. 413; M. CAPPELLETTI, *op. cit.*, p. 71; F. ERMACORA, «Procédures et techniques de protection des droits fundamentaux. Cour Constitutionnelle autrichienne», in L. FAVOREU (ed.) *Cours constitutionnelles européennes et droit fundamentaux*, 1982, p. 189.

54 Arts.137-148, Constitution of I May 1945. See a Spanish version of the Constitution in I. MÉNDEZ DE VIGO, «El Verfassungsgerichthof (Tribunal Constitucional Austríaco)», *Boletín de Jurisprudencia Constitucional*, Cortes Generales, 7, Madrid 1981, pp. 555-560.

55 Law N° 85, 1953. See in T. OHLINGER, *Legge sulla Corte Costituzionale Austriaca*, Firenze, 1982.

56 Art. 148 of the Constitution. The Internal Regulation of the Tribunal of 1946, can be seen in T. OHLINGER, *op. cit*, p. 137.

57 See the general considerations made in this respect by H. KELSEN, *loc. cit.*, pp. 226-227.

58 F. ERMACORA, *loc. cit.*, pp. 190-191.

«If this danger is particularly important, it is preferable to accept the legitimate participation of the political parties in the formation of the Tribunal, rather than its hidden and uncontrollable influence...»[59]

Nevertheless, the constitution has established various restrictions to secure the impartiality of the Tribunal members establishing a marked participation of the legal profession,[60] and forbidding the members of the government or of the legislative organs or the principal leaders of the political parties to be members of the Tribunal. In particular, concerning the President and Vice-President of the Tribunal, they must not have occupied a political position for at least four years previous to their appointment.[61]

In a different way to the Czechoslovakian antecedent in which the Constitutional Tribunal was conceived exclusively as a constitutional judge, the Austrian Constitutional Tribunal combines its functions of judicial review, with other powers related to political and organic matters. These other attributions are the following:

In the first place, a series of jurisdictional powers to settle controversies in which the political bodies of the Federal state are involved. Some of these controversies are derived from the Federal system and the vertical distribution of state power, and are as follows:

First, the Constitutional Tribunal has jurisdiction regarding patrimonial actions against the Federation, the States, (*Lander*) the districts, the municipalities or associations of municipalities, when they could not be resolved in an ordinary judicial procedure or by administrative resolution.[62] Therefore, these actions are exceptional and suppletory and are referred to patrimonial relations regulated by public law.[63]

Second, the Constitutional Tribunal has jurisdiction to resolve all conflicts between constitutional organs, and particularly, conflicts of jurisdiction between administrative and judicial authorities; conflicts of jurisdiction between courts, and in particular, the conflict over the distribution of state powers in the vertical way, between the Federation, and the *Lander*, or between the *Lander*.[64] It must also be said that regarding conflicts between the Federation and member states, article 138, paragraph 2 of the Constitution attributes the Constitutional Tribunal specific powers concerning the interpretation of the Constitution to determine when hearing a request of the Federal or States government before a concrete conflict has arisen, whether the regulation of a specific matter is constitutionally assigned to the Federal legislator or to the States legislatures. In this case, the decision prevents disputes over the powers attributed in the vertical distribution of state power, because it is adopted before any state act is issued, and by adopting it the constitutional tribunal is empowered to interpret the constitution on those matters.[65]

59 H. KELSEN, *loc. cit.*, p. 227.
60 Art. 147.3. *Cf.* H. KELSEN, *loc. cit.*, p. 227.
61 Art. 147.4.
62 Art. 137.
63 *Cf.* E. ALONSO GARCÍA, *loc. cit.*, pp. 421-422.
64 Art. 138.
65 *Cf.* F. ERMACORA, *loc. cit.*, p. 191. In this case it is considered that the Constitutional Tribunal exercises a «previous judicial review of status»: W.K. GECK, «Judicial Review of Statutes: a Comparative Survey of Present Institution and Practices», *Cornell Law Quarterly*, 51, 1966, p. 266.

Finally, regarding the federal conflicts of powers, the third attribution of the Constitutional Tribunal is to interpret agreements adopted between the different levels of the Federal state, particularly between the Federation and the *Lander* or between the *Lander*, all as a result of the cooperative federalism system followed in Austria.[66]

In the second place, the Constitutional Tribunal has another series of jurisdictional powers regarding elections and referenda. First the Tribunal is empowered to decide upon actions that could be brought before it against the election of the President of the Federation, of the representatives to the Assemblies, of the representatives of the organs of the Professional Associations, and against the elections of government officials to the *Lander* and at municipal level. It also has jurisdiction to resolve the loss of the respective mandate of elected representatives.[67] On the other hand, the Tribunal also has jurisdiction to decide upon any claim against the result of a referendum directed to approve certain laws.[68]

In the third place, the Constitutional Court also has jurisdiction to decide upon accusations brought before it, against the supreme organs of the Federation or of the *Lander*, based on constitutional liability derived from illegalities,[69] the decision of which could produce the loss of office and even the temporal loss of political rights.[70]

Finally, in the fourth place, the Constitutional Tribunal is empowered to act as a constitutional judge controlling the constitutionality of laws, executive regulations and Treaties, and also granting constitutional protection against the violation of fundamental rights. These final attributions are directly related to judicial review.

3. The Constitutional Tribunal and Judicial Review

In effect, among the various jurisdictional powers of the Constitutional Tribunal in the Austrian system, the Constitution assigns it the role of constitutional judge, with power to review the constitutionality of statutes, treaties and executive regulations, in a concentrated way, which can be sought by two methods: principal and incidental.

The first aspect to be noticed in the Austrian system is that the exclusive power to review the constitutionality of state acts assigned to the Constitutional Tribunal, not only includes legislative acts, but also treaties and executive regulations.

Regarding legislative acts, judicial review refers to federal and *Lander* statutes[71] and concerning international treaties, the Constitutional Tribunal has had the power to decide upon their «illicity» or unconstitutionality only since 1964.[72] In both cases, the state acts object of judicial review can be considered acts issued in direct execution

66 Art. 138.a. and 15,a.
67 Art. 141.
68 Art. 141,3.
69 Art. 142.
70 Art. 142.4.
71 Art. 140,1.
72 Art. 140.a.*Cf.* H. KELSEN, *loc. cit.*, p. 232.

of the constitution, regarding which the control of constitutionality is the consequence of the hierarchical expression of the legal order.[73] In accordance with that scheme, judicial review of executive regulations, normally subordinated to the legislation, is generally attributed in Europe to the administrative jurisdiction and not to the Constitutional Courts.

But in spite of such general trends according to H. Kelsen's thought on the matter, judicial review of executive regulations in Austria is also attributed to the Constitutional Tribunal. In this respect, Professor Kelsen said:

> «Without doubt these executive regulations are not acts immediately subordinate to the Constitution; their irregularity immediately consists of their illegality and only in a mediate way, their constitutionality. If, in spite of that, we propose to extend the attributions of the constitutional jurisdiction to them, it is not due to the mentioned relativity of the opposition between direct and indirect constitutionality but taking into consideration the natural boundary between general and particular juridical acts».[74]

Consequently, according to Kelsen, only the particular acts of state (administrative or judicial) were to be excluded from constitutional jurisdiction.[75] Thus, executive regulations, or administrative acts with general effects, were also submitted to the jurisdiction of the Constitutional Tribunal. And this happened in Austria, where the Constitution assigns power to the Tribunal to decide upon the «illegality» of the decrees of the federal or *Lander* authorities and even of the ordinances at local level and the general regulations of professional associations.[76]

4. Methods of Control and the Ex-Officio Powers of the Constitutional Tribunal

According to the Constitution, there are two basic methods for seeking the jurisdiction of the Constitutional Tribunal, through a direct petition or action and in an incidental way, although in its original 1920 feature, the only established method was the principal one, exercised through a petition reserved only to certain political organs of the state.[77] The 1929 and 1975 constitutional reforms enlarged the standing requirements to interpose the direct petition, and in 1929 the incidental method of judicial review was also established. Additionally, the Constitutional Tribunal has been empowered by the constitution to raise constitutional issues *ex-officio*. It is also possible to distinguish another method of seeking judicial review, this time, indirect, as a consequence of the exercise of the constitutional protection actions or complaints regarding fundamental rights. Thus, five different methods seeking judicial review can be distinguished in the Austrian system.

A. *Direct Petition for Unconstitutionality*

The first method is the direct petition for unconstitutionality of statutes that can be brought before the Constitutional Tribunal, as follows: regarding federal statutes, at the request of the government of the *Lander* or of one third of the members of the National Council (Parliament); and regarding the *Lander* statutes,

73 *Cf.* H. KELSEN, *loc. cit.*, pp. 228-231.
74 *Idem*, p. 230.
75 *Idem*, p. 233.
76 Art. 139, 1. *Cf.* E. ALONSO GARCÍA, *loc. cit.*, p. 434.
77 *Cf.* M. CAPPELLETTI, *op. cit.*, pp. 72- 73.

at the request of the Federal government, the Constitutions of the Lander being authorised by the Federal Constitution to give the right to petition to one third of the members of their legislatures.[78] It must be noted that by granting standing to interpose the direct petition to one third of the representatives in the legislative bodies, the 1975 constitutional reform has given the opposition a means for controlling the laws adopted by the majority,[79] following the trends developed in other European countries.

Regarding executive regulations, the direct petition of illegality can be brought before the Constitutional Tribunal, by the governments of the *Lander* if the object of judicial review is a federal decree; and if it is a decree of the Lander executive authorities, by the Federal Government and also by the municipalities regarding executive acts of local government control.[80]

Regarding international treaties, the Constitution disposes the analogous application of the previous mentioned rules, differentiating between Treaties approved by the National Council and those enacted by executive means.[81]

B. *Direct action of unconstitutionality*

Nevertheless, in the Austrian system the direct request for unconstitutionality is not only reserved to political organs. Since the 1975 constitutional reform, a direct action or recourse has also been granted to individuals who can bring it directly before the Constitutional Court, but only when they deem their rights directly violated by a statute or an executive regulation. It is necessary that the norm in question be directly applicable to them, without any other further judicial decision or individual administrative act.[82] In this case, the claimant must express in his action, how the statute, without any further judicial decision or administrative act, can really affect his rights directly. Therefore, this action or constitutional complaint, is not an *actio popularis*, which was not recommended by Kelsen for the purpose of judicial review,[83] on the contrary, it is an action submitted to specific requirement for standing.

On the other hand, the action cannot be brought directly before the Constitutional Tribunal against a statute, if there have been judicial decisions or administrative acts enforced in application of the said statute. Therefore, if any possibility of an administrative or judicial decision to be produced in a reasonable degree still exists, recourse must first be interposed against those decisions before the Administrative Court, or other Court of Justice or even the Constitutional Court itself. In those cases, the constitutional issue could be raised in an incidental way or *ex-officio* by the Constitutional Court.[84]

C. *Incidental method for judicial review*

The constitutional question concerning state acts cannot only be brought before the Constitutional Tribunal through a direct petition or action. Since the 1929

78 Art. 140, 1.

79 Art. 139, 1.

80 *Cf.* L. FAVOREU, *loc. cit.*, p. 1152.

81 Art. 140, a.

82 Art. 140, 1

83 H. KELSEN, *loc. cit.*, p. 245.

84 *Cf.* L. FAVOREU, *loc. cit.*, p. 1153.

constitutional reform an incidental method for judicial review has been established in Austria, enlarged later, in 1975.

According to the constitution, the constitutional question regarding statutes, could reach the Constitutional Tribunal by a referral formulated by the administrative court, the supreme court of justice or any court of appeal when they must apply the law in a concrete proceeding.[85] Regarding executive regulation, the constitutional question through the incidental means for its annulation, could be brought before the constitutional tribunal by any court.[86]

In such cases, the incidental referral formulated before the Constitutional Tribunal has suspensive effects regarding the concrete proceeding in which the constitutional question has been raised, which could only be continued after the constitutional tribunal's judgment has been adopted.[87]

Even though the supreme courts and the courts of appeal do not have judicial review power in the Austrian system, which is concentrated, this incidental means for judicial review gives them in a certain way, as Professor Cappelletti pointed out, not only the power but the duty «not to apply laws whose constitutionality is in doubt, without having first heard the binding judgment of the Constitutional Court»,[88] which means that those courts have the power to appreciate the unconstitutionality of legislation, though not to annul laws.

D. *Ex-Officio powers for constitutional review*

Apart from the two principals and from the incidental methods of judicial review, the Constitution empowers the Constitutional Tribunal to raise on its own initiative, any constitutional question regarding statutes and executive regulations, in cases developed before the Tribunal, in which a statute or an executive regulation must be applied for resolution.[89] This could be considered as a fourth method of judicial review in the Austrian system also envisaged by Hans Kelsen[90] although it is not unlimited. The Constitution establishes that even though the Tribunal could have the conviction that a statute is unconstitutional because it was enacted in an unconstitutional way, if the complete annulment of the statute could mean a manifest prejudice against the juridical interests of the individual claimant in a direct action, or of the plaintiff in the proceeding in which an incidental question was brought before the Tribunal, it must not annul the statute. [91]

E. *Indirect means for judicial review and the Protection of Fundamental Rights*

Finally, in the Austrian system a fifth method of judicial review can be distinguished through which the Constitutional Tribunal could be called upon to decide upon the unconstitutionality of statutes, in an indirect way, as a consequence of the exercise of a direct recourse or complaint for constitutional protection of fundamental rights.

---

85 Art. 140.1.
86 Art. 139.1.
87 Art. 57 Law of the Constitutional Tribunal.
88 M. CAPPELLETTI, *op. cit.*, p. 74.
89 Art. 139, 1 and 140.1, 3.
90 H. KELSEN, *loc. cit.*, p. 247.
91 Art. 140, 3.

In effect, the Constitution established the right of individuals to bring before the Constitutional Tribunal recourses or complaints against administrative acts when the claimant alleges that they infringe a right guaranteed in a constitutional law.[92] This is the basic rule that has contributed to the development of a special judicial means of protection of fundamental rights in Europe, although in a concentrated way which establishes the difference with the recourse for protection developed in Latin American countries.

However, the relation between this recourse for protection of fundamental rights against administrative acts of particular effect and judicial review of constitutionality, is that it could also be based on the allegation that the administrative act prejudiced the claimant because it has applied an illegal decree, an unconstitutional law or an international treaty contrary to the rule of law,[93] in which cases the Constitutional Tribunal must decide upon the constitutional issue.

5. Effects of Judicial Review

In all these five methods of judicial review of legislation the decision of the Constitutional Tribunal upon the constitutionality of statutes and decrees, when declaring the unconstitutionality of state acts, has *erga omnes* effects, thus binding on all the courts and administrative authorities.[94] The decision has also *constitutive* effects in the sense that it annuls the statute or the decree, *pro-futuro, ex-nunc*.

Nevertheless, the Tribunal has powers to annul statutes or decrees already repealed, thus without formal validity,[95] which, in principle, supposes the retroactive effects of the judicial review, this being an exception to the *ex-nunc* effects.

Anyway, according to the general rule of prospectiveness, proposed as a matter of principle by Hans Kelsen,[96] the factual situations or the situations verified before the annulment of the statute or decree, will continue to be submitted to its regulation, except in the case considered in the decision, unless the Tribunal decides otherwise.[97] Thus, the Tribunal in its own decision can temper the possible negative consequences of the *ex-nunc* rule.

But in general, the effects of the Tribunal decision only begin the day of the publication of the consequent repeal of the annulled act, by the executive authority concerned, unless the Tribunal establishes a delay for the expiration of the effects of the annulled act[98] not in excess of one year. In such cases, and on a purely

92 Art. 144.
93 Art. 144.
94 Art. 139, 6; 140, 7.
95 Art. 139, 4; 140, 4. *Cf.* H. KELSEN, *loc. cit.*, p. 234.
96 H. KELSEN, *loc. cit.*, p. 242. For instance, regarding the Austrian system, L. Adamouch stated in 1954: «To the decision of the Constitutional Tribunal which declares that the unconstitutionality of a statute, one cannot assigne a simple declarative value; it do not establishes that a concrete statute has been null from its origin, whose effects are to be nul *ex-tunc*, that is to say, as it were an act without any juridical value from its origin; on the contrary, the decision of the Constitutional Tribunal only annules the unconstitutional statute, that is to say, destroys *ex nunc* its juridical existence, exactly as it would have been abolished by a successive legislative act, and as that this act would have ended its juridical existence». in «Esperienza della Corte Constituzionale della Republica Austriaca», *Revista italiana per la scienze giuridiche*, Milan 1954.
97 Art. 139, 6; 140, 7.
98 Art. 139, 5; 140, 5.

discretionary basis, the Tribunal can postpone the beginning of the ex-nunc effects due to the annulment of the statute.

On the other hand, concerning statutes, their annulment could bring about a situation in which other statutes previously repealed by the annulled one, will restart their validity beginning the day in which the annulment is effective, unless the Tribunal decides otherwise,[99] which confirms the *ex-nunc* effects.

Finally, regarding treaties, the Constitutional Court has no power to annul them directly when unconstitutional, but must only declare their unconstitutionality which implies, first that the treaty could not be applicable from the day in which the decision is made public by the state organ which is due to execute it, unless the tribunal fixes a delay in which the treaty could continue to be applied;[100] and second, that if the treaty is due to be applied by laws or decrees, any of these will cease to have effects.[101]

III. JUDICIAL REVIEW IN THE FEDERAL REPUBLIC OF GERMANY: THE FEDERAL CONSTITUTIONAL TRIBUNAL

1. The Weimar Antecedents

Also, after the Second World War, and under the federal Constitution of *Weimar* of 11 August 1919, the basic elements for the development of a constitutional system of judicial review were established in Germany, although dispersed among a set of courts and tribunals. In particular, a limited system of concentrated judicial review can be found within the powers attributed to the Tribunal of the Empire (*Reichsgericht*), the highest court in the ordinary judiciary, which had powers to resolve the compatibility of laws passed by member states of the Federation (the *Lander*) with Imperial legislation.[102] Another special court, the Tribunal of state Justice (*Staatsgerichthof*), had the special task of resolving constitutional litigation arising within a *Lander* which lacked special courts to do so; also, public law conflicts arising between different *Lander* or between the Empire and one *Lander*, when these cases fell outside the jurisdiction of any other court of justice of the Empire.[103] This Tribunal of state Justice was also empowered to try accusations against the President, the Chancellor and the Imperial Ministers, for infractions of the Constitution.[104]

But during the *Weimar* Republic, discussions were developed regarding the powers of all courts to control the constitutionality of laws when deciding cases submitted for their decision, and the Tribunal of the Empire adopted particular judicial decisions in this respect.

The decision of the *Reichsgericht* of 4 November 1925 is famous. In it, the Tribunal in accordance with article 102 of the Constitution which established the submission of the judges to the laws, stated:

---

99 Art. 140, 6.

100 Art. 140 a, 1.

101 Art. 140 a, 2.

102 Art. 13 of the Constitution. *Cf.* the text in F. RUBIO LLORENTE, «E1 Tribunal Constitucional alemán», *Revista de la Facultad de Derecho*, UCV, 18, Caracas 1959, p. 116; J.C. BÉGUIN, *Le contrôle de la constitutionnalité des lois en Republique Fédérale d'Allemagne*, Paris 1982, p. 19; F. SAINZ MORENO, «Tribunal Constitucional federal alemán», *Boletín de Jurisprudencia Constitucional*, Cortes Generales, 8, Madrid 1981, p. 603; G. MÜLLER, «E1 Tribunal Constitucional federal de la República Federal de Alemania», *Revista de la Comisión Internacional de Juristas*, Vol VI, Ginebra 1965, p. 222.

103 Art. 19 of the Constitution.

104 Art. 59.

«The submission of the judge to the law does not exclude the power of the judge to question the validity of statutes of the Empire or of certain of its dispositions when they are in opposition to other pre-eminent dispositions that must be observed by the judge. This is the case when a statute is in opposition to a juridical principle established in the Imperial Constitution».[105]

And the Imperial Tribunal concluded in a way which can be considered as the general admission of the diffuse system of judicial review in Germany by stating in a very similar way to what was stated in the *Marbury* v. *Madison* case:[106]

«The Imperial Constitution, not containing any disposition in accordance to which the decision upon the constitutionality of a statute of the Empire would have been taken away from the judges and transferred to another specific organ, the power and the duty of the judge to examine the constitutionality of statutes of the Empire must be recognised».[107]

Anyway, the situation of the system up to 1933 was not completely clear, and judicial review of federal laws by all courts, particularly lower courts whose decisions were unable to be reviewed through appeals by the Supreme Court, was not always accepted and was frequently criticised.[108] This led to an important change in the establishment of a system of constitutional justice in West Germany, in the Constitution of the Federal Republic of Germany of 23 May 1949.

2. Concentrated System of Judicial Review in West Germany and its Coexistence with a Limited Diffuse System of Review

In effect, the Constitution of 1949 created a Federal Constitutional Tribunal which, although being part of the Judicial Power as are all other federal and *Lander* courts[109] is considered the «supreme guardian of the Constitution»[110] having «the last word on the construction of the Federal Constitution».[111] Thus it is the state organ in which all constitutional jurisdictional questions have been concentrated.

To accomplish this role of constitutional judge, the Federal Constitutional Tribunal was organised in the federal law referred to in the Constitution[112] as a constitutional organ of the Federation, «autonomous and independent regarding all other constitutional organs»,[113] even with self-regulatory powers.[114]

---

105 See the quotations in C.J. FRIEDRICH, «The Issue of Judicial Review in Germany», *Political Science Quarterly*, 43, 1928, p. 188; H.G. RUPP, «Judicial Review in the Federal Republic of Germany», *The American Journal of Comparative Law*, 9, 1960, p. 31; J.C. BÉGUIN, *op. cit.*, p. 15.

106 H.G. RUPP, *loc. cit.*, p. 31.

107 See note 4, supra.

108 *Cf.* J.C. BÉGUIN, *op. cit.*, p. 13-21; H.G. RUPP, *loc. cit.*, p. 32; M. CAPPELLETTI, *Judicial Review in Contemporary World*, Indianapolis 1971, pp. 50-51-59,64.

109 Art. 92.

110 G. MÜLLER, *loc. cit.*, p. 216; F. SAINZ MORENO, *loc. cit.*, p. 606.

111 H.G. RUPP, «The Federal Constitutional Court and the Constitution of the Federal Republic of Germany», *Saint Louis University Law Journal*, Vol XVI, 1971-1972, p. 359.

112 Art. 94,2. The Law on the Organization and Procedure of the Federal Constitutional Tribunal (FCT. Law) was published the 12 March 1951. See the whole text in F. RUBIO LLORENTE, *loc. cit.*, pp. 125-167. The Law has been modified in various opportunities: 1956, 1959, 1963 and 1970. The present text up to date is of 3 February 1971, modified in 1974 and 1976. *Cf.* F. SAINZ MORENO, *loc. cit.*, p. 604.

113 Art. 1,1 FCT Law.

114 Art. 30, 2 FCT Law, The Interior regulation of the Tribunal was published in 1975 and reformed in 1978.

The status of the Federal Constitutional Court, as a constitutional organ, is also reflected in its composition. According to the Constitution, its members are elected by the fundamental politico-representative organs of the Federation: the *Bundestag* (National Council) and the *Bundesrat* (Federal Council), in equal numbers in each case, but the elected members may not be members of both Councils or of the Federal government nor of any of the corresponding organs of a Land.[115] All the members of the Tribunal are considered to be federal judges, although only a proportion of them must be elected from active federal judges.[116]

Based on all these constitutional provisions regarding the organisation, composition and powers of the Federal Constitutional Court it has been considered by one of its former Presidents, a «neutral power» within the state. It has a constitutional pre-eminence over all other state organs, particularly because of the various powers that the Constitution assigns it related to constitutional justice and judicial review powers, and which has also been considered, as «not having been conferred to any other constitutional tribunal, or supreme court» in any other country.[117]

The Federal Constitutional Tribunal, therefore, is the expression of a concentrated system of judicial review, particularly of federal and *Lander* statutes, established to «protect the legislator against the ordinary judicial power»,[118] but its establishment did not eliminate completely the diffuse system of judicial review in West Germany, which in a limited way is exercised by all courts. In other words, according to the general trend in all concentrated systems of judicial review, the concentration of the powers of constitutional justice in one single organ, is only established regarding certain state acts, with the result that in relation to all other state acts not specified in the concentrated powers, the supremacy of the constitution allows all the other courts to control their constitutionality in a diffuse way. This general trend is followed in the West German system.

In effect, according to article 93, section 2 of the Federal Constitution, in matters of judicial review of legislation, the Federal Constitutional Tribunal has the exclusive power to review the constitutionality of federal laws and laws of the *Lander*, but considering as such, the laws that have been passed by the legislators established in the 1949 Constitution. Therefore, statutes adopted before 1949, can be the object of judicial review in a diffuse system by all courts, as well as executive regulations or normative decrees, whose constitutional judicial review is not reserved to the Federal Constitutional Tribunal.[119] Nevertheless, pre-constitutional legislation can be constitutionally reviewed by the Federal Constitutional Tribunal but only by means of the direct action which leads to the abstract control of norms [120]

Therefore, the West German constitutional system has established a concentrated system of judicial review by attributing exclusive powers to control the constitutionality of state acts, and particularly of legislation to the Federal Constitutional Tribunal. It has also established so by allowing the ordinary courts

115 Art. 94, 1. Constitution.
116 The Tribunal is divided in two Chambers (*Senaten*), each one with 8 judges, three of them elected from active federal judges. Arts. 4, 5. FCT Law.
117 G. MÜLLER, *loc. cit.*, pp. 216-221.
118 J.C. BÉGUIN, *op. cit.*, p. 93.
119 *Cf.* G. MÜLLER, *loc. cit.*, p. 233; J.C. BÉGUIN, *op. cit.*, p. 69, 94.
120 *Cf.* G. MÜLLER, *loc. cit.*, p. 234.

the power of review in a diffuse system regarding pre-constitutional legislation and executive regulations.

On the other hand, it must also be stressed that as a consequence of the federal system, the Federal Constitution has not reserved the absolute monopoly of the concentrated system of judicial review to the Federal Constitutional Court. In general, each *Lander* has its own constitutional court empowered to control the violations of the *Lander* constitutions and to settle constitutional litigations within each *Lander*.[121]

3. Federal Constitutional Tribunal as a Constitutional Jurisdiction

But at the federal level, the Federal Constitutional Tribunal as the supreme guardian of the Constitution, has the monopoly of its defence derived from a very wide range of powers attributed to it in the Constitution, and in accordance with which, in the federal law which regulates its functioning and organisation.[122] These powers, all of a jurisdictional nature, can be classified into six groups of attributions through which the tribunal guarantees the protection of the politico-constitutional order; the distribution of state powers; the electoral representative character of the political system; the protection of fundamental rights; the interpretation of the Constitution, and control of the constitutionality of all normative state acts.

The first group of jurisdictional powers of the Federal Constitutional Tribunal relates to what may be called the protection of the politico-constitutional order embodied in the Constitution, or in other words, the protection of the state against actions taken by political parties, individuals or public officials. In relation to political parties, which in the constitutional system of the Federal Republic are the main means by which «the political will of the people»[123] is formed, the Constitutional Tribunal is empowered to declare them unconstitutional, when:

> «By reason of their aims or the behaviour of their adherents (they) seek to impair or destroy the free democratic basic order or to endanger the existence of the Federal Republic of Germany».[124]

The protection of the state against individuals is regulated in the Constitution particularly as a consequence of the abuse of the exercise of certain freedoms and liberties, which could endanger the constitutional order. In this respect, the Federal Constitutional Tribunal is empowered[125] to decide upon the deprivation of the freedom of speech, especially the freedom of the press, the freedom of education, the freedom of assembly, the freedom of association, the secrecy of mail, post and telecommunications, property and the right of asylum, by those who abuse those rights by using them to fight against the fundamental and free democratic order, and who consequently make themselves unworthy of those freedoms.[126]

Finally, regarding state officials, the Constitutional Tribunal functions as protector of the state being empowered to take cognisance of accusations brought

---

121 *Cf.* J.C. BÉGUIN, *op. cit.*, p. 27, 43-46.

122 Art. 93, Constitution.

123 Art. 21, 1 Constitution.

124 Art. 21, 2. Constitution. In 1952 and 1956, the Tribunal declared unconstitutional a neo-nazi party (*sozialistischen Reichspartei*) and the communist party (*Kommunistische Partei Deutschlands*). *Cf.* he reference in F. SAINZ MORENO, *loc. cit.*, p. 622.

125 Art. 18 Constitution.

126 Art. 36-42 FCT Law.

against the Federal President by the *Bundestag* or the *Bundesrat* for voluntary infraction of the Constitution or of other federal laws;[127] and of accusations brought against federal judges who undermine the principles of the Constitution, or the constitutional order of a Land.[128]

The second group of constitutional jurisdictional powers of the Federal Constitutional Tribunal relates to the institutional functioning of the state and empowers the tribunal to resolve constitutional conflicts and litigations regarding the vertical and horizontal distribution of state powers.

In this respect, regarding the federal form of the state, the Tribunal has jurisdiction in cases of «difference of opinion over the rights and duties of the Federation and the *Lander*, particularly in the execution of federal law by the Lander and in the exercise of federal supervision;»[129] 28) and «on other disputes involving public law, between the Federation and the *Lander*, between different *Lander* or within a *Lander*, unless recourse to another court exists».[130]

But also in relation to the vertical distribution of powers, the Constitutional Tribunal has jurisdiction to resolve conflicts between the Federal and *Lander* powers and the municipalities, in the sense that it shall decide «on the complaints of unconstitutionality, entered by municipalities or association of municipalities on the grounds that their right to self-government... has been violated by a law other than a Land law open to complaint to the respective Land Constitutional Court».[131] This competence leads directly to one of the means of judicial review of legislation.

On the other hand, regarding the horizontal distribution of state power, that is to say, the resolution of conflicts between the constitutional organs of the Federation, the Federal Constitutional Tribunal shall decide upon the interpretation of the Constitution, «in the event of disputes concerning the extent of the rights and duties of a highest federal organ or of other parties concerned who have been vested with rights of their own by the Constitution or by a regulation of a highest federal organ».[132]

These «highest federal organs» whose conflicts must be decided upon by the Tribunal, are the *Bundestag*, the *Bundesrat*, the President of the Federation, the Federal Government and the Permanent Commission of the *Bundestag*. The political parties have also been considered as having quality to allege violations to their rights as participants in constitutional life.[133]

The third group of constitutional jurisdictional powers attributed to the Federal Constitutional Tribunal concerns the electoral-representative basis of the political system, in relation to which the Tribunal must resolve «the claims against the decisions of the *Bundestag* over the validity of an election or the acquisition or loss of the condition of representative to the *Bundestag*»;[134] and also, the recourses against *referenda* when a new division of the federal territory is adopted as a result of the modification of the boundaries of the *Lander*.[135]

---

127 Art. 61 Constitution.
128 Art. 98, 2 Constitution.
129 Art. 93, (1), 3 Constitution.
130 Art. 93, (1), 4 Constitution.
131 Art. 93, (1), 4 Constitution.
132 Art. 93, (1), 1 Constitution.
133 J.C. BÉGUIN, *op. cit.*, p. 40.
134 Art. 41, 2 Constitution; Art. 13, 3 FCT Law.
135 Art. 29 Constitution. *Cf.* G. MÜLLER, *loc. cit.*, p. 229.

The fourth group of constitutional jurisdictional powers assigned to the Constitutional Tribunal concerns the protection of fundamental rights and freedoms against the state. Specifically the Federal Constitution empowers the Tribunal to decide «on complaints of unconstitutionality», which may be entered by any person who claims that one of his basic constitutional rights has been violated by public authority.[136] This power of the Constitutional Tribunal established in the 1951 Statute of the Tribunal and only regulated in the 1969 amendment to the Constitution, has given rise to a very important recourse for the protection of fundamental rights against public authorities, as is the «trial for *amparo*» developed in Latin America called the «constitutional complaint» which has contributed to the consideration of fundamental rights and freedoms as a limit upon the powers of the state.

The fifth group of constitutional jurisdictional powers of the Federal Constitutional Court related to constitutional justice, concerns the interpretation and application of the Constitution and of federal legislation. Two attributions of the Constitutional Tribunal can be distinguished regarding the interpretation of the Constitution. First, the power of the Tribunal to decide cases in which a constitutional court of a *Lander*, when interpreting the Federal Constitution, intends to deviate from a decision previously made by the Federal Constitutional Tribunal or by the constitutional court of another *Lander*.[137] Second, the power of the Tribunal to resolve upon the continuity of the validity of a pre-constitutional law as federal law.[138]

Regarding the application of federal law, a third attribution of the Constitutional Tribunal may be distinguished regarding international law which in accordance with the Constitution forms part of the federal law.[139] In this respect, if in the course of a litigation before a court, doubt exists as to whether a rule of public international law is an integral part of federal law and whether such a rule directly creates rights and duties for the individual, the court shall obtain a decision from the Federal Constitutional Court.[140]

Finally, the sixth group of constitutional jurisdictional powers attributed to the Federal Constitutional Tribunal, as a constitutional judge, are the powers to control the constitutionality of normative state acts, comprising legislative acts. It is precisely this function of verifying the constitutionality of normative state acts, in which the character of the Tribunal reveals itself in full, as the constitutional organ laid down in the Constitution for the purpose of judicial review of legislation.

For the accomplishment of these functions, the constitutional questions regarding normative acts of the state can reach the Constitutional Tribunal by three methods: a direct request or complaint brought before the Tribunal; an incidental referral placed before the Tribunal by a lower court; or through an indirect way when the Constitutional Tribunal must decide upon the unconstitutionality of a state act, for the resolution of another of the constitutional jurisdictional proceedings different to the abstract or concrete control of normative acts of the state.

---

136 Art. 93, (1), 4,a). Constitution.
137 Art. 100, 3 Constitution.
138 Art. 126 Constitution.
139 Art. 2,2 Constitution.
140 Art. 100, 2 Constitution.

4. Constitutional Control of Normative State Acts Through Direct Requests or Complaints

The first method established in the Federal Constitution for the purpose of judicial review of state normative acts is through the exercise of a direct request, action or complaint brought before the Federal Constitutional Tribunal with the purpose of seeking its decision exclusively upon the unconstitutionality of a statute or other normative act of the state.

This direct means for judicial review, according to the constitution, can be exercised through two specific actions: first, by a request formulated by some state organs, called the abstract control of norms; and second, by the exercise of a constitutional complaint brought by any person who claims that one of his fundamental rights has been violated by the specific statute or act, or by a Municipality who claims that its right to self-government has been violated by a federal law.

A. *Request for the Abstract Control of Norms*

The request for the abstract control of norms (*Die abstrakte Normenkontrolle*), that is to say, the exercise of judicial review powers by the Constitutional Tribunal without reference to a particular case or process, is established in article 93, section 1, N° 2 of the Constitution, when it states that the Constitutional Tribunal shall decide:

> «In case of differences of opinion or doubts on the formal and material compatibility of federal law or *Lander* law with this Basic Law, or on the compatibility of *Lander* law with other federal laws, at the request of the Federal Government, of a *Lander* Government or of one third of the *Bundestag* members».[141]

This power attributed to the Constitutional Tribunal has led to the development of what may be called an «objective» judicial review proceeding because it has as its only purpose the ensuring of the maintenance of the hierarchy system of norms, in an abstract way.[142]

As we said, the Constitution gives the right to formulate the request only to the Federal Government, the Government of a *Lander* and to one third of the *Bundestag* members,[143] allowing in the latter case the parliamentary minorities to have access to the Tribunal, and challenge the statutes approved by the majority. It also establishes that the representatives of the interested constitutional organs that have participated in the formation of the challenged normative act must be heard[144] by the Tribunal. Nevertheless, it must be said that in the proceeding there are no proper parties.[145]

The request, in fact, is formulated against a state act, not against a state organ, and the Constitutional Tribunal must decide the constitutional question in an abstract way, being allowed, moreover, to raise other constitutional questions *ex-officio* regarding the challenged act, or other of its articles.[146]

---

141 Also see Art., *76-88* FCT Law.

142 *Cf.* J.C. BÉGUIN, *op. cit.*, p. *60;* H.G. RUPP, «Judicial Review...», *loc. cit.*, p. *35;* G. MÜLLER, *loc. cit.*, p. 231.

143 Art. 76 FCT Law.

144 Art. 77 FCT Law.

145 *Cf.* J.C. BÉGUIN, *op. cit.*, p. 61; G. MÜLLER, *loc. cit.*, p. 231.

146 Art. 78 FCT Law. *Cf.* J.C. BÉGUIN, *op. cit.*, p. 61; F. SAINZ MORENO, *loc. cit.*, p. 613.

The objective character of the proceeding and the powers of the Constitutional Tribunal as a guardian of the Constitution are, furthermore, confirmed by the fact that even when a request is withdrawn by the state organ, the Tribunal can continue the proceeding when it is justified as being in the general interest.[147]

On the other hand, it must be said that this objective proceeding for the abstract control of the norms, refers to all normative state acts. Thus, it is not a proceeding for this sole purpose of judicial review of legislative acts in its formal sense, but can be referred to any other normative act of the state, including pre-constitutional statutes, executive normative decrees and international treaties and even, constitutional amendments.[148] In particular, all the statutes through which international treaties are approved, are subject to judicial review, and it has been applied, for example, in relation to state acts concerning the laws of the European Community.[149] But even though the general trend of judicial review of legislation in West Germany is its *a posteriori* character regarding treaties an exception to this principle is established, in the sense that the Constitutional Tribunal decision upon the constitutionality of its approving statute, must be adopted after its sanction but before the treaty begins its effects.[150]

B. Constitutional Complaint Against Statutes

But the abstract control of norms, additional to the request formulated by state political organs, can also be exercised by the Federal Constitutional Tribunal as a result of a constitutional complaint that any person can bring before the Tribunal when he claims that one of his basic or fundamental rights has been directly violated by a normative state act. This «constitutional complaint» only constitutionalised in 1969 was originally established in the 1951 Federal Statute of the Constitutional Tribunal,[151] and is conceived as a special judicial means for the protection of fundamental rights and freedoms against any action of the state organs which violates them. Therefore, it is not a specific action only directed to obtain judicial review of legislation, but it can be used for that purpose, when exercised against a statute.

The constitutional complaint after the 1969 constitutional amendment is expressly established in article 93, section 1, N° 4a of the Constitution when attributing the Federal Constitutional Tribunal power to decide:

> «On complaints of unconstitutionality, which may be entered by any person who claims that one of his basic rights or one of his rights under paragraph (4) of article 20, under articles 33, 38, 101, 103, or 104 has been violated by public authority».[152]

Therefore, the constitutional complaint can be brought before the Tribunal against any state act, whether legislative, executive or judicial, but in all cases, it can only be exercised once the ordinary judicial means for the protection of the

---

147 *Cf.* J.C. BÉGUIN, *op. cit.*, p. 61; F. SAINZ MORENO, *loc. cit.*, p. 613.
148 *Cf.* J.C. BÉGUIN, *op. cit.*, p. 63.
149 L. CONTASTINESCO, «L´introduction et le contrôle de la constitutionnalité des traités et en particulier des traites européens en droit allemand», *Revue belge de droit international*, 2, 1969, pp. 425-459.
150 *Cf.* F. SAINZ MORENO, *loc. cit.*, p. 613.
151 Art. 90. FCT Law.
152 See also Arts. 90-96 FCT Law.

fundamental rights that have been violated, are all exhausted.[153] Consequently, the constitutional complaint is a subsidiary mean of judicial protection of fundamental rights,[154] and if there are other judicial recourses or actions that can serve the purpose of protecting fundamental rights, the constitutional complaint is not admissible, except when the Constitutional Tribunal considers the matter as being of general importance or when it considers that the claimant is threatened by a grave and irremediable prejudice if it is sent to the ordinary judicial means for protection.[155]

As we said, the constitutional complaint can be exercised directly against a statute or any other normative state act on the grounds that it directly impairs the fundamental rights of the claimant. In that case, it leads directly to the exercise of a judicial review of normative state acts function by the Constitutional Tribunal. As a result of this constitutional complaint, the statute when unconstitutional must be declared null.[156]

The basic condition for the admissibility of constitutional complaints against laws is, of course, the fact that the challenged statute or normative state act, must personally affect the claimant's fundamental rights, in a direct and current way, without the need for any further administrative application of the norm. On the contrary, if this further administrative application is needed, he must wait for the administrative execution of the statute and complain against it. This direct prejudice caused by the normative act on the rights of the claimant, as a basic element for the admissibility of the complaint, justifies the delay of one year after its publication established for the introduction of the action before the Tribunal.[157] It also explains the power of the Constitutional Tribunal to adopt provisional protective measures regarding the challenged statute, *pendente litis,* in the sense that the Tribunal can even theoretically, suspend the application of the challenged law.[158]

Finally, regarding this constitutional complaint, article 93, section 1, N° 4b of the Constitution, also empowers the constitutional tribunal to decide:

> «On complaints of unconstitutionality, entered by communes (municipalities) or association of communes (municipalities) on the ground that their right to self-government under article 28 has been violated by a law other than a *Lander* Law open to complaint to the respective land constitutional court».

Hence, the direct constitutional complaint against laws is not only attributed to individuals for the protection of their fundamental rights, but also to the local government entities, for the protection of their autonomy and right to self-government guaranteed in the Constitution, against federal statutes that could violate them. In these cases, it also results in a direct means of judicial review of statutes of legislation.

5. Incidental Method of Judicial Review

The second method established in the Federal Constitution for the purpose of judicial review of statutes, is the incidental method, called the concrete control of

153 Art. 90, 2 FCT Law.
154 Art. 19.4 of the Constitution establishes in general that «Should any person's rights be violated by public authority resource to the courts shall be open to him. If jurisdiction is not specified, recourse shall be to the ordinary courts».
155 Art. 90, 2 FCT Law.
156 Art. 95, 3, B FCT Law.
157 Art. 93, 1, B FCT Law.
158 Art. 32 FCT Law. *Cf.* J.C. BÉGUIN, *op. cit.*, p. *158-163;* F. SAINZ MORENO, *loc. cit.*, p. 626.

norms (*Konkrete Normenkontrolle*) established in article 100 of the Constitution, as follows:

> If a court considers unconstitutional a law the validity of which is relevant to its decision, the proceeding shall be stayed, and a decision shall be obtained from the *Lander* court competent for constitutional disputes if the Constitution of a Land is held to be violated, or from the Federal Constitutional Court if this Basic Law is held to be violated. This shall also apply if this Basic Law is held to be violated by *Land* Law or if a *Land* Law is held to be incompatible with a federal law».[159]

According to this constitutional provision, the concentrated system of judicial review of legislation in the West German constitutional system is, of course, confirmed. It is so mainly because of the implicit prohibition for the courts to control the constitutionality of statutes, although as we have seen, they retain power to control the constitutionality of pre-constitutional legislation and of executive normative acts of the state in a diffuse manner.

Therefore, contrary to the abstract control of norms, in which the petition can refer to any normative state act, the concrete control of norms only refers to statutes in its formal sense.[160]

In this incidental method of judicial review, the constitutional question of a statute always reaches the Constitutional Tribunal through the referral made by any court[161] before the Tribunal, when in a concrete proceeding being developed before it the court considers a law unconstitutional, the validity of which is relevant to its decision in the case. Therefore, the constitutional question in this case, is always of an incidental character, related to the decision of a concrete case by a court; thus it must be related to a case and be determinant to its resolution.

In this case, if it is true that the courts do not have the power to declare statutes null, and do not have *ex-officio* power to decide not to apply them, conversely they have the power to appreciate the unconstitutionality of the statutes, [162] 61) by formulating a referral of a constitutional question before the Constitutional Tribunal.

Furthermore, the judge must be convinced of the unconstitutionality of the statute, that is why he must lay the foundations of his referral to the Tribunal, by explaining in which way his decision depends on the validity of the statute, and which constitutional disposition it is incompatible with.[163]

On the other hand, the referral of constitutional questions of statutes to the Federal Constitutional Tribunal is a power attributed to the courts, which can be exercised *ex-officio*, and whose exercise is not submitted to the will of the parties. Consequently, the referral the courts may send to the Constitutional Tribunal is independent from the parties' allegations concerning the unconstitutionality of a statute provision,[164] thus the incidental method of judicial review that it may bring about is not necessarily motivated by an exception alleged by a party.

---

159 See also Arts. 80-82 FCT Law.

160 *Cf.* G. MÜLLER, *loc. cit.*, p. 233; F. SAINZ MORENO, *loc. cit.*, p. 614.

161 *Cf.* G. MÜLLER, *loc. cit.*, p. 232; F. SAINZ MORENO, *loc. cit.*, p. 614; H.G. RUPP, «Judicial Review ...» *loc. cit.*, p. 32.

162 *Cf.* J.C. BÉGUIN, *op. cit.*, p. 92.

163 Art. 80,2 FCT Law.

164 Art. 80, 3 FCT Law.

Anyway, and although being of an incidental character, the powers of the Constitutional Tribunal are limited to the consideration of the constitutional question raised in the referral. Thus the Constitutional Tribunal does not review the case on its merits and only decides the question of whether or not the statute which a lower court considers unconstitutional, is repugnant to the Constitution.[165] That is why this proceeding for judicial review, in the concrete control of norms, like the abstract control of norms, is also considered an objective proceeding.[166] Thus, once the Constitutional Tribunal decides upon the constitutional question referred to it by a lower court, the latter must resume the proceedings and render its judgment in accordance with the Constitutional Tribunal decision which has general binding effects.[167]

6. Indirect method of judicial review

As we have seen, the basic means for the concentrated system of judicial review in the Federal Republic of Germany are petitions for the abstract control of norms and constitutional complaints against laws that can be brought before the Constitutional Tribunal, in a direct way, on the one hand. On the other hand, there are the referrals made by any court before the Constitutional Tribunal through the incidental method, to seek a concrete control of statutes. Additional to these means for review, in the West German constitutional system one can distinguish a third method of judicial review of legislation, which can be considered an indirect one, due to the fact that the powers of review of the Constitutional Tribunal are not exercised as a consequence of a direct request or of a constitutional complaint against a statute or of a incidental referral made to it by a lower court, but as an indirect question that can be raised in a proceeding that is developed before the Constitutional Court, conceived as having another direct or immediate purpose, different to the sole constitutional review of a statute.

This indirect method for judicial review of the unconstitutionality of statutes, can be developed in the following principal situations:

In the first place, as a consequence of a constitutional complaint for the protection of a fundamental right when exercised, not directly against a statute, but against a judicial decision which is considered to have violated the rights and freedoms of a person because it applied a statute which is alleged to have been unconstitutional.[168] In this case, the Constitutional Tribunal must decide upon the unconstitutionality of the statute indirectly challenged before it.

In the second place, the Constitutional Tribunal can also exercise its powers of judicial review of legislation in an indirect way, when deciding upon conflicts between constitutional organs of the Federation,[169] that is to say, disputes concerning the extent of the rights and duties of the highest federal organs established in the Constitution. In cases of conflict, for instance, between the President and the *Bundestag*, the proceeding has a subjective character, thus it is developed in a contradictory way between parties, and can lead to an indirect control of the constitutionality of statutes, only when the act that causes prejudices to the rights

---

165 Art. 81 FCT Law.
166 *Cf.* J.C. BÉGUIN, *op. cit*, P. 93.
167 Art. 31, 1 FCT Law.
168 Art. 93, 1, 4,a) FCT Law.
169 Art. 93, 1, 1 Constitution.

and duties of a state organ is a statute, particularly those directed to regulate the functioning of public powers. In this case, however, it is considered that the court does not have annulatory powers regarding the statute unless the abstract control of norms method is accumulated.[170]

7. Effects of the decisions of the Federal Constitutional Tribunal on judicial review and its ex-officio powers

Now, regarding the effects of the federal constitutional tribunal decisions when exercising its powers of judicial review of the constitutionality of normative state acts, particularly of legislation, the general rule is that the tribunal declares the nullity of the unconstitutional provision of the statute or normative act. In this respect, article 78 of the Federal Law of the Constitutional Tribunal established that:

> «If the Constitutional Tribunal reach the conviction that the federal law is incompatible with the Constitution, or that the law of a *Lander* is incompatible with the Constitution or with another norm of federal law, it declares its nullity in its decision».[171]

This decision can be in accordance with the contents of the petition, the constitutional complaint or the court referral, according to the method used for obtaining judicial review, but in adopting it the Constitutional Tribunal is not bound by their respective contents, in the sense that it has *ex-officio* powers to raise another constitutional question and thus, to decide, *ultra petita*. That is why the same article 78 of the Federal Law of the Constitutional Tribunal established that:

> «If other dispositions of the same statute are incompatible with the Constitution, or another norm of federal law, the Constitutional Tribunal can declare them null at the same time».

The decisions of the Constitutional Tribunal are always obligatory for all constitutional organs of the Federation and of the *Lander*, as well as for all the authorities, the courts[172] and, of course, for the individual. Thus, courts decisions, including those adopted in a judicial review proceeding, have *erga omnes* effects. In particular, in cases of abstract or concrete control of norms, exercised through a petition of a state organ or through a referral by a lower court in which the Constitutional Tribunal declares the nullity of a statute, the decision has the same force as a statute[173] in the sense of its obligatory *erga omnes* character, including the Constitutional Court itself.[174]

However, contrary to Hans Kelsen's conception of the effects of the decision of the constitutional judge in a concentrated system of judicial review when declaring the nullity of a statute,[175] and to the Austrian model, in accordance with the German constitutional tradition [176] in cases of abstract and concrete control of norms and when deciding upon a constitutional complaint against a statute, when a statute is

---

170 *Cf.* J.C. BÉGUIN, *op. cit.*, pp. 78-81; F. SAINZ MORENO, *loc. cit.*, p. 612.

171 See also Art. 95, 2 FCT Law.

172 Art. 31, 1 FCT Law.

173 Art. 31, 2 FCT Law.

174 R. BOCANEGRA SIERRA «Cosa Juzgada, vinculación, fuerza de ley en las decisiones del Tribunal Constitucional alemán», *Revista Española de Derecho Constitucional*, N° 1, 1981, p. 269.

175 H. KELSEN, «La garantie juridictionnelle de la Constitution (La Justice constitutionnelle), *Revue du droit public et de la science politique en France et à l'étranger*, Paris 1928, p. 243.

176 J.C. BÉGUIN, *op. cit.*, pp. 209-228.

declared null, it is understood that it is declared null and void *ab initio*, that is to say, the decision of the Tribunal has *ex-tunc*, retroactive effects.[177] This traditional doctrine is confirmed by the fact that the legislator in the Federal Law of the Constitutional Tribunal has expressly limited its scope by establishing that after a statute has been declared null because of its unconstitutionality, only criminal proceedings can be reviewed in cases in which the final judicial decision would have been based on the said statute declared null.[178] All other final and non-reviewable judgments and administrative acts resting on the statute declared null, will stand unchangeable, but their enforceability, if not yet made, would be illicit.[179]

Finally, it must be stressed that in the West German system of judicial review, the criterion of the presumption of constitutionality of statutes[180] also exists as a matter of principle, according to which the Constitutional Tribunal has tended not to declare statutes null on the grounds of unconstitutionality, if it is possible to interpret them as consistent with the Constitution. In this sense, the Constitutional Tribunal, in many cases, has followed the method of «interpretation according to the Constitution» through which avoiding the declaration of the nullity of a statute, which would be unconstitutional if interpreted in a certain manner, it has nevertheless considered it valid within the ambit of another interpretation established by the Tribunal «according to the Constitution».[181]

In other cases, even though the Constitutional Tribunal has considered a statute unconstitutional, in order to avoid a possible vacuum in the legal order that could be produced by the nullity of the state act, the declaration of nullity is not adopted. Instead, the court only declares its «simple unconstitutionality» and in some cases has referred the matter to the Legislator to rectify the unconstitutional disposition.[182] Finally, in other cases, the Constitutional Tribunal, although considering a statute consistent with the Constitution, has, nevertheless, referred the matter to the legislator with indications for the rectification of the statute, so as to convert it into being «absolutely constitutional» and, therefore, avoiding any possible future declaration upon its unconstitutionality.[183]

IV. JUDICIAL REVIEW IN ITALY: THE CONSTITUTIONAL COURT

1. Constitutional compromise and the Constitutional Court as its guarantor

Immediately after the Second World War, and even before the creation of the Federal Constitutional Tribunal in the Federal Republic of Germany, the Constitution of the Italian Republic of 1st January 1948 also created a Constitutional Court, charged with controlling the constitutionality of statutes and other state acts with the same force, as the basic element of a concentrated system of judicial review of constitutionality. Nevertheless, the system only started to function in 1956 when the Constitutional Court initiated its activities. Up to that year, the pre 1948 Constitution system of judicial review persisted, being on the contrary a diffuse

177 *Cf.* F. SAINZ MORENO, *loc. cit.*, p. 624; H.G. RUPP, «Judicial Review...», *loc. cit.*, p. 37; R. BOCANEGRA SIERRA, *loc. cit.*, p. 268.

178 Art. 79, 1 FCT Law.

179 Art. 79, 2 FCT Law.

180 H.G. RUPP, «Judicial Review...», *loc. cit.*, p. 38; J.C. BÉGUIN, *op. cit.*, p. 185.

181 *Cf.* J.C. BÉGUIN, *op. cit.*, pp. 184-207; F. SAINZ MORENO, *loc. cit.*, p. 625.

182 Art. 32,2 and 79 FCT Law. *Cf.* J.C. BÉGUIN, *op. cit.*, p. 232-266; F. SAINZ MORENO, *loc. cit.*, p. 624.

183 *Cf.* C. BÉGUIN, *op. cit.*, p. 266-293; F. SAINZ MORENO, *loc. cit.*, p. 624-625.

system of judicial review according to which, all ordinary courts had the power not to apply statutes they considered unconstitutional, when resolving concrete cases to which the said statutes applied.[184]

The radical change in the system can be attributed to various factors, but above all, to the new rigid character attributed to the 1948 Constitution contrasting with the flexible one of the monarchical Fundamental Law (*Statuti Albertini*) of 1848,[185] thus the need to protect the Constitution against the legislative power particularly after the totalitarian experiment of fascism, and the need to protect and defend fundamental rights and freedoms regarding state powers,[186] give way to a concentrated system of judicial review. The constitutional court, therefore, was conceived as the organ in charge of the guarantee of the «constitutional compromise» embodied in the Constitution to establish a democratic regime in which the powers of the state organs were limited.[187] As Professor Giovanni Cassandro, former member of the Constitutional Court said:

> «The Court is the constitutional organ which secures the balance among the various powers of the state, preventing any one of them from trespassing the limits imposed by the Constitution, and thus ensures an orderly development of public life and the observance of the Constitutional rights of citizens».[188]

Therefore, the Constitutional Court in Italy, as the guarantor of the Constitution,[189] was also established as a «constitutional organ»,[190] independent from all other state organs, although not in an express positive law way as was the case of the Federal Constitutional Tribunal in West Germany[191] or of the Constitutional Tribunal in Spain.[192] Nevertheless, the position of the Constitutional Court as an independent and paritarian constitutional organ has been recognised without discussion, and is reflected in various aspects concerning the status of its members, its administrative and budgetary autonomy, the absence of any external control that could be exercised over it,[193] and its auto-regulatory powers.[194]

---

184 M. CAPPELLETTI, «La justicia constitucional en Italia», *Boletín del Instituto de Derecho Comparado de México*, 30, 1960, p. 41; M. CAPPELLETTI, *Judicial Review in the Contemporary World*, Indianapolis 1971, p. 50.

185 *Cf.* A. PIZZORUSSO, «Procedures et techniques de protection des droits fondamentaux. Cour Constitutionnelle italienne», in L. FAVOREU (ed.), *Cours constitutionnelles europeeures et droit fondamentaux*, Paris 1982, p. 195; J. RODRÍGUEZ-ZAPATA y PÉREZ, «La Corte Constitucional Italiana: ¿Modelo o advertencia?, in *E1 Tribunal Constitucional*, Instituto de Estudios Fiscales, Madrid 1981, Vol. III, p. 2416.

186 *Cf.* G. CASSANDRO, «The Constitutional Court of Italy», *American Journal of Comparative Law*, 8, 1959, p. 3.

187 *Cf.* F. RUBIO LLORENTE, *La Corte Constitucional italiana*, Caracas 1966, pp. 2-4.

188 G. CASSANDRO, *loc. cit.*, p. 12; *Cf.* J. RODRÍGUEZ-ZAPATA y PÉREZ, *loc. cit.*, p. 2417.

189 The Constitutional Court in its decision N° 13 of 1960 the Court defined its functions, as essentialy «the exercise of a function of constitutional control, of the supreme guarantee of the observance of the Constitution ... by the Constitutional organs of the state and of the Regions» (quoted by F. RUBIO LLORENTE, *loc. cit.*, p. 10, note 27); and in his decision N° 15 of 1969 has defined itself as the «highest organ for the guarantee of the republican order, to which exclusively corresponds ensure the rule of the Constitution over all the other constitutional agents». Quoted by J. RODRÍGUEZ-ZAPATA y PÉREZ, *loc. cit.*, p. 2420.

190 A. SANDULLI, «Sulla posizione della Corte Costituzionale nel sistema degli organi supremi dello Stato», *Rivista trimestrale di diritto pubblico*, 1960, p. 705.

191 Art. 1,1, Federal Law of the Federal Constitutional Tribunal (1951).

192 Art. 1,1, Organic Law of the Constitutional Tribunal (1978).

193 A. SANDULLI, *loc. cit.*, p. 718: *Cf.* J. ROGRÍGUEZ-ZAPATA y PÉREZ, *loc. cit.*, p. 2428-2441; G. CASSANDRO, *loc. cit.*, pp. 13-14.

194 Art. 14 Statute N° 87 of 11 March 1953, Norms on the Constitution and Functioning of the Constitutional Court. See the text in F. RUBIO LLORENTE, *op. cit.*, pp. 48-55.

Furthermore, the independence of the Constitutional Court regarding the traditional organs of the state guaranteed by Constitutional Law N° 1 of February 1948, also results from the paritarian form established for the appointment of its members, which is attributed not only to the politico-representative organs of the state as is the case in West Germany, but to the three traditional powers of the state: the President of the Republic, the Parliament and the Judicial Power. In effect, in accordance with the Constitution[195] and Statute N° 87 (1953) concerning the Court,[196] the Constitutional Court is composed of fifteen members, appointed in the following manner: five are appointed by the ordinary and administrative judicial order, as follows: three by the Court of Cassation, one by the Council of state and one by the Court of Accounts, chosen from among members of the judiciary, even retired members.

The second five members are elected by Parliament, both chambers sitting in joint session, by a majority of three fifths of the members of the assembly, chosen from among judges, ordinary professors of law in universities, or lawyers having practised twenty years or more before the supreme judicial organs of the Republic; and the last five members are appointed by the President of the Republic.

As we said, the Constitutional Court is conceived in the Italian constitutional system, as a constitutional organ independent from the other state organs, in charge of maintaining the power balance among them. For that purpose it was created separate from the traditional state powers, and particularly from the Judicial Power, regarding which the Constitutional Court itself established differences.[197]

But although not being a judicial organ, discussions were developed at the beginning of the functioning of the Constitutional Court regarding the nature of the powers it exercised. In this respect, its judicial character was rejected, and the idea of the negative legislator was initially accepted[198] under the influence of Hans Kelsen. But eventually, the jurisdictional character of the functions of the Court is today the predominant thesis initially due to the work of Professor Mauro Cappelletti.[199] Thus, like the other European Constitutional Courts particularly the Austrian and Spanish Tribunals, the Constitutional Court in Italy is conceived as an independent constitutional body separate from the Judiciary, which exercises jurisdictional functions when resolving and deciding upon conflicts regarding the constitutionality of state acts and the submission of all the activities of the state organs to the Constitution. Therefore, as happened in the Austrian and German experiences, the Constitutional Court in Italy not only has powers of judicial review of legislation. It can also settle other constitutional disputes particularly deriving from the vertical and horizontal systems of distribution of state powers adopted in the Constitution, although not in the wider sense of the West German system.

---

195 Art. 135.

196 Statute N° 87 (1953), Arts. 1-4.

197 Decision N° 13, 23 March 1960. Quoted by F. RUBIO LLORENTE, *loc. cit.*, p. 10.

198 P. CALAMANDREI, *La illegittimitá costituzionale delle leggi nel processo civile*, Padova, 1950, p. 57; H. FIX-ZAMUDIO, «La aportación de Piero CALAMANDREI al derecho procesal constitucional», *Revista de la Facultad de Derecho de México*, 24, 1956, p. 191.

199 M. CAPPELLETTI, *La giurisdizione costituzionale dele libertá* (Primo studio sul ricorso costituzionale con particolare riguardo agli ordinamenti tedesco, suizzero a austriaco), Milano 1955, p. 112; M. CAPPELLETTI, «La justicia constitucional ...», *loc. cit.*, p. 52; F. RUBIO LLORENTE, *loc. cit.*, pp. 10-13.

2. Jurisdiction of the Constitutional Court

In effect, three main sets of competences of the Constitutional Court can be identified in accordance with the Constitution.

The first general attribution of the Constitutional Court is related to the settlement of «conflict of attribution», which may arise among the powers of the state. These conflicts of attributions or powers can derive from the vertical distribution of state powers, particularly regarding the Regions, and the horizontal distribution of state powers among the constitutional organs.

In effect, the Italian Republic has been constitutionally organised as a «Regional State», which is a form of political decentralization very close to the federal form of state, but with its own peculiarities. Nevertheless, what both forms of political decentralization have in common is a basic distribution of state powers in the vertical sense, over territorial autonomous units, called «Regions» in the Regional State. Therefore, similar to the functions of the Federal Constitutional Tribunal in West Germany, which must settle controversies between the Federation and the *Lander*, in the Italian Republic the Constitutional Court has the power to resolve and settle conflicts of attributions that may arise between state and Regions, if the state invades the sphere of Regional authority or if a Region exceeds its own sphere[200] invading the National state powers or between the regions themselves, if they invade the attributions of other Regions.

The conflict, in such cases, arises as a consequence of administrative acts, and when deciding it, the Constitutional Court not only decides to which level of state powers the challenged attribution belongs, but has the power to annul the administrative act that brought it about,[201] also to suspend *pendente litis* its effects, when serious reasons to do so exist.[202]

It must be said that these are the only cases in which the Italian Constitutional Court can declare the nullity of an administrative act, having no other jurisdiction to judge the unconstitutionality of administrative acts.[203]

However, the conflicts of attributions between the state and the Regions can also have their origin in legislative acts of the state. In that case their resolution by the Constitutional Court is made through a direct means for judicial review of legislation exercised by the Regions and to which we will refer later on.

But as we said, in the Italian constitutional system the conflict of attributions may not only arise between the vertically distributed state powers, but also between the powers constitutionally assigned to the various national constitutional organs.

In this respect, the Constitutional Court also has jurisdiction to resolve these conflicts «for the delimitation of the sphere of attributions determined for the various powers by constitutional norms»,[204] for instance, between the Chamber of Deputies and the Senate, or between the President of the Republic and Parliament. But it is obvious that the conflict of attributions between the state powers in the horizontal

---

200 Art. 134 Constitution; Art. 39 Statute Nº 87.
201 Art. 38 Statute Nº 87.
202 Art. 40 Statute Nº 87.
203 F. RUBIO LLORENTE, *op. cit.*, p. 16.
204 Art. 37 Statute Nº 87.

distribution of the state power in the Italian constitutional system, is not only possible between the traditional three powers of the state, but can also arise regarding other state organs, not subordinated to them, for instance, the Superior Council of the Judicature, the Court of Accounts, and the National Economic Council. In this respect, Professor Aldo Saudulli, also a former Constitutional Court judge, has said that the expression «state powers» must be understood to comprise «all the bodies of the state organisation which, in accordance with the constitutional order, are in such a situation that its activities are not subject to any kind of external control by any other state organ (even constitutional state organs)».[205]

Anyway, in all these cases of conflicts of attributions between constitutional organs of the state, the Constitutional Court must resolve the sphere of attributions conferred upon the various state powers by constitutional norms, [206] and must declare to which state organ the challenged power belongs, and when an act has been produced inflicted with incompetence, the Court must also annul it.[207]

The second general competence of the Constitutional Court, in a similar way to the Austrian and West German systems, refers to cases of accusations against or of impeachment of the President of the Republic for crimes of undermining the Constitution and high treason, and against the President of the Council of Ministers and the Ministers for crimes committed by them in the exercise of their functions.[208] The accusation in these cases can only be brought before the Court by Parliament, which must vote on it in a joint session of its two chambers.

The third jurisdictional power of the Constitutional Court refers to referenda and the Constitution empowers the Court to judge upon the admissibility of derogatory referenda that can be presented for the abrogation of ordinary laws, exception being made of taxation and budget laws, laws granting amnesty and pardon, and laws authorising the ratification of international treaties.[209] Nevertheless, the statute referred to in article 75 of the Constitution, which must regulate the above mentioned admissibility conditions and modalities for the derogatory referenda, has not yet been approved.

Finally, the fourth set of jurisdictional powers of the Constitutional Court of Italy refers to judicial review of the constitutionality of legislation, that is to say, to laws (statutes) and other state acts with the same force to which we will refer next.

Thus, the Italian Court does not have jurisdiction over electoral matters and political parties[210] as the West German Federal Constitutional Tribunal has, and

---

205 A. SANDULLI, «Die Verfassungsgerichtsbarkeit in Italia», in E. MOSLER (ed.), *Verfassungsgerichsbarkeit in der Gegenwart* (Constitutional Review in the World Today), Max-Plank-Institut Internationalen Kolloquium, Heidelberg, 1961, Köln-Berlin 1962, p. 310; quoted by F. RUBIO LLORENTE, *op. cit.*, p. 36.

206 Art. 37, Statute N° 87.

207 Art. 38, Statute N° 87.

208 Arts 90, 134 Constitution. Statute N° 20, of 25 January 1962. See the text in F. RUBIO LLORENTE, *op.cit.*, p. 55-61.

209 Art. 74, 75 Constitution; Art. 2 Constitutional Statute N° 1, 11 March 1953. See the text in F. RUBIO LLORENTE, *op. cit.*, pp. 46-47.

210 Regarding political parties Professor RUBIO LLORENTE says that the Constitutional Court can only decide upon the constitutionality or unconstitutionality of them, only by indirect means when a question of constitutionality is referred to the Court concerning a statute sanctioned based on article 18 (prohibition of secret on paramilitary societies), 49 (freedom of association in political parties), or on the Transitory Disposition XII (prohibition of any form of reorganization of the fascist party) through which a party or a political organization could be dissolved. F. RUBIO LLORENTE, *op. cit.*, p. 16.

more important to notice, the Italian Constitutional Court does not have powers to act as a direct guarantor of fundamental rights and freedoms, not having attributions to decide upon constitutional complaints or recourses for constitutional protection as they exist in the West German, Austrian and Spanish systems of constitutional justice,[211] particularly, when exercised against laws. Nevertheless, the need for a direct action before the Constitutional Court was a matter of discussion during the drafting of the Constitution. Moreover, in one of the first drafts of the text, the main form of judicial review of legislation was established through a direct recourse of unconstitutionality that could be brought before the Constitutional Court, as an *actio popularis*, accessible to all citizens without the need of an injury to be done to their subjective rights, an action that needed to be exercised during a one year period after the publication of the statute.[212] This proposal for a popular action of unconstitutionality was later rejected, mainly due to political reasons,[213] the means for judicial review of legislation being reduced basically to an incidental system of judicial review concentrated in the Constitutional Court, combined with a limited principal means of review and a preventive system established only regarding certain state acts.

3. Scope of judicial review in the Italian system

Therefore, the Italian system of judicial review of constitutionality is a concentrated system according to which the Constitutional Court is the only state body to have exclusive jurisdiction to determine the conformity of legislation with the Constitution, comprising in the term «legislation», as established in the Constitution, the laws (statutes) and other state acts with the force of law,[214] either of the National state or of the Regions. As a result, formal laws are subject to constitutional control. Also the decree-laws, enacted by the executive by virtue of parliamentary delegation,[215] or in cases of urgency,[216] those considered as being «acts with force of law». On the other hand, the *interna corporis* of Parliament, issued in direct execution of the Constitution, are also subject to constitutional control by the Constitutional Court[217] taking into account their similar rank to statutes, in the hierarchy of the legal order.

Other points should be stressed with respect to these «legislative» acts, which are subject to control. The first is the admissibility of control of constitutionality in the case of laws contrary to the Constitution but passed before their enactment and which, in principle, could be considered to have been tacitly repealed by it. The Constitutional Court has accepted exercising control upon these pre-constitutional laws but only through the incidental method when the issue of constitutionality is raised before an ordinary judge in a concrete case and he refers the question for examination by the Constitutional Court.[218]

---

211 *Cf.* A. PIZZARUSSO, *loc. cit.*, p. 168.

212 F. RUBIO LLORENTE, *op. cit.*, pp. 4-5.

213 *Idem*, pp. 5-6.

214 Art. 1. Constitutional Statute N° 1, 9 February 1948.

215 Art. 75 Constitution.

216 Art. 77 Constitution. These Decree-Laws issued in emergency situations must be submitted to Parliament the following day of its enactment and only when they are convalidated by Parliament, they can be questioned on constitutional grounds.

217 *Cf.* F. RUBIO LLORENTE, *op. cit.*, p. 23.

218 Decision N° 1, 1956. Quoted by F. RUBIO LLORENTE, *op. cit.*, p. 35; *Cf.* G. CASSANDRO, *loc. cit.*, p. 5.

The second aspect refers to the actual enforcement of the laws submitted to control; and specifically as to whether it is possible to raise the issue of constitutionality with respect to repealed laws, which have already lost their force. The Italian Constitutional Court has repeatedly declared its competence to hear disputes concerning the constitutionality of these repealed laws, thus no longer in force, considering that they could have created situations, the persistence of which after their repeal, could have justified constitutional control.[219]

The third aspect has to do with the objective of this control, which is not only a substantive control in the sense of determining if the statute is consistent with the constitution in its normative contents or not, but also a formal control over acts submitted to constitutional review, regarding the procedures followed for its sanctioning.[220]

On the other hand, the jurisdictional powers of the Constitutional Court to review the constitutionality of legislation, refer not only to the confrontation of legislative acts with the constitution itself, but also to «constitutional laws» that can be enacted in accordance with article 138 of the Constitution to amend it. The *bloc* of constitutionality, therefore, is particularly composed, other than the principles, which could be deduced from the constitutional text, of the Constitution and the «constitutional laws» to which all other norms must conform. But the «constitutional laws» being regulated for their enactment by the Constitution, which establishes their scope and possible contents, can also be submitted to constitutional review by the Constitutional Court.[221]

Finally, regarding the scope of judicial review exercised by the Constitutional Court, one must stress the discussions that have arisen as a consequence of the terms used in article 134 of the Italian Constitution, in the sense that the Constitutional Court has jurisdiction to settle disputes dealing with «constitutional legitimacy» of laws and state acts with force of law,[222] which could lead to the conclusion as happened in the administrative justice field regarding the control of administrative acts, that the Court could control the merits of legislative activities.

In principle, this power attributed to the Constitutional Court deals only with matters of abstract repugnancy of state acts with the Constitution in the sense that the Court must control the submission of the legislator to the constitution and the limits to its activities established in it, the Court not being authorised to judge upon the motives and merits the legislator could have had when enacting a statute. In this respect, the 1953 Statute N° 87 of the Constitutional Court expressly states:

> «Art 28. The Constitutional Court control over the legitimacy of laws or an act with force of law, excludes any value judgement of policy nature and any judgement upon the use Parliament makes of its discretionary power. But even with a text of this clarity, the Constitutional Court, always within the ambit of this norm, since 1960, has controlled the «arbitrariness» or «non

219 Decision N° 4, 1959. Quoted by F. RUBIO LLORENTE, *op. cit.*, p. 22.
220 *Cf.* G. CASSANDRO, *loc. cit.*, p. 4.
221 G. CASSANDRO, *loc. cit.*, pp. 3–4. *Cf.* F. RUBIO LLORENTE, *op. cit.*, p. 20.
222 The term is also used in article 1, Constitutional Statute N° 1, 9 February 1948; and in arts 23–36 Statute N° 87, 1953.

arbitrariness» of the legislator concerning the legislation enacted in relation to the principle of equality and non-discrimination, and the «rationality» of the distinctions established in legislation».[223]

4. Incidental method of judicial review

As we have said, the basic means for raising questions of constitutionality of legislation before the Constitutional Court and undoubtedly, the most important means for keeping statutes and legislative acts within the framework of the Constitution in the Italian system, is the incidental method expressly regulated in the 1948 Constitutional Statute N° 1, which contained the norms related to the trials of constitutional illegitimacy and to the independence guarantees of the Constitutional Court. Article 1 of that Constitutional Statute, states:

> «The question on the constitutional illegitimacy of a law (statute) or of an act of the Republic with force of law, raised *ex officio* or alleged by one of the parties in the course of a trial, and not evidently considered unfounded by the judge, must be referred to the Constitutional Court for its consideration.

This incidental method of judicial review has been regulated in the 1953 Statute N° 87 in which its fundamental provisions are to be found, which reinforce the concentrated incidental character of the Italian system of judicial review.[224]

In accordance with this 1953 Statute N° 87, in the course of a process developed before a court, either party or the Public Prosecutor may raise the question of constitutional legitimacy in the form of a petition, indicating, firstly the provisions of the law or the act with force of law of the state or of the Region, containing defects of «constitutional illegitimacy»; and secondly, the provisions of the Constitution or of the «constitutional laws» which have allegedly been violated.

Once the issue of constitutionality is raised before the ordinary judge, he must made a decision referring the issue to the Constitutional Court, when it is a «prejudicial» question, that is to say, if the case does not allow him to take a decision avoiding the issue of «constitutional legitimacy», and also when the judge considers that the issue raised before him is not evidently unfounded.[225] In other words, if the judge considers that the issue of constitutionality has sufficient basis and its resolution is essential for the decision of the process, then he must decide upon the existence of both conditions and therefore refer the question to the Constitutional Court, sending with the referral the statement made by the parties or by the Public Prosecutor and the whole file of the case, whose proceeding must be suspended.

The judge, in a motivated decision, can reject the constitutional question alleged by the parties or by the Public Prosecutor when he considers that it has no relevance to the case or has no due foundation. However, this rejection does not prevent the parties from later raising the question in any stage of the proceeding.[226]

---

223 *Cf.* The Court Decisions and the opposite doctrine on this matter in F. RUBIO LLORENTE, *op. cit.*, pp. 17-19; and G. ZAGREBELSKI, «Object et portée de la protection des droits fondamentaux. Cour Constitutionnelle italienne», in L. FAVOREU (ed.), *Cours constitutionnelles européenes et droits fondamentaux*, Paris 1982, p. 330.

224 M. CAPPELLETTI, «La justicia constitucional...», *loc. cit.*, pp. 44, 45.

225 Art. 23, Statute N° 87, 1953.

226 Art. 24, Statute N° 87, 1953.

But as the 1948 Constitutional Statute N° 1 and the 1953 Statute N° 87 state, the issue of constitutional legitimacy may also be raised *ex-officio* by the judge hearing the case. In that event, he must also make a decision in which he must include the precise indication of the provisions of the law or of the acts with the force of law considered unconstitutional, as well as the norms of the Constitution or of the constitutional laws deemed to have been violated by the challenged statute. The judge must also justify in his decision the «prejudicial» character of the question and the reasons for considering the statute unconstitutional.

Anyway, when raising the constitutional question concerning the constitutional illegitimacy of a statute or of a state act with force of law, the judge is not bound by the will of the parties: he can reject their allegations upon constitutional issues and can raise them *ex-officio*. In all such cases, it is the judge who must decide upon the unconstitutionality of the statutes, although he has no power to annul them and his powers are limited to referring the question to the Constitutional Court.

Furthermore, neither is the Constitutional Court when considering the constitutional question referred to it, bound by the parties of the original process in which the constitutional issue was raised; therefore, even if those parties of the *a quo* process must be called upon and heard, as well as the executive authority concerned (President of the Council of Ministers or of the Regional Board),[227] the proceeding developed before the Court, is not an adversary one developed *inter partes*, rather it is of a non adversary and objective nature, developed independent of the will of the parties and even in cases of abandonment of action or when a voluntary dismissal of the case has taken place.[228]

As we have said, in the Italian system of judicial review, this incidental method is the most important mean for seeking constitutional review of legislation and, therefore, it has been considered as having limited scope, particularly regarding statutes that could directly affect individual rights. As Professor Cappelletti said:

> «The inconvenience of this system results from the fact that certain statutes, particularly those called by the Mexican constitutional doctrine auto-applicable (auto effective or auto-executive), could immediately infringe the juridical sphere of certain individuals, without the need of being «concretised» by an executive or applicative act; thus, at least regarding these laws, the sole incidental control of constitutional legitimacy, could appear as insufficient».[229]

5. Direct method of judicial review and its regional scope

But in spite of its predominant incidental concentrated character, the Italian system of judicial review also allows a direct method of judicial review, although limited, and in a certain way very closely related to the powers of the Court to resolve conflicts of attributions between state and Regions.

In effect, article 2 of Constitutional Statute N° 1 of 9, February 1948 attributes the resolution of questions of constitutional illegitimacy to the Constitutional Court

---

227 Art. 25, Statute N° 87, 1953. The parties or the public official may not appeal before the Court, Art. 26. *Idem.*

228 Art. 22, Complementary Norms of the Court. *Cf.* F. RUBIO LLORENTE, *op. cit.*, p. 24; G. CASSANDRO, *loc. cit.*, p. 6; A. PIZZORUSSO, *loc. cit.*, p. 176.

229 M. CAPPELLETTI, «Judicial Review...», *loc. cit.*, p. 45.

brought before it through a direct action that can only be exercised by a Region against national legislation or statutes of other Regions. This article states the following:

> Art 2. When a Region deems that a statute or an act with force of law of the Republic invades the sphere of competences attributed to it in the Constitution, it can present before the Court, upon deliberation of the Regional Board, the question of constitutional illegitimacy within thirty days of the publication of the statute or of the act with force of law».[230]

Therefore, the first recourse or direct action of unconstitutionality accepted in the Italian constitutional system is the one that the Regions could bring before the Constitutional Court against legislative acts of the Republic, which in fact, results in a conflict of attributions between national and regional levels,[231] not based on an administrative act, but rather on a statute or other national act with force of law, particularly decree-laws. Nevertheless, this action or recourse cannot be brought before the Court the other way round, that is to say, by the Republic against the Regional statutes, in which cases the question must be treated as a conflict of attributions in the sense already mentioned.[232]

On the other hand, the direct action or recourse of unconstitutionality in accordance with the 1948 Constitutional Statute N° 1 can also be brought before the Constitutional Court by a Region against a statute or another act with and force of law of another Region and considered constitutionally illegitimate, when it deems its competences have been violated by it.[233]

The proceedings in such cases of direct action are considered in a sense as adversary, because contrary to the situation in the incidental method, in the principal one the will of the parties carries weight in the sense that the «waiver of the action, if accepted by all parties, extinguishes the proceeding».[234]

6. Preventive method of judicial review of regional legislation

Finally, the Constitution also establishes a preventive means of judicial review but limited only to controlling the constitutionality of regional legislation[235] by the Constitutional Court, by attributing to the Council of Ministers the power to bring a direct action or recourse against regional statutes, before their enactment, before the Court, within fifteen days following the formal information that the President of the Regional Board must send when a regional bill is approved in a second vote by the Regional Council.[236]

In these cases, when the preventive judicial review request is brought before the Court, the enactment of the challenged regional statute must be suspended until a decision is adopted[237] in which case, if it is of unconstitutionality, its promulgation would be impossible.

---

230 See also Art. 32 Statute N° 87, 1953.
231 *Cf.* F. RUBIO LLORENTE, *op. cit.*, p. 25.
232 Art. 39 Statute N° 67, 1953.
233 Art. 2; See also Art. 33 Statute N° 87, 1953.
234 Art. 25, Complementary Norms of the Court. *Cf.* G. CASSANDRO, *loc. cit.*, p. 8.
235 Art. 127 Constitution.
236 Art. 31 Statute N° 87, 1953.
237 Art. 128 Constitution.

7. Effects of the Constitutional Court decisions

In all cases of judicial review of the constitutionality of legislation, the Constitutional Court must decide, «within the limits» of the action or referral,[238] which are the norms considered «illegitimate», that is to say, unconstitutional. Thus, in accordance with the terms of Statute N° 87, it has been considered that the Constitutional Court does not have *ex-officio* powers to consider other constitutional issues different to those submitted to it by the referral in the incidental method or in the action or recourse in the direct or principal method of judicial review. In this respect, the Court has powers only to declare «which other legislative dispositions whose illegitimacy is a consequence of the decision adopted»,[239] but cannot declare the unconstitutionality of legislative dispositions other than those indicated in the referral by the ordinary judge or in the direct action.

On the other hand, the Constitutional Court decision in which the unconstitutionality of a statute is declared, has *erga omnes* effects and therefore, the act «cannot be applied onwards from the day following the publication of the decision».[240] Therefore, it must be considered that the decision has a constitutive character[241] in the sense that it annuls the unconstitutional statute, its effect being *ex-nunc, pro futuro*. This rule, has been widely discussed[242] and the Constitutional Court has interpreted the constitutional norm (art 136) which states that the act declared unconstitutional cannot be applied onwards from the day after the publication of the Court decision, in the sense that:

> «The decision upon the unconstitutionality, if it is true that it leaves out all the effects irrevocably produced by the norm declared unconstitutional, on the contrary it produces effects upon the juridical situations not yet exhausted when they are still susceptible to being regulated in a different manner as a consequence of the decision. Thus, the declaration of unconstitutionality of a statute produces its inapplicability to all the relations judicially controverted as and when they are still not the object of a decision with *res judicata* force, with the consequence that in all stages of the trial, the judge even *ex-officio* must take into account the said decision of constitutional illegitimacy when deciding the concrete juridical relation of a case, in the same way and to the same extent as if it were a *ius superveniens*».[243]

This criterion of the Constitutional Court, in fact, confirms the constitutive character of the effects of the decisions declaring the unconstitutionality of statutes, whose exceptions are established in the 1953 Statute N° 87, in which the retroactive effects of the decision are only applicable in criminal cases, when a judicial condemnation has been pronounced based on a statute declared unconstitutional, in which case its execution and its criminal effects must cease.[244]Another indirect exception of the *ex-nunc* effects of the decision results from the already mentioned possibility of annulment of statutes already repealed.[245]

---

238 Art. 27 Statute N° 87, 1953.

239 Art. 27 *Idem.*

240 Art. 136 Constitution; Art. 30, Statute N° 87, 1953.

241 *Cf.* G. CASSANDRO, *loc. cit.*, p. 6.

242 *Cf.* F. RUBIO LLORENTE, *op. cit.*, p. 12 and 29-33.

243 Decision N° 3491, 1957. Quoted in F. RUBIO LLORENTE, *op. cit.*, p. 30.

244 Art. 30 Statute N° 87, 1953.

245 See note N° 1034.

Another issue, which has been raised regarding the effects of the Constitutional Court decision on issues of constitutional illegitimacy, is that of the effects of the decision, which reject the question of unconstitutionality for lack of foundation. Initially Professor Calamandrei maintained that these decisions were to be considered authentic interpretations of the Constitution, that should prevent future challenges and therefore had *erga omnes* effects.[246] Discussions have taken place regarding the matter, and today it can be said that the same Constitutional Court has limited the effects of its decisions declaring the lack of foundations of the unconstitutionality issue, to the principal process in which the issue was first raised; therefore, that decision has a binding efficacy on the concrete case, with the full authority of *res judicata*.[247] To reach this conclusion, it has been considered that because the general norm of the Italian legal system is to limit the effects of judicial decisions to the case in dispute, the norm of Article 136 of the Constitution, which attributes *erga omnes* effects to declarations of unconstitutionality has an exceptional character, which cannot be the object of extensive interpretation. The result is that this *erga omnes* character cannot be applied to decisions that dismiss or reject issues of unconstitutionality.[248]

Another criterion that have been exposed are that of the preclusive effect of the Court decision, in the sense that the incidental question of constitutionality cannot be raised twice in the same process in its original form. Nevertheless, this does not preclude the possibility of it being raised in another process, or even, that the parties could raise new issues of unconstitutionality judged negatively by the Court on a previous occasion.[249]

V. JUDICIAL REVIEW IN SPAIN: THE CONSTITUTIONAL TRIBUNAL

1. Second Spanish Republic antecedents: Constitutional Guarantees Tribunal

The third European experience in establishing a concentrated system of judicial review, after the 1920 Czechoslovakian and Austrian constitutional justice regulations, was developed in the Second Spanish Republic, in accordance with the Constitution of 9 December 1931, which created a Tribunal of Constitutional Guarantees. The system established was a concentrated system of judicial review, in which the direct influence of the Austrian experience and the thoughts of Hans Kelsen, can be found,[250] although with its own peculiarities and with its own historical antecedents in the projects of the First Republic in 1873.[251]

In effect, the 1931 judicial review system was conceived as a concentrated one, in which the Tribunal of Constitutional Guarantees had exclusive powers to judge upon the constitutionality of statutes, through two methods: an incidental and a principal one. Additionally, the Constitution regulated recourse of constitutional

---

246 P. CALAMANDREI, *op. cit.*, p. 71.

247 *Cf.* F. RUBIO LLORENTE, *op. cit.*, pp. 32-33.

248 M. CAPPELLETTI, «La justicia constitucional... «, *loc. cit.*, pp. 56-57.

249 *Idem*, p. 57.

250 J.L. MELIÁN GIL, *El Tribunal de Garantías Constitucionales de la Segunda República Española*, Madrid 1971, pp. 16-17, 53; P. CRUZ VILLALON, «Dos modos de regulación del control de constitucionalidad: Checoslovaquia (1920-1938) y España (1931-1936), *Revista española de derecho constitucional*, 5, 1982, p. 118.

251 J.L. MELIÁN GIL, *op. cit.*, p. 9; N. GONZÁLEZ-DELEITO DOMINGO, *Tribunales constitucionales. Organización y funcionamiento*, Madrid 1980, p. 21.

protection (*recurso de amparo*) also to be exercised before the Tribunal for the protection of fundamental rights.

The incidental mean for judicial review was established in article 100 of the Constitution, which stated:

> «When a court of justice would have to apply a law (statute) which it deems to be contrary to the Constitution, it must suspend the proceeding and send a consultative request to the Tribunal of Constitutional Guarantees».

Additionally, the Constitution assigned competence to the Tribunal of Constitutional Guarantees to take cognisance of the «recourse of unconstitutionality of laws»[252] conceived as an autonomous action, which could be exercised before the Tribunal by the Public Prosecutor, the Government of the Republic, the Regions and by «any individual or collective person, even if it was not directly injured»,[253] which in fact converted it into a popular action.

Nevertheless, this concentrated system of judicial review so broadly established in the 1931 Constitution was reduced in the Organic Law of the Tribunal enacted in 1933. In it, the «recourse of unconstitutionality of laws» was conceived only as an incidental mean of judicial review, sought *ex-officio* by a court or as a consequence of an exception raised in a concrete proceeding by the party whose rights could result in being affected by the application of the challenged statute, or by the Public Prosecutor.[254] In this way, the system, exclusively incidental, was distanced from the Austrian model and followed trends of the diffuse system of judicial review regarding the effects of the Tribunal decisions declaring the unconstitutionality of state acts, in the sense that they were not *erga omnes* but were reduced only regarding «the concrete case of the recourse or the consultation».[255] Thus, the statutes were not annulled by the Tribunal but only considered inapplicable to the concrete case.[256] The Organic Law of the Constitutional Guarantees Tribunal was broadly criticised for this restriction regarding constitutional dispositions, and was the first to be the object of a recourse of unconstitutionality.[257] Anyway, less than five years after the promulgation of the Constitution, it was repealed in 1936 and with it, the system of judicial control of constitutionality was eliminated. It has only been with the publication of the new democratic Constitution of 27 December 1978 that a new system of judicial review has been established in Spain, with the creation of the Constitutional Tribunal later regulated in the «Organic Law of the Constitutional Tribunal» of 3 October 1979.[258]

2. Constitutional Tribunal as a European model

Having been established after the consolidation of the main continental European experiences of constitutional justice, the Spanish judicial review system adopted the most important features of the European model, being influenced by the West German, Italian and French regulations. That is why, up to the creation of

---

[252] Art. 121. See the text in J.L. MELIÁN GIL, *op. cit.*, p. 11; N. GONZÁLEZ-DELEITO DOMINGO, *loc. cit.*, p. 22.
[253] Art. 123. *Idem.*
[254] Art. 30-33. Organic Law 1933. See in J.L. MELIÁN GIL, *op. cit.*, pp. 14, 29.
[255] Art. 42, *Idem*, p. 30.
[256] J.L. MELIÁN GIL, *op. cit.*, p. 30.
[257] *Idem*, p. 45; N. GONZÁLEZ-DELEITO DOMINGO, *op. cit.*, p. 23.
[258] Organic Law 2/1979. See the text in *Boletín Oficial del Estado*, N° 239, 5 October, 1979.

the Constitutional Tribunal in Spain, it was said that the Federal Constitutional Tribunal of West Germany had the widest jurisdiction on constitutional matters compared to any other tribunal or supreme court in the world.[259] After 1978, this assertion was no longer true, and the Constitutional Tribunal of Spain was the one generally considered as the constitutional organ with the most complete jurisdiction in constitutional matters.[260] But today, at least on the grounds of judicial review and constitutional justice, this can be said in Europe, of the Constitutional Tribunal of Portugal established in the 1982 Constitutional revision, in which a mixed system of judicial review of legislation has been established.

Nevertheless, the Spanish system can be considered as an illustrative example of the concentrated European model of judicial review[261] which has proved its workability over recent years.

Of course, not all the normative acts of the state are subject to exclusive constitutional review by the tribunal, and as in other European countries it is admitted that the pre-constitutional legislation even though reviewable by the tribunal, can be reviewed in a diffuse way by all courts.[262]

Anyway, in accordance with the Constitution, the Constitutional Tribunal is conceived as a constitutional organ, thus independent and separate from the Judicial Power, but with jurisdictional functions as the guarantor of the constitutionality of state action.[263] In this respect, article 1 of the Organic Law 2/1979 concerning the Tribunal, expressly establishes that:

> «The Constitutional Tribunal, as the supreme interpreter of the Constitution, is independent from the other constitutional organs and it is only submitted to the Constitution and to this Organic Law».

According to article 159 of the Constitution, the tribunal is composed of 12 members appointed from among magistrates and public prosecutors, university professors, public officials and qualified lawyers with over 15 years practice. The members of the tribunal are appointed by the king, in the following manner: four are appointed on the proposal of a three fifths majority of the members of Congress; four on the proposal of the same majority of the Senate; two on the Government's proposal; and two on the proposal of the General Council of the Judicial Power. Thus, as happens in the Italian system, all the three traditional powers of the state intervene in the appointment of the members of the Tribunal. As also happens in

---

259 G. MÜLLER, «El Tribunal Constitucional Federal de la República Federal de Alemania», *Revista de la Comisión Internacional de Juristas*, Vol VI, (2), 1 5, p. 221.

260 *Cf.* E. GARCÍA DE ENTERRÍA, *La Constitución como norma y el Tribunal Constitucional*, Madrid 1981, p. 137; P. BON, F. MODERNE and Y. RODRÍGUEZ, *La justice constitutionnelle en Espagne*, Paris 1982, p. 41; L. FAVOREU, «Actualité et légitimité du Contrôle juridictionnel des lois en Europe occidentale». *Revue du droit public et de la science politique en France et à 1'étranger*, Paris 1984 (5), p. 1154.

261 P. BON, F. MODERNE and Y. RODRÍGUEZ, *op. cit.*, p. 41.

262 J. SALAS, «El Tribunal Constitucional Español y su competencia desde la perspectiva de la forma de Gobierno: sus relaciones con los poderes Legislativo, Ejecutivo y Judicial», *Revista española de derecho constitucional*, 6, 1982, p. 165.

263 M. GARCÍA PELAYO, «El Status del Tribunal Constitucional», *Revista española de derecho constitucional*, 1, 1981, pp. 11-34; F. RUBIO LLORENTE, «Sobre la relación entre Tribunal Constitucional y poder judicial en el ejercicio de la jurisdicción constitucional», *Revista española de derecho constitucional*, 4, 1982, pp. 35-67, As an independent organ it also has autoregulatory powers: Art. 2,2 Organic Law 2/1979.

the other European systems, so as to avoid the politization of the Tribunal, the Constitution is quite explicit as to the incompatibilities with respect to its members. It stipulates that the status of being a member of the Constitutional Court is incompatible with any representative mandate, with political and administrative posts, with directive functions in a political party or trade union, or employment by them, with a judicial or public prosecutor career and with any other professional or commercial activity. It is also stipulated that the members of the Constitutional Tribunal have the same incompatibility as the members of the Judiciary.

The competences of the Tribunal can be classified into three main groups: the resolution of constitutional conflicts between state powers; the decision of the recourses of constitutional protection (*recursos de amparo*) of fundamental rights; and the control of the constitutionality of legislation.

The first major group of powers assigned to the Constitutional Tribunal refers to the resolution of constitutional conflicts between state organs, in accordance with the vertical and horizontal systems of distribution of state powers adopted by the Constitution. In Spain, the Constitution has organised the form of the state, as a «State of Autonomous Communities», in a similar way to the Regional state formula of the Italian Constitution; therefore, a particular system of political decentralization has been adopted, in which the Autonomous Communities are the most important pillars of the territorial organisation of the state.[264] Therefore, the Constitutional Tribunal is empowered to resolve «the conflicts of attributions between the state and the Autonomous Communities and conflicts between the latter».[265]

But within this same sort of jurisdiction, the Constitutional Tribunal has been empowered by the Organic Law that regulates it to resolve conflicts of competences or attributions between the constitutional organs of the National state, that is to say, those conflicts that confront «the Government with the Congress of Deputies, the Senate or the General Council of the Judicial Power; or any of those constitutional organs between themselves».[266] The justification of the competence of the Constitutional Tribunal in conflicts between constitutional bodies, as in all the other European constitutional justice systems, seems evident. Any conflict between political entities is, in itself, a constitutional conflict, which questions the organic system established by the Constitution itself. Consequently, the Constitutional Tribunal is the only adequate body for the settlement of such conflicts, which affect the very essence of the Constitution, the distribution of powers, which it establishes, and the competences distributed by it.

The judgments pronounced in settlement of conflicts of competence have *inter partes* effects because the content of these judgments basically consists of a declaration on the entitlement of the constitutional bodies, for example, Congress, the Senate or the General Council of the Judiciary, to the competence in dispute.[267]

However, when the declaration on entitlement implies the declaration of the nullity[268] of the normative provision issued by the body declared to be incompetent, the judgment must be published for it to have *erga omnes* effects.[269]

264 Art. 2, 137, 143 Constitution.
265 Art. 161, 1,c Constitution; Art. 60-72 Organic Law 2/1979.
266 Art. 59, 3; 73-5 Organic Law 2/1979.
267 Art. 75, 2 Organic Law 2/1979.
268 *Idem*.
269 Art. 164, 1 Constitution.

The second major block of attributions of the Constitutional Tribunal relates to the decision of the *recursos de amparo* (recourse for constitutional protection). It can be directly brought by individuals before the Constitutional Tribunal, when they deem their constitutional rights and liberties violated by dispositions, juridical acts or simple factual actions of the public powers of the state, the Autonomous Communities and other public territorial entities or by their officials.[270] This recourse for the protection of fundamental rights cannot be exercised directly against statutes, which violate fundamental rights in a direct way,[271] as in the West German system. Therefore, it can only be exercised against administrative or judicial acts and acts without force of law produced by the legislative authorities,[272] and only when the ordinary judicial means for the protection of fundamental rights have been exhausted.[273] Consequently, the recourse for *amparo* in general results in a direct action against judicial acts [274] and can only indirectly lead to judicial review of legislation when the particular state act challenged by it is based on a statute considered unconstitutional.[275]

Finally, the third group of attributions of the Constitutional Tribunal refers to judicial review of legislation, which can be exercised through a direct or principal recourse or in an incidental way. The Constitutional Court can also exercise the power of judicial review in an indirect way and regarding certain state acts, in a preventive way. Therefore, four different means of judicial review of legislation can be distinguished in the Spanish system.

3. Direct control of the constitutionality of legislation

The first of the means through which judicial review powers can be exercised by the Constitutional Tribunal, and upon which it is empowered to decide, is through the «recourse of unconstitutionality against laws and normative acts with force of law»,[276] through which «the Constitutional Tribunal guarantees the primacy of the Constitution and judges the conformity or inconformity» of the laws and normative acts with force of law with it.[277]

In a very similar way to the Italian formula, the state acts that can be the object of this direct recourse of unconstitutionality are the laws (statutes) and other state acts with the same force of laws, which include the «Statutes of Autonomy» approved by Parliament for the Autonomous Communities, and also the organic laws and the ordinary laws approved by Parliament;[278] international treaties;[279] the *interna corporis* regulations of the Chambers and Parliament; [280] the other normative acts of the National state with force of law, including the decree-laws enacted by the Government,[281] either through delegate legislation[282] or in cases of urgent and

---

270 Art. 161, 1, b) Constitution; Art. 41, 2 Organic Law 2/1979.
271 *Cf.* . GARCÍA DE ENTERRÍA, *op. cit.*, p. 151.
272 Art. 42 Organic Law 2/1979.
273 Art. 43, 1 Organic Law 2/1979.
274 *Cf.* FAVOREU, *loc. cit.*, pp. 1155-1156.
275 Art. 55,2 Organic Law 2/1979.
276 Art. 161,1,a Constitution.
277 Art. 27,1 Organic Law 2/1979.
278 Art. 27,2, a,b) *Idem.*
279 Art. 27,2,c) *Idem.*
280 Art. 27,2,d) *Idem.*
281 Art. 27,2 ,b) *Idem.*
282 Art. 82 Constitution.

extraordinary necessity;[283] and finally, the normative regulations of the legislative assemblies of the Autonomous Communities. [284]

It must also be noted that pre-constitutional laws can also be controlled on the ground of their constitutionality by the Constitutional Tribunal even though, as we said, they can be declared inapplicable by any judge when considered unconstitutional,[285] particularly because the Constitution expressly states in its Derogatory Disposition, N° 3, that «all dispositions repugnant to what is established in this Constitution are repealed».

This recourse of unconstitutionality can be brought before the Constitutional Tribunal by the President of the Government, the «Peoples Defendant», fifty Deputies or fifty Senators;[286] and also by the Collegiate executive organ and the Legislative Assemblies of the Autonomous Communities when the challenged acts are laws or other state acts with similar force of law which affect their respective autonomy ambit.[287] In any case, the recourse can only be brought before the Tribunal within a delay of three months following the publication of the challenged act.[288]

The radical difference between the direct action or recourse of unconstitutionality established in Spain, and the Italian model in which, for instance, the standing of the Government is limited to challenging only the regional laws, must be stressed. On the contrary, in the Spanish system, the standing attributed to the various political organs, including the President of Government, implies their right to challenge any law or state act with force of law on the grounds of unconstitutionality.[289]

But regarding the dispositions and decisions of the organs of the Autonomous Communities that can be challenged by the Government, what the Constitution establishes is the suspensive character of the recourse in relation to the challenged acts.[290]

Just as in the West German system, the aim of this direct action on the ground of unconstitutionality is to exercise an abstract control over normative state acts, without reference to a particular conflict in which it would be necessary to elucidate the constitutional issue. Thus, in these cases it is simply a question of an abstract discrepancy over the interpretation of the Constitution in relation to a particular law.[291] On the other hand, and although the state organs whose normative acts must be called upon and could be heard[292] the proceeding for the decision of this recourse of unconstitutionality can be considered an objective one in which the political organs which initiated it and the representatives [293] of the state organs whose statutes and acts are challenged, do not have the strict procedural position of parties[294] the abandonment of the recourse not being conceivable.[295]

---

283 Art. 86 Constitution.
284 Art. 27,2,f) Constitution.
285 Art. 27,2,f) Constitution.
286 This has been expressly admitted by the Constitutional Tribunal. *Cf.* J. SALAS, *loc. cit.*, pp. 165-166.
287 Art. 162,1,a) Constitution; Art. 32,1 Organic Law 2/1979.
288 Art. 33 Organic Law 2/1979.
289 S. GALEOTTI and B. ROSSI, «El Tribunal Constitucional en la nueva Constitución española: Medios de impugnación y legitimados para actuar», *Revista de estudios políticos*, 7, Madrid 1979, p. 125.
290 Art. 30 Organic Law
291 E. GARCÍA DE ENTERRÍA, *op. cit.*, p. 140.
292 Art. 34 Organic Law 2/1979.
293 Art. 82,1 *Idem.*
294 J. GONZÁLEZ PÉREZ, *Derecho procesal constitucional*, Madrid 1980, p. 101.
295 *Idem*, p. 197.

4. Incidental method of judicial review of legislation

The second method of judicial review in the Spanish system is the incidental one, established in article 163 of the Constitution as follows:

> «When a judicial organ considers in a process, that a norm with rank of law applicable to the case and on whose validity its decision depends, could be contrary to the Constitution, it must refer the question to the Constitutional Tribunal in the manner and with the effects established in the law, which in any case will be of a suspensive character».[296]

The first aspect that must be stressed regarding this incidental means of judicial review is that in the Spanish system, the judges are the only organs authorised to raise the constitutional question, although they can act either *ex-officio* or on the instance of a party.[297] Therefore, the parties can raise the constitutional question, at any stage in the concrete process, but it is the judge who must appreciate it in a non appealable decision,[298] and only when he considers the specific norm contrary to the Constitution, must he refer the question to the Tribunal.

In accordance with the Organic Law that regulates the Tribunal, this constitutional question can be raised by the Judge only once the proceeding in the concrete case has concluded and within the delay to decide the case, that is why the issue does not have suspensive effects, in the sense that the proceeding must continue up to the stage of possibility of the adoption of the final decision.[299]

The referral must express the statute or norm with force of law whose constitutionality is questioned, the constitutional norm that is supposed to be infringed and the judge must specify and justify to what extent the decision in the concrete proceeding depends on the validity of the norm in question, that is to say, he must justify the pre-judiciary character of the constitutionality of the statute or normative act regarding the concrete process.

Anyway, before adopting his own decision on the matter, the judge must hear the Public Prosecutor and the parties regarding the constitutional issue.[300] But once the issue of unconstitutionality has been raised before the Constitutional Tribunal, the parties of the *a quo* proceeding have no right to intervene in the constitutional process, the Constitutional Tribunal only being obliged to notify the question to the representatives of the organs whose acts have been challenged, in order to allow them to argue before the Tribunal on the matter.[301]

Regarding this incidental mean for constitutional review, different regulations that exist in the Spanish system in relation to the German model must be stressed: in the latter, the incidental constitutional question can only be raised by a court before the Constitutional Tribunal when the judge is convinced of the unconstitutionality of the particular statute; whereas in the Spanish system it is

---

296 See also Art. 35,1 Organic Law 2/1979.

297 Art. 35,2 *Idem.*

298 *Idem*

299 See J.M. RODRÍGUEZ OLIVER, «Sobre los efectos no suspensivos de la cuestión de inconstitucionalidad y la Ley Orgánica 2/79 de 3 de Octubre» *Revista española de derecho administrativo*, 25, Madrid 1980, pp. 207-222.

300 Art. 35,2 Organic Law 2/1979.

301 Art. 37,2 *Idem.*

sufficient for the judge to consider that the applicable norm «could be contrary to the Constitution» though, more similar to the Italian system in which the judge must raise the constitutional question only when he considers that it is not evidently unfounded.[302]

5. Indirect means of judicial review of legislation

Apart from the direct and incidental methods of judicial review, in the Spanish system a third method for seeking before the Constitutional Tribunal judicial review of legislation in an indirect way can be distinguished, when the constitutional question is raised in other constitutional processes developed before the Tribunal, whose objectives are not the direct review of legislation. This can happen in cases of conflicts of attributions between constitutional organs and in cases of recourses for constitutional protection (*amparo*) of fundamental rights.

The first case refers to constitutional conflicts regarding competences or attributions directly assigned by the Constitution, the statutes of autonomy and the Organic or ordinary Laws, intended to delimit the ambit of their competences. These conflicts may oppose the state and the autonomous communities, two or more of which, and the Government with the Congress of Deputies and the Senate or the General Council of the Judicial Power.[303] In such cases, the Constitutional Tribunal has admitted for instance, that if the conflict arises from an executive regulation which is additionally considered to be based on an unconstitutional statute, in those cases the constitutionality of the latter must be reviewed by the Tribunal.[304]

Anyway, the Constitution establishes that if the controverted attribution would have been assigned by a statute or a norm with rank of law, the conflict of competence must be carried out from the beginning or from when the issue of unconstitutionality is raised, in the same procedural manner established for the recourse of unconstitutionality.[305]

The other indirect means of judicial review of legislation can be found as a consequence of the exercise of a recourse for the protection (*recurso de amparo*) of fundamental rights that can be brought before the Tribunal by any person with direct interest in the matter, against state acts of a non legislative character.[306] However, if the recourse for protection is based on the fact that the challenged state act is based on a statute that at the same time infringes fundamental rights or freedoms, the Tribunal must proceed to review its constitutionality through the procedural rules established for the direct action or recourse of unconstitutionality.[307]

Regarding this indirect method of judicial review of legislation, the Constitutional Tribunal has considered that the interpretation of the Organic Law concerning its functioning, particularly its article 52,2,

> «Compels one to understand that the unconstitutionality of a statute that violates fundamental rights and liberties could be alleged by the claimant,

---

302 *Cf.* S. GALEOTTI and B. ROSSI, *loc. cit.*, p. 134.
303 Art. 59 Organic Law 2/1979.
304 Decision N° 39/1982. Quoted in J. SALAS, *loc. cit.*, p. 148, note 23.
305 Art. 67 Organic Law 2/1979.
306 Art. 161,1,b) Constitution; Art. 41,2 Organic Law 2/1979.
307 Art. 52,2 Organic Law 2/1979.

from which it can be deduced that a direct claim of unconstitutionality by individuals is admissible, although limited to the laws which violate or prejudice the rights and liberties established in the Constitution and to cases in which the claimant has suffered a concrete and actual injury in his own rights and always that constitutional protection is irrescindable from the unconstitutionality of the statute.[308]

6. Preventive judicial review system of legislation

Apart from the systems of direct and incidental control of the constitutionality of legislation, and from the indirect means of judicial review, which can be referred to laws and other acts with force of law, including, international treaties, Organic Laws and Statutes of Autonomies of the Autonomous Communities, these state acts can also be the object of a preventive system of judicial review, which can be considered, in the Spanish system, as being an important innovation compared the German and Italian models, and more along the lines of the French system.[309]

In particular, the Spanish Constitution expressly establishes that the signing of international treaties, which contain dispositions contrary to the Constitution, imposes a previous constitutional review. Therefore, the Government, or either of the Chambers of Parliament, can request the Constitutional Tribunal to decide whether a contradiction between an International Treaty to be signed and the Constitution[310] exists or not. In this case, it is evident that the constitutional review system adopted is a preventive one and regarding international treaties, it coexists with the direct, incidental and indirect means for judicial review of constitutionality that can also be exercised regarding them. All these means of review can be used not only indifferently, but also even successively.[311] Anyway, when the preventive mean of control is requested, the Court must hear the representative of the state organs concerned.[312]

However, although the preventive system of control is only established in the Constitution regarding international treaties, due to the fact that it authorises the legislator to assign any other competences to the Constitutional Tribunal,[313] the Organic Law 2/1979 has extended preventive control of constitutionality to the statutes of autonomy and to organic laws, regarding that it is possible to exercise «a recourse of unconstitutionality, with previous character», by the same political organs that can exercise the direct recourse of constitutionality against them.[314] This preventive mean of control is specifically important regarding the Statutes of Autonomy of the Autonomous Communities which must be approved by referendum.[315] Although a direct recourse could be exercised against them, it is obvious that a preventive control as established in the Organic Law, could avoid political difficulties deriving from the possible annulment of a statute after its approval by referendum.

---

308 Decisions 55/57/1981. Quoted in J. SALAS, *loc. cit.*, p. 148, note 23.
309 E. GARCÍA DE ENTERRÍA, *op. cit.*, p. 156.
310 Art. 95 Constitution.
311 M. ARAGÓN, «El control de constitucionalidad en la Constitución Española de 1978», *Revista de estudios políticos*, 7, Madrid 1979, p. 183.
312 Art. 78,2 Organic Law 2/1979.
313 Art. 161 ,1,d) Constitution.
314 Art. 79 Organic Law.
315 Art. 152,2 Constitution.

It must also be noted that regarding Organic Laws, when it is an Organic Law directed for the approval of an international treaty,[316] its preventive constitutional control produces in addition, another means of controlling the constitutionality of international treaties, this time an indirect-preventive mean of control, due to the close link between the approval law and the treaty.[317]

In such cases of preventive control of constitutionality the effects vary regarding the act subject to control: if it is an international treaty not definitively consented to by the state yet, and the tribunal declares that it contradicts the Constitution, its definitive enactment could only be possible through a reform of the Constitution;[318] regarding statutes of autonomy or organic laws, the declaration of the unconstitutionality of their dispositions has binding effects and, therefore, it implies that the procedure for their definitive adoption cannot continue unless they were suppressed by the respective state organ.[319] Anyway, in this latter case, the decision of the tribunal rejecting or declaring the unconstitutionality of dispositions of a statute of autonomy or of an organic law, does not prejudge the future decision that could be taken if direct recourses of unconstitutionality are exercised against them, after their enactment.[320]

7. Effects of the decision of the Constitutional Tribunal on Judicial Review

Now, regarding the effects of the decisions of the Constitutional Court in matters of judicial review of the constitutionality of legislation, the Spanish constitutional and legal system provides a few dispositions in which the different situations that can result are regulated.

The first aspect resolved in positive law refers to the power of the Constitutional Tribunal as a constitutional judge, and as supreme interpreter of the Constitution, in the sense that a question of unconstitutionality of a statute cannot be raised *ex-officio* by the Tribunal. However, once the issue has been brought before it, the Tribunal has *ex-officio* powers to raise other unconstitutionality questions regarding the particular challenged norm, and can «found the declaration of unconstitutionality in the violation of any other constitutional disposition, being invoked or not in the course of the process».[321] Moreover, it can also extend the declaration of unconstitutionality to other dispositions of the statute, when a partial challenge has been made, in cases of correction or as a consequence of the declaration of the challenged dispositions.[322]

The second aspect established in the Constitution relates to the force attributed to Constitutional Court decisions, as supreme interpreter of the Constitution, in the sense that they «have the value of *res judicata* from the day following its publication», and of course, as in all the European constitutional courts, against such decisions it is not possible to exercise any recourse.[323] Thus the decisions adopted by the Constitutional Court in any proceeding of judicial review, are «obligatory regarding

316 Art. 93 Constitution.
317 P. BON, F. MODERNE and Y. RODRÍGUEZ, *op. cit.*, p. 260.
318 Art. 95,1 Constitution.
319 Art. 79,4,b) Organic Law 2/1979.
320 Art. 79,5 *Idem*.
321 Art. 39,2 Organic Law 2/1979.
322 Art. 39,1 *Idem*.
323 Art. 164,1 Constitution.

all public powers and have general effects from the date of their publication in the Official Journal of the state».[324]

The third aspect expressly regulated in the Constitution and the Organic Law of the Tribunal concerns the effects of the decision regarding to whom they apply, and when they begin, and an important distinction is made between the decision that declares the unconstitutionality of a norm and those decisions that reject the alleged unconstitutionality.

Regarding the decisions that declare the unconstitutionality of a statute or other norms with force of law through any of the means for judicial review, either when the Constitutional Court decides upon a recourse of unconstitutionality, or when it decides upon a question of constitutionality raised incidentally, or when it declares the unconstitutionality of a statute through an indirect way, in all such cases the Constitution establishes its *erga omnes* effects, in the sense that they «have full effects regarding everybody».[325] Additionally, in cases of incidental means of judicial review, the Constitutional Court must immediately inform the respective court that must decide the process, which in its turn must notify the parties to it. In this case, the Organic Law of the Tribunal states that «the judge or court would be subject to the decision from when it learns about it, and the parties from when they are notified».[326]

On the other hand, according to the provisions of the Constitution, the «declaration of unconstitutionality» or «declaration of nullity» of a statute means its annulment, the guarantee of the Constitution being the annullability of the unconstitutional state acts rather than their nullity. Consequently, the statute declared unconstitutional is annulled, having the declaration *ex-nunc, pro futuro* effects.[327] That is why the Constitution expressly establishes that «the decisions already adopted in judicial proceedings will not lose their *res judicata* value»,[328] and the Organic Law of the Tribunal also establishes that:

> «The decisions which declare the unconstitutionality of statutes, dispositions or acts with force of law; will not allow the review of judicial proceedings ended by decisions with *res judicata* force in which the unconstitutional act would have been applied».[329]

However, as is the general trend in the concentrated system of judicial review in Europe, the exception to the *ex-nunc* effects is established regarding criminal cases, in which a limited retroactive effect is permitted, extended to administrative justice decisions in cases of administrative sanction cases. Article 40, 2 of the Organic Law of the Tribunal in this respect establishes the possibility of reviewal of judicial processes, in cases of:

> «Criminal or administrative justice processes concerning sanctioning proceedings in which, as a consequence of the nullity of the applied norm, a reduction of the penalty or sanction results, or an exclusion, exemption or limitation of liability also results».

---

324 Art. 38,1; and Art. 87,1 Organic Law 2/1979.

325 Art. 164,1 Constitution; 38,1 Organic Law 2/1979.

326 Art. 38,3 Organic Law 2/1979.

327 *Cf.* J. AROSEMENA SIERRA, «El recurso de inconstitucionalidad», in *El Tribunal Constitucional*, Instituto de Estudios Fiscales, Madrid 1981, Vol. I, p. 171.

328 Art. 161,1,a) Constitution.

329 Art. 40,1 Organic Law 2/1979.

Constitutional review of legislation by the Constitutional Tribunal, apart from the direct recourse or the incidental means, can also be exercised as a consequence of an indirect question that can be raised in a proceeding of a recourse for protection (*amparo*) of fundamental rights, or in cases of conflict of attributions between constitutional organs or between the state and the Autonomous Communities. In the first case, the declaration of unconstitutionality of a statute considered unconstitutional applied in a particular act that affects the fundamental rights of an individual is possible, and its effects are the same as already mentioned.[330] In cases of conflict of attributions, the Organic Law of the Tribunal authorises it to annul the acts that originate the conflicts or were adopted invading competences of other organs, and to decide what might be necessary regarding the situations created based on the annulled act as produced by it.[331]

On the other hand, the Organic Law of the Constitutional Tribunal expressly regulates the effects of the decisions in cases of rejection of the question raised before it as well, and two solutions have been given depending on the nature of the rejection. In effect, if it is a rejection based on the constitutional question in its substantive aspect, in the sense that the Tribunal considers the unconstitutional allegations are invalid, the rejection decision will prevent any other future allegation of the constitutional question «through the same means», founded in the violation of the same constitutional norm.[332] Thus, if the constitutional question was raised through a recourse or direct action of unconstitutionality, the rejection of the action does not prevent the possibility of the question being raised through an incidental means of review.

But also, in cases of recourses of unconstitutionality against statutes, dispositions or acts with force of law, if the rejection was based on formal reasons, the decision will not prevent the same statute, disposition or act being the object of a constitutional question raised when applied in other processes,[333] and of course of another recourse in which the formal questions would have been corrected.

VI. CONSTITUTIONAL JUSTICE IN THE SOCIALIST EUROPEAN COUNTRIES

The European model of judicial review, based on the attribution of the powers to control the constitutionality of statutes and other legislative acts to one constitutional organ of the state has, additional to the experiences of Western Europe, also been followed in some socialist countries, in a way that can be considered dissident insofar as the traditional socialist concept of the organisation of the state is concerned.

In effect, one of the basic principles of the constitutional systems of the socialist countries mainly derived from the influence of Soviet constitutionalism is the principle of the unity of state powers based on the assignment of all legislative and executive powers of state to its representative democratic body. Thus, this representative political organ of the state is conceived as the supreme organ of state power, and as the only one able to create the law and control the activities of all

330 Art. 55,2 *Idem*.
331 Arts 66; 75,1 *Idem*.
332 Art. 38,2 *Idem*.
333 Art. 29,2 *Idem*.

other state organs.[334] This concept, of course, implies the rejection of any form of separation of state powers,[335] at least theoretically, and in a certain way, regarding the legislative body, of the difference between the constituent and the constituted bodies of the state. The Constitutions of the socialist countries in general have a pre-eminent character over the whole legal order[336] but at the same time, the organ that can control the submission to the constitutional rule is the supreme organ of the state, which is the one that can also modify the Constitution. Consequently, an essential incompatibility exists between the principle of the unity of state power and the supremacy and sovereignty of parliament which represents the popular will, with any sort of judicial control of the constitutionality of statutes adopted by parliament, exercised by an extra parliamentary organ.[337]

Nevertheless, three socialist countries, Yugoslavia, Czechoslovakia and Poland have developed advanced systems of constitutional justice. That must be seen as a sign of departure from the principle of the unity of state power even though it is commonly rejected by socialist authors, who see those experiences more as a departure from the Soviet interpretation of the principle, than from the principle itself. For instance, referring to the Yugoslav theory and system, Vladimir Krivic, a former President of the Constitutional Court of the Socialist Republic of Slovenia, said that it:

> «Represents no departure from the principle of the unity of powers, but a departure from the rigid, formalistic, strictly dogmatic, bureaucratic Stalinist conception of the unity of authority with its wrong ideas about the function of legality and the status of the judicature under the socialist order».[338]

Nevertheless, being considered a departure or not from the principle of the unity of power, the adoption of concentrated systems of judicial review in some socialist countries is generally based on a principle of vertical distribution of state powers, normally with a federal form which, as V. Krivic said, «calls, *ipso facto*, for an agency whose independent and authoritative status the republics and the Federal authority»;[339] and it is also based on the limitations imposed upon the politic representative organ of the state in the Constitution, regarding other state bodies. Additionally, the declaration of fundamental and self-government rights, has justified the establishment of an extra parliamentary and independent state organ for controlling the constitutionality of statutes and other normative acts of the state organs.[340]

---

334 S. ROZMARYN, «La Constitution, loi fondamental de l'État socialist» in P. BISCARETTI DI RUFFIA and S. ROZMARYN, *La Constitution comme loi fondamentale dans les Etats de l'Europe occidentale et dans les Etats socialistes*, Turín 1966, p. 108.

335 P. NIKOLIC, *Le contrôle juridictionnel des lois et sa legalité. Développements récents dans les pays socialistes*, IALS, Uppsala, Colloquium, 1984, mimeo) p. 15. Also published in L. FAVOREU and J.A. JOLOWICZ ed.) *Le contôle juridictionnel des lois. Légitimité, effectivité et développements récents*, Paris 1986, pp. 71-115. P. KASTARI, «Le caracter normatif et la préeminence hierarchique des Constitutions», *Revue International de Droit Comparé;* Paris 1966, p. 843.

336 S. ROZMARYN, *loc. cit.*, p. 99; P. NIKOLIC, *op. cit.*, p. 7; P. KASTARI, *loc. cit.*, p. 841.

337 H. ROUSSILLON, «Le problème du contrôle de la constitutionnalité des lois dans les pays socialistes», *Revue du droit public et de la science politique en France et à l'étranger*, 1977, p. 76; S. ROZMARYN, *loc. cit.*, p. 108. *Cf.* P. NIKOLIC, *op. cit.*, p. 17.

338 *V.* KRIVIC, «Foreword», in B.T. BLAGOJEVIC ed.), *Constitutional judicature*, Beograd 1965, p. 6.

339 *V.* KRIVIC, *loc. cit.*, p. 4.

340 P. NIKOLIC, *op. cit.*, p. 21.

The first socialist country to establish a Constitutional Court was Yugoslavia in 1963, and, more recently, Czechoslovakia followed the example in 1968. In Poland, the 1982 Constitution has established a limited jurisdictional control of constitutionality of statutes. It means that the created Constitutional Court does not decide definitively upon their unconstitutionality but must only refer its appreciation to the decision of the legislative organ in its character as the supreme organ of power.[341] Thus, only in the Yugoslav and Czech systems, is it possible to distinguish a jurisdictional organ with powers to annul legislative acts.

1. Judicial Review in Yugoslavia: the Constitutional Court

The Constitution of Yugoslavia and the Constitutions of its Federated Socialist Republics, promulgated in April 1963 and reformed in 1975, in effect, established what can be considered an advanced concentrated system of judicial review. The main idea is «to prevent violations of the system laid down by the Constitution and usurpation of rights to the prejudice of citizens or self-governing bodies, as well as to enforce respect for law and the Constitution by all, the highest social organisms and state officials included».[342] The system brought about the establishment of a Constitutional Court of Yugoslavia, regulated by a special statute promulgated the same year 1963, as well as the establishment of Constitutional Courts in the six Republics of the Federation.[343]

A. *Jurisdiction of the Constitutional Court*

The Constitutional Court is conceived as an «independent Federal organ» whose main function is to «ensure protection of constitutionality and legality on the basis of the Constitution acting within its rights and duties as laid down by the Constitution»,[344] which it accomplishes through three basic sets of attributions concerning the settling of disputes between the socio-political communities, the protection of fundamental rights and liberties, and judicial review of constitutionality.

The first set of attributions confers the Constitutional Court powers to «settle disputes involving rights and duties between the federal authority and a Republic, between the Republics, and between other socio political communities from the territory of different Republics».[345] This power of the Court is, undoubtedly, one direct consequence of the establishment in the Federative Socialist Republic of Yugoslavia, of a series of autonomous solutions to its fundamental political, economic and social aims, which separate it from the Soviet model. In accordance to which V. Krivic said, «the autonomy of numerous organisms, including in the first place the self-governing working organisations and communes, and their extensive powers in the making of bye-laws made it imperative to set up a social agency which would ban bureaucratic interference with the competencies of the «inferior» self-governing bodies on the part of the superior ones, and

---

341 P. NIKOLIC, *op. cit.*, p. 52.

342 *V.* KRIVIC, *loc. cit.*, p. 5.

343 Law of the Constitutional Court of Yugoslavia CCY), 31 December 1963. See the text in B.T. Blagojevic (ed.), *op, cit.*, pp. 15-36; *V.* KRIVIC, *loc. cit.*, p. 3.

344 Art. 1, Law CCY, 1963. The Court is also authorized to «independently adopt its Rules of Procedures and other general acts affecting its organization and operation». Art. 16 Law CCY.

345 Art. 43, Law CCY, 1963.

which would perform the same function «horizontally» between the various self-governing organisations and bodies».[346]

When resolving these conflicts or disputes of competencies, the Court has the power to fix a particular obligation for a socio-political community and to order the elimination of the consequences brought about by the act or action which caused the violation or interference of attributions.[347]

It must also be said that besides conflicts between socio-political organs of the state, the Constitutional Court has also competence to settle all «conflicts of jurisdiction that may arise between courts of law and federal authorities, and also between courts of law and other state authorities from the territory of different Republics».[348]

The second set of attributions of the Constitutional Court relates to the protection of self governing rights and other fundamental rights and liberties granted by the Constitution, in cases where said rights and liberties are violated by a particular act or action on the part of federal or central authorities whose activities in the exercise of public powers extend to the whole territory of Yugoslavia.[349] This power of the Court is exercised when a proposal for protection is presented only when the ordinary recourse for the protection of such rights and liberties have already been exhausted,[350] and is presented «by any one who had his right of self-government or other fundamental rights or liberties as granted by the Constitution, violated», as well as by a socio-political organisation on behalf of their members.[351]

This «proposal for protection», as we said, can only be presented before the Constitutional Court against a «particular act or action of an authority or organisation».[352] Thus it is not possible against normative acts; and the ruling of the Court must consist, subject to the circumstances of the case, of the abolition of the act and of the elimination of the consequences brought about by such an act.[353]

Finally, the third set of attributions relates to the area of judicial review, the Constitutional Court is empowered to review «the constitutionality and legality of prescriptions and other general acts» with binding authority,[354] and this attribution is conceived, basically, as a power of the Court that can be exercised *ex-officio*, or when hearing a request for constitutional review presented by state organs or by individuals. This power of judicial review exercised by the Constitutional Court, allows it to make rulings concerning the compatibility of laws with the Constitution; the compatibility of a republican law with federal law; and the compatibility of other dispositions and general acts made by authorities and organisations with the Constitution, with Federal Law and with other Federal dispositions.[355]

---

346 *V.* KRIVIC, *loc. cit.*, p. 4.
347 Art. 44, Law CCY, 1963.
348 Art. 46, *Idem.*
349 Art. 36,1 *Idem.*
350 Art. 36,3 *Idem.*
351 Art. 37 *Idem.*
352 Arts 36, 39 *Idem.*
353 Art. 39 *Idem.*
354 Art. 2 *Idem.*
355 Art. 17 *Idem.*

B. *Ex-Officio Powers of the Constitutional Court*

The Constitutional Court is empowered by the law that regulates its functioning to «initiate the procedure for judging the constitutionality and legality of a disposition or other general acts on its own initiative», in which case any member of the Court may request such a procedure to be initiated and a decision to be taken thereupon.[356]

The Court can also on its own initiative give its opinion concerning «the compatibility of the Constitution of a republic with the Constitution of Yugoslavia» to the Federal Assembly,[357] and it is also authorised to «offer opinions and proposals to the Federal Assembly for the enactment and amendment of laws, for the provision of authentic interpretation and for taking measures to ensure constitutionality and legality and protect the self-governing rights and the other rights and liberties of citizens and organisations»[358]

These *ex-officio* powers of the Yugoslav Constitutional Court to initiate, in a general way, judicial review of legislation, and to give its opinion on constitutional matters without formal request to the Federal Assembly are, perhaps, the most distinguishable features of the Yugoslav system, which are not to be found in any other legal system.

C. *Request for Judicial Review and Popular Action*

The Constitutional Court of Yugoslavia can also exercise the powers of judicial review, when a request is presented before the Court by some state organs, or by any person through a popular action. In the first case, when the request is presented by «authorities of organisations specified under the Constitution» or by an assembly of a commune, a district or an autonomous province, or by Federal Secretaries or Republican Secretaries, or by authorities of a socio-political community,[359] the Court is obliged to initiate the procedure «for considering the constitutionality» of legislation.[360] In the second case, when a popular action is exercised by individuals, the Court shall itself decide whether to initiate the procedure or not. [361]

It is important to notice that this popular action established in the Yugoslavian system which authorises «anyone» to request the Constitutional Court to initiate a procedure for judicial review of legislation[362] is also exceptional in European countries, even though in such cases the Court is not obliged to initiate it, which confirms its own powers on the matter. Moreover, in cases of judicial review proceedings, when a request has been made, it must also be mentioned that the Constitutional Court is not bound by the points raised in the proposal concerned but may also examine the constitutionality of other dispositions or acts not challenged by the proponent as unconstitutional.[363]

---

[356] Art. 4 *Idem.*
[357] Art. 18 *Idem.*
[358] Art. 3 *Idem.*
[359] Art. 19 *Idem.*
[360] Arts 4, 19 *Idem.*
[361] Art. 4 *Idem.*
[362] Art. 4 *Idem.*
[363] Art. 23 *Idem.*

D. *Decision of the Constitutional Court on Judicial Review*

Finally, concerning the decisions of the Constitutional Court on judicial review of constitutionality of statutes, it must be noticed that contrary to the situation in other European countries, the decision of the Yugoslavian Court upon the unconstitutionality of a norm does not cause the immediate annulment of the normative act, and in fact, three different stages can be distinguished in the proceeding.

First of all, prior to making a decision, the Constitutional Court, having regard to the circumstances brought out within the preliminary procedure, may give an opportunity to the representative body or other authority or organisation concerned to eliminate the incompatibility of a disposition or other general act with the Constitution and/or Federal Law.[364] In this way, the Court avoids declaring an act unconstitutional, allowing the state organ to make the necessary corrections to it. In this stage and concerning the challenge of republican law when incompatible with the Constitution or with federal law or in cases of incompatibility between republican law with federal laws which the Court finds contrary to the Constitution, the Court can rule that the dispositions of the republican law or of the federal law are not to be applicable pending the issue of its final decision.[365]

Secondly, in cases of incompatibility between federal law and the Constitution, or between republican law and the Constitution or federal law, the Constitutional Court does not annul the act immediately. However, it must announce its ruling to the parties concerned and notify the Federal or the republican Assemblies concerned, allowing them to bring the challenged act into conformity with the Constitution or the Federal Law.

In the third place, the Law of the Court establishes that if the public authority does not correct the unconstitutional act within six months from the date when the Constitutional Court announced its decision, then «the Court shall issue a ruling establishing that the law involved has ceased to have effect»,[366] or in cases of incompatibility between the republican law and the Constitution or with federal law, the Court may «abolish such republican law if it involves a manifest violation of the prerogative of the federal authorities».[367] These decisions, of course, have binding authority [368] and have *erga omnes* effects.

Even though the Law of the Court uses two expressions for the qualification of its decisions, upon unconstitutionality of normative acts, abrogation or abolishment of the unconstitutional challenged act, particularly when referring to statutes at federal or republican level or in relation to other normative acts different to statutes,[369] in both cases, the general effect of the decision in time is equivalent to the annulment of the act, thus, *ex-nunc, pro futuro*. Therefore, the annulled act «shall not be applicable as from the date of publication of the Courts' ruling in the official gazette of the Federation»,[370] and neither the dispositions or other general acts

---

364 Art. 24 *Idem.*
365 Art. 25 *Idem.*
366 Art. 25 *Idem.*
367 Art. 25 *Idem.*
368 Arts 2,2; 72 *Idem.*
369 Art. 26 *Idem.*
370 Art. 29 *Idem.*

serving for the enforcement of the unconstitutional statute; shall be applicable if the ruling of the Court implies that such acts are contrary to the Constitution.[371] Additionally, regarding the future, the Court can give its opinion as to which legal rules are to be applicable pending the issue of a new statute conforming to the Constitution to replace the one invalidated. [372]

Now, regarding the particular relations originated by the statute declared unconstitutional, even when they have begun before the date of publication of the Court's decision, the unconstitutional act shall not be applicable to them if a valid settlement of the relations is still pending on that date.[373]

Regarding final and valid acts issued in particular cases in application of the unconstitutional law, the law of the tribunal establishes a general difference according to the abrogation or the abolition of the unconstitutional act. When the normative act has been abolished the law of the tribunal in a general exception to the *ex-nunc* effects, it assigns to anyone who may have had a right of his violated by a valid particular act issued in application of the unconstitutional normative act to seek review of such act by the Court of Law or other authority that issued it; and they must do so within a delay of six months after the publication of the Court decision.[374]

Additionally, the Court can also rule that a court of law or other competent authority concerned is to be bound to review all acts or certain categories of particular acts produced based on the unconstitutional statute on the demand of citizens or organisations whose rights were violated. [375]

In relation to all other Court decisions on constitutional review matters, the Law of the Court establishes a few exceptions to the *ex-nunc* effects, and allows for the retroactive applicability of the annulment, particularly in criminal cases and violations of self-governing rights.[376] In particular, in criminal cases, the Law of the Constitutional Court gives the right to whoever had criminal sanctions imposed upon him, to seek the review of such act by the Court of Law or other competent authority that imposed the sanction.[377]

Finally, it must be stressed that the powers of the Constitutional Court are also very significant in the interpretation of the Constitution in cases in which the Court does not find a law or other normative act incompatible with the Constitution but considers that in practical application such a law has been constructed in a manner contrary to the Constitution. In such cases, the Court may lay down, through a decision, the significance thereof corresponding to the Constitution to be observed when enforcing such law or other normative act.[378]

2. Control of Constitutionality in Czechoslovakia: the Federal Constitutional Court

As we have said, Czechoslovakia was the first European country to have a concentrated judicial review system established in its Constitution of 1920, which

---

371 Art. 30 *Idem.*
372 Art. 34 *Idem.*
373 Art. 29 *Idem.*
374 Art. 32 *Idem.*
375 Art. 31,4 *Idem.*
376 Art. 31,1,2 *Idem.*
377 Art. 31,1 *Idem.*
378 Art. 28 *Idem.*

created a Constitutional Court that existed until 1938.[379] After the Second World War, the Constitution of 1948 followed the Soviet model, thus without any form of judicial review of constitutionality, and it has been in the Constitution of 27 October 1968 in which not only a definitive federal form of state was adopted, but also a concentrated system of judicial review was established, following the Yugoslav model.[380] Thus, there is a Federal Constitutional Court and two Constitutional Courts in each of the Republics of the Czech federation.

Judicial review power of the Federal Constitutional Court relates to all laws enacted by the Federal Assembly and by the Czech National Councils, as well as to all the general provisions of the administrative bodies, both, of the Federation and of the Federated Republics.[381]

As happens with decisions of unconstitutionality adopted by the Yugoslav Constitutional Federal Court, the decisions of the Czech Court do not imply the immediate cessation of the effects of the challenged act, but rather, imply only the obligation, following the publication of the decision, for the bodies that passed the provisions contrary to the Fundamental Charter, or as the case may be, contrary to the Federal Law, to redraft them and make them consistent with the Constitution. They have six months to carry out this task. The challenged dispositions only cease to be effective when this time period has elapsed.[382]

The Czech Federal Constitutional Court is also empowered to settle disputes of competences between the bodies of the Federal Republic and those of one or other of the two Federated Republics, or between the internal organs of the latter.[383]

Lastly, among the most important attributions of the Constitutional Federal Court of Czechoslovakia is that of the protection of the rights and freedoms established in the Constitution against their violation by provisions or acts of the Federal Authorities, when the ordinary law does not establish any other jurisdictional safeguards.[384]

VII. CONCENTRATED SYSTEMS OF JUDICIAL REVIEW IN LATIN AMERICA

Judicial review has a long tradition in Latin America, and over the course of more than a century it has been adopted in one way or another in all Latin American countries. As we have seen, some have adopted the diffuse system of judicial review, as is the case in Argentina and Mexico. In most countries, a mixed system is followed, in which the diffuse system functions in parallel with the concentrated system of judicial review assigned to the Supreme Court or to a specially created Constitutional Court.

Nevertheless, examples can also be found of a pure concentrated system in which the powers of judicial review of constitutionality of legislation have been exclusively attributed to the Supreme Court of Justice of the country or to a specially created Constitutional Court, or in some cases, to both in parallel. This are the

---

379 *Cf.* P. CRUZ VILLALON, «Dos modos de regulación del control de constitucionalidad: Checoslovaquia 1920-1938) y España 1931-1936), *Revista española de derecho constitucional*, 5, 1982, p. 115.

380 *Cf.* H. FIX-ZAMUDIO, *Los tribunales constitucionales y los derechos humanos*, México 1980, p. 129; P. NIKOLIC, *op. cit.*, p. 46.

381 Art. 86, 1; Art. 87 Constitutional Law. See in P. NIKOLIC, *op. cit.*, p. 48.

382 Art. 93, 90 Constitutional Law. See in P. NIKOLIC, *op. cit.*, p. 49.

383 Art. 92 Constitutional Law. See in H. FIX-ZAMUDIO, *op. cit.*, p. 131.

384 Art. 92 Constitutional Law. See in H. FIX-ZAMUDIO, *op. cit.*, p. 132.

systems we will now refer to, leaving for the last part of this book the study of the concentrated systems of judicial review exercised by a supreme court or a constitutional court mixed with the diffuse system of judicial review.

1. Supreme Court of Justice as a Concentrated Organ for Judicial Review: Panama, Uruguay, and Paraguay

As we said, some Latin American countries have established a concentrated system of judicial review by assigning the exclusive power to control the constitutionality of legislation to their Supreme Court of Justice, as the judicial organ situated at the apex of the judiciary. As an example of this modality, the constitutional systems of Panama, Uruguay and Paraguay can be mentioned.

In this respect the Constitution of Panama established the exclusive power of the Supreme Court of Justice to «guard the integrity of the Constitution,[385] and to control the constitutionality of legislation, through two means: a direct action or an incidental referral sent by a lower court.

The direct action is conceived as a popular action that could be brought before the Supreme Court by «any person», denouncing the unconstitutionality of laws, decrees, decisions, or acts whether on a substantive or formal basis. In this case, the decision must be adopted by the Court after hearing the Solicitor General of the Nation.[386]

But the Constitution also establishes that when in an ordinary judicial process, the judge, *ex-officio* or at the request of any of the parties, notices that the legal or executive normative act applicable to the case is unconstitutional, he must submit the question of unconstitutionality to the Supreme Court, while being allowed to continue the proceeding of the case until the decision stage.[387]

In both cases, the decision of the Supreme Court is obligatory,[388] and non-revisable.[389]

In the Uruguayan system, the Constitution [390] attributes exclusive and original jurisdiction to declare the unconstitutionality of statutes and other state acts with force of law to the Supreme Court of Justice, whether based on substantive or formal reasons.[391] In accordance with the Constitution, the declaration of unconstitutionality of a statute and the inapplicability of the disposition encumbered by it, could be requested from the Supreme Court by all who deem their direct, personal and legitimate interests have been injured.[392] Thus a requirement of standing, very similar to the one established regarding judicial review of administrative action, is established.

---

385 Article 188, 1. Constitution.

386 Article 188, 1.

387 Article 188, 2.

388 Art. 188, *in fine.*

389 Art. 189.

390 The system was originaly established in 1934 and 1951.See H. GROSS ESPIELL, *La Constitución y su Defensa, Uruguay,* Congreso La Constitución y su defensa, UNAM, 1982 (mimeo), p. 7, 11. The system was maintained in the 1966 Constitution, in the Institutional Act Nº 8 of 1977 and in the Institutional Act Nº 12 of 1981. *Idem,* pp. 16-20.

391 Art. 256.

392 Art. 258. *Cf.* H. GROSS ESPIELL, *op. cit.*, pp. 27, 28; J.P. GATTO DE SOUZA, «Control de la constitucionalidad de los actos del poder público en Uruguay», *Memoria de la Reunión de Presidentes de Cortes Supremas de Justicia de Iberoamérica, El Caribe, España y Portugal,* Caracas 1982, pp. 661-662.

The competence of the Supreme Court on judicial review, can be sought through two means: first, through a direct action, when there is no judicial proceeding pending of decision; second, through an incidental means, through a referral made before the Supreme Court by any court.

This second mean can be exercised *ex-officio* by the lower court, or as a consequence of an exception raised by any party.[393] In this case, the judge must refer a briefing of the question to the Supreme Court and should continue with the proceeding up to the stage of deciding upon the case. After the Supreme Court has adopted its decision, the court must make its own decision in the case in conformity with the latter.[394]

In both cases, in the Uruguayan system, the effects of the Supreme Court decisions are exclusively referred to the concrete case, having effects only regarding the proceedings in which they were adopted.[395] Of course this disposition is clear regarding the incidental means of judicial review but, not in cases in which the constitutional question has been raised through a direct action. In such cases Statute N° 13747 of 1969[396] concerning the constitutional justice process establishes that the decision has efficacy to prevent the applicability of the norms declared unconstitutional regarding who has exercised the action and obtained the decision, being allowed to use it as an exception in any judicial proceeding, including the judicial review of administrative action.[397]

Following the Uruguayan model, we must also mention the system of Paraguay in which the Constitution empowers the Supreme Court to decide upon actions and exceptions in order to declare the unconstitutionality and inapplicability of dispositions contrary to the Constitution».[398] As we said, the proceeding can be initiated through an action or an exception, and in the latter case, the proceeding in the concrete case must continue until the decision stage. In any case, the decision of the Supreme Court only has effects regarding the concrete case or the petitioner.[399]

2. Parallel Concentrated System of Judicial Review Attributed to a Supreme Court and the Constitutional Tribunal: Chile and Ecuador

Among the Latin American Countries, we must refer to the cases of Chile and Ecuador, whose constitutional systems have established a concentrated system of judicial review, but attributing it to two separate constitutional organs: the Supreme Court of Justice, through incidental means, and a Constitutional Tribunal, through direct means.

A. *The Chilean Experience*

(a) Supreme Court of Justice and the Incidental Method of Judicial Review

Since the 1925 constitutional reform in Chile, the second paragraph of article 86 authorises the Supreme Court of Justice to declare the inapplicability of a law in

393 Art. 258.
394 Arts 258, 259.
395 Art. 259.
396 See in H. GROSS ESPIELL, *op. cit.*, p. 29.
397 *Idem.*
398 Arts 200, 207.
399 L.M. ARGAÑA, «Control de la constitucionalidad de las leyes en Paraguay», en *Memoria de la Reunión de Presidentes de Cortes Supremas de Justicia de Iberoamérica, El Caribe, España y Portugal*, Caracas 1983, pp. 550-551; 669-671.

force, on the grounds of unconstitutionality. This reform substantially modified the previously existing situation, in which the unanimous opinion was that the Courts could not declare the inapplicability of an unconstitutional law, since there was no constitutional provision granting them that power. Consequently, the 1925 reform represented an important step towards the control of the constitutionality of law.[400]

This norm of the Constitution still in force states as follows:

> «The Supreme Court, in the concrete cases which it is conducting or in cases which were raised before it through recourses originated in proceedings developed before other courts, can declare any legal disposition contrary to the Constitution inapplicable to that case. This recourse can be exercised in any stage of the proceeding, without its suspension».

Consequently, the Constitution establishes a concentrated system of judicial review of incidental character before the Supreme Court of Justice, through the institution called the «recourse of inapplicability of statutes».[401]

However, this system of judicial review did not, of course, resolve constitutional conflicts between state organs, many of which were originated in questions of unconstitutionality of statutes and other norms of equal force. The continuous conflict between those organs which was one particularity of political life in Chile, was one of the main factors that contributed to the establishment of a constitutional organ, other than the Supreme Court, to settle that type of conflict.[402] Thus, the constitutional reform of 21 January 1970 created a Constitutional Tribunal with a variety of functions of judicial review and relating to the settlement of conflicts of attributions between the state organs. The Tribunal was dissolved in 1973 as a result of a military coup that dissolved the Congress. Since the main function of the Constitutional Court was to settle conflicts between the executive and the legislature, and since the latter could not appear before the Court, due to the fact that the National Congress had been dissolved, the existence of the Court was no longer justified. Thus, the Court ceased to function.[403] The Constitutional court was later re-established by articles 81 and 83 of the political Constitution approved by referendum on 11 September 1980, and drawn up by the Military Junta, in the exercise of its constituent power. The Court was assigned attributions similar to those established by the Fundamental Charter of 1970, and its functioning is regulated in the Organic Constitutional Law of 12 May 1981 passed by the Government Junta.[404]

(b) The Constitutional Tribunal and its Powers

In accordance with these recent regulations, the attributions of the tribunal are the following:[405]

In the first place, it is competent to judge upon the constitutionality of organic laws, prior to their promulgation, or of those, which interpret a particular precept of the Fundamental Charter.

---

400 *Cf.* O. TOVAR TAMAYO, *La jurisdicción constitucional*, Caracas 1983, p. 103.

401 See the text in H. FIX-ZAMUDIO, *Los tribunales constitucionales y los derechos humanos*, México 1980, p. 143, note 251.

402 E. SILVA CIMMA, *El Tribunal Constitucional de Chile (1917-1973)*, Caracas 1977, p. 12-20.

403 E. SILVA CIMMA, *op. cit.*, p. 219; H. FIX-ZAMUDIO, *op. cit.*, p. 150.

404 H. FIX-ZAMUDIO, «Dos leyes orgánicas de tribunales constitucionales latinoamericanos: Chile y Perú», *Boletín mexicano de derecho comparado*, 51, 1984, p. 943.

405 Art. 82, Constitution 1980.

It is also authorised by means of a request to exercise preventive control over any issues, which may arise during the processing of ordinary project of law, or constitutional amendments, as well as international treaties submitted for the approval of Congress.

It is also competent to resolve issues of constitutionality concerning executive decrees with force of law; claims against the President of the Republic when he fails to promulgate a law, when he should have done so, or when he promulgates a different text, or issues unconstitutional decrees or regulates subjects reserved to formal law.

The Court also decides upon conflicts arising regarding decrees or resolutions issued by the President of the Republic, when the Office of the General Comptroller, on the grounds of unconstitutionality, has denied the registration of which.

In the second place, the Court is authorised to settle other issues, other than the control of constitutionality, particularly the constitutionality of the calling of plebiscites, as well as questions relating to an individual's constitutional or legal eligibility for appointment to the office of Minister of state.

These powers of the Constitutional Court were originally established in 1970, and the 1980 Constitution additionally grants it attributions not included in the 1970 Constitution, particularly the competence to judge the unconstitutionality of organisations and political parties or movements, as well as the responsibility of persons who transgress, or have transgressed the constitutional order of the Republic,[406] more in consonance with the military regime.

Now, in the area of judicial review the Chilean Constitutional Tribunal has been empowered to review the constitutionality of legislation through two specific ways: a preventive control and a limited *a posteriori* control.

(c) Preventive Control of Constitutionality of Legislation

In the first place, the Constitution establishes the power of the Tribunal to resolve constitutional questions that could arise during discussions of Organic Constitutional Laws, of statutes intended to interpret a constitutional disposition of any bill or project of constitutional amendment and of international treaties submitted to Congress for approval.[407]

In all such cases, following the French model, the control exercised by the Constitutional Tribunal is a preventive one, and can be obligatory or exercised through a petition. In the case of Organic Constitutional Laws and of statutes that interpret a constitutional disposition, the preventive control of the Tribunal is obligatory, in the sense that the President of the corresponding Chamber of Congress must always send such texts to the Tribunal within five days after being sanctioned. Thus, this preventive control is not only obligatory but is also exercised *ex-officio* by the tribunal, and that is why in this case, the proceeding is not adversary. If in its decision the Tribunal considers one or more of the text dispositions unconstitutional, it must send it back to the corresponding Chamber, where its President in his turn must send it to the President of the Republic for promulgation, but without the dispositions considered unconstitutional

406 H. FIX-ZAMUDIO, «Dos leyes orgánicas...», *loc. cit.*, p. 947.

407 Art. 82 Constitution 1980, Art. 26-37 Organic Law 1981. See the comments in H. FIX-ZAMUDIO, «Dos leyes orgánicas ...», *loc. cit.*, p. 948.

In the case of other bills, projects of constitutional amendments or international treaties, the exercise of the preventive control by the Constitutional Tribunal is only possible when a petition is formulated before the promulgation of the text, and during the discussion of the project, by the President of the Republic or by any of the Congress Chambers or by one fourth of their members. That is why the petition does not have suspensive effects over the legislative procedure and the proceeding before the Tribunal is an adversary one: the Tribunal must notify the interested constitutional organs and hear their arguments. The decision of the Tribunal considering unconstitutional dispositions of a project of a statute or a treaty, prevents its promulgation.[408]

(d) Judicial Review Powers of the Constitutional Tribunal through Direct Means

Additional to the preventive control of legislation, the Constitutional Tribunal has also powers of judicial review of an *a posteriori* character, but only exercised regarding decrees with force of law, that is to say, those issued by the President of the Republic, by virtue of powers delegated by Congress, and also regarding presidential powers when promulgating statutes. Thus, substantive judicial review of constitutionality of legislation by the Constitutional Tribunal does not proceed against statutes once in force, but only against executive decrees with force of law.

In the first case; regarding the unconstitutionality of decree laws, the powers of the Tribunal on matters of unconstitutionality are exercised when a request is brought before it after a decision has been adopted by the General Comptroller's Office regarding the registration or not of the decree. In effect, in Chile, one of the traditional functions of the General Comptroller's Office has been the control of executive decrees, which results in their registration, or rejection of it. As a consequence, controversies traditionally arise as regards the constitutionality or legality of the executive decrees, when the Office of the General Comptroller raises objections concerning there in compatibility with the Constitution.

Prior to the existence of the Court, these controversies were settled by one of the parties, that is to say, by the executive, which could insist on the registration of the decree, which, in the Comptroller's opinion, might be unconstitutional, with the backing of the signatures of all the Ministers.[409]

This situation was changed after the 1970 constitutional reform, according to which if the General Comptroller's Office rejects a decree law, the President of the Republic can no longer insist on it being registered. Instead, within a time limit of 30 days after the rejection, the President can raise the question before the Constitutional Court, which has the last word on the matter of unconstitutionality. Likewise, if, on the contrary, the General Comptroller registers a decree law, either of the Chambers of Congress, or more than one third of their active members, is authorised to raise the issue of unconstitutionality of the decree law before the Tribunal, also within a time limit of 30 days from the publication of the decree.

The procedure in such cases is of an adversary character, and the Tribunal can declare the unconstitutionality of the decree law, with binding effects, in which case it cannot be enforced. But, if the Tribunal declares that the disposition of the decree law is constitutional, the decision has also binding effects and particularly the

408 *Idem*, p. 949.
409 H. FIX-ZAMUDIO, *op. cit.*, p. 148, 149; O. Tovar Tamayo, *op. cit.*, pp. 132-133.

Supreme Court of Justice cannot declare it inapplicable when exercising its concentrated diffuse powers of judicial review.[410]

In the second place, the *a posteriori* judicial review powers of the Constitutional Tribunal can also be exercised regarding statutes but only in relation to the formalities of their promulgation by the President of the Republic. In effect, the Constitution attributes the Tribunal competence to resolve claims that can only be exercised by the Chambers of Congress, in cases in which the President of the Republic does not promulgate a statute when he should, or when he promulgates a text other than the one that proceeds constitutionally.[411] In such cases, the constitutional review control does not in fact refer to the substantive aspects of the statutes, but only to the way the President of the Republic exercises his power when promulgating statutes, the decision of the Tribunal being directed to the correction of the promulgation.

B. Parallel-Concentrated System of Judicial Review in Ecuador and the Tribunal of Constitutional Guarantees

Among the Latin American countries that have adopted a double concentrated system of judicial review attributed to two different constitutional organs, the case of Ecuador must also be mentioned, in which the Supreme Court of Justice has exclusive power to judge the constitutionality of legislation through a diffuse system, and the Tribunal of Constitutional Guarantees is empowered to exercise judicial review of legislation in a concentrated way. Both systems of judicial review are based on the principle of supremacy of the Constitution expressly established as follows:

> «The Constitution is the supreme law of the state. The secondary norms and all others of inferior hierarchy must maintain their conformity with the constitutional dispositions. The laws (statutes), decrees, ordinances, dispositions, international treaties or accords which, in any way, would be in contradiction with the Constitution or alter its disposition, will have no value».[412]

In accordance with this proclaimed constitutional supremacy, the constitution of 1909, reformed in 1983, assigns the power to exercise judicial review power in a diffuse way, to the Chambers of the Supreme Court of Justice, to the Tax Tribunal and to the Administrative Justice Tribunal by, attributing them competences to declare in concrete cases taken over from a lower court, the inapplicability of any legal norm contrary to the Constitution».[413] This decision according to the express provision of the Constitution, «does not have obligatory force but only in the concrete case in which it is pronounced», thus its effects are *inter partes*.

However, the same 1978 Constitution also established an institution called the Tribunal of Constitutional Guarantees, with a wide composition of its members in charge of watching out for the execution of the Constitution, by requesting actions from authorities and public officials.[414] The Tribunal was originally

---

410 H. FIX-ZAMUDIO, «Dos leyes orgánicas «, *loc. cit.*, pp. 949-950; O. TOVAR TAMAYO, *op. cit.*, p. 137.

411 Art. 82. See H. FIX-ZAMUDIO, «Dos leyes orgánicas...», *op. cit.*, p. 949.

412 Art. 137. Constitution of 15 January 1978.

413 Art. 138. Constitution.

414 Art. 141, 1 Constitution. The Tribunal is composed by 3 members elected by the National Chamber of Representatives; the President of the Supreme Court of Justice; the Attorney General; the President of the Supreme Electoral Tribunal; one representative of the President of the Republic; one representative of Workers; one representative of the Association of employers; and two representatives of the people, elected by electoral bodies composed by the Mayors of Cantons and by the rovincial authorities Art. 140. Constitution.

empowered to formulate observations regarding decrees, accords, regulations or resolutions dictated in violation of the Constitution or the Statutes, once hearing the authorities, which dictated them. If its observations were not followed, the Tribunal was authorized to publish them in the press and notify the National Chamber of Representatives, for them to take a resolution.[415]

This Tribunal of Constitutional Guarantees was also empowered to take cognisance of complaints that any citizen could bring before it when the Constitution had been violated. In such cases, the Tribunal could prepare the accusation against the public official involved, and was to send it to the National Chamber of Representatives, for their prosecution.[416]

But in accordance with the constitutional reform approved in 1983, in force since 1984[417] the Tribunal of Constitutional Guarantees has also been attributed the exclusive power to suspend the effects of unconstitutional legislative acts, in what can be considered a concentrated system of judicial review. This power, up to the constitutional reform of 1983 had been attributed to the Supreme Court of Justice.

In effect, since 1984, the Tribunal of Constitutional Guarantees has had the exclusive power to «suspend totally or partially, at any moment, *ex officio* or following a party's petition, the effects of laws (statutes), ordinances or decrees that were unconstitutional whether in substance ox in form».[418] This «suspension» of the effects of legislation is, undoubtedly, an important judicial review remedy regarding unconstitutional acts, although the Tribunal must submit its decision for the National Chamber of Representatives resolution. In accordance with the Constitution neither the decision of the Tribunal nor the resolution of the National Chamber of Representatives has «retroactive effects,[419] although they have *erga omnes* effects.

This can be deduced, particularly regarding the Tribunal «suspensive» decision, from what is established in the Constitution regarding the inapplicability of legislation by the Chambers of the Supreme Court, the Tax Court or the Administrative Justice Court with *inter partes* effects in processes developed before them.

In these latter cases, it must be stressed that these courts must notify their decisions to the Supreme Court, which if it accepts the criterion must inform the Tribunal of Constitutional Guarantees which could exercise its competences to suspend the effects of the challenged act.[420]

VIII. PREVENTIVE JUDICIAL REVIEW SYSTEM IN FRANCE: THE CONSTITUTIONAL COUNCIL

All the concentrated systems of judicial review that follow the European model can be characterised by the establishment of various means of judicial control of the constitutionality of legislation once in force, that is to say, once enacted and after its

415 Art. 141, 2 Constitution.
416 Art. 141, 3 Constitution.
417 G. ZAMBRANO PALACIOS, «Control de la constitucionalidad de los actos del poder público», *Memoria de la Reunión de Presidentes de Cortes Supremas de Justicia de Iberoamérica, El Caribe, España y Portugal*, Caracas 1983, pp. 677, 678.
418 Art.138. Constitution 1978.
419 Art. 138. Constitution 1978.
420 Art. 138 Constitution 1978.

juridical normative effects have begun. Only in an exceptional way do some European concentrated systems allow for a preventive means of control regarding certain state acts, as happens in Italy with regional legislation and in Spain with organic laws and international treaties.

The basis for the existence of an *a posteriori* judicial review system has been the overcoming of the dogma of the sovereignty of parliament and of the law, and of the rigidities of the principle of separation of powers. As we have seen, judicial review implies the existence of a written and rigid constitution with normative character directly applicable to individuals, through which limits are imposed upon all constitutional organs, even the legislator, whose activities must conform to its text and therefore can be subject to jurisdictional review.

Those principles overcome by the European countries that followed the concentrated system of judicial review, have been of particular importance in the development of the French constitutional system, and if it is true that the contemporary trends of constitutionalism have also affected its traditional basis, it has been only for the establishment of a preventive system of judicial review, which undoubtedly is an incomplete system for the review of legislation deemed unconstitutional.

Of course, the adoption of a preventive system of judicial review in France and the activity developed by the Constitutional Council have been considered of revolutionary character[421] because they mean the acceptance of the principle of constitutionality and the submission of the legislator to constitutional limits,[422] but if it is compared with the system of judicial review adopted in the other European countries, we must conclude by considering that the French judicial review system is a limited one,[423] the statutes once in force not being submitted to constitutional justice control.

1. Historical Background

The French preventive system of judicial review of legislation was definitively established in the Constitution of 5 October 1958, in which the Constitutional Council was regulated[424] as a constitutional organ of the state in charge of the preventive review of legislation, that is to say, of the role of establishing its «conformity with the Constitution... before its promulgation».[425] As we have said, this institutional innovation is the result of a reaction against at least two of the traditional bases of the French constitutional system: the absolutism of the law and the rejection of any judicial interference regarding other state powers, particularly parliament.

In effect, one of the most important political dogmas resulting from the French Revolution was the deep mistrust of the revolutionary legislator regarding judges,

---

421 J. RIVERO, *Le Conseil Constitutionnel et les libertés*, Paris-Aix-en-Provence 1984, p. 168.

422 L. FAVOREU, «Le principe de constitutionnalité. Essai de definition d'après la jurisprudence du Conseil Constitutionnel», *Recueil d'etudes en Hommage a Charles Eisenmann*, Paris 1977, pp. 33-48.

423 See the comments concerning the legitimacy of the *a priori* French systems of control in a comparative perspective in L. FAVOREU «Actualité et légitimité du contrôle juridictionnel del lois en Europe occidentale», *Revue du droit public et de la science politique en France etàa 1'étranger*, Paris 1984 (5), p. 1183-1187. Also published in L. FAVOREU and J.A. JOLOWICZ (ed.), *Le contrôle juridictionnel des lois. Légitimité, effectivité et développements récents*, Paris 1986, pp. 17-68.

424 Arts 56-63 Constitution 1958.

425 Art. 61.

which denying them any possibility of controlling the other state powers, particularly the legislator and the executive. This anti judicial reaction had its political grounds in the role played by the pre-revolutionary *Parlements*, as Higher Courts, when examining the laws and decrees submitted to them to ensure that they did not contain «anything contrary to the fundamental laws of the Kingdom» which gave them an important conservative political power.[426]

This distrust of the judicial power led to an extreme revolutionary interpretation of the principle of separation of powers. It resulted in prohibiting all judges not only from reviewing legislative and administrative acts, which explains why, in its origin, the Court of Cassation was a legislative organ and why the Council of state was an executive organ, but even from interpreting the laws, which power was also reserved to the legislator exercised by decree enacted at the request of the judges through the so-called *reféré législatif*, when there were any doubt about the text of a law.[427] Therefore, as Montesquieu regarded them, the judges were *la bouche de la loi*, that is to say, «the mouth that pronounces the words of the law, mere passive beings, incapable of moderating either its force or rigour».[428]

This extreme interpretation of the separation of powers, the supremacy of the law and the role of judiciary had up to this century (20th century) a tremendous influence on the shaping of continental constitutional law. That is why, as we have seen, it has only been during recent decades that a change has been introduced in Europe, particularly through the adoption of systems of judicial review of legislation, even though not by the ordinary judges or by the Supreme Courts of the countries, but by a specially created constitutional tribunal as a constitutional organ but with jurisdictional power.

The same lines were followed in the establishment of the Constitutional Council in France, but perhaps with a more political than jurisdictional character at least in its origin in which direct antecedents can be found in French constitutional history.

In effect, the French tradition before the creation of the Constitutional Council in 1958 was the attribution of the function of guaranteeing the Constitution to a special political body. This happened with the Conservative Senate of the Constitution of the year VIII of the 22 *Frimaire*, and with the attributions of the Senate in the Constitutional Charter of 1852.[429] It was repeated in the 1946 Constitution, which attributed the undertaking of the preventive control of the constitutionality of the laws sanctioned by the National Assembly to a political body called the *Comite Constitutionnel*, to determine if their promulgation required a previous amendment of the organic part of the Constitution. Consequently, it was a very limited system of constitutional control. As a result, if the Committee deemed that the law was in fact contrary to the Constitution, it was returned to the Assembly for reconsideration, and if the Assembly confirmed its first decision, then it was necessary to proceed to reform the Constitution just as if it were a

---

426 M. CAPPELLETTI, *Judicial Review in the Contemporary World*, Indianapolis 1971, pp. 33-35; F. Luchaire, *Le Conseil Constitutionnel*, Paris 1980, pp. 5-6.

427 *Idem*

428 MONTESQUIEU, *De 1'Espirit of Laws*, Book XI, Ch VI, quoted by Ch. H. MCILWAIN, *The High Court of Parliament and its Supremacy*, Yale, 1910, p. 323.

429 C. FRANCK, *Les functions juridictionnelles du Conseil Constitutionnel et du Conseil d'État dans 1'ordre constitutionnel*, Paris 1974, pp.44-46; F. LUCHAIRE, *op. cit.*, pp. 10-11.

revision explicitly requested. However, the law could not be enacted until the reform had been concluded.[430]

2. The Constitutional Council and its Jurisdiction

Based on the background of the French tradition and of the 1946 Constitutional Committee, the 1958 Constitution created the Constitutional Council,[431] which in accordance with Maurice Duverger's ideas was a kind of «supreme political jurisdiction» entrusted with power to control the constitutionality of the law and the regularity of presidential and parliamentary elections. The term «political jurisdiction» used by Duverger to describe this body expresses the rather atypical[432] and ambiguous[433] nature of the institution: it is assigned the role of a judge, but must exercise its activities in the political arena, and more important, with political motivations. Its members enjoy the independence of all Magistrates and judges but are politically recruited and appointed.

Therefore, discussions have traditionally arisen in France regarding the jurisdictional character of the Constitutional Council,[434] which today are definitively admitted even giving rise to a distinction between the «judicial power» and a more broad «jurisdictional power», the latter being constructed to comprise other than ordinary judiciary and administrative justice functions, the constitutional justice attributions of the Constitutional Council.[435]

In accordance with the Constitution, the composition of the Constitutional Council, other than by *ex-officio* members who are the former Presidents of the Republic, is composed of nine members appointed in a paritarian way, three by the President of the Republic, three by the President of the National Assembly and three by the President of the Senate.[436]

The functions of the Council members are incompatible with those of members of Government, of Parliament and of the Economic and Social Council.[437] Council members cannot be appointed to any public office[438] during their term, nor are they allowed to take political stands on issues which have been or could be susceptible to a decision by the Council.[439] They are also prohibited from accepting positions of responsibility or administrative posts in any political party or group, nor can they

430 F. LUCHAIRE, *op. cit.*, p. 13.

431 The Constitutional Council is ruled by Title VII, article 53 to 63 of the 1958 Constitution, (*Journal Official* du 5-10-1958) and by the Organic Law Nº 58-1067 of 7th November, 1958. (*Journal Officiel* du 9-11-1958). Article 61, 2 of the Constitution was modified on 21st October, 1974 by a Constitutional Reform; and the Organic Law of the Tribunal was modified by the Organic Law Nº 59-223 of 4th February 1959 (*Journal Officiel* du 7-2-1959) and by the Organic Law of 26-12-1974 that followed the Constitutional ammendment.

432 W.K. GECK, «Judicial Review of Statutes: a Comparative Survey of Present Institutions and Practices», *Cornell Law Quarterly*, 51, 1966, pp. 256-259.

433 A. HAURIOU, *Institutions politiques et droit constitutionnel*, Paris.

434 F. LUCHAIRE, «Le Conseil Constitutionnel. Est-il une juridiction», *Revue du droit public et de la science politique en France et à l'étranger*, 1979; F. Luchaire, *op. cit.*, pp. 33-56.

435 T. RENOUX, *Le Conseil Constitutionnel et l'autorité judiciaire. L'elaboration d'un droit constitutionnel juridictionnel*, Paris 1984, p. 19.

436 Art. 56 Constitution; Art. 1, Organic Law 58-1067.

437 Art. 57 Constitution; Art. 4, Organic Law 58-1067.

438 Art. 5 Organic Law 58-1067.

439 Art. 7 Organic Law 58-1067.

mention their post in any document which could lend itself to publication on any public or private activity.[440]

The Constitutional Council, in addition to its consultative attributions, in the area of judicial review is also the judge of the constitutionality of legislation and of electoral and referendum disputes. Therefore, three types of competences can be distinguished for the Constitutional Council: to act as a consultative body, to exercise electoral jurisdiction and to control the constitutionality of legislation.

The first of the competences attributed to the Constitutional Council refers to the exercise of a series of functions of a consultative nature, and indeed, of political importance. These consultative functions refer to determining when the President of the Republic is unable to perform his functions,[441] and to give its opinion regarding the situations and measures to be taken in cases of extraordinary circumstances.[442]

In the first case, the consultative functions of the Council are directed towards preventing the President of the Republic from exercising his functions, in which it wields genuine decision-making power, when requested by the government when it considers the President of the Republic unfit to carry out his functions.

We should stress that the Constitution does not define the notion of being «unfit to perform» (*empêchement*) insofar as it does not specify if it means a physical disability or unfitness resulting from sickness or an accident. Thus, the power of appreciation of the Constitutional Council is practically unlimited. If the Constitutional Council declares the unfitness or disability of the President to be of a definitive nature, it must call new elections between twenty and fifty days following its decision. Nevertheless, the Constitutional Council can confirm the existence of a *force majeure* preventing it from calling the election, in which case, as would occur in the event of temporary incapacity, the President of the Republic would be replaced by the President of the Senate, who is empowered to exercise all of the former attributions, with the exception of the right to dissolve the Assembly, or to call a referendum.[443]

The second consultative function of the Constitutional Council concerns the opinion it must give when consulted by the President of the Republic regarding the situation and the measures that must be taken when a serious and immediate threat against the institutions of the Republic, the independence of the Nation, the integrity of its territory or the execution of international accords exists, or when the regular functioning of the constitutional public powers is interrupted. In order to adopt the necessary measures in the circumstances, the President as well as the Prime Minister and the President of the Assemblies must consult the Constitutional Council, which must refer to the conditions established in the Constitution for the exercise of extraordinary powers in which case the opinion must be published.[444]

Additionally, the Constitutional Council must be consulted on all measures that the President of the Republic intends to take under Article 16 of the Constitution, in which case, the opinion of the Constitutional Council would not be published.[445]

---

440 Art. 2, Decret 13-1-1959. See in F. LUCHAIRE, *op. cit.*, p. 71.

441 Art. 7. Constitution.

442 Art. 16. Constitution.

443 Arts 7, 11, 12. Constitution. Art. 31 Organic Law 58-1067.

444 Art. 16. Constitution. Arts 52, 53 Organic Law 58-1067.

445 Art. 54 Organic Law 58-1067.

The second group of competences of the Constitutional Council deals with its role as Supreme Electoral Tribunal, not only for parliamentary elections, but also for presidential elections and referenda.[446] Regarding parliamentary elections, the Constitutional Council has constitutional powers to decide upon the regularity of elections of Deputies and Senators[447] and as a result the Council can annul any election or can amend its reported results and is even empowered to declare another candidate as having been regularly elected.[448] To this end, every parliamentary election can be challenged before the Tribunal, within a ten day period, by any elector of the respective electoral circumscription, following a contradictory procedure in which the contested parliamentary assembly and the candidate whose election is under question are entitled to make observations.[449]

Regarding the control of presidential elections[450] the powers of the Constitutional Council are not restricted to the settlement of disputes, that is to say, they are not reduced to reviewing the regularity of an election if contested, but to watch out for the regularity of the elections. To this effect, the Constitutional Council, in the case of a challenged presidential election, is entrusted with the task of adopting and proclaiming the final results of the electoral process.[451] Moreover, the Constitutional Council *ex-officio*, when it has evidence of serious irregularities which could prevent the sincerity of the election and affect its overall result, can pronounce the nullity of the election, in which case the government must fix a new date for a new election.[452]

On the other hand, the Constitutional Council also participates in the electoral process when the government deems it necessary to replace the normal vote counting procedure, carried out at the level of the heads of Departments, and of the territories, by a centralized vote count taken in Paris. In accordance with the Organic Law on the Presidential Election the decree establishing this measure must have the favourable opinion of the Constitutional Council,[453] thus granting this body the real decision-making power in the matter.

Anyway, regarding disputes over presidential elections, only the Prefects or Heads of the respective territories may exercise a recourse before the Constitutional Council within the 48 hours following the closure of the ballot count,[454] but electors have no right to exercise such a recourse. Nevertheless, this restriction of standing is balanced when considering the already questioned *ex-officio* powers of the Council to annul an election.

The third competence regarding electoral disputes of the Constitutional Council relates to the control of referenda. In this respect the Council must be first consulted on the organisation of the operations of the referendum,[455] that is to say,

---

446 Art. 58-60. Constitution.
447 Art. 59. Constitution.
448 Art. 41 Organic Law 58-1067.
449 Art. 39,40 *Idem.*
450 Art. 30 *Idem.*
451 Art. 27 Organic Law 58-1064 7-11-58 concerning the election of the President of the Republic. *Journal Officiel* du 9-11-58.
452 Art. 22 Organic Law 58-1064.
453 Art. 23 *Idem.*
454 Art. 19 *Idem.*
455 Art. 46 Organic Law 58-1067.

its technical application. Second, it must supervise both the operations and the final vote count, and then proclaim the results.[456] Third, in the case of disputes relating to the referendum, the Constitutional Council also examines and decides on every claim raised before it.[457] The Organic Law of the Constitutional Council does not clearly establish who is entitled to make such claims, but, in view of the nature of a referendum, that is to say, a popular consultation via direct votes, it could be considered that every elector has the right to request a decision from the Constitutional Council.[458] Anyway, if the Council confirmed irregularities, it must decide then, in a sovereign manner, whether to maintain the operation of the referendum or to change it, making a statement on its partial annulment.[459]

The third group of competencies of the Constitutional Council is the control of constitutionality of legislation, of a preventive character, which is conceived in the Constitution basically as a mean of preventing encroachment of competencies between the constitutional organs of the state, and particularly to keep parliament within its constitutional boundaries. Thus, in its origin, the Constitutional Council was established as the guarantor of the organic part of the Constitution and only after 1971, has it also been considered, although indirectly, as the guarantor of the fundamental rights of the citizen against the laws.[460]

This control of the constitutionality of legislation, as we said, is conceived in France as a preventive or *a priori* control in the sense that it is exercised over acts not yet enforced, because they have not been enacted. Regarding laws, the control only proceeds against statutes sanctioned by the Assemblies but not yet promulgated by the President of the Republic, and it is precisely this aspect, which brings about the great difference between the French system of judicial review and the other European systems, in which the main control of constitutionality is jurisdictionally exercised against acts that have been promulgated and that are in force.

In accordance with the French Constitution, the judicial review powers of the Constitutional Council can be classified into two groups: the preventive control of the constitutionality of non promulgated legislation; and the preventive control over the distribution of normative powers between the law and the executive regulations.

3. Preventive Control of the Constitutionality of non Promulgated Legislation

The preventive control of the constitutionality of non promulgated legislation, is exercised by the Constitutional Council in two ways: in a compulsory way regarding parliamentary regulations, and organic laws, and in a facultative way regarding ordinary laws and international treaties.

A. *Obligatory Control of the Constitutionality of Organic Laws and Parliamentary Regulations*

In accordance with article 61 of the Constitution, organic laws and the internal regulations of parliamentary assemblies before they are promulgated, must be

[456] Art. 60 Constitution. Art. 51 Organic Law 58-1067.
[457] Art. 50 Organic Law 56-1067.
[458] *Cf.* F. LUCHAIRE, *op. cit.*, p. 277.
[459] Art. 50 Organic Law 58-1067.
[460] J. RIVERO, *op. cit.*, pp. 13-14.

submitted to the Constitutional Council for its decision as to whether they are consistent with the Constitution.

In the case of Organic Laws, the Prime Minister who must state, when appropriate, if the decision is urgent, must submit them to the Constitutional Council. In the case of parliamentary regulations or modifications to the regulations adopted by one of the Assemblies, they must be submitted to the Constitutional Council by the President of the Assembly.[461]

B. *Facultative Control of the Constitutionality of Ordinary Laws and of International Treaties*

In addition to organic laws and parliamentary regulations, the President of the Republic, the Prime Minister or the President of one of the Assemblies can also submit ordinary laws before their enactment to the Constitutional Council. Moreover, the 1974 Constitutional reform adds a new option: 60 representatives or senators may submit the question of constitutionality regarding ordinary laws to the Constitutional Council,[462] thereby giving minorities the means to challenge majority decisions.

This facultative control of constitutionality also applies to international treaties and in this case, the Constitutional Council must decide whether an international treaty contains clauses contrary to the Constitution, when requested by the President of the Republic, the Prime Minister or the President of one of the Assemblies, in which case the authorisation for its signing or for its approval could only be possible after a constitutional reform takes place.[463]

The proceeding in this case is contradictory and the authority that submits an international treaty or a law to the Constitutional Council for constitutional control, must immediately notify such action to the other authorities entitled to require a decision of the Constitutional Council.[464]

C. *Suspensive Effects of the Recourses and the Decision of the Council*

In any case in which the Constitutional Council is requested for control of constitutionality before the enactment of organic laws, parliamentary regulations, ordinary laws and international treaties, as soon as the Council hears the request, it has suspensive effects and the promulgation of the normative text under challenge is suspended.[465] The Council has a month to make a decision, although in an urgent case, the government may request that this term be reduced to eight days.[466]

The decision of the Council that must be motivated and published in the *Journal official*[467] can be to declare that the challenged statute is not contrary to the Constitution, in which case the suspensive delay of its promulgation ends.[468] But the decision of the Constitutional Council may be to declare the normative text

---

461 Art. 61 Constitution. Art. 17 Organic Law 58-1067.
462 Art. 61. Constitution.
463 Art. 54. Constitution.
464 Art. 54, 61. Constitution. Art. 18 Organic Law 58-1067.
465 Art. 61. Constitution.
466 Art. 61. Constitution.
467 Art. 20 Organic Law.
468 Art. 21 Organic Law 58-1067.

unconstitutional, in which case the non-promulgated normative text cannot be promulgated nor enforced.[469]

In relation to international treaties, as we have said, if the Constitutional Council decides that an international treaty contains a clause contrary to the Constitution, the authorisation to ratify or approve it must be postponed until the Constitution has been amended.[470]

The declaration of unconstitutionality by the Constitutional Council always takes two forms regarding the text of the challenged act: if the Constitutional Council deems that an unconstitutional provision of a statute is inseparable from the rest of the text, the full text of the law therefore cannot be promulgated;[471] on the contrary, if the Council deems that the unconstitutional provisions can be separated from the text, the President of the Republic can either enact the incomplete text, or call for a second discussion by the Chambers.[472]

In any case, the decision of the Constitutional Council is not revisable and has binding effects on all public powers and administrative and jurisdictional authorities.[473]

4. Preventive Control of the Distribution of Normative Competences

Concerning preventive judicial review, another fundamental competence of the Constitutional Council is intended to protect the distribution of normative competences between the law and the executive regulations. In effect, the 1958 French constitution, deviating from the parliamentary tradition of modern states and as a result of an obvious antiparliamentary reaction, established a system for the distribution of competences between parliament and government, based on assigning parliament exclusive power over matters expressly enumerated in the Constitution, which resulted in an extreme restriction of parliamentary powers.

In effect, in accordance with Article 34 of the Constitution, a list of subjects whose regulation is attributed to the competence of parliament is enumerated covering the statutes it can dictate and Article 37 lays down that in all other matters, outside those that form the domain of the law (statute), the regulatory powers upon them are attributed to the executive, thus reducing the power of parliament to a series of clearly enumerated subjects and leaving the remainder of the normative competences to the executive power.

This system of distributing normative state powers, of course, causes innumerable disputes between the law and the executive regulations, thus between parliament and the executive power, which the Constitutional Council must settle. Therefore, to resolve conflicts, the Council must intervene to ensure the compliance of constitutional provisions, but without examining the definitive normative text. Here the Constitutional Council really intervenes at the time of drafting the respective texts, to authorise or to prohibit their continuation until the final version of the text is ready. Of course, this competence of the Council is exercised in two aspects with regard to statutes and to the exercise of the regulatory executive powers.

469 Art. 62. Constitution.
470 Art. 54. Constitution.
471 Art. 22 Organic Law 58-1067.
472 Art. 23. *Idem.*
473 Art. 62. Constitution.

A. *Preventive Control of Bills*

In the first aspect, the intervention of the Council concerns the procedure for the drafting of statutes and their reforms. In effect, the Government may be opposed to the continuation of the discussion of a bill by the Assembly, when it considers that it includes matters which are not under the domain reserved to the law in Article 34 of the Constitution, and in the organic laws adopted for their enforcement, and when it deems it contrary to the powers of normative character assigned to Government.[474]

In this case, the President of the Assembly involved can come to an agreement with the government opposition whereby neither the proposal nor the reform is discussed. If, however, it disagrees with the government, the Constitutional Council is called upon to settle the conflict by any of the interested organs and must adopt the decision within an 8-day period. In that case, the discussion of the law or of the legislative amendment to which the government is opposed is immediately suspended.[475] In addition, the authority that requests the intervention of the Constitutional Council in the conflict, must notify all other authorities with the same competence to request a decision from the Constitutional Tribunal.[476]

B. *Constitutional Control of Statutes Regarding Executive Regulations*

The second intervention of the Constitutional Council in the distribution of competences between the law and executive regulations, concerns the exercise of regulatory power by the government, when it attempts to modify statutes that can occur in two different cases. Firstly, when the statute in question has been adopted before the delimitation of the legislative domain in the 1958 Constitution but the matters concerned enter within the executive normative powers. Secondly, when the statutes have been adopted after the 1958 delimitation, invading the executive normative powers but were not submitted to the control of the Constitutional Council before enactment.

Under the first hypothesis, the government is free to modify the existing pre-constitutional statutes, which refer to matters of the domain reserved to it by the Constitution. In such cases, the Government is only obliged to adopt the corresponding decree, after it has requested and obtained a consultative opinion from the Council of state.[477]

The second hypothesis deals with the exercise of executive regulatory power to modify statutes adopted by Parliament after the 1958 Constitution, in areas that fall under the executive normative domain. In such cases, the government is empowered to pass the respective regulatory decree only when the Constitutional Council has declared the executive regulatory nature of the matter.[478] In this way, if a government, through neglect or by deliberate political will does not submit a non-promulgated statute which falls outside the domain reserved for the legislative power to the Constitutional Council before its enactment, successive governments are not bound by this decision and can submit the statute in question to the

474 Art. 41. Constitution.
475 Art. 27 Organic Law 58-1067.
476 *Idem.*
477 Art. 37. Constitution.
478 Art. 37. Constitution.

Constitutional Council, and if it declares its executive regulatory subject character, the government can modify it quite simply by decree.[479]

Therefore, in the field of the delimitation of normative competences between executive regulatory power and statutes, the control of the Constitutional Council does not really apply to executive regulations themselves, only to the statutes. Executive regulations and the possible encroachment they might make upon the domain reserved to the legislator by Article 34 of the Constitution are subject to control by the Council of State which could lead to the divergences of criterion between the latter and the Constitutional Council.[480]

5. Substantive Control of Constitutionality of Legislation and the Principle of Constitutionality

As we have seen, the fundamental role attributed to the Constitutional Council in France, in accordance with the 1958 Constitution, relates to controlling the conformity of legislation with the Constitution in a preventive way. But the 1958 Constitution being basically an organic constitution, that is to say, one in which the distribution of powers between the different state organs is its main objective, in the first decade of its functioning, the Constitutional Council acted as the guardian of the maintenance of that distribution particularly regarding the relation between parliament and government, in other words the relations between the law (Statutes) and the executive regulatory powers.

The French Constitution, as we have seen, does not have an express declaration or enumeration of constitutional rights, which led to it being interpreted as a text not directly applicable to individuals, the only declaration of the Constitution concerning fundamental rights of individuals being its Preamble in which it is stated that:

> «The French people solemnly proclaim their adherence to the Rights of Man and to the principles of national sovereignty as have been defined in the Declaration of 1789, confirmed and completed by the Preamble of the 1946 Constitution».

A similar Preamble was established in the 1946 Constitution, which the then Constitutional Committee considered as not being directly enforceable.[481] Nevertheless, no special provision in this respect was established in the 1958 Constitution.

This normative reality led the Constitutional Council to enlarge its own judicial review powers in what has been considered its *Marbury v. Madison* decision[482] the one adopted on the 16 July 1971 concerning the freedom of associations [483]63); in which to declare a statute sanctioned by parliament unconstitutional, the Council based itself on the Preamble and through it on the «fundamental principles recognised by the laws of the Republic and the Declaration of the Rights of Man and the Citizen of 1789». Within these principles and rights, the Council assigned constitutional rank to the freedom of

---

479 See also Arts 24-26 Organic Law 58-1067.

480 C. FRANCK, *op. cit.*, p. 167.

481 Art. 34. Constitution 1946. *Cf.* J. RIVERO, *op. cit.*, p. 11; L. FAVOREU, «Le principe ...», *loc. cit.*, p. 34.

482 J. RIVERO, *op. cit.*, p. 140.

483 See in L. FAVOREU and L. PHILIP, *Les grandes decisions du Conseil Constitutionnel*, Paris 1984, pp. 222-237.

associations and declared the unconstitutionality of a statute it deemed contrary to it, thus, to the Constitution.[484] Consequently, not only was the «bloc of constitutionality» enlarged by the Constitutional Council, which, since then, has comprised, other than the formal text of the Constitution, the fundamental principles recognised by the laws of the Republic and the Declaration of the Rights of Man and the Citizen of 1789,[485] but the Council has also become the guardian of freedoms.[486]

Therefore, the Constitutional council has claimed for itself the power and duty to control the conformity of non-promulgated statutes, not only according to Articles 34 and 37 of the Constitution, which govern the distribution of competences between parliament and the executive normative powers, but also according to the Constitution in full, which includes the general principles of a constitutional character as they arise from the Universal Declaration and from the Preamble, and the fundamental rights of individuals. Of course, in pursuing this task, the recourse opening the way for parliamentary minorities to seek judicial review through the 1974 constitutional amendment, has been of fundamental importance, as it has shown in other basic decisions of the Council, like the one adopted on the 16 January and 11 February 1982 in the *nationalisation* case,[487] in which the «bloc of constitutionality» was again enlarged, to comprise the «principles and rules of constitutional value»[488] to which the Legislator is also submitted.

Finally, it must be mentioned that in addition to these transformations pressured by the Constitutional Council decisions regarding submission of all state organs to the Constitution and its principles, including the legislator, the control of constitutionality of legislation has also been enlarged through the work of the other main jurisdictional organs in France, the Council of State and the Court of Cassation.

In particular, the Council of State since its decision *Sindicat General des Ingenieurs-Counceils* of 26 June 1959[489] has exercised constitutional control over executive normative acts (decree laws) adopted in accordance with the powers attributed to the executive in Article 37 of the Constitution, not regarding the possible submission of executive regulations to the statutes sanctioned by Parliament because of the equally distributed powers of both constitutional organs, but regarding the Constitution, and moreover, «the general principles of law which result basically from the Preamble of the Constitution» which «are imposed on the regulatory executive authority, even in the absence of a legislative disposition».[490]

---

484 *Cf.* other comment upon the decision in B. NICHOLAS, «Fundamental Rights and Judicial Review in France», *Public Law* 1978, pp. 82-92; J. E. BEARDSLEY, «The Constitutional Council and Constitutional Liberties in France», *The American Journal of Comparative Law*, 20, 1972, p. 431-452; C. FRANCK, *op. cit.*, p. 208.

485 *Cf.* F. LUCHAIRE, «Procédures et techniques de protection des droits fondamentaux. Conseil Constitutionnel Francais», in L. FAVOREU ed.), *Cours constitutionnelles européenes et droits fondamentaux*, Paris 1982, pp. 64-73.

486 M. CAPPELLETTI, «El formidable problema del control judicial y la contribucion del análisis comparado», *Revista de estudios políticos*, 13, Madrid 1980, p. 71.

487 See in L. FAVOREU and L. PHILIP, *op. cit.*, pp. 524-562. See the comments in L. FAVOREU (ed.) *Nationalisations et Constitution*, Aix-en-Provence, 1982; J. RIVERO, *op. cit.*, pp. 109-125.

488 L. FAVOREU, «Les decisions du Conseil Constitutionnel dons l'affaire des nationalisations», *Revue du droit public et de la science politique en France et à l'étranger*, 1982, p, 401.

489 See in *Recueil Sirey* Jurisprudence, 1959, p. 392 (note Drago). See the comments on C. FRANK, *op. cit.*, p. 200; M. CAPPELLETTI, «El formidable problema...»., *loc. cit.*, p. 70.

490 See in C. FRANCK, *op. cit.*, p. 200.

On the other hand, the Court of Cassation in a very important decision of 24 May 1975, *Administration des Douanes v Société Cafés Jacques Varbre S.A.*,[491] led the way to the exercise of a diffuse system of judicial review in France, by establishing the power of courts to refuse to apply statutes promulgated after the treaties of the European Economic Community, contrary to those treaties which in the French constitutional system (as are all international treaties) have «authority superior to statutes».[492] This possibility of a diffuse system of judicial review of course, could lead to its general admissibility, in particular regarding statutes contrary to the fundamental rights of individuals, not only because the European Convention of Human Rights ratified by France is part of the French legislation,[493] but also because of the express acceptance by the Constitutional Council of the constitutional rank, value and character of the fundamental rights contained in the 1789 Declaration. Of course, to that end, the reluctance of the courts to control the constitutionality of statutes so traditional in France, must be overcome, and that is a fundamental task they have in the future, to which achievement the three principal jurisdictional organs of the state have led the way.

IX. LIMITED CONCENTRATED SYSTEM OF JUDICIAL REVIEW IN BELGIUM: THE ARBITRATION COURT

Finally, regarding the concentrated systems of judicial review in Europe, a limited version can be identified in Belgium. In effect, due to the establishment of a decentralised political form of the state in Belgium, first programmed in the 1970 constitutional reform and later executed in the 1980 constitutional reform,[494] in a similar way to the «Regional state» organisation formula adopted in Italy and Spain, the need for the establishment of an independent constitutional organ to resolve conflicts between the various political entities, brought about the creation of an Arbitration Court for that purpose in the same 1980 amendment to the Constitution.[495]

In effect, in accordance with that constitutional reform, the Kingdom of Belgium was divided into Regions and Communities, as political decentralised units in which organisation and functioning the linguistic and ethnic divisions of the country play a fundamental role. Thus, conflicts between national power and those attributions assigned to the Regions and Communities need to be

---

491 See in *Dalloz* (Jurisprudence), 1975, p. 497. See the comments in M. CAPPELLETTI and W. COHEN, *Comparative Constitutional Law*, Indianapolis 1979, pp. 156-168; M. CAPPELLETTI, «El formidable problema...», *loc. cit.*, p. 72.

492 Art. 55. Constitution.

493 *Cf.* A.Z. DRZEMCZEWSKI, *European Human Rights Convention in Domestic Law. A Comparative Study*, Oxford, p. 71.

494 F. PERIN, *La nouvelle subdivision du Royaume: les Communautes et les Regions*, XI Congrès International du Droit Comparé, Caracas 1982, (mimeo), p. 10. See the text in *La Constitution belge et ses lois d'application*, Cabay, Louvain-La-Neuve, 1985.

495 Art. 107 Constitution (29-7-1980) See also «Loi portant l'organisation, la competence et le fonctionnement de la Cour d'arbitrage» (L.C.A.) 28-6-83, in *La Constituttion belge..., cit.*, p. 105. *Cf.* L. FAVOREU, *Le contrôle juridictionnel des lois et sa légitimité. Dévelopments récents en Europe occidentale*, AILS, Uppsala Colloquium 1984, (mimeo), p. 15. Also published as «Actualité et Légitimité du contrôle juridictionnel des lois en Europe occidentale», *Revue du droit public et de la science politique en France et à 1'étranger*, 1984 (5), p. 1166; and also in L. FAVOREU and J.A. JOLOWICZ (ed.), in *Le contrôle juridictionnel des lois.Légitimité, effectivité et développments récents*, Paris 1986, pp. 17-68.

resolved. Hence, the creation of the Court of Arbitration composed of 12 members: six French speaking members, who form the French language part of the Court, and six Flemish speaking members who represent Flemish speaking communities. The members of the Court are appointed by the king for life, from a list with twice the number submitted by the Senate, adopted by a two thirds majority of its members present. The candidates who must be over 40 years of age, must either have held posts for five years as judicial or administrative magistrates, or be professors of law, or they must have been members of the Senate or of the Chamber of Deputies for at least eight years. Both linguistic groups must share an equal distribution of the two above-mentioned categories.[496]

The Court of Arbitration has been conferred a limited competence to judge the conformity of laws and decrees only with respect to the rules established in or based on the Constitution to determine the respective competences of the state, of the communities and of the regions».[497] Therefore, the judicial review powers of the Court are referred exclusively to certain disputes of competences between state bo-dies, in a similar way to the powers attributed to the constitutional tribunals on the European model.

The powers of the Arbitration Court can be exercised through direct or incidental means. In effect, the first method of seeking judicial review regarding conflicts of attributions is through a direct recourse brought before the Court by the Council of Ministers or by the executive body of the communities or the regions, requesting the annulment of any legislative act on the grounds that it infringes the vertical distribution of powers established in the Constitution. The right of the Presidents of the legislative assemblies to bring before the Court this direct action at the request of two thirds of their members is also foreseen. In any case, the recourse must be presented before the Court within the period of one year following the publication of the challenged act,[498] and the Court can decide, when demanded by a party, to suspend the application of the challenged statute or decree, in which case it must decide the recourse within a delay of three months.[499]

The final Court decisions on the matter can declare the nullity of the unconstitutional act, «having absolute *res judicata* authority from its publication in the *Moniteur Belge*»,[500] which means that they have *erga omnes* effects. Additionally, it has been considered that such decisions have retroactive effects,[501] thus, *ex-tunc, pro praeterito.*

The second method through which a constitutional question can reach the Court of Arbitration is the incidental one, when the issue is referred to the Court by any ordinary court before which, in a concrete case, the question of conformity of a statute or a decree with the constitution, on matters of vertical distribution

496 Arts. 21, 22, L.C.A.
497 Art. 1, 1 L.C.A.
498 Art. 2, 1 L.C.A.
499 Art. 8, L.C.A.
500 Art. 7, L.C.A.
501 L. FAVOREU, *loc. cit.*, p. 1168.

of state powers, has been raised.[502] The ordinary courts do not have *ex-officio* powers to refer constitutional questions before the Court, but have an important appreciation power when considering the issue raised by a party in the case.[503]

Anyway, the decision of the Court of Arbitration in these incidental judicial review cases, has binding effects, not only upon the ordinary court that has referred the question, but also upon all other courts that must intervene in the same case.[504]

502 Art. 15, 2 L.C.A.
503 L. FAVOREU, *loc. cit.*, p. 1168.
504 Art. 17, L.C.A.

PART SIX

THE MIXED SYSTEMS OF JUDICIAL REVIEW

As we have seen, the systems of judicial review followed in comparative constitutional law can be classified into two main groups: the diffuse systems of judicial review, in which all courts have the power and duty to judge the constitutionality of legislation and to decide not to apply statutes when they deem them unconstitutional; and the concentrated systems of judicial review, in which the power to declare the unconstitutionality of statutes and to annul them is attributed to a single constitutional organ, either the Supreme Court of the country or a specially created Constitutional Court. In general, with their own particular trends, and as a consequence of the principle of the supremacy of the constitution, all the countries in the world with written and rigid constitutions have adopted one or other system.

Nevertheless, in accordance with their general trends, and having their common basis in the principle of the supremacy of the Constitution, those systems of judicial review of the constitutionality of legislation are not only compatible with all legal systems thus existing and functioning, either in countries with a common or Roman law tradition. Moreover, they can coexist in a particular country, giving rise to what we have called the mixed system of judicial review in which the maximum protection of the Constitution is established, at least formally in the Fundamental Charter. In Europe, a mixed system of judicial review exists in Portugal and in a more limited way in Switzerland, and many of the countries in Latin America follow this mixed pattern, as are the cases of Colombia, Venezuela, Guatemala and Brazil.

I. CONTROL OF CONSTITUTIONALITY IN THE PORTUGUESE REPUBLIC

The Constitution of the Republic of Portugal approved by a Constituent Assembly in April 1976 established the basis of a mixed system of judicial review of the constitutionality of legislation, in which the Council of the Revolution, its Constitutional Commission and the ordinary courts played a very important role,[1] giving birth to the most complete system of judicial review in Europe, in which the basic elements of the European model and of the French system were adopted in

1 See in general J. Campinos, *La Constitution portugaise de 1976 et sa garantie*, UNAM, Congreso sobre La Constitución y su Defensa, (mimeo), México, Agosto 1982; M. Gonzalo, «Portugal; El Consejo de la Revolución, su Comisión Constitucional y los Tribunales ordinarios como órganos de control de la constitucionalidad», *Boletín de jurisprudencia constitucional*, Cortes Generales, 8, Madrid 1981, pp. 630, 640.

parallel with elements of the diffuse system of judicial review. That mixed system of judicial review was maintained in the First Revision of the Constitution approved by the Constitutional Law N° 1/82 of 30th September 1982,[2] in which it is regulated as we said, by what can still be considered today, the most complete system of judicial review in Europe.

1. The principle of Constitutional Supremacy and its Consequences

The 1982 Constitution is not only a written and rigid Constitution,[3] but is expressly conceived as the supreme law of the *Lander*, to which all other state acts must be submitted. In this respect, Article 3 of the Constitution states:

> «The state shall be subject to the Constitution and based on democratic legality.
>
> The validity of the laws and other state acts of the autonomous regions and local authorities shall depend on their being in accordance with the Constitution».

The consequence of this supremacy clause is also expressly established in the text of the Constitution, in which article 277 states:

> «Provisions of law that infringe a provision of the Constitution or the principles laid down therein are unconstitutional».

Therefore, the supremacy of the Constitution and of the principles laid down in its provisions implies that laws and state acts contrary to them are unconstitutional and thus, invalid. Of course, the consequence of this assertion is the establishment of a complex system of judicial review of the constitutionality of state acts, in which a diffuse system exists in parallel with a concentrated system attributed to a Constitutional Court.

The Constitutional Court» was created by the Constitution, within the judicial power,[4] as a constitutional organ «competent to judge whether acts are unconstitutional and illegal» in accordance with its provisions» [5] and also competent to judge questions related to the exercise of its functions by the President of the Republic and to electoral matters.[6] The Constitutional Court is composed of thirteen judges, ten being named by the Assembly of the Republic and three co-opted.[7]

2. Diffuse system of judicial review and the direct appeal before the Constitutional Court

In accordance with article 207 of the Constitution

> «The Courts shall not apply unconstitutional provisions or principles to matters brought before them».

This constitutional provision authorises all the courts of the country not to apply unconstitutional provisions or principles, which comprise not only statutes, but also decree-laws, executive regulations, regional acts or any other normative

[2] Published in the *Diario da Republica*, 1st series, N° 227.
[3] Article 290 establishes material limits to constitutional revision.
[4] Art. 212.
[5] Art. 213,1.
[6] Art. 213,2.
[7] Art. 284.

state acts, including international treaties. Therefore, the Constitution establishes the power of all courts not to apply norms they deem unconstitutional in the concrete case, and also a real duty to do so. Thus, it is a power that can be exercised *ex-officio* by any court although any party in the concrete case or the Public Prosecutor can raise the constitutional question.

The control of the constitutionality of legislation, therefore, is a diffuse control attributed to all courts regarding the concrete cases in which the issue is raised, and which the courts must resolve when deciding the case. Thus, when they consider a norm unconstitutional, the norm is considered invalid regarding the concrete case, that is to say, with *inter partes* effects as well as *ex-tunc, pro praeterito* effects, in the sense that regarding the case and the concrete parties, the normative act is considered as never having been valid.

However, in the Portuguese constitutional systems, the most interesting feature of this diffuse system of judicial review, is the direct appeal established before the Constitutional Court against judicial decisions in which constitutional questions are decided, in a similar way to the extraordinary recourse of unconstitutionality, in the Argentinean and Brazilian systems or to the direct appeals before the Supreme Court in the United States.

In effect, in what is called the «concrete scrutiny for the constitutionality» following West German terminology, but in a very different way to the «concrete control of norms» developed by the West German Federal Constitutional Tribunal, article 280 of the Portuguese Constitution establishes the right to appeal before the Constitutional Tribunal against any court decisions when they firstly, refuse to apply any provision of law on the grounds that it is unconstitutional: or secondly, when they apply a provision of a law the unconstitutionality of which has been raised during the proceedings.[8]

This appeal must be compulsory exercised by the Department of the Public Prosecutor in cases in which a court of justice refuses to apply any provision of an international convention, a legislative act or a regulative decree on the grounds that it is unconstitutional.[9] But in cases in which a court applies a provision of law the unconstitutionality of which has been raised by a party during the proceeding, then only that party has the right to appeal before the Constitutional Court.[10]

But the powers of the Constitutional Court to hear appeals against lower court decisions in Portugal are not limited to constitutional control, but to diffuse control of legality, in the following cases:

First, when the courts refuse to apply a provision of a regional instrument on the grounds that it is illegal since it violates the statute of the autonomous regions or general law of the Republic; second, when the courts refuse to apply a provision of an instrument emanating from an organ of supreme authority on the grounds that it is illegal since it violates the statutes of an autonomous region; and thirdly, when the court applies a provision the illegality of which has been raised during the proceedings on the grounds of violating regional autonomies. In this latter case, only the interested party which raised the question has the right of appeal.[11]

---

8 Art. 280,1,a,b.

9 Art. 280,2.

10 Art. 280,4.

11 Art. 280, 3,a,b,c; 280,4.

On the other hand, the Public Prosecutor is obliged to appeal against court decisions in which a provision of law previously judged unconstitutional or illegal by the Constitutional Tribunal itself is applied.[12]

In any of these cases of appeals before the Constitutional Court, they shall be restricted to the question of unconstitutionality or illegality depending on the case.[13] Therefore, the Tribunal does not review the case on its facts, its judicial review powers being limited to the constitutional question.

The Constitutional Tribunal decisions in these cases of constitutional review through appeals have effects only regarding the concrete case, thus they are *inter partes,* and only when the Constitutional Court has judged any provision of law unconstitutional in three concrete cases, can it judge and rule with generally binding validity on the unconstitutionality of the law.[14]

3. Concentrated system of judicial review and the powers of the Constitutional Tribunal

In parallel with the diffuse system of judicial review, the Constitution of the Portuguese Republic has also established a concentrated system of judicial review of legislation, not only of promulgated state acts, thus *a posteriori* to their efficacy, but also in a preventive way, following the French model.

A. *Preventive Control of Constitutionality*

In effect, a preventive control of constitutionality is established regarding international treaties and agreements, formal laws and decree-laws, when the Constitutional Tribunal is requested by the President of the Republic; and regarding regional legislative decrees or executive normative acts, when requested by the Ministers of the Republic.

In the first case, article 278 of the Constitution establishes:

> «The President of the Republic may request the Constitutional Court to judge preventively the constitutionality of any provision of an international treaty that has been submitted to him for ratification, and acts sent to him for promulgation as a law or decree-law or an international agreement the act of approval of which has been sent to him for signature». [15]

Nevertheless, as we said, regional legislative acts and other executive normative acts can also be submitted to the Constitutional Tribunal for preventive constitutional review by the Minister of the Republic regarding «any provision of a regional legislative decree or a decree implementing a general law of the Republic that has been sent to them for signature».[16]

In such cases of preventive judicial review, if the Constitutional Court rules that a provision of any act or international agreement is unconstitutional, the act must be vetoed by the President of the Republic or by the Minister concerned, and

---

12 Art. 280,5.
13 Art. 280,6.
14 Art. 281,2.
15 Art. 278,1.
16 Art. 278,2.

must be sent back to the organ that approved it.[17] In principle, the act must not be promulgated or signed unless the organ that approved it expurgates the provision judged unconstitutional[18] the possibility of requesting another preventive control of constitutionality of the reformulated act being expressly authorised.[19]

But in cases of Treaties or laws, one can say that the Tribunals' decisions are not absolutely imperative and can be enacted in spite of their unconstitutional defect, if the Assembly of the Republic adopts a decision maintaining the provisions judged unconstitutional.

In effect, in cases in which the Assembly does not expurgate the unconstitutional provision of an international treaty found to be unconstitutional by the Tribunal, it could be ratified if the Assembly approves it by a two third majority of the members present.[20] In a similar way in cases of formal law, even when their unconstitutionality has been declared by the Tribunal through a preventive means of control, the Assembly of the Republic can confirm them by a two thirds majority of the members present.[21] In such cases, in spite of the constitutional objection the acts can be enforced, the majority required for its confirmation or ratification not being the same required for constitutional revision.[22]

B. *Abstract Control of Constitutionality*

The constitutionality of legislation can also be the object of an «abstract scrutiny» by the Constitutional Tribunal, exercised through a direct mean or action.

In effect, the unconstitutionality of any provision of law can be the object of a request that can be formulated before the Constitutional Court by the President of the Republic, the President of the Assembly of the Republic, the Prime Minister, the Ombudsman, the Attorney-General, or one tenth of the members of the Assembly of the Republic.[23] Additionally, the regional assemblies or the chairmen of the regional governments can also exercise the direct request of unconstitutionality against laws, on the grounds that the rights of the autonomous regions have been violated.[24] The Constitution also regulates this direct request or action on the grounds of their illegality, against regional acts on the basis that the statute of the region or general law of the Republic has been violated, in which case, additional to the public bodies mentioned above, the Minister of the Republic in the autonomous region is entitled to formulate it.[25]

The effects of the Constitutional Tribunal decisions in these cases of abstract control of norms are also expressly regulated in the Constitution. In effect, it stated that its decisions in cases of direct request of unconstitutionality has generally binding effects, thus *erga omnes*, «as from the entry into force of the provision ruled unconstitutional or illegal and shall determine the restoration with retroactive

17 Art. 279,9.
18 Art. 279,2.
19 Art. 279,3
20 Art. 279,4.
21 Art. 279,2.
22 Art. 288,1.
23 Art. 281,1,a.
24 Art. 281,1,a. The archipelagos of the Azores and Madeira have been organized within the state, as Autonomous Regions. Art. 227.
25 Art. 281,1,b. See also Art. 281,1,c.

effects, of the provisions that it may have revoked».[26] Regarding pre-constitutional legislation, that is to say, if the unconstitutionality of a norm is due to infringement of a later constitutional provision, the ruling of the Court shall produce effects only as from the entry into force of the new constitutional provision.[27]

These two express dispositions of the Constitution lead to the consideration that the general rule existing in the Portuguese system of judicial review is that decisions declaring the unconstitutionality of a state act, have *ex-tunc, pro praeterito* effects, except in «cases already judged», which, in principle, «shall be safeguarded, except if the Constitutional Court decides otherwise when the provision concerns penal or disciplinary matters or illegal acts in violation of mere social rules and is less favourable to the accused».[28]

Anyway, the powers of the Tribunal in this respect are very wide, and the Constitution expressly establishes that «when required by legal security, reasons of equity or public *interest* of exceptional importance, which shall be justified, the Constitutional Tribunal may fix the effects of unconstitutionality or illegality in a more restrictive way»,[29] thus, being possible to correct the inconvenient effects that could be produced by the rigidity of the retroactive general effects of the decisions.

4. Unconstitutionality by Omission

Finally, in the Portuguese constitutional system, additional to the preventive and *a posteriori* means of judicial review, the Constitution assigns the Constitutional Court powers to exercise another means of control of the constitutionality of state action, in what is called the «unconstitutionality by omission», which is not to be found in any other Western European country and follows in a certain way, the powers attributed to the Constitutional Tribunal of Yugoslavia.

In effect, the Constitution establishes that:

> «At the request of the President of the Republic, the Ombudsman or, on the grounds that the rights of the autonomous regions have been violated, the President of the regional assemblies, the Constitutional Tribunal shall judge and verify failure to comply with the Constitution by omission on the part of the legislative acts necessary to implement the provisions of the Constitution.
>
> When the Constitutional Court verifies the existence of unconstitutionality by omission, it shall communicate the fact to the competent legislative organ».

This exceptional power attributed to the Constitutional Tribunal was originally established in the 1976 Constitution as the result of the negotiations carried out by the Council of the Revolution in 1975, on behalf of the Armed Forces Movement, and the Political Parties, with a view to establishing a certain number of principles which were to be compulsorily observed and maintained by the respective parliamentary groups in the Constituent Assembly.[30]

Up to the sanctioning of the 1982 First Revision of the Constitution, in which this «constitutional control by omission» was definitively established, it was

---

26 Art. 282,1.
27 Art. 282,2.
28 Art. 282,3.
29 Art. 282,4.
30 J. CAMPINOS, *loc. cit.*, p. 35.

exercised on two occasions by the then Council of the Revolution. In 1977, it recommended the adoption of legislative measures to the Assembly of the Republic with a view to enforcing the norms of Article 46 of the 1976 Constitution, whereby, among other aspects, organisations with a fascist ideology were banned. The main contribution made by this Council decision lay in having spelt out the necessary conditions for the existence of «legislative omission». In the first place, it established that the constitutional norm could not be self-applicable and secondly, that the competent body to adopt the legislative measures must have violated its obligation to dictate norms, to a degree that it obstructed the observance of the constitutional norm by the very ones for whom the legal mandate was intended. Therefore, this condition was not verified if the legal order contained any prescriptions which made the constitutional norm applicable.[31]

In a second case, in 1978, the Council of the Revolution recommended the competent legislative bodies to adopt legislative measures for guaranteeing the applicability of Article 53 of the Constitution to domestic servants, which conferred upon these workers the right to rest and recreation, by limiting the length of the working day, establishing the weekly rest period as well as periodic paid holidays. On this second occasion, the essential contribution of the decision lay in the extensive interpretation carried out by the Constitutional Commission regarding the initiative to request control by omission,[32] which in the 1982 Constitution was reduced to the President of the Republic or the Ombudsman at the national level, and to the Presidents of the Regional Assemblies in cases of violation of the rights of the autonomous regions.

II. LIMITED MIXED SYSTEM OF CONSTITUTIONAL JUDICIAL REVIEW IN SWITZERLAND

The other European country that has adopted a mixed system of judicial review, although in a very limited way, is Switzerland, where judicial review is accepted regarding cantonal laws and federal executive regulations, but absolutely excluded regarding federal legislation.

1. The Absence of Judicial Review Over Federal Legislation

In effect, since the main constitutional reform of 1874 in which the judicial federal courts were organised, the Federal Tribunal was vested with the task of seeing that the Constitution and federal laws were observed[33] and in particular, the following clause was inserted in article 113 of the Constitution:

> «In all cases above mentioned the Federal Tribunal shall administer the laws passed by the Federal Assembly, and such ordinances of that Assembly as are of general application. It shall likewise act in accordance with treaties ratified by the Federal Assembly».[34]

This norm, even though referred to what in Switzerland are called «cases of public law», that is to say, cases arising from conflicts between the confederation

---

31 *Idem*, p. 42.
32 *Idem*, p. 42.
33 Art. 90. Constitution 1874. See the text in W.J. WAGNER, *The Federal States and their Judiciary*, The Hague 1959, p. 104.
34 Art. 113. Constitution 1874.

and the cantons or between cantons themselves, was soon interpreted by the Federal Tribunal as being applicable to all other cases, particularly to civil and criminal law cases, in the sense that in all judicial cases the Federal Tribunal was always bound to apply the laws as enacted by the federal legislature, without having any power to review or control their constitutionality. On the other hand, this was a consequence of the principle of the supremacy of Parliament and its laws over all other state organs and acts, including the judiciary and it was also a consequence of the idea that democracy demanded the recognition of the absolute character of the will of the people's representatives, or of that expressed by the people themselves. Thus, the primacy of the Legislature was unquestioned as the supreme authority, the courts not being qualified to question and discuss the validity of applicability of federal legislation».[35] That is why in a decision adopted in 1876, the Federal Tribunal stated:

> «It must be recognised as a principle of ...the Swiss federal and cantonal constitutional law that the authority of the legislative powers is supreme, and the Courts are not empowered to deny the validity and applicability of a law or decree enacted by the legislative authorities on the grounds that their content is repugnant to the Constitution; it belongs to them only to check formally whether they really face a law enacted in a way conforming to the Constitution».[36]

It can be said that this doctrine is still the one prevailing in Switzerland, in spite of efforts to modify it,[37] and a similar clause to that of article 113 was for instance inserted in the 1912 constitutional amendment, in which it was stated regarding administrative justice cases that «The administrative court shall apply federal legislation and treaties approved by the Federal Assembly».[38]

Consequently, in the Swiss system, no judicial review is admitted either by the Federal Tribunal or by any other court in the country regarding federal laws and other acts of general effects of the federal legislature,[39] and also regarding executive decrees with force of federal law adopted by the Federal Council executing extraordinary powers.[40]

Therefore, judicial review is limited in Swiss constitutional system only to cantonal laws and to executive regulations at federal level, and it can be exercised, either in a diffuse or a concentrated way.

---

35 E. ZELLWEGER, «El Tribunal Federal suizo en calidad de Tribunal Constitucional», *Revista de la Comisión Internacional de Juristas*, 7, 1966, p. 114.

36 B. GER. 2, 98, 105 (1876). Quoted by W.J. WAGNER, *op. cit.*, p. 105; and E. ZELLWEGER, *loc. cit.*, p. 126.

37 See for example, A. GRISEL, «Réflexious sur la juridiction Constitutionnelle et Administrative en Suisse», *Etudes et documents*, 28, Conseil d'Etat, Paris 1976, pp. 262-272.

38 Art. 114 A. See the text in W.J. WAGNER, *op. cit.*, p. 106.

39 The 1962 «Federal Law on Assembly procedures and on the form, publication and validity of legislative acts» defines them as follows: «Federal Laws are legislative acts of unlimited duration containing rules of law. Legislative acts containing rules of law are all general or abstract norms «which imposes obligations on, or grants rights to individuals and corporations, or regulates the organization, jurisdiction or functions of authorities, or establishes a procedure». Federal resolutions of general and binding effect are legislative acts of unlimited duration containing rules of law. See in E. ZELLWEGER, *loc. cit.*, p. 125.

40 E. ZELLWEGER, *loc. cit.*, p. 127.

2. Limited Diffuse System of Judicial Review

In effect, regarding cantonal law, which, of course, due to the federal form of the state must conform to the Constitution, and also regarding federal executive regulations, not considered as «federal legislation», all the courts have the power in the Swiss system to control their constitutionality.

Indeed, as in any diffuse system of judicial review, this verification of the constitutionality of state acts, is only of an incidental and prejudicial character, motivated by the need to apply a particular cantonal norm in a concrete case. The provision that is considered to have violated the Constitution or federal law, is not annulled by the Judge, who only declares it not applicable to the resolution of the case.[41]

On the other hand, even though, no judicial review is admitted regarding federal legislation, it has been recognised the power of all courts to verify whether a statute to be applied in a concrete case has or has not been duly published, thus, a diffuse system of judicial review is possible regarding federal legislation but only limited to formal aspects concerning its publication.[42]

3. Limited Concentrated System of Judicial Review

In parallel with the limited diffuse system of judicial review, in the Swiss system a limited concentrated system of judicial review attributed to the Federal Tribunal has also been established, exercised by means of a direct action called the «recourse of public law».

In effect, this Federal Tribunal, as the supreme judicial organ of the country, is the supreme and last instance in all judicial cases, and particularly in criminal, civil and administrative cases, for which it is divided into various sections.

One of these sections is the Public law and administrative law section, through which the Federal Tribunal acts as the court of last resort in all administrative justice cases, and as a constitutional court.[43]

In its character as constitutional judge, the Federal Tribunal through the «Public Law division» of its Public Law and Administrative Section is particularly empowered to resolve and settle conflicts of competences resulting from the distribution of state powers within the Federal system. It can also decide the public law recourses that can be brought before it on constitutional matters.

Regarding the first set of attributions of the Tribunal in the settlement of conflicts of attributions, its Public Law Division is in charge of resolving conflicts of attributions that may arise between federal and cantonal authorities, as well as those that may arise between cantons themselves in connection with the delimitation of the legal domain attributed to them.[44]

However, where the constitutional justice powers of the Tribunal are more specifically related to judicial review matters are in the second of the competences attributed to it, concerning the resolution of public law recourses that can be brought before it on constitutional matters, against cantonal dispositions.

---

41 E. ZELLWEGER, *loc. cit.*, p. 127.

42 W.J. WAGNER, *op. cit.*, p. 106; A. JIMÉNEZ BLANCO, «El Tribunal Federal suizo». *Boletín de jurisprudencia constitucional*, Cortes Generales, 6, Madrid 1981, p. 478.

43 *Cf.* E. ZELLWEGER, *loc. cit.*, p. 119; A. JIMÉNEZ BLANCO, *loc. cit.*, p. 478.

44 *Cf.* A. JIMÉNEZ BLANCO, *loc. cit.*, p. 479; E. ZELLWEGER, *loc. cit.*, p. 119.

In the Swiss system, in effect, the recourse of public law is conceived as the means for controlling the conformity of cantonal acts[45] particularly normative and other acts of the cantonal Legislature,[46] with federal law, and can be exercised by any interested individual or corporation, for the following reasons: 1°) Violation of any of the citizens' constitutional rights; 2°) violation of «concordats», that is to say, public law agreements between cantons; 3°) violation of international treaties, except in cases of infringement of civil or criminal law provisions contained in some treaties by decision of the cantonal authorities; and 4°) violation of federal law dispositions relating to the delimitation of areas of competence of the authorities.[47]

Also considered as public law recourses, are those concerning the citizens' right to vote, and those relating to cantonal elections and voting, regardless of the cantonal constitutional or federal law provisions applicable.[48]

These Public law recourses before the Swiss Federal Tribunal are essentially of a subsidiary nature, that is to say, they are only admissible when the alleged violation of the right cannot be brought before any other judicial authority through other legal means established either under federal or cantonal law.[49] Consequently, the action cannot be admitted unless all existing cantonal remedies have been exhausted. Nevertheless, this requisite of previous exhaustion of ordinary legal procedures does not apply to actions relating to the violation of freedom of establishment, the prohibition of double taxation in fiscal matters, the citizen's right to appear before his «natural» judge, and the right to legal aid,[50] which can be brought before the Federal Tribunal in a principal way.

Citizens and «corporations» whose rights are violated by cantonal acts or provisions of general binding effect or who, even in the absence of any such violation, are personally affected by the said acts or provisions, are entitled to bring a public law recourse.[51] The term «corporation» is understood by law to mean private law entities, which includes companies and professional associations.[52]

Exceptionally, a public law action could also be brought before the Tribunal by public law entities, to protect their sphere of autonomous action vis-à-vis administrative bodies of higher rank. In this respect, for example, a municipality can impugn acts of the canton of which it is a dependency, by means of a public law recourse brought, in this case, on the grounds of violation of municipal autonomy.[53]

In general, the Tribunal does not have *ex-officio* powers to consider constitutional questions other than those denounced in the recourse by the claimant, and it has refused to consider facts not alleged in the ordinary judicial proceeding previously exhausted.[54]

---

45 The conformity of administrative federal acts with federal law is also judge by the Federal Tribunal but through the recourse of administrative law. *Cf.* A. GRISEL, *loc. cit.*, p. 255.

46 The control of the constitutionality of Cantonal Constitution have been excluded. *Cf.* E. ZELLWEGER, *loc. cit.*, p. 124.

47 Art. 84 Law of Judiciary Organization. See the text in E. ZELLWEGER, *loc. cit.*, p. 120.

48 Art. 85, a Law of Judiciary Organization.

49 Art. 84,2 *Idem. Cf.* A. GRISEL, *loc. cit.*, p. 255; E. ZELLWEGER, *loc. cit.*, p. 122; W.J. WAGNER, *op. cit.*, p. 109.

50 Art. 86,2 Law of Judiciary Organization.

51 Art. 88 *Idem.*

52 E. ZELLWEGER, *loc. cit.*, p. 123.

53 *Idem*, p. 123.

54 A. GRISEL, *loc. cit.*, p. 255.

In any such case of the exercise of these constitutional justice powers, when the Federal Tribunal considers that a cantonal act is unconstitutional, it annuls the act with *erga omnes* effects,[55] thus applicable to everybody and not only to the parties involved in the proceedings.

III. MIXED SYSTEM OF JUDICIAL REVIEW IN VENEZUELA

As we have seen, a complete mixed system of judicial review in Europe only exists in Portugal; and in Switzerland it also exists but in an incomplete form. The European countries have chosen to follow either the diffuse system, or more recently, the concentrated system of judicial review, attributed to a specially established constitutional court, tribunal or council. That is why the experiences of Austria, West Germany, Italy and Spain have given rise to what has been called the European model of judicial review.

We have also seen that in other parts of the world, particularly in Latin America, the two main systems of judicial review, the diffuse and the concentrated, have also been followed, but with a particular trend, namely, that of the important role generally attributed to the Supreme Court of Justice of the country. In those which follow the American model, the Supreme Court of Justice appears as the supreme interpreter of the Constitution, through the extraordinary recourses that can be brought before it; and in those which have adopted a concentrated system of judicial review, the power to declare the unconstitutionality of legislation and to annul laws is attributed exclusively to the Supreme Court of the country, the establishment of a Constitutional Court separate from the Supreme Court, being exceptional.

But in Latin America mixed systems of judicial review established since the middle of the last century, (19th century), it can also be distinguished in a few countries giving rise to what can be considered today as a Latin American model of judicial review. This mixed system has developed particularly in Brazil, Colombia, Guatemala and Venezuela, to which we will now refer to, beginning by analysing the Venezuelan system, perhaps the most complete mixed system together with that of Colombia.

1. Constitutional Supremacy and Judicial Review

The Venezuelan constitutional system is based on the principle of constitutional supremacy, the Constitution being considered as a normative charter not only organising the exercise of public power, but also establishing the fundamental rights of citizens. Thus, it is considered an embodiment of positive norms directly applicable to individuals, a characteristic that has developed from the very beginning of our constitutional process in 1811.[56] This principle of the supremacy of the Constitution has inevitably led to the development of a system of judicial review of constitutionality of state acts, established more than a hundred years ago.[57] The Supreme Court of Justice explained the system in 1962 when

---

55 W.J. WAGNER, *op. cit.*, p. 109.

56 See Allan R. BREWER-CARÍAS, *Instituciones políticas y constitucionales*, Caracas 1985, Vol. I, p. 342.

57 See the comments regarding the mixed system of judicial review of constitutionality as a consequence of the principle of the supremacy of the Constitution, in R. FEO, *Estudios sobre el Código de procedimiento civil venezolano*, Caracas 1904, Vol. I, pp. 26-35; R. MARCANO RODRÍGUEZ, *Apuntaciones Analíticas sobre las materias fundamentales y generales del Código de procedimiento civil venezolano*, Caracas, Vol. I, pp. 36-38; BORJAS, *Comentarios al Código de procedimiento civil*, Caracas Vol. I, pp. 33-35.

deciding a popular action brought before it against the Law of approval of the Extradition Treaty signed with the United States of America, as follows:

> «The existence of a judicial control of the constitutionality of state acts exercised by the Highest Tribunal of the Republic, has been traditional in Venezuela, and is indispensable in any regime, which pretends to subsist as a state submitted to the rule of Law (*Estado de Derecho*). The unconstitutionality is always anti-juridical and contrary to the principle that compels the Public Power, in all of its branches, to subject itself to the constitutional and legal norms, which define its attributions. The unconstitutionality is an outrage against the citizen's rights and against the legal order in general, which have their supreme guarantees in the Fundamental Law of the state. In countries ruled freely, all private or governmental activities must necessarily be maintained within the limits established in the Fundamental Charter, which prescriptions, as the solemn expression of the popular will in the Public Law sphere, are norms of inescapable observance for those who govern and those who are governed, from the humblest of citizens up to the highest powers of the state. From the principles established in the Constitution, from the norms drawn up by it, whether in its organic or in its dogmatic parts, the laws and all dispositions enacted after must be simple developments; and as unconstitutional and thus, improper they would be considered if they exceed that character, as unconstitutional and also improper as would be any other act of the Public Powers which openly contravenes what is established in the fundamental Law».[58]

As a consequence of this principle of constitutional supremacy, the 1961 Venezuelan Constitution, following a constitutional tradition that can be traced back to the 1858 Constitution[59] established in article 215 the competence of the Supreme Court of Justice to review the constitutionality of laws and other normative acts of the national, state or municipal deliberative bodies, of executive regulations and acts of government adopted by the President of the Republic. That is to say, it provides for judicial review of the constitutionality of all state acts; judicial and administrative acts also being subjected to special means for reviewing their legality and constitutionality through the recourses of cassation and appeals, and through special administrative judicial actions.

In particular, judicial review of constitutionality of state acts at the national level is referred to laws and other acts with the same rank or force of law (other acts of parliament without the form of law, and Decree Laws and other government acts), and to executive regulations adopted by the national executive. At the member state level of our Federation, judicial review refers to laws issued by the Legislative Assemblies; and, at the municipal level, to Municipal Ordinances adopted by the Municipal Councils. This review power of the constitutionality of state acts allows the Supreme Court of Justice to declare them null and void when they violate the Constitution. It thus constitutes a concentrated system of control of the constitutionality of laws and other state acts.

---

58 Supreme Court of Justice in Plenary Session, 15-3-62. See in *Gaceta Oficial* Nº 760 Extra., 22-3-62, pp. 3-7.

59 See J. G. ANDUEZA, *La jurisdicción constitucional en el derecho venezolano*, Caracas 1955 p. 46.

Moreover, Article 20 of the Civil Proceedings Code allows all Courts and Tribunals of the Republic to declare all normative state acts inapplicable in a given case, when they consider them unconstitutional and, hence, to give preference to constitutional rules. Thus, the system here established is also a diffuse system of judicial review. Therefore, as now happens in the Portuguese system, it can be said of the Venezuelan system of judicial review of the constitutionality of laws and other state acts, that it is one of the most extensive in comparative law, since it mixes the diffuse system of judicial review of the constitutionality of laws with the concentrated systems.[60]

With respect to this mixed character of the Venezuelan system, the Supreme Court has analysed the ambit of judicial review of the constitutionality of laws in our country, and has pointed out that this is the responsibility:

> «Not only of the Supreme Court of the Republic, but also of the judges in general, whatever their rank and standing may be. It is sufficient for an official to form part of the judiciary for him to be a custodian of the Constitution and, consequently, to apply it's ruling preferentially over those of ordinary laws... Nonetheless, the application of the fundamental rules by the judges, only has effects in the concrete case at issue and, for that very reason, only affects the interested parties to the conflict. In contrast, when constitutional illegitimacy in a law is declared by the Supreme Court when exercising its sovereign function, as the interpreter of the Constitution, and in response to the pertinent action, the effects of the decision extend *erga omnes* and have the force of law. In the first case, the review is incidental and special, and in the second, principal and general. When this happens -that is to say when the recourse is autonomous- the control is either formal or material, depending on whether the nullity has to do with an irregularity relating to the process of drafting the law, or whether -despite the legislation having been correct from the formalist point of view- the intrinsic content of the ruling suffers from substantial defects».[61]

Consequently, the Venezuelan system of judicial review is a mixed one, in which the diffuse system functions in parallel with the concentrated system of judicial review assigned to the Supreme Court of Justice.

2. Diffuse System of Judicial Review

As we have said, the Venezuelan Civil Procedure Code since 1897 has established the following, in article 20:

> «Art. 20. When the law whose application is demanded conflicts with any provision of the Constitution, the judges will give preference to the latter».[62]

---

[60] See in general, Allan R. Brewer-Carías, *E1 control de la constitucionalidad de los actos estatales*, Caracas 1977; and also «Algunas consideraciones sobre el control jurisdiccional de la constitucionalidad de los actos estatales en el derecho venezolano», *Revista de Administración Pública*, 76, Madrid 1975, pp. 419-446.

[61] See Federal Court (which in 1961 was substituted by the Supreme Court of Justice), 19-6-1953 *Gaceta Forense*, 1, 1953, pp. 77-78.

[62] The text of the norm in Spanish is as follows: «Cuando la ley vigente, cuya aplicación se pida, colidiere con alguna disposición constitucional, los jueces aplicarán ésta con preferencia». The text was originally adopted in the 1897 Code (Art. 10), followed by the 1904 Code (Art. 10) and the 1916 Code (Art. 7). In the 1985 Code the only change introduced in relation to the previous text, is the word «judges» which substituted the word «Tribunals». See the text of the 1897, 1904 and 1916 Codes in *Leyes y Decretos Reglamentarios de los Estados Unidos de Venezuela*, Caracas 1943, Vol. V.

According to this norm, the diffuse system of judicial review allows any judge, from the lowest judicial rank to the Supreme Court of Justice, to decide not to apply a law in a concrete case that conflicts with any provision of the Constitution when the application of that law is demanded by a party to litigation. This is, no doubt, the basic consequence of the principle of the supremacy of the Constitution, as considered since the beginning of the present century by all the commentators of the Code.[63]

According to this power attributed to all judges, the diffuse system of judicial review in Venezuela can be characterised by the following trends:

A. *Pre-eminence of the Constitution and the Nullity of Unconstitutional Acts*

Firstly, as we have said, the power attributed to all judges to control the constitutionality of legislation is the natural consequence of the principle of the supremacy of the Constitution. The judges are bound by the Constitution and have the duty to apply it; therefore, if a law is unconstitutional, they cannot apply it and must give preference to the Constitution, because an unconstitutional law can have no value.

It must be said that this was the basic principle established ever since the beginning of our constitutionalism, in the 1811 Constitution in which it has been considered that an implicit diffuse judicial review system was adopted.[64]

In effect, article 227 of the 1811 Constitution established:

> «The present Constitution, the laws to be adopted in its execution and the Treaties to be subscribed under the authority of the Union Government will be the supreme law of the state in the whole Confederation, and the authorities and inhabitants of the provinces are bound to religiously obey and observe them without excuse or pretext; but the laws enacted against the text of the Constitution will have no value unless they fulfil all the required conditions for a just and legitimate revision and sanction».[65]

According to this norm, in the same sense as the American model, unconstitutional laws were considered null and void, as they could have no effect whatsoever.

The guarantee of the Constitution in that case was the nullity of the unconstitutional act, and not its annullability. Thus, the judges were not bound to apply unconstitutional laws and acts, the contrary, as established in the 1830 Constitution, all public officials had the duty not to «obey or execute orders evidently contrary to the Constitution or the laws».[66]

Now concerning fundamental rights and freedoms, ever since the 1893 Constitution the *nullity* of the laws, which violated or harmed them, as their basic guarantee has been expressly established.[67] That is why the present 1961 Constitution expressly establishes that

---

63 See note 2, Supra.

64 H. J. LA ROCHE, *El control jurisdiccional de la constitucionalidad en Venezuela y Estados Unidos*, Maracaibo 1971, p. 24; T».El recurso de inconstitucionalidad en la Constitución venezolana de 1811», in *El pensamiento constitucional de Latinoamérica* 1810-1830, Congreso de Academias e Institutos Históricos, Actas y Ponencias, Caracas 1962, Vol. 3, p. 208.

65 See in Allan R. BREWER-CARÍAS, *Las Constituciones de Venezuela*, Madrid 1985, p. 203.

66 Art. 186. See in Allan R. BREWER-CARÍAS, *Las Constituciones ..., cit.*, p. 353.

67 Art. 17. See in Allan R. BREWER-CARÍAS, *Las Constituciones..., cit.*, p. 531.

«Art.46: Every act of the Public Power which violates or impairs the rights guaranteed by this Constitution is void, and the public officials and employees who order or execute it shall be held criminally, civilly or administratively liable, as the case may be, and orders of superiors manifestly contrary to the Constitution and the laws may not serve as an excuse».

Consequently, it can be said that since the 1811 Constitution, the diffuse system of judicial review of legislation, based on the principle of the supremacy of the Constitution and the nullity and infectivity of unconstitutional acts, has existed in Venezuela following the implicit North American constitutional trends, particularly until 1897, when it was expressly established as a power of all judges in the Civil Procedure Code.

It must be mentioned also that in the 1901 Constitution, following the approval of the 1897 Civil Procedure Code, the power of all judges to control the constitutionality of laws was ratified. In that Constitution, competence to declare which disposition would prevail in a concrete case, when a lower judge *motu proprio* or at party instance, would have referred a constitutional question to the Supreme Court, was attributed to the Supreme Court. Nevertheless, it was expressly established that this referral did not have suspensive effects on the procedure, and that the lower judge was empowered to decide the constitutional question if through the opportunity of adopting his own decision, the Supreme Court opinion was not received by the lower court.[68]

Anyway, historically and in the present constitutional system, our country has always had, following the American model, a diffuse system of judicial review according to which all courts have the power to examine the constitutionality of laws and not to apply them when considering them to be unconstitutional, giving preference to the Constitution. Of course, the expression «laws» used in the Civil Procedure Code has always been interpreted in an extensive way, comprising not only formal laws approved by Congress, but also all normative state acts, including executive regulations.

B. *Incidental Character of the System and the Ex-Officio Powers of the Judges*

Following the general trends of all diffuse systems of judicial review, the Venezuelan system also has an incidental character, that is to say, the judge can only review the constitutionality of a law and decide not to apply it, when deciding a concrete case brought before him by a party, in which the constitutional question is not, of course, the principal issue submitted for his decision, but only an incidental question regarding the law which the judge must apply for the resolution of the case as required by a party.

Therefore, the power of judges to control the constitutionality of legislation can only be exercised within a concrete adversary litigation, regarding the law whose application is demanded by a party, and when the constitutional issue is relevant to the case and necessary to be resolved in their decision. But in the Venezuelan system, the constitutional issue itself can be raised *ex officio* by the judge when deciding the concrete case it not being required, as happens in the North American system, to be alleged by a party. Therefore, the Venezuelan diffuse system of judicial review although incidental, is not a control that it is exclusively exercised

[68] Art. 106, 8 in Allan R. BREWER-CARÍAS, *Las Constituciones ..., cit.*, pp. 579-580. See the comments regarding this norm in R. FEO, *op. cit.*, Vol. I, pp. 32-33.

through an «exception of unconstitutionality»[69] rose by a party. On the contrary, it can be exercised by the judge, *motu proprio* as stated in the 1901 Constitution.[70]

C. *Effects of the Judicial Decision and the Absence of Extraordinary Means of Appeals or Recourses*

On the other hand, the nullity of unconstitutional laws, particularly those that violate fundamental rights; being the guarantee of the Constitution, the decision of the courts in the diffuse system of constitutional control has declarative effects. That is to say, the judge when deciding not to apply a law in a concrete case declares it unconstitutional and, therefore, considers it unconstitutional ever since its enactment (*ab initio*), thus as never having been valid and as always having been null and void. Consequently, the decision of the court in the concrete case evidently has *ex-tunc* and *pro pretaerito* or retroactive effects, preventing the unconstitutional and inapplicable law from having any effect in the case. Thus, the judge's decision is not a declaration «of nullity» of the law he considered unconstitutional, but rather a declaration that the law «is unconstitutional». In declaring the law inapplicable to the concrete case, he plainly judges that the law could never have produced effects in the particular case; he judges it not to have existed and never to have done so. In other words, when he declares that the law is inapplicable to a particular case which was supposed to have been governed, in the past, by a law whose applicability is demanded by one of the parties to the case, the Judge is «ignoring» the -in his opinion- unconstitutional law, and thus considering it never having had effects on the particular case brought before him.

Of course, these declarative and *ex-tunc* effects of the decision, only refer to the concrete parties, in the concrete process in which the decision is adopted.

Thus, the decision only has *in casu et inter partes* effects,[71] as a consequence of the incidental character (*incidenter tantum*) control. Therefore, if a law has been considered unconstitutional in a concrete judicial case decision, and the judge decided not to apply it to the case but gave preference to the Constitution, this does not mean that the law has been invalidated and is not enforceable and applicable elsewhere. According to the Civil Procedure Code, judges have no competence to make declarations of the nullity of the unconstitutional law, or to annul it, these attributions being exclusively assigned in the Constitution to the Supreme Court.[72] Thus, in the diffuse system of review, the decision in which the judge decides not to apply a law in the concrete case only means that concerning that particular process and parties, the law must be considered unconstitutional, null and void, but with no effects regarding other cases, other judges or other individuals.

Therefore, the fact that a law is declared inapplicable by reason of unconstitutionality by a judge in a particular case does not affect its validity nor is it equivalent to a declaration of nullity. The law as such continues to be valid and will only lose its general effects if repealed by another law [73] or if annulled by the Supreme Court of Justice.[74]

---

69 See a contrary opinion in H.J. LA ROCHE, *op. cit.*, pp. 137, 140, 150, 162; and in J.G. ANDUEZA, *op. cit.*, pp. 37-38.

70 Art. 106, 8.

71 See the Federal Court decision of 19-6-1953, in *Gaceta Forense* N° 1, 1953, pp. 77-78.

72 *Cf.* R. MARCANO RODRÍGUEZ, *op. cit.*, Vol. I, p. 37.

73 Art. 177, 1961 Constitution.

74 Art. 215, 3, 4, 1961 Constitution.

In any case, in the Venezuelan procedural system, the *stare decisis* doctrine has no application at all, the judges being sovereign in their decisions, only submitted to the constitution and the law. Therefore, decisions regarding the inapplicability of a law considered unconstitutional do not have binding effects, neither regarding the same judge who may change his legal opinion in other cases, nor regarding other judges or courts, even if the decision is made by a higher court. On the other hand, unlike the American or Argentinean systems, in the Venezuelan system of constitutional judicial control, there are no extraordinary means of appeal or recourses against judicial decisions in which constitutional questions are involved that could be brought before the Supreme Court.

On the contrary, judge's decisions are only subject to the ordinary means of appeal and to the recourse of cassation, following the general rules established in the Civil Procedural Code. It was only in the 1901 Constitution that the Federal Court was assigned the power to establish general criterion in constitutional matters referred to by lower courts, when a constitutional issue was raised in concrete judicial cases, which power was eliminated in the subsequent constitutional reform of 1904. In effect, article 106, 8 of the 1901 Constitution established as an attribution of the Federal Court, to

> «Declare in the shortest possible delay which disposition must prevail in the special case which is referred to it *motu proprio* or at the instance of the interested party by the authority, which is due to apply the law, in the delay established for adopting its decision, when the said authority considers that a collision exists between the Federal or state Laws with the Constitution of the Republic».[75]

Notwithstanding this consultative power of the Federal Court, when a referral was made before it, it had no suspensive effect in the concrete process, which, said the 1901 Constitution, was not to be stopped and when the opportunity to decide it came without having received the Federal Court opinion, the lower court was to decide in accordance with the Civil Procedure Code, that is to say, reviewing by itself the constitutionality of legislation, in the concrete case.

Nevertheless, the possible contradictions that could arise between different court decisions, with the consequent uncertainty in the legal order, have been corrected ever since 1858 in Venezuelan constitutional system, through the establishment, in parallel with the diffuse system of judicial review, of a concentrated system of constitutional control assigned to the Supreme Court of Justice.

3. Concentrated system of judicial review

A. *Historical antecedents*

In effect, in parallel with the diffuse system of judicial review a concentrated system of judicial review has existed in Venezuela ever since the 1858 Constitution by attributing the power to annul laws and other normative state acts, with general effects, when declared unconstitutional, to the Supreme Court.

The 1858 Constitution in effect, attributed competence to the Supreme Court to

> «Declare the nullity of legislative acts sanctioned by the Provincial Legislatures, when petitioned by any citizen, when they are contrary to the Constitution».[76]

---

75 Art. 106,8. See the text in Allan R. BREWER-CARÍAS, *Las Constituciones de Venezuela, cit.* p. 579.

76 Art.113, 8. *Idem*, p. 392.

Thus, in 1858 a popular action was established to seek the control of the constitutionality of legislative acts adopted at provincial level. It was a limited concentrated judicial review system, which did not refer to the national legislative act, but it can be considered the direct antecedent of the current popular action established after 1893. It was originally intended to protect the invasions by the Provinces of the competences of the Central Power, and that is why in the 1864 Constitution that consolidated the Federal form of the state, the principle of protection was reverted so as to sanction the invasions of the competences and rights of the Member States by the Federal level. In this sense, the 1864 Constitution expressly established that:

> «Art. 92. Any act of Congress or of the National Executive which violates the rights of the Member States guaranteed by the Constitution or which harm its independence, must be declared null by the High Court, when the majority of the Legislatures demand it».[77]

Thus, the 1864 Constitution eliminated the popular action and limited the standing to seek judicial review of legislation to the legislatures of the state members of the Federation. Nevertheless, that same Constitution attributed competence to the Federal High Court to declare which law was in force when collisions existed between the national laws, these and the member states legislation, and between the laws of the various member states[78] which authorised some sort of judicial review regarding the legislation of the member states in relation to federal regulations.

This situation stood invariable until 1893, when the constitutional reform of that year extended the powers of judicial review of legislation of the Supreme Court to a point very similar to the present one.

The 1893 Constitution attributed competence to the Federal High Court to:

> «Declare which is the law, decree or resolution in force when a collision exists between the national acts, or those with one of the States, or between the acts of the States, and any of those acts with the Constitution».[79]

In this way, the Supreme Court powers of judicial review of constitutionality were re-established, extended not only to laws, but also to decrees and resolutions, and maintaining the protective norm of the rights of the member states against the invasions of their competences by the federal or national power.[80]

On the other hand, in the same 1893 Constitution, the guarantee of the fundamental rights of citizens was established for the first time in our constitutional history in an express form, by stating that:

> «The rights recognised and established in the Constitution will not be harmed or damaged by the laws which regulate their exercise, and those which do so will be considered unconstitutional and will have no effects».[81]

Finally, the same 1893 Constitution assigned the Federal High Court powers to declare the nullity of all state acts that could be dictated by a usurped authority

---

[77] Art. 92. *Idem*, p. 422
[78] Art. 89, 9. *Idem*, p. 422
[79] Art. 110, 8. *Idem*, p. 540
[80] Art. 123. *Idem*, p. 541
[81] Art. 17. *Idem*, p. 531

or as a consequence of a direct or indirect request by force or by a subversive people's gathering,[82] acts which were expressly declared null in the text of the Constitution.[83]

Therefore, as a result of all these constitutional dispositions, we can say that it was in 1893 that a complete and effective concentrated system of judicial review was established in Venezuela, followed by the diffuse system of judicial review expressly established four years later in the Civil Procedural Code of 1897.

The system of the 1893 Constitution, with the only exception of a short period of three years between 1901 and 1904,[84] has more or less been maintained in all subsequent constitutional texts and reforms but with a tendency to widen the means of control. In effect, in 1925 the possibility of also declaring the nullity of the Municipal ordinances that violated the Constitution was added to the powers of the Supreme Court,[85] and in 1936, Executive Regulations were added to the list of acts submitted to constitutional judicial review.[86] Anyway, it was in the 1936 Constitution adopted after the end of a 35 year dictatorship, that the concentrated system of judicial review was definitively established when the Constitution assigned the Supreme Court, then the Federal and Cassation Court, power to declare the nullity of all acts of the Public Powers which violated the Constitution.[87]

Finally, it must be said that in parallel with the regulations of judicial review of the constitutionality of legislation (national, state and municipal legislation), after the 1925 Constitution[88] the system of judicial review of administrative action was also expressly established giving way to the development of the judicial control of administrative acts through an administrative jurisdiction established within the Judiciary.[89] Constitutional jurisdiction, therefore, was reserved to the Supreme Court and in general terms, is only concerned with legislative acts whether at national, state or municipal level, or national acts enacted in direct execution of the Constitution, like Decree-Laws and other acts of government.[90]

In this respect, the 1961 Constitution in force today establishes as a competence of the Supreme Court of Justice the power to declare in the first place, the total or partial nullity of national laws and other acts of the legislative bodies that are in conflict with the Constitution. In the second place, it can declare the total or partial nullity of state laws, Municipal Ordinances and other acts of the deliberative bodies of the States and Municipalities that are in conflict with the Constitution; and third, the nullity of regulations and other acts of the National Executive when they violate the Constitution.[91]

---

82 Art. 110, 9. *Idem*, p. 540.

83 Arts. 118, 119, *Idem*, p. 541

84 The 1901 Constitution eliminated the atributions of the Supreme Court to control directly the constitutionality of legislation and only established and incidental diffuse control based in a referral of the constitutional question to the Supreme Courts by the lower courts. Art. 106, 8. See the text in Allan R. BREWER-CARÍAS, *Las Constituciones... cit.*, p. 579.

85 Art. 34 and Art. 120,11. *Idem*, p. 705-706.

86 Art. 34 and Art. 123, 11. *Idem*, p. 824

87 Art. 123, 11. *Idem*, p. 824.

88 Art. 120, 12. *Idem*, p. 715.

89 Allan R. BREWER-CARÍAS, *E1 control de la constitucionalidad... cit.*, pp. 27-29.

90 *Idem*, pp. 33-114

91 Art. 215, ord. 3,4 and 6.

These attributions have been developed by the organic Law of the Supreme Court of Justice of 1976,[92] in which it can be said, all state acts of a normative character (legislation of the three territorial levels and executive regulations) and all other state acts issued in direct execution of the Constitution are submitted to judicial review of constitutionality by means of a direct popular action.[93] This action or recourse of unconstitutionality leads, indeed, to an *a posteriori* judicial review, exercised after the challenged acts have come into effect, which is the most important and most commonly exercised. But in the Venezuelan constitutional system, an *a priori* judicial review, particularly of national legislation, can also be distinguished, exercised by the Supreme Court at the request of the President of the Republic, before the promulgation of the laws. Therefore, the concentrated system of judicial review can be both preventive and *a posteriori*.

B. *Preventive control of constitutionality of laws*

In effect, since 1945, the Venezuelan Constitution has expressly established the possibility of a judicial preventive control of the constitutionality of national laws, including the special laws through which Congress approves international treaties, by the Supreme Court of Justice, at the request of the President of the Republic, and as a consequence of its powers of veto regarding legislation approved by Congress.[94] The present 1961 Constitution in article 173 establishes, in effect, the procedure for the enactment of laws, and in particular the possibility of the Presidential veto to legislation, in the following way.

The President of the Republic shall promulgate the law within ten days after the date of receipt, but within that period, with the approval of the Council of Ministers, he may ask Congress for its reconsideration, giving an explanation with reasons, in order to amend certain provisions or withdraw its sanction of all or part of the law. The Chambers in joint session shall decide on the points raised by the President of the Republic and may write a new text for the provisions objected to and those connected therewith.

When a decision has been adopted by two thirds of those present, the President of the Republic shall proceed with the promulgation of the law within five days following its receipt, and he may not offer new objections. But when a simple majority has reached the decision, the President of the Republic may choose between promulgating the law or returning it again to Congress within the same five-day period for a new and final reconsideration. In this latter case the decision of the Chambers in joint session is definitive, even by a simple majority, and promulgation of the law must be made within five days following its receipt.

In any case -adds article 173 of the Constitution- if the objection is based on unconstitutionality, the President of the Republic may, within the period fixed for the promulgation of a law, that is to say, within five days following the receipt of the law after Congress' reconsideration, have recourse to the Supreme Court of

92 Art. 42, ord. 1,2,3,4,11,12 of the Organic Law of the Supreme Court of Justice (LOCSJ), 30-7-76, *Gaceta Oficial* Nº 1893 Extra, 30-7-76.

93 Nevertheless, the Supreme Court has established in a decision of the Plenary Session of 29-4-1965 that the Laws of approval of international treaties could not be submitted to judicial review. See the decision and critics in Allan R. BREWER-CARÍAS, *El control de la constitucionalidad... cit.*, pp. 48-52.

94 Art. 91, Constitution 1945. See in Allan R. BREWER-CARÍAS, *Las Constituciones... cit.*, p. 850. In the same sense, Art. 90, Constitution 1953, *Idem*, p. 947.

Justice, requesting its decision as to the alleged unconstitutionality.[95] The Court shall decide within a period of ten days, counted from the date of receipt of the communication from the President of the Republic. Nevertheless, if the Court denies the complaint of unconstitutionality, or does not decide within the aforementioned period, the President of the Republic must promulgate the law within five days after the decision of the Court or the expiration of the period indicated.[96]

On the contrary, if the Court accepts the alleged unconstitutionality it must decide the case and that will prevent the sanctioned law from being promulgated.[97]

Although the Constitution does not establish the possibility and consequences of a delayed decision of the Court upon the unconstitutionality of a law at the request of the President, after the expiry of the delay of ten days established in the Fundamental text, it can be considered that the expiry of that delay and the subsequent compulsory promulgation of the law, do not prevent the Court from the possibility of declaring the nullity of the law once in effect, based on its concentrated powers of judicial review of promulgated legislation.

C. *Direct Control of Constitutionality*

Additionally, to the diffuse and preventive systems of judicial review in the Venezuelan constitutional system, the control of the constitutionality of legislation -national, state and municipal legislation- and other state acts issued in direct execution of the Constitution, can also be exercised in a concentrated way by the Supreme Court of Justice at the request of any body, through a popular action, whose antecedents can be traced back to 1858.

(a) Popular action and the principal character of the process

In effect, the fundamental feature of the judicial review powers of the Supreme Court to control the constitutionality of legislation is that it has been set up as a consequence of a popular action, that is to say, of a recourse open to any inhabitant of the Republic in full possession of his rights.[98]

Thus, the concentrated system of judicial review in Venezuela is always of a principal character, which can only be exercised by the Supreme Court when a popular action is brought before it. This popular action, as stated by the Supreme Court in 1971, is open to:

> «Any member of the general public (hence its name) is intended to defend a public interest which is, at the same time, the simple interest of the petitioner who, for this reason alone, need not be vested with any other standing or judicial interest».

95 Art. 42,2 LOCSJ attributed powers to the Court to «decide upon the Unconstitutionality of laws requested by the President of the Republic before its promulgation».

96 Art. 173. 1961 Constitution.

97 Thus, in this case, Article 175 of the Constitution which confers the President and Vice-President of the Congress to promulgate laws not promulgated by the President of the Republic, within the prescribed delay, does not apply.

98 See the decision of the Federal Court (CF) of 2-2-60 in *Gaceta Forense* N° 27, Caracas 1960, pp. 107-108; and the decision of the Supreme Court of Justice, in Politico-Administrative Chamber (CSJ-SPA) of 3-10-63, *Gaceta Forense* N° 42 Caracas 1963, pp. 16-20; of 6-4-64, *Gaceta Oficial* N° 27.373 of 21-2-64; of 30-5-63 *Gaceta Forense* N° 52, Caracas 1968, p. 109; and of 25-9-73, *Gaceta Oficial* N° 1643 Extra. 21-3-74.

For this reason, the popular action in Venezuela is instituted, the Court has added:

> «To contest the validity of an act by the Public Power, which by virtue of its normative and general character, acts *erga omnes* and thus its validity affects, and is of interest to all, equally».[99]

From this stem one of the great differences between the popular action of unconstitutionality and actions seeking judicial review of administrative acts. The first requires no special standing: a «simple interest» in legality is sufficient. By contrast, if an administrative act with individual effects is contested in the administrative jurisdiction, it is required that the petitioner is entitled to some subjective right, or have a personal, - legitimate and direct interest in the legality of the act.[100]

But regarding the popular action, it must be pointed out that its popularity, traditionally wider, has been restricted in some way since 1976 by the Organic Law of the Supreme Court of Justice, which requires that the challenged law must violate «the rights and interests of the petitioner» in some way.[101]

In this way, the traditional, absolutely «popular» nature of the action of unconstitutionality has been legally restricted, but, without it ceasing to be a «popular action».

In effect, this restriction can be considered reasonable, and can only affect standing in extreme cases: for instance, if the challenged law is a law of a member state, at least it is required that the petitioner be resident of the said state or has some particular interest located in that state.[102]

Anyway, doubts about the extent of the restriction to the popularity of the action have been clarified by the Supreme court, which has considered that the legal reference to the need that the challenged law affected ''the rights and interests» of the petitioner does not mean that the popular action has been eliminated, and that a special standing requirement has been established to bring such action before the Court. The object of the popular action, the Court has said, is the «objective defence of the majesty of the Constitution and its supremacy» and if it is true that the Organic Law of the Supreme Court requires that the petitioner is affected in his rights or interests, this expression must be interpreted in a «restrictive way». Thus, the Court has concluded that when the popular action is exercised against legislative acts,

> «A presumption exists that at least relatively, the challenged act of general effects, affects the rights or interests of the petitioner in his condition as a Venezuelan citizen in some way unless the contrary shows itself evident from the text of the complaint».[103]

Anyway, from this popular character of the recourse of unconstitutionality another difference results regarding the recourses established for reviewing

99 See CSJ-SPA, 18-2-71 in *Gaceta Oficial* Nº 1472 Extra. 11-6-71. *Cf.* CSJ-SPA, 6-2-64 in *Gaceta Oficial* Nº 27373, 21-2-64.

100 See, for example, CSJ-SPA, 18-7-71 in *Gaceta Oficial* Nº 1472 Extra. 11-6-71. See article 121 LOCSJ.

101 Art. 112 LOCSJ.

102 Allan R. BREWER-CARÍAS, *El control de la constitucionalidad... cit.*, p. 122.

103 See decision of the Supreme Court of Justice in Plenary Session (CSJ-CP) of 30-6-82 in *Revista de Derecho Público* Nº 11, Caracas 1982, pp. 135-138.

administrative action. As the action of unconstitutionality refers to legislative acts, thus with general effects or those with the same rank as laws, it is not subject to any expiry period; it is inextinguishable.[104] However, judicial actions against administrative acts, when referred to acts with particular effects must be exercised within a delay of six months,[105] after which they expire.

In relation to the popular nature of the action of unconstitutionality, it is also clear that, as it is open to any person whose rights and interests have been violated, the fact that deficiencies may exist in the petitioner's legal representation is no impediment to acceptance of the recourse, since the supposed legal representative could equally well bring the action in a personal capacity.[106]

On the other hand, not only individuals and public corporations have standing to bring a popular action of unconstitutionality before the Supreme Court, but the Prosecutor General is also entitled to do so[107] and, in general, any public officer. Thus, even the President of the Republic has been recognised by the Supreme Court as having standing to bring a popular action against legislative acts before the Court.[108]

(b) Objective character of the process

The direct consequence of the popular character of the action for requesting judicial review of legislation by the Supreme Court in the Venezuelan system is the objective character of the process developed before the Court. The action is not presented against a state organ, for example, the Congress or the President of the Republic at all but is only directed against a state act: the law. Thus, there are no parties to the process in the strictest sense. The petitioner is not a plaintiff and there is no defendant in the strict sense. The process is a judicial process against a state act, for instance a law, which can be initiated by any individual or corporation, or by any public official, even a member of the Supreme Court in his personal capacity. Thus, if it is true that the Court in itself does not have self-initiating power to act as a constitutional judge, and an action must be brought before it for exercising its powers of judicial review,[109] this popular action could personally be exercised by a member of the Court.

On the other hand, as there are no defendants in the process it is not required that any person be summoned;[110] and only the head of the legislative body and the Prosecutor General are notified, the latter in cases in which he himself is not the petitioner.[111] In any case, the Court must order the publishing of a notice requesting the intervention of any interested person in the process. Thus, in the same way that any citizen whose rights and interests have been prejudiced may exercise the action of unconstitutionality of laws and other state acts of legislative rank, so any citizen

---

104 See CSJ-SPA, 3-10-63 in *Gaceta Forense* Nº 42, 1963, pp. 20-21.
105 Art. 134 LOCSJ.
106 See CF 12-6-52, *Gaceta Forense* Nº 1, Caracas 1953, pp. 48-50; CF 22-2-60, *Gaceta Forense* Nº 27, 1960, pp. 107-108; and CSJ-SPA, 25-9-73, in *Gaceta Oficial* Nº 1643 Extra. 21-3-74.
107 Art. 116 LOCSJ.
108 See CSJ-SPA 3-10-63 in *Gaceta Forense* Nº 42, 1963, pp. 19-20.
109 Art. 82 LOCSJ
110 See Federal and Cassation Court in Politico-Administrative Chamber (CFC-SPA) 20-11-40, in *Memoria de la Corte Federal y de Casación*, 1941, pp. 264-268.
111 Art. 116 LOCSJ.

with the same simple interest has the right to present writs and briefs to the Court, against or in defence of the law or act being challenged.[112]

In any case, the popular action of unconstitutionality must be brought before the Supreme Court by means of a petition for remedy in which the petitioner must clearly state the act which he is impugning[113] and indicate precisely the breach of the Constitution denounced - that is to say, both the grounds for the petition and the constitutional rules that are said to have been violated.[114] However, given that this is a popular action in which the validity of a law and the supremacy of the Constitution are at stake, in our opinion the Court is able to appraise by virtue of its function, whether the contested act is in breach of the Constitution, as a result of defects not alleged by the petitioner,[115] and does not have to limit the hearing to the unconstitutionality denounced by it.[116] Therefore if it is true that the popular action must be brought before the Court by a petitioner[117] the Supreme Court is not totally subject to his will, and if the petitioner for instance, abandons the action once undertaken, the Court is empowered to continue with the hearing.[118]

(c) Grounds for the action

The only grounds that can be claimed for the action of unconstitutionality are violations or collisions with the Constitution; that is to say, grounds of unconstitutionality[119] whether of a substantive or of a formal or adjective character.

The Supreme Court of Justice, however, has maintained that not all constitutional rules, when violated, provide grounds for the exercise of judicial review.

On the contrary, it has frequently been required that a directly operative rule is at issue, and the Court has not annulled a law when violations of a programmatic rule have been alleged.[120] This does not mean, however, that judicial review of legislation cannot be exercised based on constitutional principles.

For instance, article 50 of the Constitution expressly establishes that:

> «Art. 50. The enunciation of rights and guarantees contained in this Constitution must not be construed as a denial of others which, being inherent in the

---

112 Art. 137 LOCSJ. Before the promulgation of the 1976 LOCSJ, see in contrary sense CSJ-CP, 12-6-68 in *Publicaciones del Senado*, 1968, p. 190; and CSJ-SPA, 27-5-70, *Gaceta Forense* Nº 68, 1970, p. 111.

113 Art. 113 LOCSJ. *Cf.* CSJ-SPA, 23-1-69 in *Gaceta Forense* Nº 63, 1969, p. 95.

114 Art. 113 LOCSJ. *Cf.* decision of the Federal and Cassation in Plenary Session (CFC-CP), 14-12-50 in *Gaceta Forense* Nº 6, 1950, pp. 46-47; CSJ-SPA, 11-8-64, *Gaceta Forense* Nº 45, 1964, pp. 185-186.

115 In this respect, the Attorney General's Office has indicated that the constitutionality of legislative acts is a matter of prime public interest. Thus, in cases in which such matters are considered, the judges powers are not, nor can be, limited by what is alleged or proven in the complaint. See *Doctrina de la Procuraduría General de la República 1963*, Caracas 1964, pp. 23-24.

116 As has been held by the Supreme Court. See CSJ-CP, 15-3-62. *Gaceta Oficial* Nº 760 Extra, 22-3-62. In this respect, J.G. ANDUEZA holds that the decision of the Court may not contain *ultra petita, op. cit.*, p. 37.

117 Art. 82 LOCSJ

118 Art. 87 LOCSJ, *Cf.* J.G. ANDUEZA, *op. cit.*, p. 37

119 Reasons of illegality may not thus be alleged. See CSJ-SPA, 13-2-68, in *Gaceta Forense* Nº 59, 1969, pp. 85-86.

120 See CSJ-CP, 12-6-69, in *Gaceta Forense* Nº 65, 1969, p. 10; CSJ-SPA, 27-4-69, in *Gaceta Forense* Nº 64, 1969, p. 23; and CSJ-SPA, 13-2-68 in *Gaceta Forense* Nº 59, pp. 85-86.

human person, are not expressly mentioned herein. The lack of a law regulating these rights does not impair the exercise thereof».

Thus, the Supreme Court of Justice could exercise judicial review control of legislation, on the grounds of violations of rights inherent in the human person, not enunciated expressly in the Constitution.

Anyway, the complaint of unconstitutionality must necessarily involve a «logical link -by way of a serious and necessary motivation- between the act contested and the rule which is said to have been broken by it».[121] For this reason, the Court has considered complaints of infractions of constitutional rules to be formally insufficient when such a link does not appear in the petition.

In any case, it is clear that the act, which is challenged, may constitute a breach of the Constitution when it contradicts the spirit and purpose of a constitutional rule,[122] and not only when there is a literal contradiction between the rules and the challenged act.

(d) Content of the Court's decision

According to the provisions of the Organic Law of the Supreme Court of Justice, in its final decision, the Court, once the grounds on which the action has been founded have been examined, shall declare the nullity of the challenged act or of its articles when accepted.[123]

Accordingly, the Court is under an obligation to examine *all* the grounds on which the action founded, but the Organic Law does not limit this appraisal solely to those grounds alleged by the petitioner. In view of the issue of unconstitutionality involved in these popular actions, in my opinion as the procedure is in the nature of an inquiry, the Court is able to assess grounds for unconstitutionality, which are not alleged by the petitioner.

Regarding the contents of the decision, the Supreme Court pointed out in 1966 that:

> «It is the function of the Court, when exercising its power to review the constitutionality of acts of the legislative bodies, to declare the nullity of the act which is challenged if it is in any way in conflict with the precepts of the Constitution, and as a consequence of that declaration, to proclaim the legal annulment or, alternatively, to sustain it in full force instead of the assumptions which were advanced».[124]

---

121 See CSJ-SPA, 21-12-67, in *Gaceta Forense* Nº 58, 1968, p. 68.

122 See the decision of the Federal Court, 25-3-58, in *Gaceta Forense* Nº 19, 1958, p. 58. To the contrary, the Attorney General's Office has maintained that an infraction of the «motives» of the Constitution cannot be the cause for the annulment of a legal text. See *Doctrina de la Procuraduría General de la República 1964*, Caracas 1965, p. 158. Elsewhere, however, the same Attorney General's Office has held that the Constitution is being violated when the law intends to achieve ends different to those proposed by the Constitution, and not only when there exists some literal contradiction between the rule in the Constitution and the legal rule. See *Doctrina de la Procuraduría General de la República 1969*, Caracas 1970, p. 111. In general, on the various grounds for unconstitutionality of laws, see *Doctrina de la Procuraduría General de la República 1966*, Caracas 1967, pp. 170-174.

123 Articles 119 and 130.

124 See CSJ-SPA, 20-1-66, in *Gaceta Forense* Nº 51, p. 13. *Cf.* CFC-SPA, 2-12-41, in *Memoria de la Corte Federal y de Casación*, 1942, pp. 335-338, and 13-7-42, in *Memoria de la Corte Federal y de Casación*, 1943, pp. 174-175.

In 1976, however, the Organic Law of the Supreme Court of Justice, in the provisions common to the popular action and to the recourses for judicial review of administrative action, includes an article which after insisting that «In its final decision, the Court shall declare whether or not the nullity of the act which is being contested is admitted, and shall determine the effects of its decision over time»,[125] it adds the following:

> «Art. 131. ...Also, according to the terms of the corresponding petition, the Court may order the payment of sums of money and the restitution of damages, for whose origin the Administration has responsibility and may also make the necessary provisions for re-establishing the subjective legal situations prejudiced by the activity of the administration».

The placing of this rule might lead us to think that the Court's verdict when deciding upon a popular action may have a condemnatory content. However, the references the article makes to «the Administration» and to «administrative activity» would make it inapplicable to any supposed responsibility of the state for a legislative act. This shows the legislature's intention of confining the damages claimed only to cases of judicial review of administrative action.

Finally, it must be said that the decision of the Supreme Court can also be that of rejecting the action when without grounds, and in particular, if the Court considers that the action was rash and obviously unfounded, it can impose a fine on the petitioner,[126] through which the possible inconveniences that can be produced by the popular character of the action, can be overcome.

D. *Effects of concentrated control decisions*

As we have seen, the Court decision in the concentrated system of judicial review can be that of accepting the petition and thus, declaring the nullity of the unconstitutional challenged law, or it can also be that of rejecting the action dismissing the alleged unconstitutionality of the law. The effects of those decisions, are, of course, different, as the Supreme Court has established.

(a) Effect of the dismissal decisions

In effect, in cases in which the Court decision is to declare the action unjustified, thus considering the reported unconstitutional defects to be without basis, the effects of the decision are *erga omnes* with respect to the constitutionality of the law, at least as far as it concerns the challenged articles and the defects reported.[127] Moreover, in relation to these rejected defects, the decision has the force of *res judicata*, which, of course, does not extend to other similar legislative acts, which may be contested for the same defects. In this respect, the Civil Cassation Chamber of the Supreme Court of Justice has analysed this problem when considering the effects of a decision of the Politico-Administrative Chamber of the same Supreme Court in which a Municipal Ordinance was annulled on the grounds of unconstitutionality. The situation was as follows: the Politico Administrative Chamber of the Supreme Court in a previous decision had dismissed a popular action exercised on the grounds of unconstitutionality against a Municipal Ordinance of one Municipality of the

---

125 Art. 131. Repeating what is expressed in article 119.

126 Art. 119.

127 See CSJ-CPA, 20-1-66, in *Gaceta Forense* N° 51, 1966, p. 13.

Republic (in the case of the *Bocono* District); and in a civil and different procedure in which a Municipal Ordinance of another Municipality (in the case of the *Valera* District) -but similar to the former- had to be applied, a party alleged its constitutionality, bringing before the Cassation Chamber of the Supreme Court the previous decision of the Politico-Administrative Chamber.

In this respect the Cassation Chamber stated that:

«It is to be observed that, although said decision produces *res judicata erga omnes*, this is limited strictly to the matter itself which was decided on, that is, the constitutionality of the ordinance of the *Bocono* District, and there can be no question of extending it to that of the *Valera* District, nor to any other, despite the fact that they deal with the same matter and that their regulations are, by chance, similar.

In this case, the question of the constitutionality of the *Valera* District Ordinance was raised, both as incidental and as an exception, and the lower courts which decided in this case were completely at liberty to consider and decide, under Article 7 of the Civil Procedures Code, whether or not the Ordinance brought before them was unconstitutional, without being bound to any *res judicata* whatever, because there was no such thing. They found that the Ordinance in question is not unconstitutional, and ordered that it be complied with.

The same occurs with this Civil, Mercantile and Labour Cassation Chamber , which is not bound in the least by the *res judicata* pronounced in some different matter, in which a decision was reached on the constitutionality of an Ordinance, different from the one which is required to be complied with here. Had the decision of the Political and Administrative Chamber dealt with the *Valera* District ordinance, then for this Chamber -as for all- the constitutionality of that Ordinance would have been beyond discussion, as it would have been covered by *res judicata.*

As it is not precisely that Ordinance which is at issue, but another different one, this Chamber has the full and absolute jurisdiction, liberty and discretion to decide, for the purposes of these proceedings, whether the Ordinance that is in question here is in conflict with the National Constitution or not, in terms of the infractions of which the challenged judicial decision is accused, as a result of the lower judge having complied with the provisions of that Ordinance which, according to the appellant, are unconstitutional.

The criterion established by that Politico Administrative Chamber when setting out the grounds for its decision, merits the greatest respect and attention from this Civil Cassation Chamber when reaching verdicts on similar matters, but does not bind it -in the same way that its own criterion on matters decided previously does not bind it- if it finds sufficient reasons to modify it».[128]

A few basic principles can be deduced from this Supreme Court decision of 1963:

First, the absolute powers of all judges to control the constitutionality of legislation through the diffuse system of judicial review.

---

[128] See Civil, Commercial and Labor Cassation Chamber of the Supreme Court of Justice, (CSJ-SCCMT), 12-12-63, in *Gaceta Forense* N° 42, 1963, pp. 667-672.

Second, the power of the Supreme Court to control the constitutionality of legislation in a concentrated way, the decisions adopted in this case, having *erga omnes* effects.

Third, the *res judicata* effects of the decisions of the Supreme Court concerning the constitutionality of legislation, either when a legislative act is annulled or when a popular action of unconstitutionality is dismissed, only refers to the particular and specific law challenged before the Court, and cannot be extended to other legislative acts.

Therefore, the decision of the Supreme Court dismissing a popular action against a legislative act, and thus, admitting its constitutionality, has *erga omnes* and *res judicata* effects in the sense that the constitutionality of the act must be accepted by all courts who are bound to follow the criterion established by the Supreme Court. Hence, they cannot through their diffuse judicial review powers decide not to apply the law on the grounds of its constitutionality. Particularly in another decision of the Civil, Mercantile and Labour Cassation Chamber of the Supreme Court of Justice of 1971, the Court was even clearer. It established that a decision by the Politico Administrative Chamber of the Court in which it dismissed a popular action of unconstitutionality should necessarily be applied by the Cassation Chamber, as well as by all Courts, as it was a pronouncement with *erga omnes* force. By virtue of this, the Cassation Chamber allowed a remedy for cassation, sought with respect to a lower court decision which had not applied a Politico Administrative Chamber's decision which had considered a municipal act valid, disallowing a petition for its annulment.[129]

(b) Effects of decisions declaring the nullity of the legislative act

The decision of the Court when declaring the challenges legislative act annulled -either totally or with respect to those of its articles against which action is lodged- it produces cessation of the effects of the act, and the Court being also authorized to declare null all other acts carried out based on the act which is declared null.[130]

In such cases, the effects of the Court's decision, as we said, are of general value that is to say, *erga omnes* and the Supreme Court itself has always maintained this. For instance, in 1938, the former Federal and Cassation Court sustained the following:

---

[129] See CSJ-SCCMT, 11-8-71, in *Gaceta Forense* N° 73, 1971, p. 477. In this respect, the Attorney General's Office has described the effects of a declaration denying a popular action of unconstitutionality, in the following terms: «The decision on constitutionality grounds like any other judicial decision, produces *res judicata*. That... obtained in objective jurisdiction, whether it be favourable or unfavourable, always produces effects *erga omnes*. Consequences of great interest, such as that of irrevocability, follow from this principle. When the Federal Court declares the action inadmissable because the state act which is challenged lacks the defects which are denounced against, this decision may not be reviewed as it enjoys all the characteristics of any decision which produces *res judicata*: it may not be discussed nor changed». «In a case in which the Federal Court has denied a popular action of unconstitutionality, and nonetheless, this is brought again, for the same reasons and supported by the same constitutional provisions, the Court must disallow the new action as this is already *res judicata*. In consequence, the Court should apply *ex-officio* the previous decision or decide the exception of *res judicata* filed by the Attorney General. (J.G. ANDUEZA, *La Jurisdicción Constitutional en el derecho venezolano*, Universidad Central de Venezuela, Facultad de Derecho, Vol. II, Caracas, p. 99)». See *Doctrina de la Procuraduría General de la República 1963*, Caracas 1964, p. 199.

[130] See CSJ-CP, 4-4-74, in *Gaceta Oficial* N° 1.657, Special, 7-6-74.

«The Federal and Cassation Court is the highest level in the judicial hierarchy; *res judicata* established by it, even supposing it were mistaken doctrinally, is the last word by the Judiciary, against which nothing and nobody can prevail in law, neither the Court itself, nor the other two Powers (of the state). As it is a federal institution with exclusive power to annul -*erga omnes*- the laws and acts of the Public Power, which are in violation of the Constitution, it thus constitutes the sovereign interpreter of the constitutional text and of ordinary laws, and the sole judge of acts by the Public Powers and high officials of state. Any official, however high ranking he may be, or any of the other Public Powers which seek their own interpretation of the Law to prevail over the interpretation and application established by the Court when reaching decisions and verdicts on the same matter, usurps power and violates the Constitution and the laws of the Republic».[131]

In this respect, the same former Federal and Cassation Court described its decisions in 1939 as «provisions complementary to the Constitution and Laws of the Republic, which produce *erga omnes* effects»;[132] and in a decision in 1949 it indicated that its decisions «come to form a special legislation, arising from the secondary Constitutive Power which this High Court exercises in these matters».[133]

The former Federal Court that followed the latter as the constitutional body for judicial review of legislation agreed with this criterion, and in 1953, indicated that as its decisions have *erga omnes* effects, they «take on force of law».[134]

More recently, the Civil, Mercantile and Labour Cassation Chamber of the Supreme Court of Justice was precise in this respect in a decision on 12 December, 1963:

«Absolute review of constitutionality is exercised firstly by the full-court session of the Supreme Court of Justice (*Pleno* Court) when it declares the nullity of a national law by reason of its unconstitutionality. This decision deprives the law, or that part of it which is annulled, of effect, and has the force of *res judicata, erga omnes*. This nullity is declared as a result of what is known as a popular action.

A similar power is exercised by the Politico-Administrative Division of this Supreme Court, also by popular action -but only with respect to state laws and Municipal ordinances- and its verdict also produces *res judicata, erga omnes*.

This is to say that the declaration of the constitutionality or unconstitutionality of a law by principal (popular) action is definitive and produces effects against everyone, since that supposed law ceases to be such from the moment it is declared unconstitutional. The same occurs with state Laws and Municipal Ordinances which are pronounced unconstitutional».[135]

---

131 See CSJ-SPA, 17-11-38, in *Memoria de la Corte Federal y de Casación 1939*, pp. 330-334.

132 See CFC-SPA, 21-3-39, in *Memoria de la Corte Federal y de Casación 1940*, p. 176.

133 See CFC-SPA, 16-12-40, in *Memoria de la Corte Federal y de Casación* 1941, p. 311.

134 See CF, 19-6-53, *Gaceta Forense* Nº 1, 1953, pp. 77 and 78. The Supreme Court has also held in a decision of its Politico Administrative Chamber that «the effects of the decisions issued by the Court when exercising this power only extend to the time during which the constitutional precet on which they are based continues valid». See in *Gaceta Forense* Nº 62, 1968, p. 106-113.

135 See CSJ-SCCMT, 12-12-63, in *Gaceta Forense* Nº 42, 1963, pp. 667 to 672.

Consequently, according to the doctrine established by the Court, the verdict declaring the unconstitutionality of a law, and thereby annulling it, has *erga omnes* effects and an absolute character as *res judicata.*

E. *Question of the temporal effects of concentrated constitutional review*

In the context of the effects of Supreme Court decisions declaring nullity of laws by reason of unconstitutionality, the fundamental problem that doubtlessly arises in Venezuela is that of the moment in which these are produced. In other words: Is the law which is declared null considered to have produced effects until declared null by the Court, or is it considered, on the contrary, never to have produced effects? From another point of view: Does the Court's decision have effect from the moment it is published, or are its effects retroactive to the moment the act that has been annulled was first published?

The Organic Law of the Supreme Court of Justice of 1976, as we have seen, does not resolve the question. It only establishes that in its decision, the Supreme Court must «determine the effects of its decision in time».[136] Now, with, two systems of judicial review: the diffuse and the concentrated systems, existing in parallel in the Venezuelan constitutional system, the confusion about the judicial review decision effects in both cases, and the application of the doctrine of the nullity guarantee of the diffuse system to the concentrated system, ignoring the difference between them, has been frequent.

Of course, in order to define this problem accurately, it is necessary to clearly distinguish the effects of the diffuse system of judicial review of constitutionality of state acts totally different from the effects of the concentrated system of judicial review of constitutionality. As we have said, the confusion, which has existed between the effects of these two types of review, has lead to error even within the Supreme Court Chambers themselves.

(a) Principles referring to both systems of judicial review

We have said, in effect, that under the diffuse system of judicial review, any judge in a concrete case may appraise the constitutionality of a law, decide it is unconstitutional, and thus, not apply it to the resolution of the case in question, with *inter partes* effects. In this way, all judges of the Republic are constitutional judges. We have also pointed out that, in Venezuela, a concentrated system of judicial review assigned to the Supreme Court of Justice, also exists. In this role, it is considered the supreme interpreter[137] and defender[138] of the Constitution, responsible for being the balancing point in the application of the principle of the separation of powers, [139] (84) when deciding whether the «juridical extinction» of legislative acts challenged through a popular action or when maintaining them in full force.[140]

---

136 Art. 119 and 131 LOCSJ

137 This implies the irreversibility of its decisions. See Article 211 of the Constitution. The doctrine has, however, been established for many years by the Court itself. See, for example, CFC-SPA, 17-11-38, in *Memoria de la Corte Federal y de Casación 1939*, p. 330.

138 See CFC-SPA, 4-3-41, in *Memoria de la Corte Federal y de Casación* 1942, p. 128-130.

139 See CFC-SPA, 3-5-39, in *Memoria de la Corte Federal y de Casación 1940*, p. 217; and 17-4-41, in *Memoria de la Corte Federal y de Casación 1942*, p. 182.

140 See CSJ-SPA, 20-1-66, in *Gaceta Forense* N° 51, 1968, p. 13.

The effects of constitutional review differ in the two cases, and in the absence of a law specifically governing constitutional jurisdiction,[141] solutions must be found in comparative law, which have frequently been utilized by the Supreme Court of Justice when reaching its decisions. But, indeed, it is neither appropriate nor possible to apply the characteristics of constitutional review of laws in the American model, which is exclusively diffuse in nature, to constitutional review of laws as exercised by the Supreme Court of Justice of Venezuela, which is a concentrated one.

As we have said, in the diffuse system of judicial review of the constitutionality of law assigned in Venezuela to all Courts, the decision declaring the inapplicability of a law considered unconstitutional in a concrete case does not affect its validity. Thus, it has only a declarative effect, extended only *inter partes*, and *pro pretaerito*. In the words of André and Susan Tunc in their masterful analysis of the North American constitutional system, with respect to decisions in the diffuse system of judicial review:

> «The law is neither repealed nor annulled. It is purely and simply not recognized, as if it were not a law, but rather, it could be said, a simple appearance of law, and the rights of the parties are regulated as if it had never been approved... The Court is limited, purely and simply, to ignore the law ... From (which)... stems the retroactive effect of the declaration of unconstitutionality».[142]

Consequently, the «retroactivity» of the declaration of inapplicability of a law only makes sense when we bear in mind that the judge considers it never to have produced effects, in which case the declaration of unconstitutionality operates *ex tunc*, as it is simply a decision declaring pre-existing unconstitutionality or nullity. In this respect, for instance, we have said that it is justified to deliberate on the constitutionality of a law, which, although already repealed, was applied while still in force to the particular case, which the judge is hearing. Although the law may already have been repealed at the time of the decision, the declaration that it is inapplicable is important to the proceedings.[143]

However, as we already know, these effects of the diffuse system of judicial review are quite different to those of the concentrated system of judicial review, as have been clearly developed in comparative law. In the concentrated system of judicial review as exercised by the Supreme Court in the Venezuelan system, the Court «declares the nullity» of the law[144] that is to say, annuls it. Up to the moment when the Court's decision is published, the law must be considered valid and effective, producing all its effects despite its unconstitutionality.

In fact, as Professor Cappelleti indicated, when emphasising the difference between the concentrated and diffuse methods of constitutional review:

---

141 See, for example the Draft Constitutional Jurisdiction Law in Comisión de Administración Pública, *Informe sobre la reforma de la administración pública nacional*, Caracas 1972, Vol II, p. 47 et seq. See the text also in Humberto J. LA ROCHE, *op. cit.*, pp. 215-238.

142 See A. and S. TUNC, *Le système constitutionnel des Etats Unies d'Amerique*, Paris 1954, Vol. II, pp. 294 and 295.

143 It has thus been said that, if the judicial verdict passed in constitutional review of laws has retroactive effects, as occurs with diffuse review, then clearly reapealed laws may be annulled, since this puts an end to the effects which the law may have produced while in force. See J.G. ANDUEZA, *op. cit.*, pp. 56-57.

144 Art. 215, paragraphs 3 and 4. 1961 Constitution.

«It can be said that, while the United States' system of judicial review of constitutionality of laws has a purely *declaratory character*, conversely, the Austrian system has the nature of a *constitutive* control of invalidity, and consequent inefficacy of laws contrary to the Constitution. From this, it is quite coherent to conclude that while in the first system, the effects (purely declarative) operate *ex tunc* that is, retroactively -it is, in effect, a simple declaration of a pre-existing nullity-, in the Austrian system, on the contrary, the effects of the decision of unconstitutionality (which are constitutive, that is to say, of annulment, operate *ex nunc*, and thus *pro futuro*, which excludes retroactive effects of the annulations».[145]

To this difference between the diffuse and concentrated constitutional judicial review systems of legislation, another fundamental one must be added - in the latter, the «general» nature of the annulment, which while lacking retroactive effects (since, as has been said, these are *ex nunc* or *pro futuro*), as we have seen do however operate *erga omnes*.[146]

Anyway, what can definitively be said in comparative law is that in general the most important systems of concentrated constitutional judicial review of laws attribute general effects backwards to the past (that is, *ex tunc, pro praeterito*) to all decisions in which unconstitutionality and nullity of laws is declared.

Hence, those decisions are not merely declaratory, nor do they have retroactive effects, but are solely constitutive. In systems like those Italy and Germany, as we have seen, which do attribute certain effects backwards to the past to the Constitutional Courts decisions in which a law is annulled, in general, these are fundamentally restricted to criminal matters. The solution adopted by these legislations is logical. It would have monstrous repercussions on juridical stability to maintain that the effects of decisions declaring the nullity of a law considered unconstitutional are merely declaratory, and that acts, which took place before the law was declared null, are thus taken as never having been passed. It might, however, be equally unjust in criminal cases, if decisions passed under a law, which is subsequently annulled, were not affected by its annulment. This is why the Italian and German legal systems establish an exception, regarding criminal cases, to the principle that the effects of decisions declaring the nullity of laws deemed unconstitutional only produce effects towards the future.

Moreover, the situation of conflict that could arise between juridical stability and criminal decisions, as we have also mentioned, has led the North American Supreme Court to establish the programmatic exceptions to the opposite principle. We have seen that constitutional review being diffuse in character in the United

---

145 See Mauro CAPPELLETTI, «El control judicial de la constitucionalidad de las leyes en el derecho comparado» *Revista de la Facultad de Derecho de México*, 61, 1966, p. 58-59.

146 See, for example, CFC-SPA, 17-11-38, in *Memoria de la Corte Federal y de Casación 1939*, pp. 330 334; CF. 19-6-53, in *Gaceta Forense* N° 1, 1953, p. 77; CSJ-CP, 29-4-65, published by the *Imprenta Nacional*, Caracas 1965, pp. 113-116. *Cf. Doctrina de la Procuraduría General de la República 1963*, Caracas 1964, pp. 199-201. In other words, as CAPPELLETTI points out, «once the decision of unconstitutionality is pronounced, the corresponding law is deprived of effects in a general manner, exactly as if it had been abrogated by a subsequent law, and vice versa, all the legislative provisions prior to the unconstitutional law regain their validity» (*loc. cit.*, p. 59). Thus, the effects of the concentrated constitutional review system are radically different from the particular, *inter partes* effects of the diffuse constitutional review system.

States, the effects of decisions declaring laws unconstitutional are merely declaratory and thus retroactive in nature. Despite this, however, case law has extended this retroactive nature only to criminal cases. On the contrary, it respects the effects produced in civil and administrative matters on the basis of a law, which is declared unconstitutional.[147]

Now, as the constitutional judicial review power that the 1961 Venezuelan Constitution attributes to the Supreme Court of Justice[148] is similar to that termed concentrated in comparative law, it is evident that, in the absence of any constitutional or legal positive rule, the effects of the declaration of nullity of a law on the grounds of its unconstitutionality can only be produced *erga omnes*, but towards the future. That is to say, in principle, Supreme Court decisions are constitutive, *pro futuro* with *ex nunc* effects, which cannot generally be extended backwards to the past, thus they cannot be retroactive. This criterion can be said, is followed not only by authors on constitutional law,[149] but also by decisions of the Supreme Court of Justice, although the Court has not been consistent in the matter.

In effect, the Supreme Court of Justice in Venezuela is divided into three Chambers: the Politico-Administrative, the Civil Cassation and the Criminal Cassation Chambers, and can also act in *Pleno* or Plenary session. According to the Constitution, the concentrated system of judicial review is exercised only in *Pleno* and by the Politico-Administrative Chambers, which sustain the criterion of the constitutive effects of their decisions. This criterion has been contradicted by the Civil Cassation Chamber, which does not have powers of concentrated judicial review, when it has interpreted the effects of the decisions of the former.

(b) Criterion of the constitutional organs with powers to annul laws: The Supreme Court in Pleno and its Politico-Administrative Chamber

In effect, the Supreme Court has expressly maintained that:

> «Laws are made to be executed, and should thus be accomplished even when, contingently, they may be declared constitutionally null, as the result of a sufficient action. They are only rendered invalid by the definitive decision declaring their nullity».[150]

In other words, in the corresponding decision by the Supreme Court, declaring the nullity of a law on the grounds of its unconstitutionality, it limits itself to «proclaiming the juridical annulment» of the law to which objection is made.[151]

147 *Cf.* M. CAPPELLETTI, *loc. cit.*, pp. 63-64.

148 Article 215, Paragraphs 3 and 4.

149 In his book on *La jurisdicción constitucional en el derecho venezolano*, (*cit.*), José Guillermo ANDUEZA has abundantly and finally demonstrated that the decision declaring nullity by reason of unconstitutionality which all acts by the Public Powers enjoy, means that these produce all their legal effects until such time as they are pronounced null by the Court. Consequently, the Court's decision should necessarily respect the effects which the state act produced while it was in force» (p. 93), since «it produces a change in the effects of a state act. That is to say, the sentence renders ineffective a previously valid act». (p. 94). According to ANDUEZA himself, and following the most orthodox doctrine, «what characterizes constitutive sentences is the absence of retroactive effects. These continue always *pro-futuro, ex nunc*; that is to say, that the decision produces its effects from the day of its publication», (p. 94). Then, we do not share the opinion of J. J. LA ROCHE, *El control jurisdiccional en Venezuela y Estados Unidos*, *cit.*, p. 153.

150 CFC, 20-12-40, *cit.*, by J.G. ANDUEZA, *op. cit.*, p. 90.

151 See CSJ-SPA, 20-1-66 in *Gaceta Forense* N° 51, 1966, p. 13.

That is to say, the Supreme Court has maintained that laws produce all their effects until they are annulled since, as it indicated in another decision, «acts which are annullable are valid and, once passed, fully produce all their effects until they are declared null».[152] and, while the effects of decisions declaring nullity by reason of unconstitutionality are general and *erga omnes* in nature,[153] it is clear that, when it declares a law to be null, the Supreme Court's decision comes to form part, *mutatis mutandis* -as the Supreme Court has said- of «a special legislation arising from the secondary Constitutive Power which this High Court exercises»,[154] since such decisions «are complementary provisions of the Constitution and laws of the Republic».[155]

In other words, as the Supreme Court, it has stated the effects of these decisions «extend *erga omnes* and have the force of law».[156]

Thus, if a law, declared null on the grounds of its unconstitutionality, is deprived of effect in a general manner by the respective decision, just as if it had been abrogated by a later law, it is clear then that just as the law cannot have retroactive effects, so neither can the decision declaring the law's nullity which is deemed to have «force of law» as the same Supreme Court has considered. This affirmation is so logical that, in some Latin American constitutional systems, the classic principle of the lack of retroactivity of laws[157] has been expressly extended to decisions of the Supreme Court or of the Tribunal of Constitutional Guarantees as happens in Ecuador.[158]

This principle that the effects of the Supreme Court's decisions declaring the nullity of laws considered unconstitutional are not retroactive, stems from the nature of the decisions, which are *constitutive* and not declaratory. It was expressly recognized by the Politico Administrative Chamber of the Supreme Court itself when, in 1965, it decided to declare the nullity of a Municipal Ordinance which created a tax contravening a prohibition contained in paragraph 4 of Article 18 of the Constitution,[159] and rejected the petitioner's request «that the Municipality be ordered to repay the sums of money which it had received by collecting the contribution under discussion ...» as it was considered unfounded.[160]

---

152 See CSJ-SPA, 15-2-67 in *Gaceta Forense* Nº 55, 1967, p. 70.

153 *Cf.* CFC-SPA, 17-11-38, *Memoria de la Corte Federal y de Casación 1939*, p. 330; 21-3-39, *Memoria de la Corte Federal y de Casación 1940*, p. 176; 16-12-40, *Memoria de la Corte Federal y de Casación 1941*, p. 311; and of the CF, 19-6-53, in *Gaceta Forense* Nº 1, 1953, pp. 77 and 78.

154 See CFC-SPA, 16-12-40, in *Memoria de la Corte Federal y de Casación 1941*, p. 311.

155 See CFC-SPA, 21-3-39, in *Memoria de la Corte Federal y de Casación 1940*, p. 176.

156 See CF, 19-6-53, in *Gaceta Forense* Nº 1, 1953, pp. 77, 78.

157 Article 44 of the Constitution.

158 Art. 141,4. Constitution of Ecuador 1983. See the comments of J.G. ANDUEZA, *op. cit.*, p. 94.

159 Art. 18,4. 1961 Constitution.

160 See CSJ-SPA, 18-11-65, *Gaceta Forense* Nº 50, 1967, p. 111. This was also the criterion of the former Federal and Cassation Court in Cassation Chamber when, in a decision in 27 February, 1940, it expressly decided the following: «The decision which is appealed, to deny the action, is founded on the fact that the Municipal Ordinance which gave rise to the fine being placed to the plaintiff for an infraction of one of its Articles, was issued by a competent authority and produced all its effects until the day it was declared null by the Federal and Cassation Court, which was the Tribunal which was competent for this purpose. The effects of the verdict of cassation cannot be made retroactive to the date that Ordinance expired, but rather they are produced from the date of that decision. As, on the other hand, the plaintiff did not appeal against the fine, he agreed to the fiscal sanction that was imposed on him, and the decision appealed concludes that there was no undue payment. The

In this way, the Court acknowledged the nature of its decision to annul the ordinance, as being constitutive and having effects towards the future, since otherwise, had it had considered the effects of the decision to be merely declaratory, *ex tunc*, it would have proceeded to order the Municipality to repay as requested.

Later, in 1968, the Court emphasized the presumption of the constitutionality of laws when it pointed out that:

> «National legislative acts, once passed and published, keep their effectiveness and validity until such time as they are repealed by the body which passed them or are annulled by the Court and, meanwhile, their legitimacy also extends to actions taken by other authorities under powers which the laws attribute to them».[161]

For this reason, once a law is declared null on the grounds of its being unconstitutional, if retroactive effects were granted to the decision, this would be equivalent to depriving all acts taken in compliance with the law of their effects, thus severely prejudicing juridical stability.

In the same year, 1968, the Supreme Court incidentally recognized that its decisions were constitutive and not declaratory, when it maintained that:

> «The effects of the decisions passed by the Court when performing its function of judicial review of the constitutionality of laws, only extend for the duration of the validity of the constitutional rule on which... (the Court's decisions) are based. Consequently, it is possible that a legal provision which is annulled because it is unconstitutional- but which in fact has continued to form a part of some legal instrument which has not been so repealed recover legal force with the coming into effect of some other norm which repeals the constitutional rule on which the Court had founded its decision to declare the law null, or one which radically changes the previous legal system».[162]

If the situation described by the Court in its decision is possible, it is precisely because the effects produced by the law, before the decision to annul it, remain intact, as a result of its constitutive effect. Otherwise, the disturbance of the legal order would be unbearable, since if the decisions of the Court in which it exercises constitutional review of laws were retroactive, that is to say, merely declaratory, *ex tunc*, not only would those acts performed under the law declared null be rendered without effect, but if the unconstitutional law were non-existent, this would leave no room for the possible case in which it recovers its validity if the Constitution under which it was declared unconstitutional were modified, as pointed out by the Court. We thus insist that, in our opinion, the effects of decisions in which the

---

damages claimed as a consequence of that payment are thus denied. This Court considers that the grounds stated, on which the lower court bases his decision are according to the legal principles which govern this matter. In our Administrative Law, Municipal Ordinances issued under the powers which the National Constitution grants the Municipalities «have the character of local laws, and as such, it follows to apply to them the rule of the non-retroactivity of their provisions. As these Ordinances are the work of an administrative authority, invested with a part of the Public Power, these acts retain all their legal validity even in the case in which they suffer from defects which would make them anulable, until such time as their nullity is declared by the competent Court». See CFC-SPA 27-2-40 in *Memoria de la Corte Federal y de Casación*, 1941, p. 20.

161 See CSJ-SPA, 13-2-68, in *Gaceta Forense* Nº 59, 1969, p. 85.

162 See CSJ-SPA, 19-12-68, in *Gaceta Forense* Nº 62, 1969, p. 112.

Supreme Court declares laws null on the grounds of their being in breach of the Constitution are those proper to constitutive judgements, that is to say, they only produce effects towards the future.

This statement may also be inferred from other decisions of the Supreme Court of Justice itself in relation to petitions for the annulment of laws already repealed. In fact it can be said, as Professor Andueza indicated, «that the position adopted with respect to these petitions depends on the position taken with respect to the effects of the decision upon constitutionality».[163] If retroactive effects are attributed to these clearly, laws, which have been repealed, may be annulled, thus putting an end to the effects, which the law may have produced during the time it was in force. If the decision is only binding *pro futuro*, however, it becomes then contradictory to annul a non-existent law, since by virtue of the principle of the presumption of constitutionality -which covers all acts of state- the effects produced while the law was in force cannot be destroyed.[164]

On the basis of this alternative, we can say that ever since 1949, the Court has denied petitions for the annulment of laws, which have been repealed. In fact, although in 1940 the Supreme Court held that there was reason to demand the annulment of a law which had been repealed, since «the annulment works retroactively and suppresses all the effects which had been produced by the application of the voided law»[165] this opinion changed radically as of 1949, not only in relation to the dismissal of actions of unconstitutionality of laws which had already been repealed, but also in relation to the solely constitutive effects of decisions in which the Court declared laws null on the grounds of their being in breach of the Constitution.

In effect, the Court held in 1949 that «this High Court's constitutional powers to review the constitutionality of laws refer only to laws in force», thus when a petition is made for it to annul a law which has already been repealed, «the Court lacks any matter on which to decide».[166] In 1966, the Politico Administrative Chamber of the Supreme Court of Justice upheld the same criterion when it specified that, among the decisive circumstances with respect to proceedings in actions of unconstitutionality, «the very existence of the act challenged as being in breach of the Constitution and which is to constitute precisely the matter or object of the process, is especially important», and that if the action applies to the annulment of an act whose validity has expired, it thus «lacks an object».[167]

Now, according to this criterion, it is clear that in Venezuela, generally speaking, Supreme Court decisions declaring laws annulled on the grounds of unconstitutionality have general effects, *erga omnes*. However, these effects only extend towards the future in the sense that they annul a law that, while it produced effects up to the moment when the decision was published, it is legally suppressed as of that moment. The effects of the Court decision, in this respect,

---

163 See J.G. ANDUEZA, *op. cit.*, pp. 56-57.

164 *Idem.*

165 See CFC-SPA, 13-1-41, in *Memoria de la Corte Federal y de Casación* 1941, p. 102.

166 See CFC-CP, 21-12-49, in *Gaceta Forense* N° 1, 1949, p. 15.

167 See CFC-CP, 20-01-66, in *Gaceta Forense* N° 51, 1968, pp. 13 and 14.

cannot be retroactive, which effects are reserved to merely declaratory decisions, but only *pro futuro* as is the case with constitutive judgements.[168]

There is no doubt, in our opinion, that in Venezuela, the aims of the constitutional review powers exercised by the Supreme Court of Justice under paragraphs 3 and 4 of Article 215 of the Constitution, as a concentrated system of judicial review, are to annul laws (the Constitution says, «declare the nullity», and not «declare the unconstitutionality»). This annulment is performed with *erga omnes* effects that extend *ex nunc* (*pro futuro*), by means of a decision termed «constitutive», in contrast to «declaratory»,[169] unless dealing with cases of absolute nullity under express constitutional provisions, as we shall see.

(c) Contradicting criterion of the Civil Cassation Chamber of the Supreme Court

However, this criterion that has been followed uncontested by the Supreme Court in *Pleno* Court and in its Politico-Administrative Chamber through which the Supreme Court exercises its competence to annul laws and other acts of state with general effects, has been contradicted by the Civil, Commercial and Labour Cassation Chamber of the same Supreme Court of Justice, in a decision passed on 10 August 1978, in which, while hearing a recourse of cassation, this Chamber broached the matter of deciding and determining the effects of *Pleno* Court decisions when declaring the annulment of laws.

In effect, the Cassation Chamber decision was adopted after a *Pleno* Court decision of 15 March 1962; it declared the nullity of an article of a Law approving a contract for the fulfilment of the National Treasury auxiliary service, signed between the Republic and a private bank.

---

168 This, and none other, for example, was the opinion of the Court in the decision which declared the nullity of Article 20 of the law approving the Contract signed between the National Executive and the Banco de Venezuela, S.A., passed on 15 March, 1962 (See CSJ-CP in FC, in *Gaceta Oficial* N° 760 Extra, 22-03-62 and to realize this it is sufficient to take the opinion of the presiding judge in that verdict, SARMIENTO NUÑEZ, as expressed in his dissenting opinion from the Supreme Court of Justice decision which denied the petition for nullity by reason of unconstitutionality of paragraph 14 of Article II of the Law approving the Extradition Treaty signed between Venezuela and the United States of America on 29 April, 1965. In his dissenting opinion, the presiding Magistrate in the sentence declaring the nullity of Article 20 of the law approving the contract signed between the National Executive and the Banco de Venezuela, S.A., insisted on the distinction between diffuse and concentrated constitutional review systems of laws in Venezuela, and indicated that, in the former, as exercised by the Courts under Article 7 of the Civil Proceedings Code (now Art. 20), the decision is relative in nature, since it affects only the particular case in question, and does not bind future cases of this or other Courts». By contrast, decisions of the Supreme Court of Justice, (in concentrated review systems) are absolute in nature; the nullity of the law is proclaimed *erga omnes,* that is, with respect to all cases, and produces effects *ex nunc,* that is to say, as of the decision». See CSJ-SPA, 29-7-65, published by the *Imprenta Nacional,* 1965, p. 74).

169 In this respect, it must be pointed out that this general principle which is universal in comparative law and accepted by Venezuelan case law and doctrine, was followed by these who drafted the Law of Constitutional Jurisdiction, when they established, in Article 19 of the draft that: «The laws which are declared unconstitutional may not be applied nor shall have any effect whatsoever, from the day following the publication in the Official Gazette or, failing such publication, as of ten days after it is signed. When a definitive criminal decision has been pronounced on the basis of these, and is being executed, it shall cease, as shall all other penal effects». (See Draft Law of Constitutional Jurisdiction drawn up by Profs. MARTÍN-RETORTILLO, RUBIO LLORENTE and Allan R. BREWER-CARÍAS in Comisión de Administración Pública, *Informe sobre la reforma de la administración pública nacional,* CAP, Caracas 1972, Vol. II, p. 551).

The article in question exonerated the bank from paying municipal taxes, which was considered unconstitutional. Thus once annulled by the Supreme Court the Federal District Municipality brought a civil suit against the private bank for payment of taxes incurred during the ten years previous to the Court's decision -which is the expiry period for claims for municipal taxes-, interpreting the decision in which the annulment was declared, as producing *ex tunc* effects, that is, declaratory and retroactive. The bank alleged that these were constitutive in nature, and the Civil, Commercial and Labour Cassation Chamber of the Supreme Court, when it heard the case for the cassation of the decision made by a civil court which had ordered the bank to pay the taxes as required, applied what it called «its own doctrine» as follows:

> «Laws are constitutional or unconstitutional. The former are so because they conform to the rules of the National Constitution. The latter are unconstitutional when they include violations or breaches, which would contradict the content of constitutional rules. Until such time as they are declared unconstitutional, they are rendered obligatory by a presumption of their legitimacy. If so declared however, -that presumption is removed by the declaration of nullity and everything they meant in the past is erased. That is to say that the decision declaring nullity is declaratory in nature, and its effects are, in principle, backwards to the past; retroactive, *ex tunc*. This conclusion follows freely from logical principles, since the declaration of nullity seeks to re-establish the legal order disturbed by an unconstitutional law. This Chamber does not hesitate to follow this doctrine, which is upheld by leading authorities, both national and foreign. Thus the decision which is being appealed against is correct in considering as declaratory the decision passed by the Supreme Court of Justice on 15 March, 1962, in which it annulled Article 23 of the Law approving the extension of the contract signed between the Federal Executive and the *Banco de Venezuela*, as being unconstitutional. As that Law was contested by means of a principal and direct action of unconstitutionality, the annulment pronounced by the Supreme Court is without question absolutely declaratory in nature, and thus its effects extend both backwards to the past (*ex tunc*) and towards the future (*ex nunc*). Leading authorities indicate that «that law which is declared unconstitutional should be regarded, to all intents and purposes, as if it had never possessed legal force». This doctrine stems from precise constitutional texts, which endow the Supreme Court with power to «declare the total or partial nullity of national laws», without indicating therein what the nature or character of such nullity is. Within this doctrine, however, one must accept the possible existence of limiting cases, such as when considerations of higher justice or overriding public interest make it advisable to temper the rigour of its effects. Among the cases in which this occurs is the immutability of the *res judicata* arising from firm, final verdicts, which should, in principle, be maintained. In the case in question, however, this exceptional situation does not arise, since the interest at issue is eminently private by nature. Thus, as the decision of 15 March 1962- in which the Supreme Court of Justice declared the nullity on the grounds of unconstitutionality of Article 20 of the above law approving the contract signed between the National Executive and the *Banco de Venezuela*, is declaratory in nature, its *ex tunc* effects are correct and normal to this type of decision. The appellate decision thus did not violate the legal provisions mentioned in the petition when it ordered the bank to pay the taxes which had been demanded».[170]

[170] See CSJ-SCCMT, 10-8-78 in *Gaceta Forense* N° 101, 1978, pp. 591-592.

In this way, as a result of decisions by its component Chambers, the Supreme Court of Justice itself has established contradictory criteria. In *Pleno* Court, and in the Politico-Administrative Chamber, it has maintained the constitutive nature, *pro futuro* and *ex nunc* effects of its decisions to annul on the grounds of unconstitutionality, laws and other state acts with general effect, which may be contested by means of popular action. By contrast, the Civil, Commercial and Labour Cassation Chamber - which incidentally has no competence for declaring laws null on the grounds of unconstitutionality, but rather has a reduced competence for hearing recourses of cassation, attributed to the *Pleno* Court and the Politico-Administrative Chamber decision different effects from those accepted by themselves by deciding that those decisions declaring nullity on the grounds of unconstitutionality were declaratory in nature (not constitutive) with *pro praeterito* (not *pro futuro*) and *ex tunc* (not *ex nunc*), effects.

This is, without doubt, an inadmissible contradiction, since not only is the Civil, Commercial and Labour Cassation Chamber of the Supreme Court not competent to declare the nullity of laws, but also, in attributing *ex tunc* effects to the decisions of another Chamber and to those of the *Pleno* Court, contrary to their own criterion, it has done so erroneously. The Cassation Chamber has resorted to doctrinal criteria, which relate to the diffuse systems of judicial review, their application to the concentrated systems of judicial review, being absolutely inadmissible.

In any case, since 1976, Article 131 of the Organic Law of the Supreme Court of Justice has been central to both interpretations, because it endows both the *Pleno* Court and the Politico-Administrative Chamber with power to establish «the effects of their decisions with time». Thus, even though the effects of their decisions declaring the nullity of laws on the grounds of unconstitutionality should, in principle, continue to be constitutive, *pro futuro ex nunc*,[171] the Court may correct the unfavourable effects that may be produced by the rigidity of this principle, particularly in matters of constitutional rights and guarantees, and give its decision retroactive *pro praeterito, ex tunc* effects.

In our opinion, even in cases relating to constitutional rights and guarantees, the problem of the rigidity of the principle of the *ex tunc, pro futuro* effects of decisions annulling laws, which could mean that a law that violates a constitutional guarantee, despite its having been declared null, could have produced effects up to the time of that declaration, is resolved, since the Constitution itself guarantees against this situation. It declares the absolute nullity of «acts by the Public Power» -including laws- which prejudice constitutional rights and guarantees».[172]

Thus, it is the absolute nullity of certain acts, as provided for in the Constitution, which allows certain decisions in which the Court declares the nullity of a law to have retroactive effects, backwards to the past, and for them to be considered declaratory and *ex tunc* in nature.

---

171 Fox example, in a decision of the Politico Administrative Chamber of the Court on 23-2-84, declaring the nullity by reason of unconstitutionality of an act installing the Legislative Assembly of a state of the Federation, the Court provided expressly that «this decision shall have no retroactive effects whatsoever in relation to procedures carried out in the Legislative Assembly». (Consulted in original).

172 Art. 46. 1961 Constitution.

(d) Objective Guarantee of the Constitution: Absolute or Relative Nullity

In fact, in relation to the effects, with time, of Supreme Court decisions declaring the annulment of laws on the grounds of their unconstitutionality, what must be clarified in the Venezuelan constitutional system is the objective guarantee of the Constitution established in the Fundamental text, particularly regarding the concentrated system of judicial review. In other words, when the Supreme Court of Justice declares the nullity of a law, which violates the Constitution, does the Court adopt its decision based on the annullability or relative nullity of the unconstitutional law, or, does it annul the law based on the grounds of absolute nullity, because the Constitution provides for cases of absolute nullity? To resolve this dilemma, it is necessary to determine whether all unconstitutional laws are «annullable acts» or whether, on the contrary, the possibility exists of unconstitutional acts with defects such that they are considered by the legal order, as «null and void acts».[173]

As we have said, the general rule in Venezuela is that Supreme Court decisions declaring the nullity of laws are constitutive. Thus the unconstitutional laws are, in principle, state acts liable to relative annulment, that is to say, annullable acts, setting aside only two possible cases, and here we have the exceptions to the rule.

In fact, despite the power legally attributed to the Supreme Court to determine the effects with time of its decisions, the Venezuelan Constitution only allows the interpreter to infer that Supreme Court decisions that declare the nullity of a law, have *per se* the character of a declaratory judgement, producing full effects backwards to the past, in such cases in which the Constitution itself declares a law or state act as «null and void» or without effects. This possibility is provided for only in Articles 46 and 119 of the Constitution. In effect, article 46 of the Constitution establishes the following:

> «Art. 46. All acts of the Public Power that violate or impair the rights guaranteed by this Constitution are null, and public officials and employees who order or execute them shall be held criminally, civilly and administratively liable, as the case may be, and orders from their superiors evidently contrary to the Constitution and the laws may not serve as an excuse».

According to this first express exception, a law, which, for example, establishes discrimination, based on «race, creed, sex or social status», expressly violates the right to equality guaranteed in Article 61 of the Constitution, and is «null» under the text of Article 46. The defect is such that the nullity is absolute, and the act can produce no legal effect and should not even be applied by any authority, the contrary originating responsibility. In such cases, the Court's decision declaring the nullity of the law on the grounds of its being unconstitutional can be no more than merely declaratory, by virtue of the express text of the Constitution. It is a question, in fact, of certifying a nullity already established in the Constitution, which extinguishes the law in the past and into the future, in the sense that, as the law is declared

173 As pointed out by J.G. ANDUEZA, «the difference which exists between an act null and an anulable one should be seen in the nature of the judicial pronouncement. If the decision is solely declaratory, with retroactive effects, when the act is anulled *pro-praeterito*, we may affirm that we are in the presence of absolute nullity. By contrast, when the judge passes a constitutive judgement with effects *ex-nunc, pro futuro*, the defect produces only the anulability of the state act», *op.cit.*, pp. 92-93.

«null» by the Constitution itself, it is considered as never having been able to produce effects. In the possible cases in which rights guaranteed by the Constitution are at stake, and which are regulated by Article 46 of the Constitution, the Supreme Court decision declaring the nullity of the unconstitutional law cannot have constitutive effects, neither can it consequently leave the effects produced by an unconstitutional law which violates fundamental rights prior to its being declared null by the Court intact.

The second exception to the principle of the constitutive effect of the Supreme Court's decisions declaring the nullity of unconstitutional laws is expressly regulated by Article 119 of the Constitution, which establishes that:

«All usurped authority is without effect, and its acts are null».

By usurpation of authority should be understood «the defects accompanying all acts decreed by a person totally lacking authority»,[174] that is to say, «the usurper is he who exercises authority and puts it into effect without any type of investiture, either regular or established. The concept of usurpation, in this case, arises when a person who has no *auctoritas* acts as an authority»,[175] in the sense in which the Constitution employs the term «authority». Thus, as the Constitution states, usurped authority is without effects and its acts are null. This second case in which the express text of the Constitution declares an act of state «null» and without effect, a defect such that the nullity is absolute, that the Supreme Court decision declaring the nullity for example, «of a law of a government organised by force»,[176] can only have the effect of declaring a nullity already expressly established in the Constitution itself.

We must emphasize, however, that apart from these two express provisions of the Constitution by which the text of the Constitution itself declares a law absolutely null, with the consequence that the Supreme Court of Justice's decisions declaring the nullity of an unconstitutional law have merely declaratory effects, when in other cases the Supreme Court of Justice declares the nullity of an unconstitutional law it is considered, as a general rule, to be defective in such a way as to entail its relative annulment, and the only cases that are admissible as exceptions to this general principle adopted in our constitutional system, are those cases in which the Supreme Court itself expressly establishes absolute annulment in its decisions,[177] which may be based on Article 131 of the Organic Law of the Supreme Court of Justice, in certain cases, for example, of the usurpation of functions, which is an entirely different constitutional concept from that of the usurpation of authority.[178]

If, however, the Supreme Court omits to characterize the law whose nullity is declared defective to the point of absolute nullity, extending the effects of its: annulment backwards to the past, the general principle of relative nullity is taken

---

[174] See Allan R. BREWER-CARÍAS, *Las instituciones fundamentales del derecho administrativo y la jurisprudencia venezolana*, Caracas 1964, p. 62.

[175] *Idem*. p. 59.

[176] Article 250, 1961 Constitution.

[177] In certain isolated sentences in this respect, the Court has annulled a Municipal Ordenance as contrary to equality under tax, and indicated that the infractions invalidated all its provisions to the point of absolute nullity». See CFC-SPA, 28-3-41, in *Memoria de la Corte Federal y de Casación*, 1942, p. 158. *Cf.* J.G. ANDUEZA, *op. cit.*, p. 93.

[178] See Allan R. BREWER-CARÍAS, *Las instituciones fundamentales... cit.*, p. 60

to apply, and neither the ordinary courts nor even the Cassation Chambers of the Supreme Court may substitute the powers of the *Pleno* Court or the Politico-Administrative Chamber, and judge for themselves the effects of the latter's decisions.

In accordance with what has been said, thus it can be concluded, as the general principle in the Venezuelan constitutional system that any Supreme Court decision passed in *Pleno* Court, or in its Politico-Administrative Chamber[179] in which it declares the nullity of a law considered unconstitutional has *erga omnes* effects, the decision being in nature (*ex-nunc*) and producing relative annulment, unless the text of the decision itself declares the law absolutely null, with *ex tunc* effects or the Court bases its pronouncement on the provisions of Articles 46 and 119 of the Constitution, in which case it is declaratory by nature.

However, even in these cases the retroactive character of the decision is not absolute, but rather entails that all the concrete situations arising from the application of the law declared null are susceptible to objection,[180] and thus that in many possible instances it could be held that legal situations would continue intact if they were not challenged by the interested parties.

Lastly, it should be pointed out that whatever the effects of a law being declared null on the grounds of its being unconstitutional are, it is evident that the effects towards the future continue for as long as the Constitution that gave rise to the annulment is in force. Thus, as the annulment is declared based on the violation of a particular constitutional rule, if that rule were to lapse as the result of constitutional reform, it would cause the decision declaring unconstitutionality to lose its *erga omnes* effects, and the law declared unconstitutional would regain its validity. The Supreme Court has expressly accepted this possibility.[181]

---

179 Under article 215, paragraphs 3 and 4. 1961 Constitution.

180 This is the opinion, with which we agree, of the Office of the Attorney General of the Republic. We differ in that the Attorney General's Office considers that all sentences declaring the nullity of a law are declaratory in nature, and thus have effects towards the past. See the opinion in *Doctrina de la Procuraduría General de la República*, 1968, Caracas 1969, p. 20, in particular p. 25.

181 This has been expressly decided by the Supreme Court of Justice in a decision of 19 December, 1968, in the following terms: «It is as well to warn, moreover, that the effects of the decisions which the Court passes when exercising this power only extend for the time for which the constitutional precept on which they are based continues in force. In consequence, it is possible that a legal provision which is anulled because it is contrary to the Constitution -but which in fact has continued to form part of a legal instrument which has been revoked- recover its legal effect when a reform comes into effect repealing the Constitutional precept on which the Court rested in order to declare it null, or when the previously established regime changes radically./ Such was the situation created when -after the Federal and Cassation Court passed the verdict mentioned by the petitioner, on April, 1951- the constitutional order in force at that time was reformed by the Constitutions published respectively in 1953 and 1961. In 1951, the restrictions which provided the basis for the Federal and Cassation Court to declare null the rules which the plaintiff refers to in his petition still served as a basis for the federal and Cassation Court to deny municipal competence over the tax on industrial and trade permits and subjected the power of local authorities to levy taxes. But when the Constitution was reformed in 1953, those restrictions were removed, and among the categories taxable by the Municipal Power it included those indicated in the current National Constitution, and in particular, the tax on industrial and trade permits. This being the case, the Municipal Council of the Federal District was not subject to the aforementioned constitutional limitations when, in the exercise of its autonomy and of the power granted to it in the Fundamental Charter, to levy taxes it sanctioned the current Ordinance on the Permit for Industry and Trade in 1958, and if the activity of that body could not be bound by provisions, which like those of the 1936 Constitution,

4. Judicial Review and the Fundamental Right to Constitutional Protection (*Derecho de Amparo*)

As we have said, the Venezuelan system of judicial review has been developed as a mixed system, in which the diffuse and concentrated systems of judicial review perform in parallel. But in addition to the constitutional and legal provisions specifically related to judicial review of the constitutionality of legislation that we have previously analysed, as far as judicial review is concerned, we must also consider the right to constitutional protection (*derecho de amparo*) as a fundamental right established in the Constitution, through which judicial review of legislation can also be obtained.

In effect, one of the most important democratic innovations in all Venezuelan constitutional history was the establishment of the right to protection (*Amparo*) in Article 49 of the 1961 Constitution. It not only extended the adjective system for the protection of fundamental rights and liberties set up in an incomplete form in previous constitutional texts[182] that had culminated in the establishment in 1947 of the writ of *habeas corpus*[183] as a protection for personal liberty, but led to the creation of a special institution. This right to protection (*amparo*) established in the 1961 Constitution as a legal protection, presents peculiarities that distinguish it from similar contemporary institutions for the protection of constitutional rights and guarantees established, both in Europe and in Latin America.[184]

A. *Constitutional basis of the right to protection*

In effect, article 49 of the Constitution declares the following:

> «Article 49. According to the law, the Courts will protect all inhabitants of the Republic in the enjoyment and exercise of the rights and guarantees established in the Constitution.
>
> The procedure will be brief and summary, and the competent judge will be empowered to immediately re-establish the infringed legal situation».

Despite this being, as said, an innovation in our constitutional tradition, the document explaining the motives of the constitutional project in 1960 limited its comments on the matter by saying in Section III on «Rights, Duties and Guarantees», that the right to protection «was sanctioned» and subsequently adding that «with respect to protection, only the general principles were established, which the law must regulate; but so as not to suspend its effects until the respective law is passed, the right of *habeas corpus* was sanctioned in the constitutional Temporary Provisions, thus regulating it provisionally». In this respect, the Fifth Temporary Provision of the Constitution established the rules of procedure for «the protection of personal

had already been revoked, less could it be so bound by what was decided in a decision whose effects are limited to the duration in force of the legal provisions which served as its basis». See CSJ-SPA, 19-12-68, in *Gaceta Forense* Nº 62, 1968, pp. 106 to 113. *Cf.* CSJ-SPA, 29-10-68, in *Gaceta Forense* Nº 62, 1968, pp. 37-39.

182 See the historical analysis of these constitutional rules in E. AGUDO FREITES «Estado actual de la acción de *amparo* en Venezuela», *Estudios sobre la Constitución. Libro Homenaje a Rafael Caldera*, Universidad Central de Venezuela, Caracas 1979, Vol. II, pp. 659-773.

183 Art. 32, Constitución 1947

184 See in general H. FIX-ZAMUDIO, *La protección procesal de los derechos humanos ante las jurisdicciones nacionales*, Madrid 1982.

liberty, until such time as the special law regulating it is passed, as stipulated in Article 49 of the Constitution».[185]

Thus, according to these rules, the 1961 Venezuelan Constitution sanctioned the» right to protection as a fundamental right that can be exercised by recourse to a variety of legal means, aimed at protecting all constitutional rights and guarantees, including that of personal liberty, so as to ensure that they are enjoyed and exercised by all inhabitants of the Republic. The document explaining the motives of the Project of Constitution in 1960 thus described the «right of *habeas corpus*» as a specific means of the broader «right to protection».

According to the Constitution, the protection (*amparo*) has been consequently sanctioned *as a constitutional right* of the inhabitants of the country, to require of *all* the Courts within their own jurisdiction and according to the provisions of the law, that they protect and ensure the enjoyment and exercise of *all the rights and guarantees* established by the Constitution or inherent in the human person, against any distress, whether by public authorities or individuals, by means of proceedings that should be brief and summary, and that allow the judge to restore the infringed legal situation immediately.[186]

Hence, the Constitution does not establish only «one» action or writ of protection as a particular means for legal protection, but rather a «right to protection» as a fundamental right which can, and in fact is exercised through a variety of legal actions and recourses, including a direct «action for protection» of a subsidiary nature.

Thus, article 49 of the Constitution does not establish a particular constitutional *adjective* «guarantee» of constitutional rank to protect constitutional rights, but moreover, what it has established is a true «constitutional right», the right of everyone to be protected by the courts in the enjoyment and exercise of their constitutional rights and guarantees. This character of the *amparo*, as a «constitutional right» is the basic element that identifies the Venezuelan institution[187] and that leads to its consideration not as a single action or complaint, but as a right. This criterion was the one that in our opinion, led the Supreme Court in 1983, to change its criterion established in 1970, regarding the possibility of the exercise of the action for protection, even in the absence of the law regulating and developing the constitutional dispositions on the matter.[188]

The question could be stated as follows: If the norm of article 49 were to establish an «action or recourse» for protection, then article 50 of the Constitution which lays down that the absence of laws regulating the exercise of «constitutional rights» would not impede their exercise, would not be applicable[189] on the contrary,

---

185 See the «Exposition of Motives» of the Constitution, *Revista de la Facultad de Derecho*, Universidad Central de Venezuela, N° 21, pp. 371-420; particularly pp. 380-381.

186 The right of protection (Art. 49 Constitution) is thus different to the broader right to access to justice specifically regulated in Article 68 of the Constitution.

187 See Allan R. BREWER-CARÍAS, «El derecho de *amparo* y la acción de *amparo*», *Revista de derecho público,* N° 22, Caracas 1985, pp. 51-61.

188 See Supreme Court of Justice in Político-Administrative Chamber, 20-10-83, *Revista de Derecho Público,* N° 16, Caracas 1983, p. 169.

189 See the opinion stated by the Attorney's General Office in *Doctrina de la Procuraduría General de la República 1970,* Caracas 1971, p. 35.

if article 49 of the Constitution was to establish a «fundamental right», as it is done, then article 50 of the Constitution would be applicable,[190] and even without the law of the right of *amparo*, this right could be constitutionally exercised. The latter is the predominant criterion followed by the courts, and in our opinion is the most distinguishable feature of the *amparo* institution in Venezuela.

B. *Amparo as a Right to Judicial Means for Protection*

The consolidation of «constitutional protection» as a fundamental right to judicial means for protection, has as a direct consequence, namely that the *amparo* is neither exactly an «action» nor a «remedy», since the Constitution does not identify the right to protection with any specific legal means. Thus, as conceived in the Constitution, «protection» (*amparo*) may take the form of recourse in the strict sense of the review of judicial or administrative decisions, or it may take the form of an «autonomous action» which does not necessarily entail the review of a given state act. For this reason, the protection may consist equally of a «recourse» or of an «autonomous action». This depends on the legal regulations.

However, as conceived in article 49 of the Constitution, *amparo* is established not only as a right of the inhabitants of the Republic to be protected in the enjoyment and exercise of the rights and guarantees established by the Constitution, but it really also takes on the nature of «a duty» of the Courts to protect all inhabitants of the Republic in the enjoyment and exercise of such rights and guarantees. For this reason, article 49 begins by stating, «The Courts shall protect...» This is why we have indicated that *amparo*, as it appears in the text of the Constitution, is not conceived as a single judicial recourse or action, nor as a single autonomous action, necessarily independent of all other judicial remedies and actions contemplated for the defence of constitutional rights and guarantees. Rather, the Constitution is sufficiently broad and flexible to allow the legislator to organize a variety of legal means for the defence of civil rights and guarantees, whether these are by means of ordinary legal actions, or in cases where these do not allow adequate protection of rights, through the general and subsidiary means, «action for protection».

Thus, many legal means can, and indeed do exist that afford protection to individuals in the enjoyment and exercise of their constitutional rights, by means of brief and summary proceedings, in which the judge is empowered to immediately re-establish infringed legal situations. In all such cases, it is not that the ordinary means substitute the right of protection (or diminish it), but that they can serve as the judicial means for protection. For this purpose, in many cases they need to be perfected, which is the legislator's future task.

Despite the several means for the legal protection of constitutional rights and guarantees that ensure the «right to protection» contemplated in the Constitution, there is no doubt that, given the all inclusive nature of the protection which the Fundamental Text establishes «according to the Law», for the real effectiveness of that right to protection, it is evident that a subsidiary «action for protection» must be identified, and accepted, but only if those other ordinary legal means that can

[190] See J.R. QUINTERO «Recurso de *amparo*. La cuestión central en dos sentencias y un Voto Salvado» in *Revista de la Facultad de Derecho*, Nº 9, Universidad Católica Andrés Bello, Caracas 1969-1970, pp. 161-162-166. See the judicial decision and its dissident opinion in pp. 180-206. See the text also in O. MARÍN GÓMEZ, *Protección procesal de las garantías constitucionales de Venezuela. Amparo y Habeas Corpus*, Caracas 1983, pp. 229-250.

serve for the protection of constitutional rights and guarantees, formally established by law, are insufficient.

Thus, the «right to protection» can be ensured by a variety of existing legal means (actions and recourses), in which case, the «right to protection» is not identified with any specific legal action. But in the case of the «action for protection» -which, as it has been said, is of a subsidiary nature in that it is admissible only when there is no other means of protection or relief formally provided for in the legal system, this subsidiary «action for protection» does appear as differentiated from other means for the legal protection of rights and guarantees, and for the defence of the Constitution itself.

Indeed, this leads us to point out the substantial difference that exists between the Venezuelan «right to protection»- and even the subsidiary «action for protection» contemplated in the Constitution, and the Mexican «trial for *amparo*», which is really a mixture, under one name, as we have seen, of five legal actions which in the Venezuelan legal system are completely distinct. These actions that in Mexico are covered by the heading *juicio de amparo* are: firstly, the protection of personal liberty, which is basically the remedy of *habeas corpus*; secondly, what is known as the «*amparo* against laws», which substitutes the direct action of unconstitutionality of laws; thirdly, the «*amparo* cassation», which is really the same as the recourse of cassation; fourthly, what is known as «administrative protection», which leads to judicial review of administrative acts; and fifthly, the Mexican system of protection also includes what is known as «agrarian *amparo*» for the protection of the rights of peasants.[191]

By contrast with the Mexican situation, the right to protection contemplated in article 49 of the Venezuelan Constitution, as we have pointed out, firstly ensures the possibility of protection when fundamental rights are infringed by state acts by means of the action of unconstitutionality of laws (popular action), or through the decision of any judge not to apply a law in the diffuse system of judicial review of constitutionality; by means of the recourse of cassation with respect to judicial decisions; and by means of the administrative remedies against administrative actions. Additionally, it ensures the possibility of protection of fundamental rights against infringement by other individuals through ordinary judicial means. To ensure the effectiveness of all these ordinary judicial means to serve as means for protecting fundamental rights, the legislator must of course perfect them. For instance, in cases of popular action, when its grounds are the infringement of a constitutional right or guarantee, due to the absolute nullity implied, the Supreme Court might be empowered to suspend the effects of the impugned law while the case is being decided. In the procedure of the recourse of cassation, when the complaint against the impugned judicial decision is based on the violation of a fundamental right, the motives for the admissibility of the recourse could be widened, as well as the judicial decisions that could be impugned. In the proceeding of judicial review of administrative action, when the grounds of the actions are the violation of fundamental rights, the expiry delay for the actions to be exercised could be eliminated, due to the absolute nullity involved, and the judge must be allowed to use his powers more freely to declare the emergency situation of the process, shortening

---

191 Héctor FIX-ZAMUDIO, «Algunos aspectos comparativos del derecho de *amparo* en México y Venezuela», *Libro Homenaje a la Memoria de Lorenzo Herrera Mendoza*, Universidad Central de Venezuela, Caracas 1970, Vol. II, pp. 344-356.

delays, and to suspend the effects of the challenged administrative act while the final decision of the case is produced.

C. «*Action for Protection*» *as a Subsidiary Means*

However, as we have said, additional to all the ordinary means, the right to protection allows adequate protection to be achieved for constitutional rights and guarantees, by means of an «action for protection», as a subsidiary judicial means. It, of course, appears in the legal system as completely different from the popular action of unconstitutionality of laws, the recourse of cassation, and from actions for judicial review of administrative actions.

In this case, the «action for protection» appears as a much broader subsidiary action for protecting absolutely all constitutional rights and guarantees including the enjoyment and exercise of personal liberty.

Now, one of the features of this autonomous subsidiary legal action, called the «action for protection», is that it does not presuppose that other previous legal means have to be exhausted before it can be exercised. This differentiates the institution of the «action for protection» in Venezuela from the «recourse of protection» (*recurso de amparo*) or the «constitutional complaint» which has recently developed in Europe, particularly in Germany and in Spain. In these countries, the protective remedy is really an authentic «recourse» that is brought, in principle, against judicial decisions. In Germany, for example, to bring a constitutional complaint for the protection of constitutional rights before the Federal Constitutional Tribunal, the available ordinary judicial means need to be previously exhausted, which definitively entails a recourse against a judicial decision, even though, in exceptional cases, a direct complaint for protection may be allowed in certain specific cases and with respect to a very limited number of constitutional rights.[192] In Spain, all legal recourses need to be exhausted in order to bring a «*recurso de amparo*» of constitutional rights before the Constitutional Tribunal, and, particularly when dealing with protection against administrative activities, the ordinary means for judicial review of administrative decisions must be definitively exhausted. For this reason, the recourse for protection in Spain is eventually a means for judicial review of decisions taken by the Administrative Judicial review courts.[193]

On the contrary, the subsidiary «action for protection» in Venezuela is not conditional upon the previous exhausting of other legal means, and thus it does not result as recourse against judicial decisions either.

It is, as it has been pointed out, a subsidiary legal action in that it is only admissible when no other legal action in the legal system exists to seek the protection of fundamental rights and their immediate reestablishment by means of brief, summary proceedings.

In this sense, in order to adequately understand the subsidiary character of the «action for protection», as an autonomous action, we must bear in mind what we

---

192 K. SCHLAICH, «Procedures et techniques de protection des droits fondamentaux. Tribunal Constitutionnel Fédéral allemand», in L. FAVOREU (ed.), *Cours constitutionnelles européenes et droits fondamentaux*, Paris 1982, pp. 105-164.

193 See, J.L. GARCÍA RUÍZ, *Recurso de amparo en el derecho español*, Madrid 1980. F. CASTEDO ALVAREZ, «El recurso de *amparo* constitucional» en Instituto de Estudios Fiscales, *El Tribunal Constitucional*, Madrid 1981, Vol. I, pp. 179-208.

have said about the protective character of other judicial means, among which are the actions for judicial review of administrative acts. It is not the case that the action for protection requires the previous exhausting of the actions for judicial review of administrative acts, when these violate fundamental rights, but that the action for judicial review can be itself considered in that case, as a means for protection of fundamental rights. Thus, only when no judicial means for protection exists, and in the case of administrative acts, when actions for their judicial review are not effective as a means for protection due to the particular circumstances of the case, the «action for protection» would be admissible.

On the other hand, it should be noted that according to the Constitution, the right to protection may be exercised according to the law, before «the Courts», and thus, as it has been said, the organization of the legal and procedural system does not provide for one single judicial action to guarantee the enjoyment and exercise of constitutional rights to be brought before one single Court.

The legal system may, and indeed does, regulate systems for the protection of constitutional rights and guarantees by means of ordinary actions, through brief and summary proceedings in which the judge has power to re–establish the infringed subjective legal situations immediately, which differentiates the system from those in Europe, particularly from the action for protection in Germany or in Spain which is one, single action, to be brought before one, single Court, and which serves as a mechanism for the protection of certain constitutional rights and guarantees.[194]

On the contrary, the right to protection in Venezuela is expressed in several legal judicial means which may be brought before all the Courts, and which may serve as a protection by means of pre–existing actions and remedies, so long as provision is made for brief, summary proceedings with powers for the judge to restore the infringed subjective legal situations. For this reason, and given this all-inclusive characteristic, the «action for protection» as such is subsidiary in nature, which implies that it is not the only action or recourse admissible for protection but that, rather, it may also be obtained by other legal means regulated by the legal system.

D. Protection of all Constitutional Rights and Guarantees

However, whether by use of pre-established legal means or through subsidiary autonomous action, the right to protection as expressed in the Constitution is to protect all the rights and guarantees that the Constitution establishes. This protection constitutes a fundamental guarantee of human rights, which in turn entails certain implications. Above all, the objective of the right to protection, according to the Constitution, is to protect the enjoyment and exercise of constitutional rights and guarantees, and thus, it applies not only to individuals as holders of such rights, but also to cases in which these rights are exercised by companies or corporations. There can be no doubt that, given the scope with which article 49 of the Constitution declares the «right to protection», the expression «all the inhabitants» cannot be understood to refer solely to individuals, rather that it also refers to all entities or organizations, since the rights established in the Constitution are moreover not only rights of individuals, but many of them are also rights of collective entities.

---

194 *Cf.* H. FIX–ZAMUDIO, «El derecho de *amparo* en México y en España. Su influencia recíproca», *Revista de estudios políticos*, Nº 7, Madrid 1979, pp. 254–255.

At the same time, however, the protection of the enjoyment and exercise of constitutional rights and guarantees is embodied in the Constitution not only regarding public actions, which may disrupt the enjoyment and exercise of such rights, but also regarding disruptions, which may originate from other private individuals. The Constitution makes no distinction in this respect, and thus an action for protection is perfectly admissible against actions by individuals, the action for protection has doubtlessly been conceived as a traditional means of protection against actions by the state and its authorities. However, despite this tradition of conceiving the action for protection as a means of protecting rights and guarantees against public actions, we consider that, in Venezuela, the scope with which this is regulated by article 49 allows the action for protection to be brought against individual actions, that is to say, when the disruption of the enjoyment and exercise of rights originates from private individuals or organizations.

This also differentiates the Venezuelan system from that which exists in other systems such as those in Mexico or Spain, in which the «action for protection» is solely conceived against public actions.[195] For this reason, as we have said, in Spain the action for protection is expressed as a review of decisions by the administrative judicial court when reviewing administrative acts.[196]

On the other hand, in the case of protection from disruption originating from public authorities, it should be affirmed, without doubt, that as regulated by article 49 of the Constitution, this protection is admissible against all public actions, that is to say, against all state acts as well as against any other action by public officials. The right to protection has, of course, been regulated, in many cases in this field, by judicial means already established in the legal system. For example, as far as unconstitutional laws, which affect constitutional rights and guarantees, are concerned, it is admissible to bring a popular action before the Supreme Court of Justice, which can be considered as a means for protection. Also, when a judge decides not to apply a law, under article 20 of the Civil Procedural Code, because he decides that it infringes a constitutional right, he also ensures protection of that right.[197] The same occurs with actions brought before the administrative judicial Tribunals against administrative acts, which constitute a means for the protection of constitutional rights and guarantees when the basis for impugning the administrative act is the violation of the enjoyment and exercise of such rights and guarantees, and the judicial suspension of the effects of the impugned act may be obtained immediately, and is admissible against any type of administrative act, both express and implied.[198]

Additionally, it must be said that the subsidiary action for protection is admissible against any action by the administration, even when this does not constitute a formal administrative act and is thus not open to actions before the administrative jurisdiction. That is to say, it would be admissible, for example,

---

195 *Idem*, pp. 254-255. On the contrary in Argentina is accepted the recourse of «*amparo*» against individual actions. *Kot* case of 5.9.1958. See G.R. CARRIO, *Algunos aspectos del recurso de amparo*, Buenos Aires 1959, p. 13.

196 *Cf.* J. GONZÁLEZ PÉREZ, *Derecho procesal constitucional*, Madrid 1980, p. 278.

197 See Allan R. BREWER-CARÍAS, *El control de la constitucionalidad de los actos estatales*, Caracas 1978.

198 Allan R. BREWER-CARÍAS, «Tipos de acciones y recursos contencioso-administrativos y el tema de la legitimación», in *Conferencia sobre la reforma de la justicia administrativa en Costa Rica*, Corte Suprema de Justicia, Marzo, 1986.

against material acts by the administration; its *de facto* methods; its failure to act or to fulfil an obligation; in short, against any action or omission by the administration, and even, of course, against specific acts which may not be contested before the administrative judicial courts.

Indeed, the subsidiary action for protection may also be admissible against actions by the legislative body against which there are no legal means for objection and may even be brought against judicial decisions against which no legal means of appeal exist or have been contemplated, or the recourse of cassation could not be exercised.

We have said, however, that the action for protection also constitutes a means for the protection of the enjoyment and exercise of *all* rights and guarantees established in the Constitution. To support this, it is sufficient to mention that article 49 is placed under Chapter I containing the «General Provisions» of Title III, which refers to «Constitutional duties, rights and guarantees», bearing in mind that the remaining five chapters separately regulate: duties; and individual, social, economic and political rights.

By virtue of its position in the Constitution, there is nothing to suggest that the right to protection in Venezuela constitutes a means for the protection of certain rights only but that rather, it relates, on the contrary, to all rights and guarantees established in the Constitution. This, of course, leads to the assertion that the right to protection and the subsidiary «action for protection» are means for protecting, not only those rights and guarantees listed in articles 43 to 116 of the Constitution, but also all the rights inherent in the human person, even when not specified in the Constitution, and in this respect, the full value of article 50 of the Constitution can be appreciated. This provides that:

> «Article 50. The declaration of rights and guarantees contained in the Constitution is not to be taken to mean the negation of others, such which, as they are inherent in the human being, do not figure expressly therein. The lack of a law regulating these rights does not prejudice its exercise».

The action for protection also protects all those rights that are inherent in the human being, but which do not appear expressly in the Constitution, as it is not necessary to pass a law to guarantee their exercise. One result of the provisions of Article 50, is, of course, to give substantial importance to the series of human rights listed in the U.N. Universal Declaration of the Rights of Man, and in the International Conventions that regulate human rights, such as those of the American Human Rights Convention, or the International Pacts on Civil and Political, and Economic and Social Rights, which are, moreover, laws of the Republic, because they have been approved in Congress by special laws.[199] But, though limiting our comments to the rights described in the Constitution, however, we must stress the fact that what is termed *amparo* is the right to a legal means for protecting the enjoyment and exercise of absolutely all those constitutional rights, which means that a difference is established with respect to other *amparo* institutions particular to Latin America.

In fact, if the situation in Latin America is analysed comparatively, the following criteria can, in general, be identified. In the first place, the system that

[199] See *Gaceta Oficial* N° 31.256 de 14-6-77 and N° 2.146 Extra. de 28-1-78.

identifies *amparo* with judicial protection from arbitrary detention (*habeas corpus*) always entails a writ requiring that the person detained be shown. This was the legal tradition, for example, in Chile. Secondly, there is the system, that identifies *amparo* as a means for the protection of all rights, except that of personal liberty, which is granted a special means of protection, such as the remedy of *habeas corpus*. This system, in fact, distinguishes between the two types of action, the action for protection and the writ of *habeas corpus*, and is the tradition in the Argentinean, and Brazilian systems.

Thirdly, *amparo* is also seen as a means for the protection of all rights and guarantees enshrined in the Constitution, and it has been the tradition in Central America, particularly in Guatemala, Honduras and Nicaragua, in contrast to the situation in Europe, for example, in which the remedy is established for the protection of certain rights only.[200] This happens, for example, in Spain, where the recourse of protection is reserved for the protection of a limited group of constitutional rights only, equivalent to what the Venezuelan Constitution has characterised as «individual rights».[201]

We have pointed out that *amparo* is conceived in Venezuela as the right to a legal means (action or remedy) for the protection of all constitutional rights and guarantees absolutely, not only, of course, of individual rights, but also of the social, political and economic rights expressed in the Constitution. Also, as *amparo* is intended for the protection of all the rights and guarantees expressed in the Constitution, this implies that what is known as the right of *habeas corpus* is really a part of the right to protection, or if preferred, one manifestation of *amparo*. This is made clear by the regulation in the Fifth Temporary Provision of the Constitution, which lays down that «until such time as the special law is passed, according to Article 49, protection of the right to personal liberty shall proceed according to...» a series of procedural rules laid down therein, aimed at protecting individuals against the loss of or restriction to their liberty, in violation of their constitutional rights. When this Temporary Provision speaks of «protection for personal liberty» and refers to Article 49, it is simply affirming that the right to protection expressed in Article 49 is also intended to protect personal liberty, and that a special temporary procedure is established in this provision, but without really setting up the right of *habeas corpus* in Venezuela, as distinct from the general right to protection regulated by Article 49 of the Constitution.

E. *The Meaning of Violation of the Rights and Guarantees Protected by the Right to Amparo*

From the terms of Article 49 of the Constitution, it can be said that the objective protected by the right to protection is the enjoyment and exercise of constitutional rights and guarantees, and of course, protection for the enjoyment and exercise of such rights and guarantees is admissible, not only when some *direct* violation of a

---

200 Allan R. BREWER-CARÍAS, *Garantías constitucionales de los derechos del hombre*, Caracas 1976, p. 69.

201 Art. 53, ord. 2. Spanish Constitution 1978.

202 See the decision of the Supreme Court in Politico-Administrative Chamber of 28-10-83 in *Revista de derecho público*, N° 16, Caracas 1983, p. 169.
See the comments of René DE SOLA, «Vida y vicisitudes del recurso de *amparo* en Venezuela», *Revista del Instituto Venezolano de Derecho Social*, 47, Caracas 1985, p. 58, (also published in *Revista SIC*; 472, Caracas 1985, 74.

constitutional rule occurs, but also of course, when there is a violation of the legal rules that regulate the enjoyment and exercise of such rights. We consider that, there is no foundation whatsoever in Venezuela for wishing to restrict the exercise of the subsidiary action for protection only to cases in which a «direct violation» of the Constitution occurs.[202]

In effect, we must bear in mind that the regulation of constitutional rights and guarantees in Venezuela is not uniform, and that the manner in which they are embodied in the Constitution gives rise to differing effects of such rights and guarantees.[203] In fact, we may identify, in the first place, the «absolute rights», among which are the right to life, the right not to be held incommunicado, not to be subjected to torture or other procedures that cause moral or physical suffering, which is the same thing as the right to the integrity of the person, and the right not to be condemned to prison for life, or to punishments that are defamatory or that restrict personal liberty for more than thirty years.[204] These rights are expressed in the Constitution in such a way that it can be said that they are rights that can neither be limited nor regulated even by the legislator, and that are, moreover, the only rights which may not be restricted or suspended by executive decision based on the powers attributed to the President of the Republic in cases of emergency or disturbances that may disrupt the peace of the Republic, or in serious circumstances which affect its economic or social life. With the exception of these absolute rights, all other rights and guarantees, by contrast, are liable to limitation or regulation by the Legislator, and may be subject to measures for their restriction or suspension.[205]

A second type of constitutional right comprises those whose exercise may be restricted or suspended by the President of the Republic, even though, in principle, the legislator may not limit them. This stems from the manner in which the Constitution expresses the rights, for example, to protection of honour, reputation and privacy; the right not to take an oath or to make self-incriminating statements; not to remain imprisoned once officially released from jail; not to be punished twice for the same crime; the right to equality and freedom from discrimination; the right to religious freedom and to freedom of thought; the right to petition and to receive timely response; the right to be judged by one's ordinary judges; the right to defence; the right of association; the right to health protection; the rights to education and to work; and the right to vote.[206]

A third category of rights, stemming from the Constitution, is that composed of those rights which may be limited by the legislator, even though in a limited way. This category contains, for instance, the prisoner's right, before being sentenced, to be heard «as indicated by the law»; the right to inviolability of the home, except in cases of search «according to the law and the decision of the courts»; the right to inviolability of correspondence, except in cases of inspection or fiscal supervision of accounting documents «according to the law»; the right to take public office, with the only restrictions being conditions of aptitude «required by law».[207]

The fourth category comprises a series of constitutional rights that can be regulated and limited by the legislator in a wider form. Among such rights would

[203] Allan R. BREWER-CARÍAS, *Instituciones políticas y constitucionales*, Caracas 1985, Vol. II, p. 491.
[204] Art. 58; 60,3; 64,7.
[205] Art. 241 Constitution.
[206] Arts. 59; 60,4; 60,6; 60,8; 61; 65; 66; 67; 68; 69; 71; 76; 78; 84; 111.
[207] Arts. 60,5; 62; 63; 112.

be the right not to be detained unless caught *in fraganti*; «in the cases and with the formalities established in the law»; the right not to be conscripted «but within the terms established by law»; the freedom of movement «with the condition established by law»; the right to follow a cult under the «supreme inspection of the National Executive according to the law»; the right to carry on economic activities with no other limitations than those established by law by reasons of security, health or other social interests; the right to property, submitted to the «contributions, restrictions and obligations established by law based on public or social interests»; the right to political association and to public demonstration «according to the formalities established by law».[208] In all such cases, the exercise of rights is definitively subject to what the legislator stipulates, and within quite considerable margins.

The fifth and final category of constitutional rights and guarantees is formed by those established in such a manner that their exercise is definitively subject to legal regulation. Among such rights would be, for example, that of using the organs for the administration of justice «under the terms and conditions established by the law»; that of joining associations «according to the law»; the right to strike «under the conditions set by the law», and in the public services, «in those cases permitted by the law»[209] all such cases, the manner in which the Constitution expresses the rights and guarantees requires that, they be regulated by the Law so as to be exercised at all. From this classification of rights and guarantees into five groups, according to the Constitution,[210] it is evident that there is no sense in holding that the right to protection, and in particular, the subsidiary «action for protection», is admissible only when the Constitution is «directly violated», since many rights are not only embodied in the Constitution, but rather, by virtue of the Constitution itself, their exercise is subject to provisions and regulations established by the Legislator. The right to protection is thus also admissible against violations of laws, which regulate the enjoyment, and exercise of rights.

F. *Object of the Right to Protection: The Enjoyment and Exercise of Constitutional Rights and Guarantees*

We have pointed out that the right to protection, as regulated by the Constitution, has the definitive aim of ensuring the *enjoyment and exercise* of constitutional rights and guarantees. Precisely for this reason, the Constitution grants the power to immediately «re-establish the infringed juridical situation» to the competent judge, and precisely for this reason also provides that «the procedure should be brief and summary».

This aim of the remedy of ensuring the enjoyment and exercise of constitutional rights and guarantees entails that the judge, of course, has power to adopt preventive and cautionary measures, but bearing in mind that the legal means of protection, and even the subsidiary action for protection, are not necessarily exhausted thereby.

In other words, the protection for the enjoyment and exercise of constitutional rights and guarantees does not only entail, nor is it exhausted by the adoption of some immediate measure, by means of a brief and summary proceeding which re-

208 Arts. 60,1; 60,2; 60,9; 64; 65; 96; 99; 114; 115.
209 Arts. 68; 70; 92.
210 Allan R. BREWER-CARÍAS, *Instituciones políticas..., cit.*, Vol. II, pp. 492-490.

establishes the infringed legal situation, but rather that the action or remedy for protection by means of legal proceedings -whether through subsidiary action for protection, or by means of the actions available under ordinary law- needs the judge in the case of *amparo* to decide on the substantive issue and give a verdict as to the legality and legitimacy of the «violation» of the right in question, without prejudice to the fact that, by means of brief and summary mechanisms, decisions may be adopted during the proceedings to immediately re-establish the infringed legal situation.

G. *Amparo as a Right and not as a Single «Recourse» or «Action», and its Consequences*

In our opinion, and after analysing the constitutional text, the following conclusions can be formed:

First, the Constitution consecrates a *right to protection*, and not any particular «action» or «remedy» before a particular Court. This right is established as a fundamental right of individuals and collective persons.

Second, the right to protection implies an *obligation* of all Courts to protect according to the law, against disturbances of the enjoyment and exercise of rights and guarantees. Thus, the development that the legislator may, and has done with this right to protection may take the form, as has happened, of pre-existing actions or remedies, or may consist of a subsidiary action for protection, which is admissible when actions and remedies for protection cannot be effective by means of a brief and summary procedure with powers for the judge to protect fundamental rights and immediately re-establish the infringed legal situation.

Third, the right to protection may thus be guaranteed by means of *actions and recourse* contemplated in the legal order, (the popular action of unconstitutionality; the power of all judges to decide not to apply a law considered unconstitutional; actions for judicial review of administrative actions; the provisional system of *habeas corpus*), or by means of the subsidiary and autonomous action for protection, whose development by the courts has recently begun[211] and that can be brought before any court according to its subject of attributions.

Fourth, the right of protection is admissible to guarantee the enjoyment and exercise of *all* constitutional rights and guarantees. It may be put into effect with respect to disturbances of individual rights, as well as those of social, economic and political rights.

Fifth, the right to protection seeks to assure protection of constitutional rights and guarantees against *any disturbance* in their enjoyment and exercise, whether this is originated by *private* individuals or by *public* authorities. In the case of disturbance by public authorities, the right of protection is admissible against legislative, administrative and judicial acts, by means of the actions and recourses contemplated in the legal order (the action of unconstitutionality, the recourse of cassation, or actions for judicial review of administrative actions) when they allow a legal situation which has been infringed, to be re-established by means of a brief and summary procedure, or by means of the subsidiary autonomous action for protection.

---

[211] Allan R. BREWER-CARÍAS, «La reciente evolución jurisprudencial en relación a la admisibilidad del recurso de *amparo*», *Revista de derecho público*, N° 19, Caracas 1984, pp. 207-218.

Moreover, this action for protection is admissible against material acts or courses of action of the administration, thus it is not then admissible against administrative acts only.

Sixth, by virtue of the different ways in the Constitution for regulating fundamental rights, the right to protection can be exercised to protect the enjoyment and exercise of constitutional rights and guarantees, *not only when there has been some direct violation of the Constitution*, but also when what has been violated are the legal developments which, by virtue of the Constitution, regulate, limit and even allow the exercise of such rights. Of course, protection must be exercised against an activity that directly violates a fundamental right established in the Constitution, whether it be regulated by law or not, and whether or not the violation is contrary to what the law developing the right establishes.

Seventh, the decision of the judge as a consequence of the exercise of this right to protection, whether this be by means of pre-existing actions or recourses means of the subsidiary and autonomous «action for protection», should not limit himself to precautionary or preventive measures, but should re-establish the infringed legal situation. To this end he should make a pronouncement on the substantive issue brought before him, namely the legality and legitimacy or otherwise of the disturbance of the constitutional right or guarantee that has been reported as infringed.

Eighth, as we have seen, the Venezuelan system of judicial review, being a mixed one, in which the diffuse system of judicial review has been fully developed, that is to say, it can be exercised by all Courts in whatever kind of judicial proceeding, it is obvious that judicial review of legislation is a power that can be exercised by the Courts as a consequence of any action or recourse for protection of fundamental rights and of course, when deciding an autonomous «action for protection» of fundamental rights, when for instance, their violation is infringed by a public authority act based on a law deemed unconstitutional. In such cases, if the judge gives the protection requested through an order similar to the writs of mandamus or to the injunctions, he must previously declare the law based on which the challenged action was taken, inapplicable on the grounds of it being unconstitutional. Therefore, in such cases, judicial review of the constitutionality of legislation is also exercised when an action for protection of fundamental rights is exercised as a consequence of the diffuse system of judicial review.

IV. MIXED SYSTEM OF JUDICIAL REVIEW IN COLOMBIA

A mixed system of judicial review has also been established in Colombia since 1910. In it, the power attributed to all courts to declare the inapplicability of laws they deem contrary to the Constitution performs in parallel with a concentrated system of judicial review attributed to the Supreme Court, also through the exercise of a popular action.[212] Although it has been qualified as non-systematic, disperse and incongruous,[213] when this system is analysed in

---

212 Concerning the mixed character of the system see: J. VIDAL PERDOMO, *Derecho constitucional general*, Bogotá 1985, p. 42; D.R. SALAZAR, *Constitución Política de Colombia*, Bogotá 1982, p. 305; E. SARRIA, *Guarda de la Constitución*, Bogotá, p. 78.

213 See L.C. SACHICA, *E1 control de constitucionalidad y sus mecanismos*, Bogotá 1980, p. 59, 66; L.C. SACHICA *La Constitución y su defensa*, Congreso Internacional sobre la Constitución y su Defensa, UNAM, México 1982, (mimeo), p. 38.

comparative law, it can be considered like the Venezuelan, as one of the most complete constitutionally established systems of judicial review in contemporary constitutionalism.

As we have said, the system as a mixed one, was originally established in the 1910 Constitutional Reform in which the principle of the supremacy of the Constitution was expressly adopted with the consequent jurisdictional control of the constitutionality of laws assigned to the Supreme Court of Justice.[214] It was in the 1910 Constitution in which the role of «guardian of the integrity of the Constitution» that it is still today in the Fundamental text, was attributed to the Supreme Court of Justice for the first time[215] and it was also in the same Constitution that the principle of the diffuse system of judicial review acquired constitutional rank, established today in article 215 of the Constitution, which states:

> «Art 215. In all cases of incompatibility between the Constitution and a law, the Constitution rule must be applied in preference».

Nevertheless, even before the constitutional reform of 1910, we can say that the basis of the diffuse system of judicial review according to the North American and Latin American models, during the 19th century had already been established with a legislative rank in article 5 of Law N° 57 of 1887. It prescribed in a very similar way to the present article 215 of the Constitution, that «when there was incompatibility between a constitutional provision and a legal one, the former will be preferred».[216]

Anyway, since 1910, the Colombian constitutional system has mixed both the diffuse and the concentrated systems of judicial review, but with two other mechanisms of control: a preventive one, as a consequence of the veto powers of legislation given to the President of the Republic, and an obligatory one, concerning executive acts adopted in a state of emergency.

1. Diffuse System of Judicial Review Through the «Exception of Unconstitutionality»

As we said, article 215 of the present Colombian Constitution provides the basis of the diffuse system of judicial review, according to which all judges have the power to decide not to apply a law in a concrete process, when they deem it contrary to the Constitution. The system, as it has been developed, functions entirely according to the North American model, particularly, because it has been conceived as an «exception of unconstitutionality».

In effect, the text of the Constitution does not exclude the possible *ex officio* powers of all judges to decide themselves and without party requirement, not to apply a particular law to the resolution of the case when they deem it to be unconstitutional, as happened in Venezuela. However, the unanimity of the Colombian commentators understands that what is established in article 215 of the Constitution, is an «exception of unconstitutionality», in the sense that in all cases, the constitutional question must be raised in a process by one of the parties

214 *Cf.* L.C. SACHICA, *La Constitución* ... p. 38; L.C. SACHICA, *El control* ..., *cit.*, p. 73.

215 *Cf.* D.R. SALAZAR, *op. cit.*, p. 304.

216 See the text in J. VIDAL PERDOMO, *op. cit.*, p. 40; and in E. SARRIA, *op. cit.*, p. 77.

through an exception regarding the applicability of a law;[217] a party that must show a personal and direct interest in the non-application of the law in the concrete case.[218]

Of course, in these cases of diffuse constitutional control, the judges cannot annul the law or declare its unconstitutionality, nor can the effects of their decision be extended or generalized. On the contrary, as happens in all other diffuse judicial review systems, the court must limit itself to deciding not to apply the unconstitutional law to the concrete case, of course only when it is pertinent to the resolution of the case. That decision only has effects concerning the parties to the case. Therefore, as with similar systems elsewhere, the law whose application has been denied in a concrete case, continues to be in force and other judges can moreover continue to apply it. Even the judge who chose not to apply it in a concrete case, can change his mind in a subsequent process.[219]

However, regarding the text of article 215 of the Constitution, in which the diffuse system of judicial review has its basis, we must mention the doubts that have arisen in Colombia concerning the scope of its regulations. In effect, some authors have considered that the power regulated in that norm, concerns not only judges but all public officials, an interpretation that has been rejected by others.[220] We really think that this is an inadmissible discussion. In our opinion, it is logical and the only interpretation compatible with juridical certainty, the one that considers the text of such a norm, as conferring review powers only to the courts and judges. In a state submitted to the rule of law, only the judges can be judges of the constitutionality of legislation. On the contrary, the attribution of constitutional review powers to all public officials particularly of the executive power, with the task of applying the law, could lead to anarchy, and is inadmissible in a *État de droit*.

2. Direct Control of Constitutionality of Legislation through a Popular Action

In addition to the diffuse system of judicial review, the Colombian Constitution also provides for a concentrated system of judicial review attributed to the Supreme Court of Justice. In this respect, article 214 of the Constitution establishes under Title XX related to «Constitutional Jurisdiction», the following

> «Art 214. The guarding of the integrity of the Constitution is assigned to the Supreme Court of Justice. Consequently, in addition to the attributions assigned to it in this Constitution and the laws, it shall have the following: [...]
>
> 2. To definitively decide the unconstitutionality (*inexequibilidad*) of all laws and Decrees enacted by the Government according to the attributions referred to in articles 76, paragraphs 11 and 12, and 80 of the Constitution (Decrees with the force of law), when denounced before it as unconstitutional by any citizen...».[221]

---

217 *Cf.* J. Vidal Perdomo, *op. cit.*, pp. 47-48; L.C. Sachica, *El control ... cit.*, p. 64; E. Sarria, *op. cit.*, p. 77; D.R. Salazar, *op.cit.*, p. 307; A. Copete Lizarralde, *Lecciones de derecho constitucional*, Bogotá, pp. 243-245.

218 A. Copete Lizarralde, *op. cit.*, p. 246.

219 *Cf.* L.C. Sachica, *El control...cit.*, p. 65.

220 *Cf.* the various opinions in A. Copete Lizarralde, *op. cit.*, p. 244; E. Sarria, *op. cit.*, p. 78; J. Vidal Perdomo, *op. cit.*, p. 48; L.C. Sachica, *La Constitución ... cit.*, p. 44.

221 Through the Legislative Act N° 1 of 1979, this article was reformed, and it assigned the Supreme Court the rol not only to «guard the integrity of the Constitution», but its «supremacy». *Cf.*

Thus, according to this article, a concentrated system of judicial review is attributed to the Supreme Court of Justice, which exercises it when required through an action that can be brought before it by any citizen. That is to say, through a popular action, that can be based on any grounds of unconstitutionality, whether substantive or formal.

A. Objective Character of the Process

As a result of the «popular» character of the action of unconstitutionality, that is to say, that it can be exercised by any citizen without any particular requirement of standing, the subsequent process developed before the Supreme Court can be considered as an objective one. It is not the result of an action brought before the court against the state or any state organ, but against a law or a state act with the force of law, and that is why, in principle, any citizen can intervene in the procedure whether aiding the petitioner's position or as defender of the challenged law.[222] Due to its popular character, in any case of action of unconstitutionality, the Attorney General of the Nation must also intervene as head of the Public Prosecutors Office.[223]

The objective character of the process also results from the fact that the Supreme Court of Justice can consider any other defects of a constitutional nature to the one denounced by the petitioner or by the citizens, that have participated in the process, and can declare the unconstitutionality of the law submitted to control.[224] Thus, the defects of unconstitutionality that were contained in the action do not limit the powers of the Court as guardian of the integrity of the Constitution, being authorised to examine *ex officio* the impugned act and to confront it with all the constitutional dispositions.[225] On the other hand, also as a consequence of the role assigned to the Court, the withdrawal of the action by the petitioner has no effect, and the Court must continue its constitutional examination.[226]

Finally, and also as a result of the «popular» character of the action, in principle there is no precise delay in which it must be exercised, thus, it is inextinguishable and that is why it has been considered a political right of the citizens.[227] Nevertheless, the constitutional reform of 1979, later ineffective, sought to establish that when the grounds of the action were based on procedural or formal defects of the challenged law, the action could only be brought before the Court within a delay of one year after its enactment.[228]

L.C. SACHICA, *E1 control... cit.*, p. 142. Nevertheless, that reform resulted ineffective 'because the Supreme Court in decision of 3-11-81 declared the unconstitutionality of that Legislative Act N°1 of 1979, based on defects of procedure. See the reference in J. VIDAL PERDOMO, *op. cit.*, p. 49. The power attributed to the supreme court as constitutional judge has been regulated by the Decree 432 of 1969. See the text in J. ORTEGA TORRES (ed.), *Constitución Política de Colombia*, Bogotá 1985, p. 148.

222 This was expressly established in the constitucional reform sanctioned by the Legislative Act N° 1 of 1979. *Cf.* L Carlos SACHICA, *El control...* p. 150. The present Constitution only establishes the free intervention of any citizen when the state Act impugned is a Decree of Emergency. See Art. 215,2 and Arts. 121 and 122 Constitution; and Art. 14 Decree 432 of 1969.

223 Art. 215,2. Constitution.

224 Art. 29. Decree 432 of 1969.

225 L.C. SACHICA, *El control..., cit.*, p. 106.

226 A. COPETE LIZARRALDE, *op. cit.*, p. 246.

227 L.C. SACHICA, *La Constitución..., cit.*, p. 45

228 *Cf.* L.C. SACHICA, *El control..., cit.*, pp. 73, 151.

B. *Object of the Concentrated Judicial Review System*

As stated in article 215 of the Constitution, the object of the popular action as a means for judicial review of constitutionality, is «all the laws» and decrees with force of law, that is to say those issued by the executive as a consequence of the attribution of extraordinary powers or special legislative authorizations by Congress,[229] and also those issued by the executive on matters concerning the economic, social and public works plans when Congress fails to sanction them within a particular delay.[230]

Thus, the judicial review powers of the Supreme Court refer to legislative acts and decrees with the force of law, executive regulations also being submitted to judicial review of constitutionality, but by the Council of State.[231]

Nevertheless, despite the very wide constitutional review powers assigned to the Supreme Court concerning «all the laws» of the Nation, which for instance, comprise legislative acts containing constitutional reforms by formal defects,[232] the Court itself has restricted the scope of its review powers and has excluded certain laws from being examined on the grounds of unconstitutionality. This is particularly true regarding laws of approval of other state acts, such as administrative contracts and international treaties. In these cases, the Supreme Court by case law has limited its judicial review powers and has abstained from exercising constitutional control over those laws.[233] In particular, concerning international treaties and contrary to the general trend, for instance in continental Europe, the Colombian Supreme Court has considered that controlling the constitutionality of a law of approval of an International Treaty would mean the breaking of the international obligations of the state, additional to the criterion traditionally followed in Colombia, regarding the superior hierarchy of international treaties regarding internal public law.[234]

C. *Compulsory Judicial Review of Executive Emergency Decrees*

Within the state acts submitted to judicial review through the exercise of a popular action, we must also mention decrees issued by the President of the Republic when a state of siege is declared as a consequence of an external war or of internal commotion or when the economic and social order of the country is gravely altered.[235] In such cases, the Colombian Constitution establishes a compulsory judicial review proceeding according to which the day following their enactment, the President of the Republic must submit them to the Supreme Court, which must then «definitively decide upon their constitutionality».[236] As we mentioned, in the proceeding, any citizen is allowed to participate whether in defence of or in the attack on the constitutionality of such Decrees.[237] Once the Court has pronounced its decision, it has *erga omnes* effects and the value of *res judicata*, thus no further action of unconstitutionality can be exercised against those acts.[238]

---

229 Art. 76, paragraphs 11 and 12. Constitution.
230 Arts. 76 paragraph 4; 80 and 215, paragraph 2.
231 Art. 216 Constitution.
232 *Cf.* L.C. SACHICA, *El control... cit.*, p. 144; J. VIDAL PERDOMO, *op. cit.*, p. 49.
233 *Cf.* L.C. SACHICA, *El control... cit.*, pp. 79-84
234 *Cf.* L.C. SACHICA, *El Control... cit.*, p. 80
235 Arts. 121, 122 Constitution.
236 Arts. 121, 122 Constitution. Art. 13 Decree 432 of 1969.
237 Art. 215 Constitution. Art. 14 Decree 432 of 1969
238 As was established in the constitutional reform sanctioned by the Legislative Act Nº 1 of 1979, later annuled. See J.C. SACHICA, *El control... cit.*, pp. 148-149.

D. *Role of the Constitutional Chamber of the Supreme Court*

As we have said, the powers to control the constitutionality of state acts are assigned in the Constitution of Colombia, following the general trend of the Latin-American systems, to the Supreme Court of Justice, which exercises it in Plenary session.[239] Nevertheless, in the 60's and influenced by the European model of judicial review, attempts were made to create a Constitutional Court to substitute the Supreme Court in its role of Supreme Guardian of the Constitution.[240] The project was rejected, and in the 1968 constitutional reform, within the Supreme Court of Justice, a Constitutional Chamber or Division was created instead, composed of four members of the Court specialising in public law,[241] with the special task of studying cases of unconstitutionality previous to the decision of the Plenary session, and proposing projects of resolutions to it.[242] Thus, the Constitutional Chamber has merely an advisory character and no power of decision on constitutional questions. It must be mentioned that the constitutional reform adopted by the Legislative Act N° 1 of 1979, tended to give the Constitutional Chamber self-decision powers in almost all matters of unconstitutionality, except those regarding the unconstitutionality of constitutional reforms due to formal defects and that of executive decrees issued in cases of state of Siege or economic emergency.[243] Nevertheless, Legislative Act N° 1 of 1979 was itself declared unconstitutional by the Supreme Court in 1981[244] and consequently, the 1979 constitutional reform ceased to be effective.

E. *Effects of the Supreme Court decision on judicial review*

As happens in all concentrated systems of judicial review, the Supreme Court decisions, when declaring the unconstitutionality of a legislative act, have general and *erga omnes* effects.[245] Additionally, the decision has *res judicata* value, and its contents are obligatory to everyone. In particular, the value of *res judicata* to the Supreme Court's decisions rejecting the action, and thus, declaring the constitutionality of the challenged law, has been recognized, in which cases, the courts through their diffuse control powers cannot declare the inapplicability of the law on the same grounds of unconstitutionality rejected by the Supreme Court.[246]

On the other hand, regarding time, the endless discussions of the *ex tunc* or *ex nunc* effects of the Supreme Court decision on judicial review, has also taken place in Colombia, even though the majority of authors tends to assign them only *ex nunc, pro futuro* effects.[247] Thus the laws declared unconstitutional by the Supreme Court due to their presumption of constitutionality, in principle are effective until their annulment is declared by the Court, the juridical situations originated by the law prior to its annulment being only submitted to review through ordinary judicial means.[248]

---

239 Art. 215 Constitution. Art. 1, Decree 432 of 1969

240 See the comments of H. FIX–ZAMUDIO, *Los tribunales constitucionales y los derechos humanos*, México, 1980, pp. 151-152.

241 Art. 1. Decree 432 of 1969.

242 Art. 3. Decree 432 of 1969.

243 *Cf.* L.C. SACHICA, *El control... cit.*, p. 59.

244 Décision of 1-11-81. See in *Revista Foro Colombiano*, N° 151-152, 1982. See the comments in J. VIDAL PERDOMO, *op. cit.*, p. 49.

245 *Cf.* A. COPETE LIZARRALDE, *op. cit.*, p. 245; L.C. SACHICA, *El control..., cit.*, p. 68.

246 *Cf.* A. COPETE LIZARRALDE, *op. cit.*, p. 246; L.C. SACHICA, *El control... cit.*, p. 172

247 *Cf.* L.C. SACHICA, *El control... cit.*, p. 68; E. SARRIA, *op. cit.*, p. 83

248 E. SARRIA, *op. cit.*, p. 83

Anyway, regarding legislative acts containing constitutional reforms, when declared unconstitutional, they become totally and definitively inapplicable after the declaration. However, the effects produced by the act declared unconstitutional are intangible. Consequently, in such cases, the decision has no retroactive effects; and the constitutional rules revoked or amended by the constitutional reform declared unconstitutional are revived,[249] thereby returning to the constitutional system in force prior to the enactment of the annulled reform.

3. Preventive Judicial Review of Legislation

Finally, it must be mentioned that in addition to the *a posteriori* concentrated judicial review system, since 1886, the Colombian Constitution has established a preventive judicial review method of laws, as a consequence of the veto powers of legislation assigned to the President of the Republic.[250]

When a law is vetoed based on substantive or procedural constitutional issues, if the legislative chambers insist on its promulgation, the President of the Republic must send the project of law to the Supreme Court, which must take its decision within a six-day delay.

In the event of the Supreme Court declaring the bill unconstitutional, the project must be filed, but if the Supreme Court rejects the constitutional objections raised by the President, then he is obliged to promulgate it.[251]

V. MIXED SYSTEM OF JUDICIAL REVIEW IN GUATEMALA

Also following the North American model based on the principle of the supremacy of the Constitution[252] the 1921 Guatemalan Constitution established the power of the Court to declare in their decisions the inapplicability of any law or disposition of the other state powers when contrary to the norms contained in the Constitution of the Republic.[253]

This power of the Courts, which can be termed a diffuse power of judicial review, was maintained in all constitutional texts up to the present Constitution of 1965 in which a concentrated system of review attributed to a specially created Constitutional Court was established in addition to the diffuse system. Thus, the Guatemalan system of judicial review can also be considered a mixed one.

1. Diffuse system of Judicial Review

In effect, the 1965 Constitution expressly establishes the principle of the supremacy of the Constitution and the subsequent nullity of all state acts contrary to it, prescribing the duty of the judges to give preference to the Constitution in cases of laws conflicting with the Constitution.

In particular, article 77 establishes the general norm by stating that:

> «The laws, government dispositions, and any other order which regulates the exercise of the rights guaranteed in the Constitution shall be *ipso jure* null if they diminish, restrict or distort them».[254]

---

249 J. VIDAL PERDOMO, *op. cit.*, p. 46

250 Arts. 90 and 215,1. Constitution. Art. 11, Decree 432 of 1969.

251 Art. 90 Constitution.

252 See the comments regarding the constitutional process of Guatemala during the 19th Century in J.M. GARCÍA LA GUARDIA, *La defensa de la Constitución*, México 1983, pp. 52-53.

253 Article 93, c. Constitution 1921.

254 See also Article 172 Constitution 15-9-1965.

Additionally, article 246 establishes:

«The Courts of Justice will always observe the principle that the Constitution must prevail over any law or international Treaty».

Consequently, according to these norms, the judicial review power attributed to all courts of justice, is conceived in the Constitution as a duty of the judges, which they can therefore exercise *ex officio*,[255] in deciding a concrete case, that is to say, without the requirement of a party to the case. Nevertheless, when a party to the case raises a constitutional question regarding a law or a part of it, the judges must decide upon the question.[256] Anyway, due to the purely incidental character of the review, article 246 of the Constitution states:

«If the unconstitutionality of a law is declared, the decision must limit itself to establishing that the legal disposition is inapplicable to the case and the question must be sent to Congress».[257]

The party requirement regarding constitutional questions can be brought before the ordinary Court in the concrete case, either through the concrete claim or as an exception in the process. In any case, prior to the judge's decision of the case and thus, prior to the decision of the constitutional question, the judge must hear the parties and the Public Prosecutor.[258]

As in all diffuse systems of judicial review, judge's decision when declaring the inapplicability of a law on the grounds of unconstitutionality, has declarative effects, in the sense that it establishes a pre-existent nullity with retroactive or *ex tunc* effects, but exclusively related to the parties to the case[259] (*in casu et inter partes*).

2. Concentrated System of Judicial Review and the Constitutional Court

However, the 1965 Constitution, following the European model and additional to the diffuse system of judicial review, also established a concentrated system, by assigning the exclusive power to declare the unconstitutionality of laws, and thus, to annul them with *erga omnes* effects, to a Constitutional Court.[260]

This Constitutional Court, although created in the Constitution,[261] is not conceived as a permanent organ, but as a temporal one that only functions when required to exercise judicial review. It has 12 members, appointed as follows: four by the Supreme Court of Justice, and the rest designated by the Supreme Court of Justice, by a draw from within the members of the Court of Appeals and the Administrative Justice Tribunal. The President of the Constitutional Court is the President of the Supreme Court of Justice.[262]

255 J.M. GARCÍA LA GUARDIA, *op. cit.*, pp. 56-57.
256 Art. 246 Constitution.
257 This norm has been developed in the legislative Decree Nº 8, Articles 96-104. See J.M. GARCÍA LA GUARDIA, *op. cit.*, p. 58.
258 J.M. GARCÍA LA GUARDIA, *op. cit.*, p. 58.
259 *Idem*, p. 59.
260 See H. FIX-ZAMUDIO, *Los tribunales constitucionales y los derechos humanos*, México 1980, p. 136
261 Art. 262 Constitution. The Court and the recourse of unconstitutionality is regulated in the Law of *amparo, habeas corpus* and constitutionality of 3-5-1966. See the reference in H. FIX-ZAMUDIO, *op. cit.*, p. 137.
262 Art. 266 Constitution, Art. 105 Law

The judicial review powers of the Constitutional Court are exercised when requested through a «recourse of unconstitutionality» conceived as a direct action[263] that can be exercised against «laws and governmental dispositions of general effects when considered to be totally or partially unconstitutional».[264]

The standing to bring the action before the Constitutional Court is a specific one, thus differing from the popular action that can be brought before the Supreme Courts of Venezuela and Colombia. In particular, this «recourse of unconstitutionality» can only be brought before the Court by the following: the Council of state, conceived in the Guatemalan constitutional system, as a consultative institution; the Public Prosecutor, when requested to do so by the President in a decision adopted in the Council of Ministers; and finally, by any individual or entity directly affected by the unconstitutionality of the law or the challenged governmental act, assisted by ten lawyers.[265] Thus, the standing has been considered extremely limited.[266]

In the proceeding of the recourse of unconstitutionality, if the Public Prosecutor does not bring the action before the Court, he must be notified and in principle, he must defend the constitutionality of the challenged act, even though he can express his conformity with the alleged unconstitutionality.[267]

We must also mention, as an important feature of the proceeding before the Constitutional Court of Guatemala, that the Court can provisionally suspend the effects of the challenged law or executive act during the process, when the unconstitutionality is notorious and could produce irreparable damage.

This decision of suspension of the effects of the law or executive act of general contents has general effects and an *erga omnes* character and must be published in the official Journal.[268]

The final decision of the Court if it is of declaring the unconstitutionality of the law, has also *erga omnes* effects, but as in all concentrated systems of judicial review, with *ex nunc* effects. Thus, the decision has a constitutive character, with *pro futuro* consequences, and without any effect back towards the past.[269] Only when a temporal suspension of the effects of the law has been decided by the Court during the procedure the final decision declaring the unconstitutionality of the law can have *ex tunc* effects, but back to the date of the suspensive decision of the effects of the challenged law.[270]

3. Judicial Review and the Constitutional Protection (*Amparo*)

Finally, it must also be mentioned that in Guatemala, a special judicial means for constitutional protection (*amparo*) of the fundamental rights established in the Constitution, following the Mexican model,[271] has been established.

[263] H. FIX-ZAMUDIO, *op. cit.*, p. 138.
[264] Art. 263 Constitution. Art. 106 Law.
[265] Art. 264 Constitution. Art. 107 Law.
[266] H. FIX-ZAMUDIO, *op. cit.*, p. 64.
[267] J.M. GARCÍA LA GUARDIA, *op. cit.*, p. 63
[268] Art. 263 Constitution. Art. 106 Law.
[269] Art. 108 Law.
[270] J.M. GARCÍA LA GUARDIA, *op. cit.*, p. 67; H. FIX-ZAMUDIO, *op. cit.*, p. 140.
[271] H. FIX-ZAMUDIO, *op. cit.*, p. 136

The main purpose of this *amparo* as all the institutions of this kind in Latin America is to seek «the maintenance of or the restitution to the aggrieved person of the enjoyment of the rights and guarantees established in the Constitution».[272] Nevertheless, according to the Guatemalan Constitution the *amparo* is also admissible in order «to declare, in concrete cases that a law, an executive regulation or any other act of an authority is not obligatory for the petitioner, because it contravenes or it restricts any of the rights guaranteed in the Constitution».[273] Thus, through the *amparo* action, the judge can exercise his powers of judicial review in an incidental way *incidenter tantum*, in accordance with the diffuse system, and declare a law deemed unconstitutional because of violation of fundamental rights inapplicable.

The concrete effect of the judge's decision granting *amparo* to the petitioner, is to suspend the application of the law or executive regulation regarding the petitioner, and restore when necessary, his juridical situation previously infringed.[274]

VI. MIXED SYSTEM OF JUDICIAL REVIEW IN BRAZIL

The Brazilian system of judicial review, like the Argentinean, can be thought of as one of the Latin American systems that had followed the North American model more closely,[275] although it can now be thought of as a mixed system, after the establishment in the 1934 Constitution, of a direct action of unconstitutionality that can be brought before the Supreme Court of Justice to impugned laws.

1. Historical Background

In effect, the Federal Constitution of 1891 clearly influenced by the North American constitutional system[276] assigned the Supreme Federal Tribunal the power to review, through an extraordinary recourse, the decisions of the federal courts and of the courts of the Member States, in which the validity or the application of the treaties or Federal Laws was questioned, and the decisions were against; or in which the validity of laws or government acts of the states was questioned on the grounds of being contrary to the Constitution or to the federal laws, and the decisions considered the challenged laws or acts valid.[277] As a consequence of this express constitutional attribution, the Federal Law 221 of 1894[278] assigned the power to judge upon the validity of obviously unconstitutional laws and executive regulations, and to decide their inapplicability in concrete cases, to all federal judges. Thus, the diffuse system of judicial review of legislation was established in Brazil as from the end of the last century, and was perfected through the subsequent constitutional reforms of 1926, 1934, 1937, 1946 and 1967.[279] Therefore, we can say that the main feature of the Brazilian system of judicial review is its diffuse character, with all its consequences according to the American model.

---

272 Art. 80,1 Constitution.
273 Art. 80,2 Constitution.
274 J.M. GARCÍA LA GUARDIA, *op. cit.*, p. 50; H. FIX-ZAMUDIO, *op. cit.*, p. 136.
275 H. FIX-ZAMUDIO and J. CARPIZO, «Amerique latine» in L. FAVOREU and J.A. JOLOWICZ (ed.), *Le contrôle juridictionnel des lois*, Paris 1986, p. 121.
276 O.A. BANDEIRA DE MELLO, *A teoria das Constituiçoes rigidas*, Sao Paulo 1980, p. 157; J. Alfonso DA SILVA, *Sistema de defensa da Constituiçao brasileira*, Congreso sobre la Constitución y su Defensa, UNAM, México 1982, p. 29. (mimeo).
277 Art. 59, III, 1. 1981 Constitution.
278 Art. 13,10. Law 221 of 20 November 1984.
279 O.A. BANDEIRA DE MELLO, *op. cit.*, pp. 158–237.

In addition to the diffuse system of judicial review, a concentrated system of review was established in the 1934 Constitution, by attributing power to the Supreme Federal Tribunal to declare the unconstitutionality of member state Constitution or laws (state laws) when required to do so by the Attorney General of the Republic.[280] Thus, a direct action of unconstitutionality was established as from 1934, to defend federal constitutional principles, against Member state acts,[281] later developed in subsequent Constitutions [282] up to its extension after the 1965 Constitutional Amendment, to control all normative acts of state, whether federal or of the Member States.[283]

Consequently, the Brazilian system can be considered a mixed one in which the diffuse system of judicial review operates in combination with a concentrated system.[284]

2. Diffuse system of judicial review

In the American Model and in the Argentinean experience the powers of the courts to control the constitutionality of legislation were derived from the principle of constitutional supremacy as applied by the Supreme Court. Contrary to that, the diffuse system of judicial review arose in Brazil from express provisions in the 1891 Constitution, and[285] it is still based on constitutional norms. In this respect, the present Constitution establishes the competence of the Supreme Federal Tribunal to judge through extraordinary recourses, cases decided in the last resort by other courts or judges, when the challenged judicial decisions: first, were against any disposition of the Constitution or denied the enforcement of a Treaty or federal law; second, when they declared the unconstitutionality of a Treaty or of a federal law; and third, when they deemed a law or other local government act challenging the Constitution or a federal law valid.[286]

According to this norm, not only is the diffuse system of judicial review established, but the power of the Supreme Tribunal to intervene in all processes in which constitutional questions have been resolved, is also established.

A. *Incidental character of the system and the exception of unconstitutionality*

As we mentioned, the diffuse system of judicial review in Brazil follows the general trends of the American model also developed in Argentina. Therefore, all the courts of first instance have the power not to apply laws (federal, state or Municipal laws) they deem unconstitutional, when a party to the process has raised the question of constitutionality. Thus, the judges have no *ex officio* power to judge the constitutionality of the laws and can only exercise it when the question of constitutionality has been raised by the interested party as an exception or defence in the process.[287] The constitutional question, once raised, has a preliminary character regarding the final decision of the case, which the judge must decide beforehand.

---

280 Art. 12,2. 1934 Constitution.

281 J. Alfonso DA SILVA, *doc. cit.* p. 29.

282 Also in the Law Nº 2271 of 22 July 1954.

283 *Cf.* J. Alfonso DA SILVA, *doc. cit.*, p. 31.

284 A. BUZAID, «La accion directa de inconstitucionalidad en el derecho brasileño», *Revista de la Facultad de Derecho*, UCAB, Nº 19-22, Caracas 1964, p. 55; O.A. BANDEIRA DE MELLO, *op. cit.*, p. 157.

285 *Cf.* J. Alfonso DA SILVA, *doc. cit.*, pp. 32, 34; J. Alfonso DA SILVA, *Curso de direito constitucional positivo*, Sao Paulo 1984, p. 17.

286 Art. 119, III b,c, Constitution. J. Alfonso DA SILVA, *Sistema... doc. cit.*, p. 43; O.A. BANDEIRA DE MELLO, *op. cit.*, p. 215.

287 J. Alfonso DA SILVA, *Curso...* p. 18; J. Alfonso DA SILVA, *Sistema... doc. cit.*, pp. 33, 37, 58.

Of course, the decision of the courts on constitutional matters has only *in casu et inter partes* effects, and the unapplied law is considered null and void *ab initio*. Thus, the decision has *ex tunc*, retroactive effects.[288]

The constitutional question can also be considered in a second instance, through the normal appeals process, in which case, when the court of second instance is a collegiate court, the decision upon matters of unconstitutionality of legislation must be adopted by a majority vote decision of its members.[289]

B. *Extraordinary recourse before the Supreme Federal Tribunal*

The Brazilian Constitution, ever since the establishment of the constitutional review judicial system in 1891, has always expressly regulated the power of the Supreme Court to review lower courts decisions on matters of constitutionality, through an extraordinary recourse that can be brought before the Tribunal, by the party to the process who has lost the case.[290]

This extraordinary recourse of unconstitutionality, as we mentioned, proceeds only when the Superior Courts of Appeal have made decisions that are considered contrary to the Constitution or that deny the validity of a treaty or federal law; when the decisions declare the unconstitutionality of a treaty or of a Federal Law; and when they deem a local government law or act that has been challenged as unconstitutional or contrary to a federal law valid.[291]

It must be mentioned that due to the constitutional questions that are the object of the proceeding before the Supreme Federal Tribunal, the Attorney General can always intervene; and can also intervene in any process pending decision, to raise constitutional questions, which must be decided by the Tribunal.[292]

Finally it must be said that when deciding constitutional questions, the Supreme Federal Tribunal must adopt its decision with the vote of the majority of its members.[293] The decision, as the first instance one, when declaring the unconstitutionality of a law, has *inter partes* and *ex tunc* effects.[294] In such cases, the Tribunal in fact recognises the *ab initio* unconstitutionality of the law, in a decision which has declarative effects, but does not annul or repeal the law, which continues in force and to be applicable.

In the Brazilian system, an additional feature can be distinguished: once adopted by the Tribunal the decision must be sent to the Federal Senate which has the power, according to the Constitution, to «suspend the execution of all or part of a law or decree, declared unconstitutional by the Supreme Federal Tribunal through a definitive decision,[295] in which case the effects of the Senate decisions have, of course, *erga omnes* and *ex nunc* effects.[296]

---

288 J. Alfonso DA SILVA, *Sistema... doc. cit.*, pp. 41,64; A. BUZAID, *loc. cit.*, p. 91.

289 This qualified vote was first established in the 1934 Constitution Art. 179), and is always required. See O.A. BANDEIRA DE MELLO, *op. cit.*, p. 159.

290 J. Alfonso DA SILVA, *Sistema... doc. cit.*, p. 44.

291 Art. 199. III, b,c. Constitution.

292 J. Alfonso DA SILVA, *Sistema... doc. cit.*, p. 44.

293 D.A. BANDEIRA DE MELLO, *op. cit.*, p. 218.

294 J. Alfonso DA SILVA, *Sistema... doc. cit.*, pp. 69, 71.

295 Art. 42, VII Federal Constitution.

296 J. Alfonso DA SILVA, *Sistema..., doc. cit.*, p. 73.

Anyway, it must be said that in Brazil, like in the North American system, a presumption of constitutionality also exists regarding laws and other state acts. Consequently, only when the unconstitutionality of a law appears to be without doubt, the Tribunal can declare its unconstitutionality. Thus, in case of doubt, it must reject the question and consider the law constitutional, and applicable in the concrete case.[297]

3. Concentrated system of judicial review

Additional to the diffuse system of judicial review, as we have said, the Brazilian Constitution has since 1934 also adopted a concentrated system of review attributed to the Supreme Federal Tribunal, through a direct action that can be brought before the Tribunal only by the Attorney General of the Republic. This direct action of unconstitutionality can be of two types: the intervention direct action and the generic direct action.

The so-called «intervention direct action» was originally established in the 1934 Constitution as a means for the protection of the federal constitutional principles regarding States legislation.[298] The Constitution in effect established the possibility for the Federal Government to intervene in the Member States, to secure the observance of the following principles: republican form of government; independence and harmony of powers; temporal character of electoral functions; non re-election of governors for the next term; municipal autonomy; submission of administrative accounts; and guarantees of the Judicial Power.[299].

Now, when any of these principles are violated by a member state, the federal power can intervene in it. But previous to that intervention, the Attorney General must submit the question of unconstitutionality of the member state acts when contrary to those principles, for examination by the Supreme Federal Tribunal, through a direct action.[300] If the final decision of the Tribunal is to declare the unconstitutionality of the challenged Member state law or act, it must be published and sent to the President of the Republic for it to suspend, by Decree, the execution of the challenged act, and if necessary, to order federal intervention in the Member state.[301] Thus in this case, the effects of the Tribunal decision are considered to be declarative[302] and with *erga omnes* effects.[303]

Only when the act is declared unconstitutional by the Tribunal, federal intervention can take place.[304]

In the 1946 Constitution, in addition to the interventive direct action, what is called a generic direct action of unconstitutionality[305] was established. This action

---

297 *Cf.* T.B. CAVALCANTI, *Do controle de constitutionalidade*, Rio do Janeiro, 1966, p. 69.

298 Art.7 Constitution 1934. O.A. BANDEIRA DE MELLO, *op. cit.*, p. 170; J. Alfonso DA SILVA, *Sistema... doc. cit.*, p. 31.

299 Art. 10 Constitution. O.A. BANDEIRA DE MELLO, *op. cit.*, . 221.

300 Art. 11,1 Constitution. Art. 1 Law N. 2271 of 22-7-1954 and Law Nº 4337 of 1-6-1964. A BUZAID, *loc. cit.*, pp. 76-78.

301 Art. 11,2 Constitution. Art. 9 Law Nº 4337 of 1-6-1964. A. BUZAID, *loc. cit.*, p. 53.

302 See O.A. BANDEIRA DE MELLO, *op. cit.*, p. 212; A. BUZAID, *loc. cit.*, p. 95. In contrary sense see J. Alfonso DA SILVA, *Sistema... doc. cit.*, p. 76.

303 J. Alfonso DA SILVA, Sistema..., *doc. cit.*, p. 76. In contrary sense see A. BUZAID, *loc. cit.*, p. 96.

304 A. BUZAID, *loc. cit.*, pp. 79, 97; O.A. BANDEIRA DE MELLO, *op. cit.*, p. 222.

305 J. Alfonso DA SILVA, *Sistema... doc. cit.*, p. 31; A. BUZAID considers this action as the only one in Brazil whose principal object is the declaration of the unconstitutionality of a law, *loc. cit.*, p. 84.

differs from the one already mentioned by the fact that it is intended not to protect certain constitutional principles regarding member state laws and acts only, but any of the dispositions of the Constitution.

The Constitution, in effect, attributes competence to the Supreme Federal Tribunal at the request of the Attorney General of the Republic, to decide upon the unconstitutionality of any law or act of a normative character, either federal or of a Member state.[306] In this case, if the Supreme Federal Tribunal declares the unconstitutionality of the federal or state law or normative act, a copy of the decision must be sent to the Federal Senate, which has the power to «suspend the execution of all or part of the law or decree declared unconstitutional by a definitive decision of the Supreme Federal Tribunal.[307]

Discussions have taken place among Brazilian constitutional law authors regarding the effects of the Supreme Federal Tribunal decision declaring the unconstitutionality of a law, as a consequence of a generic direct action, particularly due to the fact that the Constitution assigns the aforementioned power to the Federal Senate. It has been considered, in effect, that the Supreme Federal Tribunal decisions in such cases of generic direct actions of unconstitutionality do not have, in themselves, *erga omnes* effects[308] their contents being only to verify the existence or not of a defect of unconstitutionality in the challenged act.[309] Thus, it has been thought to have declarative effects, thus, with *ex tunc* repercussions.[310] Only the Senate decision of suspension of the execution of the law is considered to have *erga omnes* effects.[311]

4. Indirect Means for Judicial Review of Legislation

Additional to the diffuse and concentrated systems of judicial review, an indirect means for judicial review, through the actions for protection of fundamental rights and liberties and through a popular action established to seek the protection of public assets, can also be identified in the Brazilian constitutional system.

A. *Mandado de segurança and habeas corpus actions and judicial review*

In effect, since 1934,[312] the Constitution of Brazil has expressly established the *mandado de segurança* as a special means for the protection of fundamental rights, other than personal liberty, which is protected through the recourse for *habeas corpus*. Thus, in the Brazilian constitutional system there are two special actions for the constitutional protection of fundamental rights: the *mandado de segurança* and the *habeas corpus* actions.

In particular, the *mandado de segurança* is intended to protect actual individual rights not protected through *habeas corpus*, whoever the authority responsible for

306 Art. 119, I, 1. Constitution; Law N. 4337 of 1-6-1964. J.A. Alfonso DA SILVA, *Curso... cit.*, p. 18.

307 Art. 42, VII, Constitution.

308 J. Alfonso DA SILVA, *Sistema... doc. cit.*, pp. 54,64,69; In contrary sense see O.A. BANDEIRA DE MELLO, *op. cit.*, pp. 201, 213.

309 J. Alfonso DA SILVA, *Sistema.., doc. cit.*, p. 74.

310 O. BANDEIRA DE MELLO, *op. cit.*, p. 201; A. BUZAID, *loc. cit.*, p. 96.

311 J. Alfonso DA SILVA, *Sistema... doc. cit.*, pp. 54,64,69,73; In contrary sense see A. BUZAID, *loc. cit.*, p. 95.

312 Art. 113,33 Constitution 1934. A. RÍOS ESPINOZA, Presupuestos constitucionales del mandato de seguridad», *Boletín del Instituto de Derecho Comparado de México*, UNAM, 46, 1963, p. 71. (Also published in H. FIX-ZAMUDIO, A. RÍOS ESPINOSA and N. ALCALÁ ZAMORA, *Tres sstudios sobre el mandato de seguridad brasileño*, México 1963, pp. 71-96.

the illegality or abuse of powers may be.[313] Nevertheless, it has been traditionally considered that the laws or any other normative act of state, cannot be the object of an action requesting either *habeas corpus* or a *mandado de segurança.*[314]

In this respect, as happened with the Argentinean recourse for *amparo* until recent changes within the Supreme Court decisions, the abstract control of the constitutionality of laws is not possible through the exercise of the actions for a *mandado de segurança*, or *habeas corpus*. In other words, no direct action against laws can be exercised through the *mandado de segurança*, or *habeas corpus* actions, even if they are what the Mexican system calls auto applicative or self-executing laws.[315] Nevertheless, such actions can serve as an indirect means of judicial review, according to the diffuse system, when they are exercised against an act of any authority when executed based on a law deemed unconstitutional. Thus, it is only the concrete situation that results from the execution or application of the law or normative act, the one that can be directly impugned by means of these actions for protection of fundamental rights, and only in an indirect way and in accordance with the diffuse method of review, that laws can be controlled by the courts on the grounds of their unconstitutionality.

B. Popular Action for the Protection of Public Assets and Judicial Review

Also, ever since the 1934 Constitution[316] in the Brazilian constitutional system, a *popular action* as a special means devoted to invalidating illegal acts, which could affect the assets of public entities, has been instituted.[317] In particular, it is an action open to any citizen and principally directed to impugn administrative acts, which, therefore, cannot be brought before the courts to impugn, in a direct way, laws or normative acts on the grounds of being unconstitutional. Nevertheless, in this case, the popular action can be an indirect means of judicial review of legislation, if the concrete administrative act which causes damage to the assets of any public entity, is based on a law deemed unconstitutional. Nonetheless, it has been considered a direct means of judicial review of legislation, in cases in which damage to the assets of public entities is directly caused by the law or decree.[318] In such cases, the powers of review of legislation exercised by the judges, of course, follow the general pattern of the diffuse system of review.

VII. THE TRIBUNAL OF CONSTITUTIONAL GUARANTEES AND THE MIXED SYSTEM OF PERU

Finally, a mixed system of judicial review can also by the distinguished in Peru, where the 1979 Constitution established the basis for a diffuse system of judicial review and additionally created a Tribunal of Constitutional Guarantees, with concentrated powers of judicial review, following the Spanish model.[319]

313 153,21 Constitution.

314 *Cf.* A. Alfonso DA SILVA, «*Sistema... doc. cit.*, p. 47; H. FIX-ZAMUDIO, «Mandato de seguridad y juicio de *amparo*», *Boletín del Instituto de Derecho Comparado de México*, UNAM; 46, 1963, pp. 11, 17. Also published in H. FIX-ZAMUDIO, A. RÍOS ESPINOSA, N. ALCALÁ ZAMORA, *op. cit.*, pp. 3-69; A. RIOS ESPINOSA, *loc.cit.*, p. 88.

315 H. FIX-ZAMUDIO, *loc. cit.*, p. 16; A. Alfonso DA SILVA, *Sistema... doc. cit.*, pp. 46,47.

316 O.A. BANDEIRA DE MELLO, *op. cit.*, p. 174.

317 Art. 153, 31 Constitution.

318 J. Alfonso DA SILVA, *Açao popular constitucional. Doutrina a proceso*, Sao Paulo 1968, p. 129; J. Alfonso DA SILVA, *Sistema... doc. cit.*, p. 49.

319 See D. GARCÍA BELAUNDE, «La influencia española en la Constitución peruana (a propósito del Tribunal de Garantías Constitucionales)», *Revista de derecho político*, UNED, 16, Madrid 1982-1983, p. 201.

In effect, the Constitution of Peru of 12 July 1979, in force since the 28th July 1980,[320] following a long tradition, has established in article 23 the diffuse system of judicial review as follows:

> «Art. 236. In case of incompatibility between a constitutional norm and an ordinary legal one, the judge must prefer the former. In similar way, he must prefer the legal norm above any other inferior norm».

According to this constitutional disposition, all judges can exercise their power of judicial review of legislation, deciding not to apply a law, which they deem unconstitutional. This must by done in an incidental way when required by a party to the case, and with *inter partes* effects.[321] This power of judicial review, without doubt, can be considered a diffuse one, even though not commonly exercised by the courts.[322]

Additionally, to the diffuse system of judicial review, a concentrated system of judicial review has also been established in Peru since 1980. In effect, another example of a specially created constitutional organ for judicial review of constitutionality of legislation in Latin America, is the Tribunal of Constitutional Guarantees created by the Peruvian Constitution of 1979 as a «control organ of the Constitution» made up of nine members appointed in a partisan way (three each) by the Congress, the executive power and the Supreme Court of Justice.[323] Its functioning has been regulated by the Organic Law of the Tribunal of Constitutional Guarantees of 19 May 1982.[324]

This Tribunal of Constitutional Guarantees, with jurisdiction throughout the territory of the Republic, is competent in two basic aspects, relating to constitutional supremacy: first, it has jurisdictional power to control the constitutionality of legislation; and second, it is competent to decide, in the last resort, as a cassation court, recourses regarding lower courts decisions on *habeas corpus* and *amparo* recourses[325]

As a jurisdictional organ for judicial review, the Tribunal of Constitutional Guarantees is competent

> «To declare, on the petition of a party, the partial or total unconstitutionality of laws, legislative decrees, regional norms of a general character, and municipal ordinances which contravene the Constitution as a matter of form or substance».[326]

The «parties» that are authorised to interpose an action of unconstitutionality are the President of the Republic, the Supreme Court of Justice, the Public Prosecutor of the Republic, sixty members of Parliament, twenty Senators, or fifty thousand petitioning citizens whose signatures must be certified by the National Electoral Board.

---

320 See D. GARCÍA BELAUNDE, «La nueva Constitución peruana», *Boletín mexicano de derecho comparado*, 40, 1981.

321 See D. GARCÍA BELAUNDE, «La influencia española...», *loc. cit.*, pp. 205-207.

322 *Idem*, p. 205.

323 Art. 296. Constitution 28-7-80.

324 See the comments in H. FIX-ZAMUDIO, «Dos leyes orgánicas de Tribunales Constitucionales latinoamericanos: Chile y Perú», *Boletín mexicano de derecho comparado*, 51, México 1984, p. 943.

325 Art. 298 Constitution.

326 Art. 298,1 Constitution.

The power of the Tribunal on judicial review is not bound by the will of the parties contained in the action requests, and can exceed them, by declaring the unconstitutionality of dispositions other than the challenged ones, when the ruling is a consequence or is in connection with the action contents and also by declaring the unconstitutionality of the statute or norm based on the violation of any other constitutional disposition, even not invoked in the proceeding.[327]

In the case of statutes, the effects of the ruling upon its unconstitutionality are not immediate regarding their validity. In effect, similar to the Yugoslavian solution, once the decision is adopted it must be communicated to the President of the Congress, so that the latter may pass a law repealing the provision contrary to the Constitution. When 45 days have elapsed with out the new derogatory rule having been promulgated, the unconstitutional provision is understood to have been nullified and the Tribunal must publish the decision in the Official Gazette.[328]

On the other hand, when the ruling of unconstitutionality relates to other normative state acts, different to formal laws, the Tribunal must order the publication of the ruling in the Official Gazette, and it becomes effective the day following publication[329]

In both cases, the Tribunal decision declaring the unconstitutionality of a statute or other normative state acts, once published, has *erga omnes* effects, and in accordance with an express provision of the Constitution, they «do not have retroactive effects»[330] thus they are only *ex nunc, pro praeterito*. Therefore, the Organic Law of the Tribunal establishes that decisions declaring the unconstitutionality of a normative state act, cannot serve as support to review judicial processes already concluded in which the unconstitutional norms were applied. Nevertheless, in accordance with the general exception principle of the possible retroactivity of statutes in penal, labour or taxation cases,[331] the Organic Law allows the retroactive applicability of the Tribunal decision in proceedings in which its effect could be favourable to the convicted person, the worker or the taxpayer.[332]

But additional to the concentrated means of judicial review that can be exercised before the Tribunal of Constitutional Guarantees, the 1980 Constitution also establishes the actions of *habeas corpus* and *amparo*, as special means for the protection of fundamental rights. The former directed to protect personal liberty and the latter, as a means for the protection of all other fundamental rights recognised in the Constitution.[333] Through the exercise of these two actions the ordinary judge can also exercise judicial review powers when the alleged violation of the fundamental right is based on a norm incompatible with the Constitution. In such cases, the judge can declare the said norm inapplicable.[334]

---

[327] Art. 40 Organic Law.
[328] Art. 301 Constitution.
[329] Art. 302 Constitution.
[330] Art. 300 Constitution.
[331] Art. 187 Constituion.
[332] Art. 41 Organic Law.
[333] Arts 295, 298,2 and 305. Constitution 1980.
[334] See H. FIX-ZAMUDIO, «Ley peruana de *habeas corpus* y *amparo*», *Boletín mexicano de derecho comparado*, 50, 1984, p. 575.

Thus, a limited principle of a diffuse system can also be distinguished in Peru, as a consequence of the exercise of the actions for protection of fundamental rights, and which performs in parallel with the concentrated system.

Anyway, the ordinary courts decisions on matters of constitutional protection (*habeas corpus* and *amparo*) are subject to ordinary appeals before the Superior Courts, and against the decisions of the latter, recourse based on reasons of nullity, which can be exercised before the Supreme Court. The decisions of the latter can additionally be the object of a recourse of cassation before the Tribunal of Constitutional Guarantees in order to examine whether or not the Supreme Court has violated or erroneously applied the law.[335]

---

335 *Idem*, p. 579.

ADDENDUM

CONSTITUTIONAL COURTS AS POSITIVE LEGISLATORS IN COMPARATIVE LAW*

PRELIMINARY REMARKS

- ***The subordination of Constitutional Courts to the Constitution***

In all democratic countries, Constitutional Courts[1] have the same role of interpreting and applying the Constitution in order to preserve its supremacy testing the constitutionality or conventionality of statutes,[2] and in order to assure the prevalence of the democratic principle and of fundamental rights they even have the role of adapting the Constitution when changes and time imposes such task.

And this is true in all systems of constitutional judicial review, where a progressive convergence of principles and solutions has been consolidated over the past decades,[3] being nowadays very difficult even to draw in a clear way the classical distinction between the concentrated and the diffuse systems of judicial review[4] so commonly used during many decades.[5]

---

* Synthesis of the General Report, Subject IV.B.2, «Constitutional Courts as 'Positive Legislators», *XVIII International Congress of* Comparative *Law,* International Academy of Comparative Law, Washington, July 27, 2010. See Allan R. Brewer-Carías, «Constitutional Courts as Positive Legislators», in Karen B. Brown y David V. Snyder (Editors), *General Reports of the XVIIIth Congress pf the International Academy of Comparative Law- Rapports Généraux du XVIIIème Congrès de l'Académie Internationale de Droit Comparé,* Springer, 2012, pp. 549-569. The full text of the General Report (as well as the text of the National Reports) in Allan R. Brewer-Carías, *Constitutional Courts as Positive Legislators,* Cambridge University Press New York, 2011, 933 pp.

1 For the purpose of the *General Report,* due to the variety of solutions, I have used the expression «constitutional court» in a general sense, as referring to any court acting as constitutional judge.

2 For the purpose of the *General Report,* I used the expression «control of constitutionality» as comprising not only judicial review of statutes regarding their conformity with the Constitution, but also comprising «control of conventionality» in the sense of their conformity with International Conventions, particularly on matters of Human Rights, as is the case, for instance, in The Netherlands, in the U.K., in France and in many Latin American countries; as well as their conformity with «Constitutional Conventions», called by John Bell, the *British National Reporter,* as «constitutional review». See in general Ernesto Rey Cantor, *El control de convencionalidad de las leyes y derechos humanos,* Ed. Porrúa, Mexico 2008; Juan Carlos Hitters, «Control de constitucionalidad y control de convencionalidad. Comparación (Criterios fijados por la Corte Interamericana de Derechos Humanos), in *Estudios Constitucionales,* Año 7, N° 2, Santiago de Chile 2009, pp. 109-128.

3 See Lucio Pegoraro, «Clasificaciones y modelos de justicia constitucional en la dinámica de los ordenamientos», in *Revista Iberoamericana de Derecho Procesal Constitucional,* No 2, Instituto Ibero-americano de Derecho Procesal Constitucional, Editorial Porrúa, Mexico 2004, pp. 131 ff.; Alfonse Celotto, «La justicia constitucional en el mundo: formas y modalidades», in *Revista Iberoamericana de Derecho Procesal Constitucional,* No 1, Instituto Iberoamericano de Derecho Procesal Constitucional, Editorial Porrúa, Mexico 2004, pp. 3 ff.

In all the systems, the basic principle that can be identified is that Constitutional Courts, when accomplishing their roles, must always be subordinated to the Constitution, not being allowed to invade the field of the legislator or of the constituent power, The contrary would be, as asserted by Sandra Morelli the *Colombian National Reporter*, to develop an «irresponsible judicial totalitarianism»,[6] which of course is a chapter of the pathology of judicial review.

That is to say, Constitutional Courts can assist the legislators in the accomplishment of their functions, but they cannot substitute the Legislators and enact legislation, nor they have any discretionary political basis in order to create legal norms or provisions that could not be deducted from the Constitution itself.

It is in this sense that it is then possible to affirm as a general principle, that Constitutional Courts, still are considered to be -as Hans Kelsen used to say- «Negative Legislators»[7] or that they are not «Positive Legislators» in the sense that, as affirmed by Richard Kay and Laurence Claus, *the American National Reporters*, they are not able to consider, propound or create *ex novo* pieces of legislation «of their own conception», or to introduce «reforms» on statutes conceived by other legislative actors.[8]

---

4 See for example, Francisco Fernández Segado, La justicia constitucional ante el siglo XXI. *La progresiva convergencia de los sistemas americano y europeo-kelseniano*, Librería Bonomo Editrice, Bologna 2003, pp. 40 ff.; Francisco Fernández Segado, «La obsolecencia de la bipolaridad 'modelo Americano-modelo europeo-kelseniano' como criterio analítico del control de constitucionalidad y la búsqueda de una nueva tipología explicativa», in his book *La Justicia Constitucional: Una visión de derecho comparado*, Tomo I, Ed. Dykinson, Madrid 2009, pp. 129-220; Guillaume Tusseau, *Contre les «modèles» de justice constitutionnelle: essai de critique métodologique*, Bononia University Press, Edition bilingue: français-italien, 2009; Guillaume Tusseau, «Regard critique sur les outils méthodologique du comparatisme. L'example des modèles de justice constitutionnelle», in *IUSTEL, Revista General de Derecho Público Comparado*, No 4, Madrid, enero 2009, pp. 1-34.

5 See Mauro Cappelletti, *Judicial Review in Contemporary World*, Indianapolis 1971, p.45; Mauro Cappellettiy and J.C. Adams, «Judicial Review of Legislation: European Antecedents and Adaptations», in *Harvard Law Review*, 79, 6, April 1966, p. 1207; Mauro Cappelletti, «El control judicial de la constitucionalidad de las leyes en el derecho comparado», in *Revista de la Facultad de Derecho de México*, 61, 1966, p. 28; Allan R. Brewer-Carías, *Judicial Review in Comparative Law*, Cambridge University Press, Cambridge 1989; Allan R. Brewer-Carías, *Étutes de droit pubic comparé*, Bruilant, Bruxelles 2000, pp. 653 ff. Regarding the distinction, it can be said that the only aspect of it that nowadays remains is the one referred to the organ of control, in the sense that in the diffuse system of judicial review all courts are constitutional judges without the need for their powers to be expressly established in the Constitution; whether that in the concentrated system, it is the Constitution the one that must expressly establish the Constitutional Jurisdiction, assigning to a single Constitutional Court, Constitutional Tribunal or Constitutional Council, or to the existing Supreme or High Court or Tribunal of Justice, the power to control the constitutionality of statutes and to annul them.

6 See Sandra Morelli, *La Corte Constitucional: un papel por definir*, Academia Colombiana de Jurisprudencia, 2002; and «*The Colombian Constitutional Court: from Institutional Leadership, to Conceptual Audacity*», Colombian National Report, XVIII International Congress of Comparative Law, Washington, July, 2010, p. 3. See also, Allan R. Brewer-Carías, «*Quis Custodiet Ipsos Custodes*: De la interpretación constitucional a la inconstitucionalidad de la interpretación», in *VIII Congreso Nacional de derecho Constitucional, Perú*, Fondo Editorial 2005, Colegio de Abogados de Arequipa, Arequipa, Septiembre 2005, pp 463-489, and in *Revista de Derecho Público*, Nº 105, Editorial Jurídica Venezolana, Caracas 2006, pp 7-27; *Crónica sobre la «In» Justicia Constitucional. La Sala Constitucional y el autoritarismo en Venezuela*, Editorial Jurídica Venezolana, Caracas 2007; and *Reforma Constitucional y Fraude a la Constitución*, Academia de Ciencias Políticas y Sociales, Caracas 2009.

7 See Hans. Kelsen, «La garantie juridictionnelle de la constitution (La Justice constitutionnelle)», in *Revue du droit public et de la science politique en France et a l'ètranger,* Librairie Général de Droit et the Jurisprudence, Paris 1928, pp. 197-257 ; Hans Kelsen, *La garantía jurisdiccional de la Constitución (La justicia constitucional)*, Universidad Nacional Autónoma de México, Mexico 2001.

8 See Laurence Claus and Richard S. Kay, «*Constitutional Courts as 'Positive Legislators' in the United States*», U.S. National Report, XVIII International Congress of Comparative Law, Washington, July 2010, pp. 3, 5.

- ***New role of Constitutional Courts and the question of acting as Positive Legislators***

This continues to be the general principle in comparative law, notwithstanding the fact that during the past decades the role of Constitutional courts has dramatically changed, due to the fact that their role is not limited to declare the unconstitutionality of statutes or to annul or not to annul a statute on the grounds of its unconstitutionality.

In all systems, new approaches have been developed, for instance, based on the principle of conservation of statutes, due to their presumption of constitutionality, empowering Constitutional Courts not to annul or declared them unconstitutional (even though being contrary to the Constitution), but to interpret them according to the Constitution or in harmony with the Constitution. This has allowed the Courts to avoid creating any legislative vacuum, and in some cases, to fill permanently or temporarily the vacuums that could be originated by the nullity.

In addition, nowadays is more frequent to see Constitutional Courts, instead of dealing with existing statutes, to deal with the absence of statutes or with absolute or relative omissions or abstention incurred by the Legislator. By controlling these omissions, Constitutional Courts in many cases have assume the role of legislative assistant or auxiliaries, creating norms they normally deduct from the Constitution; and even, in some cases, substituting the Legislator, by assuming an open role of «Positive Legislators», issuing temporary or provisional rules to be applied on specific matters pending the enactment of legislation.

One of the main tools to trigger this new role of Constitutional Courts, has been the principles of progressiveness and of the prevalence of human rights,[9] as has occurred in many cases with the rediscovery of the right to equality and nondiscrimination. In these cases, in the interest of the protection of citizens' rights and guaranties, there have been no doubts in accepting the legitimacy of Constitutional Courts' activism interfering with the Legislative functions, applying constitutional principles and values.

In these matters, the main discussion today is directed, not to reject these legislative activities by the courts, but to determine the extent and limits of Constitutional Courts decisions, and the degree of interference allowed regarding Legislative functions, as expressed by Francisco Fernandez Segado, the *Spanish National Reporter*, in order to avoid «transforming the guardian of the Constitution into sovereign».[10]

My analysis of the subject of «Constitutional Courts as 'Positive Legislators,'» in comparative law,[11] has allowed me to identify four main trends regarding the

---

9 See Pedro Nikken, *La protección internacional de los derechos humanos: su desarrollo progresivo*, Instituto Interamericano de Derechos Humanos, Ed. Civitas, Madrid 1987; Mónica Pinto, «El principio *pro homine*. Criterio hermenéutico y pautas para la regulación de los derechos humanos», in *La aplicación de los tratados sobre derechos Humanos por los tribunales locales,* Centro de Estudios Legales y Sociales, Buenos Aires, 1997, p. 163.

10 See Francisco Fernández Segado, «Algunas reflexiones generales en torno a los efectos de las sentencias de inconstitucionalidad y a la relatividad de ciertas fórmulas esterotipadas vinculadas a ellas», in *Anuario Iberoamericano de Justicia Constitucional,* Centro de Estudios Políticos y Constitucionales, No. 12, 2008, Madrid 2008, p. 161.

11 For the preparation of the *General Report* I received 36 **National Reports** from 31 counties: 19 from Europe (including 6 from Eastern Europe), 10 from the American Continent (3 from North America, 5 from South America, and 2 from Central America); one from Asia, and one from Australia. The **National Reports** are listed in the *Appendix* of this article.

relations of the Constitutional Courts not only with the Legislator, but also with the «Constitutional Legislator», that can be considered as expressions of their activities acting as been positive legislators. These are:

First, the role of Constitutional Courts interfering with the Constituent Power, enacting constitutional rules and even mutating the Constitution;

Second, the role of Constitutional Courts interfering with existing legislation, assuming the task of being assistants to the Legislator, complementing statutes, adding to them new provisions, and also determining the temporal effects of legislation;

Third, the role of Constitutional Courts interfering with the absence of Legislation due to absolute and relative legislative omissions, acting in some cases as Provisional Legislators; and

Forth, the role of Constitutional Courts as Legislators on matters of judicial review.

FIRST TREND: CONSTITUTIONAL COURTS INTERFERING WITH THE CONSTITUENT POWER

The first trend that comparative law shows us is the role of Constitutional Courts, interfering with the «Constitutional Legislator», that is with the Constituent Power, in some cases enacting constitutional rules, for instance, when resolving constitutional disputes between State organs; when exercising constitutional control over constitutional provisions or over constitutional amendments; and when mutating in a legitimate way the Constitutions by means of adapting their provisions to current times, giving them concrete meaning.

- *Constitutional Courts Resolving Constitutional Federal Disputes and Enacting Constitutional Rules*

The first case refers to the Constitutional Courts interfering with the Constituent power, when they resolve constitutional conflicts or disputes between State organs, which is a common role in Federal States, as has been highlighted by Konrad Lachmayer, the *Austrian National Reporter,* referring to the Austrian Constitutional Court, saying that it has acted as a «positive legislator», «enacting constitutional law» when exercising positive powers regarding the division of competences between the Federation and the «*Länder*», having the final say on the matter.[12] It has also been the case in the United States, where the Supreme Court has been progressively determining the powers of the federal government regarding the states, based on «commerce clause», being difficult nowadays to imagine anything that Congress could not regulate.[13] By means of these case law on matters related to the federal State, the Supreme Court's decisions, without doubt, eventually have enacted constitutional rules; although in some cases, they have distorted the constitutional frame of power distribution, as has been the case in Venezuela.[14]

---

12 See Konrad Lachmayer, «*Constitutional Courts as 'Positive Legislators,'*» Austrian National Report, XVIII International Congress of Comparative Law, Washington, July, 2010, pp. 1-2.

13 See Erwin Chemerinsky, *Constitutional Law. Principles and Policies,* Aspen Publishers, New York 2006, pp. 259-260.

- ***Constitutional Courts Exercising Judicial Review on Constitutional Provisions***

The second way in which Constitutional Courts can participate in the enactment of constitutional rules is when they are empowered to review the Constitution itself, as is also the case in Austria, where the Constitutional Court is empowered to confront the Constitution with its own basic principles, like the principle of democracy, the federal state, the *Rechtsstaat*, separation of powers and the general system of human rights.[15]

- ***Constitutional Courts Exercising Judicial Review Constitutional Reforms and Amendments***

The third way Constitutional Courts interfere with the Constituent Power, is when they are empowered to review constitutional amendments, as is the case of Colombia, Ecuador and Bolivia, although limited to its procedural aspects.[16]

In other countries, discussions have been developed regarding the powers of Constitutional Courts to exercise judicial review powers on the merits of constitutional reforms or amendments, for instance, regarding the unchangeable constitutional clauses (*cláusulas pétreas*) expressly defined in the Constitutions. The basic principle here is that in such cases, the courts' powers derive from the supremacy of those constitutional clauses. In such cases, in order not to confront the will of the people and not to substitute the constituent power, the control must be exercised before the reform has been enacted through popular vote, when this is the case.[17]

Nonetheless, even in the absence of constitutional authorization, there are cases in which Constitutional Courts have exercise judicial review regarding constitutional amendments. It was the case, a few months ago, in Colombia where the Constitutional Court (February 26, 2010) annulled a Law convening a referendum for the purpose of approving a reform of an article of the Constitution directed to allow the reelection for a third period of the President of the Republic, by considering that such reform contained «substantial violations of the democratic principle», introducing reforms implying the «substitution or subrogation of the Constitution».[18]

---

14 Decision of the Constitutional Chamber N° 565 of April 15, 2008, Case: Procurador General de la República, *Interpretación del artículo 164.10 de la Constitución de 1999*, available at http://www.tsj.gov.ve/decisio-nes/scon/Abril/565-150408-07-1108.htm. See the comments in Allan R. Brewer-Carías, «La ilegitima mutación de la Constitución y la legitimidad de la jurisdicción constitucional: la «reforma» de la forma federal del Estado en Venezuela mediante interpretación constitucional», in *Memoria del X Congreso Iberoamericano de Derecho Constitucional*, Instituto Iberoamericano de Derecho Constitucional, Asociación Peruana de Derecho Constitucional, Instituto de Investigaciones Jurídicas-UNAM and Maestría en Derecho Constitucional-PUCP, IDEMSA, Lima 2009, tomo 1, pp. 29-51.

15 Decision of the Constitutional Court, VfSlg 16.327/2001. See in Konrad Lachmayer, «*Constitutional Courts as 'Positive Legislators,'*» Austrian National Report, XVIII International Congress of Comparative Law, Washington, July, 2010, p. 6 (footnote 20).

16 See the references in Allan R. Brewer-Carías, *Reforma Constitucional y Fraude a la Constitución. Venezuela 1999-2009*, Academia de Ciencias Políticas y Sociales, Caracas 2009, pp. 78 ff.

17 See Allan R. Brewer-Carías, *Reforma Constitucional y Fraude a la Constitución. Venezuela 1999-2009*, Academia de Ciencias Políticas y Sociales, Caracas 2009, pp. 78 ff.; and «La reforma constitucional en América Latina y el control de constitucionalidad», in *Reforma de la Constitución y control de constitucionalidad. Congreso Internacional, Pontificia Universidad Javeriana, Bogotá Colombia, junio 14 al 17 de 2005*, Bogotá, 2005, pp. 108-159.

18 The Decision, in September 2010, have not been published. See the Communiqué of the texto f the decision published by the Constitutional Court, No 9 of February 26, 2010, available at

In other cases, like in India, it has been the Supreme Court the one that has imposed «implied» limits on the power of Parliament to amend the Constitution, excluding basic features or basic structure of the Constitution,[19] like for instance, the scope of judicial review powers, [20] the Supreme Court being converted, as said by Surya Deva, in the *Indian National Report*, «as probably the most powerful court in any democracy».[21]

- **The Role of Constitutional Courts Adapting the Constitution on matters of fundamental rights**

The fourth case Constitutional Courts interfering with the Constituent Power, is when they assume the role of adapting constitutional provisions by means of their interpretation, particularly on matters of fundamental rights. In these cases, as said by Laurence Claus and Richard S. Kay, the *U.S. National Reporters*, Constitutional, Courts «engage in positive constitutional lawmaking» particularly when the rule they «formulate, creates 'affirmative' public duties».[22]

This role of Constitutional Courts has been the result of a «discovering» process of fundamental rights not expressly enlisted in the Constitutions, enlarging the scope of its provisions in order to maintain the Constitution «alive».[23] Referring to the U.S. Supreme Court role in the elaboration of constitutional principles and values, as mentioned by Laurence Claus and Richard S. Kay, «provides perhaps the most salient example of positive lawmaking in the course of American constitutional adjudication».[24] It was the case, for instance beginning *Brown v. Board of Education of Topeka*, 347 U.S. 483 (1954), when trhe Supreme Courts interpreted the «equal protection» clause of the Fourteenth Amendment in order to expound the nature of equality; or when having argued about the constitutional guarantee of «due process» (Amendments V and XIV), or the open clause of Amendment IX, in order to construct the sense of «liberty». This process has converted the Court, they have said, in «the most powerful sitting [constitutional] lawmaker in the nation».[25]

The same has happened in France, where the Constitution does not have at all a declaration of fundamental rights, the role of the Constitutional Council during

---

www.corteconstitucional.com. See the comments in Sandra Morelli, «*The Colombian Constitutional Court: from Institutional Leadership, to Conceptual Audacity*», Colombian National Report, XVIII International Congress of Comparative Law, Washington, July, 2010, pp. 13-16.

19 Case *Kesvananda Bharti v State of Kerala*, Supreme Court of India, in Surya Deva, «*Constitutional Courts as 'Positive Legislators: The Indian Experience», Indian National Report, XVIII International Congress of Comparative Law, Washington, July, 2010*, pp. 5-6.

20 Cases *Waman Rao v Union of India* AIR 1981 SC 271; *S P Sampath Kumar v Union of India* AIR 1987 SC 386; and *L Chandra Kumar v Union of India* AIR 1997 SC 1125, in *Idem*, p. 6 (footnote 41).

21 *Idem*, p. 6.

22 See Laurence Claus and Richard S. Kay, «*Constitutional Courts as 'Positive Legislators' in the United States*», U.S. National Report, XVIII International Congress of Comparative Law, Washington, July 2010, p. 6.

23 See Mauro Cappelletti, «El formidable problema del control judicial y 1a contribución del análisis comparado», in *Revista de estudios políticos*, 13, Madrid 1980, p. 78; «The Mighty Problem» of Judicial Review and the Contribution of Comparative Analysis», in *Southern California Law Review*, 1980, p. 409.

24 See in Laurence Claus and Richard S. Kay, «*Constitutional Courts as 'Positive Legislators' in the United States*», U.S. National Report, XVIII International Congress of Comparative Law, Washington, July, 2010, pp. 12-13.

25 *Idem*, p. 20.

the past decades has been precisely of mutating the Constitution, enlarging the *bloc de constitutionnalité*, by giving constitutional rank, through the Preamble of the 1958 Constitution, to the Preamble of 1946 Constitution, and eventually to the 1789 Declaration of Rights of Man and Citizens.[26]

This role of Constitutional Courts adapting the Constitution in order to guaranty fundamental rights can be nowadays considered as a main trend in comparative law, which can be identified in many countries with different systems of judicial review, as is the case of Switzerland, Germany, Portugal, Austria, Poland, Croatia, Greece, and India, where Constitutional Courts have introduced important changes in the Constitution, expanding the scope of fundamental rights.[27]

- **The Mutation of the Constitution on Institutional Matters**

On the other hand, on matters different to fundamental rights is also possible to find legitimate constitutional mutations made by Constitutional Courts referred to other key constitutional matters related to the organization and functioning of the State. The German Federal Constitutional Tribunal, for instance, in the case *AWACS-Urteil* of July 12, 1994,[28] ruled on the deployment in time of peace, of missions of German Armed Forces to foreign countries, detailing a substitute legislation (provisional measures) ordering the Legislator and the Executive to proceed according to it, imposing the formal participation of the Legislator.

The Constitutional Court of Austria has even created new constitutional framework to be followed by Parliament in areas not expressly provided in the Constitution, like the privatization process, imposing rules to all State authorities.[29]

---

26 See Louis Favoreu, «Le principe de Constitutionalité. Essai de definition d'apres la jurisprudence du Conseil Constitutionnel», *Recueil d'étude en Hommage a Charles Eisenman*, Paris 1977, p. 34. See also in comparative law, Francisco Zúñiga Urbina, *Control de Constitucionalidad y sentencia*, Cuadernos del Tribnal Constitucional, No. 34, Santiago de Chile 2006, pp. 46-68.

27 See Tobias Jaag, «*Constitutional Courts as 'Positive Legislators:' Switzerland*», Swiss National Report, XVIII International Congress of Comparative Law, Washington, July 2010, p 11; I. Härtel, «*Constitutional Courts as Positive Legislators*», German National Report, XVIII International Congress of Comparative Law, Washington, July 2010, p. 12; Marek Safjan, , «*The Constitutional Courts as a Positive Legislator*», Polish National Report, XVIII International Congress of Comparative Law, Washington, July 2010, p. 9; Sanja Bariæ and Petar Baèiæ, "*Constitutional Courts as positive legislators. National Report: Croatia*», Croatian National Report, XVIII International Congress of Comparative Law, Washington, July 2010, p. 23 ss; Julia Iliopoulos-Strangas and Stylianos-Ioannis G. Koutna, «*Constitutional Courts as Positive Legislators. Greek National Report*», XVIII International Congress of Comparative Law, Washington, July 2010, p. 14; Joaquim de Sousa Ribeiro and Esperança Mealha, «*The Constitutional Courts as a Positive Legislator*», Portuguese National Report, XVIII International Congress of Comparative Law, Washington, July 2010, pp. 9-10; Surya Deva, «*Constitutional Courts as 'Positive Legislators: The Indian Experience*», Indian National Report, XVIII International Congress of Comparative Law, Washington, July 2010, p. 4.

28 Cases: BVferG, July 12, 1994, BVeffGE 90, 585-603, in Christian Behrendt, *Le judge constitutionnel, un législateur-cadre positif. Un analyse comparative en droit francais, belge et allemande*, Bruylant, Bruxelles 2006, pp. 352-356.

29 Cases: «Austro Control» VfSlg 14.473/1996; «Bundeswertpapieraufsicht» (Federal Bond Authority) VfSlg 16.400/2001; «E-Control» VfSlg 16.995/2003; «Zivildienst-GmbH» (Compulsory community service Ltd), VfSlg 17.341/2004, in Konrad Lachmayer, «*Constitutional Courts as 'Positive Legislators'*» Austrian National Report, XVIII International Congress of Comparative Law, Washington, July, 2010, p. 11 (footnote 31).

The Council of State of Greece has also imposed limits on matters of privatization excluding for instance police powers.[30] The Constitutional Court of the Slovak Republic, has reshaped the constitutional provisions regarding the position and authority of the President of the Republic within the general organization of the State, being the Court considered by Ján Svák and Lucia Bertisová, the *Slovak National Reporters* as «the direct creator of the constitutional system of the Slovak Republic».[31]

Finally, the Supreme Court of Canada, through the very important instrument of the «reference judgments» has created and declared constitutional rules, for instance, governing important constitutional processes as the patriation of Canada's constitution from the United Kingdom (*Patriation Reference*, 1981)[32]; and the possible secession of Quebec from Canada (*Quebec Secession Reference*, 1998),[33] laying down as mentioned by Kent Roach, the *Canadian National Reporter*, some basic rules to guide constitutional change and to advert potential constitutional crises.

In these matters, unfortunately, there are also examples of Constitutional Courts mutating the Constitution but with the purpose of destroying the democratic principle, as happened in Venezuela with the Constitutional Chamber implementing a rejected 2007 constitutional reform by mean of constitutional interpretation.[34]

SECOND TREND: CONSTITUTIONAL COURTS INTERFERING WITH THE EXISTING LEGISLATION

The most important and common role of Constitutional Courts is developed regarding existing legislation, not only declaring their unconstitutionality but

Decision of the Council of State No. 1934/1998, *ToS* 1998, 598 (602-603), in Julia Iliopoulos-StrangasyStylianos-Ioannis G. Koutna, «*Constitutional Courts as Positive Legislators*, Greek National Report, XVIII International Congress of Comparative Law, Washington, July, 2010, p. 16 (footnote 125).

30 Decision No. I. ÚS 39/93, in Ján Svák and Lucia Berdisová, «*Constitutional Court of the Slovak Republic as Positive Legislator via Application and Interpretation of the Constitution*», Slovak National Report, XVIII International Congress of Comparative Law, Washington, July, 2010, p. 4.

31 Decision [1981] 1 S.C.R. 753, in Kent Roach, «*Constitutional Courts as Positive Legislators:* Canada Country Report», XVIII International Congress of Comparative Law, Washington, July, 2010, p. 9.

32 Decision [1998] 2 S.C.R. 217, in Kent Roach, «*Constitutional Courts as Positive Legislators:* Canada Country Report», XVIII International Congress of Comparative Law, Washington, July, 2010, p. 9.

33 See the comment son some Cases in Allan R. Brewer-Carías, «El juez constitucional al servicio del autoritarismo y la ilegítima mutación de la Constitución: el caso de la Sala Constitucional del Tribunal Supremo de Justicia de Venezuela (1999-2009)», in *Revista de Administración Pública*, No. 180, Madrid 2009, pp. 383-418; «El Juez Constitucional vs. La alternabilidad republicana (La reelección continua e indefinida), in *Revista de Derecho Público*, No. 117, (enero-marzo 209), Caracas 2009, pp. 205-211; «La ilegítima mutación de la constitución por el juez constitucional: la inconstitucional ampliación y modificación de su propia competencia en materia de control de constitucionalidad», in *Libro Homenaje a Josefina Calcaño de Temeltas*, Fundación de Estudios de Derecho Administrativo (FUNEDA), Caracas 2009, pp. 319-362; «La ilegitima mutación de la Constitución y la legitimidad de la jurisdicción constitucional: la «reforma» de la forma federal del Estado en Venezuela mediante interpretación constitucional», in *Memoria del X Congreso Iberoamericano de Derecho Constitucional*, Instituto Iberoamericano de Derecho Constitucional, Asociación Peruana de Derecho Constitucional, Instituto de Investigaciones Jurídicas-UNAM and Maestría en Derecho Constitucional-PUCP, IDEMSA, Lima 2009, Vol. 1, pp. 29-51.

34 See F. Fernández Segado, «*El Tribunal Constitucional como Legislador Positivo*, Spanish National Report, XVIII International Congress of Comparative Law, Washington, July, 2010, pp. 8 ff.

interpreting statutes in conformity to or in harmony with the Constitution, giving directives or guidelines to the Legislator.

- ***Constitutional Courts Complementing Legislative Functions interpreting Statutes in Harmony with the Constitution***

This role of Constitutional Courts has resulted from the surpassing of the classical binomial: *unconstitutionality / invalidity-nullity* that conformed the initial activity of Constitutional Courts as «Negative Legislators»,[35] having Constitutional Courts, on the contrary, progressively assumed a more active role interpreting the Constitution, and the statutes in order not only to annul or not to apply them when unconstitutional, but to preserve the Legislator actions and the statutes it has enacted, interpreting them in harmony with the Constitution;[36] molding these Constitutional Courts as important constitutional institutions in order to assist and cooperate with the legislator in its legislative functions.

These sorts of interpretative decisions have been widely used by the Constitutional Court in Italy, Spain, France and Hungary,[37] where in many cases they have decided not to annul the challenged law, and instead have ruled modifying its meaning by establishing a new content, making the law constitutional as it result from the constitutional interpretation.[38]

In all these cases, the interference of Constitutional Courts with existing legislation has followed two main courses of action: first, complementing legislative functions as provisional Legislators or by adding rules to existing Legislation through interpretative decisions; and second, interfering with the temporal effects of existing legislation.

- ***Constitutional Courts Complementing the Legislator by «Adding» to the Existent Legislative Provision New Rules when giving it a New Meaning***

Regarding the process of interpreting statutes in harmony with the Constitution, when testing their unconstitutionality, Constitutional Courts, in order to avoid their invalidation, have frequently create new legislative rules, in some occasions altering the meaning of the particular provision, and adding to its wording what is considered to be lacking.

---

35 Case Ashwander v. TVA, 297 U.S. 288, 346-48 (1936), Supreme Court of the United States (Justice Brandeis). The principle was formulated for the first time in the Case Crowell v. Benson, 285 U.S. 22, 62 (1932). See «Notes. Supreme Court Interpretation of Statutes to avoid constitutional decision», in *Columbia Law Review*, Vol. 53, No. 5, New York, May 1953, pp. 633-651.

36 See Gianpaolo Parodi, «*The Italian Constitutional Court as 'Positive Legislator,'*» Italian National Report, XVIII International Congress of Comparative Law, Washington, July, 2010, p. 3; Francisco Fernández Segado, «*El Tribunal Constitucional como Legislador Positivo*, Spanish National Report, XVIII International Congress of Comparative Law, Washington, July, 2010, p. 34; Bertrand Mathieu, «*Le Conseil constitutionnel 'législateur positif. Ou la question des interventions du juge constitutionnel français dans l'exercise de la function legislative*», French National Report, XVIII International Congress of Comparative Law, Washington, July, 2010, p. 13; Lóránt Csink, József Petrétei and Péter Tilk, «*Constitutional Court as Positive Legislator. Hungarian National Report*», XVIII International Congress of Comparative Law, Washington, July, 2010, p. 4.

37 See Francisco Javier Díaz Revorio, *Las sentencias interpretativas del Tribunal Constitucional*, Lex Nova, Valladolid 2001, pp. 59 ss; and in José Julio Fernández Rodríguez, *La justicia constitucional europea ante el Siglo XXI*, Tecnos, Madrid 2007, pp. 129 ff.

38 See Gianpaolo Parodi, «*The Italian Constitutional Court as 'Positive Legislator,'*» Italian National Report, XVIII International Congress of Comparative Law, Washington, July, 2010, p. 6.

These are the so-called «additive decisions» that have been extensively issued by the Italian Constitutional, as explained by Gianpaolo Parodi, the *Italian National Reporter*, through decisions in which although leaving unaltered «the text of the provision that is declared unconstitutional,

the Court have «transformed its normative meaning, at times reducing, at others extending the sphere of application, not without introducing a new norm into the legal system», or «creating» new norms.[39] These additive decisions have also been applied for instance in Germany by the Federal Constitutional Court and in Peru by the Constitutional Tribunal.

These additive decisions have been regularly applied in cases related to the protection the right to equality and non-discrimination, seeking to eliminate the differences established in the law. This is the case in Spain, where the Constitutional Tribunal for instance, has extended to «sons and brothers», the benefit of Social Security pensions granted to «daughters and sisters;»[40] to those living in a marital de facto and stable way, the right of those married;[41] cases in which Francisco Fernandez Segado, the *Spanish National Reporter*, has said that is possible to consider the Spanish Constitutional Tribunal as a «real positive legislator».[42]

A similar situation can be found in Portugal, where the Constitutional Tribunal, for instance, has extended to the widower, the allowances assigned to the widow; [43] to the *de facto* unions, rights of married persons; and legal protection given to children of *de facto* unions, similar to the one given to legitimate children.[44]

In similar way, in South Africa, the Constitutional Court has extended to the same sex partner in a stable condition, some rights assigned to married couples. [45]

In Canada, the Ontario Court of Appeal to strike down a definition of marriage as a union of a man and a woman substituting it with the gender-neutral concept of a union between persons, in order to allow same sex marriages. These decisions, as affirmed by the *Canadian National Reporter*, Kent Roach, «amount to judicial amendments or additions to legislation». [46]

---

39 Decision STC 3/1993, January 14, 1993, in Francisco Javier Díaz Revorio, *Las sentencias interpretativas del Tribunal Constitucional,* Lex Nova, Valladolid 2001, pp. 177, 274; F. Fernández Segado, «*El Tribunal Constitucional como Legislador Positivo*», Spanish National Report, XVIII International Congress of Comparative Law, Washington, July, 2010, p. 42.

40 Decision STC 222/1992, December 11, 1992, in Francisco Javier Díaz Revorio, *Las sentencias interpretativas del Tribunal Constitucional,* Lex Nova, Valladolid 2001, pp. 181, 182, 275; F. Fernández Segado, «*El Tribunal Constitucional como Legislador Positivo*», Spanish National Report, XVIII International Congress of Comparative Law, Washington, July, 2010, p. 41.

41 See F. Fernández Segado, «*El Tribunal Constitucional como Legislador Positivo*», Spanish National Report, XVIII International Congress of Comparative Law, Washington, July, 2010, p. 48.

42 Decision No. 449/87 del Tribunal Constitucional, in Joaquim de Sousa Ribeiro and Esperança Mealha, «*Constitutional Courts as «Positive Legislators»*, Portuguese National Report, International Congress of Comparative Law, Washington, July, 2010, p. 8.

43 *Idem*, p. 9.

44 See in Iván Escobar Fornos, «Las sentencias constitucionales y sus efectos en Nicaragua», in *Anuario Iberoamericano de Justicia Constitucional*, Centro de Estudios Políticos y Constitucionales, No. 12, 2008, Madrid 2008, pp. 111-112.

45 See Kent Roach, «*Constitutional Courts as Positive Legislator*», Canadian National Report, XVIII International Congress of Comparative Law, Washington Julio 2010, p. 7.

46 See for example, Marek Safjan, «*The Constitutional Courts as a Positive Legislator*», Polish National Report, XVIII International Congress of Comparative Law, Washington, Julio 2010, pp. 13-14;

A similar solution of additive decisions to enforce the right to equality and non discrimination can also be found in many similar cases in the Netherlands, in Peru, Costa Rica, Argentine, Poland, the Czech Republic and France, [47] where, in a particular case regarding the right to respond on matters of TV Communications, as mentioned by Bertrand Mathieu, the *French National Reporter*, he Constitutional Council has substituted the will of the legislator.[48]

- ***Constitutional Courts Complementing Legislative Functions by Interfering with the Temporal Effects of Legislation***

The second role of Constitutional Courts interfering with existing legislation refers to the power of said Courts to determine the temporal effects of legislation. Decades ago, the matter of the temporal effects of the decisions issued by Constitutional Courts was one of the main aspects of the distinction between the diffuse and the concentrated system of judicial review. Nowadays, this distinctive element has completely disappeared, and a process of convergence can be found between all the systems, so the role of Constitutional Courts on matters of interfering with the temporal effects of legislation is common.

This can be seen, in comparative law, regarding three different situations: in postponing the effects of the Courts decisions; in extending retroactively or prospectively the effects of the Courts decisions and on reviving repealed legislation as a consequence of the constitutional control.

Lóránt Csink, Józef Petrétei and Péter Tilk, «*Constitutional Court as Positive Legislator. Hungarian National Report*», Hungarian National Report, XVIII International Congress of Comparative Law, Washington, Julio 2010, p. 5; Zdenek Kühn, «*Czech Constitutional Court as Positive Legislator*», Czech National Report, XVIII International Congress of Comparative Law, Washington, Julio 2010, p. 9; J. Uzman T. Barkhuysen & M.L. van Emmerik, «*The Dutch Supreme Court: A Reluctant Positive Legislator?*», Dutch National Report, XVIII International Congress of Comparative Law, Washington, Julio 2010, p. 14; Fernán Altuve Febres, , «*El Juez Constitucional como legislador positivo en el Perú*», Peruvian National Report, XVIII International Congress of Comparative Law, Washington, Julio 2010, pp. 14-15; Rubén Herández Valle, «*Las Cortes Constituitonales como Legisladores positivos*», Costa Rican National Report, XVIII International Congress of Comparative Law, Washington, Julio 2010, p. 38; Alejandra Rodríguez Galán and Alfredo Mauricio Vítolo, «*Constitutional Courts as «Positive Legislators»*, Argentinean National Report, XVIII International Congress of Comparative Law, Washington, Julio 2010, p. 17.

47 See in Bertrand Mathieu, «*Le Conseil constitutionnel 'législateur positif. Ou la question des interventions du juge constitutionnel français dans l'exercise de la function legislative*», French National Report, XVIII International Congress of Comparative Law, Washington, Julio 2010, p. 16.

48 See Konrad Lachmayer, «*Constitutional Courts as 'Positive Legislators,'*» Austrian National Report, XVIII International Congress of Comparative Law, Washington, Julio 2010, p. 7; Julia Iliopoulos-Strangas and Stylianos-Ioannis G. Koutna, «*Constitutional Courts as Positive Legislators. Greek National Report*», XVIII International Congress of Comparative Law, Washington, Julio 2010, p. 20; Christian Behrendt, *Le judge constitutionnel, un législateur-cadre positif. Un analyse comparative en droit francais, belge et allemande*, Bruylant, Bruxelles 2006, p. 87, 230, 235, 286, 309; P. Popelier, «*L'activité du judge constitutional belge comme législateur*», Belgium National Report, XVIII International Congress of Comparative Law, Washington, Julio 2010, pp. 4-7; Zdenek Kühn, «*Czech Constitutional Court as Positive Legislator,*" Czech National Report, XVIII International Congress of Comparative Law, Washington, Julio 2010, p. 12; Sanja Bariæ and Petar Baèiæ, "*Constitutional Courts as positive legislators. National Report: Croatia*», XVIII International Congress of Comparative Law, Washington, Julio 2010, p. 17; Jairo Gilberto Schäfer and Vânia Hack de Almeida, «O controle de constitutionalidade no dereitto brasileiro e a possibilidade de modular os efeitos da decisão de inconstitutionalidade», in *Anuario Iberoamericano de Justicia Constitucional*, No. 12, 2008, Centro de Estudios Políticos y Constitucionales, Madrid 2008, p. 384; Domingo García Belaúnde and Gerardo Eto Cruz, «Efectos de las sentencias constitucionales en el Perú», in *Anuario Iberoamericano de Justicia Constitucional*, No. 12, 2008, Centro de Estudios Políticos y Constitucionales, Madrid 2008, pp. 283-284.

- ***The Power of the Constitutional Court to determine in the future when an Annulled Legislation will Cease to have Effects: the Postponement of the Effect of the Courts' Ruling***

The first of the cases in which the Constitutional Courts interfere with the legislative function modulating the temporal effects of its decision declaring the unconstitutionality or nullity of a statute, is when the Court establishes a *vacatio sentenciae,* determining when an annulled legislation will cease to have effects in the future by postponing the beginning of the effects of its own decision and extending the application of the invalidated statute. This is the situation in Austria, Greece, Belgium, the Czech Republic, France, Croatia, Brazil, Poland and Peru[49] In Mexico, if it is true that in principle, the Court's decisions have general effects since the date of its publication, the Court can establish another date in order to avoid legislative vacuums, giving time to the Legislator to enact a new legislation in substitution of the annulled one.[50]

The same solution is found in Germany, although without a clear provision and based in the Constitutional Tribunal Law provision that gives it the power to establish the way in which the execution of the decision will take place. [51]

Also, in Italy, although the Constitution establishes in a clear way that when the Constitutional Court declares the unconstitutionality of a statutory provision it ceases in its effects the following day after its publication (Article 136),[52] there are important decisions of the Constitutional Court of deferment of the effects in time of the declaration of unconstitutional provision.[53] The same has happened in Spain and Canada, in the absence of any legal rule on the matter, the Constitutional Courts have assumed the power to postpone the beginning of the effects of its nullity decisions;[54] and also in Argentina, having a diffuse system of judicial review.[55]

---

49 See «Tesis jurisprudencial» P./J 11/2001, in SJFG, Tomo XIV, Sept. 2001, p. 1008, in Héctor Fix Zamudio and Eduardo Ferrer Mac Gregor, *Las sentencias de los Tribunales Constitucionales*, Ed. Porrúa, México, pp. 69; and in «Las sentencias de los tribunales constitucionales en el ordenamiento mexicano», in *Anuario Iberoamericano de Justicia Constitucional*, No. 12, 2008, Centro de Estudios Políticos y Constitucionales, Madrid 2008, pp. 247-248.

50 Case BVferG, May 22, 1963 (Electoral Circuits), in Christian Behrendt, *Le judge constitutionnel, un législateur-cadre positif. Un analyse comparative en droit francais, belge et allemande*, Bruylant, Bruxelles 2006, pp. 299-300. Case BVferG, November 7, 2006 (Impuesto sucesoral), in I. Härtel, «*Constitutional Courts as Positive Legislators*», German National Report, International Congress of Comparative Law, Washington, July, 2010p. 7.

51 The non approved constitutional reform draft seek to authorize the Constitutional Tribunal to postpone up to one year the effects of its nullity decisions. See Francisco Javier Díaz Revorio, *Las sentencias interpretativas del Tribunal Constitucional,* Lex Nova, Valladolid 2001, p. 125 (footnote 166).

52 Decision Nos. 370/2003; 13 and 423/2004 (on matter of education), in Gianpaolo Parodi, «*The Italian Constitutional Court as 'Positive Legislator,'*» Italian National Report, XVIII International Congress of Comparative Law, Washington, Julio 2010, p. 13.

53 Case *Manitoba Language Reference* [1985] 1 S.C.R. 721, in Kent Roach, «*Constitutional Courts as Positive Legislator*», Canadian National Report, XVIII International Congress of Comparative Law, Washington Julio 2010, p. 7 (footnote 8).

54 Case *Rosza, Jurisprudencia Argentina,* 2007-III-414, in Néstor P. Sagües, «Los efectos de las sentencias constitucionales en el derecho argentino», in *Anuario Iberoamericano de Justicia Constitucional,* Centro de Estudios Políticos y Constitucionales, No. 12, 2008, Madrid 2008, p. 352.

55 Case *Norton v. Selby County,* 118 US 425 (1886), p. 442. See the critic to this decision in J.A.C. GRANT, «The Legal Effect of a Ruling that a Statute is Unconstitutional», in *Detroit College of Law Review,* 1978, (2), p. 207.

- **The Power of the Constitutional Court to Determine since when an Annulled Legislation Will Have Ceased to Have Had Effects: the Retroactive or Non Retroactive Effects of its Own Decisions**

Another aspect regarding the temporal effects of the Constitutional Courts decisions, refers to their retroactive or non-retroactive effects, in which a process of convergence has occurred between all systems of judicial review, where is not possible now to find rigid solutions.

- ***The Possibility of Limiting the Retroactive Ex Tunc Effects Regarding Declarative Decisions***

The classic approach to these matters was that as a matter of principle, in a diffuse system of judicial review, the judicial review decisions were considered to be declarative ones, with *ex tunc, ab initio* and retroactive effects. This was the traditional principle for instance in the United States, assigning the U.S., the Supreme Court decisions' retroactive effects, particularly in criminal matters.[56] Nonetheless, the principle has been progressively relaxed, due to its possible negative or unjust effects regarding the effects already produced by the unconstitutional statute; so the former «absolute rule», has been abandoned, recognizing its authority to give or to deny retroactive effects to its ruling on constitutional issues. The same solution has been followed in Argentina,[57] and in the Netherlands, regarding the control of «conventionality» of statutes.[58]

The same relaxation of the principle has occurred in countries with a concentrated system of judicial review where the same retroactive principle was adopted for decisions annulling statutes. It is the case of Germany, where although being the declarative effects of the Federal Constitutional Tribunal the applicable rule, in practice is uncommon to find decisions annulling statutes with purely *ex tunc* effects. [59] In Poland, and Brazil, the Constitutional Courts are authorizes to restrict the retroactive effects of their decisions and to give them *ex nunc, pro futuro* decisions».[60]

---

56 Case Itzcovich, *Jurispudencia Argentina* 2005-II-723, in Néstor P. Sagües, «Los efectos de las sentencias constitucionales en el derecho argentino», in *Anuario Iberoamericano de Justicia Constitucional*, Centro de Estudios Políticos y Constitucionales, No. 12, 2008, Madrid 2008, p. 351.

57 Case *Boon v. Van Loon* de 27 de noviembre de 1981, *NJ* 1982/503, in J. Uzman T. Barkhuysen & M.L. van Emmerik, *The Dutch Supreme Court: A Reluctant Positive Legislator?» Dutch National Report*, XVIII International Congress of Comparative Law, Washington Julio 2010, p. 42 (footnote 138).

58 See Francisco Fernández Segado, «*El Tribunal Constitucional como Legislador Positivo*, Spanish National Report, XVIII International Congress of Comparative Law, Washington, July, 2010, pp. 8, 14.

59 See for instance, Marek Safjan, «*The Constitutional Courts as a Positive Legislator*», Polish National Report, XVIII International Congress of Comparative Law, Washington, July, 2010, p. 5; Maria Fernanda Palma, «O Legislador negativo e o interprete da Constitucão», in *Anuario Iberoamericano de Justicia Constitucional*, Centro de Estudios Políticos y Constitucionales, No. 12, 2008, Madrid 2008, p. 174; 329; Francisco Fernández Segado, «Algunas reflexiones generales en torno a los efectos de las sentencias de inconstitucionalidad y a la relatividad de ciertas fórmulas esterotipadas vinculadas a ellas», in *Anuario Iberoamericano de Justicia Constitucional*, Centro de Estudios Políticos y Constitucionales, No. 12, 2008, Madrid 2008, p. 174; Iván Escovar Fornos, *Estudios Jurídicos*, Tomo I, Ed. Hispamer, Managua 2007, p. 493; Joaquim de Sousa Ribeiro and Esperança Mealha, «*Constitutional Courts as «Positive Legislators»*, Portuguese National Report, XVIII International Congress of Comparative Law, Washington, July, 2010,pp. 6; Thomas Bustamante and Evanlida de Godoi Bustamante, «*Constitutional Courts as «Negative Legislators:» The Brazilian Case»*, Brazil National Report, XVIII International Congress of Comparative Law, Washington, July, 2010, p. 26.

60 See Konrad Lachemayer, «*Constitutional Courts as 'Positive Legislators,'» Austrian National Report*, XVIII International Congress of Comparative Law, Washington, July, 2010, pp. 7-8.

- ***The Possibility of Giving Retroactive Effects to Ex Nunc Constitutive Decisions***

On the other hand, in countries with concentrated systems of judicial review, although the initial principle following Kelsen's thoughts adopted in the 1920 Austrian Constitution was the constitutive effects of the Constitutional Courts decision annulling a statute, having in principle *ex-nunc, pro futuro* or prospective effects,[61] such principle has also been mitigated particularly in criminal cases, accepting the retroactive effects of the annulment decision. This general trend is today the common principle applied for instance in Spain, Peru, France, Croatia, Serbia, the Slovak Republic, Mexico and Bolivia. [62] In other countries like Venezuela, Brazil, Colombia and Costa Rica, the principle is that Constitutional Court is authorized to determine the temporal effects on its judicial review decisions, which according to the case, can have or not retroactive effects.[63]

- ***The Power of Constitutional Courts to Revive Repealed Legislation***

Finally, although as a matter of principle, also according to Hans Kelsen 1928 writings,[64] judicial review decisions declaring the nullity of a statutory provision adopted by a Constitutional Court, does not imply the revival of the former legislation that the annulled statute had repeal, the contrary principle has been the one adopted in Austria, and is the one applied in Portugal and Belgium.[65] In other countries like in Poland, Mexico and Costa Rica, it is for the Constitutional Courts to decide on the matter.[66]

---

61 See for instance, Francisco Javier Díaz Revorio, Las *sentencias interpretativas del Tribunal Constitucional,* Ed. Lex Nova, Valladolid, 2001, pp. 104-105; 126-127; Francisco Fernández Segado, «Algunas reflexiones generales en torno a los efectos de las sentencias de inconstitucionalidad y a la relatividad de ciertas fórmulas esterotipadas vinculadas a ellas», in *Anuario Iberoamericano de Justicia Constitucional,* Centro de Estudios Políticos y Constitucionales, No. 12, 2008, Madrid 2008, p. 192-194; Domingo García Belaúnde and Gerardo Eto Cruz, «Efectos de las sentencias constitucionales en el Perú», in *Anuario Iberoamericano de Justicia Constitucional,* Centro de Estudios Políticos y Constitucionales, No. 12, 2008, Madrid 2008, p. 281-282.

62 See for instance, Allan R. Brewer-Carías, «Algunas consideraciones sobre el control jurisdiccional de la constitucionalidad de los actos estatales en el derecho venezolano», in *Revista de Administración Pública,* Nº 76, Madrid 1975, pp. 419-446; and in *Justicia Constitucional. Procesos y Procedimientos Constitucionales,* Universidad Nacional Autónoma de México, Mexico 2007, pp. 343 ff.; Jairo Gilberto Schäfer and Vânia Hack de Almeida, «O controle de constitucionalidade no dereito brasileiro e a possibilitade de modular os effeitos de decisão de inconstitucionalidade», in *Anuario Iberoamericano de Justicia Constitucional,* Centro de Estudios Políticos y Constitucionales, No. 12, 2008, Madrid 2008, pp. 383-384; Héctor Fix Zamudio and Eduardo Ferrer Mac Gregor, *Las sentencias de los Tribunales Constitucionales,* Ed. Porrúa, Méxcio, pp. 69; and «Las sentencias de los Tribunales Constitucionales en el ordenamiento mexicano», in *Anuario Iberoamericano de Justicia Constitucional,* Centro de Estudios Políticos y Constitucionales, No. 12, 2008, Madrid 2008, p. 248

63 See Hans Kelsen, *La garantía jurisdiccional de la Constitución (La justicia constitucional),* Universidad Nacional Autónoma de México, Mexico 2001, p. 84.

64 See for instance, Christian Behrendt, *Le judge constitutionnel, un législateur-cadre positif. Un analyse comparative en droit francais, belge et allemande,* Bruylant, Bruxelles 2006, pp. 280, 281; 436-437.

65 See for instante, Héctor Fix Zamudio and Eduardo Ferrer Mac Gregor, *Las sentencias de los Tribunales Constitucionales,* Ed. Porrúa, Méxcio, pp. 63-64, 74; and «Las sentencias de los Tribunales Constitucionales en el ordenamiento mexicano», in *Anuario Iberoamericano de Justicia Constitucional,* Centro de Estudios Políticos y Constitucionales, No. 12, 2008, Madrid 2008, p. 252.

66 See Iván Escovar Fornos, *Estudios Jurídicos,* Tomo I, Ed. Hispamer, Managua 2007, p. 513; and in «Las sentencias constitucionales y sus efectos en Nicaragua», in *Anuario Iberoamericano de Justicia Constitucional,* Centro de Estudios Políticos y Constitucionales, No. 12, 2008, Madrid 2008, p. 114.

THIRD TREND: CONSTITUTIONAL COURTS INTERFERING WITH THE ABSENCE OF LEGISLATION OR WITH LEGISLATIVE OMISSIONS

In contemporary world, one of the most important roles of Constitutional Courts is not to control the constitutionality of existing legislation, but the absence of such legislation, or the omissions the statutes contain, when the Legislator does not comply with its constitutional obligation to legislate on specific matters, or when the legislation has been issued in an incomplete or discriminatory way.

Two sorts of legislative omissions are generally distinguished: absolute and relative omissions, being both subjected to judicial review.[67]

- *Constitutional Courts Filling Absolute Legislative Omissions*

Regarding judicial review over absolute legislative omissions, Constitutional Courts have carried out constitutional control through two judicial means: First, when deciding a direct action filed against the unconstitutional absolute omission of the Legislator; and second, when deciding a particular action or complaint for the protection of fundamental rights filed against an omission of the Legislator that in a particular case prevents the possibility of enjoying such right.

- **The Direct Action against Absolute Legislative Omissions**

The direct action in order to seek judicial review of unconstitutional absolute legislative omissions was first established in the 1974 Constitution of the former Yugoslavia, and two years later, was incorporated in the 1976 Constitution of Portugal, giving standing to sue to some high public officials.[68] The decisions of the Constitutional Tribunal in these could only inform the competent legislative organ of its findings conduct.[69]

A few years later, the direct action for judicial review of absolute unconstitutional legislative omissions was adopted in a few Latin American countries, in particular in Brazil (1988),[70] Costa Rica, Ecuador and Venezuela, where it has been used extensively. Nonetheless, the main difference regarding these countries is that in the case of Venezuela, the action is conceived as a popular action, [71] and Constitutional Chamber has been granted express powers to establish not only the unconstitutionality of the omission but the terms, and if necessary, the guidelines for the correction of the omission. Nonetheless, the Constitutional Chamber has enlarge its powers controlling the legislative omission regarding non-legislative acts, and in 2004, after the National Assembly fail to appoint the members of the National Electoral Council, the Chamber not only

---

[67] See José Julio Fernández Rodríguez, *La inconstitucionalidad por omisión. Teoría general. Derecho comparado. El caso español, Civitas*, Madrid 1998, pp, 33, 114 ff.

[68] See Jorge Campinos, «Brevísimas notas sobre a fiscalizacão da constitucionalidade des leis em Portugal», in Giorgo Lombardi (Coord.), *Constituzione e giustizia constitutionale nel diritto comparato*, Maggioli, Rímini, 1985; and *La Constitution portugaise de 1976 et sa garantie*, UNAM, Congreso sobre La Constitución y su Defensa, (mimeo), México, Agosto 1982, p. 42.

[69] See in José Julio Fernández Rodríguez, *La inconstitucionalidad por omisión. Teoría general. Derecho comparado. El caso español, Civitas*, Madrid 1998, pp. 265-266.

[70] See for instance, Marcia Rodrigues Machado, «Inconstitutionalidade por omissão», in *Revista da Procuradoria Greal de São Paulo*, No. 30, 1988, pp. 41 ff.

[71] See Allan R. Brewer-Carías and Víctor Hernández Mendible, *Ley Orgánica del Tribunal Supremo de Justicia*, Caracas 2010.

declared the unconstitutionality of the omission, but proceeded to appoint directly those high officials, usurping the Assembly's exclusive powers, assuring in this way the complete control of the Electoral branch of government by the National Executive.[72] A case, also, for the Chapter of the pathology of judicial review.

Also, in Hungary, the Constitution grants the Constitutional Court to decide *ex officio* or at anyone's petition, upon the unconstitutionality of legislative omissions, being able to instruct the Legislator to fulfill its task within a specific deadline, and even defining the contents of the rules to be sanctioned.[73] This power has also been attributed in Croatia to the Constitutional Court, which can also proceed *ex officio*.[74]

- **The Protection of Fundamental Rights against Absolute Legislative Omissions by Means of Actions or Complaints for their Protection**

The other mean commonly used for Constitutional Courts to exercise judicial review regarding unconstitutional legislative omissions are the specific actions of amparo[75] or of complaints for the protection of fundamental rights that can be filed against the harms or threats that such omissions can cause to such rights.

In this sense, it is the case in Germany, where the complaint for the constitutional protection of fundamental rights (*Verfassungsbeschwerde*),[76] has been used by the Federal Constitutional Tribunal as a mean for judicial review of absolute legislative omissions, applied, for instance in cases regarding rights of illegitimate children, imposing the application of the same conditions referred to the legitimate ones, exhorting the Legislator to reform the Civil Code in a giving specific term.[77]

In India, also, the Supreme Court has controlled the legislative omissions, ruling in cases of complaints for the protection of fundamental rights, like in the important case regarding ragging (bullying) menace at Universities, in which the Court not only urged the Legislator to enact the omitted legislation, but prescribed detailed steps to curb the practice, and outlined diverse modes of punishment that educational authorities may take. The Indian Supreme Court even directly

---

72 See the commenst regarding Decisions No. 2073 OF August 4, 2003 (Case: *Hermánn Escarrá Malaver y otros*) and Nº 2341 of August 25, 2003 (Case: *Hermánn Escarrá M. y otros*), in Allan R. Brewer-Carías, «El secuestro del Poder Electoral y la confiscación del derecho a la participación política mediante el referendo revocatorio presidencial: Venezuela 2000-2004», in *Boletín Mexicano de Derecho Comparado*, Instituto de Investigaciones Jurídicas, Universidad Nacional Autónoma de México, Nº 112. México, enero-abril 2005 pp. 11-73.

73 See in Lóránt Csink, Józef Petrétei and Péter Tilk, «*Constitutional Court as Positive Legislator*», Hungarian National Report, XVIII International Congress of Comparative Law, Washington, July, 2010, pp. 5-6.

74 See Sanja Bariæ and Petar Baèiæ, "*Constitutional Courts as positive legislators*»,Croatian National Report, XVIII International Congress of Comparative Law, Washington, July, 2010, pp. 12-13.

75 See in general in comparative law, Allan R. Brewer-Carías, *Constitutional Protection of Human Rights in Latin America. A Comparative Study of Amparo Proceeding*, Cambridge University Press, New York 2009, pp. 324 ff.

76 See in general, Francsico Fernández Segado, «El control de las omisiones legislativas por el Bundesverfassungsgericht», in *Revista de Derecho*, No 4, Universidad Católica del Uruguay, Konrad Adenauer Stiftung, Montevideo 2009, pp. 137-186.

77 Decision of the Federal Constitutional Tribunal No 26/1969 of January 29, 1969, in I. Härtel, «*Constitutional Courts as Positive Legislators*», German National Report, XVIII International Congress of Comparative Law, Washington, July, 2010, p. 19.

appointed, in 2006, a Committee to suggest remedial measures; ordering in 2007, the implementation of its recommendations.[78]

In a similar orientation, and also through equitable remedies like the injunctions, the U.S. Supreme Court progressively developed the protection of fundamental rights filling the gap of legislative omissions, particularly using coercive and preventive remedies, as well as structural injunctions.[79] This was very important after the Supreme Courts decision in *Brown v. Board of Education* case 347 U.S. 483 (1954); 349 U.S. 294 (1955 declaring the dual school system discriminatory, allowing the courts to undertake the supervision over institutional State policies and practices in order to prevent discrimination.[80] This injunction activism was later applied in other important cases of civil rights litigations involving electoral reappointments, mental hospitals, prisons, trade practices, and the environment. Also, deciding these equitable remedies for the protection of fundamental rights, the U.S. Supreme Court has also created complementary judicial legislation, for instance, regarding the conditions for lawful search and arrest in connection with investigation and prosecution of crime.

In Latin America, these complaints for the protection of legislative omissions have also been used.[81] It has been the case of the Brazilian *mandado de injunção*, as writ of injunction granted whenever the lack of regulatory provision makes the exercise of constitutional rights and freedoms, unfeasible. If these injunction the courts can given the Congress not only a term to repair its omission, but established the rules, some time by analogy, to be applied if the omission persist. As has occurred on matters of social security regime and strike Rights of public sectors employees.[82]

The same general approach of the Constitutional Court complementing the Legislator on matters of protection of fundamental rights deciding actions of amparo can be found in Argentina.[83] Also, in Colombia, deciding actions of *tutela*, in the case of massive violations of human rights regarding displaced persons, the Constitutional Court has created even ex officio, what it has called factual a «state of unconstitutionality» (*estado de cosas inconstitucionales*) used in order to substitute the ordinary judges, the Legislator and the Administration in the definition and coordination of public policies.[84]

---

78 Cases *Vishwa Jagriti Mission v Central Government* AIR 2001 SC 2793, and *University of Kerala v Council of Principals of Colleges of Kerala,* in Surya Deva, «*Constitutional Courts as 'Positive Legislators: The Indian Experience*», Indian National Report, XVIII International Congress of Comparative Law, Washington, July, 2010p. 9 (footnote 58).

79 See William Tabb and Elaine W. Shoben, *Remedies,* Thomson West, 2005, p. 13; Owen M. Fiss, *The Civil Rights Injunctions,* Indiana University Press, 1978, pp. 4-5; Owen M. Fiss and Doug Rendelman, *Injunctions,* The Foundation Press, 1984, pp. 33-34; and Allan R. Brewer-Carías, *Constitutional Protection of Human Rights in Latin America,* Cambridge University Press, New York 2009, pp. 69 ff.

80 Case Missouri v. Jenkins, 515 U.S. 70 (1995), in Laurence Claus and Richard S. Kay, «*Constitutional Courts as 'Positive Legislators' in the United States*», US National Report, XVIII, International Congress of Comparative Law, Washington, July, 2010, p. 31 (footnote 104).

81 See Allan R. Brewer-Carías, *Constitutional Protection of Human Rights in Latin America,* Cambridge University Press, New York 2009.

82 See Thomas Bustamante and Evanlida de Godoi Bustamante, «*Constitutional Courts as «Negative Legislators:» The Brazilian Case*», Brazil National Report, XVIII, International Congress of Comparative Law, Washington, July 2010, p. 19.

83 See in Alejandra Rodríguez Galán and Alfredo Mauricio Vítolo, «*Constitutional Courts as «Positive Legislators»,* Argentinean National Report, XVIII, International Congress of Comparative Law, Washington, July, 2010, p. 17.

84 See in Sandra Morelli, «*The Colombian Constitutional Court: from Institutional Leadership, to Conceptual Audacity*», Colombian National Report, XVIII, International Congress of Comparative Law, Washington, July, 2010, p. 5.

In Canada, in a very similar way to the Latin American amparo proceeding for the protection of constitutional rights, according to the Charter the courts have the power to issue a wide variety of remedies including declarations and injunctions requiring the government to take positive actions to comply with the Constitution and to remedy the effects of past constitutional violations. These judicial powers have been widely used for instance enforcing protection on minority language in order to assure bilingualism obligations of the Provinces; on matters of criminal justice, due to the absence of legislative response to enact statutory standards for speedy trials and disclosure of evidence to the accused by the prosecutor; and on matters of extradition of person that could face death penalty in the requesting state.[85]

In a certain way, in the United Kingdom, although the basic principle is that the courts does not substitute itself for the legislature, it is also possible to identify important activity developed by the courts on matters of constitutional review regarding the protection of human rights, by issuing decisions with guidelines that supplement the jurisdiction of the legislator or the administration, as has occurred on matters related to sterilization of intellectually handicapped adults, and persons in a permanent vegetative state, providing rules for future application.[86]

Also in the Czech Republic the Constitutional Court has filled the gap derived from legislative omission on specific matters like the one related to rent rising in apartment houses, in which the Court considered that «its role of protector of constitutionality, cannot limit its function to the mere position of a 'negative' legislator».[87]

- *Constitutional Court Filling the Gap of Relative Legislative Omissions*

In the case of judicial review regarding relative legislative omissions, when dealing with poor, deficient or inadequate legislative regulations affecting the enjoyment of fundamental rights, during the past decades, particularly in concentrated system of judicial review, Constitutional Courts have developed the technique of declaring the unconstitutionality of the insufficient provisions but without annulling them, sending instead to the Legislator, directives, guidelines and recommendations, and even orders, in order to seek for the correction of unconstitutional legislative omissions. In all these cases, the Constitutional Courts have developed a role of assisting and collaborating with the Legislator, particularly in order to protect the right to equality and nondiscrimination. These instruction or directives sent by Constitutional Courts to the Legislator are in some cases non-binding recommendations; in other cases they have an obligatory character; and in others, they are conceived as provisional pieces of legislation.

---

85 Cases: *Reference re Manitoba Language Rights* [1985] 1 S.C.R. 721; [1985] 2 S.C.R. 347; [1990] 3 S.C.R. 1417n; [1992] 1 S.C.R. 212; *R. v. Stinchcombe* [1991] 3 S.C.R. 326, in Kent Roach, «*Constitutional Courts as Positive Legislators: Canada Country Report*», XVIII, International Congress of Comparative Law, Washington, July 2010, pp. 11-12.

86 Cases *Re F (Mental Patient: Sterilisation)* [1990] 2 *AC 173; and Airedale NHS Trust v Bland,* in John Bell, «*Constitutional Courts as 'Positive Legislators': United Kingdom*», British National Report, XVIII, International Congress of Comparative Law, Washington, July, 2010, p. 7.

87 Decision Pl. ÚS 8/02, *Rent Control II*, no. 528/2002 Sb. Of November 20, 2002; and Pl. ÚS 2/03, *Rent Control III*, no. 84/2003 Sb, of March 19, 2003, in Zdenek Kühn, «*Czech Constitutional Court as Positive Legislator*», Czech National Report, XVIII, International Congress of Comparative Law, Washington, July 2010, p. 14 (footnote 58).

- **Constitutional Courts Issuing Non-Binding Directives to the Legislator**

In general terms, regarding the noncompulsory judicial recommendations, called in Italy, exhortative decisions, delegate decisions or *sentenze indiritzzo,*[88] the Constitutional Court declares the unconstitutionality of a provision but does not introduce the norm to be applied through interpretation leaving this task to the Legislator. In other cases, the instruction directed to the legislator can have a conditional character regarding the judicial review power of the Constitutional Court, so that in Italy, through the so-called *doppia pronuncia* formula,[89] if the Legislator fails to execute the recommendations of the Court, in a second decision, the Court will declare the unconstitutionality of the impugned statute.

This sort of exhortative judicial review is also accepted in Germany, and is called «appellate decisions», where the Federal Constitutional Tribunal can issue «admonitions to the Legislator», containing legislative directives giving a term to enact the omitted provision.[90]

This same technique has been applied in France and Belgium, where the Constitutional Council and Court have also issued these directives addressed to the Legislator, which and even without normative direct effects, can establish a framework for the future legislative action.[91] A similar technique has been applied in Poland, called «signalizations», through which the Constitutional Tribunal directs the legislator's attention to problems of general nature;[92] and has also been applied in Serbia, the Czech Republic and Mexico.[93]

Also in countries with diffuse systems of judicial review, like Argentina, these exhortative rulings have also been issued by the Supreme Courts, in cases related to collective habeas corpus petition, exhorting the involved authorities to sanction new legal provisions in order to take care, for instance, of the overcrowding and dreadful situation in the prisons system.[94] These powers have also been used in cases of judicial review of «conventionality» regarding the American Convention of Human Rights. A similar position has been adopted by the Supreme Court of the Netherlands giving its «expert advice» to the Legislator.[95]

---

88 See L. Pegoraro, *La Corte e il Parlamento. Sentenze-indirizzo e attivitá legislativa*, Cedam, Padova 1987, pp. 3 ff.; and Francisco Javier Díaz Revorio, Las *sentencias interpretativas del Tribunal Constitucional*, Ed. Lex Nova, Valladolid, 2001, p. 268.

89 See Iván Escovar Fornos, *Estudios Jurídicos*, Tomo I, Ed. Hispamer, Managua 2007, p. 504.

90 See Francisco Javier Díaz Revorio, *Las sentencias interpretativas del Tribunal Constitucional,* Ed. Lex Nova, Valladolid, 2001, pp.264; and Iván Escovar Fornos, *Estudios Jurídicos*, Tomo I, Ed. Hispamer, Managua 2007, p. 505.

91 Decision BVerfG, de 19 de Julio de 1966, BVerfGE 20, 56 (114-115), in Christian Behrendt, *Le judge constitutionnel, un législateur-cadre positif. Un analyse comparative en droit francais, belge et allemande*, Bruylant, Bruxelles 2006, pp. 176-179, 185 ff.

92 See for instance the «signalization» regarding tenents'protection of June 29, 2005, OTK ZU 2005/ 6A/77, in Marek Safjan, «*The Constitutional Courts as a Positive Legislator*», *Polish National Report*, International Congress of Comparative Law, Washington, July, 2010, p. 16 (footnote 45).

93 See por ejemplo, Héctor Fix Zamudio and Eduardo Ferrer Mac Gregor, «Las sentencias de los tribunales constitucionales en el ordenamiento mexicano», in *Anuario Iberoamericano de Justicia Constitucional*, No. 12, 2008, Centro de Estudios Políticos y Constitucionales, Madrid 2008, p. 252.

94 Case *Verbitsky*, CSIJ, Fallos. 328:1146, in Néstor P. Sagües, «Los efectos de las sentencias constitucionales en el derecho argentino», in *Anuario Iberoamericano de Justicia Constitucional*, Centro de Estudios Políticos y Constitucionales, No. 12, 2008, Madrid 2008, p. 340.

95 Case *Harmonisation Act de 1989, in J.* Uzman T. Barkhuysen & M.L. van Emmerik, «*The Dutch Supreme Court: A Reluctant Positive Legislator?*», Dutch National Report, XVIII, International Congress of Comparative Law, Washington, July 2010, p. 6.

- **Constitutional Courts Issuing Binding Orders and Directives to the Legislator**

In many other cases of judicial review referred to relative legislative omissions, generally based on the violation of the right to nondiscrimination and to equality, Constitutional Courts, when declaring the unconstitutionality of a provision without annulling it, have progressively assumed a more positive role, issuing regarding the Legislator, not only directives, but orders or instructions, in order for it to reform or correct pieces of legislation in the sense indicated by the Court. This has transformed Constitutional Courts into some sort of auxiliary of the Legislator, imposing them certain tasks, and establishing a precise term for its performance.

This judicial review technique has been used in Germany, where the Federal Constitutional Tribunal, through injunctive decisions has issued orders to the Legislator on matters related of the regime of alimony, professional incompatibilities, reimbursement of electoral expenses in electoral campaigns, status concerning professors, abortion, and alternative civilian service, even indicating the Legislator what not to do that could aggravate the unconstitutional inequalities.[96] A similar sort of decision of the Constitutional Court can be found in Belgium, Austria and Croatia, and Colombia.[97]

In the case of France, due to the traditional a priori judicial review of legislation system exercised by the Constitutional Council, one of the most important means in order to assure the enforcement of the Council's decisions have been the directives called «*réserves d'interprétation*» or «*réserves d'application*» although directed to the administrative authorities that must issue the regulations of the law and to the judges that must apply the law.[98]

- **Constitutional Courts as Provisional Legislators**

Finally, in many other cases facing relative legislative omissions, Constitutional Courts have not limited themselves to issue orders to the Legislator seeking the enactment of legislative provisions, but have assumed the direct role of being «provisional Legislators» by including in their decisions when declaring the unconstitutionality of statutes, provisional measures or regulations to be applied in the specific matter considered unconstitutional, until the Legislator sanctions the statute it is obliged to produce.[99] In these cases, the Court immediately stops the application of the unconstitutional provision, but in order to avoid the vacuum that a nullity can originate, temporarily establishes certain rules to be applied until the

---

96 Decisions BVerfG, of July 14, 1981, BVerfGE 57, 381; BVerfG, of February 15, 1967, BVerfGE 21, 183; BVerfG, of March 9, 1976, BVerfGE 41, 414, in I. Härtel, «*Constitutional Courts as Positive Legislators*», German National Report, XVIII, International Congress of Comparative Law, Washington, July, 2010, p. 9.; and Christian Behrendt, *Le judge constitutionnel, un législateur-cadre positif. Un analyse comparative en droit francais, belge et allemande*, Bruylant, Bruxelles 2006, pp. 259-288.

97 See for instance, Mónica Liliana Ibagón, «Control jurisdiccional de las omisiones legislativas en Colombia», in Juan Vega Gómez and Edgar Corzo Sosa, *Instrumentos de tutela y justicia constitucional. Memoria del VII Congreso Iberoamericano de Derecho Constitucional*, Universidad Nacional Autónoma de México, México 2002, pp. 322-323.

98 See Bertrand Mathieu, «*Le Conseil constitutionnel 'législateur positif. Ou la question des interventions du juge constitutionnel français dans l'exercise de la function legislative*», French National Report, XVIII International Congress of Comparative Law, Washington, July, 2010, p. 10.

99 See Christian Behrendt, *Le judge constitutionnel, un législateur-cadre positif. Un analyse comparative en droit francais, belge et allemande*, Bruylant, Bruxelles 2006, pp. 333 ff.

enactment of a new legislation. Constitutional Courts, in these cases, in some way act as «substitute legislators» although not in order to usurp its functions but in order to preserve its legislative freedom.[100]

This technique has been applied also in Germany by the Federal Constitutional Tribunal, assuming «an auxiliary legislative power», and acting as a «parliamentary reparation enterprise»,[101] on a matter like the one resolved in 1975, on the partial decriminalization of abortion. In the case, after declaring unconstitutional the provisions of the Criminal Code, the Tribunal considered that «in the interest of the clarity of law» it was suitable to establish «provisory regulation» that was to be applicable until the new provisions would be enacted by the Legislator»,[102] and proceed to enact a very detailed «provisional legislation» on the matter that was applied for nearly 15 years, until 1992. In 1993, after the corresponding reform, the Federal Constitutional Tribunal issued a new decision considering it to be contrary to the Constitution,[103] and establishing once more in an extremely detailed way, as «real legislator», all the rules applicable to abortion in the country.

In Switzerland, the Supreme Court in various cases has also provided for rules in order to fill the gap due to legislative omissions concerning enforcement of constitutional rights, as has happened, for instance, regarding the proceedings concerning the detention of foreigners; the right of asylum; and the rules on expropriation.[104]

Also in India, the Supreme Court has assumed the role of provisional legislator, also on matters of protection of fundamental rights related to police arrest and detention, issuing notices to all state governments, establishing very detail «requirements to be followed in all cases of arrest or detention till legal provisions are made». In this case, even though the requirements were seemingly intended to be temporary, they have continued to be the main rules applicable on the matter.[105] The Supreme Court has also exercised the same powers protecting these rights of working women against sexual harassment at workplace, issuing «for the protection of these rights *to fill the legislative vacuum.* [106]

---

[100] See Otto Bachof, «Nuevas reflexiones sobre la jurisdicción constitucional entre derecho y política», in *Boletín Mexicano de Derecho Comparado*, XIX , No 57, Mexico 1986, pp. 848-849.

[101] See Christian Behrendt, *Le judge constitutionnel, un législateur-cadre positif. Un analyse comparative en droit francais, belge et allemande*, Bruylant, Bruxelles 2006, p. 341, footnotes 309 and 310.

[102] Decision BVerfG, of February 25, 1975, BVerfGE 39, 1, (68), in Christian Behrendt, *Le judge constitutionnel, un législateur-cadre positif. Un analyse comparative en droit francais, belge et allemande*, Bruylant, Bruxelles 2006, pp. 342 ff; and I. Härtel, «*Constitutional Courts as Positive Legislators*», German National Report, XVIII International Congress of Comparative Law, Washington, July, 2010, p. 14.

[103] Decisions BVerfG, of March 25, 1993 (*Schwangerrschaftsabbruch II*), and BVerfGE 88, 203, de of February 25, 1975, in Christian Behrendt, *Le judge constitutionnel, un législateur-cadre positif. Un analyse comparative en droit francais, belge et allemande*, Bruylant, Bruxelles 2006, pp. 346-351.

[104] Decisions BGE 91 I 329 ff. (Sustantive expropriation); BGE 94 I 286 ff. (Taking Neighbors rights). See in Tobias Jaag, «*Constitutional Courts as 'Positive Legislators:' Switzerland*», Swiss National Report, XVIII International Congress of Comparative Law, Washington, July, 2010, p. 16 (footnote 89).

[105] Case *D K Basu v State of West Bengal*, (1997) 1 SCC 416, in Surya Deva, *Constitutional Courts as 'Positive Legislators: The Indian Experience*», Indian National Report, XVIII International Congress of Comparative Law, Washington, July, 2010, pp. 6-7.

[106] Case *Vishaka v State of Rajasthan*, 1997 SC 3011, in Surya Deva, *Constitutional Courts as 'Positive Legislators: The Indian Experience*», *Indian National Report*, XVIII International Congress of Comparative Law, Washington, July, 2010, p. 8 (footnote 49).

Within these sort of judicial review decisions including provisional regulations by interpreting the Constitution, it is possible to mention the cases of «*súmula vinculante*» issued by the Federal Supreme Tribunal of Brazil, for instance, regarding the prohibition of nepotism in the Judiciary, and the demarcation of indigenous people land.[107]

Also in Venezuela it is possible to find cases in which the Constitutional Chamber of the Supreme Tribunal, in the absence of the corresponding statutes, has issued decisions containing legislation, when exercising what the Chamber has called its «normative jurisdiction», establishing complete regulations for instance regarding the *de facto* stable relations between men and women, and on matters of in vitro fertilization.[108]

FOURTH TREND: CONSTITUTIONAL COURTS AS LEGISLATORS ON MATTERS OF JUDICIAL REVIEW

Finally, the fourth trend that can be identified in comparative law regarding the role of Constitutional Courts as «positive legislators», is related to matters of legislation on judicial review, not only regarding the powers of the Court when exercising judicial review and the actions that can be filed before them, but regarding the rules of procedure applicable to the judicial review proceedings. This situation varies according to the system of judicial review adopted.

- ***Constitutional Courts creating their own judicial review powers***

- **The Judge-Made Law Regarding the Diffuse System of Judicial Review**

In the diffuse or decentralized system of judicial review, being a power attributed to all courts which derives from the principle of the supremacy of the Constitution and the duty of the courts to discard statutes contrary to the Constitution, such power does not need to be expressly established in the Constitution. This was the main doctrine established by Chief Justice Marshall in *Marbury* v. *Madison* 1 Cranch 137 (1803). Consequently, in the U.S., due to this essential link between supremacy of the Constitution and judicial review, judicial review was a creation of the courts, as was also the case a few decades later in Norway, in Greece, and in Argentina,[109] where judicial review was also a creation of the respective Supreme of High Courts.

- ***The extension of judicial review powers in order to assure the protection of fundamental rights***

Also in the same sense, and in particular regarding the protection of fundamental rights and liberties, Constitutional Courts in many Latin American countries,

---

107 *Súmula vinculante* No. 13, STF, *DJ* 1°.set.2006, ADC 12 MC/DF, Rel. Min. Carlos Britto, and STF, *DJ* 25.set.2009, Pet 3388/RR, Rel. Min. Carlos Britto, in Luis Roberto Barroso et al, «Notas sobre a questão do Legislador Positivo» (*Brazil*), XVIII International Congress of Comparative Law, Washington, July, 2010, pp. 33-37; 43-46.

108 Decision No. 1682 of July 15, 2005, Case *Carmela Manpieri, Interpretación del artículo 77 de la Constitución*, available at http://www.tsj.gov.ve/decisiones/scon/Julio/1682-150705-04-3301.htm; and Decision No. 1456 of July 27, 2006, Case *Yamilex Núñez de Godoy*, available at http://www.tsj.gov.ve/decisiones/scon/Julio/1456-270706-05-1471.htm See Daniela Urosa Maggi, «*Cortes Constitucionales como 'Legisladores Positivos:' La experiencia venezolana*», Venezuelan Nacional Report, XVIII International Congress of Comparative Law, Washington, July 2010, p. 19-20.

109 See Allan R. Brewer-Carías, *Judicial Review in Comparative Law*, Cambridge University Press, Cambridge 1989.

in their character of supreme interpreter of the Constitution have created in the absence of legislation, the action of amparo, as a special judicial mean for the protection of fundamental rights. This was also the case in Argentina in 1957, in Dominican Republic in 1999,[110] and in the Slovak Republic, where the Constitutional «created» a specific means of protection.[111]

In Venezuela, the Constitutional Chamber has admitted the direct amparo action for the protection of diffused and collective rights and interests established in the Constitution,[112] and in India, the Supreme Court has also expanded the action for the protection of fundamental rights for the protection of collective or diffused rights, called «public interest litigation» (PIL).[113]

- **The Need for the Express Provision in the Constitution of Judicial Review Powers of the Constitutional Jurisdiction and its Deviation**

Nonetheless, and specifically referring to the concentrated system of judicial review, the power to judge the control of constitutionality of legislative acts when reserved to a Supreme Court of Justice or to a Constitutional Court must be accomplished as expressly provided in the Constitution; and cannot be developed by deduction through court's decisions.[114]

Notwithstanding, regarding their judicial review powers, in some cases, Constitutional Courts have extended or adapted them, as happened for instance, when applying the technique of declaring the unconstitutionality of statutes, but without annulling them, including the powers to extend the application of the unconstitutional statute for a term, and to issue directives to the legislator for him to legislate in harmony to the Constitution. This was a technique developed in Germany, as mentioned by Ines Härtel, the *German National Reporter*, «without statutory authorization, in fact *contra legem*»;[115] and in Spain, where the Constitutional

---

110 See Allan R. Brewer-Carías, *Constitutional Protection of Human Rights in Latin America*, Cambridge University Press, New York, 2010.

111 Decision of the Constitutional Court No. III. ÚS 117/01, in Ján SvákyLucia Berdisová, «*Constitutional Court of the Slovak Republic as Positive Legislator via Application and Interpretation of the Constitution*», *Slovak National Report*, XVIII International Congress of Comparative Law, Washington, July 2010, p. 9.

112 Decisions No. 656 of June 30, 2000, Case *Dilia Parra Guillen (Peoples' Defender)*, in http://www.tsj.gov.ve/decisiones/scon/Junio/656-300600-00-1728%20.htm; No. 1395 of November 21, 2000, Case *William Dávila* Case, in *Revista de Derecho Público*, No. 84, Editorial Jurídica Venezolana, Caracas, 2000, pp. 330; No. 1571 of August 22, 2001, Case *Asodeviprilara*, available at http://www.tsj.gov.ve/decisiones/scon/Agosto/1571-220801-01-1274%20.htm. See Daniela Urosa Maggi, «*Cortes Constitucionales como 'Legisladores Positivos:' La experiencia venezolana*», Venezuelan National Report, XVIII International Congress of Comparative Law, Washington, July, 2010, p. 11-12.

113 Cases *S P Gupta v Union of India* AIR 1982 SC 149; *PUDR v Union of India* AIR 1982 SC 1473; *Bandhua Mukti Morcha v Union of India* (1984) 3 SCC 161, in Surya Deva, «*Constitutional Courts as 'Positive Legislators: The Indian Experience*», Indian National Report, XVIII International Congress of Comparative Law, Washington, July, 2010, p. 2, 4-5.

114 See Allan R. Brewer-Carías, *Judicial Review in Comparative Law*, Cambridge University Press, Cambridge 1989, pp. 185 ff.; and Jorge Carpizo, *El Tribunal Consitucional y sus límites*, Grijley Ed, Lima 2009, p. 41.

115 See I. Härtel, «*Constitutional Courts as Positive Legislators*», German National Report, XVIII International Congress of Comparative Law, Washington, July, 2010, p. 8; Francisco Fernández Segado, «Algunas reflexiones generales en torno a los efectos de las sentencias de inconstitucionalidad y a la relatividad de ciertas fórmulas esterotipadas vinculadas a ellas», in *Anuario Iberoamericano de Justicia Constitucional*, Centro de Estudios Políticos y Constitucionales, No. 12, 2008, Madrid 2008, p. 162.

Tribunal, has applied the technique in spite of the provision on the contrary contained in the Organic Law of the Constitutional.[116]

But in other cases, Constitutional Courts have created their own judicial review powers not established in the Constitution, as has been the case in Venezuela, where the Constitutional Chamber of the Supreme Tribunal has created as a new means of judicial review not envisaged in the Constitution, the so called «abstract recourse for constitutional interpretation»,[117] through which at the Attorney General requests, the Constitutional Chamber has distorted important constitutional provisions. It was the case, for instance, of the decisions adopted regarding the consultative and repeal referendums between 2002 and 2004, where the Chamber transformed the repeal referendum into a ratification referendum not established in the Constitution.[118] Anyway, these are cases for the chapter of the pathology of judicial review.

- ***Constitutional Courts Creating Procedural Rules on Judicial Review Processes***

Finally, regarding Constitutional interfering upon the legislative functions, the process of creating rules of procedures for the exercise of their constitutional attributions, when not established in the legislation regulating their functions, must also be mentioned.

For such purpose, Constitutional Courts, as is the case of the Constitutional Tribunal of Peru, have claimed to have «procedural autonomy» having exercise their extended powers developing and complementing the procedural rules applicable in judicial review process not expressly regulated in the statutes.[119]

---

116 See F. Fernández Segado, *El Tribunal Constitucional como Legislador Positivo», Spanish National Report*, XVIII International Congress of Comparative Law, Washington, July, 2010, p. 6, 11.

117 Decision No. 1077 of September 22, 2000, Case *Servio Tulio León*, in *Revista de Derecho Público*, No. 83, Editorial Jurídica Venezolana, Caracas 2000, pp. 247 ff. See Allan R. Brewer-Carías, «Le Recours d'Interprétation Abstrait de la Constitution au Vénézuéla», in *Renouvau du droit constitutionnel. Mélanges en l'honneur de Louis Favoreu*, Paris 2007, pp. 61-70; and «La ilegítima mutación de la constitución por el juez constitucional: la inconstitucional ampliación y modificación de su propia competencia en materia de control de constitucionalidad», in *Libro Homenaje a Josefina Calcaño de Temeltas*, Fundación de Estudios de Derecho Administrativo (FUNEDA), Caracas 2009, pp. 319-362.

118 The constitucional mutación occurred precisely for the purpose of preventing repealing the mandate of President Chávez in 2004. He was elected in August 2000 with 3,757,744 votes; being enough in order to repeal his mandate according to the Constitution, that the votes dor the revocation be more that such figure. The number of votes in favor od the repeal of the President cast in the August 15 2004 voting was 3,989,008, so the mandate was constitutionally repealed. Nonetheless, the national Electoral Council on August 27, 2004, due to the fact that the votes No for the revocation were 5.800.629, decided to «ratify» the Presdient in his post, until the end of his term in January 2007. See *El Nacional*, Caracas, August 28, 2004, pp. A-1yA-2. See the comments on this case in Allan R. Brewer-Carías, «La Sala Constitucional vs. El derecho ciudadano a la revocatoria de mandatos populares o de cómo un referendo revocatorio fue inconstitucionalmente convertido en un «refrendo ratificatorio», in *Crónica sobre la «in» justicia constitucional. La Sala Constitucional y el autoritarismo en Venezuela*, Colección Instituto de Derecho Público, Universidad Central de Venezuela, No. 2, Editorial Jurídica Venezolana, Caracas 2007, pp. 350 ff.

119 Decisión of the Constitutional Tribunal, Exp. N.° 0020-2005-AI/TC, FJ 2, in Francisco Eguiguren and Liliana Salomé, «*Función contra-mayoritaria de la Juridicción Constitucional, su legitimidad democrática y los conflictos entre el Tribunal Constitucional y el Legislador*», Peruvian National Report, XVIII International Congress of Comparative Law, Washington, July, 2010, p. 14; and Fernán Altuve-Febres, «*El Juez Constitucional como legislador positivo en el Perú*», *Peruvian National Report II*, XVIII International Congress of Comparative Law, Washington, July, 2010, pp. 22-23.

In Germany, the same principle of procedural autonomy has been used (*Verfahrensautonomie*) to explain the powers developed by the Federal Constitutional Tribunal to complement procedural rules on judicial review process based on the interpretation of article 35 of the Law of the Federal Constitutional Tribunal related to the execution of its decision.

In other cases, judicial interference on legislative matters related to rules of procedures on matters of judicial review has been more intense, as in Colombia, where the Constitutional Court has assumed the exclusive competency to establish the effects of its own decisions.[120] And in Venezuela, the Constitutional Chamber of the Supreme Tribunal of Justice, has also invoked its «normative jurisdiction» in order to establish the procedural rules for judicial review when not regulated in statutes, in particular regarding the action for controlling absolute legislative omission,[121] and on matters of the habeas data, establishing detail procedural regulations «in order to fill the existing vacuum».[122]

FINAL REMARKS

The main conclusion that we can deduct from this comparative law study on «Constitutional Courts as Positive Legislators», is that in contemporary world, Constitutional Courts have progressively assumed roles that decades ago only corresponded to the Constituent power or to the Legislator, in some cases, discovering and deducting constitutional rules particularly on matters of human rights not expressively enshrined in the Constitution, and that could not even be considered to have been the intention of an ancient and original Constituent when sanctioning a Constitution conceived for other society.

In other cases, Constitutional Courts have progressively been performing legislative functions, complementing the Legislator in its role of lawmaker, in many cases, filling the gaps resulting from legislative omissions, or sending guidelines and order to the Legislator, and even issuing provisional legislation resulting from the exercise of their functions.

These common trends, found in different countries, and in all legal systems, are of course more numerous and important than the possible essential and exceptional differences that could exist. That is why, in these matters of judicial review, Constitutional Courts in many countries, in order to develop their own

120 See Decision C-113/93, in Germán Alfonso López Daza, «***Le juge constitutionnel colombien, législateur-cadre positif: un gouvernement des juges*** *Colombian National Report I*, XVIII International Congress of Comparative Law, Washington, July, 2010, p. 9.

121 Decision No. 1556 of July 9, 2002, Case *Alfonzo Albornoz y Gloria de Vicentini*, available at http://www.tsj.gov.ve/decisiones/scon/Julio/1556-090702-01-2337%20.htm. See Daniela Urosa Maggi, «*Cortes Constitucionales como 'Legisladores Positivos:' La experiencia venezolana*», Venezuelan National Report, XVIII International Congress of Comparative Law, Washington, July, 2010, pp. 10-11.

122 Decision No 1511 of November 9, 2009, Case *Mercedes Josefina Ramírez, Acción de Habeas Dat*, available at http://www.tsj.gov.ve/decisiones/scon/Noviembre/1511-91109-2009-09-0369.html. See Allan R. Brewer-Carías, «El proceso constitucional de las acciones de habeas data en Venezuela: las sentencias de la Sala Constitucional como fuente del Derecho Procesal Constitucional» in Eduardo Andrés Velandia Canosa (Coordinador), *Homenaje al Maestro Héctor Fix Zamudio. Derecho Procesal Constitucional. Memorias del Primer Congreso Colombiano de Derecho Procesal Constitucional* Mayo 26, 27 and 28 de 2010, Bogotá 2010, pp. 289-295; and Daniela Urosa Maggi, «*Cortes Constitucionales como 'Legisladores Positivos:' La experiencia venezolana*», Venezuelan National Report, XVIII International Congress of Comparative Law, Washington, July, 2010, p. 13.

competencies and exercise their powers to control the constitutionality of statutes, to protect fundamental rights and to assure the supremacy of the Constitution, have progressively begun to study and analyze the similar work developed in other Courts and in other countries, enriching their ruling.

Consequently, it is possible to say that nowadays, perhaps with the exception of the United States Supreme Court, is common to find in Constitutional Courts' decisions, constant references to decisions issued on similar matters or cases by other Constitutional Courts, so it can be said that in general there is no aversion about using foreign law, to interpret, when applicable, the Constitution.

On the contrary, in the United States is possible to hear voices like those of Justice Sonia Sotomayor at her Senate confirmation hearings a few month ago, affirming that «American Law does not permit the use of foreign law or international law to interpret the Constitution» being this a «given» question regarding which «There is no debate».[123] On the contrary, on these matters, Justice Ruth Bader Ginsburg, has said that she: «frankly don't' understand all the brouhaha lately from Congress and even from some of my colleagues about referring to foreign law», explaining that the controversy was based in the misunderstanding that citing a foreign precedent means for the court to considers itself bound by foreign law as opposed to merely being influenced by such power as its reasoning holds. That is why she formulated the following question: «Why shouldn't we look to the wisdom of a judge from abroad with at least as much ease as we would read a law review article written by a professor?[124]

And this is precisely what is now common in all Constitutional Jurisdiction all over the world, were Constitutional Courts commonly consider foreign law, when they have to decide on the same matter and based on the same principles. In such cases, in the same sense as of studying the matter according to authors' opinion and analysis in books and articles, they can also rely on courts' decisions from other countries, which can be very useful because they dealt not only with a theoretical proposition, but with a specific solution already applied by a court in the solution of a particular case. And it is here, precisely, where comparative law is a very important and useful tool.

New York, September 2010

NATIONAL REPORTS RECEIVED FOR THE PREPARATION OF THE GENERAL REPORT:

For the purpose of the General Report on the subject «Constitutional Courts as Positive Legislators», presented in the International Congress of Comparative Law, I received the following National Reports, all published in the book: Allan R. Brewer-Carías, *Constitucional Courts as Positive Legislators*, Cambridge University Press, New York 2010, 933.pp.: **ARGENTINA I:** Alejandra Rodríguez Galán and Alfredo Mauricio Vítolo, «*Constitutional Courts as «Positive Legislators» (Argentina)*, pp. 18; **ARGENTINA II:** Néstor Pedro Sagües, «*La Corte Suprema Argentina como legislador positivo*» (pp 24); **AUSTRALIA**: Cherryl Saunders, «*Interpretation and review*» (pp. 54

123 See the xomments of Justice Sonia Sotomayor, in the Senate confirmation Hearings on July 15, 2009, in «Sotomayor on the Issues», *The New York Times*, 16 de Julio de 2009, p. A18.

124 See Adam Liptak, «Ginsburg Shares Views on Influence of Foreign Law on Her Court, and Vice Versa», in *The New York Times*, 12 de abril de 2009, p. 14.

pp.); **AUSTRIA**: Konrad Lachmayer, «*Constitutional Courts as 'Positive Legislators'*» (13 pp.); **BELGIUM**: Patricia Popelier, «*L'activité du judge constitutional belge comme législateur*» (16 pp.); **BRAZIL I**: Thomas Bustamante and Evanilda de Godoi Bustamante, «*Constitutional Courts as «Negative Legislators:» The Brazilian Case*» (29 pp.); **BRAZIL II:** Marcelo Figuereido, «*Judicial remedies aimed to fill the Legislative Gaps resulting from State Omissions under Brazilian Law*» (12 pp); **BRAZIL III**: Luis Roberto Barroso, Thiago Magalhães and Felipe Drummond, «*Notas sobre a questão do Legislador Positivo*» (pp.47); **CANADA:** Kent Roach, «*Constitutional Courts as Positive Legislators: Canada Country Report*» (25 pp.); **COLOMBIA I**: Germán Alfonso López Daza, «***Le juge constitutionnel colombien, législateur-cadre positif: un gouvernement des juges*** (16 pp.); **COLOMBIA II:** Sandra Morelli, «*The Colombian Constitutional Court: from Institutional Leadership, to Conceptual Audacity*» (20 pp.); **COSTA RICA**: Rubén Hernández Valle, «*Las Cortes Constituitonales como Legisladores positivos*» (43 pp.); **CROATIA**: Sanja Bariæ and Petar Baèiæ, "*Constitutional Courts as positive legislators. National Report: Croatia*» (29 pp); **CZECH REPUBLIC**: Zdenek Kühn, «*Czech Constitutional Court as Positive Legislator*» (17 pp.); **FRANCE**: Bertrand Mathieu, «*Le Conseil constitutionnel 'législateur positif. Ou la question des interventions du juge constitutionnel français dans l'exercise de la function legislative*» (18 pp.); **GERMANY**: Ines Härtel, «*Constitutional Courts as Positive Legislators*» (22 pp); **GREECE**: Julia Iliopoulos-Strangas and Stylianos-Ioannis G. Koutna, «*Constitutional Courts as Positive Legislators. Greek National Report*» (24 pp.); **HUNGARY**, Lóránt Csink, Józef Petrétei and Péter Tilk, «*Constitutional Court as Positive Legislator. Hungarian National Report*» (7 pp); **INDIA**: Surya Deva, «*Constitutional Courts as 'Positive Legislators: The Indian Experience*», (11 pp.); **ITALY**: Giampaolo Parodi, «*The Italian Constitutional Court as 'Positive Legislator'*» (13 pp.); **MEXICO:** Eduardo Ferrer Mac Gregor, «*La Corte Suprema de Justicia como Tribunal Constitucional*» (27 pp.); **NETHERLAND:** J. Uzman, T. Barkhuysen & M.L. Emmerik, «*The Dutch Supreme Court: A Reluctant Positive Legislator?*» (54 pp); **NICARAGUA:** Sergio J. Cuarezma Terán and Francisco Enríquez Cabistán, «*La estructura normativa de la Constitución Política de Nicaragua y sus mecanismos de tutela*» (55 pp.); **NORWAY**, Eivind Smith, «*Constitutional Courts as 'Positive Legislators:» Norway*» (7 pp.); **PERU I:** Francisco Eguiguren and Liliana Salomé, «*Función contra-mayoritaria de la Juridicción Constitucional, su legitimidad democrática y los conflictos entre el Tribunal Constitucional y el Legislador*» (18 pp.); **PERU II:** Fernán Altuve Febres, «*El Juez Constitucional como legislador positivo en el Perú*» (30 pp); **POLAND**, Marek Safjan, «*The Constitutional Courts as a Positive Legislator*» (18 pp.); **PORTUGAL**: Joaquim de Sousa Ribeiro and Esperança Mealha, «*Constitutional Courts as «Positive Legislators», (Portugal)*» (11 pp.); **SERBIA**: Boško Tripkoviæ, «*A National Report for Serbia on the topic Constitutional Courts as «Positive Legislators*» (19 pp); **SLOVAKIA**: Ján Svák and Lucia Berdisová, «*Constitutional Court of the Slovak Republic as Positive Legislator via Application and Interpretation of the Constitution*» (14 pp.); **SPAIN**: Francisco Fernández Segado, «*El Tribunal Constitucional como Legislador Positivo (Spain)*» (48 pp); **SWEEDEN**: Joakim Nergelius, «*Human Rights and Judicial Review*» (29 pp.); **SWITZERLAND**, Tobias Jaag, «*Constitutional Courts as 'Positive Legislators:' Switzerland*» (23.pp); **UNITED KINGDOM**: John Bell, «*Constitutional Courts as 'Positive Legislators': United Kingdom*» (8 pp.), **UNITED STATES**: Laurence Claus and Richard S Kay, «*Constitutional Courts as 'Positive Legislators' in the United States*» (38 pp); **VENEZUELA**: Daniela Urosa, «*Cortes Constitucionales como 'Legisladores Positivos:' La experiencia venezolana*» (30 pp.).

JUDICIAL REVIEW IN COMPARATIVE LAW.
COURSE OF LECTURES, CAMBRIDGE 1985-1986,
de ALLAN R. BREWER-CARÍAS, se imprimió
en la República Argentina en marzo de 2021.

www.ingramcontent.com/pod-product-compliance
Ingram Content Group UK Ltd.
Pitfield, Milton Keynes, MK11 3LW, UK
UKHW040229290926
15471UKWH00001B/79

9 789563 929737